Henry Whitney Bellows

A History of the Unitarian Church
of All Souls, Vol. II

Henry Whitney Bellows

Walter Donald Kring

SKINNER HOUSE • BOSTON

A Skinner House Book published under the auspices of the
Unitarian Universalist Association

Printed in the United States of America

ISBN 0-933840-03-9

Contents

Preface   ix

1. *The Church Is My First Bride*   1

   Born and Bred an Unitarian   1
   Candidating in New York   10
   I Accept Your Invitation   18
   My Old Flame   26

2. *The Channing of His Time?*   35

   We Never Worshipped There Again   35
   The Walls Are Very Insecure   48
   A Changing Minister in a Changing New York   58
   Putting His Stamp on the Parish   70

3. *Indications of Reality*   78

   Revolution in France, Riots in England   78
   She Sank Very Suddenly   88
   Trembling and Rejoicing in Responsibility   94
   Unagitated by Abolitionist Fever   102

4. *Going Beyond Channing*   110

   Four Long Nines   110
   Beautiful Garments of Real Belief   116
   Our Church Was Sold Last Night   124
   A Friendly Criticism   134

5. *Seasons of Duty*   146

   Cupolas Here, Cornices There   146
   Father of All! Thy Children Come   153
   Present Excitements   166
   My Track Made of Iron   176

6. *The Suspense of Faith*   183

   The Weakest Part of My System   183
   A New Catholic Church   189
   A Sequel to the Suspense   199
   A Church of the Unchurched   204

7. *Our Commission Is Ordered by
    the Government*   213

   Last Days of Peace   213
   A Crisis of Extreme Interest   218
   The Air Is Thick with Bayonets   224
   Just a Fifth Wheel?   231

8. *The Making of a Marvel*   240

   Things in a Higgledy-Piggledy State   240
   Great Events Are Happening Every Day   246
   Some Hard Nuts to Crack   256
   Only a Drop in the Bucket   261

9. *Approaching Its Natural Conclusion*   274

   How Heavy the Harness Is   274
   California Calls   280
   West Coast Interlude   287
   Looking Toward New Fields   299

10. *Morning is Breaking All Around*   305

    Finding a Creed   305
    The Triumph of Our Denominational Life   314
    The War Has Left Things Changed   322
    Radicals Outside Our Camp   331

11. *Troubles and Strife*   340

    Tired Down to the Bottom   340
    A Rich Rewarding Journey in the East   347
    The Osgood Affair   354
    I Don't Like to Mix In   362

12. *A Green Old Age*   371

    Never Fully at Home in the Flesh   371
    The Life of a Widower   378
    The Hepworth Affair   384
    The Pillow and Staff of My Remaining Pilgrimage   391

13. *As Life Wears to Its Close*   403

    The Sweetest of Cries   403
    Sort Of a Fossil   409
    Mine Eyes Have Seen the Salvation   418
    Saving the Second Church   427

14. *The Old Warrior*   436

I Begin to Feel My Limits   436
The Wade School of Religious Philosophy   444
Our Generation Is Thinning Out   456
That Glorious and Inspiring Beyond   463

Appendix A: Officers of the Unitarian Church of All Souls, 1837–1881   475

Appendix B: Church Membership Criteria   479

Notes   483

Bibliography   521
Bibliographical Note   521
Note on Bellows's Magazine Publishing and Editing   522
List of Publications by Henry Whitney Bellows   522

Index   531

Henry Whitney Bellows, All Souls Archives

Preface

Dr. Henry Whitney Bellows, one of the most important American figures in the nineteenth century, deserves an adequate biography. Lesser men have been well treated by biographers, but Bellows has been so forgotten that many students of American history scarcely know his name.

There have been intentions in the past to write the story of his life, but somehow these have all foundered—perhaps because of the great mass of material that is available. Henry Bellows's son, Russell Nevins Bellows, undertook to write a "Memoir" of his father's life, and fortunately for posterity put a notice in the *Christian Register* asking all of his father's correspondents to send him any letters from Henry Bellows that might be in their possession. Many persons responded, and since Russell Bellows never returned the letters to their owners, they are now in the Bellows Papers at the Massachusetts Historical Society. This makes the collection very rich, for it often contains both sides of a correspondence.

Russell Bellows never completed more of his projected biography than the brief sketch of his father's life which appeared in *The Bellows Genealogy*.[1] Henry Bellows's grandson, Thomas Robinson, a dear friend of mine, considered for many years writing his grandfather's biography, but a busy life precluded the time necessary for research. So it has fallen on me as Henry Bellows's successor (with five other ministries between his and mine) to finish the task. This never would have been possible if my parishioners at the Unitarian Church of All Souls in New York City had not given me a nine-month sabbatical in 1975 to go to Boston to read the entire corpus of the Bellows Papers which relate to Bellows's lifetime.

Henry Bellows has until recently been forgotten even by Unitarians. Yet no less a scholar than Dr. George Williams of the Harvard Divinity School has pointed out that Unitarians love to "identify worthy triumvirates . . . the most famous is that which can come to the lips of any Unitarian: Channing, Emerson, and Parker . . . The ritual naming of these three early Unitarians has become a convention." Dr. Williams would retain Channing in his own triumvirate of great Unitarians. But "for the middle of the nineteenth century" he would "put down Henry Bellows of New York, organizer and spokesman of the Sanitary Commission during the Civil War, and the prime mover (1865) of the National Conference of Unitarian Churches in which his vision of a broad liberal church of America would in the end at least profoundly reshape the individualistic AUA (American Unitarian Association) on the basis of a powerfully wrought theology, including a well-articulated ecclesiology." Williams feels that "Bellows was a tireless promoter and organizer with continental vision."[2] It is my hope that the readers of this volume will agree with Dr. Williams on the importance of Henry Bellows in the annals of American history, and that he will now appear in the scholarly literature where he rightfully belongs.

I am indebted to many people for help with this book, and without their encouragement it would not have come into being. First, the members of the Bellows family. Henry's daughter, Ellen Derby Endicott, was a constant source of help until her death in 1972. The three surviving Bellows grandchildren, Mrs. Anne Tower, Thomas Robinson, and Kay Robinson, have given me extensive and constant support. Mrs. Tower opened up the attic of the Bellows's estate in Walpole for me to search for materials which resulted in some of the pictures in this volume (reproduced here for the first time). I am also deeply indebted to the Massachusetts Historical Society in whose friendly reading rooms I spent many days with the constant help of all present, particularly Miss Winifred Collins. For permission to publish such an extensive portion of the Bellows Papers I am deeply grateful to the Society. To Jack Holzhueter who helped with much of the original research I am indebted, as well as to my wife who helped with much of the initial research and gave constant criticism, but most of all who listened to me talk about Henry Bellows and Herman Melville day after day when she probably had better things to do and to think about. I am in debt to my secretary, Mrs. Rita Savides, who did much of the typing of the manuscript over the years, and to Monona Rossol and Mrs. Mildred Pelmont who helped in typing the final manuscript. I am indebted to Jeannette Hopkins who gave me a critical reading of the manuscript at an early stage. I particularly owe thanks to Dr. Conrad Wright of the Harvard Divinity School, who has done so much in his own writing to put Bellows into proper historical perspective. Dr. Wright volunteered to read the original manuscript, gave unstintingly of his vast knowledge, and helped me to fill in the gaps of the source materials. I am indebted to Carl Seaburg for his careful editorial work, to Jocelyn Riley for copy-editing and to Burnell O'Brien of the Beacon Press for pulling the whole thing together.

My thanks also to Dr. Donald Yannella and Dr. Hershel Parker of the Melville Society who gave me encouragement when the Melville material contained in this book came to light. I owe thanks also to Drs. Joyce and Frederick Kennedy who encouraged me to dig into the church records to find previously unknown things about Herman Melville's relationship to All Souls Church. To my student assistant at the church for two years, the Reverend Jonathan Sinclair Carey, who helped to stimulate me intellectually about these matters, I express my appreciation.

In his autobiography Loren Eiseley tells of the difficulties of the scholar working over a mass of material that seems more and more endless. He suggested that two things threaten the researcher, "First, he may become so lost below ground, trail leading on to trail, that he may never emerge to publish." A second danger is that "publishing comes to seem a heresy."[3] I have felt that way about the preparation for this book. But I have vowed that this biography will not suffer the fate of previous attempts to tell the story of Bellows's life. The material is endless. It would please me if this volume were to become the authoritative biography of Henry Bellows. But this biography is published as a beginning of what I trust will be much further in-depth research into the life and ideas of this amazing man.

Because it was necessary to cut this manuscript by fully one-third for publication, copies of the complete original manuscript may be found in the Harvard Divinity School Library and at the Unitarian Church of All Souls in New York City.

May 1979   Walter Donald Kring

CHAPTER ONE

The Church Is My First Bride

Born and Bred an Unitarian

His name was not supposed to be Henry Whitney Bellows. He was one of twin boys born to John and Betsy Eames Bellows.[1] They named him Edward Stearns Bellows. The twin brother was called Henry Whitney Bellows. But when they took him to be christened at the First Church in Boston, the minister got the names mixed up, so Edward was baptized as Henry and Henry as Edward. Out of deference to the clergyman, the parents never corrected his mistake. So Henry Whitney Bellows he became. In an odd way the mistake was to haunt him all his life.

The twins had been born on 11 June 1814 in Boston. Their father was a wealthy and important Boston merchant with an active interest in civic affairs and local politics. He was the head of the firm of Bellows, Cordia, and Jones, importers of English dry goods, and the president of the Manufacturers and Mechanics Bank of Boston. John Bellows also served as an alderman on the City Council. The family lived on Tremont Street, near West Street, among other affluent families living in "Colonnade Row." Only three of the Bellows's five children were alive when the twins were born, the oldest being ten-year-old Eliza Eames; nine-year-old John Nelson; and six-year-old Alexander Hamilton. The first child born to the Bellows had died in infancy, and older sister, Mary Anne Louisa, had died at the age of two just before the twins were born.

The twin who was supposed to have been named Edward Stearns was of extremely delicate constitution, while the other was robust and had vigorous energy. Thus, Henry grew up as the smaller shadow of Edward, who was always getting himself into scrapes, leaving his fragile, nervous, intensely loyal brother to cover for him. Edward was always considered the more promising of the two, and according to Henry Bellows's daughter, Anna, little stock was placed in Henry's ever becoming a man of importance.[2]

Betsy Eames Bellows was in poor health when the twins were born, and her health failed rapidly thereafter. She died when Edward

1

and Henry were barely two years of age, and John's maiden sister, Louisa, came to care for the five children. Later, John Bellows married Anne Hurd Langdon, who adopted the children as her own, and the children always thought of her as their real mother. She soon gave birth to five more children, a daughter (also named Mary Anne Louisa) arrived on 22 May 1818, shortly before the twins's fourth birthday. The following year, Francis William Greenwood was born and named for Francis William Pitt Greenwood—the minister of King's Chapel. Harriet Augusta arrived on 15 April 1822, Percival Langdon on 16 May 1825, and George Gates on 14 October 1827. Thus the twins lived a happy relatively carefree life in a large family surrounded by brothers and sisters. The twins were especially devoted to each other, and spent many days playing on the Boston Common and sailing their toy boats on the Frog Pond.

Shortly after his marriage to Anne Langdon, John's sister, Louisa, who had been a second mother to the twins, married Jacob Newman Knapp, a schoolmaster in Jamaica Plain, Massachusetts. John Bellows immediately sent his two older boys and the seven-year-old twins to be educated at Mr. Knapp's school. Thus, once again the Bellows's boys were under the care of their Aunt Louisa. For the next two years the twins studied and played at Mr. Knapp's school in Jamaica Plain. The lively Edward—or Ned, as he was called—distinguished himself by getting into all sorts of mischief, but when Ned was punished, Henry always tried to shield and protect him, standing in his brother's stead whenever he could get away with it.

When the twins were nine years old young Henry's health appeared to be so precarious that the parents decided to send them to Walpole to live with John's brother Thomas for a year. This was Henry's and Edward's first real contact with the open country as opposed to the city of Boston, and the lush greenery, the magnificence of Bellows Falls, and the softness of the winter snows left a profound mark on young Henry for the rest of his life. It was this experience which made him wish to live in Walpole later in his life.

Henry Bellows's cousin, Emily R. Barnes, tells of the arrival of the twins on "a certain bright morning in May." "Two little passengers from Boston, ticketed for Walpole." She wrote, "This was the first time they had left their city home." Edward ran away the next day but was "soon induced to return willingly." They planted a garden which "proved a source of lasting enjoyment." Mrs. Barnes noted that they were very curious youngsters "showing at this period an unusual desire for knowledge."[3]

When the twins were ten years old they were sent to the fashionable Round Hill School at Northampton, Massachusetts. Their politically active father was very busy in Boston now, for as an alderman, John Bellows had aligned himself with Josiah Quincy, the mayor of Boston, and was participating energetically in helping to effect badly needed reforms in the municipal government. At Round Hill School the boys were not only prepared for college, but were thoroughly instructed in the gentlemanly arts, from horseback riding to manners.

Near the end of his life Henry Bellows wrote an account of the Round Hill School.[4] He called it "a very famous but short-lived school" which lasted for only ten years, from 1823 to 1833. Bellows was in the school from 1824 until 1828 "when both the founders and principals, Joseph Cogswell and George Bancroft, were still connected with it." Shortly after Bellows left the school George Bancroft went on to other things, and Cogswell conducted the school alone for the last half of its existence. Bellows wrote, "Seldom have two men of such power and intelligence united in establishing and carrying on together a school for boys. They aimed to found a private school with the character of a great public school, without any public foundation, and to supply its wants from its annual receipts." Bellows termed it "a romantic enterprise." He believed that "there never was before, and probably never will be again, such a school in America, or perhaps in the world." Its students were largely the sons of rich men and many came from the Southern states. "There were as many Southern boys as Northern ones, and the mixture gave a special flavor to the social and school atmosphere."

Bellows believed that the aim of the school was above all "to make gentlemen,—gentlemen rather than scholars or citizens. To ride on horseback, dance gracefully, to speak the truth, to be chivalric in manners and temper, to observe the best table manners, —these things had first attention." There was great attention paid to modern languages in the school as well as the usual Latin and Greek. "Indeed, there was nothing connected with the culture of the mind, or the care and development of the body, or the elevation of the character, that was not contemplated by the founders of Round Hill School." However, Bellows believed that it was very difficult "to make much, at school or college, out of the sons of rich men."

There is some question as to just how good a student Henry Bellows was in these early years at Round Hill School. He seems to have had the necessary intellectual capacity to be a good student and lacked only the necessary confidence. His teachers, Joseph Cogswell and George Bancroft, hoped to improve his temperament as well as his mind at Round Hill. At the end of the summer term in 1828 he was actually kept in school somewhat longer than the rest of the boys. In a letter to Henry's father in Boston, Cogswell explained the detention and said that Henry "was not quite ready in all things."[5]

Despite the required athletics that made up a substantial part of the training of his four years at Round Hill School, Henry was graduated at the age of fourteen still a significantly undersized boy. He immediately entered Harvard College, looking like a mere child. Henry's older brothers, John Nelson and Alexander Hamilton—both now in their twenties—had also entered Harvard, but had not completed their studies there. Henry's twin brother, Edward, chose not to enter college but went directly into the business world, leaving Henry lonely and unsure of himself. Having little else to occupy his loneliness Henry concentrated on his freshman studies, for which he had literally been too well prepared at Round Hill, with the result that he went far beyond most of his classmates, and his attention was not engaged fully for most of the freshman year. His health remained delicate, and he continued to be timid and shy, with a passion for being good.

Fortunately, Professor Thomas Nuttall, an ornithologist and Henry's professor of Natural History, took an interest in the boy and, believing that outdoor life would do more for Bellows than sitting in study halls, encouraged Henry to go hunting in the Cambridge woods. Henry responded enthusiastically to this activity. In a defiance of college laws, an action which was more characteristic of his twin brother than of himself, he went tramping about the woods with his gun hung over his shoulder. Harvard then had a strict rule forbidding any student to keep or to shoot firearms in the town. During his early college years, Henry also developed an interest in the theater. When the French actress Rachel played in Boston, he frequently played truant to see her. This interest in show business was to remain with him for the rest of his life. Despite his diminished interest in his studies, however, Henry Bellows managed to keep at the head of his class.

Henry might have continued this rather frivolous attitude in regard to college if it had not been for a series of family tragedies which began during his junior year. A manufacturing crisis in 1830 had begun to make its impression on John Bellows's fortune. In June of 1831, the second Mary Anne Louisa died at the age of thirteen. Bellows had never known his older and full sister with that name, but the loss of his younger half-sister had a profound effect upon the family. At any rate, Henry settled down to serious study in his junior year, and continued this attitude of concentration through his senior year. His health had greatly improved, and he shot up to a normal height of 5 feet, 11 inches, so that he no longer carried the name of "little Bellows" which his classmates had pinned upon him.

In his junior year at Harvard, Henry became avidly absorbed in reading and reflection, and he began seriously to contemplate the profession of the ministry. He also suffered doubts at this time. He questioned whether the Spirit had really settled upon him and whether he was truly fit for such a demanding calling as the Christian ministry. To overcome these anxieties, he developed a regular habit of prayer, seeking for enlightenment. His efforts were rewarded, and Bellows himself recalled: "I conquered these [anxieties] by a habit of prayer, which I formed with great difficulty and obstinate persistence, led to it by reading the autobiographies of the Saints, Brainerd among others, and by gradually acquiring a sense of God which set aside the childish images of a form and put me in possession on my spiritual senses."[6]

By the time of Henry's graduation from Harvard in 1832, John Bellows's ample fortune was all but gone. He had lost money rapidly in various enterprises, and four small children had to be supported on what remained. Francis William Greenwood Bellows was thirteen, Harriet was ten, Percival seven, and George only three. The two older boys were not really prepared to do much in the way of contributing to the family income. Brother John Bellows, running a school in Cooperstown, never had anything left over to help at home. Alexander Hamilton Bellows was something of a dilettante and probably was earning little if any income. After leaving Harvard he had studied medicine for a while at Dartmouth College in Hanover, New Hampshire, but now at twenty-four years of age he was living with relatives at Walpole. Edward Stearns, who had chosen to go into business rather than go with Henry to Harvard, had now left the world of commerce and was studying law with the firm of Sprague and Loring in Boston. The oldest daughter, Eliza Eames Dorr, had married Joseph Dorr only the year before and had gone with her husband to Buenos Aires where Mr. Dorr was busy making—and losing—fortunes.

Thus, upon graduation, Henry Bellows was unable to enter the

Divinity School immediately for there were no funds. Instead, he went to Cooperstown to assist John in the girls' school. For the next year Henry taught eighteen-year-old girls five different languages and mathematics. These damsels were very close in age to their teacher. Despite these allures, Henry left his brother's school the next year. He helped to move his family, now utterly ruined financially, from Boston to the ancestral home at Walpole. He seemed to have reached a dead end: a college graduate literally unprepared for any career except teaching and with no funds available for further education.

At this propitious time, Henry was invited to be the private tutor of a young man, Isaac Baldwin, whose recently deceased father owned a large plantation named "Baldwin" near Alexandria, Louisiana. As both the salary and the "fringe benefits" were enticing, Henry accepted the proposal. To get to Louisiana he had to make a long trip which gave him his first real contact with the wider world beyond Boston. His comments about this first visit to New York City illustrate his parochialism at this stage of his life. He felt it was not comparable to Boston. It "is a bustling city with a great many elegant public buildings—but dirty & restless and insubstantial." Broadway he found a babel, for "every other man is a foreigner." He went to the theater several evenings, and wrote to his brother, "I fear you will think I am quite dissipated—but one's evenings in a strange place hang so heavy without amusement, that the theaters become a solace and a boon to sweep dark care away."[7]

When Henry first reached Pine Woods near Alexandria, Louisiana, and saw the Baldwin home, he was very happy. He described the plantation on the Red River about twenty miles from Alexandria in these words, "Imagine a little village of log houses, one story high, located in the immense solitude of a pine forest, surrounded with a rude fence with everything in accordance with this rusticity." He found Mrs. Baldwin, "one of the most kind and motherly ladies in the world. The loss of her husband affected her very much." Isaac, her son whom he was to tutor, he described as "a boy of 15, rather undersize—thin & delicate—but yet enjoying fine health and has *never been sick*. He has a most remarkably intelligent face—sparkling eyes—of a most mature and manly bearing—intelligent—a lover of books." He had received "a broken education with little system to it—is entirely ignorant of Latin & Greek."[8]

By the middle of March Henry's initial happiness had changed to skepticism about his ability to remain with Mrs. Baldwin and Isaac. He slowly began to realize that the beautiful house in the pine woods which had so impressed him was not all that it had seemed to be in the way of elegance. Further acquaintance with Isaac led him to call the boy "a queer compound of talent & ignorance." Isaac had improved his mind considerably under Bellows's tutoring, but Henry felt that his progress would be much improved "if he would be industrious." He also felt that another young man whom he called "that snake in the grass" was poisoning the mother's mind against him. One thing that really disturbed his Protestant mind was the difference between the Protestant customs of New England and the Roman Catholic customs of Louisiana. He wrote, "The Catholic way of keeping the Sabbath gives an unhallowed air to the whole manners and customs."[9]

By the end of April Henry was back in Walpole. He had made the long journey home and was now planning to enter the Divinity School in Cambridge. He told his brother that he had "left Mrs. Baldwin and the south forever . . . Mrs. Baldwin's conduct towards me had turned from the warmest regard to the coldest reserve and apparent dislike." At first he thought that it was a decline in her health that had altered her attitude toward him, for he felt that he was doing well in tutoring Isaac. But he soon realized that there were other factors in his dismissal. On the first day of April, Mrs. Baldwin had sent for him. She "told me that I did not suit her and that she was sufficiently pleased with my mode of instruction and her son's progress—but did not like my manners, or my principles (Unitarian) & that she thought that we had better separate."[10] Henry was totally unprepared for this curt dismissal. Mrs. Baldwin even refused to pay his passage back to Boston, and said that the $250 which he had originally received would take care of that. Somehow, he managed to find enough money to pay for his passage by ship, and returned to Walpole penniless.

By the time that Henry Bellows entered the Divinity School in 1834, the institution had been established for two score years, and had earned its reputation as a distinguished and respectable school for training liberal ministers. In 1829, Josiah Quincy—the former mayor of Boston and a friend of Henry's father—replaced Kirkland as the President of Harvard College. In the faculty of the Divinity School were John G. Palfrey, who served as Dean, and both of the Wares, Henry and Henry, Jr.

One has only to look at the fellow students of Henry Bellows at the Harvard Divinity School[11] to see the tremendous influence that these men had on him throughout his life. When Henry entered his first year, Cyrus Augustus Bartol was a senior. Perhaps Bellows's longest friendship was with Bartol who held only one pastorate in Boston at the West Church. Bartol never professed to see eye to eye with Bellows in all of his projects and endeavors, but they were sincere and lifelong friends. Another senior that year was Charles Timothy Brooks who held a single pastorate throughout his life at Newport, Rhode Island. Also in that senior class was Samuel Osgood, a high-church Unitarian who was Bellows's co-worker in New York City at the Second Church for two decades.

Another lifelong friend in the middle class in the Divinity School when Bellows entered was Abiel Abbot Livermore who later was president of Meadville Theological Seminary from 1863 until 1890. In that class also was the controversial Theodore Parker who is usually regarded as a social radical because of his attitudes on the slavery issue. But Parker was also a very distinguished scholar, the brains of his class. Bellows was never close to Parker although he respected him. In the junior class also was William Silsbee, a very close and dear friend. He corresponded with Bellows incessantly, but Silsbee did not have the mental or driving power of Bellows and their friendship tapered off with the years.

In Bellows's own class of 1837 only one man was a lifelong friend. Rufus Phineas Stebbins (not to be confused with Horatio Stebbins) later professor at Meadville Theological Seminary for a dozen years between 1844 and 1856. Thus it was the older students of the seminary with whom he felt an affiliation and formed friendships.

Henry Whitney Bellows entered avidly into the life of the Harvard Divinity School. During part of this time he had the good fortune to live in the same house with Orville Dewey who was then at the height of his powers as assistant to William Ellery Channing at the Federal Street Church in Boston.[12]

Very early in his studies at the Divinity School Henry Bellows showed the promise of the great preacher that he was one day to be. The first practice sermon that he mentions was delivered in a meetinghouse identified only as Mr. William Neweles's Meeting House. He wrote, "I found it delightful, exhilerating beyond every thing and unaccountable as it may be, I was never more at ease in my own room."[13]

During Henry's third year at the Divinity School he suffered what was to be one of the most traumatic and ironic tragedies of his life. His twin brother, Edward, had become a promising young lawyer and appeared to be on the threshold of a brilliant career. He had gone to Michigan to become an apprentice in a law office. A very dramatic letter from a Mr. Orange Butler of Adrian, Michigan, where Edward had gone to work, gives the vivid details of the death of Edward in a snowstorm.

Mr. Butler was a member of the Michigan State Legislature so that he was away in Lansing when the tragedy took place. It seems as if it was necessary for Edward to make a trip to Cold Water to secure a "demand." Edward took the stage for most of the sixty miles, and then tried to cross some woods to get to the home of the person against whom the demand was being filed. But he lost his way and returned. "Tuesday morning," wrote Mr. Butler, "he started out again and borrowed a rifle as he said he did not like to go through the woods unarmed . . . Nothing was heard of him until Thursday when the owner of the rifle started to go to the place where Mr. Bellows was to go, went there, and he had not been there." An alarm was immediately made, and a colleague in the law office, a Mr. Halsey, went out to Cold Water where he learned "that Mr. Bellows had been found by the side of the road, dead, about ten feet from the track, and some miles from the place he was destined to go. No mark of violence was discovered . . . Everything except the rifle was about his person."[14]

Thus the young man who had originally been named Henry Whitney, who had passed all of his twenty-three years in robust health, and who had always been thought of as the more confident and brilliant of the twins, was suddenly and shockingly no more, leaving his fragile, timid, and relatively unpromising shadow—the original Edward Stearns—to rise to brilliant fame in his stead.

Looking back on his own personal religious life, Henry Bellows wrote in 1860: "I was born & bred an Unitarian, of Unitarian parents, rich & prosperous; in an Unitarian city, Boston, educated at an Unitarian school (Round Hill, Northampton); & afterwards graduated at an Unitarian college, Harvard. I never had any Calvinistic notions in my mind, or any early doubts or difficulties, touching the simple fatherhood of God, the subordinate nature of Christ, or the erectness of human nature. I read the Bible in all simplicity, & found it an Unitarian book, that, is to say, I found nothing in it to give me a moment's distrust of the opinions in which I was educated."

But even at this early age he had the doubts of most teenagers. "I passed through an earnest religious experience in my college course, beginning at about my sixteenth year, in which I struggled with my own apathy, ignorance, & conventional righteousness, & attained what I then believed, & still believe, to be a conscious, personal relation of filiality to God, a habit of prayer, & a grateful & willing discipleship to Jesus Christ, as my Savior & Lord." Henry Bellows noted that at this time, "I was so poorly acquainted with ecclesiastical history . . . that until my 14th year, I thought all the various kinds of so-called orthodoxy & trinitarian principles confined to ignorant people; as the only persons entertaining them within my immediate observation, were the kitchen maids & men servants in my father's *house*, & other houses. You will imagine my surprise in my college-course to learn what an insignificant minority we Unitarians were, & how *local* our importance."

He concluded, "On leaving college at 18 years of age, (much too early!) I spent two years in travel and in the discipline of tutorship, and with warm & earnest & *happy* religious feelings, commenced my divinity studies in Cambridge in 1834. These studies, conducted by large, candid & devout men, confirmed me unwaveringly in my Unitarian faith, & dismissed me to my work in the ministry in 1837."[15]

In the middle of July of 1837 Henry Bellows finished his work at the Divinity School and addressed his class at the graduation exercises. He wrote about this occasion: "A larger assembly than usual did themselves the honor of listening to us. The exercises were of an *unusually high order*."

Bellows left Cambridge with great regret. He said that he would miss the quiet and contemplative atmosphere. "Shall I ever find a castle like my room—so entirely & sacredly my own?" He dreaded the candidating that lay ahead of him to secure a pulpit. He was worried about being thrown into some great city with very little preparation for life, and wondered "if a man could continue to grow intellectually and spiritually when he actually got out into the ministry."[16]

Candidating in New York

Where would Bellows begin his ministry? Reverend Ephraim Peabody, in charge of the supplying of pulpits in the American Unitarian Association, told him there were prospects in Washington, D.C., Mobile, Alabama, and Toledo, Ohio. Bellows replied that he "should prefer going to Mobile rather than Toledo, as I could do more good there."[1] In a fashion that was to be typical of Bellows all of his life he armed himself with more than sixty letters of introduction from the best persons to the best persons, and he set out for Mobile, Alabama, after receiving their invitation for a trial in the pulpit.

On this second trip south Bellows stopped in Philadelphia and made the acquaintance of the Unitarian minister of that city, William Henry Furness, who was to be another lifelong friend and close associate.

He enjoyed his six-month stay in Mobile, and made a great many friends there. He had no leisure time because of the press of his ministerial duties. "From dinner 'til tea time, i.e. from 4 till 6, I occupy myself in visiting the merchants & clerks in their stores and counting rooms. The evenings I devote to the visiting of families." He found the people "open-hearted and generous." He was received very kindly and felt that among these people of the aristocratic south he could be perfectly natural. He wrote, "Piety does not need here to be clothed in sackcloth and fed on locusts and wild honey to be considered genuine. The minister is not expected to be different from other men. They treat me like a man & not like a woman, as is too much the case in the north."[2]

He also rediscovered what he already ought to have known— that he was a natural-born preacher. The pulpit was his real home. The importance which he gave to the sermon gives one clue as to why he became a famous preacher. He commented that "Each [sermon] is an endeavor to give definiteness to some religious truth or rather to religion itself . . . I always write as if the whole subject [were] perfectly new to the audience—as if 'faith' or 'rejuvenation' or 'love of God' were perplexing terms which they had heard mentioned, but attached no meaning to."[3] He added a thought that is familiar to most ministers: "My sermons, after I finish them, are new to myself." He was able by this fresh approach to sermon writing and delivery to give his sermons a sincerity coupled with common sense, which aroused and attracted. "I preach them with an earnestness and zeal which makes me feel as if I should fly out of my body, and they are listened to with an interest & silence which tells me they go to the right place."[4]

Bellows saw everywhere the fruits of slavery. "The more I see of it the more I deplore it. It seems to me quite as bad for the people as for the slaves." He made another judgment: "The slaves are the most degraded, vicious, miserable race . . . when this great moral error takes possession of the mind, it tends to confound all moral distinctions & to undermine the virtues of the whites . . . Slavery taints the whole southern character."[5]

When his father expressed concern about the views of slavery which he expounded, Bellows assured his father that he had no intention to preach about slavery in the pulpit. He felt that in the North there was a great ignorance upon the whole subject. "You don't know half the perils or the evils of slavery there. The Whites are more the slaves of the Blacks than the contrary. Cruel treatment is rare, but such debasement was never known." He expounded at that time a policy which was to be typical of his attitude toward all extreme positions. He commented, "The Slave-owners are as blind as the Abolitionists. A few years will show them the viper they are warming in their own bosoms. You can hardly imagine the intense enmity which most Southerners feel towards the North. I sense nothing but disunion and civil war before us."[6] This was prophetic, for it was twenty-three years before the outbreak of the Civil War.

Eventually Henry Bellows decided that he did not want to accept a pulpit in the South. He told the trustees of the Mobile church of his decision. Yet, after he left Mobile the trustees of the church met and resolved. that the chairman of the board, Mr. Dellingham, should "address the Rev. H. W. Bellows inviting him to return to this city next autumn to take charge of this congregation as its pastor with the view to remaining here permanently." The trustees, expressing their inner uncertainty about his acceptance, wrote that they did not wish to submit this request to a vote of the congregation unless they received a favorable reply from him. They requested an early reply so as to be able to have a meeting of the congregation soon.[7]

Bellows must have been flattered by this generous offer. Meanwhile, he traveled to Cincinnati to preach in the Congregational (Unitarian) Church there. By August second he was back home in Walpole. He turned down the offer of the Cincinnati Church to be its minister largely because of the declining condition of his father's health. He contemplated going to Boston to talk with the Unitarian people there and hoped to candidate for a New England church.[8] The offers from Mobile and Cincinnati had been most appealing, but he had decided that he did not want to live in the South. In spite of a very persuasive letter from Mr. Dellington, the chairman, Bellows turned down the offer from the church in Mobile.[9] The Cincinnati trustees had asked him to be their pastor for six months with the object of seeing if at the end of that time "a more interesting communion might be formed between us."[10]

In April the trustees of the New York church had written to Henry Whitney Bellows in Mobile, Alabama. Bellows received an

invitation to "preach in New York as a candidate." He "presumed it
was in Wm. Ware's old pulpit." He told his uncle that he had written
to New York and that "he could make no engagements before
reaching the North and consulting my friends." Evidently the
invitation was not of great import to Bellows, for he wrote that he
"should prefer to be nearer home [Walpole] for the summer."[11]
Bellows was not attracted by the lure of the great city which was
rapidly becoming the largest metropolis of the nation. He appears to
have desired a small parish in a New England town where he would
be forever. "But heaven only knows where I shall be pitched. I shall
try to be content anywhere."[12]

His friend, Henry Ware, Jr., had encouraged him to preach in
the New York pulpit, and wrote to Bellows about the deep
attachment he had to the society and the people there. He recalled, "I
was their first stated preacher. I gathered the Ch. [Church]. I first
administered the Lord's Supper. I laid the cornerstone of the building
& have dearer feelings to it than to any except my own Ch. [Church]
in Boston. There are few so important fields as New York."[13]

Bellows's friend, Mrs. Saint John, whose husband was a ship
captain, wrote to him from her home in Newport that she would
arrange for him to meet the famous Dr. William Ellery Channing
who summered in his birthplace at Newport. "I can promise you a
warm reception from Dr. Channing—he is so anxious to meet you.
He is desirous that you should go to New York," she wrote. "The
happiness and welfare of your family is your first consideration," she
counseled him but asked that "before making any engagement I hope
that you will see and consult with him."[14]

By September Henry's older brother John who was living in
New York urged Henry to consider settling there. John said that he
found the activity on the streets and the movement in the harbor
most interesting. In New York there "may be great, but there are no
petty annoyances."[15] But Bellows was loath to leave New England.
Walpole had always seemed to him to be a place of healing.

The pressures were too strong for Henry to resist, and New
York City was not as far away from Walpole as Mobile or even
Cincinnati. He accepted Mrs. Saint Johns's invitation to visit
Newport, met Dr. Channing, and preached the ordination sermon
for his fellow student at the Divinity School, George Frederick
Simmons. He offended some of the worthy ministers from Boston in
that sermon by what were considered to be his heretical views. "Dr.
Parkman came to me almost in tears to say how grieved he had been
to hear such sentiments from a Christian minister." Bellows recalled

that "the most objectionable remark was that a sincere worshipper of idols, or a pious heathen, might be acceptable in the sight of God as a Christian."[16]

Simmons had preached at the New York church, and described for Henry the conditions as he saw them there. It was most discouraging. "Their Sunday School has ceased. Their library is wholly disused. Their tracts lie on the shelves, and the attendance at church is irregular & in the evening for the most part very small." He added this comment: "In truth I am hardly satisfied that Mr. Dewey should be the only representative of Unitarianism in New York. His happiness-principle is so bad & his ambition gives such a taint of unholiness. And then, does he preach the gospel to the poor? Has he the lowliness and impartiality of the Christian?" Simmons also speculated that when the new church that Mr. Dewey was building was finished that some might be drawn away from the First Church. The trustees of the Chambers Street church were confident, however, that this would not be the case for the pews in Mr. Dewey's church were too dear (none cost less than fifty dollars per annum). He wished that Bellows would consider the New York church. "My only doubt is whether you are strong enough for the place." But, he added, "Your naturalness would be peculiarly appreciated . . . Mr. Dewey's voice is not sufficient, for Mr. D. cannot preach to all of N.Y., and besides there are & always will be, those who dislike him."[17]

"New York from Brooklyn Heights," by J.M. Hill, engraved by W.J. Bennett, and published by L.P. Clover, Courtesy of the New-York Historical Society, New York City.

By the end of October Bellows was headed for New York City to preach at the First Church for a month's trial, and to make an analysis of the church's situation in regard to its future and his. He felt that he was going perhaps for a month, perhaps for the winter, perhaps forever. The young theologue, twenty-four years of age, not even ordained, was going to the fastest-growing city in the nation, candidating for his first church in a large metropolis when what he said he really wanted was a small New England parish.

What was New York City like in that fall of 1838, and what was "William Ware's old pulpit" like? What kind of a Unitarian Church would Henry Bellows find in New York City? If one in imagination stood on the shore of the East River at Brooklyn Heights in that year 1838 when Henry Bellows arrived, and looked across the river to the skyline of Manhattan Island, it would be a very different silhouette from that of the present day. Fortunately we have the colored drawing of just such a scene executed in 1837 by J. W. Hill which shows a great deal of shipping in the East River; boats with sail of all kinds, cargo ships of all sizes and riggings, slender clipper ships which sailed the Seven Seas. The silhouette of Manhattan Island was so low that on a clear day one could readily see the shores of Staten Island and New Jersey in the distance. There were some large buildings, but usually not over six stories. And there were churches, several dozen of them with steeples pointing toward the heavens which were scattered along the various streets of the city. Broadway had just been extended to Fourteenth Street, and everything above that was farmland entirely rural in character with small scattered clusters of farm buildings and dwellings. The population of Manhattan had gradually been moving to the northward.

But if one viewed Manhattan Island from Brooklyn Heights in that year 1838 the steeple of the First Congregational Church—as it was then called—would not be among those of the skyline of Manhattan. The congregation in that year was still worshiping in the original Federal-style building on Chambers Street, and the congregation was not affluent enough to afford the elegance of a steeple. Instead, there was a round glass-domed skylight, scarcely visible above the roof. It was a squat small church of no particular architectural elegance. The people who had founded the church in 1819 and had built this first building in 1821 were largely young men who had left important families in New England to come to develop their fortunes in the growing port of New York.

During the two decades between 1819 and 1839 the church was served by two ministers. The first was William Ware, son of the

famous Henry Ware, Sr., of Harvard whose appointment caused
such a stir between the religious liberals and the orthodox at Harvard
College. Ware served the congregation well although his primary
interests were artistic and literary rather than the rigorous duty of
preaching twice every Sunday and the multifarious activities in
overseeing a growing parish. Ware finally resigned a discouraged
man in 1836 after serving the growing church for fifteen years. He
had never been very successful in his preaching because of a certain
shyness. He was a magnificent artisan with the English language and
made his real success as a writer of three historical novels: *Zenobia,
Aurelian,* and *Julian,* which secured his fame in the field of the
American novel.[18]

After Ware left the ministry of the First Congregational Church,
the congregation heard a German refugee, Dr. Charles Theodore
Christian Follen, a protege of Channing. Follen held the post of
acting pastor for almost two years. But the congregation could never
unite on calling Follen to be the permanent pastor. One reason was
that he tended to alienate people with his abolitionist ideas. Another
was that they found it difficult to penetrate his thick German accent.
Follen left the church discouraged (later in January of 1840 he lost his
life when the steamship *Lexington* burned in Long Island Sound).
It was very important that this congregation, which was increasing
in social and intellectual importance in the community, should find a
new minister who would have qualities of leadership that neither
Ware nor Follen had possessed.

Unitarianism, like the city, had also moved northward during
this first decade after the founding of the First Church. In the same
year in which the Erie Canal was opened, 1825, a group of
Unitarians who were members of the First Church but who lived too
far north of the building on Chambers Street to conveniently attend
decided to start a second church. At first this was conceived to be a
partnership with the First Church in the collegiate tradition of the
Dutch Reformed Churches. It was planned that there would be two
buildings and a minister for each church but the ministers would
trade pulpits every other Sunday—thus making the preaching
burden lighter for each of them. What began as a collegiate dream
did not turn out that way, and the Second Church became a
completely independent entity. It built an edifice at Prince and
Mercer Streets and called a young man, William Lunt, as its first
minister. Lunt, who was just out of the Harvard Divinity School,
never realized his potential in New York, although he did later in a
long pastorate in Quincy, Massachusetts.

In October of 1835 Orville Dewey, praised as one of the finest of the Unitarian preachers, accepted a call to become the minister of the Second Church. This powerful preacher began to attract many of the members of the First Church to the new church. Then disaster hit the Second Church. On 26 November 1837 Dewey's church was completely destroyed by fire. In a sense, however—and Dewey believed this—the fire was a positive factor in the growth of the Second Church, for while the congregation temporarily worshiped at the Stuyvesant Institute the seats were free, and this attracted many persons to hear the preaching of the great Dewey. The inability of the congregation of the First Church to decide about whether they wanted Dr. Charles Follen to be their settled minister also strengthened the Second Church. The Second Church built a new edifice on Broadway which was completed in less than a year.[19]

In these two decades the people who comprised the two congregations had changed in many ways. No longer were they social or religious outcasts. Some of the men had been highly successful. Orontontes Mauran owned the Staten Island Ferry. John Thomas owned the Plymouth Rock. Elihu Townsend, who had recently moved to the Second Church, was a successful merchant. William Cullen Bryant who had come to the city in 1825 at the urging of the Sedgwick family and joined the congregation shortly thereafter was not only a famous poet but the prosperous and influential editor of the *New York Evening Post*. His greatest success, however, was in real estate speculation which made him a wealthy man. Peter Cooper also had joined the church a few years after its founding, and he was beginning to amass a great deal of wealth. Nathaniel Currier was becoming a successful lithographer.

The professional and business success of these men also meant that their social position in the city had changed radically. When men become successful they are no longer "strangers from inland and outland" as Catharine Sedgwick had dubbed the original members of the church. They had become accepted by the community. Literally in 1819 they had been religious liberals set among the more orthodox Episcopalians, Presbyterians, and members of the Dutch Reformed Churches. In the early years they had been treated in the manner that later immigrants from Ireland were to be treated in regard to their religion. But this alienness in the big city was now a thing of the past, and by 1838 the congregations of both the First and Second churches were well on their way to becoming upper crust socially. They had not attained their position because of birth. This distinction was left to the Dutch Reformed and the Episcopalians. These Unitarians were upper crust economically and socially because of their strenuous efforts to get ahead in the world. In many ways they typified the successful men of the first half of the nineteenth century. As the years went by, the congregation, as it grew in numbers, became more and more middle upper class and upper class together with a few intellectuals who had made it socially.

New York City, even in 1838, was a complicated city—growing geographically and in economic power, but even then showing some cracks in the seams—if anyone thought of the city as a Utopia. As the members of the First Congregational Church thought about a new minister they had high hopes that under the right man Unitarianism in New York City would take its rightful place among the other prominent religions.

I Accept Your Invitation

Arriving in New York in early November, Henry Bellows settled in a rented room at 51 Greenwich Street, now part of Greenwich Village. He described his room as cooping him "up between walls 6 feet by 8 or 10." He had a comfortable fire burning in the grate and he tried "to feel at home."[1] Fortunately, he was staying at the same rooming house where Orville Dewey lived with his wife and daughter. He wrote about his good fortune, "Here have I been passing day after day & evening after evening with him in the most intimate intercourse imaginable. Dewey is as different a man from what I fancied as possible—the most joyous, jocund, natural, playful, sensitive person in the world, open as a child, assuming nothing, free from cant, professional peculiarities & all other objectionables . . . Now isn't this worth coming to New York for—alone—without other purpose?"

Bellows's first impressions of the city, however, were not at all favorable. He called it "a heartless place in appearance . . . amid all the business & bustle & tear & hustle—there are human hearts, I suppose."[2] He found it difficult to believe that human beings, fathers, mothers, sisters, brothers, and children could live in such a busy bustle in the same way as they did in rural Walpole.

His first reaction to the congregation was a little more pleasing to him than his impression of the city. It could be summarized in his statement to his sister after the first Sunday (which was rainy) when there was what Bellows called "a thin audience." He found people very cordial and encouraging. He already expected that they would want him to remain, but then added significantly and almost ominously, "but it takes two to make a bargain. I can't say anthing with confidence—except that I shall come home when my month is up with great joy."[3]

A week later he wrote to his sister in Boston to say that he was confident that he would receive a call from the church. Since he had been in the city for a week "everything has improved." He found it a "delightful congregation, fine people, great earnestness, refinement, etc. a good salary & an immense field of usefulness."[4]

He found the society, however, in the rather run-down condition which George F. Simmons had suggested to him. Bellows wrote, "It [the church] has been in a most despondent state since Mr. Ware left." Dr. Follen had divided it with his abolitionism which had drawn off some of the members of the church. Yet he found a sincere and dedicated nucleus of "clear grit." He found "a number of families admirable for intelligence & refinement, more particularly the Sedgwick and Schuyler families." He further believed that in this city of 300,000 people there were enough liberal Christians for half a dozen churches.[5]

He had already indicated that he expected a call, and his father gave his son some very practical advice about making an adequate contract with the church. This advice seems a bit gratuitous since his father had not been a very successful businessman. Henry should not make "a hasty contract," and he should make "provision for occasional absence, as health and strength may require, say eight or ten Sabbaths in the year,"[6] which was to prove good parental advice.

For perhaps the first time since William Ware's resignation the congregation united its interest in a particular minister in the person of Henry Bellows. The young man was a natural and unaffected speaker who when preaching was utterly sincere. Although Bellows himself claimed to have been shy and anxious about speaking and relating to strangers, he struck all with whom he came in contact as having a relaxed confidence and quiet strength. The congregation was quickly stirred from its depressed apathy, and rallied to persuade Bellows to settle as their minister. Some of the members may even have enlisted Orville Dewey's support in convincing Bellows to accept the pulpit.

The congregation met on 26 November 1838, and resolved *unanimously* to call Henry W. Bellows to be their second full-time installed minister. In spite of the severe financial situation which then prevailed, the Society fixed Bellows's salary at $2,500 per year.[7] Bellows was, of course, already prepared to receive the call as he had correctly understood his impact upon the members of the congregation. Bellows accepted their call on the thirtieth of November, asking only for a six to eight week summer vacation.

Robert Ainslee, the president of the board of trustees, acknowledged this acceptance with much pleasure. "It will be my duty to have it read from the pulpit next Sunday to the Society," he wrote, and he spoke of the need for Mr. Bellows to be ordained, and enclosed a hymn which he had written for the occasion.[8] Bellows's letter to the congregation had been a masterpiece of deference to the honor done to him by the unanimous call of the congregation. But it also revealed the candor and confidence which were such marked characteristics of his personality. He had no illusions as to the immensity of the task before him. His doubts were rational and objective rather than doubts created by the personal insecurity that had disturbed William Ware. Nor did he bring any unpopular causes to New York as did Charles Follen to divide the congregation. The prospects of his ministry in the great city were truly immense.

The society in New York acceded to Mr. Bellows's request for the vacation time, and immediately set about planning for the ordination service to be held on January second, according to Mr. Bellows's wishes.[9] When William Ware had been ordained in 1821 there were very few nearby churches that could be invited to the ordination service. Thirty or more societies, however, had been invited. But only six churches were invited to Bellows's ordination. In addition to the Second Church and the Brooklyn society, Ephraim Peabody's church in New Bedford, William Furness's in Philadelphia, and Samuel K. Lothrops's Brattle Street Church in Boston were invited. William Ware was also invited to participate.

In spite of the financial crisis, which had not yet finished its disastrous course on the city's economy, the society went to great expense and trouble to prepare for the occasion. In addition to making needed repairs on the building, the pulpit was repaneled and carpeted, the organ was repaired, and the interior of the church was painted and gilded. A chandelier was specially hung for the occasion in the center of the church. An account written by Mary Hustace Hubbard, Benjamin Hustace's daughter, tells of these efforts which can also be gleaned from the treasurer's report of 1839. Mrs. Hubbard wrote, "An elegant chandelier was placed in the center . . . a very rich crimson damask drapery had been arranged over the window behind the pulpit [which] was paneled in highly polished mahogany." Mrs. Hubbard also stated that an Egyptian-marble baptismal font—which had been given to the church shortly after

William Ware's ordination seventeen years earlier by Elbert Anderson of New York—stood on the table in front of the pulpit.[10]

In addition to these renovations the congregation had prepared a printed program.[11] Unfortunately, Mr. Lothrop and Edward B. Hall, William Ware's brother-in-law, were not able to attend the ordination, and the program had to be altered in pen. On Wednesday morning, 2 January 1839, the ecclesiastical council met and, having read and approved Bellows's qualifications—his record of graduation from the Divinity School, and his being a member of Henry Ware's Church in Cambridge—set about changing the program. In place of the absent Mr. Lothrop, William Furness of Philadelphia gave the introductory prayer; he was also assigned the reading from the Scripture, a substitution for Reverend Hall's previously scheduled "Address to the People." Mr. Furness also delivered the ordination prayer. Ephraim Peabody—who was a good friend of Bellows, and who had persuaded him to spend the previous year at Mobile—preached the ordination sermon. Orville Dewey gave the right hand of fellowship to his colleague, and the charge to the minister was appropriately given by Bellows's predecessor, William Ware. The Reverend Frederick W. Holland— who had been ordained only the previous April as Pastor of the Brooklyn Church—offered the concluding prayer. Nathaniel Frothingham of the First Church in Boston had written two hymns for the occasion, presumably replacing Mr. Ainslee's proffered hymn (which he had sent Bellows).

According to Mrs. Hubbard, the ordination took place on a bright, clear, but crispy cold morning. "The ladies were in gala costume, the church was crowded, and the music was superb."[12] Jonathan Goodhue, the noted merchant, wrote in his diary that "the service on the occasion was of the most satisfactory character, and the event is held to be full of promise of usefulness and gratification to the people."[13] Thus, except for the last-minute changes which were made in the program, the event went off smoothly and was a festive occasion, betokening the more fortunate years that lay ahead for the First Congregational Church under Henry Bellows's ministry.

Recalling the ordination service many years later Bellows spoke of his emotions on this occasion: "I can never forget the solemnity, the mingled fears and hopes, the overwhelming emotions of that occasion of self-consecration, of ordination to the ministry, and of union with a congregation, which for me had all the sentiment, sanctity, and permanency of a marriage. I brought into the ministry something of the awful sense of its peculiar obligations and requirements which marked the older time."[14]

After the ordination service a most gala social event had been planned at the luxurious home of Mrs. Philip Schuyler. Bellows wrote: "In the evening Mrs. [Philip] Schuyler . . . opened her magnificent house for me to hold grand levee for the parish, and such a crowd. Full of friends, such confrontations & hand pressings & yearnings. Boston can't furnish the like . . . It was the gladdest evening of my life."[15]

Thinking back upon the service of ordination itself Bellows found some of the events particularly touching. He remarked to his father, writing the very evening of the ordination, that "Mr. Ware who loved & was loved by his people to an exceeding extent was there in his own pulpit to charge his successor. He had to set his face like a flint to prevent himself from being perfectly overpowered with emotion."[16] His own feelings, too were deep. "They were all my heart could wish . . . I got along pretty well with everything 'till Mr. Dewey's Right Hand of Fellowship. And here was such an outpouring of affection & confidence, of natural emotion & tenderness and pathos, that my heart was stirred from its foundations & poured itself out in floods from my eyes. Unmanly it was. But I have not wept so since I was a child."[17] Having written these two letters to his father and his sister that evening after the events, Henry Bellows woke the next morning with a rather strange feeling. "To wake up in the morning & find myself the pastor of a church in this great city. I don't know how I got here. It is a dream. And what is not? My world is a dream land."[18]

On Sunday morning, 6 January 1839, the newly ordained minister of the First Congregational Church mounted the pulpit to deliver his first sermon. Bellows used a text from II Corinthians 4:5, "For we preach not ourselves, but Christ Jesus the Lord & ourselves your servants for Jesus' sake." Bellows made a few remarks about the recent ordination service, mentioned that he had spoken in the pulpit twice before, but only as "fellow creatures and fellow Christians. I now look upon a congregation of friends—whose hearts are open to me—whose homes will welcome me, whose warmth will support me." Then he spoke with "the voice of a stranger" but now he spoke "with the voice of a shepherd." Bellows told of the sorrows that they would share together as minister and people when even the Christian Gospel offered little consolation. But he saw in the future more joy than sorrow. "I feel that my profession is one of peculiar beauty &

happiness . . . The profession is a joyous one. It has the smile of heaven & the smile of man upon it."[19]

After Dr. Follen's experience in trying to collect his salary on time and with any sort of regularity, the more practical Henry Bellows was more cautious. Five weeks after his ordination, eight of the trustees of the society drew up a document which Bellows kept in his possession which certified that the trustees of the society would pay Bellows "the sum of Twenty-five hundred Dollars, and the same amount annually thereafter, payable quarterly." Dated 8 February 1839, the document was signed by Robert Ainslee, Thomas Tileston, Benjamin Wheelwright, W. W. Russel, Winthrop Gray, Joel Stone, Daniel Stanton, and Charles I. Francis, who also placed the seal of the church on the document to make it official. This document made the relationship in regard to salary very formal. Informality of payment had plagued the church previously.[20]

The work of the church went well. Bellows believed that "his sermons have assumed a new character." Each week he poured out his whole soul in a sermon to his people. "But I am sure it has not been in vain. My people are alive, the church full, everything flourishing."[21] Yet he had spells of depression, probably from overwork. He was not well for a fortnight, "overworked with sermon writing & visiting, dining out & passing the late evening hours in crowded rooms & getting to bed at a time not before twelve or one o'clock is enough to beat any man out." He felt that he was "suffering from a reaction to this tremendous excitement." He was possessed of "an obstinate gloom" which was "excluding every ray of light from heaven or face of man or woman."[22]

Bellows appeared to be a great success in his position as minister of the church. "I only pray for strength to judge myself not as the world judgeth. Every pew in the body of the house is already sold or let. My galleries which were never occupied are fast filling up. I find myself very unexpectedly quite famous . . . But Mr. Dewey tries to make me see that I have to be resigned."[23]

To improve his living conditions Bellows moved out of his single room on Greenwich Street to a larger suite of rooms at Mrs. Eaton's on nearby Houston Street. He described his new apartment as "a large square room of lofty ceiling . . . a white marble fireplace . . . a carpet of a genteel sort of buff & black—whose beauty you may reckon by its cost of about $60." On this carpet in the center of the room was a large "mahogany study table covered with a black cloth, able to sustain a cart-load of books of reference & papers—

while the drawers contain all the private writings." He possessed "a curious black-walnut study chair" which adorned the center of the room, and he also had a small French bedstead and a large washing apparatus. "In form," he said, "the whole thing is perfect & will reconcile one to a bachelor-state till—I get married."[24]

It was well that Henry Bellows's efforts at success were met reciprocally by the members of the congregation, for the church had fallen on difficult days. On the positive side, however, the climate for Unitarianism in New York City was more affirmative than the atmosphere of anti-Unitarianism which had prevailed in the city when William Ware made his pioneering effort. When Ware came to the city in 1821 the Unitarian controversy which had waxed hot in New England while he was a boy had died down in New England. But New York City was not New England, and the heat of the controversy had spread to the Middle Atlantic States and the rest of the country. Ware had been a brave pioneer. Even when Orville Dewey came to the Second Church in 1835 the situation had radically changed and Unitarianism by that time had taken a more respectable place among the older and more conservative denominations of the city's inhabitants. Follen had gotten into controversies largely about social and political issues rather than strictly theological ones, and the more orthodox clergy were beginning to thaw toward their Unitarian brethren. That was certainly not the case during the period of the founding of the church. Bellows, therefore, found himself swimming with the tide of public opinion rather than against it.

When Bellows came to New York a reform movement within the Unitarian denomination had already begun to manifest itself. This new movement involved primarily that most interesting doctrine called Transcendentalism. Follen had been a Transcendentalist and was well known to the leaders in Boston and Concord. But Follen's influence was not important in this area of spiritual idealism in New York City. In July of 1838, just three months before Henry Bellows came to New York City at the invitation of the board of trustees of the First Church to "be heard in the pulpit," Ralph Waldo Emerson had rocked the Unitarian world— and the academic world in addition—with his radical "Divinity School Address," in which he claimed that Unitarianism and orthodox Christianity, alike, were too concerned with the established institutions of religion. Emerson told the seniors of the Harvard Divinity School to look within themselves to find religion. This movement of inner mysticism begun by Emerson was to be a subject of deep concern for the next two decades. Bellows himself was deeply moved by this eloquent address which was so influential in changing the thinking of many Unitarian ministers. But over the next two decades he reached some conclusions in opposition to the anti-institutionalism and the looseness of Transcendentalism which came forth in a very mature statement in the "Suspense of Faith," which he delivered in 1859 at the same Divinity School.

Many years later Bellows was to state that his early success in the city was due to the fact that he did not take sides in these religious controversies. He had to preach to convince, to convert, and to fight the worldliness, bigotry, conformity, and materialism around him.[25] Thinking about these early days forty years later Bellows was to say that "I had from the beginning a great sense of the duty of making every sermon the best I could write, and of preaching a new sermon at least every Sunday morning." He felt the Sunday evening service was not as important, and he was willing to use an old sermon for this service. "During the first ten years of my ministry I was an indefatigable visitor; knew every family, I might almost say intimately, and laid the foundations of personal friendships that have never declined."[26] He believed that God was the source of his strength: "The truth is, Divine Providence has led me by a way I knew not, and blessed me with a rigid discipline, a furnishing of rich opportunity, a fulcrum of influence in my pulpit, a position as your minister in this central seat of power, New York, that have elicited every faculty, aptitude, affection, sympathy I possessed, and enlisted every drop of blood in my veins, and every throb of my heart, in a most rewarding service."[27]

The strain on Bellows's physical and intellectual energies as a result of all of this activity were severe. While his native physical weakness had been largely overcome during his college days, Bellows was still not of a vigorous constitution. He appears to have been subject to tonsilitis and at least two major illnesses a year which would keep him in bed for several weeks. Sometimes he was so exhausted from the nervous tension of writing his sermons and straining for new ideas that he would pace up and down in his study for days without writing down a single idea. He continually drove himself, refusing to give way to what he conceived to be his own weakness, intellectual emptiness, and ineptitude. It never seems to have occurred to him that his difficulties might have been simple and normal nervous exhaustion, the best cure for which would have been to let up on the pressures and to find some sort of relaxation. As he looked back on these early years, he said, "I wonder now that I did

not kill myself by this ignorant persistence in attempting to work
when I ought to have been in bed or at play, and I mention it only as
a warning to others."[28]

My Old Flame

Marriage was very much in the mind of Henry W. Bellows. Not
much has been known of his days of courtship or of the various
women who interested him. The short biographies of Bellows simply
mention that he married Eliza Townsend, the daughter of one of his
prominent parishioners, in August of 1839. But the love trail which
Mr. Bellows pursued which ended with Miss Townsend is far more
complicated, and is documented by letters on the face of which Dr.
Bellows in later years wrote these words: "To be burned without
being opened in case of my death," and "Confidential and not to be
read by anyone. HWB" They revealed nothing scandalous, but show
the more human side of the young minister.

His mature romances probably started after his brother Edward
was lost in the snow in Michigan, when Stella Hayward, who had
been engaged to Edward, for very understandable reasons turned
some of her thwarted affections to Henry after the death of his twin
brother. Here again is an example of how the two brothers were
substituted for each other. After Edward's death Stella wrote many
letters to Henry, and although we do not possess Henry's letters to
her, Stella's letters to him are filled with devotion and well wishes.
How far the romance progressed one can only surmise. Stella died
shortly after Henry moved to New York. Henry's father wrote him
on a sad day of 17 May 1839 "that the village bell is now tolling for
Stella, 'poor and much beloved Stella.' We rejoice at her release from
bodily and mental suffering."[1] But knowing Henry's concepts about
what marriage ought to be, it is easy to surmise that little Stella
scarcely would have filled his criteria for a wife. She was a small-
town girl and Henry had once said that the only woman he would
ever marry would be "a highly educated and intellectual female."[2]

It is unknown how his Boston love affair came about. At the
beginning of December Henry had been invited to preach to the
Young Men's Benevolent Society in Boston,[3] and had pleaded,
unsuccessfully, for the hand of a Miss "C." Miss "C" does not mean
very much until one realizes by a perusal of the Bellows Papers that
Miss "C" was none other than Miss Mary Channing, the daughter of
William Ellery Channing, the minister of the Federal Street Church
in Boston, and the founder of Bellows's church in New York.

Mary Channing Eustis, Oil Portrait, Courtesy of Mary Channing Schumacher, New York City

Evidently Henry had decided to ask for the hand of this seemingly beautiful twenty-year-old girl without ever having discussed this matter with her, by writing a letter to her through her father. This may appear to be incredible, but Henry tells the story in a letter dated from Boston 27 December 1838. "I kept my appointment with the Doctor at 4 o'clock . . . As luck would have it just as I was approaching the house, I met the fair author of all these troubles, herself. *I had not seen her before.* She greeted me very unsuspectingly, asked when I arrived, how long I should stay, whether I was coming to see them etc. . . . I replied that I was just

going to see her father! She regretted that she must be absent and
said—'Do come again.' " Bellows describes how with trembling
hands he rang the bell and the "everlasting delay" with which the
porter answered the call. He was ushered into the parlor. There were
"some interesting conversations about the weather" and then "the
Dr. proceeded to state the substance of his letter to me" which had
been directed to Walpole and which Henry had not yet received.
Doctor Channing said that "both he and his wife thought this
daughter too young to marry, that they could not bear the thought
of parting with her, that they had cherished the expectations of
having her with them for some years—*still* that they thot themselves
bound to respect their daughter's rights—that their happiness was &
should be a secondary consideration—that they felt themselves
bound neither to *encourage* nor *discourage* any person who should
aspire to her hand—that they had no personal objections to me—
that they should leave the matter entirely with me & their daughter."

Bellows protested to Doctor Channing that his daughter at
twenty was of marriageable age. He also said that he would pursue
the matter further. "I intend taking all future steps . . . I mean to
satisfy myself fully as to the character & disposition of this young
creature, and if she proves to be what I think she is, no effort of mine
will be spared to secure her."[4]

After his ordination, Bellows commented on the events of late
December in Boston and reported that he was now attempting to
bring this matter with regard to Mary Channing to a satisfactory
conclusion. "I have determined after deliberate consideration, that if
this fair creature is adapted to my wants & I to hers, she knows it by
this time, altho' she may not have confessed it to herself. And if she
says 'No' to my proposals, I shall think it sufficient evidence that we
are not made for each other."[5] On 7 January the Boston writer, Mrs.
George Lee, indicated for the first time in a letter that the mysterious
Miss "C" was none other than Mary Channing. Bellows obviously
asked the romantically inclined Mrs. Lee to be the intermediary in
his suit for the hand of Mary. In January he got back an answer that
obviously did not please him although he accepted it
philosophically. He wrote, "I received just such an answer as I
should have expected, one that raises the girl in my estimation &
gives me as much encouragement as I ought to receive. She pleads
her youth and present happiness . . . ignorance of me, etc." She
"can't say what a long time acquaintance might do, thinks that I
should be dissatisfied to receive any other answer . . . asks whether
I cannot draw my own conclusions from the statements." Henry did

draw his own conclusions, and in spite of several more communications from Mrs. Lee who acted as a devoted intermediary nothing came of this "love affair." Finally Bellows admitted, "I believe I have acted like a fool, but I don't know."[6]

The letter from Mrs. Lee that Bellows indicated was to be burned in case of his death implicates Mrs. Lee more than Henry Bellows. The part that bothered him about this letter was not his unsuccessful suit for the hand of Mary Channing but the fact that Mrs. Lee made some rather disparaging remarks about the Channings to give some solace to the young unsuccessful suitor. She wrote: "Whoever married Mary will marry all the whimsies & peculiarities of her family—& hard enough to bear they will be. . . . You can submit to all the delays and requisitions & cross-questionings that will be eternally taking place. You can serve twice seven years . . . & what will you be, during that time? A poor, spiritless, cringing lover—broken down in the glorious right of acting independently—of feeling on a perfect equality with the lady of your choice."[7]

Bellows finally admitted that what had happened was for the best. To his sister, Mrs. Dorr, he wrote: "it has blown wholly over & left me without a scar. I am somewhat ashamed of myself for having been so much deceived about my own heart, for really I thought myself the victim of a true passion. But I had only been dazzled by the circumstances about this fair creature, who is really worthy of great regard, but who would not I think make me truly happy."[8]

While the love affair in Boston was still in its climactic moments Bellows was also aware of the attention which an eligible young minister could receive from the young women in the metropolis of New York. He found "the young ladies . . . the most enthusiastic, dear creatures." And he commented with true valor, "I cannot marry them all." He stated that the whole parish—except the standing committee—was interested in his marital status. As a young minister he created a flurry among the mothers of prospective brides.[9] Evidently Henry did a few things to encourage this amorous interest among some of the young women. One letter in the Bellows Papers is somewhat mystifying. It is a letter from a Mrs. Ireland who has just lost her husband and who had several children. Perhaps the language is only the enthusiastic sentimental language of the day, and perhaps Henry did nothing to encourage her. But the letter shows at least how she felt about the matter, and it must have been rather typical of the eligible New York ladies. "My breast was so full yesterday, that I could not say half I wished to—and even now I can not say what I

Mrs. Eliza Townsend Bellows, Oil Portrait at Walpole, Courtesy of Mrs. Anne Tower

feel. . . . You cannot know how much your love and sympathy are to me, and how grateful I am to God that he has so permitted us to love each other."[10] One ought not to draw conclusions, but one might ask whether or not these are the sentiments of a widow being consoled or thoughts of love deeper than mere consolation.

It was on the evening of his ordination on 2 January 1839 that Henry Bellows met Eliza Nevins Townsend. We know about this meeting only because in 1869 on the thirtieth anniversary of their meeting Henry wrote Eliza a letter and recalled their first meeting three decades previously. (It was also to be the last anniversary of

*Henry Whitney Bellows. Oil Portrait at Walpole, Courtesy of Mrs.
Anne Tower*

their meeting that they celebrated because Eliza died in August of
1869.) The first meeting took place at the reception after the
ordination at the home of Mrs. Philip Schuyler. "I recall every
circumstance connected with the event that fixed so happily my
destiny," Bellows wrote. He went on to describe his first vision of
Eliza. "The pale lilac dress, the long curls in front, the modest &
spiritual expression, the mingled elegance & unworldliness, the
large, soft eyes, the clear red & white complexion; the gentle sadness,
the unspoiled, aspiring, nunlike qualities that marked you out in my
esteem for a young minister's wife. What an eventful evening for us

both." Bellows added, "My introduction to you was indeed the beginning of my life in New York, now so far advanced, & perhaps so nearly complete."[11]

Henry Bellows was in a romantic mood since his expression of love to Mary Channing had been unrequited. Some might call his new love for Eliza Townsend a "rebound." It began in February 1839, and after a few meetings it was carried on by correspondence for a time. The first indication that something had smitten Henry is in a letter dated 22 February 1839 to Eliza Townsend in which Bellows says, "I have watched you through the short period of our acquaintance with the eye of an eagle looking for his nest." But he also wanted Eliza to know that his "eye has been sharpened by long reflection upon woman's nature," and added, "I feel more respect for myself, that I have loved you." The young preacher also commented upon her suitability not only as *his* wife, but as a *minister's* wife. "My daily pursuits are those that you love. There is no part of my profession in which you could not support and assist me."[12]

It took Eliza just three days after the writing of Henry's letter to pen an answer. She still addressed him properly as "my dear friend." She spoke properly of her appreciation of his regard for her. But then she egged him on. She wanted them both to "drink at the fountain of truth and wisdom," and she wrote that she would "hear with gratification and pleasure whatever you may impart to me of the fruit of your studies and meditations." Then, not showing her hand too much, in the fashion of a devoted parishioner, asked him if he would loan her "at a convenient time, your sermon on the text 'I am not ashamed of the Gospel'."[13]

Henry, this time, was really smitten, and love letters flew back and forth. Henry was busy writing to his correspondents and close friends about this latest passion of his heart. To William Silsbee he wrote, "She is what you have always heard me say I should love. Born & educated in luxury & refinement and yet a child of nature — gentle & decided, bookish & retiring, musical, spiritual, quiet & deep feelings . . . fair haired, blue, long loose eyes, Blonde, neither short nor tall . . . not handsome but better than this."[14] To his sister in Boston he added a few more details. "She is a decided person & looks, thoughtful & even anxious. Her life for three years has been stormy. She has the expression of one who has been tried & who finds her happiness within."[15] Writing to his mother in Walpole he further expressed himself. "She is the eldest daughter (there being one other) of a most admirable & well-known merchant in this city, a man of great wealth & consideration, having done more for public improvement perhaps than any other man in the country." He also told his mother that she must keep the secret for several weeks.[16] By the end of May he felt that September would be the time selected for the wedding and he must be content to wait. "The only objection I have is that courting takes up so much time . . . that I want to soon have it over with."[17]

Bellows went away for the summer months, probably to Walpole. His good friend Samuel Osgood preached for him in the New York church where Osgood met Eliza Townsend. His first feeling of distrust of what Henry was doing in getting engaged was overcome. Osgood wrote: "I feared somewhat for you when I heard the report of your engagement. Rumor said you had bound yourself to a New York fashionable & although I did not believe you had wedded yourself to folly and superficiality I thought you might have been somewhat dazzled by some showy beauty who in spite of her fascination would never be a rational wife. But at a glance I saw my mistake & knew, that it was a character of reality and not of mere show that had charmed you."[18]

The date of the wedding had now been set for 13 August. The exact time was uncertain because Orville Dewey, whom Henry wished to have perform the ceremony, was still in the West. But if Dewey was not heard from he believed he would ask William Ware to come down from Boston to perform the ceremony. Promising to come to Walpole after the wedding he wrote his mother that although Eliza was brought up in luxury "she is a sensible & simple-hearted girl who measures things by their true worth,"[19] alluding no doubt to the fact that the Bellows's home in Walpole would be much simpler than the Townsend mansion on Bond Street.

On the eve of his marriage Bellows has some thoughts about his bride and himself. He felt more for her than for himself in regard to this marriage, "How do women find the courage to marry?" Yet he had some self doubts, healthy ones, no doubt, "I have learned more and more to distrust myself. I observe weaknesses in my own character which have only developed themselves under the warmth of this hot climate of love which makes me start and resolve upon more watchfulness."[20]

Henry and Eliza were married on the evening of 13 August 1839 in New York—a simple ceremony. On August twenty-third they were in Trenton Falls on their honeymoon, then on to Walpole where the happy young groom proudly introduced his bride to the Bellows clan. Henry was pleased at how easily Eliza fit into the Walpole scene. He waxed romantic: "I thought I loved her pretty well before we were married, but it seems to me as if I had just discovered how lovely she is. She makes me completely happy & I do not think that I am easily satisfied."[21]

CHAPTER TWO

The Channing of His Time?

We Never Worshiped There Again

After forty years of perspective, Henry Bellows characterized the caliber of the people who made up his original congregation of All Souls:

> The enlightened, high-toned, dignified men and women who first gathered around Dr. Channing and Henry Ware, when in 1819 they first raised the banner of our unpopular faith in New York, gave from the beginning not only a special and a vigorous character to this congregation: they stamped it with a type it has never lost, but has only more and more perfected, as a church where intellectual life was to subsist in the closest amity with religious faith and reverence, where false arts and mere popularity-making policies were not to enter, where numbers were not to be mistaken for weight, and where personal character, measured by universal standards, and not by any technical scale or test, was to be honored and trusted above all professions or subscriptions to articles of faith.[1]

But even in such a congregation Bellows had to face practical matters almost immediately. When Bellows took up his pastorate in New York the society was heavily in debt, and now that they had to pay a regular salary to a settled minister, the financial burdens upon the church's substantially reduced income were intolerable. As it had in 1823, the church was again running at an estimated annual deficit of $1,000. There was also the nagging problem of the church building itself. Some wanted to move immediately, probably arguing that the cost would, in the long run, be less than attempting to maintain the present edifice. Some were convinced that the building was not safe. But others did not agree. In light of the church's present financial state, they felt, it would be best to make do with the building until the financial prospects were brighter, and when truly suitable land and architectural design could be found. There were also those who were sentimentally attached to the present building, and who simply did not want to leave it.

Almost from the beginning, Henry Bellows was involved in these arguments. Fully aware of the enormous dimensions of the task before him—in cementing the society back together and rallying all of its resources; in leading it toward the wisest decisions; in providing spiritual, moral, and intellectual leadership for the members; in giving out a wide range of pastoral care; in helping to broaden its membership, and to establish its good name in the community—Bellows doubted his capacity to meet the challenge. It would have been a major task for a much stronger and more experienced man; and Bellows, only twenty-four and only just embarking on his ministry, claimed no surety about being able to realize all of his hopes for the church, particularly in the face of the severe competition that his esteemed colleague, Orville Dewey, represented. Nevertheless, Bellows did have high hopes, and having committed himself to the cause, he plunged himself into exhausting labors.

Bellows dutifully preached twice each Sunday, but as he stated, only to a handful of worshipers in the evening. This represented a substantial contrast to the fully attended evening lectures of Charles Follen. Bellows did not attempt to write two sermons a week as Ware had done. Instead, he labored hard over a new one for each Sunday morning. In between his sermon-writing and his diverse administrative duties—such as overseeing the music, the free school, and discussing various matters with the trustees—Bellows made it a deliberate practice to visit every family in his growing congregation frequently each year.

Few, if any, of his congregation were aware of the supreme exertion their pastor was making on their behalf. In the pulpit he appeared to be a natural orator, "his voice was sonorous and musical, his gestures natural, and his imagination kindled as his subject developed under the heat of his earnest thought and feeling."[2] There was nothing perfunctory about his preaching, and every sermon was a serious treatment of some real question that was on people's minds. To his hearers, Bellows always "came into the pulpit full of animation and enthusiasm . . . he made everything so vivid that he captivated everyone."[3] Even out of the pulpit Bellows's easy but earnest sociability and dedicated efforts to visit and entertain his parishioners soon solidified the members of his church in affection and loyalty to him, and more and more they joined together in turning to him for leadership. Moreover, the arduous pains he took to labor over his sermons began to draw others to the church.

The financial situation also steadily improved. By the annual meeting in 1839 the year's deficit was down $540 through new subscriptions and other revenues; the special collection fund for the benefit of the church was discontinued, and assessment rates increased. This latter action holds special significance, for it reveals the society's confidence that pews could be sold and rented even at the higher rate. Further, though many times during the previous years the trustees had tried to raise assessments to 15 percent, the membership could never agree on the matter, and the existing 12½ percent rate had been maintained through repeated voting on the matter. The board of trustees adopted some procedures for making the collection of pew rentals and assessments more businesslike. The treasurer, John T. Balch, was authorized to collect subscriptions to help the church meet its financial deficiency, and a new campaign to sell or rent empty pews was mapped out.

The campaign was eminently successful, and by October 1840, over 124 of the church's 161 pews were sold or rented. Many of the defectors to the Second Church returned: in addition to the Elihu Townsends, George Dummer, Moses Grinnell, and George Holland, among others, had returned by 1840 and, by 1845, Benjamin Armitage had returned.

There can be little doubt that the "friendly rivalry" between Dewey of the Second Church and Bellows of the First afforded Dewey the worst of the bargain. Though Bellows never deviated in his expressed admiration for the older man, even long after Dewey removed from the city the steady and rapid waxing of Bellows's popularity cannot but have threatened Dewey's prestige which the latter had enjoyed for about seven uninterrupted years.

By contrast with his ministry in New Bedford, Orville Dewey had enjoyed great popularity and success ever since he had come to New York in the fall of 1834. Measured against the preaching style of his predecessor, William Lunt, Dewey's orations from the pulpit were a thrilling relief to the small and struggling congregation of the Second Church. Dewey's only competition was William Ware, whose sermon delivery was decidedly inferior to his own, and even before he was installed permanently in the Prince Street Church, Dewey had drawn eager listeners from the First Church. Spurred by the unequivocal evidence of his success, Dewey waxed even more eloquent in the pulpit, and his social mingling among his parishioners was touched with an almost puffed-up air of confidence. He was asked to join the Sketch Club—a small group of eminent artists and writers—by some of his distinguished congregation, and thus became socially acquainted with other prominent citizens in the metropolis. The social isolation which their Unitarianism had caused Lunt and Ware became far less of an obstacle to Orville Dewey, and new converts to Unitarianism were

Orville Dewey, D.D., All Souls Archives

quickly gained through this widening of Dewey's social circle. Less than a year after Dewey's installation, Ware had abdicated his pulpit, and his temporary successor soon proved to be an even better boon for Dewey than Ware had been, for Follen's premature antislavery views had brought a bonus of members into Dewey's congregation. When his church burned to the ground in 1837, Dewey found that it was a blessing in disguise, for his sermons at

Stuyvesant Institute drew large crowds from the non-Unitarian population and gained many new converts.

It was while Dewey was preaching at Stuyvesant Institute that the young, wet-behind-the-ears Henry Bellows came to New York to candidate, and Bellows lived at the same rooming house as the Deweys'. Dewey liked the young man's modest, self-effacing manner, particularly since it was accompanied by a greatly admiring attitude toward himself as senior Unitarian minister of the city. Treated thus as an esteemed "Master," Dewey quickly adopted the young man as his protege, and encouraged him to accept the permanent pastorship of the Chambers Street church. After all, Dewey could do worse than to have a novice fresh out of theological school as his only "competition." Dewey probably never dreamed that underneath the young Bellows's humble and worshipful manner lay an intense ambition coupled with an indomitable confidence and canny sophistication about just what was what. In his paternal insistence that the twenty-four-year-old fledgling, Henry Bellows, take on the small, divided struggling church on Chambers Street, Dewey could not have foreseen that his own career would be severely altered as a consequence.

The young Bellows was a diplomat par excellence. With the same candid and amiable charm that united the congregation of the First Church, he cemented friendly ties between his own and Dewey's church. As Dewey began to lose some of his members to his junior colleague, Bellows took care to continue to seek out Dewey's advice, counsel, and direction, in all matters, as though Dewey were immutably the master. Thus, there grew up between Bellows and Dewey what became known as a "friendly rivalry." But there can be little doubt that this "friendly rivalry" afforded Dewey the worst of the bargain. On 3 May 1839—just four months after Bellows's ordination—Dewey and his expanded congregation dedicated their fine new building—which they had named "The Church of the Messiah"—on Broadway, just below Astor Place. Dr. Dewey gave the sermon, and the former pastor, William Lunt, Dr. Parkman of Boston, and Henry Bellows also participated in the service. At that time, Bellows's powers had in no way come to light.

Within the next year or so, though, the results of Bellows's labors were revealed, and put a heavy strain on Dewey. Dewey worked harder, but doubted himself more. As early as 1841, there were signs that Bellows's ambitious confidence and seemingly tireless efforts were beginning to wear on Dewey, for, in October of that year, Dewey suffered a breakdown of mental health in which he found himself unable to write sermons and suffered what may have been severe migraine headaches. His symptoms were an exact duplicate of his performance ten years earlier under pressures at The New Bedford Church. He left his pulpit temporarily to recuperate,

The Church of the Messiah, Engraving by J.W. Orr, Courtesy of the New-York Historical Society, New York City

spending the next two years traveling about Europe and returning in August of 1843 to his country home in Sheffield, Massachusetts.

There was also another difference between Henry Bellows and Orville Dewey. Dewey tended to lecture on politics in the pulpit much to the discomfiture of some of his parishioners. Bellows, on the other hand, typical of his attitude that there is truth in almost every position, refused to pontificate politically from the pulpit. In 1840 he felt that some people were trying to get him to commit himself on politics. "But they are mistaken quite in their man." He wrote, "I have no party opinions, but speak entirely without reference to Whig or Tory upon the merits of every question . . . If one looks at all questions from a moral point of view, he will be apt to blend the maxims of all parties and confound various policies."[4]

After the burning of the steamship *Lexington* in January 1840 in Long Island Sound,[5] Bellows had the difficult responsibility of comforting Mrs. Follen and her small son Charles who had remained in New York. They had been ill when Dr. Follen went back to Lexington, Massachusetts, to dedicate the new church which he had designed and of which he was the pastor. Bellows said that "the dreadful disaster has overwhelmed our community with sorrow . . . Dr. Follen is gone. What a loss for our country & our denomination. He was a marked man, an altogether peculiar spirit; so single hearted a lover of truth & of man." Bellows had two long interviews with Mrs. Follen. The first, he stated, was "the most painful of my life, the other more calm and supportable." He termed Mrs. Follen a noble woman but commented that she is "too loving, too true, too closely bound to her husband to feel or affect a cheerful submission." He had his own doubts at this time about the value of resignation to what is called the will of God. But he admired her courage.[6]

Just after Follen died, Bellows's father passed away peacefully in Walpole where Henry traveled by way of Boston. As this was just a few weeks later over the same water route that had been fatal to Dr. Follen, one can sympathize with the expressed fear of Eliza Bellows that he should make this trip in the middle of winter, over the Sound and over rough roads at night by stagecoach. But she trusted "Providence & my Henry's discretion."[7] Eliza was now pregnant, and Henry went to Walpole with some misgivings.

During her pregnancy Eliza went through a medical procedure often used at that time. She had a severe cough, and the doctor bled her to cure the cough. Due to her cough, bleeding, and subsequent weakness she had to miss church while Henry was in Walpole. A minister's wife's duties weighed heavily upon her. But she wrote

Henry that dutifully she got two of his sermons from a drawer and read them in the course of that Sunday. "I regret much that I could not take my wonted church seat, but church is really one of the worst places for a cold."[8] She also expressed strong feelings to Henry about the supply preachers while he was in Walpole. Mr. Holland had preached on the third Sunday in February on "Duty." She went further to comment about Mr. Day, "If there be necessity to close Chambers St. doors for once, I wouldn't have *Day* preach if he would."[9] Henry, meanwhile, was furious that Eliza has been bled to cure her cough, "It is a practice our best Boston physicians repudiate except in extreme cases," and added, "I shall not consent to it again without further advice than Dr. W's."[10]

By the second week in June Eliza was in labor, and Henry penned a letter while the long process of labor was taking place. At the end of the letter there is a joyous postscript, "Dear William! All is well. I, too, am a father. . . . Lizzie has given birth to a fine fat boy of near 10 pounds weight within 20 minutes, I have not yet been permitted to see Mother or child. I am wild with gratitude & joy."[11] The boy, born on 8 June 1840, was named Edward Stearns Bellows after Henry's deceased twin brother.

In February of 1841 it was necessary for Henry to make the trip to Walpole to pay up his father's debts and to settle the estate. His absence made him contemplate the role of his wife in the parish. He missed Eliza deeply. He wanted to increase their attachment and help organize her life better. He gave some typical advice: "I think that you should methodize your cares a little more. Make household duties more methodical & throw off anxieties & feel as if the *business* of each day, were reading, thought, spiritual intercourse, that we might be more together in thought & in person . . . For aught I see, you might have your regular hours of reading & study with me . . . You wear yourself out with anxiety. Your body would not be weary if your intellect was occupied, instead of your nerves . . . I think we ought to visit more together. Somehow I find myself going about my pastoral work as if you had little to do with it. This is not well. It stops up our common source of sympathy & erects our partition wall."[12]

June was to bring another tragedy to the Bellows family. Edward Stearns Bellows, named for his uncle lost in the snows of Michigan, died a year and a day after he was born—on 9 June 1841. Edward had convulsions and never came out of them. Many friends and relations wrote letters of sympathy. But there was no visible reaction from Henry until the end of June. "We hardly yet realize our desolation . . . We wonder that we miss him so little, we wonder that we can be as happy as we are; but the mind soon accommodates itself to what is irrevocable and unalterable. We would give all that we have or hope in this world to have him back . . . & yet knowing that this is impossible, we strive to enjoy what remains to us. Life is at best a torrent that soon runs out."[13]

By the end of November 1841, Henry Bellows was writing to Dewey, who again was away from New York in Paris, that Bellows's parish had about decided to build a new church edifice. "You have seen the last of Chambers Street, I think,"[14] he wrote.

Some gossip was going around New York about a change in the position of Mr. Dewey in regard to the church. Bellows shared this gossip with Dewey, "It forms the staple of conversation when Unitarians meet the enemy, 'Episcopalian or Presbyterian'—that 'Dr. Dewey has turned Epis[copalian], is about returning home to take orders.' I have been anxiously applied to by dozens to trace the origin of this slander & one of my chief occupations lately has been to deny it point blank and heap suitable epithets upon that supposition."[15]

In March of 1842 the New York community had a series of lectures by Ralph Waldo Emerson. His topic was, "The Times." Bellows said that Emerson "was greatly surprised & gratified by the reception he met in this very heart of custom and materialism. His lectures were well and choicely attended & I never felt his power and purity so much." Henry was also gratified to have had one personal conversation with the Sage of Concord. "He opened himself unreservedly & made me ashamed of the light words & suspicion with which he is assessed by men so infinitely his inferiors in faith & love & hope."[16]

Eliza was again in labor in April. Writing became a kind of custom of Bellows to relieve his anxiety. He told of the birth of his second son. "Eliza is this minute delivered of a beautiful boy. I have not yet seen her or the child. . . . I hear the little blessing's hearty lungs striving to catch the breath of life. It is the sweetest sound my ears have known since our dear Eddy's voice was in there. . . . I have wished for a boy, another boy, as if it were to fill the earthly place, but not to displace the memory of our innocent in Heaven."[17] This boy, born on 12 April 1842, was bequeathed three given names, two from Eliza's family and one from Henry's; Russell Nevins Townsend Bellows.

On his sixty-second birthday, 7 April 1842, William Ellery Channing preached his last sermon in the Federal Street Church in

Boston. He took a tour of the Berkshires for his health that fall and on October second he breathed his last in Bennington, Vermont, with these audible words, "I have received many messages from the spirit."[18] There was a funeral service in the Federal Street Church in Boston and the bells of the whole city (including those on the Catholic cathedral) tolled as Channing's coffin passed on its way to the cemetery. Jonathan Goodhue wrote in his diary, "A character justly and very extensively honored and admired."[19]

The Unitarians of the New York area naturally wanted to plan a service to honor the "Great Doctor." Three men were appointed from each of the three churches—the First and Second Churches in Manhattan and the Unitarian Society of Brooklyn. They met on October ninth to plan a memorial service. Present were Robert Ainslee, William F. Cary, and Benjamin F. Wheelwright from the First Church, Zebedee Cook, Jr., Isaac Green Pearson, and David Felt from the Second Church, and Joseph L. Lord, J. Henry Farley, and Luke W. Thomas from the Brooklyn Society. They voted to hold the special service at the Church of the Messiah on Thursday evening, 13 October at 7 P.M. Since the logical person to deliver the eulogy, Dr. Orville Dewey, was in Europe at that time they voted to ask Henry Bellows to make the address; Frederick A. Farley of the Brooklyn Society and the Reverend Andrew Preston Peabody, who was officiating at the Church of the Messiah, were asked to assist. William Cullen Bryant, who at this time was an attendant at both the Manhattan churches, composed a hymn for the service.

Bellows was quite apprehensive about his talk. He knew that Channing's memorial service would draw large crowds. The honor bestowed upon the young minister was outweighed, in Bellows's mind, by the tremendous responsibility it imposed upon him. Nevertheless, Bellows set himself to composing as sincere and worthy a eulogy of the great man as he could muster in the short time alloted him. Bellows was very much like Channing in his view of Unitarianism, so he felt empathy with his idol, and all who heard his sermon that Thursday evening were deeply impressed.

The discourse was full of youthful enthusiasm. It was quite oratorical and flowery even compared with Bellows's later style. He spoke of Channing's love of liberty, his various services to the community. But Bellows also spoke of Channing "as a Christian, and a Unitarian Christian. He looked to the gospel as the only regenerating influence in society, and to his own peculiar views of Christianity, must we attribute the force and direction, of his philanthropy."[20] But although Channing's views were Unitarian and he had been a controversialist, "he rose above barriers of sect. . . . Philanthropy belongs to no sect—goodness is of no party," said Bellows.[21] He further declared that "Dr. Channing's public character was his private character. He knew no distinction between public and private morality . . . An undisturbed serenity reigned over his soul."[22]

When Bellows had concluded the long address, the reaction of the congregation left no doubt that he had succeeded in his public responsibility to deliver a fine and intelligent discourse. The board of trustees of his church met subsequently, wrote a formal letter of commendation to Bellows, and requested a copy of the sermon for publication. This was the first of Bellows's sermons to be published by the society since his ordination nearly four years before.

Bellows kept up his correspondence with Orville Dewey as the latter made his journey through Europe. Of great interest is Bellows's attempt to bring Orville Dewey up to date on what was happening in the Unitarian denomination in 1843. "You will find a very great change in our denomination when you return," he wrote. Just five years after Emerson's "Divinity School Address," "Transcendentalism has come to a head, I think. There is a strong reaction in favor of Historical Christianity, a conservative spirit has awakened & the Old is engaging attention & reverence." Bellows noted that preaching had taken an evangelical turn among the best of the Unitarian preachers. He also noted that he believed that "a truly religious spirit is diffusing itself through our churches."[23] He had been more encouraged in this regard than in all the years before.

Dewey returned to his pulpit at the start of the fall season in 1843. A vacation of two full years should have been more than ample for a man ostensibly suffering from a case of overwork and no fundamental organic disease. Yet upon his return, the forty-nine-year-old Dewey found his labors as arduous as before he left. While the bulk of Dewey's congregation remained loyal to him, more and more of the members of the Church of the Messiah were coming over to the First Church.

Late in the fall of 1843 Bellows accepted an invitation to go to Savannah, Georgia. He planned to be away only for one Sunday, but in his final plans he took much longer, leaving on November seventeenth and actually missing three Sundays in the pulpit. His trip had been occasioned by the invitation of Dexter Clapp to preach the sermon at his ordination into the Unitarian ministry on 26 November 1843.[24]

On a side trip with Mr. Gilman to Charleston, South Carolina,

Bellows had met "Mrs. Dr. Channing & my old flame Mrs. Eustis
. . . Our voyage lay among the rice plantations, the Sea Islands, &
the creeks & rivers of the coast." It was, he felt, the most picturesque
sail he had ever made.

To his wife, he wrote: "I had an opportunity of renewing my old
intercourse [not the modern meaning] with Mary Channing, a thing I
have always wished. I confess I took some pains to make her feel a
little regret that matters had turned out as they did!" Was this
malicious on Bellows's part? "But interesting as she is & was, I speak
from the bottom of my soul, my darling Lizzy when I say that the
comparison I could not help but initiate was most largely in favor of
my own darling wife. I bless every day the kind Providence that has
given you to me." Later in the letter after speaking of all of the
beautiful women with whom he had conversations, he wrote, "Mary
& I sat up near midnight upon the guards in deep converse. She
seemed to labor to do away all painful feelings between us."[25]
Bellows's ego is showing. He had been repulsed only four years
before by Mary and her parents. Now he was trying to show Mary
what a bad mistake she had made, and at the same time write to his
wife that he was much happier with her.

The society had thought about selling the church building on
Chambers Street to search for a more suitable location as early as
1836. But for various reasons nothing came of this. At the annual
meeting in 1840, again the issue was raised, this time to be accepted
tentatively by the membership—provided a really suitable location
could be found. A committee was appointed to search for such a
property. But the committee was most unfruitful in finding a
location during the ensuing year, and when the society met again a
year later especially for the purpose of deciding a location, the
committee reported that it had made inquiries, but could arrive at no
satisfactory conclusions. At the 1841 annual meeting a few weeks
later, the society finally authorized the trustees to sell the present
church if ever a suitable new location could be found. The members
had agreed on the general location: it was to be on or near
Broadway, not above Grand Street nor below Franklin Street. So,
once again, the church on Chambers Street was advertised for sale.

This time the search for new premises was undertaken with
more determination. A few months later, in February 1842, Robert
Ainslie, the president of the board, located four lots on Mercer Street
which seemed to fit specifications, and the trustees authorized him to
bid $30,000 for the property. But the property was *not* purchased,
nor a buyer found for the Chambers Street building. The matter

seems to have been dropped entirely for most of the next year, until—in August 1843, just before the church was to open for its fall season—the trustees gathered to resolve that, "in consequence of the state of the roof of the church it is considered unsafe to congregate within for the present"[26] and that, therefore, a temporary hall should be hired.

Earlier in the summer, Mr. Burgyess—the sexton who had replaced Mr. Cochran when the latter resigned in 1840—had attempted to make some repairs on the roof, and he advised the trustees of its precarious state. But a hall was *not* hired for opening Sunday, there still being some contention over the matter among the members of the society. The undecided congregation had their minds made up for them once and for all by a dramatic incident which occurred on one of the first Sundays in September 1843.

In a letter to a ministerial friend Bellows gave the first extant account of the cataclysmic reason for leaving the Chambers Street Church. He wrote, "We have forsaken the old church in Chambers St. (which came near killing me by a fall of plastering during service time)."[27] In 1879, thirty-three years later, he gave a more extended explanation of the church which began to fall apart.

> In September, 1843, when our church had just opened for the season, and the question of leaving it for a hall, pending the erection of a new house of worship, was undecided, there suddenly fell, just toward the close of the public service and in the presence of a full congregation, at least fifty pounds' weight of the cornice of the ceiling, enough to have killed any persons on whom the fragments might have fallen. I remember that I had just concluded the reading of the first line of Andrews Norton's well-known hymn,
> "My God, I thank Thee. May no thought,"—when down, within a foot of my face, fell this thundering mass, lighting upon the communion table below, and in fact, we never worshipped there again.[28]

Mrs. Hubbard was among the astonished worshipers, and reported later that Bellows was seated at the time; having just finished the sermon with the prayer, he was leafing through the hymnal to find the concluding hymn when the huge mass descended: "He arose very much excited and apparently alarmed, announcing the propriety of the congregation dispersing at once as it was unsafe to remain longer in the building."[29] The worshipers immediately disbanded before finishing the remainder of the service, but even then,"no one realized that the congregation were leaving the building for the last time."[30]

The congregation moved to Apollo Hall, a large public auditorium which was used for any and all purposes by anyone who hired it. For this reason, it was less than the most desirable quarters in which the religious society of the First Congregational Church found itself: "frequent evidences of use by Negro minstrels and dramatic companies on Saturday evening were painfully evident on the Sunday morning following."[31] The Apollo Hall was located at 410 Broadway on the East Side between Canal and Walker Streets and could seat 700 persons. The New York Philharmonic Society had held its inaugural concert in the hall only the year before the congregation moved in to make it their temporary quarters.

Henry Bellows was obviously happy to be out of the Chambers Street Church, and even if Apollo Hall was not a church it did provide a temporary home for the congregation. He wrote, "I am now in a large Hall (the Apollo) on Broadway. There I am thronged with hearers—& have commenced a series of doctrinal lectures to last through the winter, Tuesday evening is the third. I endeavor to cram my mind with the subject and then speak extemporare . . . The prospects of a new church brightens."[32]

At the close of the month, the society gathered one evening expressly to discuss whether to sell or to repair the church on Chambers Street. There were many who wished to preserve the original building. "But Mr. Bellows was young and ambitious— perhaps a little impulsive and hasty— and the society had become so much attached to him that they took *pleasure* in gratifying him."[33] Thus, after a somewhat fervent debate, the majority finally decided in favor of selling the building, and for at least the third or fourth time since 1836, the trustees were authorized to sell the church and to look for suitable premises on which to erect a new one.

After deciding that they might as well stay in Apollo Hall rather than look for more dignified quarters, the members initiated a subscription campaign to finance the new enterprise. Again the sale of the church was advertised, but when no takers appeared during the next month, the trustees put the building up for public auction. The minimum price was set at $12,000.

The Walls Are Very Insecure

Although the trustees had hoped to get substantially more than $12,000 when the building was sold at public auction on 15 November 1843, it went to the New York Bank for Savings at the comparatively low price of $12,200.[1] Evidently the weak roof and cornices frightened others as well as the church people.

During the next three months the trustees diligently undertook to find suitable lots within a preferred area, but without success. The matter was postponed until 16 December 1843 at a meeting of the society held shortly after Bellows returned from preaching in Savannah. Additional lots were proposed outside the area originally prescribed by the congregation. This afforded a wider field of uptown possibilities.[2]

The committee then spent the next month arguing about the best site. Finally deciding that that committee never would resolve its differences, the trustees in mid-January 1844 replaced it with another. The new committee consisted of Robert Schuyler, Moses Grinnell, and William Taggard (who by this time had left Orville Dewey's church). Schuyler's choice of the lots on Broadway and Crosby Street (between Prince and Spring Streets) prevailed, and, in February, the agreement with Elihu Townsend for the purchase of this site was closed for the sum of $32,000.[3] The wisdom of purchasing property from a member of the society, and Bellows's father-in-law at that, was questioned when the building project grew into a grotesque and costly comedy of errors. Later, in a moment of

Broadway, New York City, Looking South from Central Park, (1840's), Lithograph by Nathanial Currier, Courtesy of the New-York Historical Society, New York City

great financial peril for the church, Townsend refunded $4,000 of the payments due him on the property.

The search for a new site was also affecting Henry Bellows's purse; he was in financial distress. "On account of the 'transition state' of my society, the church is without any income from pew rents & my salary has been for the present *stopped*. It will all be paid undoubtedly sooner or later, but I am now living upon my father-in-law until I get paid up."[4]

Robert Schuyler headed the building committee, which inquired specifically and expressly into the construction of walls which this time would *support* the roof. Stone walls, the committee felt, would be the most desirable, but these would place the estimated building cost to well above the planned $21,600. Minard Lafever, who was bidding for the architectural business, had called for hollow bricks in the plan he had submitted, and, when he saw the trustees' dilemma, he recommended strongly that hollow bricks be used for the walls— that they were *abundantly* adequate to the support of the building. With this confident assurance, the board hired Lafever for $600. The firm of Frasee and Pierson was hired to do the principal masonry work, and Job Male was hired for the carpentry. Construction was launched as soon as these details had been worked out, some time in late August or early September 1844.

The large audience that Bellows was drawing in Apollo Hall did little to offset the church's growing financial deficit; having barely recovered from its financial ails of 1838, the church now found itself again in a financial hole. At the annual meeting in 1843, operating expenses were estimated to be $3,800 in the red for 1844. Although the society had not been in debt to any *outside* lenders since 1838, it owed a sizable sum to various members who had loaned money to the church over the years, notably to Benjamin Wheelwright. When it had so rudely been forced out of its church building on Chambers Street, the society not only lost the revenues on which it had relied from pew assessments, but also had acquired new out-of-pocket expenses in the hiring of Apollo Hall. With the purchase of the new property and construction costs, the drain on the fiscal resources of the congregation as it approached its annual meeting in 1844 were severe indeed!

The new property was mortgaged for $28,000, $14,000 of it to Elihu Townsend, and another $14,000 to no less a person than John Jacob Astor. To meet the interest payments on these mortgages and to pay the building costs, the trustees juggled the odd and sundry sums which were dribbling in from the sale of the Chambers Street building. Charles Francis gave the treasurer's report at the annual meeting on 23 December 1844, the main issue of which was to rally stronger efforts behind the campaign to raise subscription loans for the building fund.

Minard Lafever, the architect of the new building, was at this time at the height of his powers in New York City. He was born 10 August 1798 near Morristown, New Jersey, a descendant of French Huguenots. When he was nine years of age he moved with his parents to the Finger Lakes region of New York State, near the head of Seneca Lake. When he was eighteen, Lafever walked fifty miles to Geneva, New York, to purchase his first treatise on architecture. There is no evidence that he was anything but self-trained in architectural design. At the age of twenty-six he moved to Newark, New Jersey, and supported himself by working as a carpenter and joiner in the daytime, devoting his evenings to drawing plans for houses and other buildings. In 1829 he published his first book, *The Young Builder's General Instructor*, about the same year that he moved to New York City, 1827 or 1828. He was listed in the city directory as a builder and carpenter until 1831 when he was listed as an architect.

Lafever's biographer, Jacob Landy, says that "Lafever's religious affiliation was Unitarian."[5] This may have been one of the important reasons why he was selected as the architect of the proposed church. Landy also believes that because Lafever was a Unitarian and therefore presumably broad-minded, he was willing to design churches of other denominations. Some of the architects of New York simply would not have designed a church for such a heretical sect as the Unitarians. Richard Upjohn, his contemporary, withdrew from the competition for the design of the Brooklyn Unitarian Church and he refused to design the Arlington Street Unitarian Church in Boston on religious grounds.

When Minard Lafever arrived on the New York architectural scene in the 1830s there was a great acceleration of building activity in the city. Lafever's first major work in New York City was the First Reformed Dutch Church (1834/35) in Brooklyn. Of all the buildings definitely known to have been done by Lafever this was the only one to be done in Greek Revival style. At this time the Grecian mode was being firmly established as the national style in America and was reaching the height of its development in New York. Lafever then designed the Dutch Reformed Church on Washington Square which was an example of early Gothic Revival. The First Baptist Church on Broome Street (built in 1841/42) was an example of more mature

Gothic Revival. His finest church in full Gothic Revival is the Church of the Savior (Unitarian) in Brooklyn. This church is still in use by the congregation today although the name "Church of the Savior" has been changed to the "First Unitarian Church in Brooklyn." Work on this building began in 1842, when the trustees of the church accepted Lafever's design and his estimates of cost.

It was shortly after this church was in the process of building that the First Church trustees began to think in terms of hiring Minard Lafever as the architect of their new church. The church minutes are somewhat obscure as to exactly when Lafever was asked

The Church of the Savoir, Brooklyn (1844), All Souls Archives

to be the architect. The first mention of his name comes after the builders had submitted their estimates of $21,000 "according to the plan and specifications prepared by Mr. Lafever."[6]

The society was threatened with a lawsuit in October 1844 because the builder allegedly was encroaching upon the neighboring property. The society paid $126 in additional title-search fees. All proceeded nicely on the building project until February 1845, when the trustees found it necessary to send a committee over to the building site to examine the walls which were going up. Apparently there were some doubts already that the barely started edifice was going to be able to support its roof.

The trustees' doubts were justified, for another building company, Tucker and Dodd, which was specially consulted, warned the trustees that the building would fall before it stood. Although Tucker and Dodd found no fault with Frasee and Pierson (the company which had been hired to *build* the church), nor "any material deviation from the plans and specifications" (Lafever's), their unbiased report stated that the building could not be occupied with safety and

> . . . that the dangerous state of the building has been produced by a want of strength in the frame of the roof which has settled and forced the walls from a perpendicular position. We do not hesitate to say that it was assuming a fearful responsibility to execute that plan and form of roofing upon a building of so great width without other support than the exterior walls. . . . We are of opinion that the time for applying support to the exterior walls has gone by.[7]

Tucker and Dodd's only recommendation was that columns passing through the pendants to the rafters might be built, but the company freely admitted that this would ruin the appearance of the building. Outside of this sort of measure, said Tucker and Dodd, the company felt that any means suitable to rectify the problem would be tantamount to tearing the whole thing down and starting all over again.

Utterly dismayed, the trustees called upon the society's old friend and founding father, Isaac Greene Pearson, who had by this time entered the field of architecture. Hints indicate the Pearson's countinghouse firm had failed, perhaps in the panic of 1837. Pearson —who had remained with the Second Unitarian Church since he had helped to found it in 1825—agreed that the new building had been deplorably designed, and recommended the changes he would make.

In March Henry Bellows "feared [the] church dedication was a good ways off. . . . An architect has made such a horrible mistake in the planning of the roof that we are seriously doubting whether it may not be necessary to take the Church wholly down and begin 'de novo'. Was there ever such a disgrace to Builder, or such a misfortune to Congregation? We are covered with chagrin and dismay. The loss will doubtless be from $10,000 to $15,000. Lafever. . . is our architect."[8]

Needless to say, Lafever was called in. Apparently perfectly calm and undaunted over the matter, Lafever had the courage to agree with Tucker and Dodd's report, and even with Pearson that "the walls are very insecure and dangerous."[9] Yet it had been Lafever who had strongly recommended this faulty architecture "without other support than the exterior walls," and hollow brick walls at that! What is more, Lafever now calmly recommended *his* way of remedying the situation! The trustees icily requested that Lafever put his plans in writing, and submit them to Tucker and Dodd. The consultants shook their heads; no, the new plan was *not* considered sufficient for the purpose. Whereupon Isaac Pearson's architectural firm was hired to patch up the bungled design.

Meanwhile, Frasee and Pearson were upset about Tucker and Dodd's part in all of this, and soon launched a suit against the church. This legal action cost the society $2,808.48. But apparently they finished the job; at least, all that Tucker and Dodd got out of it was $35 for their consultation services, while the financial records for 1844 show that, in addition to the compensation, Frasee and Pearson received a total of $8,450 in construction fees. Various other construction companies are listed in the financial records for this period, but these appear to have been contractors for the interior work. Isaac Pearson got $120 for submitting his restorative designs.

George Templeton Strong, the lawyer and diarist, had rather harsh words for the architecture of the new church building. On 1 August 1845 he took an "Architectural Tour." The first church he described was Bellows's new church. "First, there's the new Unitarian meetinghouse on Crosby Street's show front on Broadway—Gothic in the Chinese style, and a more deplorable exemplar of infatuated vulgarity trying to look venerable and medieval." He next visited Grace Church and wrote of "the unhappy straining after cheap magnificence." Pott's meetinghouse was undergoing embellishment "by the addition of something elongated." And the First Presbyterian Church "grows uglier and uglier, and when the tower is finished will represent a corpulent Chinese gander with its neck rigid, stout and tall, and its square-built rump and broad expanse of back, sturdy, squat, and not easily to be shaken."[10] So perhaps by the architectural standards of the day the new Unitarian church was not too bad!

So far as is known there are no drawings or pictures of the interior of the second edifice. But Charles S. Francis, a trustee and secretary-treasurer of the First Church, published *A Picture Guide of New York in 1846*. In this volume there is a description of the interior of the church.

> The lot occupied by the church runs through from Broadway to Crosby Street, and the main building is placed on the rear of the lot, which removes it from the noise of the great street to a place of comparative quiet. It is built of brick and is 130 feet long and 75 feet wide. It cost $82,000. It is a very lofty building, being about 70 feet from the floor to the apex; but standing back from the main street, and having large buildings all around it, it is scarcely seen from Broadway. The entrance is all that would be noticed in passing it. The front of the entrance is 27 feet wide, of elegantly carved reddish free stone, with one large Gothic door, with pillars on each side, running up some forty feet. Entering the front door there is a long passage-way of the same width as the front, and about 200 feet long, which brings us to the main body of the church. Over this covered passage-way is a suite of rooms, intended to be leased as offices. The interior of the church is finished in more complete Gothic style, probably, than any other building in the city. The material used for the pews is pine, with black walnut capping; and the pulpit, organ case, and all the other fine carved work is pine, painted a beautiful dark oak colour. There are 140 pews on the lower floor, and about 60 in the gallery. There are six windows on each side, of ground glass, admitting a soft and pleasant light. The walls are painted drab color. The side galleries are rather narrow, so that the large pillars supporting the roof stand off about five feet from the front of the gallery, which has a very fine effect. The gas lights are attached to these pillars. Taken as a whole, the house is beautiful and well worthy of attention.[11]

A British Unitarian, Henry Arthur Bright, visiting New York in 1852, adds this further comment about the interior of the Church of the Divine Unity:

> "I hardly ever saw—never indeed out of Belgium—such a splendid wooden pulpit, and noble organ screen through the woodwork of which shone the rich red of a painted window. The pews were also carved wood, and the perfect taste of everything (not forgetting the slight clustered pillars supporting the roof) made the greatest impression, as we were so entirely unprepared for any architectural beauty in the States."[12]

Henry Bellows said of the new name chosen for the church, "The Church of the Divine Unity": "We named our new church 'the Church of the Divine Unity,' probably the first time the title had ever

The Church of the Divine Unity (completed 1845), Courtesy of the J. Clarence Davies Collection, The Museum of the City of New York

been applied. It has been copied in Boston, Chicago, and many other places at home and abroad."[13]

In 1839 the Second Church had changed its name to The Church of the Messiah. This name also had theological connotations, but the name Divine Unity made the church more Unitarian than did a name like "The Messiah." It has often been said that Bellows himself named the church. Actually on 18 October 1845 the trustees voted to recommend to the society that the new church "be styled and known as 'The Church of the Divine Unity.' "[14] At another meeting on 22 October the trustees stated that the name had been submitted to the society, and that the pastor could use the name in the dedicatory services. The trustees had met at 11 A.M. to make the name official so that it could be used at the services of dedication at noon.[15] Whether the society ever really voted to confirm the name is something of a mystery. Evidently the necessity for the congregation to vote on the new name was forgotten. So the church remained officially the First Congregational Church in the City of New York, and the new building was called "The Church of the Divine Unity."

With these legal preliminaries more or less taken care of, the Church of the Divine Unity was dedicated on Wednesday noon, 22 October 1845. The dedication was planned to coincide with a convention of Unitarian clergymen and lay delegates that met in New York from Tuesday through Thursday, and thus a good attendance was assured for the dedication. Bellows's fellow ministers could also examine the new church. There was a lot of preaching at conventions in those days. Reverend Dr. Ezra Stiles Gannett, Channing's successor at the Federal Street Church in Boston, preached at the church Tuesday evening. Henry Bellows preached at the service of consecration on Wednesday at noon, The Reverend Dr. George Putnam of Roxbury preached there that evening, and The Reverend Ephraim Peabody of New Bedford on Thursday evening.

In spite of having a cold Benjamin Armitage attended the convention. He wrote that both churches were used, and that about forty ministers were in attendance. The impact of the convention, he reported, caused "such a sensation amongst the faithful Orthodox as has never been known in New York. Some of the exclusives were so alarmed at the progress of error, & the departure from Creeds and Confessions and the Crowds that pressed to hear the Hereticks that many Sermons have since been preached to guard their Flocks from being led astray from the true Christian Doctrine & the ancient oracles of the Church."[16]

A Changing Minister in a Changing New York

One of Henry Bellows's closest friends at Harvard Divinity School was Cyrus Augustus Bartol. In very much the same way as Bellows, he was called as a very young man of twenty-four to the West Church in Boston located at the corner of Cambridge and Lynde Streets. Bartol remained as minister and minister emeritus until his death in 1900. A year after he was settled in Boston he married Elizabeth Howard on 7 February 1838.

Bellows and Bartol were close friends all their lives. When Bellows was in Boston he would stay with the Bartols whose home was visited by the great and near-great of the metropolis. Visiting the Bartols late in 1845, Bellows evidently paid a great deal of attention to Elizabeth Bartol, so much so that it aroused the suspicions of her husband. When Bartol discovered his wife writing an answer to a letter that Bellows had written to her, he was shocked. In a gentlemanly fashion he wrote to Mrs. Bellows to tell her about the situation, thereby hoping of course to put an end to the matter.

> My dear Mrs. Bellows—The melancholy duty has devolved upon me,—of informing you that I have discovered a secret correspondence between your husband & my wife. Mr. Bellows, I think (not *knowing* the origin of this intimacy I cannot be confident) is chargeable with the guilt of having opened this correspondence. —Yes,—your own *Henry*, as I was charmed to hear you so often & so affectionately style him,—*he* it is, that has so resisted all the strong motives which (I well perceived) he has of fidelity to his own home.
>
> In his repeated lodgings at our house, I had noticed, it is true, the animated, & not seldom ardent pleasure which his conversations expressed. But, fond & undiscerning man that I was, I attributed this to myself as the chief exciting cause. The course of things has shown that the true steel lay elsewhere, & that all this electric fluid was gliding away by a hidden conductor out of my sight. It gives me now a thousand regrets, that I sent to him so respectful a letter, after my return from your house. For I begin to feel, as Dr. Dewey was saying when we were together, & as I remember the late Dr. Channing in substance say—that *indignation* has its uses.
>
> My feelings have been wrought up to the highest pitch by observing that your husband seems to have made the first move in this matter. Yet my wife is promptly sending him a letter under her own hand & seal (a very poor letter, she told me, which she had hardly a mind to send, evidently sticking by this affected reluctance to stave off my suspicions as to the contents). Your husband, counting on some remains of honor in my wife, urges in excuse of his own conduct—that he had observed marked attentions on my part to you.

Cyrus Augustus Bartol, D.D. (in later life), Courtesy of the Unitarian Universalist Association

After what he has done I feel that I am quits with him. He has taken off from me all obligation of reserve, & I beg leave to assure you, Madam, that my attentions were the weakest manifestation of the depth & warmth of my feelings.

I have since often thought how little I said that could at all indicate the sentiments I entertained. If I could venture to presume that you cherished in the remotest degree, the regards towards *me*, which I am so strongly conscious of towards you, we should have in case our legal partners carry their unfaithfulness further, indeed a signal revenge.

This is a fascinating letter, straightforward, and to the point—
let us say several points. Bartol makes it quite clear that the
infatuation is not limited only to Bellows and Elizabeth but also, if he
were to have anything to say about it, between himself and Eliza.
The letter is further complicated by a note at the bottom of the last
page:

> N. B. let your husband see only this corner. My dear Bellows
> Peabody's letter of acceptance was read Sunday at King's Chapel. He
> was at New Bedford only about three weeks. I miss you very much.
> We unite in love to you & your wife. Remember me to your brother &
> kiss (for once by proxy) the children.[1]

It is also interesting that while Bellows was flirting, Bartol still
relished his friendship and wanted to share the latest gossip with him
about the King's Chapel pulpit.

Charles G. Ames in writing of the life of Cyrus Bartol
characterized him in this way, "Unable to equivocate or conceal, he
could apply to himself a saying of Charles Sumner: 'If he could not
prevail by openness, he could not prevail at all.' "[2] This must have
been the spirit which prevailed in this relationship, for soon Bellows
was writing "My dear Bartol," and staying again in the Bartol home
whenever he went to Boston. We hear nothing more of Henry's
flirting, and we must just imagine that open sensible-minded men
and women worked out the problem in trust and in faith.

On 7 January 1846 Bellows explained to Bartol that he was
indisposed after the New Year's celebrations. It was not that he had
imbibed too much or stayed up greeting the New Year. People in
New York City made a great deal of the New Year with visiting and
the sending of greetings. The doorbell was worn out from some two
hundred visitors who had made their appearance in the Bellows's
household on that day. "All my male parishioners call upon their
pastor & some whom I never see at any other time," Bellows wrote.

While he was indisposed and in bed Henry Bellows read the life
of Henry Ware, Jr. [*Memoir of the Life of Henry Ware, Jr.*, by his
brother, John Ware, M.D. (Boston: James Munroe and Company,
1846).] The book "raised some questions in my mind of a very
important character," and Bellows wished that he and Bartol could
read the book together. He found that he differed so much from
some of the ideas of Henry Ware that it made him question some of
his basic assumptions about religion. He also was questioning his
position in the New York community. "I am beginning to find that

my social & domestic position in New York, stands somewhat in the way of my usefulness."

The reading of Dr. John Ware's biography of Henry Ware, Jr., prompted Bellows to again realize the "Christian character" of Mr. Ware who had also been so influential in the early days of the Chambers Street Church. Ware deemed that "God was as easy & natural an object of his meditation & communion, as an Earthly Parent. No doubts seem to have disturbed his mind in reference to any thing." Bellows contrasted Ware's simple faith with his own lack of faith. "It angers me. My whole life has been a consolation. To me God becomes no more present in prayer than in nature. I do not fly to his presence, as to his character for support. My prayers are communion with his attributes. . . I feel that presence only in the power which great thoughts of his character exercise over my mind in hours of express devotion."[3]

Bartol, on the other hand, found prayer a more direct and personal thing than did Bellows. He believed in "prayer—private and direct,—the Divine presence in it, & our consciousness of that presence," he wrote. But Bartol qualified his belief in prayer with these words, "It is the mark of fanaticism to pretend having received distinct messages from Heaven for particular things. God does not send us on errands, but gives us his great will & good spirit for our guide wherever we may go, whatever we do—the universal index of duty, the sure touch-stone of right & wrong."[4] It was obvious that Bartol believed in a more personal God than did Bellows, who used the same words as Bartol for Deity but related to God in a less personal way than his friend.

By 1846 Bellows felt that he had never been busier in his life. He had finally gotten his laymen into a mood "to awake this community up to an interest in simple & primitive theology. It is impossible for you Bostonians to understand our position. You could not believe the . . . bigotry of the religious world about us. . . the orthodox theology of your region is as the chicken to the small pox when compared with ours."

Bellows felt that his own religious ideas were changing and growing. "When I compare such a sermon as I gave at Hill's ordination with such as I gave at the dedication of my church, it seems impossible that they could have had the same author, & yet I am thoroughly sincere and ernest in both." He also believed that "the new church has helped our zeal for true and undefiled religion. I have an excellent and deeply interested Sabbath School & weekly meeting on Tuesday for conversation at the vestry. Our social meetings are well attended on Wednesday. There is a band of young men in the Society of a most promising character. I depend exceedingly upon them."[5]

Bellows was correct in his estimate that religious ideas were changing. The festivities surrounding the dedication of the Church of the Divine Unity marked a turning point in New York Unitarianism. For one thing, the convention of Unitarians from New England and elsewhere which had met at the time of the dedication testified to the significance of the city along with Boston as a major center of Unitarian thought. Further, the establishment of a statewide Unitarian Association in the metropolis revealed the growing importance of a denomination which, only fifteen years earlier, was but an irksome thorn in the sides of the orthodox and entrenched religions in the country and in New York.

It was a lucky accident for both the denomination and the First Church that Bellows accepted the New York pastorate which he had been so reluctant to take. For Bellows, more than any other Unitarian minister, was the intellectual heir of the great Channing. Channing had been a happy combination of liberal and conservative; when, in 1815, liberal Congregationalist ministers had rallied around the word Unitarian, Channing had taken the lead, yet unlike his fellows, he argued fervently to keep the Congregational denomination intact. His theology rarely offended orthodox believers, and after his famous Baltimore sermon, he settled down to preaching less controversial sermons. By contrast with many of his contemporaries, Channing was not out to inflame the world with upsetting ideas, but only to expound the simple Christian truth which, as he had repeatedly made evident, was all there in the Gospels. His heartfelt middle position could easily accommodate the essential truths contained in arguments which lay on either side of his own, and while far from being compromising and hypocritical, Channing's views permitted of a wide latitude for rational flexibility.

So it was also with Henry Bellows, who soon became the Channing of his time. Like Channing, Bellows was deeply humanitarian in his outlook, and his primary focus was upon the simple Christian truths contained in the Gospels. When the new wave of controversy broke out over Transcendentalism, Bellows was neither for or against either view, but felt that, in essence, both were true. Fully human as Emerson claimed, or fully divine as the old guard insisted, Jesus was an exemplary model after which all men should pattern their lives. Whether one wanted to think in terms of the Spirit of God or the Spirit of Christ, the important thing Bellows emphasized was that divine spirit could mingle with the human spirit to illuminate earthly existence and deeds. Thus, just as Channing had simultaneously provided the impetus for the acceptance of Unitarian ideas and the centered weight which prevented it from going too far toward the extreme, so Bellows served to maintain the stability of Unitarianism in a new age of controversy, and to make it acceptable for new and old adherents alike.

The character of the people of New York City was also changing rapidly. With the flowering of the clipper-ship trade and the opening up of the port of New York to be one of the greatest in the world, there were now many wealthy people in the city. In 1846 the Editor of *The New York Sun*, Moses Yates Beach, compiled a list of the wealthy people of the city and published their names in a small book. There were fourteen millionaires, nineteen with more than half a million dollars and a further 137 were rated as having more than a quarter million dollars. There were over 800 persons worth over $100,000. A business directory published in the same year listed thirty-one general merchants, 138 shipping and commission merchants, and eight shipping and importing merchants. There were ninety-one specialists in dry goods, eighty-six in flour and other produce, eight in domestic hardware, and 317 general commission agents.[6] Poverty was also rampant in the city. This was the period of the greatest immigration from Ireland when the potato famine hit that impoverished land. In 1846 one out of every seven citizens was a pauper or on "relief." Irish and Negro women found themselves in competition for work as house servants, although the work only paid room and board and six dollars a month.[7]

The dedication of the new church symbolized the termination of the First Congregational Church's long period of struggle and what looked like the beginning of a promising and prosperous future. Its troubles, however, were not entirely over. The trustees devoted their energies to the final details of pew sales and assessments. In selling the old building, the original plan had been to divide up the profits deriving therefrom among the pew owners so that those who had paid substantial sums for pews in the Chambers Street Church would not lose their investments. There was a large deficit accrued especially from having to tear down and rebuild the faulty side walls on the new edifice, to say nothing of the outlays made for various consultants, legal fees, and other costs in connection with the near-collapse of the partially erected building! Nevertheless, it was only fair to make some form of reimbursement to the original pew owners, and so the trustees decided to issue scrip to all former pew owners entitling them to a proportionate discount on the equivalent pew space in the new church. The trustees set the total value of the new building's 198 pews at $71,500, some $16,000 of which would be issued in scrip. Until the pews were sold and rented, the church would be in deep financial waters.

Then a minor miracle occurred. After the annual meeting, the trustees repaired to their own meeting to review the problem. A loan of $25,000 must be raised on the mortgage. But such a loan could not be had! The property was already mortgaged twice. The brand-new and luxuriously outfitted new church was standing on financial quicksand, and no banker would touch it. The board was able to arrange private and temporary loans totaling $5,000, because two of its members were themselves presidents of banks—William B. Allen of the Phoenix Bank, and John Ward of John Ward & Co. But this amount made hardly a dent in the gaping financial hole which threatened to sink the church into oblivion. Desperate, the trustees called another meeting of the society on 23 March, at which another urgent plea for funds was made. The following month, the Phoenix Bank and John Ward & Co. each gratuitously discounted their notes and raised another $3,000 between them.

This generosity did not render the Church of the Divine Unity instantly solvent, but it did help to put it on somewhat more solid financial footing. Pews worth $5,000 were sold during the year, and finally, in October, the members agreed to accept the 10 percent pew assessment. Most of the construction bills were paid off, and the interest due on the mortgages was met on time. By the end of 1846, the church had reduced its overall debt by a substantial margin. But the turning point came in February 1847, when a letter Henry Bellows had written to the trustees was laid before the society. With great enthusiasm the members unanimously resolved that "the means to pay the debt of the church shall be raised forthwith." Exactly two weeks later, on 28 February, $23,825 in subscriptions were in the hands of the trustees—enough to pay off all of the society's creditors except the two who held the original mortgages.

During the remainder of 1847, the church was on perhaps the soundest financial footing it had ever attained in the twenty-eight years of its existence. An additional $9,200 worth of pews had been sold, and together with those which were being rented, pew assessments and rents brought in $6,000 annually. Sunday services were becoming increasingly more crowded.

After it had furnished the large hall over the Broadway entrance to the building of the Church of the Divine Unity, and outfitted it with the necessary supplies with which to conduct its various denominational affairs, the Unitarian Association of the State of New York settled down industriously to print and disseminate voluminous quantities of tracts and other literature and to organize and hold public meetings and lectures. Bellows and his church were more than willing to cooperate, and almost immediately after both organizations gained occupancy to the building in the fall of 1845, the trustees voted to loan to the Association the library that the society had accumulated.

During the Association's second year at the Church of the Divine Unity, in October 1846, Bellows established a Unitarian paper called the *Christian Inquirer*, intended to circulate in New York State and other middle Atlantic states. It was to be a weekly paper of four six-column pages. Bellows's intention was in part to give useful occupation to Professor William Kirkland (the author Caroline Kirkland's husband). Professor Kirkland was to be the editor of the new journal, with Bellows contributing some of the articles and helping in some of the administrative work connected with its publication. He was assisted by Samuel Osgood, James Freeman Clarke, and Frederic Henry Hedge.[8]

But after a single issue of the *Christian Inquirer* had been published, William Kirkland met with a tragic accidental death. He had visited his son Joseph who was in school in the vicinity of Newburgh on the Hudson River. Late in the evening Mr. Kirkland, who was nearsighted and deaf, left the hotel in Newburgh to go down to board the boat back to New York City. In the darkness he missed his footing in getting on the boat, fell into the water, and was drowned.[9] By November Bellows was able to write that "Mrs. Kirkland is singularly calm & reasonable. The *circumstances* of her husband's death do not appear to *prey* upon her imagination, & her recollections of him seem to be wholly of the live & well & cheerful man."

Those responsible for the *Inquirer* agreed to "carry on the paper among ourselves." "Mrs. Kirkland has expressed a strong desire to continue connection with the *Inquirer* & will take the principal drudgery of the paper on herself—such as selecting, reading proof & making up the sheet." Bellows "expect[ed] to furnish a leader weekly, that Frederick Farley would do his part."[10] Bellows asked Orville Dewey (who was now temporarily at the Washington church) to make some contributions of articles or comments to the paper and to be the Washington correspondent. Bellows never conceived of himself as a writer, although he wrote a good many articles for the *Inquirer*. He believed he "ought to prune, elaborate & anvil beat my style for purposes of print, but I do not think it bad for preaching."[11]

The liaison with the Unitarian Association went well at first, but as time wore on, the plans and needs of the two organizations began to conflict. The church needed to use the premises rented to the association for its rapidly expanding Sunday school, and this doubling up worked to the disadvantage of both enterprises. Further, the association availed itself of the public utilities at the society's expense, a source of constant annoyance to the latter, and there were other annoyances and inconveniences. So when, in December 1847, the association announced that it would not renew its lease, the trustees of the church were quietly delighted. (I. G. Taylor continued to pay his rent on the basement space until August 1849; a Mrs. Burns rented the room thereafter.)

By the beginning of the summer of 1846 Orville Dewey's health was again on the decline. Some decision had to be made about his relationship with the Church of the Messiah. Bellows wrote, "Dewey is about to make an important change in his relation to his parish. He will either leave wholly, or preach for 3 months out of the 12, in connection with a colleague, the last probably. His health is wholly inadequate to his duties & his disease would end in apoplexy in another year under the pressure of his present labors . . . I dread another kind of co-worker. Any thing short of just such another man would dissatisfy me."[12]

Toward the end of November Bellows was able to give Orville Dewey (who was away) a report about what was happening at the Church of the Messiah. "Mr. Clapp is preaching very acceptably to your congregation. They have engaged him two Sunday's more. I have seen considerable of him and like him very much. I doubt his vigor of body or mind. He does not appear to possess a commanding spirit . . . but his soul is broad, genial, teachable." Mr. Clapp "might stay the next two Sabbaths."[13]

The problem of a minister at the Second Church was not to be easily solved and Henry Bellows worried about the situation in the sister church. This was but the beginning of his lifelong concern about the ministers of the Second Church.

Education was, as it is now, a major issue in nineteenth-century current affairs. The religious education of children had always been conducted on a small scale by the First Congregational Church, but in the new building the enrollment greatly increased. On 16 December 1845, George Woodman was appointed superintendent, and a Sunday school religious education committee was set up consisting of Bellows, E. Paine, Pierre M. Irving, and John R. Bartlett. The main task before this committee was to raise funds for the school, as the teachers were given *carte blanche* to instruct the children as they deemed best. Among the teachers were F. W. G. Bellows (Henry's brother), Miss C. M. Wheelwright, Mrs. George Schuyler, and William Taggard's daughter. Classes started on Sunday, 4 January 1846, and were held for an hour beginning at three o'clock.

On opening Sunday, there were as many as fifty or sixty pupils at the "Unity Sunday School," as it was named. But during the ensuing weeks, enrollments increased so rapidly that, by the first of February, eighty-six children were attending. A few of their names are worth noting: Annie and Lydia T. Wheelwright; Andrew and Augusta Thorp; Mary and Martha Brooks; George S. Haven, the son of George Woodward Haven; Martha Ward, John Ward's daughter; and Philip and Louisa Lee Schuyler (who became a woman of great prominence in charitable and social work, and came to play a major role in the history of the church). But many of the children were from poor immigrant families who could have no hope of providing their offspring with a sound academic education except at the Unity Sunday School. The Free School which had been initiated by members of the society some twenty-five years previously had disbanded as the congregation moved to Apollo Hall. The teachers of the Unity Sunday School spent much of their energies between classes collecting clothing for these children.

The high point of the 1845/46 season came on 9 June, when the Unity Sunday School joined with the classes from the Church of the Messiah for a Sunday-school picnic. It was the first time that either of the New York churches had held a Sunday-school picnic. About 300 people boarded the steamer *Boston* which took the gathering up the Hudson to Fort Lee—at that time open countryside atop the magnificent Palisades. The account preserved in the Sunday-school records for that year speaks eloquently of the occasion:

> We arrived at Fort Lee about 1/2 past 12 (noon) . . . and commenced our journey up a steep hill, the children carrying up the baskets of eatables which had been most bountifully provided by their parents. At the top of the hill we found ourselves in the midst of a beautiful grove in the midst of which was spread a tent and on one hill was set a table more than fifty feet in length.

After the whole company were assembled and had become rested the services of the day were commenced with a prayer by Rev. Mr. Bellows which was followed by him with a short address to the children. Previous to the prayer the first hymn selected was sung commencing with "Summer, glorious summer." After the address, another hymn was sung and the children were sent off to play. While they were at play, the teachers arranged the eatables upon the tables under the strict superintendance of the ladies so that everything was not only done 'decently and in order,' but also with great taste. The children were then again called together by the superintendent of the party, Mr. Warren, and after singing a hymn we all partook of the bountiful supply from the table . . . .

. . . At 1/2 past 4 o'clock we were again on board of the Steamboat *Boston* bound for home, having spent a most delightful day, having met with no accident—the expectations of the most sanguine having been more than realized and the whole party excepting but one feeling that the day had been too short. The excursion had been got up for the amusement of the children but all, both old and young alike, enjoyed it; in fact all were children for the day . . . .[14]

The outing was so successful that when the Church of the Savior in Brooklyn (the Brooklyn Unitarian Society), invited the Unity children to share their picnic with them on 24 June, the invitation was heartily accepted. The group got an earlier start for Brooklyn, leaving at 9 A.M., and spent the day on the grounds of Mr. Judd's estate in Brooklyn. The school closed early in July because of the heat and because so many of the members' children were away with their families in the country, and though classes no doubt resumed, as promised, early in September, here is where the quaint records abruptly leave off.

In 1847 Henry Bellows wrote a tract on "The Alleged Indefiniteness of Unitarian Theology," which was published by the Unitarian Association on the State of New York. It was a time when religious ideas were in great flux and there was inquiry on the part of many as to what Unitarians believed. It was this kind of questioning that inspired Henry Bellows to write the tract. He posed the question as to what Unitarians believe, and then noted that "insinuations, if not direct charges, are made, that they have no definite and settled opinions, or else want frankness and courage to declare them." He felt that these insinuations came from enemies, "half-confessed friends," and from "honest and earnest inquirers." The Universalists were hard at work trying to decide what Unitarians believed to see "how far union with us is possible." He admitted that it was difficult to find out what Unitarians believed, and then proceeded to probe the matter.

Unitarians, he declared are "not bound together solely by agreements of a doctrinal sort." Originally they had focused their protest against the doctrine of the Trinity. But they had resolved to keep the field of theology open. They developed the doctrine of individual independence. "There was to be no formal creed; and the largest Christian liberty, the broadest charity were their professed principles." Bellows professed that no denomination can exist "without some distinctive, avowed, and well-defined views; in short, without a belief or creed." But Unitarians, Bellows claimed, wanted it to be quite clear that no creed should become "narrow, oppressing, and enslaving." He believed that if churches adopt very rigid creeds they deprive themselves of the right of religious liberty.

Bellows stated that the views of Unitarians "are as definite as the Gospel from which we profess to derive them," and thus the alleged fault of indefiniteness belongs to Christianity itself. He believed that the church by enforcing dogmas upon itself had created an artificial Christianity which had little to do with the Christ who inspired the foundation of the church. "He [Jesus] concerned himself more with the quality than the quantity of his followers, and depended more upon a few thorough and intelligent disciples than on a crowd of hasty and half-informed, and easily convinced adherents." The definiteness, then, which others demand of Unitarianism "is precisely what our fidelity to Christianity forbids us from possessing."

Bellows was also aware that Unitarians are charged with indefiniteness "in the view we entertain of the nature and position of Jesus Christ." Unitarians are asked "to choose and defend some one of the positions that have been taken between High Arianism and the lowest Humanitarianism. We confess the charge, and decline the challenge." He believed that "the Scriptures do not settle the question of Christ's nature." Unitarians do not understand the sinlessness of the Christ, "we hover between a conviction of his proper and unmixed humanity, and his super-angelic nature." The answers to these questions are not to be found in the Bible.

He also discussed the Atonement and stated that Unitarians do not believe that Christ's death had anything to do with the salvation of the world. Bellows felt that the idea of the Atonement unsettled "all natural ideas of moral responsibility . . . [and relegated] the plain and simple teachings of Christ to the rhetorical obscurities of

Paul and the unknown author of the Epistle to the Hebrews."[15]

What Bellows had done in spite of the title of his tract was to admit that the alleged indefiniteness of Unitarianism was a fact, but a worthy fact. He did not deny the charges. He simply felt that indefiniteness was closer to the truth than the over-definiteness of typical orthodox Christianity. It was an essay that still breathed a great deal of the argumentation of Channing, but Bellows was beginning to more and more speak for himself and his own theological ideas. It also showed that this early period of transition in his ministry had made him not only a leader but also a religious thinker who was now striking out on his own to develop a theology of reconciliation among the various Unitarian opinions.

Putting His Stamp on the Parish

Bellows did not know it at the time but very important in his life was his first meeting with Thomas Starr King in New York in September 1847. "A slender, boyish stranger called at my door in New York, and introduced himself to me, without circumlocution or mediator, under the then unsuggestive name of Thomas Starr King." Bellows was used to young preachers and theological students seeking his acquaintance in this manner. King announced himself as a Universalist minister who knew almost none of the Unitarian clergy in Boston though he was settled at Charlestown, Massachusetts, in the Universalist Church. Bellows took to the young man with much enthusiasm and he did something unusual—he invited the young man to preach for him at the evening service the following Sunday. Bellows found that Starr King "was very reluctant to encounter a cultivated Unitarian congregation, and nothing but the most resolute persuasion at length overcame his scruples."

It came time for the evening service and Bellows and Starr King ascended the pulpit together. "He [Starr King] conducted all the exercises, and with such perfect self-possession, that in a very few moments I discovered that in place of a novice, a promising young minister, we had a finished thinker, scholar, and master, in those youthful proportions, at the altar of God. A universal surprise and admiration filled the congregation." Bellows's congregation wanted to know in what Unitarian church Starr King was settled, when did he graduate from Harvard? Bellows had to tell them that he was not a Unitarian minister at all, but a Universalist, that he had never been

Thomas Starr King, Oil Portrait, Courtesy of the First and Second Church in Boston

to college, let alone Harvard, had never been to theological school and was unknown to the Unitarian clergy in Boston where he preached.

The congregation was delighted with Starr King. In fact, since Orville Dewey had just resigned the pulpit at the Church of the Messiah, Bellows persuaded the trustees of that society to invite Mr. King to occupy their pulpit for two Sundays. He preached "to the continued delight and wonder of all the congregation." The question of Starr King succeeding Dewey was raised "and if it had been left to the spontaneous voice of the congregation, it would have been at once decided affirmatively. But the trustees, experienced and wise men, thought it their duty to inquire into Mr. King's antecedents." They learned nothing from the leading Unitarian ministers. They found his name in no college catalog or roster of any theological school. He was not on a list of Unitarian clergy. Bellows added, "I agreed to become sponsor for the soundness of his creed, the worth of his character, and the success of his ministry." Bellows also told the trustees of the Second Church that "they sacrificed the substance to the show of things." But the trustees were not willing to take "so unusual a course as calling . . . a man who had not in his pocket the parchment of Harvard College and the letters patent of a Unitarian council or a theological school, a young man unknown to fame and only twenty-two years old."

Instead, the trustees of the Second Church wrote a letter to King praising his abilities and his character, and they recommended that he attend the theological school at Cambridge for a year, "at which time they promised themselves, the pleasure of hearing him again, and probably asking him to become their permanent pastor."[1] King's dander rose against these conditions, and he told Bellows with tears in his eyes why he had to write to the trustees declining such conditions.

The Church of the Messiah probably made a bad mistake in not calling this brilliant young orator to be their minister, judging by his later success in Boston and San Francisco. Thomas Starr King, with letters from Henry Bellows in his pocket introducing him to the Unitarian greats in Boston, never forgot what Bellows had done for him. One wonders what would have happened to the Church of the Messiah if Starr King had become the pastor, for they had ministerial problems for the next thirty-five years.

On Wednesday, 6 October 1847, Henry Whitney Bellows preached the sermon at the ordination of his cousin, Frederick Newman Knapp, at the First Congregational Church in Brookline, Massachusetts. Knapp was the son of Henry's father's sister, Louisa Bellows, and had been born in Jamaica Plain, Massachusetts, on 19 November 1821. He graduated from Harvard College in 1843 and the Harvard Divinity School in 1847. Immediately after his graduation he was called to the Unitarian Church in Brookline (which retained the legal name of the First Congregational Church) as the colleague of and eventual successor to Rev. Dr. John Pierce. He held this position for only six years because of declining health due to a knee injury. He then moved to Walpole where his parents lived, and taught school for some years (Henry Bellows later called upon him to be the Special Relief Agent of the United States Sanitary Commission). On the occasion of Knapp's ordination, Henry Bellows gave a long sermon that gives us our best concept of his early ideas of human nature and the minister's aim.

Bellows began by quoting Paul in the letter to the Romans about the tension between the law of sin in man and the aspiration to righteousness (Romans 7:22–25). Yet, throughout the sermon there is an obvious conflict in Bellows's mind between Paul's concept of sin and the concept of man as sacred because he is believed to be the incarnation of God, a typical conflict in the minds of Unitarians of that era. At the beginning of his sermon Henry Bellows must have put his audience to sleep. There was a long discussion of the history of the early concepts of Christianity in Paul and the Gospels. Bellows later learned to tackle his subject immediately so as not to lose his audience. He made the mistake common to many young preachers of rehashing his seminary notes.

But on page ten (in the printed version) he began to talk about the subject. He told his audience that they were gathered "to ordain over this people a minister of the Gospel." Bellows affirmed that "to be an effective preacher, [he] must know how to preach and what to preach. He must have a theology. He must know to what frame of mind Christianity aims to bring the soul committed to his watch and care." To be more specific he must know something "of human nature, in its ordinary, and characteristic condition." He must know how to rectify these shortcomings of human nature and how to bring his hearers to the change required of Christians to ennoble them above their human nature.

Bellows developed his three main points in typical style. The first point was regarding the aim of the preacher about human nature. Here Bellows asserted that "it is a new heart that he is to create. His object is not so much to form the Christian character, as to beget the Christian nature. His aim is the regeneration of man, not his development." Bellows rejected the idea that a "Christian preacher is to keep in view only the general improvement of his people; the culture of their minds and hearts; the elevation of their tastes." Bellows felt that this was the aim of the school, not the pulpit, and he believed that a misinterpretation of the pastor's role had reduced the effectiveness of the preacher. He further suggested that the definite aim of the Christian preacher is "conversion." He believed that the moral strength and salvation of man "depends upon his coming into conscious and direct relations with God," and that the only way that a man could get rid of his human pride and self-sufficiency was to recognize his own sinful nature and bring it directly to the bar of God. This is a very early theological opinion of Henry Bellows, an idea about sin which he was later to modify considerably and shows the influence of his conservative Harvard theological training.

Bellows's next concern was "what constitutes the permanent and settled obstacles to the sovereignity of God in the soul of man." In this area he stated, "Man is pronounced an alien from God." He appeared more or less to agree with Paul in this area. Yet he had his own interpretations, "It is one thing to call human nature depraved and another to call it prone to evil." Bellows took his stand with the latter definition—separating him from the Calvinists. Christianity when it first reached the heart of man found the ground unprepared. To round out his beliefs he stated that God "does not give him this weak and imperfect nature in order that he may sin and suffer, but with reference to ulterior and glorious results. . . . Do you ask if man can be responsible for his own nature? I answer 'yes.' " The duty of the preacher is "to address him as a sinner, as having a measure of corruption at heart, as having a false bias, as in need of a new birth."

His third question was, "How to reconcile man to God, how to graft the Gospel upon the wild olive tree; how to make sinners, Christian; the prodigal the penitent child; the rebel a loyal subject; the natural man, a spiritual creature." Bellows expressed something anti-Pauline in his theology, for he asserted, "When we speak of human nature in its native sentiments, its moral instincts, we speak of that which cannot fall—for it is God in us." Here we begin to see Bellows's later theological ideas creeping in, for Bellows is beginning to assert the God-power in man—closer to Quakerism than to Calvinism. The conclusion to this sermon was that the minister should "stand in Christ's stead to his people, dispensing the gifts he gave to men; communicating the strength with which he strengthens you."

This sermon at the ordination of his cousin is significant in the development of Bellows's theology for one can see that his soul and mind are in struggle. It was probably the most complete statement of his own theological ideas—which were developing—until the publication of his twenty-five sermons on Christian doctrine in 1860.[2] This sermon at the ordination of Frederick Knapp[3] preceded the publication of those twenty-five sermons by thirteen years, and in those years Henry Bellows was to think a great deal more about the subject of human sin and Christ's redemption of it.

Henry Bellows was somewhat upset about the way that the Second Church had dealt with Thomas Starr King as a possible successor to Orville Dewey. In spite of not taking Bellows's advice about King, the Second Church still leaned on Henry to help them select a minister. They appointed him as a member of a committee to go to Boston to present a call to the pulpit of the Church of the Messiah to the Reverend Frederick Dan Huntington. Coincidentally, Isaac Green Pearson, one of the founders of the First Church in 1819 and the man who had rescued the second church building of the First Church from falling down, was also a member of the committee. Huntington was approached about taking the Second Church pulpit, but even the persuasive Bellows could not move him from Boston, and the committee had to continue its search.

In the first years of his ministry, Bellows had his hands full in just bringing together and strengthening the existing congregation of the First Church. No sooner had he managed this feat when the move from the first house of worship launched him into ceaseless activity on behalf of increasing the numbers of his congregation, and in making the most of the opportunities presented to him by the large audience that flocked to Apollo Hall. By the time the new building was ready for occupancy, denominational affairs were added to Bellows's responsibilities. In addition to his activities connected with the Unitarian Association which shared the Church of the Divine Unity for two years, Bellows became actively interested in the Unitarian theological school that was established in Meadville, Pennsylvania, in 1844. The Unitarian denomination was expanding rapidly in the number of its constituents, in its geography, and in its constant shifts of theological insights, so that Bellows was forced to read voluminously just to keep up with all that was going on within the denomination. The launching of the *Christian Inquirer* was but a part of his denominational activities and, coupled with his parochial duties, constituted an overwhelming burden even for a man of robust health.

Furthermore, various interests in the larger community had lured Bellows's attention. He had joined a small but prominent group of men known as the Sketch Club who met to create and to discuss artistic works. Unlike his predecessor, William Ware, Bellows was not particularly talented at sketching and painting, but he had an acute aesthetic sense and his fellow members appreciated his critical appraisals of art (for which he was well known all of his life). The group—which included such men as William Cullen Bryant, Orville Dewey, Thomas Cole, Asher Brown Durand, and Charles

Cromwellingham,—increased his prestige in the community, and thus his church's prestige and size, but fellowship with the other men also afforded him rare moments of relaxation and social enjoyment. In January 1847, the group formed, with ten members from The Column, the famous Century Club, which is now located at 7 West 43rd Street just west of Fifth Avenue. Bellows was among the founders.

Meanwhile, Bellows's own family was increasing, thus adding a host of parental responsibilities upon his shoulders. When the dedication services for the Church of the Divine Unity took place, little Russell Nevins Townsend Bellows was three, his sister Eliza was two, and Anna Langdon—who had been named for Henry's stepmother, Anne Hurd Langdon—had been born only the previous March. Two years later, on 13 April 1847, a fourth child was born and named Mary Davis. Mrs. Bellows's delicate nervous system was not up to coping with all of these toddlers around the parsonage, and while the Bellows had servants (the Townsends having considerable wealth), Henry fully enjoyed relating to his growing family and took on many parental duties.

But, despite the large and growing demands upon him, Bellows was unwilling to relinquish any measure of his pastoral duties and, indeed, began to enlarge upon them. For example, the music for worship services had always been left in the hands of a music committee appointed by the board. While William Ware had sometimes served on this committee, his part of it had been mostly to suggest and to approve of selections used in each service. The hiring and firing of musicians and the type of music performed had always been left up to one or two lay members of the congregation. By the end of 1847, however, Bellows began to have different ideas. During two years at the Church of the Divine Unity, the society relied on a professional organist and several professional choristers to perform the musical aspects of the services, all under the expert administration of Jeremiah Smith who comprised the music committee. Mr. Smith had been given a budget of $1,000 a year, and he had used it mainly to pay Clare Beames, the organist, and Nathaniel Sawyer, Israel Brown, Mary Dobson, Julie Huntington, and Emily Clark, the choir members. Bellows very likely thought that $1,000 was a lot of money to expend on music for a congregation which owed $28,000 in mortgages. In any case, on 19 December, he preached a sermon in which he expounded on the merits of congregational singing. The idea was that a member of the society should voluntarily play the organ while all hymns would be sung by the congregation itself.

Surprised but willing, the congregation met the following Monday evening to discuss the matter, and voted to comply with their pastor's suggestion. The only apparent dissenter was Jeremiah Smith, who promptly resigned his post. A new three-man committee was appointed. Even Nathaniel Sawyer and his wife stayed on to become members of the church after all the choristers had been let go. The talents of William Scharfenburg were discovered buried among the less prestigious members of the society, and Scharfenburg, a German immigrant, who was a sometime conductor and ran a music store, was promptly elevated to the prominent position of organist. At the end of 1848, Scharfenburg was effusively thanked for his voluntary services and given the added distinction of membership on the music committee with John Thomas, George Ireland, and Horatio Allen.

No sooner had Bellows accomplished this innovation, when he suddenly fainted dead away in the pulpit from sheer overwork. Alarmed, the society heard Bellows's suggestion that he be granted a six-month leave of absence during which he might regain his health. On 18 February 1848 the trustees of the Church of the Divine Unity met and unanimously agreed to give Bellows a leave of absence. During his "contemplated absence" they agreed that his salary should be continued and that the pulpit would be supplied "& parochial duties performed at the expense of the society."[4] Although Bellows had offered to supply the pulpit during his absence at his own expense, the trustees had insisted that the society would pay Bellows's full salary of $2,500 and see to it that the pulpit was supplied.

Mr. and Mrs. Bellows promptly readied themselves for a leisurely trip to Europe beginning in April 1848. The children were taken in by the Elihu Townsends, and Eliza and Henry went off on a second honeymoon, leaving the trustees to cope with such details as the last-minute needs of the Unitarian Association, which was then in the process of moving out, and leaving the congregation to struggle through with its new form of music.

CHAPTER THREE

Indications of Reality

Revolution in France, Riots in England

Henry Bellows took his journey to Europe because of his health, but he could scarcely have chosen a poorer year for traveling in peace and tranquillity than 1848, a year of ferment and revolution in most of Western Europe. Cyrus Bartol was reluctant to see his friend tour the Continent at such a turbulent time. He wrote Bellows: "There is revolution in France, riots in England, ominous heaving around ancient volcanoes in Italy & Sicily—all Europe trembling & darkened at the shadow of what is to come—absolutism & freedom, after portentiously eyeing each other from afar & some preliminary playing with & petty passing at each other, getting now close together & terribly measuring their swords & *you* in a few days going to walk on hot soil, *feel* a little tottering of the nations."[1] But his worries did not deter Bellows from making his proposed trip.

Bellows felt that he was not asking for the leave only for reasons of health. His entire family needed a change. "My father [Mr. Townsend] is a great invalid, my wife has been in a condition of great nervous discomfort for nearly a year—broken down in short with child bearing, & my own health altho not visibly impaired or specifically invaded, I myself inwardly feel to require a positive cessation from care and routine. My labors for ten years have been unintermitted. I feel that my brain requires rest, my spirits recuperation & my whole physical & moral man, a change of diet." He also admitted that there were reasons other than health for making the trip. "I have not asked leave of absence on the score of health; but simply because I felt I had a right to gratify my own personal inclinations, & my parish have conceded it, by acclamation." He indicated that he wished to make a general "survey of the continent as six or eight months would allow."[2] The plans were flexible, and although there were political problems on the Continent he hoped that he could avoid them.

The party for the European trip was to have included the Bellows, Mrs. William Kirkland, and Mrs. Bellows's father, Elihu Townsend. Mr. Townsend fully intended to make the trip until just a few days before sailing when a business complication made it seem wise that he should not leave New York because of the press of his "affair" with a Mr. Holford, a bad business situation. He had hoped to get the matter settled and sail with his family. But this was not to be. The day before the *Hibernia* sailed, he wrote to his daughter and son-in-law that he had not been able to settle the Holford "affair" and remained in New York.[3]

Henry and Eliza Bellows accompanied by Mrs. Kirkland left New York on 6 April 1848. Bellows wrote many letters to the *Christian Inquirer* about the trip which were published in the paper.[4] The crossing of the Atlantic took just sixteen days, the ship arriving off Cork, Ireland, the day before Easter. The weather had been fortunate, the winds fair, and "the sea only moderately agitated." The ship had "proved an excellent and most comfortable residence." Bellows found the daily table "truly sumptuous, and no necessary dependence appeared upon salt provisions." But the winds were not favorable for the landing in Liverpool, and the ship was mired in the Irish Sea for several days. It was not until the morning of April 25th that the ship sailed into the Mersey River and anchored off the Liverpool docks.[5]

Bellows was looking forward to seeing "Merry England, the country of Alfred, and old Canute, and Robin Hood, and Mother Goose—the land in which Jack the Giant-killer flourished . . . the land of Shakespeare, and of Shakespeare's creatures . . . England the *Old*-country, the Mother-country—land of our fathers, fountain of our liberties, source of our laws . . . England! the home of the noblest race earth has ever bourne; and the scene of a civilization without parallel since time was."[6]

After running around Liverpool Bellows wrote that he was "never weary of staring at the life, and manners, and customs, and houses, and equipages of a foreign people. To us, every thing is new, and strange, and exciting."[7] He found Liverpool a city made of stone, the style of the buildings reminding him most of Philadelphia. He thought the edifices "splendid" and wondered why so many Americans were contemptuous of Liverpool.

Thence the party went on to Birmingham and a view "of the face of England, in a ride on the stagecoach from Warwick to Oxford." It took five-and-a-half hours to cover the forty-five miles which included at least an hour's stop for rest. He found the country charming in the springtime. Bellows waxed eloquent, "There is but one word descriptive of English scenery—England is one great garden. . . . It all looks much like the immediate neighborhood of Boston."

His social conscience was moved in spite of the beautiful scenery, "Amid all this perfection of agriculture, all this order and solidity, and finish of structure, it is painful to see how little room the people take up; how inferior their accommodations are; how small a feature the homes of the million form in the landscape. . . ." He looked around for spacious farmhouses as in America but "the common people dwell in *cots* that make a surprisingly small figure in the prospect, and give the agricultural districts almost the appearance of being uninhabited. We could not help continually asking where are all the people, and where do they live, who did all this work."

Oxford to him was a most impressive place, and he doubted whether Rome would impress him more. He described the village as consisting of 30,000 people living in an area two miles square, "of which far the largest part is taken up by buildings and grounds." He found Oxford not a university but a group of independent colleges which were "as independent of each other as Harvard, Yale, Columbia, and Union." When one realized that there were twenty-four of these colleges each with its own refectory, library, chapel, and so on, one realized how great was the extent of this university town. "There are twenty-four chapels, each a magnificent temple, within this university, and full of the most costly work in stone, or oak carving, or painted glass, or monuments of antiquity, or painted ceilings, or invaluable memories of the past—as many libraries . . . as many halls, full of portraits, by the best masters, of the most celebrated scholars or statesmen of England for a thousand years past." The travelers left Oxford with great regret; "one might pass a month here, and see something new and interesting every day."[8] But they were compelled to leave for London.

They spent the first two weeks of May in London. Bellows was impressed with London's size. "Of this no description gives any adequate idea." In 1848 London was ten times the size of New York City. Yet he did not find it "a crowded place." He was impressed with the great open spaces within the city, the public parks an influence that was later to make him so active along with his parishioner William Cullen Bryant influencing public opinion for the establishment of Central Park. He was impressed with the public buildings, but he did not like the architecture. "It would often seem as if the Old World, where room is so much needed, never refuses it to a public edifice, while the New, where room is so abundant, rarely or never allows sufficient around any building, however splendid or important." He commented that in America as yet we know nothing about "the value of elbow room." He was impressed with the statues and monuments in the public places. He felt that "the irregularity of London adds much to its beauty,"⁹ finding there no long streets like Broadway in his adopted city of New York. Even with map in hand the party lost their way frequently.

Then the party went on to Paris which he said, "almost all travelers greatly prefer to London." He found a better climate in Paris, "the absence of coal-smoke, the cheerfulness and abandon of the people, the easiness of access to all places of amusement or instruction, the central position of the public walks and gardens, and above all, to the greater independence of the stranger as it affects his social position." He had been impressed with the caste system of England, "where a considerable . . . class of persons hold themselves too good for [one's] company." He felt that in London "everything seems made for the nobility. . . . When the court is in town everything is alive." But it was very different in Paris. "It is always in season here." "The people possess Paris, and constitute its interest. The city is made for the citizens, for the people, and . . . the privileged class do not constitute the life of the social world."

Somehow he felt more at home in London than in Paris. "Paris is a great show-box compared with London. It is as filagree work to solid gold. London is evidently built for use, and not show." "In Paris . . . the impression is fixed that everything has been designed for effect." He did not even find that the Tuilleries, the Champs-Elyssees, or the Bois de Bologne compared in richness with the great parks of London. He concluded, "Paris is a device, London, a growth."

There had been a recent revolution in France, and Bellows commented that he had not realized until he stood on the spot "the extraordinary crisis of affairs . . . Everything seemed at loose ends, nobody appears to have any business on hand—a sort of non-plused, what-is-to-come-next expression was on most faces." The lower class appeared "to think something very pleasant had happened." The middle class was either in a state of alarm or lacked sympathy for the revolutionary movement. He felt that the revolution was "a very accidental affair," "having no leaders or plotters to guide it." He did not believe that anyone in France was prepared for the revolution. The upper class certainly did not want it because the limited monarchy benefited them considerably. The foreigners doing business in France did not want it because of the uncertainty which it created. "The mob of Paris, the poor people throughout the country, naturally desire something better, and are willing to suppose that the Republic stands for it." Bellows felt that no one could oppose this idea of the republic, "All that the wisest can do, is to take advantage of this most unexpected state of things, and turn it to the very best account." Yet he did not despair nor deplore the coming of the republic in France. He felt that "no Republic is built without pangs."[10]

Bellows commented that when he set foot in a land where everyone was jabbering in a strange language he "for the first time fully realized his distance from home," and he began to appreciate the trials that attend a curiosity to see the world! "Truly it is further from Calais to Dover, than from Liverpool to New York." He found his boarding school knowledge of French not a "suitable preparation for chattering with custom-house officers, cab-men, and inn-keepers." He had not found the trip by railroad from Boulogne to Paris interesting. "The country is flat, and after leaving England, seems poorly cultivated." However, the cathedral at Amiens repaid him for taking this route. He was experiencing what so many travelers feel, that the small poor towns of France put such major efforts for centuries into building their magnificent cathedrals. He was impressed with the devotion of the common people to their religion, though it was Catholic and quite out of keeping with his own beliefs. "It is impossible not to respect and admire the devoutness of a large part of the common people."

Traveling from Amiens to Paris on the railroad he saw many signs of the recent revolution. He found every statue of the late king, Louis Phillippe, dishonored, and no public building was without a recent inscription, "Liberte, Egalite, Fraternite." Even the churches were inscribed with the motto. He found that the buildings destroyed by the mob were in the process of reconstruction.[11]

There was a martial air in revolutionary France. "Every other soul is a soldier. Parents clothe their little children in the uniform of the National Guard, and babies that cannot speak plain, mock the patrol of the sentry as they totter, with a stick at their shoulder, forward and back at their father's door. The everlasting red pantaloons of the French soldiery set the streets of Paris in a blaze."[12]

On 25 May the Bellows's party left Paris for Italy. He found the crossing of France very exciting. It is usually felt to be "a flat dull country without diversity of scenery, or even a pleasing monotony . . . . On the contrary, France between Paris and Chalons well justifies the title the whole country has earned, 'La Belle France'. . . . It rolls with beautiful swells of land, is carefully cultivated, and, towards Chalons rises into noble heights, affording the most extensive and pleasing landscapes. The French villages are clean and comfortable." As they approached Lyons he saw the beauty of the Jura mountains covered with snow; he enjoyed Lyons. The Bellowses then moved on to Avignon and Nimes to cross Mount Cenis into Italy.[13]

The party spent five days at Genoa, a day at Pisa, and a week in Florence. Bellows found the streets of Genoa "the narrowest we have ever seen, being usually mere alleys of eight or ten feet width. The houses run up to an enormous height on both sides so that the sky is hardly seen between their tops." Even the seemingly unromantic Henry Bellows was captivated by the Genoese women, "The women of Genoa seemed to us to possess an uncommon share of beauty." He found Pisa charming and compact. "There is not within the same space four such interesting edifices in the world," referring to the cathedral, its campanile, its Campo-Santo, and its baptistery. He particularly liked the cathedral of Pisa.[14]

Bellows attempted to understand the complicated political situation in Italy. The party attended a military mass in the cathedral at Chambery in Savoy where thousands of soldiers of Charles Albert of Sardinia were quartered. There were two thousand soldiers in the cathedral, and instead of a bell to call the faithful to the parts of the mass "a dozen drums marked the periods and progress of the Catholic ritual. There seems to be the most cordial union between the profession of arms and the profession of religion in Italy." The country of Italy was alive "with military and political enthusiasm." Some in Italy hoped for a republic; Bellows wrote that the first step toward this end would be the expulsion of the Austro-Hungarians from Lombardy and Venice. "It is upon this that Italy is now engaged. These provinces called the rest of Italy to their aid, and Charles Albert, an able monarch, took up the cause. Even the Pope sent his quota of soldiers to the frontiers. There were impressive successes of Italian arms . . . . The Pope had recently granted a constitution to the people of the Papal States." But Bellows realized that Italy was a country in transition, for he remarked, "It is impossible to conjecture what a year or a month may bring forth in Italy."[15]

Bellows developed a real fondness for the Italian churches (no wonder that a few years later the third All Souls edifice was patterned after the cathedral of Monza, Italy). He found the churches to be galleries of art. The "first place to which the traveler directs his steps in every considerable town is to the cathedral." In small miserable cities he found magnificent cathedrals, "and this brings us to remark how different a purpose the churches serve in Catholic countries and Protestant ones." He was not impressed with worship in Rome. "In the ceremonies at Rome, the worship of man is far more apparent than the worship of God. Human dignitaries are recognized with a scrupulous gradations of honors . . . . The precise rank of every official is to be inferred from the amount of incense he receives, and from the rank of the person who carries the censer." Bellows felt that "the study of Romanism" was one of the most interesting parts of his journey.[16]

Bellows nevertheless felt very much at home in Rome. "There is no city in the world where one is so much at home at first sight, or which retains its strangeness for so long a time." He felt that this familiarity was due to all the pictures of Rome which had become so familiar to him as a schoolboy. "A few weeks at Rome must send most persons away with a feeling that their visit has only served to make them acquainted with their ignorance."[17] He went to Saint Peters in great expectation. "There is no building in the world which disappoints so little at first, or at last . . . . It was as large and as lofty as we expected to find it; but it was far more beautiful in details, and exquisite in finish." He believed that fifty thousand people could stand in Saint Peters without it seeming crowded, "which is to say, that it is thirty times as large as our own church." He found that the church had a satisfying beauty. "Nothing has been spared to perfect this wondrous work." He found the church light and airy in spite of its size. "We have felt a thousand times more awe in Westminster Abbey than in Saint Peters," and yet he found that the dome of Saint Peters seen from the inside was like "the vault of heaven."[18]

The Bellows party left Rome for Naples on the fourth of July. The first view of the Mediterranean came at Gaeta. Thence the party proceeded along the seacoast to Naples, seeing the island of Ischia out in the Mediterranean. Bellows was somewhat disappointed in Naples, for although it was a city of 450,000 persons, Bellows noted that "there are very few striking buildings or public squares, or interesting monuments." He found the hue of Naples an intense white rather than the soft rust-colored hue of Rome. Bellows found few churches in Naples, but they inspected a macaroni factory and Bellows wrote at length about the process of its manufacture. In Naples Bellows suffered a letdown from his Roman experience for he found the city teeming with beggars: "Every form of sickness and misery is paraded to move the compassion of the merciful." He visited the crater, the Naples Museum, Pompeii, and Herculaneum.

He was impressed with the archeological activity. While the Bellows's party was at Naples, Mount Vesuvius had a period of fiery activity, so it was the center of attention while they were there. "It is beautiful and singular from below; it is awful in the stage in which we saw it, from above." He found the struggle up the mountain on foot to be an arduous one.[19]

After nine days at Naples and Paestum, the party boarded the French steamer *Sesostris* at Naples on 14 July and headed for Milan via Genoa. Bellows was interested in the Milan cathedral, but he was disappointed by it, for he wrote that "the narrowness of the nave, and the smallness of the dome, are fatal to a very fine effect." He found that he liked the outside of the cathedral better than the inside. "It is as light, ornate, and elegant, without, as it is heavy, bold, and melancholy within." Here he also saw what he described as "all that remains of the magnificent picture of the Last Supper, by Leonardo da Vinci." The masterpiece had faded, but neither time nor "the more fatal carresses of the restorers, have been able to obliterate its extraordinary merits." Milan was the neatest city in Italy, and its museums were fine. He was also impressed with the public parks and wished that "some intelligent and right-minded despot would seize the public purse and executive chair in every great city in the Union, for a sufficient space to pull down, with a decision like Napoleon's, whatever renders great central or circum-ambient promenades and parks impossible."[20]

From Milan the party entered Switzerland by way of Lake Como and the pass of the Splugen. In Switzerland Bellows found that nature rather than art and history was the central object of a visit. "We entered Switzerland as boys go from their lessons to their play."[21]

At Zurich Bellows found himself in what he described as "the first Protestant town we saw on the continent," and he enjoyed "breathing again a Protestant atmosphere." Here he found the old churches, once Catholic but now Protestant, stripped of everything beautiful so that "the plainest old New-England meetinghouse surpasses it in display and convenience." He found "the preaching dull, the hymn singing truly good, simple, tasteless and unintelligible to us, as the whole service was, we nevertheless enjoyed it highly, because it was *Protestant*." But Bellows also had a word to say for the Catholicism that he had enjoyed in Europe. "We have enjoyed Catholicism too, exceedingly; its architecture, art, music, splendor; its rich costumes, and its magnificent ritual," and then he added, "but not at all as Christianity."[22]

His appreciation of the Alps was increased by an overnight horseback trip with his party which consisted "of four ladies and three gentlemen." They then walked down to Lake Lucerne and a boat transported them to that city. Looking back on the Swiss mountain and lake scenery Bellows wrote "we hope to enjoy the recollection of it far more than we were able to enjoy the actual vision . . . for we possess the power of storing away the elements of them for future use and enjoyment." The journey continued from Lucerne to Interlachen—about fifty miles—and Bellows described how the ladies were carried up to a village in "chaises porteur; chairs, resting on poles, which were borne each by two men, and on which ladies are conveyed without peril or fatigue over the steepest and most inaccessible paths of Switzerland." The bearers even sang their Tyrolean songs as "they skimmed along with their burdens."[23]

Arriving at Fribourg Bellows had an opportunity to hear the celebrated organ played, its "admirable organist" performing several pieces of difficult music. "Some of the stops were so much like the human voice that we could hardly persuade ourselves that a woman was not lending her aid to the deception. The imitation of stringed instruments was so wonderful that a whole orchestra seemed often to break in upon a harmony which a band of wind instruments appeared to be making." From Fribourg the party moved to Vevey on Lake Leman. "From the terrace of our hotel . . . we looked upon the mountains, the woods, the blue waters, the villages, the vines, the dove-winged boats that had animated the genius of Rousseau and Byron.[24] Following the valley of the Rhone the party made its way to Matigny and approached the neighborhood of Mont Blanc. But they were not able to visit the mountain, although they did catch a glimpse of it as they passed from Switzerland into Savoy. "Nothing can surpass these peaks in elegance and effectiveness," Bellows wrote. "Towering far above these stands Mont Blanc himself, gaining from this point of view a special grandeur." He was tempted to try to scale the mountain but better sense prevailed. At a little chalet high up on the Montanvert he had the pleasant surprise of meeting an English Unitarian minister and some students of divinity at Geneva. Bellows broke in upon the discussion. "We had a very interesting reunion."[25]

Leaving the valley of Chamonix with great regret the party moved to Geneva situated at the foot of Lake Leman. This was the city of John Calvin, and although the churches were still in operation, Bellows wrote, "It was not easy to discover just what the state of religious opinion is." He wanted to know how far anti-

Trinitarianism prevailed, and he called upon one of the ministers for an answer. The church in Switzerland was a state church, but he found it allowed far more freedom than the English church. "The people listen in time to ministers of widely different opinions, whom, however, a mutual deference restrains from the expression of dogmatic peculiarities." He found three schools of thought which he termed the "orthodox, semi-orthodox, and liberal parties." The most popular preacher in Geneva was semi-orthodox. He was described not as a Trinitarian but as one whose theology started from the fact of human depravity. He could not learn in what proportion these three schools existed among the ministers. He concluded that in a national church there were handicaps to freedom of belief, and "we judge that nothing very favorable to the reputation of liberal views can proceed from their half-suppressed, inactive, or rather only negative existence in an established church."

The party went by steamboat to Lausanne and by carriage and boat to Neuchâtel which Bellows recalled was the birthplace of Louis Agassiz, and who now taught at his alma mater. From Neuchâtel to Basel took one day. Here Bellows found that the cathedral had been daubed with red paint over the rich old stone, inside and out. But "the tomb of Erasmus consecrates this edifice." From Basel to Strasbourg it was five hours by rail, and Bellows was impressed with the German railroads. He found the depots "tasteful" and the flower beds around the station "add a peculiar charm." The second-class railroad cars were as comfortable as the English first class. Bellows felt that the third-class cars were superior to the English second class.

Bellows was taken by surprise "by the attractive appearance of Strasbourg." The cathedral equally impressed him, "Certainly no building we had ever seen so instantly justified its reputation, and met the demands of our excited imaginations. It was grander in its proportions, more suitably placed, more unique in its effect, than anything we had conceived . . . . Nothing can exceed the airiness and delicacy of the ornamental work, the grace and richness of the parapets, the tracery of the windows, the interlacing of the exquisite lines that veil the facade. True it is a naked building, and lacks the furnished air of Saint Peters. But in religious effectiveness it far surpasses it."[26]

While Bellows was traveling around Europe the pulpit was filled largely by George Ware Briggs, who at that time was an associate minister to the Reverend James Kendall at Plymouth, Massachusetts. Bellows coaxed him away from Plymouth and he served the congregation well.[27] After two months had passed Henry's brother

Frank was able to tell Henry that he knew it would be "a great source of satisfaction to you to be told how much your people are pleased with Mr. Briggs. They have taken him into their homes and hearts *all over*, while he is delighted with the people, moved by theih kindness, and warmed by their sympathies, and he already knows about the entire parish, and has *dined & teaed* with any number. His preaching gives universal satisfaction & pleasure, and were you not so indelibly stamped upon the hearts of your people, I should fear for your continuing to occupy that place much longer."[28] Things had obviously gone well in Bellows's absence.[29]

She Sank Very Suddenly

But if things had gone well at the church it was an entirely different aituation for the Bellows's family. Refreshed and exhilarated by their journey, the Bellowses and Mrs. Kirkland set sail for home in early September, oblivious to the blow they would receive upon their return. Little Eliza—or Lilla as she was called—had become seriously ill just as the Bellows were embarking for the United States, and nothing could be done to save her. Her grandparents, the Townsends, had no means of reaching the Bellowses while they were at sea, and when the parents disembarked in New York, they were greeted with the shocking news that the healthy little girl whom they had left six months before was now dead.

Eliza, the third child and the first girl, was born on 11 September 1843. She died on 30 September 1848, and thus had just passed her fifth birthday at the time of her death. Lilla had taken sick on the fifteenth of September with what appeared to be a simple headache. They had been riding in a carriage and Russell Nevins, her uncle, felt at first that her ailment was only a sickness caused by the jouncing of the carriage. The next morning, however, she did not appear for breakfast, which was most unusual. Mrs. Townsend sent for Dr. Gates, who stayed with her for three nights, and described her as being in a precarious situation. She seemed alternately better and worse for another week. By Saturday night it was apparent that the 'end was near. The next morning at five minutes after nine o'clock, she sank "very suddenly & died peacefully." Uncle Nevins described his feeling: "It is difficult indeed, & nearly impossible to be reconciled to the departure of one so sweet, & lovely, & promising as she was." He concluded, "I have never ceased to hope that your return to us would be exempt from such a calamity as this, but God has ordered it otherwise, & we must submit."[1]

Anna Bellows (age 3½) and Mary Davis Bellows (age 1½), Courtesy of the Bellows Family

The first words that Henry Bellows wrote after the tragedy were appropriately to his mother. His brother Frank had met the Bellows's party at the wharf when the ship docked on 20 October "& broke in the most gentle and considerate manner the painful intelligence. I hope you know us well enough to believe that we could receive even this distressing announcement with calmness & submission. It has not been our misfortune to lack faith, fortitude or support at this trying hour."[2]

The greatest tragedy of Lilla's death was what it did to Mrs.

Bellows. She had been sickly for several years, but now she felt the death of her namesake more than anyone else. It had more lasting effects on her for she found that she could not bounce back like the rest of the family from Lilla's death. Henry Bellows wrote to Bartol, "Since our return my wife has flagged a good deal. Her mind works slowly and deeply. She is feeling the stroke more and more every day, and her intelligence, affections & the restored relations & habits of home bring the reality of our loss more distinctly before her." Yet Bellows was hopeful. "I am satisfied that she will triumph & be all the better for the trial & the experience."[3]

Bellows often meditated about his own destiny in his letters, but no writing is more meaningful in understanding him than this which he wrote on 1 November 1848. "At times I will confess to you, I have felt myself called to a more than common place in the world, to possess a more than ordinary discernment & to be capable of a wider & more permanent influence. A certain passion for relations with manhood in general, for a sphere as wide as the world & for an influence as broad as the race, has possessed me." Yet his call had not come "in the shape of ambition. No professional or literary success satisfies me or particularly excites or gratifies me. But I have felt a sort of confidence that there was something in me that would one day come out & enable me to do a substantial & abiding work for mankind." He continued in this vein: "You will not suspect me of mere egotism in these observations . . . for I confess that the lowest estimate I have of my mission is probably higher than my repute even with my most partial judges. He concluded, "The recent trial we have had, has called my attention anew to the operations of my nature, & connected with the renewal of my ministry. The consideration of what could be my special aim, has moved me to review my fitness, my duties, my powers . . . . Am I fitted for or do you discover in me the materials for any special influence?"[4]

During the second week of November Henry Bellows, Cyrus Bartol, and Samuel Osgood got together for a good talk session. Osgood felt that the three of them should study the dialogues of Plato together, one dialogue each session. Osgood also had informed Bellows that the Church of the Messiah wanted him to preach as a candidate. In the light of his future decision his attitude at this time is interesting, "I should like to serve the Church of the Messiah in every way possible, My going there now could not much serve them. If they are looking for candidates, I feel sure that they would not agree upon me . . . . It does not seem to me that I could be on the whole as serviceable there as here [Providence, R.I.]." He was pretty well convinced "that I am not upon the whole to their taste so much as are many men to whom kind friends do not think me inferior . . . I have had no reason to believe that the minds of the majority of the Messiah people have been or ever will be inclined towards me."[5]

At the beginning of December the angel of death again struck— twice—very close to Henry Bellows. This time it was not in his own parish, but the wife of his divinity school friend, William Silsbee. Shortly after this, Jonathan Goodhue died, and Bellows devoted the sermon the following Sunday, 3 December, to speaking of Goodhue's character. Jonathan Goodhue had been a prominent merchant and civic-minded citizen of New York City since the turn of the century. The son of the Honorable Benjamin Goodhue, formerly a Senator from Massachusetts, Jonathan Goodhue had married the daughter of General Matthew Clarkson. He joined Trinity Church and was an exemplary Episcopalian. He was particularly interested in the education of children, and taught Sunday school classes at Trinity for many years. When Unitarianism got its start in New York City, however, and Goodhue had ample opportunities to witness the unchristian attitudes his fellow Episcopalians held toward the new sect, he perceived the simple and earnest devotion inherent in Unitarianism, and finally joined with the First Congregational Church. There he had helped to establish the free school, among his other contributions to the church. He was also active in other community affairs, and his passing was observed by his fellow businessmen at a special meeting called by the Chamber of Commerce and merchants of New York. The shipping vessels in the harbor displayed their flags at half-mast.

Still suffering from the loss of his own little daughter, Bellows poured himself nobly into an eulogy for the distinguished merchant and member of the Church of the Divine Unity. Bellows mentioned something of Goodhue's background.[6] He had come to New York City "about forty years ago, and entered upon mercantile life." The public knew Goodhue only as a merchant. He had filled no public offices and had not made himself conspicuous in any philanthropic causes. He had not "distinguished himself by brilliant success." He felt that Goodhue's life would offer meager matter for a biographer. Bellows styled Goodhue essentially as a "private person," yet he was so highly regarded that there had been an outpouring of sorrow at his death. "It is the recognized worth of private character which has extorted this homage. It is not what he has done, but what he has been." Bellows also spoke of some other traits of Jonathan Goodhue, and one of these was his love of freedom. It was on this occasion that Bellows told the story of how Goodhue actually became a Unitarian.

Bellows completed his eulogy by reading a letter which Jonathan Goodhue had left for his family.[7] This letter concluded with the thought, "I am not conscious that I have ever brought evil on a single human being." Bellows's eulogy was indeed a remarkable testament to a remarkable man.[8]

In December 1848 Bellows developed plans for the expansion of the weekly newspaper which he had been editing for two years since the death of William Kirkland, the *Christian Inquirer*. He proposed to his board of directors that they raise the sum of $10,000 "to start a religious paper such as this country has never seen." He expected to have paid correspondents in the United States and abroad. He proposed to spend the capital over a period of two years, and during that time the paper would become so highly recognized, he believed, that the additional subscriptions would provide money for running the paper. He had preached in the church about the plan and $3,000 had already been subscribed. He asked Dewey if for "an adequate salary" he would become the editor of the paper, but Dewey was no more ready to accept this task than that of being a settled minister.[9]

On one of his excursions to his pulpit shortly after Bellows had returned from Europe, Orville Dewey had been implored by many of his congregation to remain among them as their minister. Dewey had been thinking of resigning because he felt he no longer had enough sermons in him nor the desire to make pastoral calls on his parishioners. When some of the congregation thus approached him, Dewey understood them to mean that his church was still very satisfied with him, despite his many absences. Thus, he said nothing of quitting his post to Bellows or to his own church members. Many of his friends, including Bellows, urged him not to be dismayed by New York, but to continue in the ministry, perhaps at a smaller church in a smaller town. To these encouragements, Dewey replied: "And here I may as well dispose of what you and others say and urge with regard to my continuance in the profession. To your question whether I have not sermons enough to last me for five years in some new place, I answer, NO, not enough for two." He continued, "I cannot enter into these affecting and soul-exhausting relations again and again, any more than I could be married three or four times. The great trial of our calling is the wrenching, the agonizing, of sympathy with affliction." He added, "I almost feel as if nobody but an intimate friend had any business in a house of deep affliction. In a congregation ever so familiar there is trial enough of this kind. If my friend is sick or dying, I go to his bedside, of course, but it is as a friend." He did not like to come to a bedside "in an official capacity—there is something in this which is in painful conflict with my ideas of the simple relations of man with man. Now all this difficulty is greatly increased when one enters upon a new ministration in a congregation of strangers . . . ."[10]

In contrast with Dewey's attitude toward pastoral visiting, Bellows fully enjoyed people, and was always ready with compassion and sympathy for anyone who needed it. He was adept at spontaneous conversation, and could be gay or serious, as the occasion warranted. During the first ten years of his ministry, he made it a practice to visit every family in his large congregation at least once a year, and at any time when there was sickness or suffering. As his interests in and acceptance among the broader community expanded, however, he necessarily cut down on the number of parish calls he made each year; yet he seldom passed up a chance to help someone in difficulty if he thought he could be of service. In this respect Henry Bellows and Orville Dewey were temperamental opposites.

A week before Christmas in 1848, Orville Dewey at last decided that he could not for reasons of health and temperament continue to vacillate between Sheffield and New York. The church concurred and his relationship with the Church of the Messiah was terminated. Bellows wrote to Dewey, "I have not known how to speak of the seeming separation in our fellowship in this field of Christian labor, how to refer to your withdrawal from New York, how to express my own sorrow that such a change should be deemed necessary. Bellows felt "dreadfully isolated" in his position in New York. He had many friends and acquaintances but "with almost no one whose intellect & heart combine to supply the needs of my own." Bellows himself had no difficulties adjusting to the ministry. He wrote to Dewey "I am just beginning to preach . . . I see how all-essential, simplicity & reality of thought, of feeling of tone & manner are to the effectiveness of the pulpit. It seems to me that I am taking wrappage after wrappage of artifice from the very tones of my voice, & falling back upon the utterance of nature & truth, and as it respects subject & matter." He continued "it seems to me that the great message we hear [. . .] ever filling our souls with a desire for opportunities to devour it, & to supply in itself the perrenial subject of our preaching,

& to gather about it all that is most animating, earnest, interesting & vivid. I confess I have no longer difficulty about subjects for sermons. The reality of religion itself is a perpetual theme."[11]

Orville Dewey said very little about his final abandonment of the pulpit of the Church of the Messiah. He had served the Washington church during the winter of 1846/47 evidently seeking a change of scene. Then he struggled through the duties at the Church of the Messiah for another year. He wrote, "In the spring of 1848 I sold my house, and retired to the Sheffield home, continuing to preach occasionally in New York for a number of months longer, when early in 1849, my connection with the Church of the Messiah was finally dissolved." Dewey lived without a salary most of the rest of his life with occasional lecturing and preaching duties. He attributed his ability to survive financially to having always put aside a portion of his salary for just such a situation. "On leaving New York I was not reduced to utter destitution."[12]

At the annual meeting of the society, which was not held until 2 January 1849, the society voted to raise Bellows's salary to $3,000, even though they still owed the full $28,000 of the original mortgages on the land under the Church of the Divine Unity. Bellows, unlike Dewey, was getting ahead in the professional world.

Trembling and Rejoicing in Responsibility

When Meadville Theological School was being incorporated, in 1845, Rufus P. Stebbins, the Dean, asked Henry Bellows to serve on the initial board of trustees of the school. It was a duty to which Bellows devoted much time and energy all of the rest of his life. Stebbins informed Bellows that "our students are not men of education, but I think something valuable can be made out of most of them."[1] There were fourteen in the Junior Class, seven in the Middle Class, and three in the Senior Class. When the official incorporation took place Rufus Stebbins and Mr. Frederic Huidekoper[2] were the faculty, and a Mr. Brookes had made a liberal donation of books for the library.

Now, four years later, in April 1849, Professor Huidekoper informed Bellows of the precarious state of the finances of the school. A plan for raising funds had been adopted, but Huidekoper insisted that neither he nor Rufus Stebbins could really leave the campus to try to raise funds. He did not know where Mr. Stebbins's salary for the next year would come from. "Are there not friends in

Elizabeth Shaw Melville, Courtesy of the Berkshire Athanaeum

New York who are persuaded of the importance of the matter sufficiently and who without adding to their subscriptions will *guaranty* that the contribution from the three churches in N.Y. and Brooklyn shall not in any case fall below $500 per annum for the next five years unless endowment enables us to dispense with it?" Professor Huidekoper's father was going to Boston to try to effect a subscription in New England of $1,000 for the next five years. But he was not optimistic that his father would be able to do this. "If he cannot effect a subscription what are we to do? Stop! We must not do this." It was a precarious way to insure continuity of the school, but since endowments were hard to come by, annual giving was the next best thing.[3]

In 1849, the novelist Herman Melville took a pew in the Church of the Divine Unity, and paid a fee of $14.15 for the privilege. The young novelist had married Elizabeth Shaw of Boston on 4 August 1847. Her father was the Chief Justice of the Supreme Court of the State of Massachusetts and a Unitarian. Melville was known for his South Sea adventures, and for some early novels about those adventures. He had published *Typee* in 1846, *Omoo* in 1847, and during the year that he attended the church he was to publish two more books, *Mardi* and *Redburn.* In 1850 the family moved off to Pittsfield for thirteen years during which time Herman Melville would publish *White-Jacket* and write his famous *Moby-Dick.* Their children were baptized by Orville Dewey while the family lived in Pittsfield. Herman recorded the baptisms in his family Bible.[4]

The Church of the Messiah had been through the difficult process of choosing a successor for Orville Dewey. Many in the society had wanted to call Thomas Starr King who had been preaching at the church. But he could not agreeably leave his parish, and there was strong opposition to him because he was a Universalist. Bellows wrote to Dewey that "Mr. Tileston thinks there never was such preaching in that pulpit." After these rather untactful words to Dewey—who considered himself a great preacher— Bellows explained that his good friend Samuel Osgood had been given an unenthusiastic call by the Church of the Messiah.

Yet, there was not much enthusiasm at the Messiah for Osgood. "With full knowledge of his defects as a preacher, & of the unattractiveness of his manner, but with a deep sense of the excellence of his character, the largeness of his attainments, the variety of his accomplishments, his parochial efficiency, social talents, general usefulness, & wide reputation (for his age) he was called, not merely by the society, but by *our religious public* in this place!" Bellows wanted Dewey to advise Osgood about accepting the call, for Bellows felt that with Osgood he could work fraternally, "no one would take off so many of my cares, no one would do as much for the Paper [*Christian Inquirer*] & the general cause as Osgood."

Bellows was, however, deeply concerned. "The upper church is utterly reckless & thoughtless of my rights. It imposes all its necessary duties upon me without so much as saying 'I thank you.' I am out of all patience with its lukewarmness, its caprice, its injustice.

*Herman Melville, in 1861, Photo by Rodney Dewey, Courtesy of the
Berkshire Athanaeum*

I do not envy the man who goes there & were I to advise Osgood
simply for his own happiness, I would say, 'Stay where you are. Do
not connect yourself with a people without gratitude, discernment,
constancy, or justice!' "[5] These were pretty strong words from
Bellows who obviously was sick and tired of the equivocation of the
parish in calling a new minister.

However, the same day Samuel Osgood wrote to Bellows that
"the die is now cast & I come to you." Mr. Curtis and Mr. Warren
had written to him that the so-called opposition to him in the church
was not significant. Therefore he had resolved to accept the call; "my
mind is clear, humble, & I hope not unsustained by a faith not of this
world."[6] He had meanwhile received a cheering word from Dewey
before Bellows's letter reached Sheffield. And he was putting the
matter to his parish as to whether they would let him go to New
York.

On 10 May 1849, there occurred in the city of New York, not far from Bellows's home, the famous Astor Place riot. Partisans of the American actor Edwin Forrest, in resentment of the appearance of his rival and competitor, William Charles Macready, stoned the Astor Place Opera House. Paving blocks, bottles, stones, anything that was available, were used by both sides. The riot got completely out of hand, and in desperation the militia was called in. The mob promptly attacked the soldiers, and finally the commanding officer ordered that the mob be fired upon. The result was that the mob was dispersed but twenty-two persons were killed and thirty-six injured. The ability of the lowest classes of the city and the foreign "elements" to incite such a riot and to flaunt law and order upset the more solid citizens of New York City.

Bellows took the occasion the following Sunday, 13 May, to preach "A Sermon Occasioned by the Late Riot in New York." "It is impossible," he said, "to fix our thoughts this morning upon any subject not connected with the recent dreadful events which have shocked our community." He proposed to preach a philosophical sermon on "Our conceptions of the nature of Liberty." Government, he said, in its essence is a grouping of people to prevent the tyranny of disorder. "There is no freedom where law does not reign . . . . True liberty, then is not—the absence of government." He professed that "the beauty and glory of our free institutions is, that we have installed Justice in our place of power." In America we have more to fear "from the weakness than from the strength of the government; from contempt or defiance of law, than from its severity or unequal pressure."

Bellows spoke about religion and its application to law. "Christianity does not recognize any condition of complete emancipation from law. We are always under law, and the only question is, whether the law shall be a law of liberty, or a law of bondage." Bellows believed that if man is left to himself that "he is the most helpless of beings, and the most sure of quick destruction." In this helpless state man needed Christianity, for Christianity "proceeds upon the hypothesis that human nature is built upon a plan." Our institutions "grow out of the domination of Christian principles in the hearts of their founders. They are based upon Christian ideas; upon human equality in the sight of God, and upon the idea that education and religion are a better police than standing armies and an ever-watchful surveillance."

He mentioned the riots and termed them "a social and civil war in the city of New York, the most horrible form of calamity that can befall a community." He held that "a secret hatred of property and property-holders has been the main-spring of the riot." His real feeling emerged, "We have arrived, indeed, at petty notions of Liberty, when a few hundred of the worst portions of our people possess the power of disgracing the whole city, braving the authorities and defeating the rightful will of ninety-nine hundredths of the people."

Bellows was no pacifist. He believed that the outcry that the soldiers should not have fired upon the mob was misplaced. "To have hesitated on a recent occasion to fire upon the mob, would have been to endanger thousands of valuable lives for the sake of saving twenty—many of which paid the just penalty of their violence and folly." He implored his congregation to "hate and shun all liberty which consists in spurning authority." Bellows probably expressed in an eloquent way the less verbal feelings of his own middle and upper-class congregation.[7]

In May Henry Bellows attended the annual meetings of the American Unitarian Association in Boston. He wrote to Eliza that he was "far less . . . excited & physically exhausted by the meetings than usual." He spoke a great deal at the convention; five speeches, in fact. He was excited by what he felt was the growth of significant religious sentiments among Unitarians. "Never was [there] before such deep, calm, & spirit in our body, ministers, & laymen as at this season. God is manifestly in the heart of our denomination. I see & feel on every side indications of reality, sensibility, to divine truth & to the reception of views deeply cherished in my own head, as they have grown out of the solitary experience of my own ministry."

"Ought I," he asked Eliza, "to breathe the thought pressed upon me by my experiences here this week—that God has fitted & educated me in a peculiar manner to lead the coming generation of our portion of the Christian flock. But I truly tremble at the responsibility while I rejoice in it, tremble to see that I possess a peculiar power over my brethren and over the people." Having been a constant speaker at the meetings Bellows was especially happy that he had been asked to give the sermon at the closing communion service on 31 May.[8]

Bellows, true fundraiser that he was, decided that he could not possibly raise money for the Meadville Theological School unless he had seen it with his own eyes. He also had another idea in his mind. He wanted to visit the spot near Adrian, Michigan, where his twin brother, Edward, had died, and if possible ship the remains back to the family tomb in Boston. He suggested to Bartol whom he had

Anna Langdon Bellows (age 4½), Russell Nevins Bellows (age 7½), Mary David Bellows (age 2½) who died shortly after this picture was taken. Original Daugerotype, Courtesy of the Bellows Family

asked to join him, that he was "long ago reconciled to my noble Brother's departure."[9]

Bellows made the trip without Bartol. He was satisfied with what he saw at Meadville. Ready to go further on his journey he penned a letter to Eliza just before the stagecoach left, writing, "I am entirely satisfied with the results of my visit thus far. It has been justified by events . . . . The exercises yesterday were of a very interesting character, and we have had constant meetings of the board of trustees, transacting very important business."[10] Bellows boarded with the Huidekopers and found everything agreeable except for Eliza's absence. He expected to reach Buffalo three days later but he doubted that he would be able to make the trip to Michigan.

Samuel Osgood was installed as minister of the Church of the Messiah on 3 October 1849, and Bellows was able to tell Orville Dewey by the end of October about the situation at the church. "Osgood is well received; too well, that is, prejudices melt away so fast. It is always desirable that the weather should clear away, without the wind's bucking round It doesn't hold in such a case." He believed ''that after the New York furore is past, Osgood's substantial merits will justify the calm confidence of the people."[11]

Bellows reported new anxiety and sadness in the family to Orville Dewey on 24 October 1849: "Today, alas! *Mary* is seriously attacked with *dysentery* and we have the shocking prospect of that long & uncertain disorder before us."[12] Two weeks later Henry Bellows reported to his sister, "I do not feel any longer like withholding the apprehension that we are about to lose our little Mary. She has been sick with the dysentery for a fortnight." The case had appeared to be a manageable one, but a "tendency to dropsy in the brain" had developed, "under which our precious child will undoubtedly sink. Nothing but a miracle can save her, and you may safely conclude, I think, by the time this letter reaches you, that she is no more."

He wrote in anticipation of little Mary's death, "It is impossible to realize the extent of this new bereavement. I seem to see my family melting away like snow drifts in spring. It would hardly surprise me to see either of my other children called away suddenly, or my wife, or to be summoned myself. Out of five beautiful and promising children, when Mary is gone, there will be only *two* left, and one of them, our darling Annie, has been always regarded as the least sturdy of them all." Bellows seemed to be content to adopt a philosophy of "submission to the perfect will of God." God, he said, "knows perfectly the pain & loss he is occasioning us, he has his own reasons for it. They are good ones & they have our best welfare in view." Henry continued, "Do not grieve for us. We shall both try to turn our great desolation into spiritual food. I fear sometimes lest my poor wife should break down under the repeated blows, but she grows wiser and more submissive under these experiences, and one blow prepares us for another."

Bellows wrote to his sister that he held the letter for thirty-six hours before posting it. On Wednesday morning, he wrote that it was now 8:30 A.M. and that Mary had died at 7:15 A.M. 'We shall commit her ashes to the tomb that holds our little Edwards' & our precious Lilla's dust tomorrow afternoon."[13] Mary Davis Bellows who had been born on 13 April 1847 now was dead at the age of two and one-half years.

Henry was wise in worrying about his wife more than being concerned about his own sorrow, for from this time on Eliza became more delicate in health. These deaths of three of her children seemed to be more than her mental or physical nature could bear. To Bartol Henry wrote, "Eliza is sadly shattered at heart but calmer & more resigned than anybody who did not know her well could expect . . . But we never can be, we do not wish to be the same persons, we have too much in the grave, too much in heaven, to love this world too well."[14]

The same day Henry Bellows probed a little more into his concept of the will of God in the light of his loss. "I have been examining myself to see how to face submission & acquiesence in bereavement as, a great Christian grace. . . . How much necessity does to reconcile us to the loss of our friends! A sensible man sees the absolute folly of contending with a hopeless misfortune. We have nothing to do but *submit* & it is easy, comparatively, after natural grief has had its short sway." Bellows did not believe that he had the right to criticize God, "or to oppose his ordinations . . . What I long for is the wisdom, strength, obedience, that shall enable me to drive out of my heart all selfish, coarse, untruthful, worldly, ambitions & self-seeking feelings. These I am deeply conscious possess too large a place in my heart. I have great temptations from . . . pride, a sense of power which I pray to be enabled to control or overcome."[45] To his mother Henry wrote that seeing the little "coffins of my *three* dear children lying side by side in the family tomb" was the worst experience of all. And he added, "It is impossible to grieve *twice* with the same bitterness."[16]

Unagitated by Abolitionist Fever

The year 1849 was a difficult and traumatic one for New Yorkers. New York City was changing. Broadway between the Battery and Chambers Street was being paved with granite blocks. Fifth Avenue above Eighteenth Street was a bumpy unpaved road. The village of Yorkville held about one hundred houses. G. T. Strong marveled in his journal, "How this city marches northward,"[1] and William Washington Russel and Lucy Channing Russel, pillars of the church, had moved to Staten Island. The Astor Place riot had most of the city in an uproar. For days thereafter the city lived in the tense aftermath of the riot, while almost suffocating from an intense and unseasonable heat wave. A cholera epidemic broke out and reached its peak toward the end of July, taking the lives of many New Yorkers.

For Henry Bellows it had been a year of trauma with the death of little Mary and Eliza's increasing withdrawal as she lost the third of her five children. Bellows's own personality was changing after a decade in the New York church. "I don't believe much in new friendships," he wrote. "It is harder as we go on to become interested in fresh people. The wax loses its 'melting mood,' we neither stick to others nor they to us. We become so fragmentary, live in so piece-meal a way, are so divided up among a thousand interests & people, that we have not a whole heart to give to anybody." His conclusion is somewhat startling, "I make no friendships & hardly expect to make any more. I must cling to those I have."

Bellows was changing in other ways also. "I am beginning to find out that I am a less social person than I supposed. Every year the social claims of society & indifferent people grow more irksome. I find I am fastidious, see few characters that interest me, & mingle in the world in rather a forced or abstemious form, keeping a sort of outer robe of courtesy & companionship for common use."

He was also growing inside his own being, his spiritual life. "Every stage of life and of spiritual development has its besetting & peculiar dangers. We are always between Scylla & Charybdis, just on the verge of ruin." He believed that "Spiritual life is like tightrope dancing. Its perils & the first condition of its excellence, its *spring*, is derived from the precarious footing it possesses, & the performer is bounded up to heaven by just escaping prostration to the earth." He stated that "Nothing could have persuaded me five years ago that so many battles lay between me & the kingdom of heaven. But I find a new crop of dragon's teeth springing forth in every new field I tread. This winter has been very eventful with me *inside*."[2]

But it was not just New York City nor the interior personality of Henry Bellows that was changing. National issues such as the question of slavery were in the forefront of the minds of thoughtful Americans. Bellows had lived for two short periods in the Southern States. The first was the rather brief stay in Louisiana when Bellows tutored young Isaac Baldwin near Alexandria, Louisiana. Bellows did not stray far from his tutorial duties to see any consequences of slavery in its operation in the South. But his six-month stint as the acting minister in Mobile, Alabama, in 1838 was a different kind of experience. Here he was in the midst of Southern society, and he witnessed Southern economics—based upon the slave trade— firsthand. Bellows at that time felt the slave trade confounded all moral distinctions. He also made the decision not to take the pastorate that was offered him in Mobile. He voiced no dissatisfaction with the congregation nor the church at Mobile. One must assume that his opposition to a slavery-based society played a large part in this decision not to settle in the South.

As the years went by the slavery issue was increasing in intensity in New York with the controversy waxing hot between the conservative merchant class and the abolitionists. In November of 1845 George Simmons, whom Bellows had known at the Divinity School and who was soon to become minister of the Springfield, Massachusetts church, wrote a critical letter to Bellows about Unitarian ministers' lukewarm opposition to slavery. Simmons noted that in the list of names appended to a recent document called "the Unitarian Ministers' Protest" that "hardly one of the names by which our denomination is known abroad, & in which it may be said to have blossomed, is among them." He listed the missing names: Gannett, Dewey, Parkman, Putnam, Peabody, Bartol, Lothrop, Huntington, Walker, and Bellows. "How does this happen? Have you not those antislavery convictions expressed in the Protest? Or are you biased & fettered by your relations to the people you influence?" Simmons posed the possibility: "are you wiser & do you discern an impropriety in such an expression, to which the rest of us are blind? Do let me know how it is in your case. Why did you not sign it? Did you not believe or did you not hope? Or is it prudence? Or do you reckon the matter not in your sphere?"[3] Simmons indicated that he was not criticizing. He was only asking for information. There is no record of Bellows's response.

In the intervening years until 1850 many things happened in the country which made moderate antislavery people feel that the slave interests were going too far. In the debate over the Compromise of 1850 it was the Fugitive Slave Law—the return to the owners of a runaway slave—which alarmed these moderates. It was in the midst of the debate on this law in Congress that Henry Bellows decided that he must speak from his pulpit. He believed that slavery had definitely become a moral issue and that no Unitarian could any longer pass the issue over as just economic in nature. The context of the delivery of this sermon is important in understanding it.

On Sunday morning, 3 March 1850, Bellows announced from his pulpit that he was going to speak on the question of slavery at the evening service. Bellows summarized the situation: "all subtle ecclesiastical and theological discussions were silenced by the angry voice of public debate over the threats of nullification and secession made by Southern legislatures and in the open Congress of the nation." Bellows claimed that "the abolitionist fever had never greatly agitated our congregation, chiefly because moderate and constitutional views had always been maintained in the pulpit and the right of open discussion upheld without being abused. We did not stifle the question and conveniently excuse ourselves from having any opinion about it because it was a political question and politics did not belong in the pulpit." He suggested the answer "we did not as a congregation sympathize with the abolitionists pure and simple, who thought the Constitution a 'compact with hell' and that slavery was to be abolished at the cost of Union or the breaking of our constitutional vows."

He said, "once only did I have any conflict with the congregation on this subject," and Bellows told the story of his conflict with some of the members of his congregation over the issue of slavery. "I had announced in the morning . . . that I should give a careful lecture in the evening on American slavery. I had been anxiously considering my duty, and was under solemn bonds to speak out on the subject." He further explained what then took place. "We had many merchants connected by shipping lines with Southern ports, who were naturally sensitive even to the least agitation of the subject." But "in the afternoon I was waited on by a committee of the trustees to advise me to break my engagement and suppress my discourse on grounds of policy and peace. I was not able to yield my deliberate sense of duty to their counsel, and was obliged to decline their request." Bellows explained, "I gave my discourse, and it freed our pulpit from that moment from any expectation or suspicion of silence or complicity with those who defended or excused slavery as right in itself because politically we were entangled with it and had given away our right to destroy it by any methods except those of law and moral persuasion."[4]

What Henry Bellows was referring to was a note written to him on Sunday afternoon, 3 March 1850, by Moses Grinnell. This very prominent layman, whose shipping interests gave him a concern in avoiding conflict with the Southern states, expressed a hope that Bellows would not carry out his promise made that morning to preach on the issue of slavery in the evening. Grinnell wrote: "In my judgment it will be productive of much evil in our society, and I cannot myself as an individual, see these matters introduced into the pulpit."[5]

But Bellows was not to be deterred from preaching about an issue in which he honestly believed there was a moral concern, even if the advice of one of his leading laymen, and the president of the board of trustees, had been against it. Having largely left political affairs out of the pulpit, he believed slavery to be a moral issue. It would take more than a letter from one of his richest, most prominent, and most loyal parishioners to keep him from speaking what he believed to be the truth. He commented: "I have been intensely interested in the political attitude of affairs, & preached on the crisis last Sunday evening [3 March 1850], after receiving a sort of official recommendation that I would not. But I heeded not, as a clear & sober conscience made me feel it a broader duty to contribute my truth to a current public Sentiment." He explained the nature of his opposition. "In this community the commercial view of Slavery prevails, & is to be withstood. My views are not ultra, but I maintain the necessity, not only of no compromise, but of an *avowed intention* to change the constitution by constitutional means, as soon as we have the power." He knew that this point of view was "considered very bad doctrine. I can hold no other."

He was also shocked at how some politicians were equivocating on the issue. "Mr. Webster has disgraced himself, I think *ruined* himself by his polite bid for the Presidency. His speech seems to me to be far less creditable to him, than Calhoun's. I am grieved, shocked at the position he takes." Bellows had hoped "that he would redeem his character by coming out upon high & holy ground, & speaking the voice of the northern conscience. There seems nobody to do it in the Senate."[6]

Mr. Grinnell was not the only one who disapproved of Bellows's position on slavery. When Bellows wrote an editorial in the 16 March issue of the *Christian Inquirer* expressing the same views, a meeting of the Directors of the Unitarian Association of the State of New York (which sponsored the *Inquirer*) was called and the Directors resolved:

That the leading editorial in the Christian Inquirer of the 16th instant, is not satisfactory to the Directors of the Association.

That the Christian Inquirer was not established for the dissemination of ultra Abolition doctrines.

That the President & Vice President of the Association be a Committee to present a copy of these resolutions to Rev. H. W. Bellows.[7]

A week later Bellows added some further information about the stir his slavery sermon had caused: "Here am I now, a plain, blunt man in a peck of trouble because I don't like slavery or its defenders & choose to say so in my pulpit & paper. For the last fortnight I've had a dreadful buzz about my ears." He briefly enumerated what had happened: "Trustees officially entreating silence, Proprietors of *Inquirer* passing votes of censure . . . & I poor conscience ridden man unable to oblige or give heed to any of them."[8] But he was optimistic, "it will come out right I suppose. I am apt to light on my feet even in the boldest business, but this is the first time I have had any serious trouble with my people." His dislike of the vacillation of Webster had gotten him into trouble, "Daniel Webster is so tremendous a favorite with the mercantile interest, that a word against him, seems like putting your hands into the commercial pocket & stealing a year's thrift. I rejoice to see the unanimity with which the religious press of the country has spoken out against the low-toned morality of that self-seeking speech." And he added, "I hope Massachusetts will disown it & him."[9]

Bellows threatened to resign from his position as editor of the *Inquirer*. He received an answer from the editorial board. They acknowledged his letter and accepted his resignation with earnest regret.[10] Later the matter was patched up and Bellows remained as editor of the *Inquirer*, with more freedom to operate.

Actually, when it came to the issue of slavery Henry Bellows was a moderate. Dr. Conrad Wright, a Unitarian historian, has divided the ministers of the Unitarian churches into three categories regarding their stand on the slavery issue. Since there were only nine Unitarian churches in the Southern states, and since most of the ministers had been trained in the North, it was natural that few Unitarians were preaching for the retention of slavery. Only Theodore Clapp of New Orleans could be classified in this category. He was known as an apologist for slavery.

There were other Unitarian ministers who took somewhat less strong a stand, but their sense of compromise sometimes led them to be considered as proponents of slavery. Orville Dewey was one of these. "Deeply concerned for the preservation of the Union and constitutional processes, he sought the containment and gradual abolition of slavery within that framework. Persuaded that Southern threats of secession were more than bravado and bluster, he accepted the compromise of 1850, deeming the Fugitive Slave Law a lesser evil than disunion."[11] It was this willingness to go along with Daniel Webster that caused some friction between Dewey and Henry Bellows.

Opposed to these men who either condoned slavery (Clapp) or believed that the law of the land ought to be obeyed (Dewey) there were men at the opposite abolitionist extreme. Charles Follen had been one of these, but he was no longer on the scene. Probably Samuel J. May, who successively served churches in Brooklyn, Connecticut, South Scituate, Massachusetts, and Syracuse, New York, was the most appealing figure among this group. Unlike some of the abolitionists, he never became abusive in criticism of those who disagreed with him. He was a good friend of Henry Bellows, and they wrote many friendly letters to each other, May always holding staunchly to his abolitionist point of view with Bellows representing the point of view of conciliation. May also preached the doctrine of nonviolence. Unlike John Brown he would not fight to free the slave, he believed like Bellows that the emancipation of the slaves could be accomplished by peaceful means, perhaps by purchase by the government and a subsequent freeing of the slaves.[12]

As Samuel J. May was the best type of the Unitarian abolitionist, so "Henry W. Bellows of New York may serve to exemplify the moderate antislavery preacher. In his antislavery, as in his doctrinal preaching, Bellows was very much a middle-of-the-roader, trying to encompass as much as possible of the positions of those on both sides of him, sympathizing at least partially with each in turn, without identifying himself with any extreme." Bellows "had a good word to say about abolitionists on more than one occasion, especially when others were attacking them. But he would characteristically couple praise with blunt criticism, or conversely, temper his criticism with a heavy acknowledgment that unpopular prophets are needed to keep the line of march on the move." Yet, "He was equally quick . . . to defend Orville Dewey from abolitionist attacks, even though Dewey took a position on the Fugitive Slave Law for which he himself had no sympathy."[13]

After the Mexican War, which Henry Bellows opposed as did so many other Americans, Bellows adopted a more outspoken position. His position could be broadly called from that period until the opening of the Civil War a "free-soil position." He believed that slavery was an evil without qualification, but he despaired that a solution to the problem was within the reach of the legislatures. He felt that the country had to abide by the Constitution, "until we have legal power to change it."[14] Meanwhile he believed that the country must be concerned about liberty, not slavery. He felt that the extension of slavery must be prevented at any cost.

CHAPTER FOUR

Going Beyond Channing

Four Long Nines

Family and personal problems also concerned Henry Bellows. Mrs. Bellows's health was not good. "She is sensitive, easily excited, often depressed. The loss of her children, her ceaseless aspiration after the unattainable, natural fastidiousness, constitutional delicacy, child-bearing, & the society or non-society of a busy husband, have all combined to try her constitution to the utter-most." Yet he was hopeful for "she keeps up . . . & has many good days & hours & I am always hoping to find the panacea which will cure her; either moral or material medicine, I can't say which she requires."[1]

Henry felt that a new home might help the situation, so early in April 1850 the Bellowses moved to a new house at 56 Irving Place, "just one street back of where we lived in Irving Square, a delightful & quiet residence."[2]

All through the thirty years of their marriage Mrs. Bellows's health was of constant concern to Henry. He would plan trips on which she was to be his companion, and then her health would become so "delicate" that she had to be left at home. This weakness on her part brought out a tenderness in Bellows seldom seen by his contemporaries and scarcely realized by moderns who do not know Bellows personally. On one such trip he wrote to her: "I don't want to be separated, my darling, from you. We are mutually necessary to each other's daily happiness. I never know how much so 'till I get away from home. You would be entirely satisfied, I am sure with the space you occupy in my thoughts during absence. Nothing 'without thee is sweet.' Oh, my dear Lizzy how I wish & pray that I could see you well & happy!" Henry then asks the question he was constantly asking, "Are we making any grand mistake in our mode of life? Or is it that your clay is of so delicate a texture that the fragile vase that carries your spirit is not able to bear even the ordinary jars of this world? If even that could be made *certain*, it would be something fixed to act upon in the future." He concluded, "There is no sacrifice of ambition, convenience, preference, professional or personal, that I could not make to secure your intrinsic happiness. Do not think these to be words—for upon every good opportunity I will prove them to be deeds."[3]

During the summer of 1851, he and Eliza spent five weeks vacationing at Nahant Beach in Massachusetts, a fashionable resort for the well-to-do at that time. They had, he wrote his mother, a cold week "in this outpost of terra-firma" but with "promenading, bowling, flirting, and gossiping they made it a pleasant one."[4] Thanks to some of his wealthy parishioners who were also summering there he met many famous people: Henry Wadsworth Longfellow, William H. Prescott, President Jared Sparks of Harvard, Senator Charles Sumner, "& a host of Boston lawyers & fashionables." He was particularly impressed with the historian William Prescott whom he had not known before. His colleague, Samuel Osgood, commented, "You certainly were in intellectual clover at Nahant."[5]

They surrendered themselves to the delights of hotel life. "Here are forty or fifty nice people, all in a heap, free from care or anxieties, passing a month together in a delightful, cool, breezy *prospective* hotel, all anxious to please, & amicably coquetting with manners, dress, gossip, & frolic, with each other." Even Bellows, who was quite conscious of his ministerial calling, found himself slipping. "I was desperately in love consequently with most of the ladies."[6] Such a vacation from the cares of the parish and from the tragedies of their private lives was what both of them needed.

But his professional cares were never far from his mind. One concerned the name of his church. The first indication of the name All Souls being applied to the First Congregational Church is in a letter to Cyrus Bartol dated 1 November 1850, in which Henry Bellows uses the words "All Souls Parsonage" at the top of the page.[7] It was not until the dedication of All Souls Church in December 1855 that this title of the church was used officially. But already five years before this time, Bellows was using the title in regard to the parsonage. "The Church of the Divine Unity" was an outdated name for him only five years after it had been adopted.

Another concern was the developing Unitarian movement in New York. A new Unitarian Society (the Third Unitarian Society) had been founded in Brooklyn, and was to be launched on the twentieth of April. This was a split-off from Brooklyn's First Church, whose pastor was Frederick A. Farley. This incident shows Bellows's tremendous ability at healing festering wounds—an ability that was to grow as the years went by. Bellows had been quite interested in this new movement in South Brooklyn, "1st on account of the general interests of religion & our own particular view of it, in that community, 2nd, on account of Farley, to whose safety it has seemed indispensable to colonize the disaffection in his society before it cankered the whole mass."[8]

The committee came to Bellows with a request that he should preach the opening sermon. He declined "on the score of avoiding the appearance of forwardness, or of competition with Bro. Farley, which I thought ought to prevent the New York brethren from being publicly prominent in the new movement." He then advised them to "ask *Farley* himself to do it, & in place of him (should he decline, which he undoubtedly will) his nearest clerical friend, Dr. Gannett, which would publicly commit him to extremely kindly relations with the new movement—which he now professes." Bellows explained that "what is necessary is not to secure his influence or favor, but simply to save his feelings & put him *right* in the eyes of the public. He is unquestionably *sore* about the new church & that can't be helped, the soreness comes from his unconscious inadequacy to his position."[9]

Another concern was his relationship with Samuel Osgood, the other Unitarian minister in Manhattan who had replaced Orville Dewey. The summer of 1851 was almost over and Samuel Osgood of the Second Church was thinking about returning to New York from his summer haven in Fairfield, Connecticut. He wrote to Bellows that he felt that they had not carried out the good relations between the two churches which they had promised each other when Osgood came to New York in 1849. "You & I have had pleasant society to ourselves, but have done next to nothing for our people in concert. We have not even had the exchanges which custom sanctions & our good fellowship should call for . . . I believe that it would be better for ourselves & people to give & have a more frequent sight of the brother pastor." Osgood went on to suggest that Bellows himself had proposed the plan that "we were to exchange—every alternate time in the morning & every alternate time in the evening. Let us begin this immediately, the evening of the second Sunday in September & follow it up regularly."[10]

Bellows was put in a very embarrassing position by this letter. He needed exchanges because two sermons every Sunday involved too much preparation and to use an old sermon often made sense. Undoubtedly the people at the Second Church would have been gratified with Osgood's suggestions to Bellows. His problem was that his own people would not have been as happy with the constant exchanges with Samuel Osgood. This called for some tact on Bellows's part.

The one thing Bellows did constantly, regardless of his problems, was to write letters. Steadily through the years his pen scratched away. He and Bartol would write each other friendly criticism of each other's literary style. Bellows felt that much of his friend's writing was "artificial and unmusical." He complained that he had to labor over one sentence for five minutes to know what Bartol meant.[11] Bartol agreed that his style was "quaint" but felt that Bellows sometimes went "into excess & extravagances, losing the fair & comprehensive statement of truth, & obliged afterwards to take back what he has said & contradict himself." Yet he enjoyed Bellows's "epistolary style" which was "amiable and seldom equalled."[12]

Yet in spite of differences which often were very serious, Cyrus Bartol respected Bellows and was impressed with his abilities: "I believe in you, & if without losing the variety and versatility of your powers, you can gather them up into single & total effort, you will come to do truly great things." He added, "I know of no one who so much as you affects me as being in a still growing condition. Yet, in the gristle, the sutures of your skull not yet closed, only let them not be, as with some children."[13]

Or Bellows might write his friend William Silsbee discussing the Scriptures. Bellows did not believe in the careful exegesis of the Scriptures as the place to find the truth of religion. In a somewhat Emersonian mood he expressed his ideas. "The doctrines of the universal Church seem to be flying about the world, like seeds which have been shaken from the lives of the saints, and as they lodge, they spring up or perish, according to the soil they light on. I find my soul responding to certain great Catholic ideas of Christianity." He explained why, "When I go to the Scriptures, not with an unprejudiced mind . . . & if I am confirmed, my faith is strengthened, if not, corrected. But I cannot understand what is called the scholastic method of teaching the Scriptures . . . But I am not a little perplexed with doubts & fears" and he added that he held "many of my views in suspense, or without a legitimate authority. But then my taste for exegesis is small."[14]

Another occasion might find him discussing one of his brother ministers. In Bellows's day even the most friendly of Unitarian ministers were apt to be very critical of one another, perhaps overly critical. The Reverend William Furness of Philadelphia spent a few days with Bellows while preaching at the Church of the Messiah. He preached "very offensively to many of the Messiah-ites . . . a real antislavery sermon. Some of our folks heard it, said it was eloquent, simple, genuine." Bellows explained that Furness was "in a high state of excitement, has his martyr's blood up, & really seems to think that there is not other subject worth talking about & no other test of Christian fidelity." He felt that his friend's spirit was very commanding in its earnestness of conviction. Then he added: "The great defect of his mind is its purely lyrical nature. He seems to despise history, institutions, experience, philosophy, coherency, & to think that no obstacle ought to be opposed to the prophecyings of any spontaneous man."[15]

In the year 1850, Henry Bellows described to Bartol on the day of his thirty-sixth birthday his poor prospects when he was a lad, and what had subsequently happened to him, "A *puny* boy, with a *timid* heart, & *womanish* taste who excited no expectation in any quarter, who seemed doomed to an invalid life or an early death." Yet a devine hand had guided him. "I have been led along by the hand of heaven! Sometimes bright, encouraging, happy always opening before, health & strength pouring in my veins, courage into my head, manhood into my spirit."[16]

On that same day he also wrote to Orville Dewey: "It is my birthday! 36! four *long-nines* of my life, I have smoked away! not in an utter offense, I humbly trust, in the nostrils of heavenly wisdom." Then he thought as usual about his twin brother, "the anniversary always reminds me in the review of my life, of him with whom I began it, my partner in the womb, the cradle, the school; the twin-brother of my heart & head up to the age of twenty-three! His miniature is open before me—a noble youth—far the best & loftiest son of his mother." Bellows always considered himself inferior to his twin. "He was my superior in all respects—unspeakably so in person—having the most commanding post of any young man I ever saw, & in intellect, aspiration, genius, not only far raised beyond the most flattering estimates of his twin-brother, but without exaggeration, the most gifted person of his age I ever knew." Yet he did not intend to exaggerate. "You will think I speak the language of partial love, and it has always been one of the bitterest griefs in thinking of him, that the world could never know what it had lost. But God knows." He wrote, "[It] will remain one of the incitements of my life, to run on earth a course parallel to his in heaven, that I may not be wholly unworthy to claim my place when we meet again."[17]

But his greatest concern was for his profession of the ministry and his place in it. Like all great men, he keenly felt and reflected on his doubts and his own limitations. Returning to work in the fall of 1851 after passing so much time at Nahant in doing nothing significant, his mind was riveted on the deeper meanings of the ministry. His reminiscences and self-searching show the true quality of his greatness and a constant search for what is meaningful in his life. He wrote about this self-searching: "I am three sermons deep in the fall business, & begin to take it quite naturally . . . I am usually much *depressed* after the first flush of the return is over." He was full of doubt, "It seems to me as if my ministry were to recommence with all the pangs & misgivings of a new birth. The old & primitive questions come up of personal fitness & of ways & means, nay even the more radical ones of the origin & authority of revealed religious institutions." He was led to even doubt "my usefulness, my fitness to preach, or the very use of preaching. Old methods disgust me, all machinery grates on my nerves, & I am ready to fly from a port to which I seem so little competent." Yet this was nothing new. "These feelings I have had many times, & got over them so many times, that I don't pay much practical attention to them. Still they annoy, & I suspect they have some reality at the bottom, which it were quite as well, I did *not* get over so regularly." But, he had found a positive use for these doubts, "The use I try to make of them is to give greater *reality* to what I do, & to determine to counteract all opposing influences by a more earnest & at the same time more honest ministry.[18]

But in spite of his doubts Bellows was a leader not only in his church but in the wider New York community. He was the chairman of a committee to receive the revolutionary patriot Louis Kossuth on his visit to the United States in December 1851. Bellows's sentiments were expressed thus: "we hope to make a good deal of money. It costs me worlds of work, real work of the hands, such as numbering, cutting, sorting, selling . . . tickets & keeping everybody else at work."[19] And this kind of work gave him a kind of satisfaction which he did not find in the work of the mind.

There could be no doubt that Bellows was maturing in his thinking about religion in spite of all the labors in the church and in his personal life. In January 1852 he wrote to William Silsbee that he believed as time went on he became "less orthodox & more confiding in liberal views all around." He said "I've tried hard to be conservative, but see that I'm a born radical by disposition & insight. & must take my place among the rough & ready pioneers of thought, not with the dainty & elegant gentry who tread the beaten road." Bellows also felt that he was growing "increasingly jealous of theology, which seems a poor substitute for religion." And he asked, "Is there any thing by which the world is more hag-ridden than by the popular theology?" He felt that what might be the best action would be "start out on a grand itinerary tour through the states, blowing a long trumpet against the dogmas which scare & stultify the public mind." He believed that "the only true doctrines are those which a thoughtful mind cannot *help believing*, & it is not of much consequence whether a man *knows* what he believes or no. Beef is beef, whether you know what you're eating or not, & faith is faith whether you've got a name for it or no."[20]

Beautiful Garments of Real Belief

In the fourth week in January 1852, Henry Bellows set off on one of his periodic exhausting speaking tours. He suffered from the extremely cold weather in the Boston area where he spoke on three successive nights at West Cambridge (Arlington), Beverly, and Salem. But in spite of all the speaking and the cold air he held out very well. He then had engagements at Haverhill, Medford, and Charlestown, Massachusetts. He wrote to Eliza that "there is nothing exciting in this work in which I am engaged! The repetition of the same stuff makes it nauseous . . . If my body [audience] thinks as meanly of my lectures as I do after two or three utterances of them, they must think me a very *stupid* fellow." He wrote that he went "into the hall to find an expectant crowd, with a hang-dog sort of feeling which I hope does not appear in the performance. I perform a *duty* in a dutiful spirit—but the pleasure, if there be any, must be wholly with the audience for I have none of it."[1] Yet Bellows persisted in wasting his strength in these lecture tours year after year. One of his concerns was the money which the lecture tours produced, another was that his national reputation depended upon many such appearances. But he detested every minute of it, or at least he claimed such!

After a quick trip to Walpole to see his ailing mother, whom he found better than he had expected, he went back to the Bartols in Boston. He had dinner one evening with Mr. and Mrs. Ralph Waldo Emerson and Dr. Frothingham. He found Emerson to be "as genial as possible." He believed that "Emerson is perhaps the first thinker in this country. The seriousness & truth of his *un*believing mind puts to shame the levity & uncandor of many believing folks. He seemed to me much nearer a skeptic, tho always asserting more confidence in

Henry Whitney Bellows, Engraving by A.H. Ritchie, Courtesy of the New-York Historical Society, New York City

rec'd opinions." He found Mrs. Emerson "a sad, not handsome, thoughtful, heroic looking person, very Yankeeish and inelegant without being a bit vulgar in her manners." Henry thought Mr. Emerson was "a thorough Yankee sublimated." And Bellows commented that he "never saw so fine an intellect in so small a *shell*. This man must somehow be condensed—made of the finest stuff rammed together with hydraulic power."[2] That evening after the dinner with the Emersons he went to Charlestown to lecture.

Two weeks later, in February 1852, he was off on another speaking/preaching trip, this time to Baltimore and Washington. Very proudly he wrote: "I preached yesterday to the President of the United States [Millard Fillmore], Senators & Honorables, & I was not afraid a bit. The greatest monarch on earth—the elected head of the American republic—walks a mile to church through a back street, & sits in a little Unitarian chapel—a member of the smallest & most assailed of all Christian sects." He saw that Washington was growing fast; it "has now 40,000 people. No business but sucking Treasury pap."[3] One thing which pleased him was that the bookseller he was staying with, Mr. Hudson Taylor, remembered his brother John Bellows as one of the best preachers and ministers the Washington Church had ever had and stated he wished they had called him. But he found "Congress . . . dull; the Senate, full of great men—the House monstrous . . . Perhaps mediocrity is . . . better . . . than genius." He termed "President Fillmore . . . the very Prince of Moderation. He looks neither wise nor foolish, neither proud nor humble, neither inspired nor besotted, a sensible, practical sober sort of personage, exactly expressive of the national character in its average, & I dare say providentially suited to the times." But the life of a President of the United States was not so hectic then. "His daughter tells me that he is not burdened with affairs & eats his three meals a day in the quiet of his family, without any thing to distinguish him, either in humor or style, from a retired merchant in Colonnade Row."[4]

On 22 February, Henry Bellows preached again at the Unitarian church in Washington, D.C. It was George Washington's birthday and Bellows appropriately preached on the subject of "Religious Liberty." He began by noting that Martin Luther, the "modern representative of *religious* liberty," was buried on 22 February 1546, "and although nearly two hundred years separated the men [they] had very much in common in their aims and aspiration of liberty . . . Both were [more] men of action than men of thought . . . Luther and Washington, together, represent the great idea of modern times —practical freedom, civil and religious. Their influence was never more potent, their inspiration never more precious, than now." He traced the history of the Reformation briefly, and indicated that Protestantism had its failures as well as its successes. "It expected to have a church as catholic, as popular, as engrossing as the Roman, without its Pope, its ritual, and its tyranny." But "its creed has broken into a thousand pieces—its church into a thousand sects." Its theological doctrines did not become popular, and were "as much aside from the actual mind and heart of the world, as is the discarded house of a shell-fish from its track to the sea."

Henry Bellows felt that "the attention of the world has been far more occupied with the liberty it [Protestantism] gave than with the dogmas it preached." He continued, "The consequence has been that more and more latitude, indefiniteness and inefficiency have characterized the doctrine and discipline of the Protestant Church, while the heart of its people has gone into other channels than purely religious ones." He termed the Unitarians "the Protestants of the Protestants." But Bellows asserted "our work hitherto (so far as the world is concerned) has been essentially a negative one—denying error, contending for entire freedom, disowning dogma and discipline." He believed that "every form of orthodoxy will pass through some phase of skepticism, and every form of church government not purely congregational and democratic, be broken up."

Bellows hoped that someday we would hear very little about either Catholicism or Protestantism. "The true faith will no longer be a Protestant, but an affirmative faith. Men will begin to put on beautiful garments of real belief, instead of throwing off ugly chains of prescription. The world will have set earnestly about the inquiry, not what is to be doubted, but what may be credited. Instead of fearing religious bondage, we shall dread spiritual nakedness." He relished the idea of the return of a positive faith to the religious world.

But this positive religion would not "appear without the use of means. Freedom, whether political or religious, has no power to produce anything. It merely leaves the faculties free to act." If people look out only for their own interests, then "freedom is worse than tyranny." He affirmed that "in maintaining schools and churches, we make a positive contribution to liberty, as in beating down monarchies and ecclesiastical pretensions and institutions, we make only a negative one. The same spirit which destroys the arm of spiritual and civil despotism, upholds the arm of the teacher . . . . Here, in this free land, let education, religious and secular, have our most generous support."[5] Bellows was beginning to affirm a more positive faith. Gradually being freed from even the shackles which Channing Unitarianism had imposed upon him, he, like Channing, was beginning to speak about a positive religion and not one of simple reaction against the excesses of the past. It was one of his greatest sermons.

There is one letter in the Bellows Papers addressed to "My dear Friend," and unfortunately there is no possible way of identifying this person. Sometimes portions of Bellows's letters make clear who "My dear Friend" is, but not this one. In this letter Bellows pours out his heart more than in any other on the subject of friendship. My own presumption is that the recipient is the manufacturer in Providence, William Weeden, because Bellows speaks of their "disparity of ages," and William Weeden was a much younger man, being twenty years Bellows's junior. Bellows had been talking with Mrs. Kirkland about friendship, and he wrote, "I had a sort of feeling that I was not grateful enough for the gift of such a cultivated, thoughtful, faithful & affectionate friend as you are." Bellows went on to say that he had three very good friendships with Dewey, Silsbee, and Osgood in addition to "excellent relations with fifty men of sense," and added, "But I find my manly heart really won wholly only by you." Then he commented about his other friends: "Dewey is too selfish—he is always thinking about himself—not in a mean temper—but so exclusively as to have only fragments of interest for his best friends." As for Silsbee he was "slow & sometimes tiresome, though pure as snow & strong, too, in many ways." As for Osgood he was "affectionate & faithful—& really" Bellows suspected, "loves me truly, as much as he can any one—& I him." But Bellows added that this unidentified friend, met him "at every point, pique my intellect, match my heart."[6]

In the middle of April 1852, Henry Bellows went south for his health accompanied by his sister Mrs. Dorr. "I have been experiencing some painful nervous symptoms for some weeks which necessitated immediate change of scene," he wrote to his friend Orville Dewey. He expected he might be gone as long as six weeks.[7] Five days later he was able to report to his wife from Richmond, Virginia, "We are both doing very well. My health is, I think, steadily mending. I have my occasional moments or hours of despondency & nervousness particularly if I . . . get too fatigued." They spent Wednesday at Washington with the Deweys where Dewey was supplying the Washington Church, and they did some sightseeing. They visited Mount Vernon by steamer. At Alexandria, Kossuth, Pulasky, and Governor Seward came aboard the boat and created some excitement. The two Poles welcomed Bellows as a faithful friend. Bellows visited Washington's tomb at Mount Vernon, but he was somewhat ashamed that his friend Kossuth should see "the neglected tomb of Washington which must have spoken to him of the ingratitude of republics."[8]

At Richmond Henry Bellows and his sister decided to take a stagecoach trip into western Virginia to visit Charlottesville and the Natural Bridge. However, they ran into the spring floods that devastated the region that year and had to return to Richmond. The rising waters threatened to cut them off from their return trip, and according to Bellows they had to stay in "some miserable log-tavern waiting for the deluge to subside." They returned to Washington where the Potomac was also swollen with the spring rains. They pushed on to Baltimore, and then decided to go to Cincinnati. Bellows was "decidedly better" in health. He had had his ups and downs, his healthy feelings and his morbid ones, but they were "decidedly lessening."[9] He felt that his lessening of mental exertion had helped with the healing process. The travelers went as far as Mammouth Cave, but here they were summoned home by a telegraphic account of Eliza Bellows's ill health. Bellows arrived home to find "Eliza not so sick as I apprehended, & now almost well from the medicine of a returned husband."

It had been a month since he had first had the "distressing symptoms." The parish had voted him a vacation until the first of September, and he wrote to Bartol, "Tomorrow, I go into the country to live with my family to *live for a year.*"[10] The family decided to go to Riverside to spend this year with Mrs. Bellows's parents while Mrs. Bellows's uncle, Russell Nevins, occupied the house in New York. Bellows felt that he must slow down and not test his endurance so much.

At the Townsends' farm in Riverside Henry tried "the effect of quietude & absolute abstinence from mental toil," but could not say that he was "materially better as yet." He rode horseback a great deal and did some manual work on the farm. His complaint was "a feeble digestive system acting in & with an enfeebled nervous system." He would have gone off to Europe if Eliza's health would have warranted it. But he could not dare to leave her, "for she is quite as sick as I, & needs my care." He had spent a whole day "without looking into a book" which was something of a Henry Bellows record.[11]

When his birthday arrived on 11 June, even the presence of Mrs. Dorr who came out to visit him every day at Riverside was too much. He wanted to spend the day in "self-examination, & to the memory of my dead but cherished brother Edward, who came into the world with me 38 years ago, & [who] left it without me 15 years since."[12]

To add to the complications of the household, Henry's mother-in-law, Mrs. Townsend, had been put on opiates by her doctor, suffered from a bad stomach, and was addicted to the opiates. Henry had a long talk with her about her problem and she promised, like most addicts, to use more self-control. But it was to no avail.[13] Many people, especially women, were put on opiates in the nineteenth century by their doctors and then suffered extreme guilt the rest of their lives because they could not shake their dependence on the drug.

Bellows's mother-in-law would wax and wane in her physical condition. One day she tried to vomit so hard that Bellows "actually feared that she would break a blood vessel." The doctor then ordered a dose of morphine, and Bellows had to go to Yonkers to get it. He sat up all night with her until she gradually became quiet. Bellows spent the days in her room, "having become so deeply interested in her case as to feel it to be no irksome duty, but a real privilege to be with her. She opened her mind & heart with great simplicity & fullness & gave me reason to hope that a deep impression had fallen upon her of the moral & spiritual horrors connected with her weakness." Mrs. Townsend was very upset when they got a nurse for her, claiming that the nurse was spying on her. The nurse was to prevent her from taking her medicine.[14]

Bellows poured out his concerns about the health of his family. He had come to Riverside worried about his own nervous condition and had been thrown into a maelstrom of health problems with Mrs. Townsend who was "very ill *in body & soul.*" He loathed the "terrible drugs." She had "a heart all love & a soul all pride." It had been an eye-opener to Henry who had assumed that she was a sick woman until his stay at Riverside where he learned about the horror of drug addiction. But discipline and prayer did very little for her condition of dependence upon opiates. Her brother and Henry were even "thinking of incarceration in an asylum." To add to the excitement and horror the ship *Henry Clay* had burned on Long Island Sound within a quarter of a mile of the Townsend farm at Riverside, and their "house was the shelter of many of the escaped."[15] Henry was in New York at the time, but returned to Riverside the next morning.

Bellows felt the intense pressures again when he returned to the church in the fall. "The truth is, this New York life to sensitive folks, is a killing life. It wants repose so much. One's nerves are positively scraped by the friction of its excitements, until they are destroyed." "After six month's absence," he felt "the return to the city very painfully." He commented, "I am preaching only *once a day* & think it likely I shall not undertake anything more for the present—so perfectly concerned am I of the necessity of a more quiet & sober life, that I am cutting down my duties on every side & seeking to secure rest & moderation." Then Henry Bellows indulged in wishful thinking: "I hope to be as notorious for calmness & repose of character in the future, as I have been for excitability & activity in the past." The mixing of the Bellows's life with the Townsends at Riverside had been too much, and the Bellows family would seek *"pleasant lodgings* out of town, *say at Yonkers,* free from housekeeping & other interruptions."[16]

To his brother John he confided how hopelessly he felt about his mental state. "I was never more miserable in feeling—subject to the most suicidal depression of spirits, irresolute, timid, disheartened." He commented that he did *"not* find preparation for the pulpit particularly trying—but the business of *preaching* is very burdensome." And he added ominously, "I am afraid that I shall break down in every part of the exercises. There is little or no comfort for me in any thing I undertake, reading, society, or domestic affections—all is stale, flat, unprofitable." But, in typical Bellows fashion, he added that he felt the necessity "to stick by the ship this winter, & I mean to nail my colors to the mast."[17] He had given up the idea of taking lodgings in the country and had taken a suite at 71 Irving Place, and Eliza and Joseph Dorr were in the same place.

Henry also felt that "one of the worst effects of the mind of ill health I am suffering—brought on doubtless by too much dealing with spiritual themes—is, that it obscures the only prospect that can illuminate the darkness of sorrow & trouble—i.e. the face of God." In this mood he wrote, "If we have blinded ourselves with excess of light, what sun can cheer us? If to dwell on divine truth only increases our disease, what else shall enable us to support our sickness cheerfully?" Perhaps his feelings came about because he was a professional religionist, "I do think that a man of sensibility runs an immense risk in making a *profession* of religion—becoming a sort of conscience, heart, soul, for hundreds of human beings." He found that he was "supplying them want of feeling by the excess of one's own & in the end turning into a sort of piety-machine, at which any body in need of devout feelings, a religious patience comes . . . until the worn out soul, the breaking heart loses its grit on drops from the axle."[18]

Our Church Was Sold Last Night

In spite of his longing for a respite, Henry Bellows buried himself still more deeply in his work. He campaigned among his parishioners to get the mortgage paid off, and to build a better church. By 1850, the Church of the Divine Unity was barely five years old, yet it already required periodic roof repairs. Several of the society's wealthier members had died, Jonathan Goodhue among them, and the rush to the "suburbs" uptown was in full swing now as the downtown area was becoming increasingly the scene of riots, begging, and other urban blights. Many pew holders would no longer come down as far as Broadway and Crosby Street to go to church. Still other members had been lost to the mounting Gold Rush in California. New pew holders were becoming increasingly hard to find, and total pew assessments and rentals, which had reached a peak of $6,200 in 1848, had declined steadily to about $4,500 in 1850. Once more the trustees were faced with having to collect arrears.

Bellows's solution to these problems was to sell the present church building and move uptown where the congregation's numbers were sure to be increased. But the trustees were cautious. They went as far as to consolidate the two mortgages of $14,000 each to one of $28,000, but they saw no hope of paying off the principal. In 1851, they had seen a hint of a possibility of selling the building to the Mercantile Library Association, but that possibility never materialized, and the matter was dropped. The following year, Bellows suggested initiating a special fund to pay off the mortgage, but the trustees vetoed this on the grounds that the regular expenses of the church were too great.

In April 1852, the trustees had called a meeting of the society to get a concensus of opinion on moving from the Church of the Divine Unity. The members were somewhat ambivalent; the present building was not yet seven years old and, while it was in frequent need of repair, the extent of this need was not anywhere near what the first building had required for most of its twenty years. On the other hand, the neighborhood was deteriorating at a rapid rate, and the society could see that its present address would not benefit the church. Finally the members empowered the trustees to dispose of the present property and to find new premises, providing that the society would really gain substantially all the way around. Not only did it wish to rid itself of the mortgage once and for all, it also wanted to possess a really handsome and suitable building in the best locality. As it turned out, it got none of these benefits.

In October 1852, the trustees sold the Church of the Divine Unity to the Fourth Universalist Church, then under the pastoral care of Dr. Edwin H. Chapin. The Universalists agreed to pay $90,000 for the package of the building and the land, excluding only the furniture in the hall and the basement. Of this total, $28,000 was the value of the mortgage (which they assumed), so the Unitarians received actually only $62,000, or two-thirds of what it had spent to build the church edifice itself. Further, since the Universalists were to gain immediate occupancy of the building, they would be entitled to all the rents received from the front hall and the basement. In return, they were to allow the First Congregational Church to share the premises until 1 June 1853.

Henry Bellows wrote, "our church affairs are in a fluctuating state. . . . Our church was sold last night to Chapin's society. . . . I bought last week (with authority from the trustees) *the site for our new church*, at the corner of 20th and 4th avenue, that is just above Union Square, one block this side of Dr. Hawk's Calvary Church." Bellows hoped that they would begin to build that fall. "In any ordinary state of mental health, this would be a great comfort to me, who knows how much our prosperity will be enhanced by this move, but just now I care little about it."[1]

On the occasion of the death of Daniel Webster on 24 October 1852, Henry Bellows preached a sermon which was not too flattering to the man held by some to be the greatest statesman of the pre-Civil War period.[2] George T. Curtis of Boston was offended by it. The sermon gave Mr. Curtis "great pain." He wrote, "Even if the gross charges of personal vice, and self-indulgence in his appetites which you make against that great man were true, I know not what feeling of Christian charity or duty would permit you to send them to one, who had just come with a bleeding heart from his death-bed and his grave." Curtis went on to state that Bellows's charges were not true. "I contradict them on a personal and somewhat intimate acquaintance of ten years." Curtis had lived under Webster's roof and had made inquiries of those whom Bellows had quoted as authority. "I must add therefore that I think as a clergyman, you should not have cited 'publick rumours' as your authority, when bringing such charges against a man who has served this nation as Mr. Webster has served it, and whose reputation cannot be seriously touched, without injury to the national character."[3]

George Ticknor Curtis was a classmate of Bellows's at Harvard. After a brief law practice in Worcester he set up a law practice in

Boston. An expert on constitutional law and a great friend of Webster's, he was one of Webster's "Cotton Whigs." Just prior to Webster's death, as United States Commissioner he facilitated the return to slavery of Thomas Sims, under the Fugitive Slave Act of 1850, thereby incurring the hostility not only of the abolitionists, but also of more moderate opposers of the slavery system such as Henry Bellows.

In his reply to Curtis, Henry Bellows wrote that he was "very sorry to be charged with such mingled inhumanity & recklessness & ignorance." Curtis had accused him of having affronted him, "wronged the memory of a great man, and done violence to my own office." In regard to sending Curtis the sermon at all he pleaded that because of "its substantial tenderness, candor & truth" he did "not suppose it would be otherwise than acceptable to anyone, not personally connected with Mr. Webster." He added that he *did not know* that your relations with him were close & affectionate."

As for his recklessness in speaking about the lacks of Mr. Webster's character Bellows wrote that he assumed that this was general acknowledge. He added that Mr. Curtis's denial of these lacks of character had great weight with himself. He would "leave no stone unturned to correct the injury accruing from my part of the offence." However, he gently chided Curtis for taking a superficial view of Webster's character. "As a reader & student of the Scriptures, as an ethical teacher, as a Christian minister, I have not learned to consider either true piety, or essential worth, or exalted usefulness, wholly compromised by infirmities of even vices. Mr. Webster at the worst had done nothing so bad as David or Peter."[4] It was an appropriate reply to a man who felt that the memory of Webster would somehow be better if all his vices were discounted.

Henry Bellows summarized the seven years at the Church of the Divine Unity thus: "The seven years we passed in the Church of the Divine Unity were very important years in our society." He noted his change of mood over the years, "I never realize the change from youth to age more than when I compare the enthusiasm, the hopefulness, the confidence, of that period of my ministry,—when all things seemed possible, and no toil was insupportable or uninviting,—with the chastened expectations, the sobered interest, the prudent economy of power and strength, which later years have necessarily brought with them."[5]

Except for some initial disagreement over the best site, the trustees proceeded with dispatch, as we have seen, to purchase a new set of lots on the corner of 20th Street and Fourth Avenue. This property belonged to Elihu Townsend's brother-in-law and business partner, Russell Hubbard Nevins, who was Eliza Bellows's uncle, and was purchased from him for $26,000. The trustees paid $13,000 in cash and obtained a mortgage for the balance. With legal and title-search fees, the society was left with less than $50,000 with which to erect a new church.

The selection of an architectural plan proceeded with considerably less haste than had the purchase of the land; presumably the wiser for the church's past experience with architect Minard Lafever, the building committee examined a wide array of suggestions. The committee comprised John Thomas (the owner of Plymouth Rock), John E. Williams, Horatio Allen, and Robert Schuyler (who had engineered the previous building enterprise of seven years ago). Schuyler had earlier taken special pains to make sure that the society had no more roof trouble, but his efforts were in vain when the incomplete edifice began to cave in at the roof. Now Schuyler was *doubly* determined that the committee should examine all possible designs before deciding. But there was the problem of funds; the most suitable plans greatly exceeded what the society had available for building.

In January 1853 Bellows wrote that there had been only "hesitating about plans." He realized as they planned the new church how much his own personality had changed in the seven years since they had built the Church of the Divine Unity. Bellows wrote, "I went into it all over then, & thought the world depended on the shape of every finial & the color of the pew linings. Now, I stand aside, with a general indifference to the architecture, the details, the time to begin & the time to finish." Bellows felt that it was "enough for me to preach & prepare to preach; the people must make the *place* & I take their procrastination most patiently."[6]

A group of the members of All Souls decided to make a subscription list in March 1853 to try to put life into the project. It is an interesting list. John E. Williams, Moses H. Grinnell, George Schuyler, and Elihu Townsend gave $1,000 each. John Allen, Paul A. Curtis, William F. Cary, Peter Cooper, James O. Ward, Benjamin F. Wheelwright, Robert Sedgwick, "a lady," and Mrs. C. M. Kirkland gave $500 each. William Rider contributed $350, and Nicholas Dean, Nathaniel Currier, and B. G. Arnold gave $300 apiece.[7] This was an act of good faith to get the new church off on the right financial foot.

Finally in March 1853, after five months of examining plans, the trustees approved a design submitted by C. F. Anderson, and took it before the congregation. The society—perhaps because by now it had had its fill of constructing churches—readily agreed to the plan, and authorized the board to execute it immediately.

But Henry Bellows was *not* pleased. The Sunday morning immediately following this meeting of the society, he preached a pointed sermon on the society's past experiences with building churches, taking as his text, "The Lord hath chosen thee to build a sanctuary; be strong and do it."

Those attending the morning service quickly gathered after the service, Nicholas Dean assuming the chair. Bellows voiced his further opinions in the matter, and a lively discussion ensued. Apparently Bellows felt that the society should not let money stand in the way of their building a really suitable house of worship, for all present rallied to form a subscription, the goal of which was to raise an additional $20,000.

Doubtless there were many who saw Bellows's incessant attempts to raise large sums from among the members of the congregation as sheer impractical folly; what worked so well the first time eight years ago, and even fairly successfully after that, could surely not keep on being successful. But there were others who were captured by Bellows's enthusiastic faith; thus the conflict was resolved by addition of the provision that all funds would be returned to their donors in the event that the full $20,000 could not be raised.

Bellows, who had previously said that he really felt that the laymen should take care of building the new church, and that he was "disinterested," rushed into the fray with a particularly Bellowsian action. To Bartol he wrote that he found that there were "two very lively parties in the field" as to what type of church should be built. With splendid partiality he called one "parsimonious" and the other "generous." In the previous vote the parsimonious party had carried the day, "& had actually accepted & adopted plans which were straightway to be executed—plans which I felt to be impolitic, unwise, & certain to injure the Society." Bellows deserved what happened: "Sunday week I affected a coup d'etat; rushed into the field alone, upset the whole scheme, & called the Society to the rescue of their own interests from the tyranny of the Trustees, who have full legal powers in our Society to build & commit the parish to what in their wisdom they may choose. The step was startling & somewhat perilous." But, said Bellows, "I had the right on my side & swept every thing before my revolutionary banner. It has taken me all the week to bury the dead & heal the wounded & fairly take possession of the field." Bellows realized that having taken this step he could not simply leave the completion of the new building to the building committee. "I expect to be full of out-door business for some time now," he wrote, "for I have 'rolled up my sleeves' & shall do any thing from hod-carrying up to altar-carving until the work is done."[8]

To his brother he called his action, "a regular Louis Napoleon *coup d'etat.*"[9] Bellows's own plans were presented and accepted on 17 April. He felt now that there would be no further trouble. During the week, Bellows put aside most of his other activities and projects to take upon himself the locating of plans; he may even have drawn them up himself. He announced a meeting following services on Sunday, 17 April at which he presented the congregation with his proposals. The society referred the whole matter to the trustees whom Bellows had bypassed! But Bellows's influence among his parishioners was strong, and the membership's resolution included a recommendation that the board seriously *consider* Bellows's architectural plan.

It was a daring presumption on Bellows's part, and no doubt would have ended the career of any lesser clergyman. The building committee resigned en masse. Finding themselves in something of a dilemma, the trustees decided to get some more architectural plans before making any decision. By the end of April 1853, no decision had been reached, except that the trustees finally agreed to scrap their original recommendation altogether, and to start all over again in the search for a suitable architect. A new building committee was appointed—Moses Grinnell, James G. Dale, George Schuyler, and Bellows himself. Robert Schuyler had met his match in Bellows.

But Bellows had other preoccupations. He received a prestigious invitation which came early in April from the literary committee of the Harvard Chapter of Phi Beta Kappa[10] to deliver the oration at the approaching anniversary of the Phi Beta Kappa society on 21 July. The members of the society felt that their fellow member Bellows would perform "this favor." But to Bellows the task became a great challenge, and during the next few months he was to produce one of the outstanding orations of his career for the occasion.

Then Elihu Townsend, Bellows's father-in-law, who had been ill most of the spring, died on 26 June 1853, at the age of sixty-seven years. He had been born in New Haven, Connecticut; and after coming to New York had formed a banking partnership with his wife's brother, Russell Hubbard Nevins, under the firm name of Nevins & Townsend. This firm was in business until his death.[11]

On Thursday afternoon 22 July, Henry Bellows gave the Phi Beta Kappa oration on which he had been working ever since the invitation arrived in April.[12] He wrote to his son Russell about the affair: "[He] had an excellent time, & . . . every thing went off quite as well as [he] could desire." As to the crowd, "there was a famous show of people, crowds of ladies & gentlemen, &, after the oration, a capital dinner, at which fun & nonsense flowed very freely."[13]

The end of the summer also brought more sadness into the Bellows family. Mrs. Bellows's uncle, Russell Nevins, was quite ill, and Henry had to take him from Saratoga Springs to New York to consult with specialists. And Henry's younger half-brother, Percival Langdon Bellows, died in Walpole in early August 1853. Percival was unmarried, and had always been the sickly member of the Bellows family. Henry wrote to his mother, "Our dear brother was not fitted to enjoy this world. He had too much simplicity, too much sensitiveness; an impaired constitution & a kind of life-weary feeling. I have not thought he could last long for some time,—and now that God has taken him, I must believe it to be wise & kind."[14] Bellows could not leave his own responsibilities to attend the funeral in Walpole. Bellows termed his summer "fragmentary," and stated that he had "hardly slept in the same bed two successive nights these six weeks."[15]

Meanwhile, the deadline for the society to give the Universalists sole occupancy of the Church of the Divine Unity was drawing near, and the First Congregational Church had not even launched its new building project. The board dropped the matter of architectural designs in order to find some place to continue worship services. Barely in time, the Church of the Messiah kindly invited the members of the First Church to worship with them.

Finding themselves homeless, the members accepted, and spent June, July, and August among their old rivals. Relations between the First and Second churches had been amicable ever since Bellows had come to the First Church. It was a practical measure for the First Church to join with the Second, for Bellows would be away on vacation for a good part of the summer, and thus the society was released from having to find substitute preachers.

The arrangement with the Church of the Messiah might have lasted until the new building was completed had it not been for the peculiar religious views of Samuel Osgood. The First Church could have saved a great deal financially, for by sharing the costs of building maintenance, the sexton's salary, and the music, it would have had only Bellows's salary to sustain on its own, and it would not have had to lay out the expenses of renting public halls. As it was, however, the members of the First Church could not tolerate Osgood's orthodox leanings. Indeed, Osgood's own congregation was somewhat less than satisfied with him and some members who had stuck it out with Dewey even when Dewey's fair-haired image had long gone, now came over to Bellows's church. Thus, in September, Bellows's parishioners abandoned the Church of the Messiah's comfortable pews and worshipful physical surroundings for the secular and theatrical atmosphere provided by Mr. Niblo's Academy Hall at Broadway and Bond Streets.

On 19 September, Bellows was back in New York to conduct the first services of the season at Niblo's Hall. It was the first time that the congregation had been together since the first of June. "It really altogether overcame me to see my now dear flock together again—to find them so faithful, so numerous & so glad to meet each other—& then to notice the vacant places which very few months will cause in a numerous company, & to miss such men as my ever-lamented Father-in-law." It was moving "to feel ourselves together under new circumstances, stripped of the old associations & all the sacred objects connected with our deserted church—altogether, it was quite too much for me & for the first time in my pulpit experience." Under the tension Henry Bellows "was unable for some minutes to go on with the service. I bless God for keeping my heart tender to such scenes & such emotions. We weep when we are happiest & best."[16]

The trustees had, by this time, finally adopted a set of architectural blueprints submitted by the well-known architect, Jacob Wrey Mould, but not without modifying them. A parsonage was planned at the rear of the church and with the church building itself, was expected to cost less than $120,000. This sum would keep the society in debt for a while, but with the enlarged seating capacity (some 1,200 people), more ample Sunday school rooms, and spacious accommodations for church offices, the expense would be more than worth it. Implicit in their expectations was Bellows's ability to increase the size of the constituency and therefore the revenues accruing to the society. By adopting Mould's design, the First Congregational Church thought it would finally have a really *sturdy*, roomy, comfortable, and attractive house of worship which would stand proudly for several generations, and which was sufficiently uptown to encourage worshipers to attend regularly, and which would also satisfy Henry Bellows's description of a generous congregation rather than a "parsimonious" one.

All Souls Church (completed 1855). This is from the architect's sketches and shows the bell tower which was never completed for lack of funds, All Souls Archives

With their hopes high, the members endured the lurid surroundings of Niblo's theater and valiantly tried to keep their spiritual sentiments as lofty and pure as possible.

In early November Eliza Bellows's uncle, Russell Nevins, much beloved by the family (Bellows's son Russell was his namesake), was on his deathbed with cancer. Bellows had to plead that he could not attend a birthday party in Walpole as he had promised. Russell Nevins was "hopelessly ill with *cancer of the stomach*,"[17] and he was very dependent upon Henry as his spiritual counselor.

Russell Nevins died toward the end of November "in a sleep which had lasted two days, without a groan or a struggle." Bellows wrote, "We were all with him & he passed away so gently that we hardly knew the precise moment. He had known for several weeks his fate; accepted it with manly & Christian fortitude & submission—made all his worldly arrangements with great sagacity & ease—& enjoyed every religious support with manifested faith & piety." Nevins was not a Unitarian, but he had seen his own pastor only once and relied on Henry Bellows for his last moments. "His last word was coupled with my name & his last act of consciousness, a smile he threw upon my eye."[18]

Bellows was often confidential with his friend Cyrus Bartol. Now he wrote about his new financial freedom:

> I know you will feel interested in the pecuniary consequences of Uncle's death. He has left about $600,000—which deducting say $50,000 in small bequests . . . is divided into 10 shares—*two* of which he leaves Mrs. Townsend [his sister] (with the house & all the moveables at the farm & in town)—being something over $100,000. —the income to be applied to her use & the principal divided among her children at her death. *Two* other shares (the same sum) he leaves to *her* four children to be immediately enjoyed. The remaining shares he distributes among his brothers & sisters—(one apeace)—or their heirs . . . Eliza . . . will have perhaps $30,000 now—& as much more at her mother's death. This, of course makes me easy about worldly affairs— which have troubled me much—but which, as infirmities & weariness begin to come upon a man, are likely to give him more concern.[19]

Uncle Russell Nevins had done quite well by his family, and it affected the Bellows's mode of living for the rest of their lives. Bellows felt that the fifty or sixty thousand dollars would put him at ease "about my children & to free me from the natural anxieties belonging to a salaried man who does not feel sure of his health & endurance.[20]

A Friendly Criticism

By the end of November 1853, the congregation had grown exceedingly restless in the unsuitable quarters of Niblo's Academy Hall. Attendance was dropping steadily, and it was becoming increasingly difficult to raise the money to pay the rent and other expenses of the worship services, to say nothing of Bellows's salary. When Erskin Mason's recently vacated church on Bleeker Street became available for rent, the trustees immediately rented it.

The building was available until May of 1854, but the society hoped their own church would be ready by then. The quarters afforded many advantages in addition to the more pleasant and suitable surroundings. Additional money could be raised by auctioning the pews for rental. The trustees fixed the rents, and then allowed the members of the society to choose the pews they wanted at the auction, the best pews going to the highest bidders.

By the time of the annual meeting, construction work on the new property was well underway, but the new building itself had barely been started because of the necessity to raze the old buildings on the site. The trustees reported progress, and the congregation realized that eagerness to move into its long-awaited, durable, and suitable quarters was not to be fulfilled for some time. The board was still toying with modifications on the design and asked the members for their approval, but, somewhat apathetically, the society delegated all such matters back to the trustees. The society also accepted—apparently without objection—a proposed raise for Bellows of $500, which set Bellows's salary at $3,500.

In April 1854, the trustees were still toying with changes in the architectural plans. They wanted their new building to be perfect. After all, Bellows had sold them on the long-term benefits of investing more than the society could afford right now in making the building perfect. Thus, when Jacob Wrey Mould suggested (and promoted) changes, the trustees accepted them. These changes and alterations in the original plans slowed down the project, and when the lease on the Bleeker Street church expired, the society was once more forced to find a public hall. The lecture room at the Medical College was decided upon temporarily.

Early in January 1854 Bellows was able to say, "I think I can safely say that Eliza & I begin the year 1854 in better health than at any previous season within five years. Our children are both well—& barring the domestic losses which have impoverished our home circle so sadly within the year, we have nothing to diminish our joy." Bellows had "exhibited the plans of the new church [to some of his parishioners]—which very few of them had seen." He also felt that his "ministry was never more acceptable than this passing season; and certainly I never labored with so much self-satisfaction. Our present church accommodations are so perfectly agreeable, as to make any undue *haste* in our building wholly unnecessary; which is a great point gained."[1]

Nicholas Dean—a very perceptive man—after seeing the drawings for the new church building had gone directly to the office of the architect to study the working plans. He liked the "originality, appropriateness, and general beauty of the design." He liked the sense of "strength and solidity" of the proposed building. But he wrote to Bellows,

> The only questionable point presented to my mind is the alternation of color in the materials of its exterior walls. Is there not danger that a display so *new to us*, may miss the beautiful, and hit the ridiculous? The masses are not well instructed in the harmony of colors, and perhaps will transfer to our *exterior* the name they have fastened upon the *interior* of Grace Church in Broadway, namely, "The Oyster Saloon."[2]

Dean realized that Jacob Wrey Mould was trying something a little new for New York City and that the general public might make the church the butt of jokes and gibes. He was certainly correct, for the third edifice of the congregation was always known as "The Beefsteak Church" or "the Church of the Holy Zebra." Nicholas Dean asked, "If the Caen stone were used only upon the angles, and to trim the openings of the doors and windows,—striking out the chequered work in the walls,—would it not be enough for ornament, and cheapen the construction?"[3] Dean raised the correct question, but he was overruled by the architect and the committee.

In January 1854 Bellows made his first trip to the newly established Antioch College to begin an interest in that institution which lasted for the remainder of his life. Horace Mann had just arrived on the scene as the first president of the college. Mann, after a distinguished career in education in the public schools of Massachusetts, had been elected in 1848 to the House of Representatives as an antislavery Whig to succeed John Quincy Adams. He was not an abolitionist, but came into direct conflict with the compromises of Daniel Webster. In 1852 Mann had met defeat as the candidate of the Free-Soilers for the governship of Massachusetts. He then accepted the offer of the presidency of

Antioch College.[4] Bellows was enthralled with Mann and very hopeful about the new educational enterprise. He had "perfectly frank and cordial conversation" with Mann for two hours before dinner. "I like his looks & sympathize with his views," wrote Bellows.[5]

At Antioch College Bellows found the trustees of the college "home spun men, rude in the extreme—but of large mental & moral build, chiefly Christian [the Christian denomination or Disciples of Christ] ministers . . . They look worn with a laborious, itinerant ministry, their faces full of emotion & simplicity. I am very much impressed with the genuineness & worth of these men," he wrote to Eliza. The college had been largely founded by these men of the Christian denomination, and Bellows was attracted to them. Although they were not Unitarian in their theology they were anti-creedal, and Bellows found much in their views with which he had deep sympathy. "In regard to the right relations of Christians & Unitarians we had the frankest utterances & formed bonds of substantial union." Bellows was impressed with the importance of being a trustee of the college and he wrote to Eliza that "yesterday was in many respects the most *pregnant & important day of my life.*"[6]

Friday evening Bellows lectured "in the chapel of the college to the students, professors and townspeople including the *Christian* brethren. It went off with sufficient éclat," he wrote to Eliza.[7] He had actually been received heartily by the Christian ministers, particularly the older men. This warmed Bellows's heart very much. He intended to return home to direct the attention of Unitarians to the support of Antioch College. A curious group of religious denominations made up the board of trustees—Unitarians and members of the Christian denomination. The Christian denomination had not been financially successful in running the college and the Unitarians and Horace Mann, a Unitarian layman, were brought in to attempt a salvage operation.

Bellows wasted no time in beginning his work for Antioch. On 6 February 1854, he was able to report to his friend Bartol that they had taken up a collection at All Souls which had netted over $8,000 for the college and he hoped to bring it up to $10,000. "We hope in all our churches here together to raise $25,000," he wrote.[8] He headed toward Boston to present the Antioch issue to the Unitarians of Boston. But this meeting with the Boston Unitarians in regard to Antioch College was to be one of the greatest disappointments of Bellows's life.

Upon his return from Boston, Bellows preached a sermon about liberals in Boston which really discussed two distinct but related subjects—first, the rejection of Horace Mann by Bostonians who were capable of giving money to Antioch, and second, some comments on the state of Unitarianism in Boston.[9]

Compared to the response which Bellows had received from his ministerial colleagues and the laity in New York who had contributed substantial sums to Antioch College, he found the climate in Boston entirely different. He first sought the cooperation of his fellow ministers by personal contact. "Here I had occasion to find how much an interest, even in the most important matters, depends upon personal observation. My brethren had not been to Antioch. I had. They felt no responsibility for the success of an institution they knew of only by hearsay." He carried what he thought was a "plan of usefulness" but he found "other plans already occupying the ground." His colleagues were already raising money for the establishment of a "Book Concern," a publishing venture, and some endowment funds for the Harvard Divinity School.

He commented, "The Unitarian ministers of Boston represent the Unitarian parishes of Boston, and their judgments, affections and tendencies must necessarily be very much influenced by the opinions, feelings, and proclivities of so weighty, sober, and decisive a class as the Unitarian laymen of that city. The 'solid men' of Boston are very generally anchored in our Unitarian harbor, and they are not men to be swept away by any freshet of clerical feeling." He found that the Unitarians of the city carry "the ballasts of great wealth," that they have "decided political convictions," and "habits of individual independence."

Bellows found all except two pulpits closed to him in which to make a special plea for Antioch. With this apparent opposition Bellows did not feel that he could approach people for money, so he made a test case by approaching a few gentlemen who he felt had the strongest opposition because of "local disaffections and painful associations." These bore partly upon feeling about the Unitarian cause but more especially as opposition to Horace Mann because of his politics. Mann was an advocate of free speech and an opponent of slavery. "I need only remind you into what deadly oppostion this soon brought him with the idol of Boston and the glory of Massachusetts," Bellows declared. He came into controversy with Senator Daniel Webster who in 1850 engineered the Kansas-Nebraska compromise which Bellows termed a "dreadful treachery." He evidently raised no funds in Boston for Antioch College.

Bellows then went on to voice his concerns about Boston Unitarianism. "Boston, by providential and traditional causes, is liberal, progressive, and versatile in its theology and philanthropy; by culture, habit, and interest, conservative, formal, and fixed in its tastes and habits; and, therefore, the more faithful representatives of its theoretical opinions have always outraged and alarmed the more faithful representatives of its practical interests." He pointed out that because of this divergent point of view, Unitarianism in Boston, unlike Universalism, never found a considerable body of people willing to back a missionary crusade with money and influence. The organization of the Unitarian movement was discouraged. "The American Unitarian Association, which represents the theoretical office and duty of our denomination, is no where in so little esteem as among the most influential men in Boston, from whose respect and support alone its sinew could be derived." He continued, "At present, a movement for the systematic diffusion of books seems to present the most promising, because the least obtrusive, form of denominational influence, and it is greatly to be hoped that its plan will succeed."

Bellows went on to state that although the Unitarian faith is based upon two great principles, respect for human nature (best represented by Channing), and faith in free inquiry (best expressed by Theodore Parker), there was a want of confidence among Boston Unitarians in these two very important principles. He found the Unitarian churches in Boston well attended and zealously administered, presided over by a devoted clergy. "But this does not at all diminish the force or truth of the statement, that a great want of faith in the distinctive principles of Unitarianism marks the community they represent." Bellows himself found these two principles just as sound as they ever were. He told his congregation,

> Liberal Christianity is just ready to begin its national career in this country. Hitherto it has been a local affair. But to commence its great and glorious race with vigor and promise, it must escape from timid hands, assume a bold and confident step, accept, without one equivocation, every fair and logical deduction from its elementary principles, and go forward conquering and to conquer. While it continues solicitous to keep on smooth terms with orthodoxy, while it seeks to disown all the unpopular followers of its camp, while it dissociates itself from the great reforms of the age, it will do nothing more than maintain a bare and wretched existence.

He concluded by telling his hearers that "this Christianity is the religion for which the world waits."

It was good for the denomination that Bellows went to Boston, for he discovered in the heartland of the movement an equivocation which explained to him why the influence of Unitarianism had been largely local and not national. He learned, and later he was to act.

Bellows had kicked up a storm with his comments in the sermon about "Unitarianism in Boston—A Friendly Criticism." To Bartol he wrote that it had "produced a good deal of stir in New York, & involved me in some very unpleasant consequences." Yet there was "no escape from the duty of publishing it, both on the score of truth & usefulness, & on the score of frankness & manhood." He claimed that he was not ready "to say anything behind the back of any community which I am not ready to say to its face. . . ." In addition, Bellows was "wholly unconscious of any personal mortification, or bad spirit [which] animates my criticism of Unitarianism at Boston." Many felt that the sermon might do Horace Mann and Antioch College serious harm. Bellows had put the sermon in the hands of a printer the day after he delivered it, but had been persuaded to send the proof sheets to Horace Mann, "for his permission to use his name so freely."[10]

Bellows sent a copy of the sermon to Bartol which now is in the Harvard Divinity School Library. On it Bellows wrote,

> My Dear Bartol: I thot it my duty to obtain Horace Mann's consent before publishing this sermon; he *declines giving* it, & without it it would hardly be lawful; so that I suppress its publication, & send a few printed copies to friends, that I may escape the dishonor of saying behind the backs of those I respect what I should not say to their faces. I shall take some other occasion & form to say my say on the subject of Unitarianism, disconnected from Antioch College—an unhappy conjunction. Yours Affectionately H. W. Bellows.[11]

On a more happy note, Henry Bellows was able to report to Bartol that he had completed the purchase of the family farm at Walpole, "& visited it last week, to set workmen at the repairs & modifications." Bellows wrote that he had agreed to set aside five acres for Bartol for his summer retreat. "Wont we have rich times?" he wrote. He hoped that securing the farm would change his life of action into one of "study & thought."[12]

What can only be described as one of the greatest disappointments of Henry Bellows's life came in the middle of March 1854. Bellows had been preaching in All Souls for over fifteen years, and the longer he was the minister the more apt he was to speak his mind freely and with perfect candor to his parishioners from the pulpit. He always allowed other opinions, but certainly the Sunday sermon was a type of discourse which could at best be called one-way. One of his most wealthy and prominent parishioners who had been active in All Souls and on very friendly terms with the Bellows family, George Lee Schuyler, wrote Bellows on 14 March 1854 that he was withdrawing from the church. He deemed it inexpedient to support Antioch College because Horace Mann was "an advocate of the religious views of Theodore Parker." He had also disagreed with some remarks that Bellows had made which were critical of Daniel Webster's speech of 7 March 1850, when the great Compromise was in the works. Schuyler termed it "the crowning glory of a political career ever true to our country, and a noble and manly sacrifice of personal considerations to a sense of duty."

In writing the letter, George Schuyler did not want to take issue with Bellows on these two matters. He did not consider the pulpit a proper place "to introduce the social, political, and personal topics of the day, which agitate and divide the community." He claimed that at one time when the population was sparse and there were few newspapers, and the clergy were about the only informed people, this made sense. But he wrote, "there is no such necessity

Bellows Family Homestead in Walpole, New Hampshire, Oil Painting by Kay Robinson (H.W. Bellows' grand-daughter)

George Lee Schuyler, Oil Portrait by Leon Bonnat, Painted in Paris in 1883, Courtesy of the New-York Historical Society, New York City

now—especially in the large cities." He felt that "the press,—the lecture room,—the public meeting give full scope to all who wish to engage in public affairs." He believed that the clergy should take part in these discussions rather than use their pulpits to express their particular views. 'To carry these subjects into the pulpit to me seems not only in bad taste and uncalled for—but decidedly injurious—more particularly, when treated with a partisan spirit." What Schuyler really wanted from the church service "after a week of excitement from the labors, pleasures and pains of an active life" was something less worldly. "I do not care to listen to one-sided arguments upon the men & measures of the day. They interfere with the frame of mind I would like to be in, during the short hour of public worship," he wrote.

Schuyler realized, however, that what Bellows did was very pleasing to others if not to himself. Gentleman that he was, Schuyler wished quietly to withdraw from the church and avoid making a fuss. "Rather therefore than contend against that which is agreeable to so many others, I prefer to withdraw, and make room for those who have different views & feelings upon this matter." He found it painful to separate himself from the association of his church, "to which I have belonged from its commencement." He wanted to avoid excitement which he could not do under any ministry of Henry Bellows. He wrote of his "strong personal regard" for Bellows, and he hoped that their social relationships "will become closer and more firmly cemented with our advancing years." He wanted to tell Bellows that the step he took came not from a pique but from a reasoned decision.[13]

In his reply several days later Bellows remarked that he had been too unwell to respond sooner. He appreciated the straightforward letter for "its courtesy, & kindness." He felt that if Schuyler left the church "it could not come in a better form." Bellows wrote to his parishioner that he was full of pain about the matter because "it never happened to me before to have the general usefulness of my ministry openly questioned, or to hear it characterized as positively injurious." He felt that this was "one of the most trying moments of my professional life." And he added that it came from "a family peculiarly associated with the prosperity, the dignity & the history of the church." Bellows wrote that he assumed that Mr. Schuyler had seriously thought about all of the consequences of his action upon his church and his minister. But if he felt the way he did Bellows wrote, "you could [not] take any other course than you now announce." For his part Bellows maintained that he would "patiently examine myself & the policy of my ministry, in the light of your objections, & endeavor to derive some benefit from your departure." Yet Bellows felt that even when he embarked upon this soul-searching process he would probably come up with the conclusion that he could not deny the all-pervading character of the religion in which he believed so that he could put it in a compartment and not speak about social and political matters in the future.[14]

The Bellows Family around 1854, (left to right), Anna Langdon
Bellows (about 9), Henry Bellows (about 40), Russell Nevins Bellows
(about 12), Mrs. Eliza Townsend Bellows (about 36), From the
Original Daugerotype, Courtesy of the Bellows Family.

George Schuyler did not take Bellows's letter kindly. He reread
a copy which he had made of his first letter to Bellows, and wrote
that he had not questioned Bellows's "general usefulness" in his
ministry. He assured Bellows that he knew his own mind, and
renewed his expressions of "personal regard."[15] This rather well-
documented incident is almost typical of the life and trials of a
prophetic preacher of Bellows's stamp. It is a constantly recurring

problem in the ministry of almost every denomination. Bellows somehow survived and so did his friendship with George Schuyler and his family.

If some were frank in their criticism of Henry Bellows, others were just as frank in their appreciation. William Ellery Sedgwick, the son of Robert Sedgwick, one of the early members of All Souls, had lost his wife and had now left New York, so that he could not attend Bellows's church any longer. He wrote a most appreciative letter in which he thanked Bellows for "the comfort and sometimes the lasting benefit I have felt, in your noble spiritual lessons, of the admiration I have felt for your opinions in all spiritual concerns. Would to God they had done more for me, as they have done much, but that is only my own fault."[16]

Another important event for the Bellows family was the installation of Henry's half-brother, John Bellows, as the pastor of the Wilton, New Hampshire, church. It was John who had run the school for girls in Cooperstown, New York, where Henry acted as his assistant in 1832. John had gone to Harvard but had never graduated. The family genealogist Thomas Bellows Peck says of him, "Mr. Bellows possessed natural intellectual gifts which if accompanied by firmer health and a better balance of faculties, should have given him distinction in his profession."[17] John had moved from church to church, and never seemed to realize his potential.

By the end of June, Henry had completed the work on the summer home in Walpole, and had settled the family there. He wrote, "It turns out more convenient & charming than I could have anticipated. Eliza is delighted with the arrangements."[18] One Sunday, Bellows described the view from his recently acquired Walpole home in these words: "This lovely village beneath the hill on which my house stands, like a sentry, is lying half hid among the greenest trees, amongst which the church-spires lift their significant fingers, a repose, without hum or motion, hovers over the spot." It was July and "the summer air is still; a delicate mist just softens the mountains; the hay-makers' half-done work stands in grassy altars all over the meadows, attesting the homage that interest pays the Sabbath." It was also a quiet village, "altho a thousand human beings are within the scope of my eye, not one is visible—so sacred is the retirement of the Lord's day morning. The birds that poured their matins at dawn, in a full choir of praise, have ceased their songs as the hour draws nigh for man to praise his maker in the 'temples made with hands'." He compared day and night, "Night itself is not so

solemn not so still, as this broad-daylight, over which a voluntary &
intentional silence of sacredness is shed by the reverence of Man."
People would soon be going to church, "an hour hence, & the elm-
shaded road,—beautiful enough to be the way to heaven—that runs
straight through the village . . . will be spotted with groups of sober
people on their way to their several places of worship." Bellows was
immensely pleased with the old family homestead and attained here
some of the peace which he so desperately sought.[19]

CHAPTER FIVE

Seasons of Duty

Cupolas Here, Cornices There

While Bellows and many in his congregation were vacationing away from the city's hot summer, New York was shocked by one of the worst scandals of the period, when it was discovered in July that the president of the New York & New Haven Railroad had issued some $2,000,000 worth of fraudulent stock. But the scandal was to have a special effect upon the members of the First Congregational Church, for the president of the railroad company was no less than Robert Schuyler, George Schuyler's brother. Schuyler managed to flee the city just before the massive swindle was uncovered; he was never caught, and died in Italy the following year.

Robert Schuyler had been a trustee of the church for six years, from 1838 to 1844, and had served as president of the board during the last year of his second term. Since then he had served on the committee to purchase the lot on 20th Street and Fourth Avenue, and until Bellows's intrusion into the matter of selecting an architectural plan, was on the building committee. The railroad could not survive the disaster and failed. George Templeton Strong predicted in his diary that the swindle would herald the beginning of an out-and-out depression.[1]

Bellows was naturally deeply distressed by the Robert Schuyler affair; "with the dreadful defalcation of my parishioner, Robert Schuyler—one of the most incredible & overwhelming facts ever known in commercial life. The whole history of the affair is wrapped in mystery. Perhaps I shall know something to satisfy a curiosity at present utterly baffled. . . . I have been greatly distressed by this affair."[2]

By contrast with this distress, Harvard's conferring on him of an honorary Doctor of Divinity degree at the 1854 commencement gave him substantial satisfaction. From this time on everyone spoke of Henry as *Dr.* Bellows, an honor which he proudly carried.

Another honor which he received was to give the address on the erection of a monument to the memory of Colonel Benjamin Bellows, the founder of Walpole. Bellows immediately went to work on the genealogy of his distinguished ancestor, and on 11 October

1854 gave an address which was printed in a book commemorating the event. It was the first significant work done on the genealogy of the Bellows family.[3]

Money was hard to come by in early 1855, for the nation, and New York with it, was suffering a severe economic setback. The steady flow of gold from California since 1850, plus the rapid expansion of industrialized manufacturing, had caused an unrealistic confidence in the nation's economy. Irresponsible speculation, rash investment, particularly in the mushrooming railroad companies, and a general extravagance among the wealthy classes had created a situation of rapidly rising prices which the country's economic balance could not withstand. As early as 1853, the country had begun to show signs of economic strain; in 1854, several business concerns went bankrupt and many others began to falter. Robert Schuyler's embezzlement, and the consequent failure of the New York and New Haven Railroad in July, had hit that company's stockholders hard. By the following autumn, unemployment was widespread, and a brief panic on the stock market had ensued. By 1855, a decided recession had settled over the nation and New York City. Many of the First Church's wealthier members were foundering financially, and no one wanted to part with any funds.

Jacob Wrey Mould, the English architect of the building presently under construction at 20th Street and Fourth Avenue, acted in oblivion of this recession. From the beginning, Mould had continuously suggested modifications in the church's design, modifications involving largely cupolas here, cornices there, and gewgaws everywhere. Further, he had imported Caen stone from Italy for the surface, a most costly procedure. Having been encouraged by Bellows's optimistic insistence, the building committee (of which Bellows was a member) had adopted many, if not all, of these proposals; consequently, the bills, as well as the building itself, were growing like Topsy. In July 1854 it had become quite clear to the trustees that a substantial sum would be needed, and *soon*, to pay for the mounting costs. The board had then decided to try for a loan of $35,000 upon the mortgage on the property. They succeeded, and the project had continued, with Mould's creative urges also continuing to wax strong. By the annual meeting it was clear that still more funds would be necessary to finance the completion of the project.

All of these expenses had to be met somehow, and the trustees laid the situation frankly before the society at the annual meeting in 1855. But no hands willingly plunged into pockets; no offers to rally to the church's desperate need came forward. Instead, the members deferred the matter back to the board, empowering it to raise the money as it saw fit. The pew holders were perfectly willing to continue paying their present rents on the pews they were currently using in New York University's chapel—to which they had just moved from the hall of the Medical College—but that was about it.

Had it not been for the courageous generosity of Moses Grinnell, the president of the board for the past year, and a member of the building committee, the society might have suffered at least a serious delay in the already well overdue completion of its new building. In spite of the bleak economic outlook for the nation, Grinnell loaned $750 to the building fund early in February, and another $1,000 in March. He also made regular loans to the society for its operating expenses.

As the year entered into its second quarter, however, the country's economy began to recover and gradually the wallets of the First Church's members began to open. By the end of June, the building fund had received over $7,000 in subscriptions; by the end of October, another $20,000 had been collected. Grinnell alone contributed over $16,000 of the $27,000 total, and in December, he loaned yet another $7,000!

Peter Cooper, too, was among the subscribers to the building fund. Cooper had become a Unitarian through the influence of Orville Dewey, during the peak of Dewey's success while the Second Church was meeting at the Stuyvesant Institute. Cooper and a friend, Joseph Curtis, neither of whom, according to Dewey, "belonged to any religious society or regularly attended upon any church,"[4] had happened along Broadway one Sunday evening in the 1830s, when they observed the crowd of people just entering the institute for the evening service. Wondering what the attraction was, Cooper and Curtis entered, too. But when they came out again at the end of the program, they had both made up their minds to become involved with such ideas as Dewey had expressed, and immediately joined the Second Church. Cooper had remained with that society at least through the time of Dewey's departure, for this subscription to the First Church's building fund in 1855 is the first time Cooper's name appears in the society's records. His friend, Joseph Curtis, also came over to the First Church about this time.

In April 1855 Henry Bellows analyzed his congregation at All Souls, "On the whole, I know not where a body of more genuine, active & thoughtful persons could be found—or one of more intelligence & culture, than in my own parish. And I have come to see this very peculiarly during the last year or two." He found that "the young people who have grown up, with & under me, seem promising, & I find, at length, a very general adoption of the special notions & current spirit of my religious & philanthropic views in the parish; so that we are a rarely united, free & genial body of folks, with no ecclesiastical ties & little machinery—but a strong spiritual bond." He begged that the recipient, Cyrus Bartol, would "excuse the fondness with which I dwell on what must needs be so precious to my thoughts."[5]

On Thursday evening 7 June 1855, Dr. Bellows gave the sermon at the installation of the Reverend Adams Ayer as the associate pastor of the Unitarian Society in Charlestown, New Hampshire, near Walpole. Thomas Starr King presided over the ceremony of the Right Hand of Fellowship. Bellows's sermon was so significant that the parish published it.[6] The title of the sermon indicated its subject matter, "Worship, the Want of Our National Church," and it pointed a persistent theme that was to be one of Henry Bellows's important themes during the rest of his life. This was an early attempt at preaching a sermon on a theme for which Bellows four years later became such an expert that this sermon suffers by comparison.

In Charlestown, Bellows argued that it was not through worship but through practical deeds that the Christian principles were triumphing in our nation. "Economy, order, law, education, morality, may flourish; social, political, and personal justice triumph, and vice decay . . . but if meanwhile the sentiments which inspire, if the noble passions which animate . . . the faith which exalts a people, die out, there will come a time when life is stale and wearisome, man mean and worldly, and civilization ripe only for decay." Bellows had made a strong case for the religious sentiment, and it was this preliminary statement which he made at the ordination of Adams Ayer which would reach its full flower in "The Suspense of Faith" at Cambridge four years later.

By the end of June 1855, Henry Bellows was able to report to Eliza that "the church is now pretty much covered with mortar inside (the scratch-coat), the gallery is up, & things begin to take shape & form. The outside is mostly cleaned & looks like a quite different building." He added, "You can hardly conceive how much the cleaning has done to bring out the beauty of the materials. People begin to talk in a very changed tone about it. We think it will be ready in *all October*; & that will answer quite well." He also reported to Eliza that the house or parsonage which was an integral part of the building was also advancing in readiness for their occupancy.[7]

Yet in spite of apparent success, Charles S. Francis wrote to Bellows that there was a large deficit in the running expenses of the church and that the building fund had interfered with the usual annual fundraising. He hoped that "the Trustees in their wisdom will devise some means to make up this deficiency before we go into the new church. I shall put the matter before them when they can be got together which is a difficult matter this warm weather."[8]

Parsonage of All Souls Church (completed 1855), All Souls Archives

Bellows returned to New York City from Walpole early in September 1855, and was able to report that "the church & house both come on well. The interior, so far as the plastering is concerned, is nearly done. But I see already it cannot be finished till December, perhaps not till 1 Jan. As I examine the remaining work I see so much yet to be done. But I am not impatient, because it goes on as fast as it can go *well*—& is done in such a beautiful & substantial way." He had visited the parsonage with Nicholas Dean, and he was impressed with the quality of the work.[9]

Meanwhile, Bellows had some problems with his minister brother John Bellows. He had met with a group of fifteen or twenty of John's parishioners at Wilton, New Hampshire, and "I was surprised to find how unanimous the people were in thinking John *insane*. They brought a great many proofs or evidence of it, & seemed to think it hopeless to continue the connexion with him longer. Nobody denied his sincerity or devotion to this work, or were disposed to think unkindly of him—but all united in the opinion that he must leave." Bellows felt the true cause of the insanity. He wrote, "The testimony of his wife & daughter is that all this excitability &

First Floor of the parsonage of All Souls Church. This is a later view after the room was turned into a church reception room, All Souls Archives

appearance of insanity is the result of the steady, moderate, various but increasing use of stimulants. In six months he has been slowly but constantly increasing his dependence on these things,—brandy & salt—stimulating medicines, tobacco (chewing & smoking), coffee, whatever else in cartons or food is most pungent & exciting." Bellows felt that John ate too much food, and that his stomach called for stimulants to digest all of it. This had all resulted in John's lack of self-control. Henry believed that if his brother went on a diet the causes would be eliminated.[10]

After preaching to his congregation on 7 October, Bellows left the next day for a ten-day trip to Cincinnati for meetings of the Antioch board of trustees and other duties in the west. At the railroad station he accidentally met Henry Ward Beecher who, somewhat to Bellows's consternation, took a seat next to him in the coach. Bellows expected that he would be in for a day "of laborious & perhaps exciting talk." But he enjoyed the encounter as Beecher "proved himself very reasonable, moderate & wise in respect to the sum & character of his talk." Bellows wrote that he was "very glad to have had this capital opportunity of forming a deliberate opinion of a man of so much mark in our day." Bellows found Beecher "unpretending, simple & genuine in his manners. His conversation boils with earnestness & bubbles with playfulness. He says many thinking & memorable things; but above all (& this surprised me) is marked by common-sense." After this talk Bellows understood the basis of Beecher's phenomenal success: "I can perfectly understand how he controls his people—not by mere boldness & self-assertion, but by having more good-sense than any & all of them." He felt that Beecher was "a very *prudent* man—& that it is prudence winged by *genius* that carries him so far ahead. He has moreover great *sweetness*, & makes you love him. . . . We parted with mutual good will, &, I hope, mutual respect. I shall want to see more of him."[11] This meeting strongly influenced Bellows in favor of the other "HWB" preacher in the New York area, but over the years his opinion of Beecher changed back again to what it had been earlier.

Bellows went from Cincinnati to Yellow Springs for the meetings of the Board of Antioch College. But he was not well. The three days he spent at Antioch "were laborious & useful & rather melancholy." He found the food "coarse, the bed hard & the company incongenial." He found his advice anxiously sought, "& taken in regard to all of the important questions that touch Antioch College at this critical moment." He was fortunately in the company of Moses H. Grinnell whom he had persuaded to go on the Antioch

Board. "He has deliberately surveyed our affairs, & *is willing to take my share of our investment off my hands,"* Bellows proclaimed. But Grinnell insisted that Bellows continue with his interest in Antioch. Bellows and Grinnell returned to New York by railroad.[12]

John Bellows had left Wilton and had been confined to an asylum at Brattleboro to try to dry him up and restore his health. Because of John, Henry Bellows was interested in the problem of alcoholism. On 6 November 1855 he spoke at "the Tabernacle [Broadway Tabernacle] in behalf of a national *asylum* for the *confinement & cure of inebriates."* He wanted this asylum to be "a place where without resorting to gaols & prisons, they may be restored to reason. Drunkenness ought to have *pathological* treatment. It is a disease and the best medical authorities say that *eighty* percent of it, like insanity of other kinds—may be cured—if it be taken in time & treated scientifically." Bellows recognized alcoholism not as moral depravity but as a disease and he thought that a national treatment center was needed. His brother Hamilton had "abandoned all use of ardent spirits." Henry hoped it would last.[13]

It had been a long and arduous fall season. "Never have I known a more busy & overwhelming season of duty." But he added that to these arduous duties has "been the sad responsibility of putting my brother John into the insane asylum, a most serious trouble, & not dismissed by struggles of doubt about keeping him there."[14]

Father Of All! Thy Children Come

Early in 1855 the congregation moved from the Medical College and, though it held its annual meeting in the library room of the Church of the Messiah, it conducted its worship services in its new temporary quarters at the New York University chapel at Washington Square for the remainder of the year 1855. As late as the end of November 1855, the building project was still incomplete, and although it had been under construction for nearly two full years, last-minute changes were still being made. No one could say for certain when the edifice would sufficiently meet the approval of the building committee and the ever-creative Mr. Mould for the long-awaited meetinghouse to be pronounced "finished."

At last, on 8 December, Mr. Grinnell called a meeting of the trustees at his office and reported, as spokesman for the building committee, that the new church would be ready for occupancy on 25

December. Although the installation of the organ had only just begun, and might not be completed by that time, the trustees thought that Christmas Day would make a fitting time to dedicate the society's new house of worship, and delegated the responsibility for arranging the program to the building committee. It was left up to Bellows, Grinnell, and Charles Butler to plan the details.

Samuel Osgood, Bellows's colleague at the Church of the Messiah, was, of course, invited to participate in the dedication, as was the other Unitarian minister from the vicinity, Dr. Frederick A. Farley, of the Brooklyn Church. Octavius Brooks Frothingham also was residing in New Jersey at this time, and was included among the clergymen asked to help consecrate the new church.[1] S.K. Lothrop from the Brattle Street Church in Boston, who on several occasions had preached at the Church of the Divine Unity, was also invited to participate.

Only two clouds marred the spirit of joyful anticipation which filled the minds and hearts of the members. One was that the organ definitely would not be fully installed by Christmas Day. The other cloud was that Nicholas Dean was not expected to be well enough to witness the consecration of the church, to whose completion he lovingly had devoted so much of his time and attention. Dean had submitted his hymn, though, and on Bellows's recommendation the committee had the words printed in the program:

Father of All! thy children come,
  And bend the rev'rent knee,
This house, from corner stone to dome
  To dedicate to Thee!

Accept our offering, Holy One!
  With humble hope 'tis given,
Make it a temple of thy Son;—
  A gate that leads to heaven.

Here let thy Gospel's purest ray
  Pierce through to every soul,
Illumine our uncertain way,
  Our erring steps control.

Thy Holy Spirit we beseech
  To live by the commands,
That pastor, people, all may reach
  "A house not made with hands."[2]

The words were to be sung to the tune of "Arlington." But Dean's hymn was also strangely prophetic of his own fate. On Saturday, 22

December, just two days away from the dedication ceremony, Dean himself passed through the "gate that leads to heaven."

Bellows had another problem weighing upon his mind. Should the new building have a new name? If so, he had a list of several possibilities. Bellows enumerated them to the trustees, adding that "All Souls" was the name *he* liked best. We have seen that Bellows in his own mind had named the church "All Souls" at least five years previously. The trustees resolved that the "Church of All Souls" be the name of the new church, and, there being no more reason to detain them, proceeded home to their Sunday dinners. Just as simply as that, the present name of "All Souls" was adopted in 1855.

The dedication service itself was held at noon on Tuesday, Christmas Day. Although the ceremony was simple, it began with great drama: all participating clergymen solemnly entered the sanctuary and, as they proceeded down the aisle, read responsively Psalm 24:

> The earth is the Lord's and the fulness thereof:
> The world and they that dwell within. . . .

When the procession had reached the chancel and the ministers had finished reading the Psalm, the choir sang, to the accompaniment of simplified organ strains, a chorus from Handel's "Messiah." Then Samuel Osgood read from the scriptures. Dr. Lothrop gave the prayer of dedication, after which the choir once more performed with the partially installed organ, this time with an anthem of dedication by Boyce: "I have surely built thee an house to dwell in, a settled place for thee to abide in forever. . . ."[3] The words expressed all of the hopes and expectations which the congregation had invested in this, their third house of worship.

The sermon had been reserved as Bellows's privilege. The sermon in its entirety apparently is lost, but a small portion of it has been preserved in an article published by the *Journel of Commerce* two days after the dedication:

> It is for others to say what success has attended our efforts to signalize, perpetuate, and adorn our fame. It has been our conscientious aim to make a building in which mean economy, superficial show, worldly artifice, and fraud, should not enter, a building religious in its structure, from corner stone to dome; and if a consumate skill, and unfailing taste, and unsparing devotion, a self-possession which neither ridicule nor blame could disturb, and a zeal which neither sickness or pain could impair, if these deserve fame, then indeed the modest architecture of this Christian temple has achieved it.[4]

By "modest architecture," Bellows was referring euphemistically, and perhaps somewhat defensively, to the elaborately ornate (and costly!) manifestation of Mould's inspiration, in which behalf Bellows himself had played an integral part.

Bellows's sermon was propitiously punctuated by the hymn which Nicholas Dean had composed. Because of Dean's recent departure, the program committee had changed the original plan calling for the congregation to sing the hymn; instead, O. B. Frothingham read its words with dramatic and reverent eloquence. As Frothingham uttered the final words of Dean's hymn, he paused, and then returned with dignity to his seat. Frederick Farley then slowly and quietly rose to give the concluding prayer. When Farley had finished, the few installed organ pipes played the opening bars of the "Christmas Anthem" from Handel's "Messiah," and the choir joined in with "For unto us a child is born, Unto us a son is given . . ." Then John Parkman (the famous Francis Parkman's less illustrious son who had once been with the Third Congregation Church in Greenfield, Massachusetts) concluded the Christmas Day dedication with a benediction.

All Souls Church (completed 1855) (Note the platform for the bell tower which was never built), All Souls Archives

The prime source of Jacob Wrey Mould's inspiration for the Church of All Souls was the Basilica of San Giovani Battista (St. John the Baptist) at Monza, in northern Italy. The Monza church was built in A.D. 595 and in 1855 was the earliest Christian edifice ever to be used as a model for a church building in the United States. The architecture of All Souls, like that of the basilica in Monza, was of the Lombardo-Byzantine (or Lombardic Romanesque) style, which belonged to the Byzantine period. Emperor Justinian I (483–565) whose empire had extended from Odessa in the East to Gibraltar in the West, had built edifices such as the Hagia Sophia in Constantinople and San Vitale in Ravenna. After Justinian's death, the structures built under his reign were taken as the main architectural style by his Lombard successors in the West.

The original design for All Souls had included a bell tower, or campanile, but both funds and time had run out before it could be built. The trustees thus postponed building the tower until more favorable circumstances prevailed, which time never came! There was a large dome over the church, and on top of this was placed a cross. At its maximum height, the building rose 106 feet to the top of

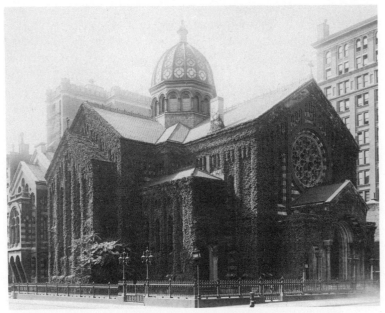

All Souls Church (completed 1855) (A later view when most of the "Beefsteak" had been covered with ivy), All Souls Archives

the cross; it was 107 feet deep, and eighty-three feet at its widest extremities. To support the heavy structure, it had been necessary to build the walls over three feet thick at the base, and two feet, four inches, thick at the top. Jacob Wrey Mould had used as his exterior material an alternating combination of Caen stone, imported from Italy, and red Philadelphia brick. The Caen stone was a light yellow; the brick "the reddest possible"[5]—with the result that there was a

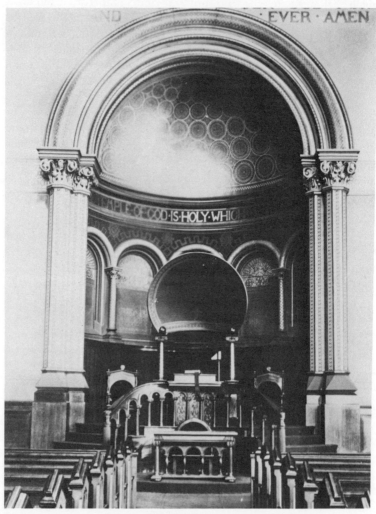

All Souls Church, Original interior (Photo taken in 1891 before extensive remodelling was done to the pulpit area), All Souls Archives

striking contrast between them and, used thus alternately, they formed a startlingly bright striped pattern.

The building represented a dramatic departure from the main themes of the city's existing architecture, and had received much attention and comment long before it was completed. There were those who felt that its vivid stripes and Byzantine design comprised a welcome relief from the monotonous brownstones that were beginning to dominate the city: "Under our brilliant and gorgeously colored skies (!), brownstone is monotonous, and white marble glaring. The eye seeks in vain for harmony and repose, where large unbroken masses of these materials are presented to it, especially in situations where they can be seen in conjunction with an expanse of atmosphere."[6] On the other hand, there were those who saw the building as the greatest architectural joke the city—even the nation—had ever witnessed. Some people named All Souls the "Holy Zebra" because of its brilliant stripes; George Templeton Strong called it the " 'pied variety' of the St. (Hagia) Sophia."[7] Others thought that the building resembled a giant piece of red meat, complete with yellow fat! It was for this latter reason that the building came permanently to be nicknamed the "Beefsteak Church."

The best description of the inside of the new church is that given by a reporter for the *New York World,* signed only "Mintwood," who visited the church for a morning service in December 1870. Written by a reporter rather than a church member, this article has some interesting insights into the church and its people. "The interior . . . is shaped like a cross," Mintwood wrote. "At the head is the pulpit, an elaborately carved walnut affair, half under the shelter of an over-arching recess. A shell-shaped sounding board rises back of the rostrum, in 'invisible' brown, relieved by a cross in red and blue and gold, surrounded with spears of gilt, to make one dream of a halo." He explained that "the walls of this cruciform enclosure are a tinted mauve, with the woodwork finished in golden brown and gilt. The carpets are red and black, and the upholstering of crimson." In the center of the roof "is a dome windowed in gorgeous hues, encased in a square of cross beams, with heavy pendants of the same dipped in gilt." The architecture pleased Mintwood: "There are innumerable lines of light and shade, of flowing tracery and carved volutes, which combine to render the interior of this ample compensation on days of worship for the infliction of the exterior on the 'unhallowed' days, if indeed one day be less hallowed than another."

The author's comments about the people who worshiped here are equally interesting. He stood near "the entrance waiting for a seat. A little white-haired usher bobbed up and down the aisles, beckoning strangers to seats." There was no suggestion of a crowded house, "but it seemed en regle to make a pretense. There were many vacant seats after all entered, which suggested a place far from popular with the average audience. Our beck came at length, and the hoary usher gave us a pleasant place." Mintwood received a cordial welcome. "When the owner of the pew came in she gave us so sweet and courteous a welcome in her benignant smile, that we concluded Unitarianism had made a Christian of at least one woman."

His description of Dr. Bellows is amusing and gives us some hints of Bellows's peculiarities in the pulpit. "If Dr. Bellows had worn a long beard, instead of being utterly devoid of all facial hirsute appendages, I should have put his portrait along with those of Moses and Aaron and Elijah." When the service begins, "he arises in his desk with his black clerical gown descending from his manly shoulders, rolls his eyes heavenward, and looks so despairing and woebegone as to make one wonder if 'tis such a dreadful thing to be a preacher after all." Mintwood suggested, "Perhaps it comes from trying to look fatherly; or perhaps words of song, of praise, of prayer ascend higher if sent upon a pitch of dolorous expression." The service continued, "After an anthem has been rendered by a quartet of accomplished singers, which sings with much understanding and little or no spirit, the pastor follows with a scriptural lesson."

Bellows's preaching style is also discussed. "He is, perhaps, better than the average pulpit orator in several essentials, but quite like them in many others: among them being that of starting off with a sentence with vim and haste and vigor, and winding up in a sort of exhausted condition." Perhaps Bellows was not the great extemporary speaker he thought he was. "He continues the service with prayer, and the attitude of the audience is devotional after the usual custom. He assumes a great deal of humility in prayer, and if he possessed a spark of magnetism or sympathetic power, he would lead his people down into a valley of despair, of hopelessness, of such unutterable worthlessness of feeling, that would be almost unbearable. As it is, however, he professes to go there himself, and a sinful hearer concludes it is better to pray on the mountain tops with joy and thanksgiving and hope." But Mintwood got restless for it was "a long prayer, full of devotional rhetoric and phraseology, and thoroughly vermiculated with head gestures that are supposed to give emphasis to the petitions as the thud of a suspended weight settles a post at every fall of the beam. His intonation and accent are peculiar, but all tending to sorrow and depression." Another Bellows peculiarity is mentioned, "After prayer he reads a hymn, something appropriate, and at the end of each verse his eyes go up to the roof of the church. The accomplished singer tenor uprolls his eyes in a similar way. The roof of the church is undeniably attractive, but it isn't heaven, and not particularly inspiring, save in an artistic and architectural way."

"Mintwood" further described the sermon: "the text chosen is full of interest, about the resurrection of the dead and the immortality of the soul." But Bellows was "closely confined to his manuscript, and his gestures and expressions partake of the confined, unnatural manner, that forever characterizes such speaking. His enunciation is very clear, his voice soft in timbre, with an undertone of kindness and pity and sympathy in it that is exceedingly doleful." He accused Bellows of being something of an actor. "There is a positive attempt at dramatic execution which is too methodically apparent for effect." However, "To those who value matter, quite regardless of manner, Dr. Bellows can hardly fail to be most acceptable. His sermons are most carefully wrought out; his rhetoric is beautiful; his words well chosen, and his reasonings, illustrations, and metaphors most happy and convincing." There was a way to avoid being bothered by the mannerisms, "to shut one's eyes, and close one's ears, save to what *is said*, one can enjoy a sacred intellectual feast that is worth remembering." But "Mintwood"'s impression was that "poor unsanctified human nature loves a speaker who looks in its wicked eyes, instead of forever over its head, up in ethereal space somewhere; it loves some by-play of voice at least; to hear interesting incidents related in a tone somewhat removed from that employed in uttering those sad, sad, words we hear at open graves." He concluded that a hearer "does not rejoice in hearing a funeral sermon fifty-two Sundays in the year."

"Mintwood" concluded with an analysis of the reasons for Bellows's popularity: "The popularity of Dr. Bellows among his people and the love and reverence in which he is held by them, is abundant proof of his possession of a large brain and a kind and generous nature. As a writer, he is everywhere popular, and it is only his depressing, despondingly forlorn manner of presenting great power and beauty of thought that is so to be deplored."[8]

In defense of Bellows one can only point to the journalistic cleverness which is apparent in "Mintwood" 's style. Also, Bellows *was* in one of the most sorrowful moods of his entire life in 1870, after the loss of his wife just a year before this time. But the description of the interior of the church, the attitudes of the people, and Bellows's mannerisms must have been much the same in 1855 as they were later in 1870.

As the Industrial Revolution took hold in New York City the startling contrast between the yellow and red walls of the "Beefsteak Church" soon faded with soot and grime. Moreover, the building was ultimately almost entirely covered with ivy. But at the time the church was dedicated, its impact upon the public was probably not unlike that made by the Guggenheim Museum, designed by Frank Lloyd Wright (a Unitarian) and completed in the late 1960s, which stands at Fifth Avenue and 89th Street.

The parsonage adjoined the church building on 20th Street, and rose four stories high. Some people considered this second edifice a masterful architectural achievement in adapting the limited space remaining after the main structure had been accounted for. Dr. and Mrs. Bellows, however, did not share these views. The parsonage was not completed by the Christmas of 1855. It was not until two months later that the board met to work out the details of space allocation in the parsonage. On 21 February 1856, the trustees resolved to *rent* the parsonage to Bellows for $1,000, with the stipulation that the basement be reserved for the church's use as a Sunday-school room, and that the Bellows family share with the society the back room, which the writer of the article in the *Journal of Commerce* called "one of the finest [drawing rooms] in the city."[9] The trustees wanted to house the church's library in this parlor, as well as to use the room as a vestry for meetings, lectures, and other mostly secular purposes. Private quarters for the Bellows family would thus occupy the remaining three floors, and the Bellowses could use the first-floor parlor for their own entertaining when the church was not using it for some official occasion.

Dr. Bellows agreed to this arrangement and the family moved into the parsonage from their house on nearby Irving Place. Anna Bellows recalled the excitement of moving from that house into the new parsonage, and her own delights with "the complicated and somewhat mysterious and inconvenient parsonage."[10] Anna was ten when she and her family made the move and she was attending "Miss Haines's well-known day school." Her brother, Russell Nevins Bellows, was nearly fourteen and was being prepared for college at the school of Theodore Weld in Eagleswood, New Jersey.

At the time that Moses Grinnell had resorted to importing Mould from England, the society was aiming for a large church, one that would seat comfortably some 1,200 people to be built for under $120,000. Contrary to these expectations, however, the rashly creative genius of Mr. Mould had produced a building that, according to the account printed in the *Journal of Commerce*, held only 900 people in its 170 pews. Bellows later insisted that its real seating capacity was barely 750, not much more than half that originally planned and hoped for by the society. The society had also originally planned to expand its Sunday-school facilities. The Unity School at the Church of the Divine Unity had become successful and too large for the space available right from the start in 1846. The sale of that building had been undertaken with the view that the new church, when completed, would provide ample space for the Sunday-school pupils and allow for future expansion. But the new building did *not* provide sufficient space for the Sunday school, nor even sufficient office facilities.

To make matters worse, bringing Mould from England and importing Caen stone from Italy had been extravagant measures; when added to the costs of the extraordinary thickness of the walls, of the materials and workmanship which went into the purely decorative aspects of the building, and of the constant additions and changes in the cornices, cupolas, and other embellishments, the project way exceeded the congregation's anticipated expense. Bellows put the final cost at over $168,000.

Almost a quarter of a century later Bellows made these comments about the hopes for the new church and the realities: "Our architect had bewitched Mr. Grinnell with his plan and his plausible estimates of expense. He was a man of genius and taste, but cared less for our interests and wishes than for an opportunity of showing his own talents." In addition, "Our debt was a millstone of portentious size when we entered the church, but let it be gratefully remembered that our people stood firm. They neither ran away nor asked assistance from others. They slowly, but persistently, rallied their confidence. They strained their ability, but they paid the debt, with the exception of $10,000, which was left unpaid under the impression that it was provided for in some testamentary form."[11]

The architect and Moses Grinnell bore the brunt of the criticism for the vast discrepancies between what the society had planned and what it finally got. Anna Bellows referred to Jacob Wrey Mould as a "talented spendthrift,"[12] and no doubt this in part was true. But it must be remembered that it was Bellows *himself* who had talked the congregation and its trustees into putting cost considerations aside, and into going all out for a really suitable church in place of just an adequate one. Yet Bellows put the onus of the cost of the building on Moses Grinnell.

Most of the members, however, were impressed with their elaborate new building. If there were any nagging doubts among some members that perhaps their long-awaited church was more a frilly showcase than the practical and enduring religious home they had been promised, these doubts probably were buried under convenient rationalizations to the effect that, surely, under all the fancy gewgaws there lay a solidly practical church, and that the trusted trustees *must* have obtained the fancy trimmings at some sort of a bargain. It probably was inconceivable to the congregation that its trustees, under the active guidance of their beloved and all-wise minister, would go to such extreme lengths of time, trouble, and expense to build merely a white elephant, especially considering the church's past painful experience with buildings!

The trustees themselves may have realized that, if the congregation were presented point-blank with the realities of what the new building *had* cost, and what the society now owed in outstanding bills, not only might this knowledge puncture all convenient rationalizations, but there might very likely be a burst of outrage and an open challenge on the part of some members. To avoid such a reaction, Grinnell announced at the annual meeting on 15 January 1856 that a verbal report on the pecuniary condition of the church "might not be understood and [would] be liable to misconstruction."[13] Grinnell then promised the members of the society that a printed statement would be forthcoming, and would include a plan of the pews in the new church with sale and rental prices.

During the next two weeks, the trustees carefully worked out a total valuation of the pews and an allocation of the price of each pew based on this valuation. Probably something like $150,000 would have been a modestly realistic sum at which to establish the total valuation, assuming that all pews could be rented and sold, and at their full proportionate value. The trustees dared not go this high, though, and established instead a sum of $90,000 as the total.

Scrip good for half the price of any pew in All Souls were distributed among those who had been pew owners in the Church of the Divine Unity and to those who had subscribed to the building fund, but pews were chosen by means of an auction, with the most desirable pews going to the highest bidders. The first sale was held on 11 February 1856, at which seventy-six pews were sold for a total of $45,900, with premiums adding to another $4,700. This was a fortunate stroke of luck for the society's finances!

Another auction was held five days later, at which seven more pews were sold, and thirty-eight were rented, making a total of 101 pews disposed of, and netting $59,000 for the society. This left only sixty-nine pews to be sold or rented. While not all of the sale prices were paid in full during the year, the amount collected enabled the treasurer to pay off Mould's and most of the contractors' remaining bills. Pew taxes and rentals helped to finance the church's operating expenses during 1856.

Bellows decided to start to make use of the new building by announcing a series of lectures. He left a slip of paper in the church vestibule and eighty-one persons signed up to "pledge [themselves] to stated attendance upon twelve weekly lectures." This was the kind of activity in which Bellows was particularly competent. He never thought of himself as a scholar, and yet he had the pastoral ability to take big subjects and make them interesting and understandable to his people.[14]

Bellows realized that he had been through a crucial struggle in the church. He wrote in March 1856: "this winter has been the Thermopylae of my life. All things had been jamming & narrowing to this pass, & a great battle of principle, policy, courage, was to be fought. *It has been fought*, & I am, thanks to God, victor, & victor over & above all my best hopes & prayers." Bellows believed that in this way he had become "the head of my society in a sense not at all common in other churches, & I suspect, in a sense in which *no other man is*. They look to me as much to guide & govern their temporal as their spiritual affairs, & with an affair of $165,000 on my heart & head, you can easily see I could not feel utterly at ease." It had not been an easy task, "to carry on the great spiritual work, & this too, has drawn all my blood." Yet, "the crisis has passed, & we are all safe & sound—nay triumphant & happy." Bellows reported that the church had sold two-thirds of the pews and had rented only about a dozen others. He also reported that "about half the parish is *new;* substantial, excellent people who have bought into our enterprise—& we have now a solid, strong permanent society, which if I died tomorrow, would give our cause in this city a corner-stone that could not be shaken."[15]

Present Excitements

In April 1856, looking forward to the annual meetings of the Unitarian Association at the end of May, Frederic Henry Hedge wrote Bellows in a "private" letter that he was dismayed and distressed by what was happening in the denomination. Hedge was concerned about "the prospects of Liberal Christianity in our land, as affected by recent developments." Articles on Unitarianism had been appearing in Frederic Dan Huntington's *Monthly Religious Magazine,* and Hedge found the tendencies avowed there "very unsatisfactory & somewhat ominous!" He believed that some kind of a demonstration, by which it "may appear that a large & respectable portion of the Unitarian body are not disposed to relinquish the results of a fifty year's struggle," ought to take place. He wanted very much to "repudiate any attempt to coalesce with orthodoxy on a doctrinal basis." Hedge felt no hope of any effective resistance to these ideas from the American Unitarian Association. In fact, he even suggested that a New Yorker ought to be the next president of the association, and he also favored moving its office to New York. But he doubted "if this could be effected without too violent a rupture." He suggested to Bellows that a dozen of those who thought similarly get together the Monday of anniversary week to draw some plans of counterattack.[1]

Bellows admitted that the tendencies in the denomination to which Hedge alluded disturbed him, too. He termed the opposition "the side-ways traveling" and "backward-looking" portion of the denomination. He felt that his "faith in the views for which we have been contending for two generations, increases yearly." He also told Hedge that although he could count on his sympathy that he himself was perhaps not yet "prepared to unite, in any *formal* way, with the friends of progress." He hated and despised the reactionary party. He found them equally weak in intellect and in will, he distrusted the sincerity and simplicity of Huntington "who appears to me like an ambitious rhetorician—without intellectual convictions, or high moral instincts." But he was not convinced that under such leadership the "semi-orthodoxy in our body" could do much that was effective. He felt that sympathy for Huntington's point of view was confined to the neighborhood of Boston, not even extending to Cambridge. Bellows believed that Huntington's sympathizers, Sears, Stearns, and Ellis, *"explode* orthodoxy by *explaining* it." He felt that Huntington's brute orthodoxy, his appeal to fear, and his superstition, which Bellows held in special dread, were antiquated.

Edward Everett Hale, D.D., Courtesy of the Massachusetts Historical Society

He believed that organizing opposition would give too much importance to Huntington. He was also afraid that the moderates would be certain that the persons named by Hedge were extremist.[2]

In the middle of May, Edward Everett Hale in a letter marked *"entirely confidential,"* asked Bellows for advice about his future career. He had been the minister of the Church of the Unity in Worcester for ten years. Now thirty-four years of age, Hale was being sought by the congregation of the South Congregational Church in Boston to be their minister. Hale preferred to preach in New York rather than Boston. He had considered the church in Brooklyn previously and Bellows had given him advice then; now he wrote asking further advice. If something were likely to develop in the New York area within the next two or three years, Hale wrote Bellows, he would be content to wait for that rather than go to Boston. He emphasized that he must have an answer by the mail that would leave New York on Sunday afternoon. We do not have Bellows's reply. But Hale did accept the pulpit of the South Congregational Church (Unitarian) in Boston where he was the minister for the next forty-three years.[3]

Looking back over the recently completed church season after she had gone to Walpole for the summer vacation period, Eliza Bellows wrote to her husband a pleading letter that he should learn better to control the business of his life. "Dr. Stone says there is nothing the matter with you, but fatigue. Well! Who authorizes & permits this fatigue? Surely not I." She quoted Bellows's own words back to him. What he needed was "a more girded & bounded life & career, simpler desires, more strictly professional tastes & narrowed devotion to details of duty." She regretted that each year there was "an increasing weight of care & complexity." She felt that it was this which had brought her "at times to the sad want of self-control I have manifested." She believed that she was not answerable for this, and was seriously alarmed "for the safety of my and your health & happiness."[4]

Henry agreed with Eliza. He was pressured in his work. But Bellows's life did not let up. He admitted that if he "could conquer what you characterize as my dependence on present excitement, & project enterprises that were animated by a lasting interest & great impersonal aim; it would very likely restore my health of body & mind, & perhaps yours too. I am conscious of great & besetting weakness in this direction." He could not doubt that some change was needed. He could lose himself willingly in his study, he believed.

He was very frank with Eliza—a trait which was to come more and more to the surface as the years went by. "But do not, my dear wife, because I am at the confessional—think that my mistake is not much complicated & greatened by *your* mistake. If I am to do for myself, what you see, & see myself to require, it must be by a better, a nobler, a more humble, & more genial ministry to my wants &

weaknesses than you have shown yourself able thus far to bestow."
He cautioned her, "You have got to struggle with & overcome this
demon of fastidiousness, of household absorption, of temper & of
pride, which is the wreck of your peace & my own. If you feel
strength for the struggle, I shall." He had a suggestion, "Let us
grapple with prayerful hearts with our common foes." He would
shut himself up and grapple with his problem but, "you shall secretly
reserve a due portion of your nervous energy, your tranquillity, your
self-sacrifice for *me*, for my personal delection & service &
support." Bellows had something of the male chauvinism of the
period in his thinking: "You shall learn to sacrifice something of
your will to a wifely submission, something of your preferences to
my tastes—& thus by mutual repentence & reformation we will solve
the problem of a wedded life in which we two true & warm hearts
with great opportunities are in part of that peace."[5]

Five years before the beginning of the Civil War the country was
agitated by what was happening in "Bleeding Kansas." Dewey asked
Bellows in June 1856, "What are we coming to?" He wondered:
"are we drifting upon the rock that is to split us asunder, & is there
nobody to do any thing, or say any thing about it?" Dewey found
fanaticism in both the North and the South on the issue of slavery
and secession. He believed that Charles Sumner was wrong and that
Emerson's stand was also wrong. Dewey did not feel that it was right
"to heap this scorn upon the whole South—upon its very character &
civilization. It is not right to speak of the 'pollution' of the slave
system—of the 'loathsomeness' of it. I know the Southern people, &
I know that this is wrong."[6]

Bellows had been in New York City (for two funerals) and he
too felt the agitated state of the country. But he was not in accord
with Dewey's thinking. He wanted to be able to get Dewey's whole
point of view since his friend had just returned from a trip to the
South. "While you speak exclusively from the Southern point of
view, & in apology for, or defence of, slavery—(tho this is very
natural for one coming freshly from the intercourse with *good*
Southern people) I do not feel much aided." Bellows believed that
"what our Northern people need . . . is not less horror of
slavery . . . but a greater sympathy with the *difficulties* of the
Southern people; more justice to their prejudices, opinions &
embarrassments—& an abstinence from insulting, coarse &
opprobrious discussion with them." Bellows felt that it was
dangerous for Northerners to look down their noses at the Southern
people. One could make allowances for the plight of the South, and

yet he said, "but this allowance must not go to the extent of compromising our convictions; & so mixing our light with their shade, our civilization with their barbarism."[7]

Ephraim Peabody, now a dying man, had said to Bellows that "the great obstacle to a right understanding between the North & the South, is, that the whole civilization, the moral code, the ideas of life, the total condition of the South are a hundred years behind those of the North." Bellows felt that this was a "deeply discouraging view, & I fear it is the right one." He agreed with what Dewey had said about the good people of the South for he himself had lived for two periods with them. But he felt that it would be equally true of a "feudal society at any age of the world." He believed that "slavery produces virtues of its own," but he compared them to a consumptive family "in which a low state of health & a serious prospect have produced gentleness, thoughtfulness & devotion."[8]

Bellows said to Dewey, "we must sweeten this controversy . . . but we cannot cool the settled determination which says 'this far & no further' to slavery." Bellows had recently had a conversation with Eliza Hamilton Schuyler, and she had finally admitted to him that he had been right all along in his views on the slavery issue. This statement on her part must have made Bellows very happy for her husband had left the church just a half-dozen years before concerning this very issue. Bellows felt that anything done to save the Union must be done by regulatory means, "not by opposing the antislavery sentiment of the country." He concluded, "I must do it as a Northerner, & with the sentiments of a Northerner, not as a Northern man with Southern principles."[9]

Shortly after Bellows returned to New York City that fall, he and Samuel Osgood decided to invite Bronson Alcott to hold a series of his noted "Conversations" in New York City, in the Vestry Room of the new All Souls church. Alcott was a famous, or infamous (depending on one's point of view), philosopher-educationist of the New England Transcendentalist persuasion, and his recently initiated "Conversations" in Boston and elsewhere were attracting large crowds. In preparation for Alcott's arrival, Bellows and Osgood publicized the "Conversations" which began at the end of September or early October 1856. George Templeton Strong was among the curious and, despite his still rather anti-Unitarian views, came to the session held on 9 October.

Strong's visit to All Souls was symbolic of the significant respectability that Unitarianism, as promulgated by Bellows, was

George Templeton Strong, Esq. (around 1857). From the manuscript Diary, Courtesy of the New-York Historical Society, New York City

gaining in the most prominent social and civic circles in the city by this time. Even as recently as the 1840s, Unitarianism had been reserved primarily for a few of the more daring of New York's upper crust; most of the leaders of the community still clustered in

orthodox circles for their professional and leisurely pursuits. But by
the middle 1850s, Bellows was increasingly among the socially
prominent and was invited to gala parties given by New York's
orthodox-Christian high society. Indeed, in May 1857, about eight
months after he attended Alcott's Conversation, Strong himself
included Bellows among the distinguished guests invited to a party at
the Strong home on 21st Street.

It was not the last party that Bellows would attend at the Strong
household, for Strong's visit to All Souls to hear Alcott also
foreshadows an important and historically significant union between
himself and Bellows that was to form six years or so hence. The
relationship between Bellows and Strong remained casual for the
first several years, but Strong was ultimately to play a vital role in
one of Bellows's major enterprises.

As the latter months of 1856 turned into the early months of
1857, the nation's economy was rushing upward at a feverish pitch.
The recession of 1854 was all but forgotten now, as industrial
manufacturing burgeoned into more and more areas of commerce,
and as more and more new factories were established. New railroad
tracks were laid, and once-isolated communities were pulled into the
expanding network of economic inlets and outlets. The wealthier
were getting wealthier, and enterprising young men of impoverished
backgrounds were streaming into the monied classes through
investment and speculation.

Still heavily shackled by mortgages and other debts, the Church
of All Souls could not boast of the same affluence as was being
enjoyed by the nation and the city. In addition to the $35,000
mortgage on the property owed to the Seaman's Bank for Savings,
the society owed thousands to Grinnell, Minturn, & Company for
loans to the building fund, at least $1,000 to Jacob Wrey Mould in
architectural fees, several thousands to the building contractors and
suppliers, and hundreds of dollars in insurance premiums. It also
had to pay the costs of using the Croton water which the city had
pumped into the reservoir at 42nd Street, on the site presently
occupied by the New York Public Library. Now that it had moved to
the Gramercy Park area, it was also assessed dues on the park.

Charles Francis, the Treasurer for the past thirteen years, had
started out the year 1856 with a "balance owed the Treasurer" of
nearly $11,000 in connection with building expenses, and of about
$3,000, also taken from his own pocket, in operating expenses.
Through careful juggling of the income from the sales and taxes on
the pews, plus Bellows's rent for the parsonage and other sundry

revenues, Francis was able to balance the budget for 1856 at a deficit to himself of only $3,122.66. But Francis's publishing company did not render his personal income so high that he could afford to lay out in 1857 all that the society would need for its budget during the coming year, and he said as much to the trustees at their first meeting in 1857, on 19 January.

This trustees meeting was held a week after the society's annual meeting, at which the members had voted that Bellows be allowed to occupy the parsonage *free* of rent. This resolution was a tidy piece of good fortune for Bellows, but it reduced the church's already too-limited income. Thus, at the subsequent trustees meeting, the board authorized Francis to obtain an additional $10,000 mortgage on the church property. Providentially, Francis was able to arrange this loan, the only means by which the society was able to balance its budget in the fateful year of 1857, for, unbeknownst to Francis and the others at the time, disaster was soon to descend.

In the meantime, the start of 1857 had brought with it a curious twist of fate for the First Church. The society had lost virtually all of its founding fathers by 1857. Wheaton, Sewall, Sedgwick, Armitage, Townsend, these and others had, one by one, succumbed to disease or old age or moved away. Benjamin Wheelwright and Nicholas Dean had joined the First Church sometime around 1828 or 1829, and now even Dean had passed away. Indeed, almost the only founding father remaining alive was Isaac Green Pearson; yet Pearson had stubbornly remained with the Second Church, of which he was also a founder, long after his fellow First-Church abdicators had returned to the original society. Now, on 13 January 1857, Isaac Green Pearson at last returned, to chair the annual meeting!

Meanwhile, the hysterically soaring economy was coming to an abrupt halt, after which it plunged immediately into an even more hysterical depression. Beginning in the last two weeks of August, large and important firms failed, leaving millions of dollars in unpaid debts. Stockholders and creditors were left bereft and helpless; panic quickly broke out in Wall Street. Immediately, railroads, banking and insurance houses, brokerages, iron mills, and numerous manufacturing companies all over the nation toppled in rapid succession like a house of cards. As vacationing New Yorkers who had escaped the emotional and thermal heat of the summer months flowed back to their city homes, they scarcely dropped off their bags before they ran to their banks to withdraw their accounts. Most of the banks could not pay, and cash, or real money, which was then gold and silver, became increasingly scarce.

At first, the banks which shut their doors to the milling throngs outside were seized by court order as in defiance of the law, but as the situation worsened, the State Supreme Court finally decided to withhold injunctions against banks which refused to issue specie, thus saving the banks, but rendering purchasing power virtually unattainable. On 14 October, Strong wrote: "we have *burst.* All the banks declined paying specie this morning, with the ridiculous exception of the Chemical which is a little private shaving-shop of the Joneses with no depositors but its own stockholders."[10]

Charles Francis and his publishing firm may have been hurt by the sudden economic crash, for he resigned as treasurer of the society on 3 November 1857. It was the custom of the trustees to appoint a wealthy man as treasurer of the society each year, for often the church's finances were so tenuous and hazy that the treasurer would have to lay out the money in advance; inevitably, the annual financial statement would carry a "balance owed the treasurer." Since Francis stayed on as secretary, a post he had already filled for twenty-seven years, personal financial disaster seems the likely reason for Francis's resignation as treasurer after years of faithful, uninterrupted service in that office. The board appointed William Prichard as Francis's replacement.[11]

The depression also seems to have hit none other than the affluent and generous Moses Grinnell, for having given nearly $25,000 to the building fund, and having taken five pews in the new church as partial repayment, Grinnell was severely in arrears on his pew assessments during all of 1858 and 1859!

On 5 April 1857,[12] Bellows preached a sermon in All Souls in which he discussed the social aspects of the time. In this discussion he admired the improvement in the legitimate theater (of which Bellows was fond) in the disappearance of some highly objectionable usages—their flavor of immorality and of contempt for religion. This particular part of Bellows's sermon was eagerly reported in the newspapers on Monday morning.

In the course of the week Bellows received a visit from a group of distinguished actors who wanted to present to Dr. Bellows a testimonial in the form of a tea service of silver plate, to express their appreciation for "the service [he] had rendered a maligned profession." Bellows was much touched, but felt that in all propriety he could not receive so lavish a gift; instead, he offered to give a public lecture expounding more fully upon the subject. As the actors and Bellows conversed, much enthusiasm for the idea developed. The actors could charge admission and donate the proceeds to the benefit fund for retired actors. It would, of course, be quite improper to use All Souls for this lecture, and the actors agreed to arrange for a theater auditorium; they also agreed to muster out a large body of their profession, and to allow Bellows to speak his entire mind on the subject, including the admonitions as well as the accolades. The actors departed warmly animated over the prospect, and immediately secured the Academy of Music on 14th Street for Tuesday evening 25 April.

This address was one of his longer endeavors, being some fifty-three pages in print which must have meant an address of between two and three hours in length.[13] It was called "The Relations of Public Amusements to Public Morality, Especially of the Theater To the Highest Interests of Humanity." It was one of Bellows's more labored attempts in the realm of lecturing. There were sections of the address which must have elicited cheers and a most favorable response from his audience of actors and their friends. But the address even in this day is boring to read, and except for certain sections is a labored and contrived attempt to justify the legitimacy of the theater from the point of view of morality.

Bellows delivered his lecture bravely and with no outward signs of shrinking, and then went home to anticipate the reactions. The newspapers printed all or part of the lecture, and soon afterward it appeared in pamphlet form both in New York and beyond, and was read even in Europe. The religious press continued to rage indignantly at Bellows, despite the lecture's moralistic and rational tone, and for some time afterward, Bellows was the object of much criticism and caricature.

But the speech won him affection and esteem from the entertainment world everywhere, and Bellows later found passages from his address recorded permanently in some German theaters. Bellows later wrote that the lecture "disabused many consciences of morbid and false self-accusation; it encouraged reform; it widened and illuminated the view of public recreations, and helped to put relaxation, spectacle and dramatic tastes, upon a new footing." He had not suffered, for "in spite of the abuse of the religious press, it did me no permanent harm, even in my clerical standing among ministers of other faiths, but drew forth sooner or later strong expressions of gratitude and of respect from the most unexpected quarters."[14]

Cyrus Bartol read a summary of the address in the Boston papers. He wrote, "I think it, in complex unity, ingenious . . . the ablest performance of yours that has come to my knowledge. . . .

You have said an admirable, useful word, which will quiver & flash long on the brain."[15]

My Track Made of Iron

Rush R. Shippen had resigned the pulpit of the Chicago Unitarian Church. Since Bellows had just been to Chicago and was in the good graces of the people there, they turned to him to find a new minister. Bellows had a letter from them "which throws the matter, too much for my peace, on to *my* shoulders." By default Bellows was acting like a settlement officer, there being no such service in the Unitarian structure then. Bellows wanted more than one church in Chicago, and he wrote to Orville Dewey to see if Dewey could be induced *"to go there for the next winter, & perhaps to undertake a five year's ministry."* Bellows was quite frank with Orville Dewey who liked to preach and detested the rest of the work of a minister. He proposed that a man of action, unlike Dewey, go at the same time, and the two of them exchange pulpits often and start a second church. Fearing that this proposition might insult Dewey, Bellows wrote, "No preaching ability, no weight of character, would take the place of executive ability, & organizing skill at Chicago, at this time. We need *generalship.* You despise it by nature & grace, are impatient of details & shrink from *assumption."* He felt that this would disqualify Dewey if he were to be the only man in Chicago. But if there were two men of completely different abilities, it might work out well. He had already written to two men of action, "William R. Alger of Boston and Charles H. Brigham at Taunton to sound them out." Bellows added to Dewey that he had "no time for circumlocution."[1]

In reply to this offer Bellows got the usual Dewey reply, that unless he could be guaranteed a position with a salary for some years he could not give up his lecture tours. He was willing to go to Chicago in the coming fall for some months provided it did not interfere with his lectures, "but to preach twice a day the year round, is, even setting aside the pastorate, a duty which I am utterly unable to master. I could not write the *sermons:* for I should *preach* in one year, about all the sermons I have." He felt that it was easy to say that two or three churches could be built in Chicago, "but it must take two or three years to bring all that about."[2]

Meanwhile Bellows had traveled to Antioch where the board of trustees had met with the new president, Horace Mann, to try to get the college on a sound footing. He wrote to Eliza, "Suffice it, that

we have made a clean sweep of the old *Adam* & begin with the *new*."
He hoped that any efforts that he might make would be helpful to
this institution. The Christian denomination (Disciples of Christ)
had started the college, but now they were no longer in control.
Horace Mann was trying to make the college not just another
denominational college but a nonsectarian one. But there still was a
rift in the board of trustees between the old Christians and the new
trustees who wanted nonsectarianism.[3]

Almost two months later Horace Mann wrote a report to
Bellows on the state of the college. The fall term had opened and
they had a larger entering class than previously, about 100; there
now were over 250 students. But Mann rightfully was worried about
the financial state of the college, a state that was to plague him until
his death. He had a plan to buy the college from the Christian
denomination, and then to seek an endowment. He felt that the
carrying out of this plan "demands the brains of all the Doctors."[4]

Bellows was in typical full swing during this fall season. He
attended the Unitarian convention in Syracuse on 13, 14, and 15
October after a special plea from Samuel May, the minister in
Syracuse, that he attend. Returning home he put the finishing touch
on the Lowell Lectures which he was to give in Boston the last week

Antioch College, Original Buildings, 1856, Courtesy of the
Massachusetts Historical Society

in October and most of November. It was a series of twelve lectures on *The Treatment of Social Diseases*, and included such considerations as crime and pauperism. It must have been a difficult chore. Not only was he away from home while Dr. Gannett preached at All Souls, but he added to the burden by giving the first lecture on the afternoon of 27 October, and the second lecture that same evening. He repeated this arduous program on 30 October with two more lectures. This schedule evidently proved too much for Bellows, and perhaps for the audience. So the rest of the lectures were spread out over the month of November on Tuesday and Friday evenings. Meanwhile he made trips back to New York, lectured at Salem, and made a side trip to Walpole for Thanksgiving.

He wrote Eliza, "My lectures are succeeding beyond my *best* expectations. They are not only crowded, but people go away in numbers. . . . I suppose a considerable portion of the clergy of the whole city are there—& the most respectable citizens give weight & dignity to the occasion."[5] He received $1,000 for the series.

No doubt Bellows had been thinking about his subject for some time, and discussing it with others as it came up at various gatherings. The time was ripe; there was nothing particularly controversial about either the subject itself or Bellows's specific ideas on the subject; certainly the flagrant immorality which had been upon the scene long before it culminated in the violence, lack of law and order, and financial disasters of the summer, was upon everyone's tongue. In his lecture series, Bellows appealed for rational and cool-headed reforms, reforms which any sane person could see were a matter of practical common sense. The combination of the times and the context from which Bellows spoke, plus Bellows's own candid and noninflammatory delivery style, served to make Bellows's Lowell Lectures much heralded, and Bellows was applauded as a wise and significant man of his times.

This incessant activity and these protracted periods away from home did not help the family situation in the Bellows household. Eliza Bellows continued to be ailing. Henry thought that her letters while he was in Boston and during his short stay in New York during the month between lectures showed that she had in her mind "a more than usual concern" about her future. He also felt that she was despairing of ever being able to do anything about her physical and mental health. He remarked to her in a letter after returning to Boston, "I said nothing, but it oppressed me." Yet, he wrote that he found "that he must not humor [his] moods. For instance, I often *feel* that I cannot go thro' a religious service, or a lecture—but I *know* that I can, & I act on my *knowledge* & not my *feelings."* He added, "I find that my moods are not at all reliable; that my nerves play me all sorts of tricks, & that if I had time to humor them, I should become their slave." But he had a solution: "I rejoice that I have no time to do it; that my duties are made for me—my time occupied by inevitable engagements & my *track* made of *iron* & not of *India-rubber."* Bellows was plainly telling Eliza that her problem was that she had too much time on her hands and that she was dominated too much by her moods.

He even offered to try to change his way of life, something that he often suggested, and then plunged right back into the thick of a busy life because he thought his work was important. But the whole psychological scene at home did not have happy forebodings.[6]

By February 1858, New York was making very slow headway in climbing out of the financial deeps. Many of the church's pew holders were severely in arrears, just when the church needed the money the most. In the city at large, the massive and burgeoning poor classes had billowed to enormous proportions virtually overnight, as laborers who had once had some form of employment now had no means of subsistence. Angry mobs milled wantonly in the streets with nothing on their minds other than their hopeless plight. Crime mounted. Mayor Wood, with his bigoted and self-seeking outlook, did not help matters, and often incited the rabble's hopes and expectations futilely in order to promote his own political maneuvers. On Monday evening, 15 February, Bellows gave a lecture in New York from his Boston Lowell Lectures on social issues, this one aptly entitled "Pauperism and Crime." George Templeton Strong attended. and reported in his diary that night:

> With Ellie [Mrs. Strong] tonight to hear one of the Rev. Dr. Bellows's lectures on "Pauperism and Crime." He blew well; his lecture was pleasant and instructive. But it is very curious to observe the un-practicality of all sermons, essays, and lectures by men of Bellows's school, Yankee-Arianism, when they undertake any practical subject. Channing, their great father, exhibits the peculiarity most distinctly. They are sensible, plausible, candid, subtle, and original in discussing any social evil or abuse. But somehow they don't get *at* it. You feel that you have heard or read a very clever and entertaining paper, embodying a good deal of clear and deep thought, and you ask *what shall I do?* and pause for a reply, and pause in vain. If you get a reply that seems definite, it is generally resolvable by analysis into some formula like "Lift yourself up by the waistband of your own breeches." "Move your limbs only once and your dead

palsy will be cured." Convince your "dangerous classes" that honesty is the best policy, and they will become useful citizens. But Bellows is far sounder and wiser than the great majority of his school. Its defects are mitigated in him by his native masculine common sense which is strong enough to neutralize a good deal of his Unitarianism.[7]

Clearly, though Strong's earlier antagonism was softening, Strong was still skeptical toward Unitarianism, but he could not help feeling a distant respect for Bellows.

Although the depression had called a dead halt to nearly all of the many building projects that had been going on in the city, it had not in any way affected the building of Cooper Union. Peter Cooper, a member of All Souls at least since 1855, had dreamed of building a free educational institution in New York for nearly thirty years. Dewey reported in his autobiography that Cooper had often discussed with him that dream, and after Dewey had taken himself off to Sheffield, it fell upon Bellows's eager ears to hear Cooper's lofty dream.

A strange combination of practicality and idealism existed in Cooper; his main emphasis in life was not to make money, but to serve mankind. Thus, he became active in civic affairs early in this successful period of his life, as an assistant alderman of New York. In this capacity, Cooper was largely responsible for the improvement of the city's water supply through the Croton project, which dammed up the Croton River in Westchester and built an aqueduct from the lake thus created all the way to the city reservoir which was built on what is now the New York Public Library on Fifth Avenue and 42nd Street.

In the meantime, Cooper was secretly preparing to realize his dream. As the money rolled in from his glue factory, his stock in the Canton Iron Works, and his Trenton wire-manufacturing enterprise, Cooper bought up real estate in the city, carefully speculating on low points in the market, and selling sometimes at market peaks. In this way, he accumulated both land and money for his educational venture. By 1852, Cooper had assembled enough parcels of land at Astor Place between Third and Fourth Avenues, and he announced his plans. The cornerstone for the building was laid the following year, and construction continued through the recession of 1854 and the depression of 1857. Throughout a good portion of this period, Cooper discussed the project with Bellows, using his pastor as a kind of sounding board for specific details. The project was completed by May 1858 and might have opened its doors to students the following autumn had the state legislature authorized the school, named

Peter Cooper, Photo by Saxony, Courtesy of the New-York
Historical Society, New York City

Cooper Union for the Advancement of Science and Art, to grant
degrees and certificates. This authorization did not come through
until 1859.

Significantly, the records of the church come to a virtual
standstill during the fateful year of 1857. Except for the annual
meeting on 13 January 1857, the subsequent trustees meeting on 19
January, at which Francis was authorized to obtain an additional

mortgage of $10,000; and the 3 November trustees meeting when Francis resigned as treasurer, no transactions are recorded in the Minute Book. The year 1858 was almost as uneventful, from the standpoint of the church's recorded activities. The trustees met on 9 January 1858 to prepare for the annual meeting, and authorized their new treasurer, William Prichard, "to take such proceedings against the pew holders who are in arrears as shall be proper to enforce the payment of their dues"[8]—for whatever good it would do in the wake of the depression.

The annual meeting itself was held on 12 January 1858, with Isaac Green Pearson presiding for the second year. Except for the annual approval of the financial accounts (which had balanced only because of the $10,000 loan), the sole business was the formulation of profuse thanks to Charles Francis for his years of service as treasurer. Only two meetings of the trustees were held after the annual meeting; one on 14 January to organize the board—with Grinnell and Francis being reelected as president and secretary, respectively—and another on 24 February, because Henry Bellows had a special request to bring before the trustees.

The depression had brought hard times upon Bellows's publishing venture of twelve years, the *Christian Inquirer*. Bellows asked the trustees that he be allowed to hold a special collection at services once each year in order to raise $400 for his religious journal. As usual, the board granted Bellows's request. But if the collection was ever taken, it does not show up among the other charity collections recorded in the financial statements for 1858. In any case, the agreement was to be regretted later.

CHAPTER SIX

The Suspense of Faith

The Weakest Part of My System

The thirty-third anniversary of the American Unitarian Association was celebrated on Tuesday 25 May 1858 in the Bedford Street Church in Boston. The program proceeded through a long day of speeches mixed with business. Henry Bellows had been chosen to make the last address of the day. His remarks in very fine print cover some eight pages. He had evidently written the speech and was determined to see it through to the end. He opened his remarks by saying "Brevity is not my forte, but I must endeavor to bring my constitutional obesity of speech within reasonable girth."[1] He congratulated the assembly on not being a sect but a denomination. "Providence has forced us into an advanced position—a position which, by theological affirmations and denials, separates us from Christendom, though it does not separate Christendom from us."[2] He felt that in spite of the fences maintained by the other denominations Unitarians were tilling fields which other Christians would presently occupy.

Then in anticipation of his address "The Suspense of Faith" to be given a year later, he stated his thesis that Unitarianism had weakened itself by dividing into schools of thought which he characterized as "The Progressive," "The Hold-Fasts," and "The Reactionaries."[3] "The Progressives," he felt, had been content to throw the denomination "utterly upon the current of the times, and trust it to the generous impulses and struggling instincts of humanity." "The Hold-Fasts," the followers of Priestley, Freeman, Ware, and Channing, "have in their way hindered our influence by localizing and confining it."[4] They do not propagandize enough, Bellows felt. "The Reactionaries have been thinking that, in the haste of our flight out of orthodoxy, we have perhaps left some of the most precious things behind us."[5] He felt that each of these groups for its own reasons had acted against denominational prosperity; these three elements "must be harmonized and united,"[6] for the instincts of all three points of view were necessary. In America, he said, the "Broad Church," by which he meant broad-scale Congregationalists, "were making a fairer and more attractive bid for the people's heart than we are. . . . After we have fought the battle, they seem likely to run away with the victory."[7]

He closed his address with a favorite theme, "No hope is more futile than the expectation of building the mere humanitarian and philanthropic instincts and passions of the age into a church, or a substitute for a church." He maintained that "the honest zeal to realize political equality, the honest indignation at the arrogance and authority of privilege, the general desire to comfort, heal, elevate, which are distinctive of our age, although commonly assessed to be based on religious convictions, and to be derived from religious aspirations, are really ideas not in or from the region of divine faith, but in and on the plane of use, of morality, of economy." He separated religion and reform: "political and social philanthropy, and Christian brotherly love, are not even similar ideas; for the most earnest, zealous, and hearty political and social reformers are often painfully deficient in, and ignorant of, the whole spirit and conduct of the second commandment."[8] Bellows pled with his brethren to seize their opportunities while they still existed.

The president asked for questions and there were none, so the meeting went on to hear a report of the nominating committee. Henry Bellows must have wondered if his words had fallen on deaf ears again in Boston as they had in regard to Antioch just four years previously.

In July 1858 an issue arose that bothered Bellows several other times in his life. He had heard through the grapevine that he was being seriously considered for the presidency of Harvard. James Walker, who had been president of Harvard since 1853, wanted to resign. He was persuaded by a unanimous faculty vote to remain, which he did until 1860 when he resigned on the plea of advancing years. But it was this proposed resignation in 1858, and the rumors that Bellows was being considered for the post, one of the most honorific in the nation, that agitated Bellows's thoughts.

He wrote a confidential letter to Cyrus Bartol from Walpole asking him if he knew anything "about this newspaper rumor of my being a candidate for the presidency of Harvard?" Bellows had treated this rumor at first as "a joke," but then he had received so many communications in regard to the matter that he decided that he had better take it seriously. He had supposed "that my age, my independence, my antecedents, would all combine to disqualify me in the judgment of such conservatives as have this appointment in hand." He was debating within himself the pros and cons of such a change of position. Often when a man is considering such a change in his life we find him expressing his truest ideas of himself and what he ought to be doing in life. He wrote Bartol none too humbly, "I humbly think that I could conduct that college with a success which it has never known—bringing the freshness of a ripe but not decaying manhood to it, a sympathy with young men; a knowledge of the world & of society, sufficient electric power: & a natural skill in leading & governing men—the gifts of a preacher, the readiness of an extempore speaker, a power of accommodativeness which would harmonize the professors, & a union of progressive & conservative tastes & sympathies."[9] This was actually a catalog of his good qualities without listing his weaknesses, of which there were few so far as being president of Harvard was concerned. Bellows asked Bartol to feel out several of his friends on the Harvard Corporation to see if there was any seriousness in the rumors. He obviously was excited about the possibilities.

Bartol wrote back from Boston the next day (mail service was better in those days) that he did not think that Bellows overestimated his capacities. "If therefore the door of influence is open, count on me as being your advocate no less than friend." He would see what he could find out about what was in the air.[10] Neither man knew, of course, that the faculty would vote unanimously to ask President Walker to remain.

Mrs. George Schuyler felt sad when she heard the rumors because she felt it was "merely a prophecy of change." From all she could hear, "Dr. Walker does not think of retiring for a year at least." Mrs. Schuyler had spoken with the oldest member of the Harvard overseers, and she wrote that if they knew Bellows would take the position probably thirty out of the forty-two were ready to vote for him immediately. She had written to her Harvard informer that she believed Dr. Bellows would accept. For the last twenty years Bellows had been trained for this post, she believed. She told Bellows not to form wishes. "We are led by the unseen Spirit to that which is best, when we throw down the reins," she preached to her minister. She felt that if he remained in New York he should take some time off during the coming winter because she was worried about his health. In fact, his health was the only thing that worried her about his taking the Harvard presidency.[11]

Toward the end of July, Henry Bellows took his young son Russell, now grown into manhood, to Cambridge to take his entrance examinations, hoping that in the fall he would be enrolled in Harvard College. They stayed with the Bartols, as usual, and spent a whole day in Cambridge where there were large crowds of boys waiting for the examinations. They attended the graduation exercises of the Divinity School and listened to an address by their host Cyrus A. Bartol. Then there was a three-hour discussion on theology which Bellows, and his son attended, and which Bellows found very interesting. They got back to Boston early in the evening. Henry Bellows was still unsure about whether he was being considered for the presidency of the college. "I have not yet said a word, or heard a word about the *subject*. Dr. Walker looks feeble—& that he will resign, is, I think pretty certain. Further than that I know nothing & of course say nothing."[12]

The next day Henry and Russell went to the Commencement exercises which Russell termed "imposing." Russell stayed for the entire exercises, but Henry Bellows sneaked away to have some private moments with Professors Child, Lowell, and Hedge. He then returned to the Commencement exercises which he termed "neither better nor worse than usual." In the course of the afternoon President Walker said to Bellows, "So, I hear you are to be my successor." Bellows was surprised that he had brought up the subject and responded, "After that, I shall hardly dane [sic] to inquire after your health for fear of being thought interested in its decline."

They went to the Commencement dinner, where Bellows introduced Russell to the members of his own class of 1832, "who welcomed him with lively interest." There were no speeches at the dinner. Those took place the next day at the Phi Beta Kappa dinner. They also attended Dr. Walker's reception.[13]

Bellows's health failed considerably in the fall of 1858, so much so that in October he consulted not one but two doctors, "*Dr. Cheeseman* & still more particularly *Dr. Parker*." Their conclusions were identical to what he might have guessed. "These gentlemen report me as having perfectly *sound* organs *in a highly exhausted condition*—due to the immense drain on my nervous energies, & declare it is suicide to continue." The doctors "propose *that I should live in the country*—& abandon for the future, all duties, but preaching. How to accomplish this is the problem." Bellows was determined to take some action, and felt that he should "bring the whole question before the congregation." Writing to Eliza he said he felt "that the turning point in *both* our lives has arrived & that your health as well as mine is involved in the course now to be adopted." He told his wife not to worry as he felt somewhat better, and that he would not do anything rash.[14]

Bellows decided with the advice of his physicians to take a horseback trip to Walpole. Henry's brother Hamilton accompanied him. Hamilton and Henry arrived at Walpole on schedule on Sunday. It was a trip of 278 miles, not bad for a man who was worried about his health.[15] During the ten days of riding with Hamilton, Henry had obviously put in a lot of thought about his future especially as it related to his health and his work. Shortly after he arrived at Walpole he wrote his wife a thoughtful ten-page letter on this subject. It was a letter written "with some care, a letter about our future." He wanted to "settle upon the policy which shall govern the residue of our lives." He was willing that Eliza's "wishes to have a fair and equitable influence in the shaping of this policy."

He worried first about his own physical nature. He ascribed his "fearful fastness" as "unquestionably the result of a *constitutional excitability of brain*, a natural fineness of cerebral organization, animated by quick spirits & strong blood, which is alike the source of my success & usefulness, & the formation of all my danger." He felt that his present physical condition was due entirely to "over-exertion of the brain." He had found his muscular system "capable of such exhausting endurance" on the horseback trip. Thus he felt that his brain was "the *weakest* part of my system."

"Providentially," he believed Eliza's difficulties "are much of the same sort." And he added "what is best for me is happily best for you. We both need retirement, freedom from over-excitement, calmness & peace." Yet he felt that with a temperament such as his he "could not safely be *too* much withdrawn from life, *too* secluded, *too* much thrown on itself, a violent & complete change in life would probably do me as much harm as none at all." His problem was to keep a balance between the outer and the inner. "I have thought, & still think, that the presidency at Cambridge would be a grand providential interposition." He did not covet the office. Yet he felt that he would "grow calm, moderate & wise under its discipline." He knew that the office probably was not to be offered. The next best course to the presidency of Harvard, he outlined to Eliza, would be "to devote what remains of my life to the same essential objects which have occupied it thus far, the moral & religious improvement of society."

He did not think that he would be justified in withholding his gifts "from the immense wants & crying ignorance of the generation . . . I *ought to preach* as long as I can." Bellows believed that preaching should be his first consideration. "To maintain health en, & calmness eno & domestic peace & contentment eno, to do this with the greatest advantage & for the longest time, ought to be my governing policy." He felt New York was "the best sphere in influence" and except for Cambridge no post could be so good. But the "life of New York" with its excitements and demands was what was turning his life upside down, "intoxicating & perplexing my brain." And he added significantly, "I feel that I cannot *live* there without some extraordinary & (to me at present) inconceivable changes of habits. My sympathies, my weaknesses do not permit it." He concluded "I must then, withdraw from the city—live in the country, & take only such a part in the charge of the society, as is compatible with a home elsewhere say at thirty or fifty miles remove." He did not feel that this would seriously injure the parish, for the outside cares of the city had "already eaten up my parochial life, & made me a poor minister out of the pulpit." He then proposed that he would resign half of his salary to an assistant. (His salary was now $4,500.)

He proposed selling the homestead at Walpole to put the money into their chosen home elsewhere. He loved the Walpole home better than any place in the world, but he was willing to consider this proposition if need be. He suggested that to look for a permanent home they might try the Hudson River Shore, the Sound, Long Island, or New Jersey. He wondered if this arrangement would not also suit Eliza's needs. The last pages of the letter are a tender expression of his love and concern for his wife and children. It was an immense effort on Bellows's part to even think of abandoning New York. But obviously his own and his wife's health were at stake.[16]

Writing to an unidentified friend a few days after his return to the city Bellows mentioned that next January he would complete twenty years of labor in New York. "I have pretty much resolved, to ask my parish to settle a colleague with me, at my expense, retaining me only as a half-day *preacher*, & allowing me to live out of New York. I suspect this is my only prudent course."[17]

It is very interesting that it should be at the end of 1858 that Henry Bellows should be going through this soul-searching and concluding that if he was to exist at all he would have to let up on the activity of his life and control his irresistible urge to do things against which his body rebelled. The next nine years of Henry Bellows's life were to be, in fact, the most active and strenuous of his career, years when he showed amazing physical power until his breakdown in 1867 when again he recuperated and was able to continue with active work in spite of physical infirmities.

Bellows observably did not slow up his pace of life. At the end of January he was in Boston to preach and to try to raise some money for Antioch College. In the vein of what he had written to Eliza in November he was still trying to justify his activity. "Stay with your dependent husband as long as you can—for he would do very badly without you. I dare say you think he is willing to kill you, with the various work he throws upon your shoulders, such as entertaining his kindred & friends." Henry reminded Eliza that he was an outgoing man: "Remember the exigencies of his position —the number of friends & of attentions he has, & his own nature, quite as imperious & tyrannical in its way, as his wife's. So don't argue, too logically, from his doings to his feelings—or from his cruelty in conduct, to his malice of heart!"[18] Bellows had evidently decided to go ahead in what he was doing even if Eliza felt his motives were selfish.

In May Henry was planning to attend the annual meetings of the American Unitarian Association in Boston, and he wrote to Bartol that he would come alone. "My prospects at home are not bright. Eliza is a broken reed, I fear. Instead of leaning on it, an atom, I must bind it with my heart strings—which are somewhat thin. But I trust every thing to the good & gracious Providence."[19]

The third week in June Henry wrote to Eliza (who had taken the family to Walpole for the summer) that he unexpectedly had to make a trip to Ohio with Charles Butler. It was a necessary trip and he begged her to understand, but above all to make the trip palatable by accompanying him. He felt that change of air, of scenes, and of people would do her more good than any other thing. He wrote that she should think of going *"by building up your confidence in your ability to do what other people do."* He felt that this *"would strengthen* [her] *nervous system & help* [her] *to a better summer."* He proposed that they stop at Trenton for a day and at Niagara Falls.[20] He was persuasive, for Eliza decided to go with him, perhaps to recapture some nostalgia for her marriage by visiting the spots of their honeymoon twenty years before.

A New Catholic Church

Unitarianism had come a long way in its approximately forty-five years of formal existence. When William Ellery Channing had delivered his epoch-making address in 1819, the word *Unitarianism* had been in common use in America for no more than four or five years, Channing himself having launched the official use of the label by publicly endorsing it in 1815. In Channing's day, Unitarianism, as radical and heretical as it had seemed at the time, had merely placed

God as supreme, although it emphasized monotheism by stressing that there was only a unity, and not a trinity, in the nature of God. It held to the tradition that Jesus was the uniquely divine Christ, and retained the worshipful reverence toward Jesus as divine figurehead. It was thus relatively little different from the Christianity of the Reformation centuries.

The advent of Transcendentalism in the 1830s, however, coupled with the mushrooming social problems that the nation had been witnessing along with its rapid industrial and economic progress, had given rise to various controversies within the Unitarian denomination, and various positions ranging from orthodoxy on the right to secularism on the left were now under the umbrella of Unitarianism. Channing's own nephew, William Henry Channing, became a Christian Socialist; Theodore Parker, who also grew out of this confused spirit of reform, emphasized that the miracles of the New Testament were no assurance of the divinity of Christ.

Ralph Waldo Emerson had helped to vocalize the ambiguously diverse range of theological positions maintained by those who called themselves Unitarian in the latter 1830s by delivering his Divinity School Address in 1838, and he simultaneously paved the way for even wider deviations from "orthodox" Unitarianism. Emerson had deposed Jesus as the theological figurehead of Unitarian and orthodox Christianity, insisting that Unitarians should bypass Jesus and the traditions surrounding him, and seek religious enlightenment directly from God through contemporary existence.

Unitarians both to the left and to the right of Emerson had totally missed his point: to the right, Henry Ware, Andrews Norton, and other of the Unitarian pioneers wished to cling to Jesus' divinity, while to the left, Theodore Parker, O. B. Frothingham, and others saw Emerson's position as a license for emphasizing secular ethics and for de-emphasizing God and worship. William Ellery Channing, and perhaps Charles Follen, were among the few Unitarian ministers who understood what Emerson was really trying to say. But as new crops of Unitarian ministers had emerged from Harvard Divinity School after 1835, the left had more and more replaced the old right wing, and now at the end of the decade of the 1850s, the main thrust of Unitarianism apparently was heading rapidly toward secularism.

It was at this point in the development of Unitarianism that Henry Bellows was asked by the alumni of the Harvard Divinity School to deliver their annual address. It was just twenty-one years since Ralph Waldo Emerson at the request of the senior class had delivered his famous address, and Bellows was to state concepts of Unitarianism almost 180 degrees different from those espoused by Emerson.

Bellows was excited about this address, which he had been asked to deliver on 19 July at the Divinity School in Cambridge. "I have written within the last fortnight my address for the alumni of the Theological School," he wrote to Cyrus Bartol. "It has interested me seriously. How much I should like your views upon many points. I won't tell you my subject till we meet." He told Bartol that when he got "back from Ohio I shall review my mss (which is frightfully long) & try to ballast, trim & paint up the ship—which is I suppose rough & freighted & dirty, after its tempestuous voyage on a new sea."[1]

Henry Bellows titled his address "The Suspense of Faith."[2] It is without doubt one of the half dozen most significant statements of nineteenth-century Unitarianism. He began his address with an apology. He was going to be critical, but he hoped that no one would imagine him "to be ungrateful to the services, insensible to the merits, or cold to the fellowship of the Unitarian body." He wanted to examine the defects of contemporary Unitarianism. He sounded the keynote (which was misunderstood): "If I show the wants of our own system, it is not as advocating a return to the systems we have abandoned; if I question the finality of Protestantism, it is not in the interest of Romanism; if I speak in the language of a Churchman, it is not as an Episcopalian, much less as one aiming at the re-establishment of a hierarchy."

Bellows then turned to a consideration of "the present condition of our Unitarian body." He conceded that numerically there was "a fair degree of prosperity." Unitarians were numerous and their ideas were popular. Yet he found "an undeniable chill in the missionary zeal, an undeniable apathy in the denominational life of the body." He found "despondency, self-questioning, and anxiety." Bellows then stated the theme of his address as given in its title: there was "a common suspense of faith." He acknowledged that the spirit of Unitarianism had spread among the other churches; "many ministers and churches, of all names and orders, are now doing our work." Sometimes he felt that they were doing it "more thoroughly than we could do it ourselves." He did not believe that the world was becoming Unitarian, in the sectarian sense of the word, nor did he feel that there would be "an inevitable abandonment of those formulas of the church against which we have openly protested." But he did believe "that the principles and sentiments, the rights of conscience, the rationality of method, the freedom of inquiry, the practical views of religion, which we have been contending for under the name and colors of our Unitarian theology, are under other names and colors so rapidly conquering the mind of our American Christendom, that it is not longer felt to be necessary to maintain a stringent denominational organization for their sake." Bellows believed that the Unitarian movement had "providentially led and historically signalized, a forward movement of the whole Protestant body." He felt that Trinitarian theology was helpful "in the times in which it arose," but that today it no longer sufficed, for it contradicted the "common sense and self-evident principles" about God's nature.

Then he returned again to "the self-distrust of our body." This self-distrust came about because of the tendencies within Protestantism itself. 'The sufficiency of the Scriptures turns out to be the self-sufficiency of man, and the right of private judgment an absolute independence of Bible or church." Bellows continued, 'No creed but the Scriptures practically abolishes all Scriptures but those on the human heart; nothing between a man's conscience and his God, vacates the church; and with the church, the Holy Ghost, whose function is usurped by private reason: the church lapses into what are called Religious Institutions; these into Congregationalism, and Congregationalism into individualism—and the logical end is the abandonment of the church as an independent institution." Protestantism had not yet reached this stage, but Bellows believed that these were the self-destroying tendencies within it.

Bellows believed that "the tendencies of political and religious sentiment, in the Universal Church of our day, are to the weakening of the external institutions of Christianity, the extinction of the ministry, and the abandonment of any special interest in religion, as a *separate* interest of man or society." It was not just the Unitarian movement that suffered from this "latitudinarianism." 'The same qualities belong to all Protestant sects," he maintained. He pointed out that three-quarters of the American population "goes to church nowhere," there was a growing hostility to established churches in all countries, and there was a "disjunction between science and faith, literature and theology." He believed that there had been a "transference of faith of the people from the church to the school-house" and it was popular to attack the clergy. Bellows worried about "the growing use of the Sabbath for recreation." He cited the growing frequency of suicide, "the increasing laxity of the marriage bond," all of these "marked indications of the decay of religious ideas." Bellows added some other indications of the secularization of American culture, such as "the peculiar interest attached to preaching in contradistinction to worship," the use of "gifted speech" in the churches, "the hostility of the philanthropy of the day to the churches, the growing number of politicians to whom the higher law in its refined form is unknown," and for whom "religious considerations of any kind seem not to sway at all."

Bellows hoped that these trends would encounter resistance. "They [must] meet and yield to other tendencies." He termed his time "an unreligious age," not an irreligious age. It was an unreligious age—"despite its philanthropy and its throes of sectarian piety, its rights of man, and its self-complacency toward God."

He felt that "it was becoming more and more unreligious." He maintained that "religious institutions and ideas in our day flourish mainly in the strength of their roots in a religious past, a strength which is constantly diminishing." He believed that the churches of the day were "lecture-foundations" in which the interest was less and less religious, and more and more political, social, and ethical. He felt that "to make a religion out of self-respect, right-living, self-culture—to insist that aspiration is worship, that truth is God, that goodness is religion—is the highest ambition of our modern pulpit." He continued, "God is too sacred a word to be lost out of the language, worship too holy a thing not to be held on to on some pretence or other; piety too profound and indestructible an instinct to be abandoned." Therefore the political and social idealism of his age used religious phraseology and forms. He believed that "the science, philosophy, and literature of the day were busily engaged in creating substitutes for religion." Bellows pointed out that the role of the church in relation to science had been completely reversed in the past several centuries. At one time "science and literature were humble suppliants of the church-gate, asking her permission to set up their conclusions within her palings." But, he pointed out, "now religion is thankful if geology, scornfully passing by, does not throw her hammer at her head, and literature lampoon her in her own pulpit."

Bellows then told his audience that "he now wished to set forth the more fundamental or psychological reason of this pause" (the suspense of faith). In this section Bellows pointed out that "there are two motions of the spirit in relation to God . . . a centrifugal and a centripetal motion." The first "sends man away from God to learn his freedom" and the second "draws him back to God, to receive the inspiration, nurture, and endowment, which he has become strong enough to hold." Bellows maintained that "man is not made acquainted with God by nature." This was the exact opposite of what Ralph Waldo Emerson had said twenty-one years before. "God does not come into his earliest stages with distinctness, because spiritual creation must precede spiritual salvation."

Man's creation is not complete at his birth. Man needs a history as a time in which to grow to his fuller potentiality. Bellows believed that these two forces can be seen at work in the church, "Romanism representing the centripetal force of Christianity, Protestantism the centrifugal." Romanism stood for external or Divine authority, Protestantism "for internal liberty and individual freedom." Bellows made some further contrasts. Romanism represented "God's condescension to man, Protestantism man's aspiration towards perfection. . . . Romanism leading to worship, Protestantism to work." He believed that "Romanism merely as religion" had fulfilled its function more perfectly than Protestantism. Protestantism's main services had not been to religion but "directly to humanity." Bellows then asked his hearers whether Protestants "are at the apogee of our orbit." He believed that Protestants had come during this cycle "nearly to the end of our self-directing, self-asserting, self-developing, self-culturing faculties." These ideas were so well established in American culture that the church no longer had to work at this task. Bellows felt that Protestantism had gone far enough in this direction. This centrifugal motion had now led to a suspense of faith, and what was needed was to emphasize the centripetal aspect of Christianity or worship.

Having spoken of the general reasons for the suspense of faith, Bellows next turned his attention "to look at the form in which we may hope that faith will rally and go on." This brought on what Bellows called "the church question." Many, he admitted, "are striving with all their might, to prove that there is no such question; that we have got by it." He claimed that many asserted that the church had no purpose, "that only priestcraft and quackery give it a seeming importance for their own ends." But Bellows believed that "the church question . . . is a real question in all Protestant countries," and that it had to be met head-on and discussed.

Bellows went on: "Have the external institutions of religion any authority but expediency?" People have said, "make your ordinary schools and colleges, your family education, *religious*, and you may dispense with the church, which has no basis but expediency." Bellows maintained that there is a common feeling "that our religious institutions are approaching their natural term of existence." He suggested that in Italy and Germany "*patriotism* is fast getting to be the only religion of the upper classes, and while their ritual is music and revolution, their immortality is to die for the fatherland." Bellows asked, "And why not, if religion means only human development and self-perfection?" People further were saying that the church had given the world the Gospel, and now that it was poured out into human society, what need was there any longer for the institution of the church?

He stated the idea in other words, "Is not that invisible church, which, without noise of hammer or saw, secretly builds itself upon the spiritual life of humanity, far more real, more life-giving, and sustaining, than the visible church, which the extant religious institutions of Christianity claim to be?" Yet, Bellows believed that we have "a great deal more of obligation to the visible than to the invisible church. The invisible church takes due care of itself and of us; the visible church is committed to our hands." Bellows was not maintaining that the visible church was as important as the invisible church, but only that "it is our charge, because of the two, it alone is within our voluntary reach." Bellows also believed that "every radically important relationship of humanity is, and must be, embodied in an external institution." He mentioned the family, society, the state, and the church.

Bellows said he realized that the term ecclesia in the New Testament probably meant a collection of individuals or a congregation, but he believed that the calling together "of human beings in any one of their radical relationships, or about any one of their essential needs or aspirations, develops at once something which none of the individual parties could have predicted or anticipated which is very different from any of the elements of which it is composed." He carried the theory further, "There is a church in humanity, as there is a family state, a social state, and a political state—a church which has always been developed, and has been the principal source of the religious life of humanity. Christianity takes advantage of a previously existent institution, which was not simply Jewish but human, when she pours her life through the church."

Bellows maintained that while the church needed reanimating, men must recognize "the existing religious institutions of Christendom as the chosen channel through which the divine Word is seeking to descend into Humanity and the world." The church, he believed, exists and is capable of receiving the Holy Spirit which animates the church. "There are faculties in man that must lay hold on God, as there are powers in God that will lay hold on man; the initiation is to be taken now by one, now by the other." He felt that any doctrine of the church which "violates or paralyzes" man's seeking of God "is false to human nature and to God."

Bellows further claimed that the church possessed "the stewardship of the Holy Ghost, and the dispensation of the Word of God" and as such it "is to be maintained and upheld in its external form as a separate and distinct, a precious and indispensable interest of humanity." And as such "the church is to be content with its *religious* function and office. It is not the source and vehicle of the general culture of society; it is not the guide and critic of science, and art, and social progress." These other interests have their own institutional protectors. The church ought to pray for the success of these other spheres of human activity, "but she has her own peculiar and precious work to do, her own sacred department to fill." Thus the church has "a sphere quite as important as it can fill . . . supplying the purely religious wants of the people." He spoke of the church as the protector of God's Word. "God talks in creation, in history, in revelation. Nations are his alphabet, epochs his syllables, humanity his discourse. The Bible is God's Word because it is the record of his dealings with nations and ages." He continued, "Christ is the Word of God" by "what he was and did and suffered" not by what he said.

Bellows believed that Christ must be formed in every man. "No lecture-rooms; no preaching-man can do this; no thin, ghostly individualism or meagre congregationalism can do this. It calls for the organic, instituted, ritualized, impersonal, steady, patient work of the church." He advocated a "new catholic church—a church in which the needed but painful experience of Protestantism shall have taught us how to maintain a dignified, symbolic, and mystic church-organization without the aid of the State, or the authority of the Pope." This, he believed "is the demand of the weary, unchurched humanity of our era." Bellows did not claim to have the wisdom to inaugurate this new church, but he believed that "it is a cry for help, which God will hear, and will answer by some new word from the Holy Ghost, when humanity is able and willing to bear it."

With this demand for the establishment of a new catholic church not dependent upon Popes or the State, Bellows closed his address. Those who felt that he would soon return to Rome read only part of the address and did not understand its meaning.

Most of the Unitarians of the day were stunned and outraged by Bellows's ideas. Not since Emerson's Divinity School address had Unitarianism, indeed the whole Protestant realm, been so astounded by a Unitarian's discourse. Bellows's alumni address ranked in importance with William Ellery Channing's Baltimore sermon of 1819 and Emerson's Divinity School address of 1838, and created every bit as much of an uproar in 1859.

Having finished his duties at Cambridge, Bellows went off to relax with his family at Walpole. While he was away, the shock wave created by his Harvard address went beyond the small circle of professional theologians who heard him, to pervade Boston. From there it radiated to Unitarian circles on the Atlantic Coast and westward; then through the religious world generally.

The impact had hit the members of All Souls. A return to *ecclesia!* A new Catholic church! What could the man be thinking of? For the first time in Bellows's tenure with the church, his congregation had questions about him, aghast that its beloved pastor could recommend a return to the very thing from which they had sought refuge. As Bellows said two decades later, in 1879, the address "was blinding to many even of my own friends and my own people, for its advocacy of institutional religion and a defence of liturgical forms of worship. This was its chief offense." He asserted that because of this "it was hastily assumed that, if I ventured to praise public and stated forms of prayer, I must be going to adopt them either by attempting to force them on my own congregation or by going into some other branch of the church."[3]

A typical example of how Bellows's address was misunderstod is a letter from an anonymous layman from Cincinnati who had read the contents in the newspapers. "What struck me as most remarkable in the address alluded to (evidently without such intention) and which I cannot refrain from telling you—is that the church you so happily & truthfully *describe,* as the one required to meet the wants of the age & times *is the American* [Episcopal] *Church*—the true catholic church of this country—not what low churchmen so-called (more properly nonchurchmen) would have it to be—but what it in reality is, a pure branch of the one catholic and apostolic church; and having (though to a certain extent now latent) all the appliances necessary for meeting the wants of all people & for all time—having all of the Roman Church that is good & true—and all that you point to as necessary to take the place of the countless sects, that have scourged our fair land."[4]

The editor of the *Quarterly Journal* of the American Unitarian Association, James Freeman Clarke, understood the meaning of the address far better than most of his contemporaries. He said that the sermon deserved "all the approbation which had been given it for its strength and sweep." He summarized the thought content of the address by saying that Bellows believed that there had been a suspension of faith because Unitarians felt no further need to modify orthodoxy—they had already done enough—the spirit of the age was working with Unitarians. Hence there was a lack of zeal, and there was a natural law of action and reaction which meant that religious liberalism was now in the saddle. Clarke called this "High Church doctrine." He felt that Bellows had overstated the doctrine and had left a one-sided impression on many points. He felt that Unitarians had not really lost any of their faith in their ideals but only in their opinions. And he challenged Bellows on the basic irreligious nature of the age. "If religion means the sense of God's presence, then there is more of it now than ever before." He believed that Bellows had yielded too much to the common error of identifying religion with its religious forms. But he felt that in one sentence Bellows had summarized the whole problem. "When he said that the church was a divine, necessary, and permanent institution, like the family and like the state, he made it divine because human, necessary because based on the nature of man, and permanent because in accordance with eternal law." Clarke continued, "When we can say that the church was made for man, and not man for the church, and that its unity is not in any forms, but in the living Christ, we shall then find that it has the keys of the Kingdom of Heaven."[5]

After the Cambridge address, Eliza Schuyler (Mrs. George) wrote to Henry Bellows addressing him "My Dear Pope." Bellows had evidently read the address to her before the Cambridge delivery, and she said, "I expected a storm upon the fundamental points." She felt that the address was a valid charge against Protestantism "But to have the world frightened by the word *catholic*" alarmed her. She was looking forward to the printed address, and was glad that he had taken the trouble to read it to her. She was evidently his sympathetic sounding board.[6]

A little over five weeks after Bellows gave his astounding address at Cambridge one of his college chums (probably the editor) wrote an article on him in *Harper's Weekly* magazine. The article was obviously written because Bellows was very much in the news after his Cambridge address. The two-page article[7] contains an engraving of "Rev. Dr. Bellows" after a photograph by Matthew Brady. It depicts him as a youngish man with his right hand resting upon a book (undoubtedly the Bible). The line drawing of the Church of All Souls shows the church with the bell tower that was in the architect's plans but never built. The author says that Henry

Bellows belonged to the order of "Bunyan's Mr. Greathearts." He terms Bellows "electric" but he finds him also a puzzle, "a strange mixture of dispassionate argument and impulsive enthusiasm." He makes further contrasts: "a devotee in prayer, and a jovial companion in society; a radical and a conservative, a democrat and an aristocrat, a transcendentalist and a churchman, a man of the world and an evangelist." The author concludes, "as to the report of Dr. Bellows going over to Rome, it is absurdity itself. He is in the very grain one of the liberals and the Liberators of our time; and if his Holiness the Pope should receive him at the Vatican as an alleged convert, after a short interview he would pronounce him as terribly Protestant even in his Catholicity, and would entreat him to depart without rehearsing his bold and romantic visions."

Clifton J. Phillips analyzed Bellows's intentions in the "Suspense of Faith" correctly when he wrote, "What Bellows was demanding was nothing less than a reversal of historical processes. . . . Bellows refused to admit the incapacity of the American churches to prevent the onrushing tendency toward debacle, and rebuild a new churchly foundation. Rather, he believed, this is the very time when we must set ourselves against the current."[8]

A Sequel to the Suspense

The opening of All Souls in the fall of 1859 was postponed three weeks because of the delay in the completion of the new gallery which it was hoped would seat the crowd that now came to hear Henry Bellows preach. This delay gave Bellows a better chance to think through his own position in regard to the reaction to "The Suspense of Faith." He was determined to give "A Sequel to the Suspense of Faith" on the first Sunday morning and evening the church was opened. "It is a very direct & frank development," he wrote to Cyrus Bartol, "of my own views on the church question, ritual, new theology in a reactionary position." He said that "the whole subject had been *simmering* for two months." He had received hosts of letters of "sympathy, inquiry, dispute." He doubted whether his views would "be any *more palatable* when they are *more distinctly* seen."[1] Bellows was determined to set the record straight not only with his own parishioners but with all of his friends and critics.

"The Suspense of Faith" had caused a furor among religious circles in the entire country and not just among those of Unitarian persuasion. It was widely believed that Bellows, in opting for the church as a necessary institution rather than relegating religion (as had Emerson twenty-one years before) into an entirely personal thing (in which the church as an institution was unnecessary), had become "High Church." Bellows had given as an affirmative example the liturgy of the Episcopal Church, and many thought that he would either end up with the Episcopalian prayerbook in a far more conservative form than that used in King's Chapel or else he would make the pilgrimage to Rome. It looked to some as if Bellows would immediately institute radical changes in the worship and liturgy at All Souls.

It was in order to reassure his own parishioners as to his intentions that Bellows felt that it was highly important to explain to his congregation on the first possible Sunday exactly what he had meant and had not meant in "The Suspense of Faith." On Sunday morning and evening, 25 September, Henry Bellows read his congregation "A Sequel to the Suspense of Faith."[2] He called it not an explanation but "an extension."

He began by saying that he had "No apologies to offer for [his] late discourse [at Harvard]. It was not the fruit of haste or moodiness, and is not a subject of repentence. It was a deliberate performance, and expressed the results of some years of patient observation and study." He apologized that he had not been able to make himself more clear. He proposed to address his audience from four different stances: 1. as an "independent congregation and church over which [he was] set as minister", 2. from the standpoint of "the Unitarian denomination", 3. from the point of view of "the Protestant world", and 4. from the point of view of "the Nineteenth Century and this new country." This was a great deal of ground to cover even for someone so broad in his interests as Henry Bellows, but he did it brilliantly in one of the finest and most significant sermons of his whole life.

The first quarter of his address was from the point of view "of the independent congregation and church over which [he was] set as minister." He allayed the fears of the congregation that he had any secret desires of "changing the forms of worship not to say the radical usages and customs of [the] congregation." Fears had been expressed that he was going to smuggle his new religious views upon the church in "a creed or ritual—a creed of the popular sort, a ritual of the Romanish kind." He hoped that his congregation understood him personally and the congregational form of government better than to believe that in any way he would even consider a ritualistic "coup d-etat," in the face of the wishes of his congregation. He stated that, "not a particle of authority lies in your minister to change your form of worship." He hoped that any improper exercise of such authority "would be properly resisted." He declared that even if he had such despotic powers he would have no desire to use them.

He then discussed a matter close to his heart which was to be his lifelong hope, that somehow the liberal church could develop a ritual and a liturgy that could bind the liberal churches together in a way that Episcopalian churches were bound together by the use of the Book of Common Prayer. He indicated that there had been a number of meetings within the Unitarian body to discuss this matter, but that it had not been productive, not from a lack of knowing "a want ourselves," but because the body had not "distinctly known how to supply it." A further poll of the "pulse of the people" had discovered "but a partial recognition of this want among them."

It was his opinion "that an important change in statement of creed and form of worship is in store for the next generation," although he could not forecast what this would mean in regard to external ritual. He felt that "the worship of the next age will grow out of wants" which are not yet felt deeply enough to be made manifest, but the idea that Christendom would revive the "mummeries and mockeries" which once belonged to the Church of Rome "is an hypothesis too absurd for contradiction." He recognized that the Episcopal Church flourished in America because of its "more perfect organization, its excellent Liturgy, and its catholic spirit." But he did not feel that the spirit of the times was "mere imitation or copying." He believed that the new worship "will organize itself from the new developments of Christianity." He continued, "It will match the heart and conscience and intellect and taste, of a new people in a new time." Yet it would also preserve the past by giving fresh meaning and organization to "every symbol, strain and idea, precious at any time to the consciousness of Christendom or the church."

He next spoke as "representing the Unitarian denomination." Bellows claimed that it has "been alleged by ill-wishers, that I have wounded Unitarianism, announced its decease, and spoken at its funeral." He felt that if there were any error it was "of too great fondness for our cause; too large an estimate of its progress; too bold a reliance on its victories." He had spoken of the triumphs of the denomination, "of our mission as successful beyond the largest hopes of its first laborers." The cause of Unitarianism had advanced to such an extent that "the time is at hand . . . when the results of the Unitarian controversy are to be reaped for the benefit of universal Christendom." The work of the critics, scholars, thinkers, and philanthropists was about to benefit the whole church. Bellows further declared that he did not believe that Unitarianism should preach "another Gospel." He did not believe that Unitarians had "the exclusive and complete truth." Rather he maintained that the contribution of Unitarians had been "the setting up of the lights of a neglected reason, of abused human nature, and of suspected science and experience . . . [that] the shadows might depart from the faces and forms of those ancient doctrines."

Bellows prophesied that the time would soon come "when the glory of Unitarianism will be to find itself true," and he suggested that this would be "*within* the lines of the Church Universal." The Unitarians had unconsciously gotten outside of this Church Universal which "hindered the influence of the church and the Gospel." But shortly the Unitarians would "lead the disfranchised millions." He believed that "even now the services which liberal Christianity has rendered to Christendom are widely acknowledged and still more widely felt."

The third section of the address was that in which Bellows spoke of himself and his audience as "representatives of the Protestant body." He claimed to be, 'a Protestant of the Protestants, and at the extreme verge of dissent from Roman or other hierarchical pretensions." He did not believe in apostolic succession "which depends on men's palms and polls, which can be broken by a fraud, interrupted by an accident, or handed down like vaccine or political legitimacy." He believed that "the church is to Christendom precisely what society is to civilization . . . the unmistakable reality, which shapes the institutions and opinions." He believed that "the church is a tradition," it is "an hereditary thing . . . it comes down in the corporal and spiritual blood of the successive generations of believers, and in the creeds and customs of the saints and sages, who have been ordained by God, and accepted by their fellows." He added that "no additions like those of the Romanist, and no subtractions like those of the Quaker . . . can cut off or exclude any of Christ's disciples from his church," an idea expressed many years previously by William Ellery Channing. He held that baptism and the Lord's supper were to be the true sacraments, "not merely expressive and interesting rites, ornamental and pleasant, but the vehicle of special and mystic influence." Thus Bellows reaffirmed the traditional Calvinistic doctrine of New England in regard to baptism and the Lord's supper.

The last portion of Bellows's address was directed to his congregation as "representatives of the Nineteenth Century and of this new country." He admitted that he was a child of the age even as he criticized the age. But he characterized the age as "to be that of essential progress in true humanity—a new faith in man, a bolder trust in truth as his glorious heritage, a legitimation of human instincts and powers." He believed that man was a son of God and not a child of the devil. He believed that his century was memorable for two events, "the discovery of vaccination, and the union of the hemispheres by the Atlantic cable." He felt that both of these inventions were "symbols of the saving powers of transmissive influences;" vaccination because it "saved America from decimation by loathsome and deforming disease," and the Atlantic cable because it saved "it from moral and spiritual barrenness of disconnection with that Europe that owns, and is, the past." Bellows thanked God that he lived in such a great day. He then concluded his two-part sermon. No wonder that Bellows is known as a churchman. He believed in the institution to which he devoted all of his adult life.

During the latter part of the year 1859 Bellows gathered together twenty-five of his sermons from the past decade which dealt with doctrinal matters.[3] The tone of "The Suspense of Faith" and "A Sequel to the Suspense of Faith" had been that of a lecture; even the two sermons which constituted the latter address were more like an address than Bellows's typical Sunday sermons. In gathering these sermons together for publication, Bellows undoubtedly felt that his theological ideas would be better presented on a simpler, more popular basis. Bellows made no claims of being a systematic theologian. But neither was he unsophisticated in matters of theology, and the sermons are something more than another routine repetition of the conventional doctrines of the times. They are little gems with theological insights which give a very different side of the thinking of Bellows than the two more ponderous addresses. Bellows put his soul into this volume and felt that it represented "the history of my religious thinking. I am tied to no sect & entertain no bodies [sic] ideas." He felt that the volume "will give the genesis & growth of my views." He did not even attempt to doctor the sermons "to a superficial agreement & consistency."[4]

Although Bellows's book of doctrinal sermons bears the imprint of 1860, copies were available by Christmastime in 1859, some of which Bellows wrapped and sent to his friends.[5] Bartol received a package of six books three days later and he distributed them as Bellows wished, to Dewey, King, Whipple, Hedge, and Clarke, keeping the sixth copy for himself.[6] Bartol sat up late and read a great deal of the book "making thorough work before going to bed." He commented, "What I have to say of it is the best thing possible—that it is true as a die to the mind it came from. The most marked characteristic is the strength always of the thought—the grip with which the one purpose of every discourse is held through all involutions, of argument. . . . Then there is abundance of fresh & original illustration—a vivid fancy works even in your style & greatly helps the sometimes abstruse complexity." Obviously Bartol, serious critic though he was, liked Bellows's book of doctrinal sermons.[7]

Frederic Henry Hedge was ecstatic about the book of sermons. "I have read the book through from beginning to end every page & every word—a thing I have not done with any volume of the kind before for many a year, a too extravagant a compliment that, if done from mere regard for the author. You must therefore set it down as not merely a friend's tribute but a critical testimony." Hedge admitted that he was "not much versed in sermons other than my own, but incline to the belief that this of yours is for thinkers the most remarkable volume of sermons in our day, excelling equally in value of thought, a vigor of statement, & aptness of illustration."[8] This was remarkable testimony from one of the most intellectual of the Unitarians.

A Church of the Unchurched

The summer of 1859 was not an easy one. Not only were there repercussions from "The Suspense of Faith," but Bellows also received alarming news from H. A. Marriner in Yellow Springs, Ohio, that Horace Mann was desperately ill with typhoid fever. "He is unable to sit up; has watchers every night; has taken no nourishment for two weeks, and is naturally enough growing steadily weaker. His tongue is very black, his pulse variable, fluttering and irregular, his stomach so irritable as to make it impossible for him to retain anything, even water."[1] Three days later Marriner again wrote, "The crisis is passed. The Old Hero is gone. . . . He died today at 5 P.M. His death was more than peaceful, it was triumphant! And it was characteristic. So much so as his Baccalaureate and last commencement." Horace Mann had "called the members of his family, the students, many of his neighbors, members of the Faculty remaining here, about him and had for each some rich word of warming or cheer. His talk was really grand and amazed us all to silence." He uttered a special message for Henry Bellows. "No one listened unmoved to a strain of talk which was worthy to come from the Other Side."[2]

It was largely out of respect for Horace Mann that Bellows had spent so much time and exerted so much labor on behalf of Antioch College. He was impressed with Mann's ideas of education, and he felt his death deeply. Like most of the others at the college after the initial grief came the question, what now could be done at the college? Antioch College had been sold that year for lack of funds, and reorganized upon a new basis. Horace Mann's death naturally left Henry Bellows, who felt responsible for the future of Antioch College, "in a great deal of anxiety." He was happy that "we had six blessed years of his life." He found it "very puzzling what to do." He wanted a "man of universal reputation for the new president." All of these questions perplexed him, but he tried to "keep cool, & eat & sleep well, & fill in all the moral *ballast* I can find."[3]

The thirty-two members of the senior class at Antioch who were slated to graduate the following June were also very disturbed by Mann's death. They appointed a committee to write to Dr. Bellows to ask him to consider becoming the president of the college. "Under these circumstances we look to you as the only man who by a single act, can repair the loss already suffered & give all full & immediate assurance that their future shall in no respect fall short of the promises & hopes of the past—our wish and expectation is that you will accept the office now left vacant."[4] Bellows must have been touched and pleased by this confidence which the students placed in his abilities. President of Harvard he would be—if asked—but it is doubtful if he wished to leave New York and take on the very difficult position of president of a debt-ridden college—particularly since he hoped to get rid of those debts from his New York base.

By the middle of August Bellows had declined the presidency of Antioch. "The seniors have heard, and are going about with *faces* as *long* as if the Union of the U.S. was going overboard," James Eastwood wrote from Antioch. Eastwood rejoiced at Bellows "non-acceptance" because no one had been able to accuse the Unitarians of trying to proselytize in the name of their particular religion. "If you *had* come probably such would soon have been inferred from the universal knowledge of your strong *denominationalism* and your influence in the Unitarian body." Eastwood preferred Bellows to any other, but he wanted to maintain, as did Bellows, the nonsectarian aspect of the college. Dr. Rufus P. Stebbins had been appointed as president, and Eastwood thought that he "ought to be supported by all the *strength* and *influence* which can be brought to his aid."[5]

Bellows had other concerns at this time. The Reverend Octavius Brooks Frothingham was among those of the new left among the Unitarian ministers. Frothingham was a forceful personality and a powerful preacher. He also displayed a great deal of strength and courage in his professional attitudes as a Unitarian minister. Often, however, what passes as courage and strength of conviction is actually largesse of stubbornness in clinging to narrow preconceived ideals. While Frothingham could not be called a bigot, he displayed a decided stubborn streak. This had been evidenced in the way he had locked horns with some in his congregation in the North Church in Salem, Massachusetts. Instead of gently and reasonably leading his semi-proslavery flock toward understanding the evils of slavery, Frothingham had precipitated the issue and had refused to budge from his position. A call from the Jersey City Unitarian Church had fortuitously arrived just as the issue had reached its peak, and Frothingham had moved to the New York area.

His departure from Salem was more than a move:

> It proved to be a break. He had slipped the traditional moorings, and henceforth was to tempt the open sea. The fact is that during his Salem ministry he had come into close touch with Theodore Parker . . . Transcendental ideas were eagerly accepted . . . conscience led him on, till one advanced position after another was fearlessly assumed, and he felt impelled to reach beyond the limits that were set by the Unitarian thought of the time.[6]

It was not long after Frothingham had been installed at the Jersey City church that his preaching eloquence became known to Unitarians in New York City.[7] Many city people told Frothingham that he merited a larger and more sophisticated congregation than the Jersey City society offered him. A group was formed expressly to hear Frothingham's preaching in New York. This following became the Third Congregational Unitarian Church of New York City, and was incorporated in 1859. The society acquired a church on 40th Street and Sixth Avenue, near the Croton water reservoir, and when that building was sold, the society moved to Lyric Hall. Frothingham drew large crowds, but mostly of abolitionist extremists and others of radical and socialistic persuasion. As Paul

Octavius Brooks Frothingham, Courtesy of the Unitarian Universalist Association

Revere Frothingham put it, the Third Church became, to a large extent, "a church of the unchurched."

Late in his life when he wrote his *Recollections*, Octavius Brooks Frothingham described his congregation in New York City as "comprised of all sorts of people. There were Unitarians, Universalists, 'Come Outers,' spiritualists, unbelievers, all kinds, antislavery people, reformers generally."[8]

If Frothingham drew large crowds of the laity there were at least two clergymen in the city who were not so enthusiastic, Henry Whitney Bellows and Samuel Osgood. They both felt that they had been deceived by Frothingham in that they had never considered that he would establish a Unitarian church which was un-Christian and for the non-churched. Dr. Osgood was particularly adamant in his denunciation of Frothingham. "We certainly did not expect him to run an opposition line, and although we knew that he did not take the supernatural ground as we do, we had his explicit assurance that he would establish a regular Unitarian congregation with the usual ordinances &, I thought, with the usual tone & policy." Osgood felt that he "appeared in New York only as a theological outlaw." He claimed that "a set of some old maids & unsexed widows & matrons appear to be his advisors." Osgood believed that "he ought to have confided in us," certainly in Bellows. "He certainly has not treated me well, for I did everything to smooth his way & his only return is a complaint of patronizing." Osgood felt that the relationship of the two Christian ministers to Frothingham "must be cleared up. . . . If he is to be the minister of a Unitarian Christian Church he is of us as brother as well as friend. If he is the head of a movement for denying Christ's Divine mission & the permanence . . . of his gospel, he may be a friend but not a brother." Osgood went on to declare that if the latter were the case he would have less to do with Octavius Frothingham than with the orthodox ministers of New York City. He had also heard that Frothingham "has talked of quitting the denomination."[9]

Evidently the Frothinghams were living with the Bellows in their home while Octavius founded his Third Unitarian Society in the city, which is somewhat surprising since Bellows felt that Frothingham had duped him into starting a nonreligious society rather than a typical Unitarian Christian Church. By February Mrs. Bellows was tired of living with the children at their school in Eagleswood, New Jersey; she had gotten somewhat sickly again, and was consulting the doctor. "She had got tired of the Frothingham arrangements & given notice to quit by May 1—when she intends to resume housekeeping. I see that she is a little unready at being less than *first* lady of the house—which is natural." Eliza had been home very little during the winter months, going to Eagleswood after spending the fall in Walpole. The Frothinghams were living in the house, and there had been the usual difficulties. Perhaps Bellows's future difficulties with Octavius Frothingham were partially due to this problem.[10]

A few months earlier Bellows had been optimistic about Eliza's health. Time away from the city at Walpole and Eagleswood had seemingly improved her condition. "Eliza is decidedly in better health, tho' still an invalid. We harmonize very much in our religious opinions & she is growing more self-controlled as to her nervous system,"[11] but it was constantly an up-and-down situation.

In addition to his problems with Frothingham, Thomas Starr King was causing Bellows some concern. King had been invited by and had turned down the pulpit of the Brooklyn Church. Now Bellows, who personally acted as a kind of Department of the Ministry for the denomination, sent him a "cubic yard or so of documents from San Francisco" to try to interest the young man in the pulpit there. King found them "very clear & strong, & I must acknowledge that they impress me seriously." He wanted very much "to be in a position where my labors would be of greater worth to the general cause than it can be in Boston." He also wanted to be relieved of the necessity to balance his budget by lecturing. He felt that the call to California seemed "like the Providential call than any position nearer home."[12] However, there were some problems; some members of his wife's family were in poor health, and the church had issued a call to Dr. Briggs of Salem to see if he was interested in the church in Boston. So he begged for several weeks' delay while Bellows stewed about getting the right man for San Francisco. King had suggested that he was taking a trip to central New York State to lecture and that he would be glad to meet Bellows and talk with him about the San Francisco situation.

Bellows therefore took the train to Albany on Wednesday 7 December; he got to Albany at five o'clock just before Starr King's train came in from Boston. They had supper together, and Henry went to hear King's lecture that evening. He then waited until 11:30 at the depot with him for King's night sleeper to the west. King spoke an hour and a quarter at his lecture "to the evident entertainment & admiration of the company." About the nature of his address Bellows wrote, "He imitates Mr. Emerson more than I knew, or even heard of. His *voice* is the best evidence of his superior abilities & quality . . . one sees after a little that he is really entitled to the place he holds as a popular lecturer. He is witty & just profound enough to be intelligible to people who can not enjoy any thing that does not go *beyond* their own ideas." Bellows added somewhat reluctantly "his ideas are too familiar to me to be interesting for any thing but their illustrations."[13]

Bellows got on the train and went as far as Rochester with King. They then went on to Batavia where he again heard King lecture. Bellows's willingness to try to persuade King to go to California is usually an overlooked part of the intimate relationship between these two men. It was to be a partnership with great historical importance.

Even after this trip and conversation with Bellows, King was still vacillating. He returned to Boston in time for Christmas, and wrote to Bellows the day after Christmas. He explained his feelings, "When under *pressure,* I feel the claim of Cincinnati; when alone, so that the attractions of the two posts play unobstructed, I find San Francisco the stronger body. . . . I still feel in the core of the heart an impulse to the more distant region." And he asked, "Must I not take it as the Providential Intimation? *Perhaps,* it is the demon in an *UnSocratic* sense." The pecuniary aspects of the Cincinnati call were better than that of San Francisco, and Starr King concluded, "I cannot but feel that San Francisco is the more crying call. If you are *inspired* to believe me wrong, I am not yet past being saved by grace.[14] It was almost as if Starr King were making up his mind while he was writing this letter.

Bellows had grown somewhat impatient with his protege's wavering between Cincinnati and San Francisco. Finally on 2 January 1860, Thomas Starr King wrote to inform Bellows that he had written his resignation which would be read to his parish that evening. "I send word to San Francisco that they can have what is left of me for two years." He would sail either on 5 March or 5 April, probably the later date. "This morning with sad pen, I sent the final word to Hosea in Cincinnati. Were I twice as strong that would be my true post."

King also told Henry Bellows that he had read his book of doctrinal sermons very carefully. "I had bought & read half your volume before Bartol, wrapped in fur, the mercury below 0, his nose a carbuncle, & looking like an Esquimaux saint, brought your gift-copy." King liked the style of Bellows's writing. "What the artists mean by broad handling you show, in a literary way, in every sermon. The lights are not spotty, but stream with the most generous & easy flush; the generalizations are ripe; while the blending of speculative originality & courage with practical intention & force is as admirable as it is rare." But King felt that the speculative thought of the book was "not worked out clearly enough for it to be titled, *Re-Statement of Christian Doctrine.* There is too much life in the volume to make it effective especially as statement. Your light runs to heat wh[ich] is *better,* but wh[ich] is *not light.*"[15]

As always there were family concerns. Both Russell, now almost eighteen, and Annie, now almost fifteen, were at Eagleswood in the preparatory school run by Marcus Spring in Perth Amboy, New Jersey. The Bellows, like many of the other parents, maintained or rented rooms at the school so that they could visit their children and also spend time at the beach resort. Mrs. Bellows often went down for a week or more at a time to get away from the pressures of the city and to be near her children. Russell was preparing for entering Harvard the next fall. Henry Bellows often wrote to his children when they were away; in fact, many of his most personal and secret thoughts were revealed during his lifetime in his letters to his children.

In January 1860, just before Mrs. Bellows went down to Eagleswood for a week while he traveled to Baltimore, Bellows wrote his children,

> Perhaps children do not know how much parents desire & even long to be *loved*. They do not expect to be loved *as* they love—for it is impossible for young folks to understand how their parent's hearts are bound up in them, & after a certain age, how much they live for them. But as much as is possible, parents desire to *have* their children's *hearts*, their society, & their devotion.

He pointed out that both Russell and Annie were in "the transition period when a few months make a great change in character & experience." He was looking to see what manner of man Russell was going to turn out to be. He pointed out to Russell that his greatest want was "the awakening of a thirst *for knowledge*—the knowledge of books—of history & literature." If he didn't possess this curiosity he had to try to cultivate it. If Russell's interest in music were going to interfere with this quest he probably ought to give up his music. But Bellows was not worried about his son's character. Only two things worried Henry about his son, his lack of love for books, and "he does not love *manly* sports, & develop physical strength & courage as he should."

In regard to Annie, Bellows wrote, "I look with great satisfaction on the development of her mind & her person—thinking them both in a very promising condition. . . . Her danger is jumping to conclusions, & not respecting enough the judgments & experiences of others." She had a strong character, Bellows believed. He wanted her to be happy in spite of this, but pointed out that she had to think more of her duty and less of her self-gratification. It was a beautiful, tender, critical, parental letter showing Bellows as so few have known him—as a warm family man.[16]

With his brother George it was a different matter. There was always the rankling problem of the estate of his father which had been so divided among the children that it was a constant family menace. Henry was one of the trustees, and also held a portion of it. Every time he needed a signature his brother George would try to wrest another loan from Henry or an advance of his interest in the estate. Eventually relations with his brother reached the breaking point. In February 1860, Henry wanted George's signature on some documents about the estate, and George tried again in his typical manner to get some money. Henry wrote, "I am sorry to say this very distinctly & emphatically, No—& moreover I will thank you not to drive me to the necessity of saying *No*, by applying further for favors, which I have no intention of conceding." He accused his brother of living mainly on brother Frank for ten years, and on himself "who paid for your education & have never rec'd a penny of comfort . . . from you, is such as I have rarely seen equalled among decent people." In regard to the estate, George could take any course he wanted, or as Bellows put it "any course, your recklessness, or folly may prompt." He noted that "whenever you pay me principal & interest for my advances, I shall be only too happy to restore your interest." He did not want to make a penny out of his brother. Since he did not really need George's signature, George could keep his begging to himself. It was a strong letter.[17]

CHAPTER SEVEN

Our Commission Is Ordered by the Government

Last Days of Peace

On Saturday afternoon, 25 February 1860, an almost unknown man named Abraham Lincoln stopped ashore from a ferryboat at Courtland Street. What little was known about him had been the result of a losing campaign he had waged against Stephen A. Douglas for a seat in the U.S. Senate from the State of Illinois in 1858. Lincoln was to speak in New York City the following Monday evening at Cooper Union—his first speech in the East. There was a snarling snowstorm Monday evening, 27 February, and Lincoln doubted that there would be many people to hear him. But two prominent New Yorkers—and members of All Souls—who had been among those who had arranged for Lincoln's New York address, Peter Cooper, who furnished the Great Hall in his newly established Cooper Union, and William Cullen Bryant, who was to introduce Lincoln to the audience, were present, although Bellows evidently was not. To Lincoln's amazement, the hall was nearly full; 1,500 New Yorkers had braved the blizzard and paid twenty-five cents in order to hear this strange man, who was already reputed to be a dark-horse candidate for the U.S. presidency in the election the following November. The tall, gangly, and almost bizzarely ugly man seemed oddly out of place with his new broadcloth frock coat which was much too small, and much too wrinkled from having been packed in his carpetbag. Indeed, Lincoln did feel out of place as he faced the large, intellectual and culturally sophisticated New York audience.

White-haired and bearded Bryant rose and introduced Mr. Abraham Lincoln of Illinois, after which Lincoln awkwardly untangled his lanky frame from his chair on the platform to face the audience. He paused, waited until the noise had subsided, and then nervously began in a falsetto voice, "Mr. Cheerman . . . " Titters fluttered through the vast hall. Lincoln gulped, and began again in his Midwestern drawl. But he spoke so softly that again he was interrupted, this time with yelling from the rear of the hall,

"Louder!" Mustering his courage again, Lincoln drew up his long frame, cleared his throat, and plunged into his well-researched and thoroughly-reasoned speech, gaining confidence and a deep resonant voice as he progressed. For the next hour and a half the sophisticated New Yorkers were held in breathless attention by this man from the West. Lincoln ended his address with the famous words, "Let us have the faith that right makes might, and in that faith let us to the end dare to do our duty as we understand it."

The next morning, the New York newspapers ran Lincoln's full text, and the address was soon appearing in pamphlets all across the land, accompanied by Brady's photograph of a statesman-like Abraham Lincoln. Republican voters and supporters were so impressed with Lincoln's Cooper Union address that soon the leading contender for the Republican nomination, William H. Seward of New York, lost his support, and that summer, Abraham Lincoln was nominated as the Republican candidate for President of the United States.

Lincoln's address had focused on the slavery question, the main social and political issue in the decade of the 1850s, and certain to be the central issue in the election of 1860. All across the nation there were divided sentiments on the matter, with the abolitionists advocating overnight freeing of all slaves, the moderates advocating the prevention of the spread of slavery, but not its abolition, and the proslavery constituents insisting on their rights as private citizens to hold slaves if they wanted to. The abolitionists and antislavery constituents objected to slavery on outright moral grounds, but there were so many other factors intricately bound up with the issue of slavery, that simple moral idealism, however correct it might be, offered no solutions to the problem; indeed had it been implemented as simplistically as the abolitionists proposed, this moral idealism would have led to far more serious and practical problems than already existed. Economics, cultural conditioning, the individual rights of private citizens and the freedom to hold personal property, states' rights, political objectives, struggles for power; all these and more, and all involving the gamut of human motives—some grossly immoral and illegal, some legal but immoral, some moral but illegal, and others quite morally and legally justifiable—intricately entangled with the issue of slavery. The federal government had been struggling along as best it could, trying to accommodate all factions, but mostly with the result that it alienated everybody on one ground or another. The Compromise of 1850, for example, had admitted California as a *free* state; established the territories of Utah and New

Mexico with *no* ruling on slavery, the inhabitants to be left to decide the question; and strengthened the Fugitive Slave Act which in effect sided with the slave owners. This and other muddled actions on the part of the federal government outraged every faction.

At the time of Lincoln's address, the Southern states were threatening secession. New York was not merely caught up in this national issue, in many ways the city was really the source of the difficulty, for New York was an underground illegal center for helping escaped slaves. At the same time, the commercial interests in the city were inextricably bound up with cotton and slavery. The Southern states had a particular grievance against New York for maintaining control of the cotton trade. New York merchants dominated every phase of this Southern business, from plantation to market. Bryant's *Evening Post* claimed that "New York belongs almost as much to the South as to the North." As a Senatorial candidate, Lincoln had perceptively declared "A house divided against itself cannot stand. I believe this government cannot endure permanently half slave and half free." It was true of the nation, but Lincoln might also have been describing the actual situation in New York City.

But Lincoln's main objective was to maintain the nation intact—a necessary first step before the slavery issue itself could be resolved. Thus, in his Cooper Union address he adopted the only practical means which existed to achieve this goal:

> Even though much provoked, let us do nothing through passion and ill-temper. Even though the Southern people will not so much as listen to us, let us calmly consider their demands, and yield to them if, in our deliberate view of our duty, we possibly can. . . . Wrong as we think slavery is, we can yet afford to let it alone where it is, because that much is due the necessity arising from its actual presence in the nation; but can we, while our votes will prevent it, allow it to be spread into the national territories and to overrun us here in these free states?[1]

Lincoln was hoping to cool the confused emotional heat that emanated from all sides of the slavery issue and to arrive at the status quo of each faction's interests.

But as is so often the case with human beings, few Americans bothered to slow their minds and emotions down long enough to follow Lincoln's careful and thorough reasoning. Written for New Yorkers in hopes of eliciting their *rational* support, Lincoln had couched his argument in cogent, but noninflammatory, terms. Consequently, too many New Yorkers construed Lincoln's address as favoring New York's position of supremacy over the recalcitrant South. The businessmen were interested in maintaining economic supremacy, while slavery dissenters were interested in enforcing their moral supremacy. Southerners, too, saw it this way, and interpreted the speech to mean only that Lincoln was *against* slavery. Thus while New Yorkers and Free Staters saw the speech to their personal advantage over the South, Southerners and slavery supporters saw Lincoln as being to their personal *disadvantage*.

The result was that, instead of cooling the emotional heat being generated on all sides of the slavery issue, the speech and the events which occurred subsequent to it actually fanned the heat into uncontrollable flames. Between 27 February, when Lincoln delivered the address before New Yorkers, and election day on 6 November 1860, Southern talk of secession grew ever louder and more threatening. The election of Lincoln in November decided the matter for the South, and in December the South Carolina legislature called a special state convention to officially dissolve the Union. The convention immediately demanded the federal government to give up all its property in the state, including the fortress situated at the harbor at Charleston. This fortress—Fort Sumter—was the strongest of the federal forts in South Carolina, and James Buchanan, who was just completing his last months of office, ordered all U.S. troups in the state moved to that stronghold. South Carolina immediately took possession of the other forts near Fort Sumter, and then determined to have Sumter, too.

Henry Bellows had not heard Lincoln's address at Cooper Union. The first indication that he was interested or knew about Abraham Lincoln is found in a letter to Mrs. George Schuyler in March 1860. He agreed with Eliza Schuyler in her estimate of a speech which William Seward had recently delivered, and then he wrote, "Did you read Mr. A. Lincoln's—which in many ways is *better*? A more solid, statesmanlike Mss, we have not had from any quarter. It *proves* what others simply grasp at, or abstract."[2] Little did Henry Bellows know what changes the reality of "a house divided" would make in his own personal and public life for the next five years.

Meanwhile, it was time to bid farewell to Thomas Starr King. He had accepted the invitation to San Francisco and had preached his last sermon at Hollis Street Church. Now he was in New York preparing to sail. There was a farewell breakfast for Starr King and his family given by the New York Unitarians at the Fifth Avenue Hotel at the end of March. About 230 persons were present, according to Mrs. Bellows. William Cullen Bryant presided. There were many tributes including that by Frederick Henry Hedge, "Happy Soul! himself a benediction wherever he goes; a living evangel of kind affections, better than all prophecy and all knowledge, the Angel of the Church whom Boston sends to San Francisco."[3] It was an appropriate send-off for a man who was in the next four years to work miracles in the Golden State.

On 29 April 1860, Robert B. Swain in San Francisco took advantage "of the first overland mail" [Pony Express] to inform Henry Bellows that Thomas Starr King and his family had arrived on Saturday afternoon, 28 April, at 3 P.M. from Panama. The people of the San Francisco church had decided that there would be no service on Sunday whether the boat arrived on Saturday or not. "Nevertheless, in accordance with Mr. King's own wish he preached this morning to a house crowded to overflowing." Men and women of every denomination were present to hear this newly arrived orator from the East. "None how highsoever were their expectations, turned away disappointed." King was "a decided hit." His *perfect success* is already assured—the question is settled beyond all peradventure." Swain concluded, "I already see a bright and glorious day for our cause upon the Pacific Coast dawning before us."[4]

The third week in June, Bellows again went to Cincinnati and on to Antioch College. Here he discovered that he was thoroughly appreciated. "The students really seem to associate me so completely with the history of the place that in Mr. Mann's absence, I am more than any one their *Father*, & I am really in danger of getting the degree of Father Bellows at this youthful period of 46." Father Edward Taylor of Boston and James Freeman Clarke had been with him at Antioch, and "both added amazingly to the interest of the occasion."[5]

Theodore Parker died in Florence, Italy, on 10 May 1860. It took several weeks for the word to get to the United States. Bellows wrote to Eliza from Cincinnati, "you see that the papers have told of some garbled report of my few words in an extempore sermon on Theodore Parker and are abusing me. I don't mind it. I said nothing untrue, or unkind, or narrow—& I am willing & anxious to be known as not in sympathy with his theology, or in chord with his spirit. So let it go." Then he philosophized about the criticism, "I sometimes think one's influence for good is to be measured by the eagerness with which one's words are perverted. I dare say Emerson had me in mind among the *fops* he speaks of in his eloquent remarks at Parker's funeral oration in Boston. What then?"[6] It is too bad that these remarks were extempore for we should like know exactly what he said about Theodore Parker, not one of Bellows's favorite Unitarian ministers.

In these last days of peace, Henry Bellows wrote something about his own appearance and physical condition. "I am forty-six years old—but twenty-two years of intensely active labor in the City of New York, have not left me unmarked, & probably I look, & perhaps speak, like an older man. . . . I am young at heart, & by no means broken in constitution, & I look forward to many years of service in the Christian field."[7]

That fall, Russell went to Harvard to join the freshman class. It had always been Henry Bellows's intention that his son would follow in his footsteps at his alma mater. A Harvard man is quoted as saying that his son could go to any college that he himself chose, but that his tuition would be paid only at Harvard; so it was with Henry Bellows. Russell found the change from Eagleswood School to Harvard College difficult. He complained to his father that Professor Peabody at the college chapel always seemed to be trading pulpits with some other minister so that he never had a chance to hear the college preacher.[8]

Bellows himself had been in college when Henry Ware, Jr., was the college preacher. He wrote that under Ware, his "religious affections were touched first, my conscience aroused, & my hunger & thirst after righteousness consciously developed." Henry felt that listening to good preaching was a vital experience. He wrote to Russell, "You will find a deepening sense of interest in preaching, & a longing even for the days to come round when your soul can be fed with the Gospel." He suggested that if he did not get this kind of preaching at Cambridge, he should go into Boston and listen to James Freeman Clarke, "whose charm for young & old is very peculiar."[9]

A Crisis of Extreme Interest

Bellows's political feelings of preference for Seward rather than Lincoln are indicated in a letter that Annie wrote to her brother. "I suppose you know that Lincoln, or 'old Uncle Abe,' as they call him, has been nominated for the presidency by the republicans. Father & I are *of course* disappointed, as *we* would have much rather had Seward, who deserves it so much more; however I dare say Lincoln will make a good president."[1] Although Bellows was disappointed that William Seward had not been nominated by the Republican Party, he still backed the Republican candidate, Abraham Lincoln. At the end of October, just before the election, he wrote, "It is really a crisis of extreme interest. I suppose there is no serious doubt how it is going. But there is a genuine fear that the *passions* of the South may induce them to take some steps *towards secession* in case of Lincoln's election which would no doubt introduce very painful results." He believed that, "sacred as the *union* is & most precious to my feelings, we are not at liberty to yield any more to Southern threats & secessionists, even to save it." He wished that the "four months were well over, Lincoln installed & the South acquiescent. I expect this, but am not without patriotic anxiety."[2]

Bellows was pleased over "the triumph of the Party of the Union,—of the inauguration of a new policy in our national affairs!" He felt that the free states were very patient with the South, "calm decision in the face of threats of disunion & blood, on the non-extension of slavery." Bellows was "very proud of the people." He felt that some important disturbance would be made in South Carolina, "But nothing that will make us regret, in any event, our present firmness." He had been reading Frederick Law Olmsted's books on the slave states, "candid, cautious, detailed & furnishing the materials of sound judgment rather than mere opinions. . . . They indicate a state of society 200 years behind ours. . . . But for the sake of humanity, I hope we shall stick together . . . I think the threatening game is played out."[3] A few days later he admitted that people in New York were not very much frightened by secessionist threats in South Carolina, and commented that "the wisest merchants seem to think that it will blow itself out. They talk too loud & too much. I hope in mercy, that civil war will not break out."[4]

Bellows's Thanksgiving sermon in 1860 was devoted to the proposition that the North ought to stand firm for the Union, and that threats from the South ought not to deter true patriots from insisting that the Union be held together. The North ought not to wilt under Southern threats.

Early in December the Bellows family was again shaken by sorrow. On 2 December, Henry's mother—actually his stepmother who had served as his mother from a time when he could remember no other—passed away "so peacefully that sister Mary who sat watching her sleeping, did not have time to call brother George from the *fire-place* to the bed, to catch her only sigh as she died!" They had been expecting her death for some hours. Bellows commented,

"I made many prayers at her bed-side at her request. She seemed full of faith & hope altho' without excitement of any kind. Her endurance astonished the doctor. . . . She remembered every body, & talked as long as her voice lasted at intervals."[5]

Political events did not take a turn for the better, and Bellows was worried. "I have been greatly tried by the state of the country," he wrote. "Really it is very threatening. I don't think New England with her older & better civilization knows how exposed the country at large is to anarchy." He feared "very much that violence may terminate the career of some of the leaders in the abolition party." Yet there was no room for concessions. "I would not counsel a back track, nor important *concessions*—but I think if we expect to hold together, it must be by hanging fast to the constitution *as it is* & by invoking all possible support for the federal power." He concluded, "God spare us from civil, servile, and internecine war."[6]

Mrs. George Schuyler added a word of hope to Henry's concern about the country: "Those who have seen Lincoln lately say, that he is a firm, straightforward, prudent man. They are most satisfied with him than they expected. This treason of the Cabinet & President is uniting the North of all parties!"[7]

At the end of the year Bellows received a printed list of the standings of the freshman class at Harvard. It must not have warmed his heart, for Russell had the percentage standing of seventy-five, and he stood thirty-third in a class of fifty-four, although he was ten names higher on the list than the president-to-be's son, Robert Lincoln, who stood forty-third.[8]

As 1861 arrived, Bellows expected the New Year to "be a very eventful one." He felt that not "improbably it may try our patriotism to the utmost & call for sacrifices of which we, in our wonted ease & security, do not dream." He felt that every young man would be tested about the freedom of his country.[9] Bellows realized that all persons with whom he came in contact did not agree with his opinions about the Union. He suggested that he had "to face the most opposite opinions & convictions in my own parish." By 8 January he expected that within twenty-four hours "we shall hear of blood-shed . . . in the collision of S. Carolina with the reinforcements sent to Maj[or] Anderson." He also feared "that general rebellion will occur in the more Southern states, & be put down with rivers of blood." But he felt that it was "time that we showed that we should know whether government means any thing but self-will, in Republican Institutions. The hour has struck for this question & if it strikes some thousands dead, it is a question that must be directly & affirmatively answered."[10]

Bellows also believed that the problem was not one that had been brought about by the recent legislation on the issue of slavery, but something that had been brewing for over twenty years. "More & more it appears that a twenty year conspiracy to break up the Union has existed South, & that they are merely carrying out (as far as they can) the pre-arranged programme." He felt that if "it can only be got into the people's heads in time, that it is not recent legislation on slavery—nor any real encroachments on Southern rights—but actual local ambition, & envy & political fraud that is breaking us up, there will be a great reaction & we shall be spared."[11]

By the end of February, Bellows was pleased with "*Lincoln's* firm tones," which he felt "encourage those who don't believe in compromise." He felt that what the North needed was courage. Lincoln was to be inaugurated on 4 March, and Bellows looked forward to this changing of the old for the new in the White House.[12]

Russell at Harvard found his classmate, Robert Lincoln, little changed because his father was now President of the United States. "Bob Lincoln has returned & is, as far as I can see, the same old sixpence. His father's position doesn't affect Bob's manner at all. He has no airs or graces, & never will have the latter. He will probably 'bleed' his father's pocket-book pretty extensively."[13]

By the middle of the month, Bellows felt that "we are essentially in a state of *war*, so far as suspended commerce . . . is concerned, & like to be so for some time."[14] The economic impact of the war was great in New York City where the banking interests were heavily engaged in financing the cotton industry and cotton growing. This involvement of the North in the mercantile business of the South bothered Bellows exceedingly. Some of his parishioners must have felt the stoppage of trade with the South quite sharply.

Although many thought that war was coming, no one knew exactly when or under what particular circumstances. When the war came, it suddenly galvanized and united the North into action and unity as nothing else could have done. Fort Sumter was fired upon—a Confederate army under General Beauregard fired upon the American flag! Such hostile action angered the people of the North and precipitated them into action. It was an expected action, but when it came it had emotional overtones that could never have been predicted before it happened. Henry Bellows was in the midst of his sermon that April day in 1861. He had debated for a long time with himself as to whether he should preach about the action that the North should take if the fort were fired upon. He had made his resolution. He was preaching about such action when it came. His own words convey the emotion of the day.

On the Saturday night before the news of the firing on Sumter reached New York, Bellows recollected "walking my study nearly all night in the agitation caused by considering the probable effect of a discourse I had carefully prepared on the duty of supporting the government with all our power, should certain contingencies then pending turn, as it was feared they would, into open rebellion on the part of the South."[15] Bellows felt that neither his congregation nor the opinion of the general public would tolerate the unqualified loyalty which he was going to propose that Sunday morning. He felt as he ascended the pulpit stairs that it might be the last sermon he would ever preach to a united congregation. But he was prepared to let the consequences be what they might.

The sermon was half over and was being received in ominous silence when Bellows became aware that some important news was spreading by whispers throughout the congregation. The news that Fort Sumter had been fired upon had reached the ears of Bellows's congregation. Bellows wrote, "Suddenly the hook and line of my discourse, which had hitherto hung loose and free, were nibbled at as by an eager school, and then seized and pulled as by some voracious fish, until I could feel the whole weight of the hearts and minds for which I had been fishing with apostolic hope fastened to the rod." He continued, "The congregation surprised at the heat of the patriotism suddenly evoked by the appalling news that the national flag had been fired at by one of our own States, accepted the discourse as the voice of inspiration, and echoed back with courage and confidence the sentiments I had almost feared to express, yet had not dared to stifle."[16]

The moment Bellows concluded his sermon the people rose and with one voice asked the choir to sing the national anthem, which was joined in by all with intense feeling. The people were united in a general sentiment of indignant patriotism and determination to avenge the insult the nation had received. "From that hour we knew that party feeling had yielded to love of country, and that trade and commerce had resolved to sacrifice their prudential scruples to the duty and passion of national self-preservation."[17] Thus the people were united, as they were also in the South, for the waging of what was to be the bloodiest war in history up to that time, a war that would rage for four long years and which would siphon into its maelstrom millions of young men, some of them from the First Church, and would involve Bellows himself in what was undoubtedly the greatest effort of his life (on behalf of the Sanitary Commission).

The South's attack upon Fort Sumter brought to a head for the Northern intellectuals a whole series of philosophical-patriotic questions which had perplexed them for several decades. If one looks at these intellectuals as a group, and certainly Bellows was one of the leaders, their responses to Southern secession were attempts to intellectually clarify the situation. Yet their responses were often diverse and contradictory. Nathanial Hawthorne's reaction to the war was unusual—he tried to detach himself from the war and the war's meaning. But elsewhere among the intellectual community there was deep thought and much expression of it in public utterances and writings.

As one of the leading spokesmen of the day, Henry Bellows attempted to work out with as much clarity as he could his own moral support of the war. We have already seen that as the news from Sumter was coming in Bellows had prepared himself for the event and was preaching a "patriotic" sermon.[18] He believed that it was God's will that men should "defend the sacred interests of society." A week later in another sermon Bellows developed his theme further. This time he claimed the church is concerned about the interests of the state. He defined the state as "nothing less than the great common life of a nation, organized in laws, customs, institutions, its total being incarnate in a political unity, having common organs and functions; a living body, with a head and a heart . . . with a common consciousness. . . . The state is indeed divine, as being the great incarnation of a nation's rights, privileges, honor and life. . . . "[19] This, as George M. Frederickson states, "was one of the ablest statements of the organic social theory to come out of Nineteenth Century America. Because he could argue that the war was being fought for the maintenance of order and in defense of an inherited way of life, Bellows had a strong position from which to attack all varieties of anti-institutionalism." Even further, "he found courage to hint at the supreme heresy—the idea that all recognized nationalities and established governments rest on the same solid religious basis as that of the United States." This put Bellows in the position of defending Napoleon III, and the Czar of Russia, among others. Frederickson concludes, "Whether Bellows realized it or not, this kind of reasoning could lead to a repudiation of the doctrines of the Declaration of Independence."[20] But in the heat of the post-Fort Sumter intellectual atmosphere Henry Bellows had not really thought it through.

Orestes Brownson, from an entirely opposite theological perspective, also echoed this sentiment of protection of the Northern status quo. He believed that materialism was the principal vice of the North, and somehow in the conduct of the war he felt that there would be a deliverance from this evil. It would enable people who were wholly interested in trade and making money to devote themselves to a more idealistic cause, the safety of the nation.

During the mobilization and after the early defeats these voices from the pulpit and in the printed page helped many Northern intellectuals to get some moral perspective on the war. After the first defeats Henry Bellows wrote in the *Christian Inquirer* on the "moral necessity of the late defeat," and he claimed that "nothing but disaster could thoroughly arouse the country to the efforts, the reforms, and the spirit essential to the proper and vigorous conduct of this war." Many even saw the war as the inevitable struggle within the newly disclosed theories of Charles Darwin as the struggle of the fittest to survive in the inevitable (it was believed) progression to the higher stages of the evolutionary process.

The Air Is Thick with Bayonets

On Monday morning after the Battle of Fort Sumter, President Lincoln put out a call for 75,000 volunteers, the small number indicating that the President, like the enthusiasts in the South, underrated the other's intentions. Men were mobilizing all over the country, developing their own colorful uniforms, and heading toward the capital. Shortly the railroads leading to Washington were overcrowded and in some instances blocked by traffic. Washington was also isolated from the East by the Confederate armies which tore up the rails from Annapolis to Washington. Thus what started out to be a struggle to regain the forts in Southern hands soon became a struggle to preserve the capital from imminent occupation by Southern troops.

Before a week had passed Bellows was fairly certain that the Northern public would respond to the emergency. He wrote, "I have never seen such an extraordinary manifestation of emotional feeling & such a revolution of public sentiment, as had occurred with[in] four or five days. Last Saturday & Sunday were blue days. We did not know where the national spirit was, or how it would act." But by Monday morning, "a generous breath of enthusiasm began to clear

Henry Whitney Bellows, Photo by Matthew Brady, Library of Congress, (probably taken during the Civil War)

the atmosphere & by this time, doubt, disaffection, division, party jealousy, everything hostile to unity & the government has been blown below the horizon." He found that "the most generous, free & consecrated determination exists, to vindicate the flag, maintain the government & hold together the Union."

He had feared that the people of commerce would react badly, but "the rich & prudent are giving the largest support to the government, & New York, I am proud to say." He continued, "Dear old Massachusetts, I could kiss her soil, for her ardor & devotion to liberty. Her regiments have rec'd a most enthusiastic welcome here. Every body is stirring in a good cause." The war was a real thing now. "I have been bidding good bye to the five young men in my own parish going to the Sacred War (not without tears & pride &

sorrow)." And he added an afterthought, "I have thought how fortunate we were in not being compelled to send our son—although willing I hope to give even him—if necessary—for the country."[1] That same day Federal troops were attacked by a crowd in Baltimore.

On the first Sunday of the war—21 April—Bellows preached a fiery sermon in favor of the war. At the climax of his sermon one can almost imagine temperatures rising in the filled church. "We have, then, a holy war on our hands—a war in defence of the fundamental principles of this government—a war in defence of American nationality, the Constitution, the Union, the rights of legal majorities, the ballot-box, the law." He maintained that "We must wage it in the name of civilization, morality, and religion, with unflinching earnestness, energy, and self-sacrifice." He begged his audience not to despise their enemies, for they were in earnest. "They have a desperate game to play." He said, "This is not a war against the South, or against its institutions, its rights, or its people. It is a war for the South, for the whole people, for the Constitution, for the Union." The South was ready to commit national suicide for their interests, and this madness "if allowed to have its way, would bury the American name, and its liberties and glories, in an ignominious oblivion."

Then came the fiery conclusion to the address, in the spirit of Patrick Henry. "March on, then, ye noble patriots from the loyal States of our sacred Union." He told his congregation that the men of 1861 were no more precious nor less brave than those at Lexington in 1776. "Go, then! ye noble sons of Massachusetts and New York, Pennsylvania and Ohio, Rhode Island and young Minnesota! Offer your bodies as the first ramparts to our invaders." He continued, "The ranks will rapidly close up behind you—for this is no time for men to hold their lives dear; no day for cowards, sluggards, or neutrals."[2]

Things were now moving very fast. On 26 April, Henry Bellows was asked if he would consider "the position of chaplain—fighting chaplain—of a squadron of cavalry to be composed of gentlemen; who are anxious to go into active service?" George E. Manning, Jr., who wrote the letter, stressed Bellows's "patriotism," but added, "Our only doubt is whether you will consider yourself at liberty & have time." Henry sent the letter on to Russell and added this note, "I send this as a curious commentary of the times. . . . It is the second overture of this sort I've rec'd!"[3] Bellows had bigger things in mind than to be a fighting chaplain.

On the morning of 25 April, Dr. Elizabeth Blackwell, a friend of Florence Nightingale, and the first woman doctor of medicine in the United States, called together a group of New York women at the New York Infirmary to organize an Aid Society. Their immediate concerns were the conditions on Staten Island where there were now many camps pitched by volunteers on their way to Washington. Ninety-two women, the top ladies of New York society, gathered at the invitation of Dr. Blackwell. They included Mrs. Peter Cooper, Mrs. William Cullen Bryant, and Miss Louisa Lee Schuyler, all members of All Souls. Dr. Elisha Harris, who was the Superintendent of Hospitals on Staten Island, told the women of the conditions of the camps there. Another man whom Dr. Blackwell had invited to this meeting was Henry Bellows, who, along with young Dr. Harris, seems to have been the only other man present at the meeting. Why Bellows was invited is not quite clear except that many of the women were members of his church and he was known to be a leader who could unite many factions in the city. The result of this meeting was a determination to publish a call for all interested women to meet at the Peter Cooper Institute at eleven o'clock the following Monday morning, 29 April. A notice appeared in the Sunday papers announcing such a meeting.

During the days between 25 and 28 April, a series of meetings were held in Bellows's study to plan the organization of a society to coordinate the work of the aid societies. Bellows preached extemporaneously on the war on Sunday 28 April, as he did not have time to write a sermon. Events were moving so rapidly that what happened the first of the week might not be very applicable at the end of the week. His sermons of the two previous weeks were already in print and being widely distributed.[4]

On Monday over 4,000 women gathered in the auditorium of the handsome new educational center so recently built by Peter Cooper for the poor boys of the city. The meeting was opened by no less a dignitary than the Vice President of the United States, Hannibal Hamlin. Two members of the garrison of Fort Sumter spoke of their experiences.

The agenda had obviously been well prepared at those meetings in Bellows's study by the hastily gathered committee, for the entire program for the meeting (in Bellows's handwriting) is contained on four sheets of paper in the Bellows Papers. Dr. Bellows called the meeting to order and asked Vice President Hamlin to take the chair. Bellows then nominated the following officers; as vice presidents: Dr. Valentine Mott, the Honorable Peter Cooper, Rev. Dr. Adams,

Louisa Lee Schuyler, Oil Portrait by Leon Bonnat, Courtesy of the New-York Historical Society, New York City

Hiram Ketchum, Esq., John E. Williams, Esq., and as secretaries: Professor Wolcott Gibbs and Henry D. Sedgwick. Dr. Bellows was then called upon to explain the purpose of the meeting.

After Dr. Bellows spoke, two resolutions were adopted: "1. Resolved, that it is highly expedient to concentrate & methodize the spontaneous & varied efforts now making by the women of New York in behalf of the sick & wounded of the approaching campaign—the better to secure proportion, economy & efficiency in their benevolent labors. 2. Resolved, that to accomplish this end, it is desirable to form a Women's Central Association of Relief; and 3. that a committee of three ladies and three gentlemen be appointed by the chair to report a plan of organization to this meeting." This committee was then appointed to consist of the following persons: Dr. Bellows, Dr. Harris, Dr. Griscom, Mrs. Kirkland, Dr. Elizabeth Blackwell, and Mrs. C. Griffin.[5]

The women present then formed themselves into the Women's Central Association for Relief with a Board of Managers, and Dr. Valentine Mott, one of the world's great surgeons and the dean of American doctors, as its president. This placed the highest authority

Women's Central Relief Association Headquarters at Cooper Union (April 29, 1861 - July 7, 1865), Courtesy of the Museum of the City of New York

of American medicine behind the women's efforts. The office of the new association, which came to be known as "The Women's Central," was in charge of Louisa Lee Schuyler, the corresponding secretary. An office was provided by Mr. Cooper at Cooper Union. Miss Schuyler wrote, "We began life in a little room which contained two tables, one desk, half a dozen chairs, and a map on the wall. . . . We sent out circulars, wrote letters, looked out of the windows at the passing regiments, and talked about our work, sometimes hopefully, sometimes despairingly."[6]

They might well despair, for it appeared as if exactly nothing was being accomplished in Washington. They had hoped to send nurses whom they would train to help in the situation, but the War Department wrote to them that no arrangements whatsoever had been made to receive such nurses. General John Dix, in command of the New York volunteers, threw cold water on the project, although his wife was a member of it. Even Henry Bellows, who looked in

Women's Central Relief Association Officers at Cooper Union (left to right: Mrs. William B. Rice, Miss Louisa Lee Schuyler, Mrs. Griffith, Mrs. d'Oremieuly, and Miss Collins), Courtesy of the Museum of the City of New York

occasionally on the office, said that he felt that in some ways the women's efforts were ill-advised. But the women were undismayed. As Miss Schuyler said, "There is one institution of government we are still privileged to use, and that's the United States Post Office."[7] She enlarged her correspondence with every mail. Women who had sent off their loved ones to a "sacred cause" soon learned of the terrible conditions into which they had been sent. There was little food, and long periods with no food; the first uniforms fell to pieces; and the conditions in the camps were beyond belief. Contagious diseases were spreading among the ill-fed exhausted men with fatalities mounting rapidly. When they were sick, these recruits were piled into churches without running water or toilets, into office buildings, or into shacks hastily cleared of Negro refugees. Here they died. The women frantically asked the army why nothing could be done.

These and other reports came to Miss Schuyler in her Cooper Union office. She intended to pass them on to those in authority. Gradually the sheer number of the letters and the protests forced Bellows and the medical advisers of the women to take steps which they feared might make them look rather ridiculous. They were determined to go to Washington and ask that the Board of Managers of The Women's Central be appointed by President Lincoln as "The United States Sanitary Commission." A special committee was to carry this petition of The Women's Central to Washington so that the effort would be able to coordinate all of the local efforts going on all over the country.

Just a Fifth Wheel?

Henry Bellows was chosen to head the committee that was to go to Washington to seek to have the federal government coordinate the aid programs of the entire country by appointing a Sanitary Commission. He had not personally met Abraham Lincoln nor William H. Seward, the Secretary of State. So Moses H. Grinnell, president pro tem of the Union Defence Committee of the Citizens of New York, wrote a letter introducing Henry Bellows to Abraham Lincoln. He hoped "for him a kind reception at the Executive Mansion." He continued, "The Doctor is alike eminent for eloquence, piety and a large acquaintance with the progress of the age in the development of humanity. He will bring to you the most reliable testimony of how universal is the feeling in support of your policy and your measures for maintaining the integrity of the Union."[1]

By Thursday evening, 16 May, Bellows was in Washington and had checked in at Willard's Hotel. His was the first train to go on the regular route through Baltimore. Some of the passengers had expected difficulty, but none had occurred. Henry wrote to Eliza that they had been subjected to some military surveillance, "but it was not unpleasant." They had their first committee meeting that very evening. He found the "committee to be a very intelligent and agreeable one." He had an interview the next morning at 9:00 A.M. with Dorothea Dix, who had been appointed head of the nurses of the Army. Later they met with the Surgeon General.[2]

Bellows found that The Women's Central and its purpose was taken seriously in Washington. "Every door has opened at our bidding from the President down all the way through the cabinet to the bureaus—& it would almost seem as if we had only to speak our will & have it done." He related to Eliza, "If you had seen your humble husband haranguing the President at the head of his committee, & then the *Generalissimo* of the Army, & then the Major Generals & the Brigadiers—(getting a colonel deposed for drunkenness, & *one* regiment out of rotten quarters into safe ones)—& then all the cabinet officers in turn,—you would really have fancied him suddenly promoted into the office of *premier*." Bellows felt that their reception gave promise of quick success. The Surgeon General of the Army suddenly died, and Bellows felt that now there was "a most providential opening for a new man who will accept our suggestions & carry them out, & we can influence the appointment."

But, he wrote, "Our most important work . . . lies in procuring the appointment of *a Sanitary Commission*, to keep the whole question of army health constantly stirred up here at head quarters, & to preside over the matter in a thorough manner after we retire." He confided to Eliza, "If you knew the vast importance of this move to the health, morals & efficiency of the army & navy you would appreciate the earnestness of my labors in bringing it about. If I can succeed in it, I shall be about ready to sing my 'Nunc Dimittis'—'Now let thy servant depart in peace, for my eyes have seen thy salvation'." Bellows expected his business to keep him in Washington most of a second week.

On 19 May, Bellows had dinner with Salmon P. Chase, the Secretary of the Treasury, "having a delightful & most profitable time." Bellows's opinion of President Lincoln continued to rise. He found the President, "a good, sensible, honest man, utterly devoid of dignity—*without that presence* that assures confidence in his adequacy to his trying position." He further described Lincoln, "His smile is sweet, his mind patient, slow, firm—but I doubt his comprehensiveness. Seward seems to me *cunning*, not frank, not gentlemanly, but able & comprehensive." He felt that "Chase is the superior of all in moral elevation, personal manners, & breadth & positiveness." He found the generals "refined, humane & cordial men. The air is thick with bayonets, sword-knots & uniforms." He was glad that he wore a white cravat and felt that it was "good to have a respectable name to precede one on grounds like this."[3]

On 20 May Bellows talked with the President privately for half an hour in a "plain manner on the subject of my mission. He appeared much better than on the last interview, & I feel that he would probably grow upon acquaintance."[4] He felt that the work was moving ahead. The next day Bellows gave up any idea of returning to New York in the immediate future. "I am so near a result that I do not dare to let go my hold." He believed that "the amount of sickness & suffering among the troops forbids my neglecting anything I can possibly do to bring the matter home to the government." Dorothea Dix had begged him to remain, and "a powerful committee from New York is expected here tomorrow evening."[5]

The committee arrived: Dr. Harris, Dr. W. H. Van Buren, and Dr. Jacob Harsen. The members of this committee were received with politeness. They presented their petition to the War Department. They were respectfully bowed in and bowed out. "The Department regarded us," said Dr. Bellows, "as weak enthusiasts, representing well-meaning but silly women."[6] For twenty days these four men cooled their heels in the capital city and visited the camps around Washington. At the end of that time Bellows and his colleagues appeared to have gone through a transformation. They had hardened into shrewd reformers whom no women would ever again have to set in motion. They had seen the utter incapacity of the War Department and the tragic demoralization of the volunteer army. They knew now that the future of the army and of the whole country depended upon immediate and drastic changes in the method of handling the volunteers.

The committee believed that the situation was one which no purely military effort could reform. What was needed was a system of civilian cooperation and reinforcement to bring the best resources of the nation to the understaffed corps of military men who naturally were concerned more about the military aspects of the struggle than about sanitation.

The committee also discovered that there were some camps that were not so bad largely because they had enlisted women in their ranks. Some regiments, especially from New England and the Northwest, had in their simplicity assumed that they would need some women for housekeeping and nursing. So they enlisted them just like soldiers. The women thus chosen were actually of a type rather well suited for these purposes. They had usually been certified by local clergymen as women of good character or as possessing nursing experience and were not "camp followers."

The War Department had no idea what could be done about the bad conditions. It had enough on its hands in the way of purely military preparations to try to defend Washington. But circumstances were working in favor of Bellows and his committee. Every day brought weeping women to Washington to recover the bodies of their dead. Every day the trains left the capital city with a load of corpses packed in ice. Bellows faced the War Department, "We understand," he said, "that on July 4, President Lincoln will go before Congress and ask for 400,000 volunteers. Our own investigations show that, of the men already recruited, one half will be dead of camp diseases by November 1. Do you think you can go before the country, and ask the wives, mothers, sweethearts, sisters, fathers, and neighbors of these men to send more of them into this shambles?"[7] The harassed officials finally gave up and told the President to let the women clean up the mess.

Bellows was also a diplomat. While Henry cooled his heels in Washington, young Russell evidently had made friends with Bob Lincoln at Harvard. Bellows wrote to Russell, "Mrs. Lincoln, the President's wife, consents to Bob's going on & spending the vacation with you. Ask him in your own & my name & press it on him."[8] Bellows expanded this idea several days later. Mentioning the invitation to Robert Lincoln, he wrote, "I hope you will bring him, as I think he would enjoy it & that it would be a good thing for you & for me. I am destined (I fear) to be more or less in Washington during the war, & it would facilitate my objects to have a *connecting link* with the President & his family. Enough said."[9]

Returning to New York Henry Bellows found himself completely tired out by his Washington endeavors. "I preached extempore this morning," he wrote Russell, "on my Washington experience—combining all I had seen, heard & felt in a discourse on the State of the Nation. Your mother did not like it very well." Mrs. Bellows never did like her husband's extemporaneous discourses. But Bellows thought it was "good, judicious & interesting, not to say eloquent & I wish you had been there to hear." There had been a reporter present, but he only had notes on the speech. "That's the mischief of extempore speech. It is spilled on the ground & gone."[10] said Bellows.

On 5 June Bellows was back in Washington still waiting for the official red tape and apparent apathy to run its course. He persisted, however. He wrote Eliza that "delays are not so dangerous, as they are arrogance in public business. The exhausting nature of waiting on these worn & over-worked officials cannot be exaggerated." He said he "would sooner fight with an alligator & a rhinocerous, than with routine & official apathy. The skins of the last are thicker. I am promised light & deliverance from suspense *to-day*—but promises are poor."[11]

On 9 June, the Secretary of War, Simon Cameron, approved a document providing for the appointment by President Lincoln of a United States Sanitary Commission with power to oversee the welfare of the volunteer army, and to serve as a channel of communications between the people and the government. At the same time Dorothea Dix, who had kept after the War Department, was finally appointed United States Superintendent of Army Nurses with authority to recruit army nurses and to oversee the housekeeping of the military hospitals. She was the first woman ever appointed to an executive position with the United States government.

Now a Sanitary Commission had been appointed. But it had no power except to make suggestions, which could be ignored, and to write reports, which could be filed away in the government files; the commission, as Bellows said, was born paralytic. The commission elected Bellows president, Professor Alexander Bache, vice president, and Dr. John Newberry, secretary for the West. The Washington office was established in the Treasury building in rooms donated by the government. Henry wrote to Russell, "Our commission . . . is ordered by the government & I am placed in the honorable post of chairman. I shall try to put off the duty to the last degree upon younger men—acting myself mainly as an adviser & regulator."[12] These were Bellows's hopes as he became the president of the United States Sanitary Commission, but vain hopes they turned out to be, for in June began the four most active years of Bellows's life, running a civilian organization approved by the government but with no government funds, and at the same time retaining his post as minister of All Souls Church.

Between 9 June and 15 June the committee met continuously, keeping in constant communication with The Women's Central in New York, and reorganized itself as "The United States Sanitary Commission" by adding to itself a number of physicians, army officers, and scientists whose reputations qualified them to be of the highest service at the moment. Bellows and The Women's Central brought to their committee a group that was probably as able as the President's cabinet. There was nothing amateurish about the list of fourteen members of the commission that Bellows proposed to present to the President, names so outstanding that the President would have to approve them. They were taking no chances with commissioners appointed by anyone but themselves. On 13 June, the reorganized commission was presented to President Lincoln. He looked over the document. "I'm afraid it's just a fifth wheel to the coach," he said. Then he took the document and wrote across it "I approve the above. A. Lincoln."[13]

The original members (in addition to Bellows) of the United States Sanitary Commission were:

Professor Alexander Dallas Bache, a grandson of Benjamin Franklin, an influential educator, and Superintendent of the United States Coast Survey. Vice President.

George Templeton Strong, Esq., a successful and public spirited New York lawyer. A diarist whose published work after his death was critical of many of his contemporaries. Secretary.

Dr. Cornelius Rae Agnew, a specialist in diseases of the eye, a front-ranking New York doctor.

Professor Oliver Wolcott Gibbs, most distinguished chemist in the United States. Also an M.D. In 1863 he moved to Cambridge to hold the Rumford Professorship in Harvard College.

Dr. Elisha Harris, a pioneer sanitarian. Practiced medicine in New York City, and in 1855 became superintendent of the quarantine hospital on Staten Island. Helped prepare the "code of marine hygiene" adopted in 1860. The only experienced sanitarian on the Sanitary Commission. He designed the famous hospital car to move the wounded.

Dr. William Holme Van Buren, thrown out of Yale for a student prank, graduated from University of Pennsylvania as an M.D., and settled in New York after a short army career. Member of the surgical staff of Bellevue Hospital, Professor of Anatomy of the University of the City of New York. Declined appointment as Surgeon General of the United States near the end of the war.

Dr. Samuel Gridley Howe, M.D. from Harvard, helped in the Greek revolution against Turkey as surgeon in the Greek fleet. For six years he raised money and sent clothing. In 1831 he was appointed to run the recently founded Massachusetts School for the Blind. He backed Horace Mann in the fight for better schools. He was a good friend of John Brown, but claimed not to have known in advance of the raid on Harper's Ferry. His wife was Julia Ward Howe.

In addition to these there were two members of the United States Army appointed as liaison: Robert C. Wood, M.D., and Major Alexander E. Shiras. During the war other members were appointed to the commission.

On 13 June "Document No. 1." of the Sanitary Commission was printed—a "Plan of Organization." The commission was termed "The Commission of Inquiry and Advice in respect of the Sanitary Interests of the United States Forces." Its duties were divided into two aspects, inquiry and advice. In regard to the first, inquiry, the commission was to decide "what must be the condition and want of troops gathered together in such masses," what is their condition, and "what ought to be their condition, and how would sanitary science bring them up to the standard of the highest attainable security and efficiency." For this branch of inquiry there were to be three committees. The first was for immediate aid. The second committee would inspect all army and navy bases and encampments, and consult with officers, chaplains, and so on, "to collect from them needful testimony as to the condition and wants of the troops." The third committee would investigate cooking, clothing, malaria and other camp and hospital diseases, ventilation, antiscorbutics, sinks, drains, and so on. This was to be a scientific investigation.

The second branch of the work of the commission was to be advice, "opinions and conclusions of the commission [which would be] approved by the Medical Bureau, ordered by the War Department, carried out by the officers and men." There were to be three subcommittees in regard to advice, one in direct relations with the government, one in relation with army men and medical officers, and the third in relation with state authorities and benevolent associations.

Bellows's duties as president of the Sanitary Commission were also vaguely described in Document No. 1. "His duties would be to call and preside over all meetings of the commission, and give unity, method, and practical success to its counsels." This was quite an order for any individual. Also listed were the duties of the vice presidents, the secretary, and the treasurer.[14]

It was also decided that the commission would have two centers, one in Washington and the other in New York. The "Committee of Inquiry" would be based in New York, the "Committee of Advice" in Washington. It was agreed that for convenience the members of these committees insofar as possible should live near the centers. The rest of that week was spent in commission meetings in Washington. They met from 11:00 A.M. to 3:00 P.M. and then from 8:30 P.M. until 11:00 P.M. for three days. They heard "a great deal of *evidence* from different persons, as to the causes of illness among the volunteers & have plans of general prevention & alleviation on foot." They made visits to camps in the Washington area.[15]

Bellows had returned to New York tired on Saturday, and, of course, there had been no time to write a sermon. So he began to draw on what proved to be a godsend during these busy years of the war—his abilities as an extemporaneous speaker. He preached on 16 June to his congregation a talk called "The Value of Life," counseling "prudence & care of it in our military affairs." He felt that he was making progress in this style of preaching. "Mother does not much encourage it," he wrote to Russell, "on account of its *greater* excitement & its *lesser* condensation & dignity. I agree with her in the main in her view of the matter." He believed that "the extempore speech is . . . more pertinent & vital, because the hearers blend their thoughts & feelings with the speaker's." He then mentioned what was reported to be one of his speaking flaws: a speaker must look at the audience and catch their eyes and their spirit. "It is very important (I don't do it) to look the audience in the face & eyes. I have made a great mistake in this—& fear I shall never acquire the power," wrote Bellows. He suggested to Russell that he ought to develop this power of extemporaneous speech, using a "little skeleton" of an outline and then not choosing language beforehand but thinking aloud in speech.[16]

The United States Sanitary Commission opened a New York office at 823 Broadway which handled the general business in the Eastern section of the country, and became a place where the executive committee often met. But the real work of making bandages and other comforts for the men at the fronts was carried on at The Women's Central in Peter Cooper Institute and in various other places. Anna Bellows says that "in All Soul's Sunday school room . . . ladies met to prepare lint, bandages, havelocks, and the thousand and one things necessary for the comfort of the soldier, whether well or wounded. As the war went on, with all its horrors, the desire to save suffering increased, enthusiasm and zeal rose high. Hospitals, ambulances, doctors, surgeons, and nurses were needed to supplement those already on the battle-field."[17]

It was a busy June. Bellows spent most of the rest of the month in Washington getting the commission's work going and obtaining personnel. He took a trip west combining a visit to Antioch College at Yellow Springs with visits to military installations. He did not get back to New York City until Sunday 7 July. The church was closed for the summer so he did not have to preach. He arrived home very tired having traveled three days and nights. He addressed the troops at Cairo, Illinois, the last Sunday evening in June. He wrote to Russell, "My principal address was on the Fourth of July at Camp Pope on the Mississippi near Alton [Illinois], where I made a semi-patriotic, & a semi-sanitary address to a Brigade formed in hollow square of 5,000 noble & earnest men, with American nationalism flashing in their eyes & tipping their bayonets with flame." He wrote that, "it was a heart-stirring scene & I wished only for the voice of Stanton, to be heard by such a vast, inspiring audience." He added that he "bent over nearly a thousand beds of manly suffering . . . in regimental hospitals—some dying, others suffering acutely, others only seriously but not mortally. I heard hardly any where a complaint! Those plain men learn to suffer & be strong. It was a great lesson."[18]

CHAPTER EIGHT

The Making of a Marvel

Things In a Higgledy-Piggledy State

Frederick Law Olmsted was led into the practice of landscape architecture by Calvin Vaux, an attendant at All Souls, in 1858. It was an embryonic profession in the United States. The two won the competition that year for the design of Central Park in New York City. Olmsted was on very friendly terms with George Schuyler, whom he found "an ardent and happy Republican."[1] About this time also, Olmsted became acquainted with Bellows. Olmsted's biographer, Laura Wood Roper, describes Bellows at this time in his life: "Success, having come to him early and easily, had given him a manner ebulliently confident and guilelessly self-satisfied; he enjoyed turning phrases, and his speech was mellifluous and elaborate." But, she wrote, "He was, however, by no means all facade; he was a man of driving energy, quick to turn it to useful social purposes and brilliantly successful in engaging others in them with him, although not businesslike in handling the routine of the enterprises he inspired."[2]

Bellows had watched the development of Central Park from the beginning, and when James T. Field asked Olmsted about someone who could write an article for *The Atlantic Monthly*, Bellows's name was one of those submitted by Olmsted. Bellows was given the assignment, and Olmsted invited him to spend a day with him in the park. The article, published in April 1861, was a success and it was obvious that Bellows understood the philosophy of the architecture of the park.

When the war began in April 1861 Olmsted at first did not find a place in the national tragedy. He had one leg two inches shorter than the other and was unfit for military duty. He was slowly recovering a recent crippling fall from his horse. He encouraged his park employees to enlist. Olmsted watched the raw recruits going to Washington and die like flies as disease took its toll. He watched the organization of The Women's Central Relief Association, and Bellows and his three doctor associates leave for Washington.

On 9 June, when the United States Sanitary Commission came into existence, Olmsted was at that time tempted to try to volunteer

Frederick Law Olmsted, Photo from the frontispiece of Frederick Law
Olmsted, Landscape Architect *(1928), Courtesy of the New-York
Historical Society, New York City*

for service in the army in spite of his ailments, but Bellows had a better plan for his talents. Bellows invited Olmsted to be the executive secretary of the Sanitary Commission and to direct its business in Washington. He invited Olmsted to meet the officers of the commission and to discuss the proposition. At noon on 20 June at Bellows's home in Stuyvesant Square Olmsted met with the commission members—Professor Bache, George Strong, Dr. Agnew, and Professor Gibbs. Unanimously they urged Olmsted to take the post of executive secretary, and when he was assured of three months' leave from his duties at the park, Olmsted at once accepted.

No one had much of an idea exactly what the work of the commission would be, but his job description was worked out as Olmsted met almost daily and nightly for a week with the committee to discuss matters. At the end of the week Olmsted was ready to leave for Washington and to feel his way into his new work. He left for Washington on 26 June and arrived there the evening of 27 June at Willard's Hotel, which was swarming with politicians, office seekers, lobbyists, and idlers.

Olmsted's first assignment was to inspect the army camps in the Washington vicinity. For the next ten days, accompanied by Dr. Harris, he inspected the camps that had sprung up in the wastelands around the capital. Early in July Olmsted drew up a report of their findings—a disheartening document which pointed out that the tents were in bad condition, nothing had usually been done about drainage ditches, latrines were usually nothing but trenches, their edges filthy, their stench unbearable. Clothing of the volunteers was dirty. The food, although usually good, was atrociously cooked, and fresh vegetables were not provided. Olmsted believed that the commission members should have some administrative powers to do something about the conditions in the camps. But the commission did not have such powers, only those of persuasion. Olmsted found that the officials did more to obstruct what ought to be done than do anything about the bad conditions.

Ensconced in his Washington office at the Treasury building Olmsted began to find out what was needed. He made the general permission of the War Department to investigate devastatingly specific. He sent out inspectors to all of the camps around Washington. They asked all of the necessary questions about sanitation and the general conditions of the men. Meanwhile Dr. Newberry and Dr. Bellows set out on a trip throughout the West to survey the troops there. They returned and made an impressive report to the War Department and to The Women's Central. But they were discouraged. The war was in chaos, and everyone's authority was uncertain.

The authorities in Washington were eager for military action against the enemy. They soon got their wish. On 21 July came the Battle of Bull Run which turned into a Union defeat. But it was not a defeat for the Sanitary Commission. They were testing their theories by going along with the army to take care of the wounded. Their ambulances and wagons, under the personal direction of Mr. Olmsted, left from Washington following the army. Sixteen wagons of the Sanitary Commission arrived at Bull Run just after the army deserted it. Under a flag of truce the inspectors and relief agents went onto the battlefield, and for days they worked there, trying to locate and care for the wounded men. The Confederates had filled the canteens of some with water, and had shared with them their own scanty bread. On the third day after the battle the wounded were released on parole and were slowly gathered into the hospitals at nearby Centerville, guided and aided by the Sanitary Commission. The Sanitary Commission was quick to point out to the army command that the very soldiers in the camps they had criticized were the ones who had broken and run. The commission called for the immediate establishment of adequate military discipline. They felt that the volunteer soldiers would welcome such discipline.

Every church, every government building, and every other building that could possibly be spared was filled with the sick and wounded. Dorothea Dix abandoned temporarily the high standards of nursing she was trying to establish and let almost any woman take her turn at nursing. Establishing friendly relations with the new commander of the Army of the Potomac, General George B. McClellan, the Sanitary Commission in league with Dorothea Dix set to work to clear up the cesspools which some of the hospitals had become. They suggested that old buildings of any kind do not make good hospitals and recommended that the "pavilion plan" originally designed by Florence Nightingale be adopted. This meant the erection of new buildings of wooden construction to provide water for washing, bathing, and water closets. Each little hospital was to provide for from thirty to sixty men. Orders were placed by the War Department for such pavilions to accommodate 15,000 men.

Henry Bellows, who had returned from Washington to New York on 17 July, was in Walpole that Sunday when the Battle of Bull Run was fought. He immediately cut short his brief vacation and rushed to New York and thence to Washington. There he found matters in complete disarray. He had been detained in Baltimore for several hours when he missed connections, and this gave him a chance to see Neddy, a young relative who had been in battle. Neddy had been under fire for an hour and a half and now was heading home with his regiment (the New York Eighth) to be mustered out of the war. Bellows thus learned about the battle firsthand. He wrote about Washington, "I find things here in a very higgledy-piggledy state. The *demoralization* of the forces is, I judge very great. It is easy to exaggerate our loss in actual life,[3] but not in discipline & tone. I fear it will take a good while to recover it." He felt that the country was "in for a serious war in which we have much to learn by adversity."[4]

Early in August Bellows finally got back to Walpole for some much-needed rest from his pressing duties. He found the life he had been leading for the past three months, "so new, crowded, responsible and hurried, so immediately in connexion, or in conflict, with the principals in our affairs, . . . so exacting towards faculties & feelings little drawn upon by our professional life—so executive, urgent and direct." But, "happily my fellow-laborers have been high & noble men, free from narrowness, jealousy, or self-seeking, their society a constant instruction, & their co-operation a real & potent support. I have never worked with any body of men, so pleasantly & profitably, & can hardly see how we were so fortunately consorted & so fitly composed." Yet the tasks were difficult: "Our labors have been truly severe—both in the strain & the judgment, in the prudence & persistency required in overcoming official obstinacy & ignorance; and in the actual use & application of our powers as inspectors & advisers in camps & hospitals."[5]

By September the work of the commission had grown larger and larger. The meetings of the commission, at which Bellows presided as chairman over a group of a dozen active and thinking men, he found challenging but exhausting. On 6 September he wrote to Eliza, "Yesterday I was *ten hours* in session, & thinking all the rest of the time. It is no joke to have these dozen active-minded men to preside over, & requires all the alertness and attention & judgment I can command."[6]

Bellows also felt that the probing inspections of the Sanitary Commission were gradually producing results. "We are coming into close quarters with Gen. McClellan and with the War Department! They have gradually felt the necessity of asking our advice & acting upon it, & now we are almost embarrassed with the extent of our power & responsibility." He had spent three hours on 11 September with the general and the Secretary of War "in warm & earnest discussion of the defects of the Medical Department of the Army, & the necessity of cutting a great deal of the red tape that now strangles the health & comfort of the troops. They are both resolved to be guided in these matters very much by the commission, & we have our duties correspondingly dignified & extended."

Bellows wrote a long description of General McClellan, and summarized by saying that "he looks like one who always had succeeded & always would succeed." Bellows also found McClellan "a product of America—a kind of bright, consummate flower of our soul-road, telegraphic & money-making system—with all that is best in young America distilled into his veins." He continued, "He is neither an Englishman, nor a Frenchman, nor a German, but an American—unreserved with those he has reason to trust, rapid in his judgments & confidences, extending little or no precedent to age or even others' expectations. He goes straight to the point & does the thing."[7]

Bellows summarized his work, "I have been in Washington for the last ten days, & go home tomorrow. Our work in the commission goes on swimmingly. We have fought through a kind of bloody campaign, with the jealousies & formalities of a little close-corporation, called the 'Regular Army'." But he added, "This purpose we have balked." They had "acted not merely as a board of military health, but as a kind of Cabinet & Counsel of War—boldly seizing anomalous powers, advising the government, & seeking to influence the men, military & otherwise who 'command the position'."[8]

Early in October the Sanitary Commission moved out of the rooms in the Treasury building, "as we were only on sufferance in the Treasury building." They moved to new quarters supplied by the government at 244 "F" Street. The government had also supplied the Commission with six saddle horses to ride about town and to inspect nearby camps.[9]

Bellows himself had an interview with Abraham Lincoln on Wednesday, 16 October. The next day the entire commission met at 9:00 A.M. with the President. Bellows called it "a very valuable & impressive interview. . . . We appeared in our whole strength—& with some extra support from a few associate-members." He "addressed the President at length on the doings of the commission & we rec'd an hour's very gracious & sympathetic intercourse with the President. It was felt we had reached an important stage when the President in this stately interview paid us such marked compliments." Bellows also "made a visit with the Secretary of State Mr. Seward & had a very satisfactory interview with him. Our affairs go on with singular success & we are in full blast."[10]

By December the Sanitary Commission had been so successful that it was beginning to be attacked in certain quarters. Henry Bellows wrote to Russell, "We begin to suffer from *attacks*, which is a proof that we are felt. You can't correct abuses without offense, & we are likely to catch some sharp words & blows; but never mind. Our motives are single, our cause sacred, our methods honorable—& we must be ready to receive, as we are ready to give blows in the cause."[11] Bellows had just returned from another stint in Washington, and the fact that the commission was being attacked more pleased than worried him.

Great Events Are Happening Every Day

Simon Cameron had aroused the wrath of Abraham Lincoln when in his annual report at the close of 1861 he recommended the arming of the slaves in the South. Although Edwin McMasters Stanton[1] was Cameron's legal adviser, he was nominated and appointed to succeed Cameron as Secretary of War on 15 January 1862, and took office on 20 January. Bellows had breakfast with Stanton and his wife two days later to talk over matters of concern to the Sanitary Commission and the War Department. Bellows found little time to open a newspaper or write letters during this period in Washington, his duties were so pressing. He wrote to Eliza, "Our relations with the new secretary are now established most strongly & cordially. I breakfasted with him yesterday & had two hours of confidential talk, which I think established a truly hearty & permanent friendship. He is a man of soul, transparent, honest, sturdy, right to the point." Bellows also found that Stanton's young wife was very "interested in the account of the commission & on whose sympathy I count."[2]

Several days later Bellows and Strong had an hour's free conversation with the President at which time Lincoln largely told stories and anecdotes. Strong's conclusions after this interview with the President, like many of his conclusions, are interesting. "He is a barbarian, a Scythian, yahoo, or gorilla, in respect of outside polish . . . but a most sensible, straightforward, honest old codger. The best President we have had since old Jackson's time at least. [Jackson was Strong's ideal President.] His evident integrity and simplicity of purpose would compensate for worse grammar than his, and for even more intense provincialism and rusticity."[3]

By the middle of February the Sanitary Commission was discussing winding up its affairs and resigning. They felt they were getting no cooperation or support from the government. Everyone was making promises but nothing was being done about the promises. Strong said, "I heartily approve of the proposition to resign. We have been shielding the Medical Bureau all this time from the hurricane of public wrath its imbecility would have raised by our volunteer work. . . . The Bureau is still imbecile, notwithstanding our remonstrances. For our own sake, we had better retire and leave the responsibility where it lawfully belongs."[4]

However, the more the members of the Sanitary Commission thought of disbanding the organization that had been put together with so much effort, the less it seemed to be the thing to do. The only thing that really hampered them were the finances. "Our experience has recently so abundantly proved our usefulnes, that we do not see how we can devise violence to humanity, give up our organization." Bellows also felt that "things are now so thoroughly organized & are working so satisfactorily, that . . . the commission members will not be so pressingly necessary."[5]

The work of the Sanitary Commission also proved to the Army that they themselves ought to take over this aspect of the military establishment. Actually, the work of the Sanitary Commission was the first medical field service ever worked out in detail for any army. An act of Congress of 11 March 1864 decreed this kind of field service as a part of the armed forces, although actually it was in effect long before Congress got around to formally recognizing the fact.

During this period General McClellan and General Lee exchanged letters and agreed henceforth to treat unarmed surgeons, Sanitary Commission agents, and other medical relief personnel as neutrals or noncombatants. The Sanitary Commission also formally adopted what had long been its practice (almost from the beginning), to draw no distinction in medical service and the relief of suffering between Union and Confederate soldiers. These formulations worked out between the medical corps of the Army and the Sanitary Commission became the basis of the Geneva Convention of the International Red Cross under which relief work and the care of the wounded and prisoners of war are more or less still carried on today among those countries that recognize the Geneva Convention. Among those who were especially concerned to watch the progress of the work of the Sanitary Commission at this time was an international committee in Geneva, Switzerland, under the leadership of a young Swiss, Henri Dunant, who was trying to evolve an international version of the Sanitary Commission.

In the middle of March Bellows, Strong, and Van Buren made a trip into northern Virginia to visit some of the camps. Conditions were primitive, and Strong says that the three of them slept in their shawls and overcoats on the floor. "Van Buren snored in a steady, severe, classical style: Bellows in a vehement, spasmodic, passionate sturm und drang Byronic way, characteristic of the Romantic School."[6]

Thomas Starr King was hard at work raising funds for the Sanitary Commission in California, and on 18 March he sent a thousand dollars to Bellows. Starr King wrote that the telegraph had brought the Californians news that "there had been a great battle at Manassas & a total rout of the enemy. Afterwards we learned that it was a *retreat* of the scoundrels." King wanted to be certain that the war would settle the slave question, "& yet if its Moloch arrogance isn't crushed, Jeff Davis will be elected next President of the nation."[7]

The spirits within the Sanitary Commission were raised considerably when Dr. William A. Hammond, a comparatively young assistant surgeon in the army, was commissioned Surgeon General with the rank of Brigadier General on 25 April 1862. Their politicking to get rid of seniority and have appointments in the Army Medical Corps based upon ability had been successful—or so it seemed.

In April 1862 the campaign began on the Peninsula, as McClellan made a strong attack in the direction of Richmond. The Sanitary Commission by this time had convinced the army that to take care of the stragglers, the sick, and the wounded was a very important part of fighting a war. The Hospital Transport Service made history on the Peninsula. Mr. Olmsted made a contract with the Army to remove all of the wounded incapable of being restored to action within thirty days. In working out the service, full use was made of "lady superintendents" who could establish the standards of housekeeping and train soldier-nurses. They did this by rebuilding old ships and making them into hospital ships. They had a fleet of six hospital ships going up the York River and making trips to Boston, New York, Philadelphia, and Baltimore, taking away the sick and wounded and bringing back stores and added personnel as needed.

On 3 May a telegram arrived in New York from the Sanitary Commission "calling for nurses, & without delay." Bellows reported that "seven or eight ladies . . . volunteered out of my own parish, and that in the course of the next day, we got together five surgeons, ten dressers, thirty-two male nurses, eight ladies, & ten servant women, & two clerks & despatched them via the Balt[imore] & Norfolk boat to Yorktown via Fortress Monroe." Bellows himself "left with nineteen women & two clerks . . . went to Easton's Hotel & felt very much like Brigham Young traveling with his harem." To Russell he also commented, "Your mother seemed to enjoy it exceedingly! I was amazed at her offer & wish to go—but encouraged it on the general principles; believing that the extra exertion in the self-sacrificing way, always *pays*, & that moral tonics are invaluable."[8]

On Tuesday 6 May, Henry Bellows took this large contingent of volunteers from New York to Baltimore to staff the hospital ship *Ocean Queen* which was near Fortress Monroe. Bellows headed the contingent. "Ladies going as superintendents of nurses" included none other than Mrs. Henry Bellows, Mrs. George Strong, and Mrs. Joseph Allen. There were eight of them. There was also a matron, assistant matron, a laundress, four upper chambermaids, and four lower chambermaids, who were servants in the homes of the superintendents of nurses.[9]

Bellows left the women in Baltimore and went on to Washington for work with the Sanitary Commission. He had time there to reminisce about the "nineteen women" in the party he had left at Baltimore. "Eliza seemed to enjoy the escape from common-place life very much. I have not seen her in as good spirits for a long time." After spending the night in Baltimore Bellows had put the ladies in charge of Lieutenants "and sent them aboard the Norfolk boat to be transferred this morning" to small boats that would take them to the Fortress. Olmsted had planned to pick up about 2,500 of the wounded men from the Peninsula and put them aboard various hospital ships. The one with the ladies on it would probably go to New York.[10]

On 9 May Mrs. Bellows wrote to "Dear Friends" a long letter describing her experiences after leaving Henry at Baltimore. She was on the steamboat *Wilson Small* off West Point, Virginia. The ladies had reached Fortress Monroe on the *Adelaide*. At Fortress Monroe they visited the hospital. "There I first saw wounded men, one with an arm off—next [to] him one apparently dying of loss of blood from [a] wound in the back—another who had been nearly a year in the room, nearly recovering." She found the hospital "clean & well ventilated." They embarked on the *Nelly Baker* for Yorktown. They were apparently not expected there and waited on the dock for three hours until several doctors appeared. They saw that the *Ocean Queen* was "crowded with fever & dysentery patients." They did not go on the *Ocean Queen* as yet but took on wounded from the recent battles on the small boat, the *Wilson Small*. Eliza remarked that they "made them so comfortable that it must have seemed like Heaven to the wounded men." The ladies "were very glad they happened to be New York men." Mrs. Strong "showed great pluck. She and Mary Gardner with their women went on board the "Stare" crowded with wounded & dying & remained three or four hours ministering to them under circumstances more trying than ours." About 150 sick and wounded were loaded on the *Knickerbocker* and the ladies accompanied them to Fortress Monroe. Mrs. Bellows's party went on the *Daniel Webster* to the same destination. They ministered to the wounded all night on the trip. Some had fever, others were moaning in distress, and some of the wounded were very near death. The weather was good and supplies were plentiful, Mrs. Bellows reported.[11]

Back in Washington Bellows was having his troubles. All his efforts had not kept the *Ocean Queen* for the continued use of the Sanitary Commission. It had been ordered to the Gulf of Mexico by the Navy. With the President and the Secretary of War still in Yorktown not much decision-making was going on in the capital. Bellows had to stay over in Washington until they returned the early part of the following week. He was, however, very optimistic. "Great events are happening every day!" he wrote to Eliza. "The feeling is growing that the enemy is on his last legs & McClelland's stock rises. The victory at N.[ew] Orleans is immense. We expect to hear before night that Norfolk is in our possession & Richmond perhaps in a day or two." His optimism was based on reports from the front where things for the moment seemed to be going well for the Union cause.[12]

Bellows had waited in Washington for the return of President Lincoln and Secretary of War Stanton because the government had been procrastinating in the appointment of the persons authorized by the Medical Bill. Bellows cooled his heels and waited. Eventually it became necessary from the standpoint of the Sanitary Commission which had worked so hard getting the bill framed and through Congress that he do something. He called on Stanton on the morning of 13 May. He had waited fifteen minutes and was starting down the stairs when Stanton came up. Stanton recognized him, and said good morning. Bellows asked, "Can you see me a minute?" Stanton replied, "Yes, walk in," amid the stares and evil looks of the several dozen other persons who were waiting in the office to see the Secretary of War.

The trip to Virginia and the Peninsula had evidently been a difficult and exhausting one. Stanton denied that he was ill, although from his testiness Bellows decided that he was putting on a good front. Bellows also felt that he was "a man who presumes on the helplessness of a clergyman." However, he felt that Stanton was "honest, *and suspicious* that other men are not so." He believed that Stanton was in bad physical condition, and he feared "an internal temper and cerebral condition which will come to some disagreeable end—if it continues to increase."

Amid obvious hostility Bellows pressed Stanton, expressing hope that the appointments under the new bill would be made as soon as possible. Stanton tested Bellows by asking what his concern was in all of this. Bellows replied, "*We know* who the proper men are, and have presented them in a letter Dr. Van Buren has left with you. There may be other men as good—but we do not feel that there are. The service is suffering immensely for prompt action in this matter, and we cannot feel easy while this action is delayed, or willingly see it take a wrong direction." Stanton told him that the government would act "as soon as it sees its way clear," and that was the end of the interview.[13]

The members of the Sanitary Commission and particularly Bellows were tired of the constant meetings in Washington. It was therefore decided in May to set up a branch office in New York. Bellows had evidently used his office at home as his headquarters, for Mrs. Bellows complained, "We are tired of being called up at all hours of the night to receive telegraphs—two a day is now no uncommon thing." As a result of these constant interruptions Bellows rented an office at 823 Broadway near Broome Street "to systematize the business as far as possible." Mrs. Bellows, however, had risen to the occasion. Forgetting her own illness for a while she had made two trips on the hospital ships from the Peninsula to New York.[14]

In Saint Louis there was a branch of the Sanitary Commission which went its separate way. Bellows had pleaded with Dr. William G. Eliot, the moving spirit and also a Unitarian minister, to unite it with the United States Sanitary Commission. On 23 May, Eliot sent a copy of a printed report of the Western Sanitary Commission to Bellows, and appended a letter in which he spoke of some of the conflicts which had arisen, particularly in the raising of money and the collection of stores for the armies. He described the situation, "though not working exactly together, I regard it as being in parallel lines, which lie so near together that it is the best mode of cooperation."[15] Bellows always considered the Western Sanitary Commission's independence to be due to the intransigence of Eliot. He was particularly perturbed that this came from another Unitarian minister. Eliot's answer was that there were really two distinct theaters of the war, and the people in Saint Louis were nearer the struggles on the Mississippi River. The people in the East should take care of the Army of the Potomac.

On a trip to Cincinnati, in company with Dr. Moore, the Medical Director of the Army, Bellows visited all of the hospitals in the city. "I saw a great deal of suffering & a great many frightful wounds, which the doctors generally taking me for a *medical* man, insisted on my *seeing critically*. So bandages were unwound & wounds exposed in a manner to have driven me distracted a year ago, but which I now stand with professional non-chalance." In Cincinnati he found a hospital which the Sanitary Commission felt was "a model of sanitary excellence."[16]

Continuing on to Chicago Bellows preached on Sunday morning at the First Church, and felt that "judging by the straining I saw" that his sermon had been well received. He had difficulty getting permission to visit the 10,000 Confederate prisoners in Camp Douglas five miles from Chicago. When he saw the camp he wrote, "I did not much wonder when I got there that the government did not want the place seen. For a more disgusting hole I never witnessed." He described the camp, "the ground is a wretched prairie, low and half swampy—the barracks are divided by narrow alleys, in which drains of stagnant, green, slimy water stand open. Rotten straw, bones, all imaginable filth & vileness are accumulated. The sinks & cooking-places are inconceivably dirty." He found that "two regiments of our troops guard these prisoners—who look sad, weary & disgusted." He said that he "carefully inspected the place, attended by a surgeon; & when I got to the hotel, wrote a full letter to Col. Hoffman, telling him what the responsibility of keeping the men in such a compound was; begging him to abandon it; to remove the prisoners & burn the barracks, as the only purification possible. I hope it will have some effect." Bellows did not want to say anything publicly in order not to embarrass the government, but his comment was, "such neglect is abominable."

Bellows then took the night train for Cleveland and visited the Women's Auxiliary of the Sanitary Commission. This group had over 200 affiliated societies, "& has furnished more than 300,000 articles" for the commission. Some of the local clergy called upon him, and in the evening he addressed a large group at the Presbyterian Church "composed of all the leading citizens, in the interests of the San[itary] Commission."[17] He found great enthusiasm accorded his address. On his way home he also found time to visit the Inebriate Asylum in Binghamton, New York.

Back in New York Bellows took the occasion of the national holiday on the Fourth of July to write to Thomas Starr King to pour out his discouragement about the conduct of the war, and particularly the defeat of McClellan's army in front of Richmond. "We have lost 50,000 men in McClellan's army since it left Washington three months ago! The best he can do is to *hold his own* until reinforcements reach him." Bellows also believed that the Confederates were at a stage of final exhaustion, and would not last too much longer. But he felt that the war would continue for a long time, and added, "Literally it would take little to drive my anxious heart to this step, & if it be necessary to give example of the sacredness of the cause, I shall off with gown & on with uniform." Bellows believed that the chief reason that McClellan had been so unsuccessful was that he constantly delayed and did not take advantage of his situation, but he felt that the war against the South must be carried on until the South surrendered.[18]

Bellows's former parishioner, now living in San Francisco, Robert Swain, wrote to Bellows to tell him that what was left over from a Fourth of July celebration, $2,400, was being sent to the Sanitary Commission. He commented on the good work of Thomas Starr King, "I cannot tell you how much good Mr. King has done and is doing here. To his exertions more than to all other influences combined is the General Government indebted for the loyalty of California." Swain stated that "before the inauguration of Mr. Lincoln and before the people of this state knew *where* they stood Mr. King stepped in the breach and *made* controlled and directed public sentiment until the election which asserted our loyalty." King had "laboured increasingly in this city and in the hottest secession mining camps of the interior, and by his surpassing eloquence and patriotic appeals *saved* us from a fierce civil war on the Pacific Coast. I hope the Government will appreciate the value of his services as the people *here* do." Swain also reported that "our new church proceeds admirably."[19] They hoped to build a fine edifice and had the necessary amount subscribed.

By the first of September Bellows decided that he must go back to Washington. The reports from the battlefields were very mixed. The Second Battle of Bull Run had just been fought and the new General of the armies, John Pope, had suffered a bad tactical defeat in a bloody battle. Olmsted was being treated for jaundice at Saratoga, and so Bellows wanted to go to the capital to see exactly what the state of things was within the Sanitary Commission. It was a low point in morale for the commission. To go to Washington, Bellows wrote, was "gall & wormwood to me, in my present frame of body & mind. . . . The position of the commission under the new Surgeon General is so stripped of importance that if I could get it to commit 'hari-kari' I should do so." He continued, "it is my hope that at our next regular meeting, we shall formally abandon all our *practical work*, if not our whole existence. We have achieved the great end of our existence, the reform of the Medical Department, & can now safely fling our once urgent duties back upon the Government."[20]

Two days later in Washington Bellows discovered the depths to which the Union cause had foundered by the recent defeats. When he reached the office of the Sanitary Commission he found it "crowded with doctors & civilians—including the Surgeon General, the Medical Director & other functionaries of importance." One of the Sanitary inspectors had been down to the battlefield at Bull Run and had been captured. He had "been suffered to escape." This agent had reported that the battle had not been as bloody as was at first supposed. He reported the dead at 3,000, the wounded at 2,000. Many of the wounded were prisoners, and "many must have died of neglect on the battlefield." He had reported that the dead lay everywhere unburied. The rebels were now advancing, and the Union Army was retreating toward Washington. The Army, Bellows reported, was "demoralized by its recent humiliating experiences." McClellan was now back in favor after both John Pope and Irvin McDowell had failed, and he felt that they could defend Washington against the rebel forces. Bellows found no panic in Washington, only "a serious feeling of doubt here as to our position." The capital had been turned into a hospital waiting for the sick and wounded. Bellows confided to Eliza that he thought "the Real North will not arise in its majesty, till Washington is actually taken & destroyed. The people seem a thousand miles in advance of the Rulers." He wrote his "faith in the wisdom of the Providence behind these clouds is perfect."[21]

But other more positive actions were in the offing. On 16 September, Bellows received an invitation from Parke Godwin and

James McKaye to be a member of a delegation "to urge upon the administration the policy of emancipation." A date for a meeting was set for Mr. McKaye's at 72 East 19th Street for Thursday 18 September.[22]

A day before this meeting came the battle of Antietam. It was the single bloodiest day of the war. Union casualties were officially put at 2,108 killed and 9,549 wounded and 753 missing. Confederate losses were put at 2,700 killed, 9,024 wounded, and about 2,000 missing.[23] It had been a terrible battle. McClellan hesitated and Lee slipped back into Virginia the next night. By many it was considered the decisive battle of the war, but the result was actually indecisive.

The concern of the Sanitary Commission was the great number of wounded simply left on the field. Bellows described the work: "After Antietam . . . nearly 10,000 of our own wounded, besides many of the enemies, were left, an immense proportion of the whole shelterless in the woods and fields, without any adequate supply of surgeons, and with not a tenth part of needed medical stores." The Union medical stores "were locked up in the block of the railroad, between Baltimore, the base of supply, and the battlefield." The Sanitary Commission, however, had sent a wagon out daily "for some time to meet this anticipated difficulty." Bellows added, "for four days the medical director received no government supplies, and the wounded were mainly dependent meanwhile on the stores of the commission."[24] The only chloroform available for amputations was that supplied by the Sanitary Commission.

On 18 September, Thomas Starr King wrote Bellows a letter containing news which Bellows had received long before through the new telegraph system. King and other gentlemen in San Francisco had pledges of $100,000 for the Sanitary Commission, a tremendous sum in the light of their small budget; the only question had been whether it was to be sent to Bellows in entirety or some to Dr. Eliot and the Western Sanitary Commission in Saint Louis. As King put it to Bellows, "we belong to the west, you know." Finally it was decided that it would all be sent to Bellows who would apportion it equitably. "Let him have a fair bite when it gets there," wrote King.[25] The donation encouraged Bellows at a time when he despaired of the Sanitary Commission, which on several occasions thought of finishing up its work and disbanding. The money arrived just at the time of the battle of Antietam.

Robert Swain wrote a letter to Bellows about the collection "for the benefit of the sick and wounded soldiers and seamen of the Army and Navy." Although King himself had written to Bellows that the work was largely done by others, Swain had a different opinion, "You must give the credit of this great movement to Mr. King *entirely.*" Swain told Bellows King had stomped from one end of the state to the other with this purpose in mind. Swain estimated that the fund would go way over $100,000.[26]

On 28 September, King again wrote to Bellows that an additional $100,000 had been collected, and that he felt that the interior cities would be able to raise a like amount. He had been speaking in these cities, and the response to the appeal was most encouraging. Again, part of the money was to go to Saint Louis to Dr. Eliot, but no amount was specified.[27] Later, the portion of the second sum that was to go to Dr. Eliot was stipulated to be $30,000. Someone telegraphed Eliot that he was to receive $50,000, and eventually Bellows was asked to send that amount to him. But King promised that from now on "you will not be hampered by our committee who are unanimously in favor of making you Commander in Chief now, & successor to Uncle Abe in 1864."[28] At the end of October Thomas Starr King sent to Bellows another $50,000 for the Sanitary Commission.

On the evening of 11 December 1862 Bellows spoke for an hour and a quarter on the work of the Sanitary Commission to a distinguished crowd at the Academy of Music in New York. Bellows described his audience as "a very weighty collection of citizens." Bellows opined that his long speech was very successful, "so far as carrying the audience along with me went." He wrote to Russell that he "had a statement to *make*" and he probably knew as much or more than anyone else on the subject of the benevolences of the nation to the soldiers and sailors. It is well to know "what you are talking about," he wrote to his son.[29]

George Strong wrote, "He was clear, compact, and forcible; kept the large audience wide awake for about an hour and a quarter . . . Dr. Bellows has a most remarkable faculty of lucid, fluent, easy colloquial speech and sympathetic manners, with an intensely telling point every now and then, made without apparent effort. A most enviable gift. The meeting was fuller and went off better than I expected."[30]

Some Hard Nuts to Crack

In spite of the war, the Sanitary Commission, his ministry, and many personal activities, Bellows was trying hard to be sure that Antioch College did not go down the drain because of the war. He was trying to secure a gift of $25,000 from Thomas Whittridge of Baltimore. There also were rumors abroad that Harvard was considering Thomas Hill, President of Antioch, to be their next President, a job that Bellows obviously coveted. A letter from Bellows to Hill is an interesting footnote to this rivalry. He wanted Hill to remain at Antioch because "your special powers, are as a *teacher* & as an *intimate influence* through *personal contact* with young men." He wrote that he felt that this personal influence was important to the highest degree at Antioch. Bellows felt that Hill would find this only to a limited degree at Cambridge. "You know what a Harvard President is—a dignified, distant gentleman, administering the *discipline* of the college in moral cocked-hat & knee-breeches—& looking after its financial interests."

Then the real message is revealed: "I would have my own ideas of what a President of Harvard should be, & carry them out with whatever amount of antagonism & contention might be necessary. But you are too peaceful & gentle to take such a course. They wouldn't have so dangerous a man as I on this account, & they would have you, I dare say, because they would expect to lead you on the same string that the rest have followed." However, if Antioch did go down he advised Hill to go to Harvard if it were offered to him.[1]

Hill answered Bellows's letter a week later. He suggested that if Mr. Whittridge did not give the sum of $25,000 to Antioch that they ought to close the college for the duration of the war. Hill does not mention Harvard at all in his letter, but said that he had now "several glorious opportunities of usefulness which may be closed against me before many weeks have past." He was therefore naturally concerned about Mr. Whittridge's prospective gift.[2]

Just a week later, Bellows wrote a fateful letter to Thomas Hill. He had had two letters from Mr. Whittridge. Both of these letters had been disappointing, and Whittridge was saying now that he might *perhaps* give $5,000 or $10,000. This simply was not enough of a promise of funds to keep Antioch going, and Bellows instructed Hill to close down the college in July for the duration of the war at least. He also told Thomas Hill that he was free to accept any other offers. Harvard picked Hill, and for a second time Bellows was passed over.

In closing Antioch Bellows suggested that they must "*surrender* to the times, to the apathy of the Unitarians, the stupidity & bad faith of the Christians.[3] God knows how it grieves my affections, mortifies my pride, disappoints my hopes, & almost embitters my heart, to give up an enterprise in which I have buried so much of my influence, my time, my money, my prayers & my good name. It is a bitter pill to swallow."[4] He didn't believe that the ten years of the Antioch experiment had been wasted, however.

Another disappointment concerning Antioch had been that a member of All Souls, Robert Clarkson Goodhue, who had recently died, had left All Souls $10,000 in his will but had not provided anything for Antioch. Bellows remarked that Goodhue "thought Antioch too uncertain to be a good investment of charity. This has destroyed my last hope." Bellows noted that "this man was one of the most generous & intelligent of my monied friends." Robert Goodhue, the son of the shipping merchant, Jonathan Goodhue, had died at the early age of forty-five—much beloved by Bellows and the congregation. Much to Bellows's surprise he had left Bellows personally $5,000 "as a token of affection." Bellows pleaded with Russell in a twentieth-birthday letter not to speak about this bequest, for "I did not know it till *after* I had spoken at his funeral." Bellows said how proud it would make him if his own son would be "like him [Goodhue] in real, fixed, Christian worth;—& justice & gratitude to God for his goodness in giving me such a son, compels me to add, on his twentieth birthday, that he is not *unlike* him whom I have praised."[5]

In May Bellows sent a check for $1,000 to Thomas Hill at Antioch. This was in fulfillment of a pledge that he had made to the college. He still owed $500 which he intended to send in July, and he wrote to Hill, "with that I hope to close my thankless experience & connexion with Antioch College. She & her belongings have cost me thousands, worlds of labor & anxiety, & oceans of abuse & suspicion." And he added, significantly, "I am pretty well persuaded that it is alike the interest & the duty of us Unitarians to *drop* the concern very much into Christian hands; boosting them no further & letting them sink to their own level."[6] He was at a loss as to whether to resign before commencement or participate and then to resign. He also congratulated Thomas Hill on being elected as the new President of Harvard.

Bellows did go to Yellow Springs, Ohio, for the meeting of the trustees of Antioch College at the end of June. The college, now completely free from debt, became a high school for the duration of the war. The Christian denomination agreed to take complete responsibility for this period, and Henry Bellows wrote to his wife that if the Christians did not succeed "then not *I*, but the Unitarian body, must take up the college."[7] He had had a change of heart.

One of Henry Bellows's best qualities, and one which made him such a fine churchman and national leader, was his inability to take a fixed position on anything until he had thoroughly looked at both sides of an issue. As the war wore on and the North had reverses, the bitterness among many Northerners grew and fanaticism increased. When Bellows tried to combat this biased view by talking about some of his experiences among Southern people when he lived in Louisiana and Alabama during his early years, his words were often greeted with anything but enthusiasm. When Bellows wrote about some of his experiences with Southerners who were at least gentlemen and human beings, Samuel P. Parkman wrote him a stinging letter. "You will doubtless have many letters of thanks from your Southern friends for your earnest praises of Southerners & Slavery. I think every Northern man & woman whose feelings you have outraged by them, ought also to write to you, to bear testimony against such sentiments." He continued, "mothers, wives, & sisters at the North can never forget how you have eulogized those traitors who have with premeditation of years—brought all the horrors of war upon their country."[8] The unforgiving spirit exemplified by Parkman made the post-Civil War period such a dark one in American history and set back the resurrection of the South and the emancipation of the blacks. This kind of righteousness was not part of Henry Bellows's nature any more than it was a part of the character of his Commander in Chief, Abraham Lincoln, whose attitude of extending the friendly hand was also misunderstood.

Bellows defended his point of view about his speech in Brooklyn which had been widely reported in the papers and had so incensed Samuel P. Parkman and others. He wrote, "would you believe that the end & object of my brief concession to Southern quality, is so wholly lost sight of—that I am belabored in the press & by private letters, with *outraging* Northern sentiment, & abused like a disloyal pick-pocket." He continued, "It must be that I overstretched prudence in my desire to make a fulcrum by which to work my lever. I wanted to take the wind out of the sails of Southern Sympathizers & resurgent democrats who are striving to turn the good qualities of the Southerners to the account of compromise & subversion, & to turn them just *the other way*—acknowledge as much as possible in their favor, & convert it into a fresh reason for fighting them more resolutely & fiercely!"[9]

The Unitarians in San Francisco, under the able leadership of Bellows's friend Thomas Starr King, were planning to build a church, and King wrote to Bellows to give him some of the details.

He had spent four days in the interior cities of California speaking about the work of the Sanitary Commission and collecting money. King had plenty of things to do, but he felt that the new church building was of prime importance. The new church was to cost $50,000 in addition to the $18,000 spent for the land. "A new organ [is] *to be built out here* (one of my hobbies)," wrote Starr King, "to cost four thousand & all to be paid for in a year. It will be a very hard pull. But I must carry it through, in spite of war & all other calls for money." King felt hurried because he felt he ought to leave San Francisco the year after next "if the war shall cease, to get a little rest, even if I return here afterwards."

King went on to say "I have promised to furnish the new organ as my gift, besides subscribing to the church building." He proposed to give a course of lectures on the subject of "Prominent American Poets,"[10] including Bryant, Longfellow, Holmes, Whittier, and Lowell. He felt that this series of lectures would help raise money for his organ fund, and he asked Bellows to secure a new poem from Bryant if at all possible. King hoped that they might break ground for the new church the following week.

The Nevada territory had supplied $20,000 of the $50,000 for the Sanitary Commission. King noted that "three years ago it was a wilderness." King had written a letter to one of his friends in the territory and the $20,000 was the result. King also wanted Bellows to consider spending a year in California when the war was over. "What a swath you could cut from Los Angeles to Cape Flattery, & from the Sierra to the sea! And what good you could do here in a year!" He wanted to show California to Bellows. "What a refreshment some portions of the state would supply to you! The Yosemite & Shasta for instance,—& Mt. Hood from the Columbia. Will you think of it?" Some of his friends had wanted to run King for the United States Senate but he had refused. "*Nothing* can induce me to turn my eyes in that direction," he wrote. "I am unfitted even by what powers I do possess."[11]

A month later King suggested to Bellows that the church would be finished by 1 June 1863. "Can't you manage to be here for the Dedication? What a reception you would have! We will line your pockets with money for some lectures, & will show you the Yosemite, Mt. Shasta, the Big Trees, the Geysers, Columbia River, Mt. Hood, & *all* our gems especially polished & brilliant for the great occasion." King wrote, "Think seriously now, if you do not owe it to the country's cause & the Unitarian interest, to make the journey then. Come by the isthmus & return overland. The state will spring to its feet to welcome you."[12]

William Cullen Bryant did respond to Thomas Starr King's request for an original poem he could read to his San Francisco audience. Bryant wrote to Bellows: "I send a little poem written a year since which has never yet seen the light of day and which will be only too highly complimented by being given to the public in the beautiful utterance of our friend Starr King." Bryant commented, "I would follow your suggestion to string a few rhymes together about the munificent charities of the Californians, but, though that would have been sure to bring down the house, I was distrustful of my power to do the thing well—and preferred to send to King a poem which I rank among the least bad that I have written. I hope you will have it in season to send to California as early as it will be wanted."[13] The poem, in Bryant's own handwriting, was "Waiting by the Gate." Evidently Bellows was better than his word to Starr King, for in addition to the poem of Bryant's he was able to send original poems by Holmes, Whittier, and Longfellow.[14]

National and local elections were held the first week in November 1862. Bellows described "the winter, foaming at the mouth, is rushing suddenly & madly upon us!" He felt that "the election was a hard nut to crack & a bitter pill to swallow! . . . It seems to be regarded as a sort of expression on the part of the people of their impatience at the slow or crab-like program of the war—a desire for *change*, without knowing what change will bring." He commented, "the election in the city, of Mr. Woods & Brooks, only show I suppose that in this Babel we have two hundred thousand people, who care not . . . for right or wrong! There seems to be no serious expression of anxiety caused by the election. Stocks have fallen under it, but not much!" He could simply not understand McClellan who had just again been removed from command of the armies and replaced by the reluctant Ambrose Burnside. He summed up McClellan in these words: "Clearly he wants the audacity demanded by the crisis."[15]

Only a Drop in the Bucket

The work of the United States Sanitary Commission was now beginning to be appreciated by both the public and the Army generals. Early in 1863 General W. S. Rosecrans wrote to Bellows from his headquarters at Murfreesboro, on the Cumberland,

William Cullen Bryant, Courtesy of the New-York Historical Society, New York City

offering any help he could give for the men of the Sanitary Commission. He was in a tough spot militarily, and he pleaded with Bellows, "Pray for me." In fact, he wanted everybody to pray for him, and added that he had "no doubt that God answers the prayers which are made in the name of Jesus Christ with humility, confidence, and perserverence."[1] This was not especially Bellows's theology, but it shows the pressure of the times, and General Rosecrans wanted God and the Sanitary Commission there when his army went into battle.

By February 1863 Strong, as treasurer of the Sanitary Commission was able to write, "the success of this Sanitary Commission has been a marvel. Our receipts in cash up to this time are nearly $700,000 at the central office alone, beside what has been received and spent by auxiliaries, and the three or four millions' worth of stores of every sort contributed at our depots." He continued, "It had become a 'big thing' . . . and a considerable fact in the history of this people and of this war. . . . Our work at Washington and Louisville, our two chief nervous centers, is on a big scale, employs some two hundred agents of every sort, and costs not much less than $40,000 a month."[2]

At the Academy of Music in Philadelphia, on Tuesday evening 24 February 1863, Bellows made a significant address regarding the work of the Sanitary Commission.[3] Its first task, he said, was to prevent sickness in the army. This was necessary in order to prevent a waste of precious life. There was a general ignorance of the laws of health. The commission sent an army of experts into the camps to make recommendations regarding sanitation and followed through on their recommendations until most sickness was alleviated. Their second task was to help to heal the sick and wounded. At this point Bellows congratulated his audience for the supplies which they had sent to the field. Discharged soldiers also somehow had to be gotten home since the government took no responsibility, and the Sanitary Commission had labored diligently in this task.

Money was also beginning to come to the commission in larger amounts, and not just from California. An unexpected bonus from an unusual quarter came when William H. Seward, the Secretary of State, turned over to Bellows for the use of the Sanitary Commission the sum of $3,688.84 which had been sent from Americans living in Chile "destined for the sick and wounded soldiers of the Union Army."[4]

During the middle of April, Bellows spent several days with the Army of the Potomac. He said that he had "not had a comfortable night since I left" Washington. He had been riding horseback, sleeping in tents, and eating army fare. He found the experience a trying one. "Young men little know what they are going to, when they go into the army. I sincerely believe it either in peace or war, the worst profession a young man can choose." In war he found it "laborious, exposing, monotonous, on account of the long waiting to which campaigns are subject, & with strong temptation to drinking." He found that "almost all officers" drank and "smoked without moderation, . . . & chew when they don't smoke." Dr. Agnew was his companion on the trip. They went down to the Rappahannock where the pickets of the enemy were on the other side of the river. "The men can talk across it—they naturally agreed *not to fire* on each other. On the bank, where I went, I was within range of the enemies' fires, & could have been picked off by a rifle." From where he stood he could see the town of Fredericksburg in the distance, the scene previously of a disastrous defeat of the Union forces under General Ambrose Burnside. He was impressed that there were 60,000 horses with the army and that they ate 800 tons of hay every day, and that 700 tons of food for the men was required.

Bellows had talked with General Hooker three times, had dined with him and his staff, and had an hour's interview with the commanding general. Bellows even listed the menu of the tent supper, "oyster-soup, Potomac Shad, roast mutton, roast chickens, puddings, pies, champagne, cigars." Bellows unfortunately was too sick to eat anything, "& indeed with great difficulty kept from vomiting at the table—a feat I accomplished successfully the moment I got home." There was a Swiss General in full regalia as a guest at the occasion, and also General Denham, his old parishioner.

He liked General Hooker, and felt him "not so much a great drinker as a man not able to drink a great deal without feeling it. He evidently uses liquor now—but not with recklessness. He chews & smokes pretty steadily." Hooker was not too complimentary about his predecessors. "He spoke of McClellan as an incompetent & of Burnside as a child." Bellows found Hooker's "moral instincts far from cultivated." Hooker had no chaplain and had had no religious services at his headquarters. Bellows told him that this was a mistake, "and one the country would not overlook, & he promised to seek out a chaplain & have regular services." Bellows felt that if he had the strength this might be the place for himself. "I should consider it perhaps the greatest of services I could render to accompany Hooker & obtain influence & exercise sway over that staff."[5]

On 26 June 1863, Henry wrote his sister that he was scheduled to have dinner with President Lincoln in Philadelphia on 4 July. Little did either Lincoln or Bellows realize what that day would have in store for the Northern and Southern armies now moving toward a little town in Pennsylvania called Gettysburg. But Bellows was aware that something important was soon to come for he wrote, "It looks a little now, as if Gen. *Lee*, thought himself asked to that feast, or meant to come uninvited. I can't say I should think Pennsylvania very ill-treated if he did; for she seems not to have the spirit of a mouse."[6]

On 1, 2, and 3 July 1863 the two great armies met in the most decisive battle of the war. There was uncertainty after it was over about what had happened or who had won the battle at Gettysburg. Mrs. George Schuyler felt that it was a defeat, and that people wanted McClellan back in power.[7] But it was really too early to know what the outcome of the battle had been. Bellows was trying to make arrangements to get his family to Walpole. He believed about the battle, "we have not only escaped a terrible calamity, but struck a tremendous blow at the Rebellion." He had just received private word that 15,000 prisoners and 100 guns had been captured at Gettysburg. But Bellows as yet did not know the terrible extent of the battle and the casualties.[8]

On 6 July Bellows left for the battlefield. He expected to be gone a week. "*Events* have changed the political prospect," he wrote. "The great *victory* wipes McClellan out clean [as a candidate for President] & strengthens the administration immeasurably. I think it both useless & wrong to attempt to remove Stanton. Interference with the President's *executive* responsibility, is in principle bad & not to be encouraged. I don't like Stanton—but I could not join in any effort to remove him."[9]

For one of the few times in his life Bellows wrote scarcely a word to anyone (that we know of) while he was at Gettysburg. The only word from the battlefield extant in the Bellows Papers was written on a tiny scrap of paper. Bellows spent better than a week there, and was appalled at the carnage of this most terrible battle. He sent Eliza the following message:

July 8th Wednesday, Gettysburg 7 o'clock P.M. Dear wife & daughter. I am well but intensely busy. The suffering here with 70,000 wounded is unspeakable! We are showing every nerve to aid—but it is only a drop in the bucket. I have not washed my face & hands today, and I am now writing in the field surrounded by a thousand wounded men, on my knee. I see no chance of getting back before Sunday. Have the pulpit supplied or have the church closed as you please. My chances of writing are very poor. I am well & rejoiced to be here. [Very] important, & I thank God I was moved to come. I am well. It has rained fearfully all day, but it is now ceased. The battle ground is fearful, & the hospitals quite as much so. I will write again the first opportunity. Do not worry about me. Your loving husband. Henry W. Bellows[10]

At Gettysburg the Sanitary Commission did its most extensive acts of mercy. This battle, which became the turning point of the war, involved 150,000 men. The Confederacy lost about 40,000 killed and wounded in the battle and the Union about 20,000. When the Confederate armies headed South in retreat after the failure of Pickett's charge, there were thousands of helpless and wounded men lying on the field of battle. These included at least 5,000 Confederates. On 4 July 1863, a call was sent out all over the East for women to go to Gettysburg and to report to the United States Sanitary Commission headquarters. At all of the main railroad stations in the North well-known women interviewed applicants. Relief trains were made up in Baltimore. On the field the army nurses worked under Dorothea Dix along with the army surgeons. The women worked for three weeks on the field of Gettysburg and cared for some 16,000 men. Their work done, they marched from the field with two army bands playing "Three Cheers for the Red, White, and Blue."

After the Battle of Gettysburg, a Sanitary Commission auxiliary unit was attached to every army corps. Into these units were absorbed most of the women who had been traveling with the army in one capacity of service or another. While none of these women was ever killed in battle, many of them died after each big engagement as the result of overwork; and many became invalids for life for the same reason. They had secondary casualties as the result of their nursing service.

The Draft Riots which wracked New York City just after the Battle of Gettysburg were one of the worst outbreaks of violence the city ever experienced. The drawing of names of conscripts under the Draft Act had commenced in the city on Saturday morning 11 July. Essentially the Draft Riots were an uprising of the Irish immigrants who felt keenly the competition of the Negro freedmen. The police having been overwhelmed at the draft headquarters the angry mob now faced soldiers who had been brought in from Gettysburg. At first they shot blanks at the rushing sea of men, and then they shot live ammunition, killing several of the mobsters. But they were overwhelmed before they had a chance to reload their rifles. These Draft Riots of 1863 stand as one of the most shameful episodes in New York history. Politicians encouraged mob violence, law and order broke down, mobs seized control of America's largest city, innocent people were tortured and slaughtered. No one will ever know how many people were killed.

Bellows wrote an account of the Draft Riots and spoke of the senselessness of the New York mob, "the experience of the mob in N. Y. All my family were there during the whole of it—& the surge of the riot ran up & down our street. My church & house, it was thought, would be an object of attack. I did not fear it, however." He continued, "whether because I had lately seen such destruction at Gettysburg & had lost the power of being amazed, I was not terrified, or even much excited—except with anger. I found my homicidal instincts very . . . stimulated." He had become emotional himself, "I verily believe I could have killed a dozen of the rioters not only *without compunctions*, but *with* unction." He found himself to be very angry. "The mortification of being in a city beleagured by its own vilest inhabitants—of having my own free movements hindered by this scum, roused my dander." But the "police behaved magnificently—so did the chief newspapers. The citizens were *craven*. There was not half, no not a tenth part the pluck there should have been among the solid men, to withstand each & every attempt of the rioters, at all costs." But he was relieved when it was over, "I think, however—considering the absence of the military—we did pretty well to put it down in three days."[11]

On 10 August Frederick Law Olmsted wrote to Bellows that the Mariposa Mining Company of California wanted him to go to California to make some sense out of its large financial empire. Olmsted was afraid that he could not afford to refuse the offer since it carried the magnificent salary of $10,000 a year with the job. He wrote that he was thinking the matter over carefully, and would let Bellows know his decision shortly.[12]

Near the end of August Henry Bellows was planning a trip to the White Mountains with his children, but his mind was very much on the affairs of the nation. He had been worried about the national affairs for several years. But now he felt that things could scarcely be better. "It is evident to me that the administration daily holds a firmer hand, wears a more confident manner, & feels that it has the Rebellion *under*." He felt that "squirming democracy . . . cannot change the direction of affairs."[13]

In his haste and the press of duties of the Sanitary Commission Bellows sometimes neglected to keep his wife informed. Eliza happened to see a notice in the *New York Tribune* that "the U.S. Sanitary Commission will hold their annual meeting at Walpole, N.H., on Tuesday and Wednesday of next week." This notice had appeared in Friday's *Tribune,* and on Saturday when Eliza happened to see the notice, she understandably was livid. She wanted to know whether it was the work of Frederick Knapp, or whether Bellows had made the arrangements himself and had simply neglected to tell her. She complained that there was not enough room in the house, and that if many men showed up they would have to stay at the local hotel. "I feel very much annoyed at the way you have got into keeping things back from me, & I beg you will discontinue doing so—You know surprises make me sick—then why allow me so unnecessarily to encounter them." It was one of the curtest letters ever written by Eliza to Henry. He probably deserved the reprimand.

The same newspaper had carried the story that "Fred. Law Olmsted has received the appointment of Superintendent of the Mariposa Mining Company, with a salary of $10,000, and will consequently leave his position in the Sanitary Commission. Dr. Jenkins will probably succeed him." With this news there was added reason that the commission should have a meeting.[14]

During the second week in October Bellows was again in Washington, again forced to stay over the weekend. He was able to send Mr. Heywood, who had been working with him on Sanitary business, to fill the New York pulpit. The Board of the Sanitary Commission had had dinner with Secretary of State Seward one evening to go over the problems of the Sanitary Commission. Bellows wrote that "our affairs have moved harmoniously & concluded satisfactorily. Our treasury is the only source of anxiety. We have over $100,000 in it—but we see small prospect of any large increase except by stirring up California, & how to do that is now our chief inquiry." He commented that "the Board are exceedingly anxious to have me go out [to California] & I may really be obliged to consider it most seriously. But do not breathe any such thot, except to Mr. Heywood."[15]

But the next day Bellows had a chill and felt feverish. He had sent word to Eliza to send him a sermon manuscript. It had not arrived, so he had to preach at the Washington church extemporaneously, and found it a difficult task for he had a "disordered stomach & a bad cold." He wrote that Olmsted had left for California, and "has taken away with his admirable genius, pure purpose & forcible will, a certain obstruction & impracticable element which always embarrassed us. I can feel that the wheels move more slowly. I hope they won't gain ease, by losing strength & reliableness."[16]

True to his belief that the Sanitary Commission could not long endure without an injection of a large amount of gold from California, Bellows on 23 October telegraphed the Soldiers' Relief Committee in San Francisco: "The Sanitary funds are low. Our expenses are fifty thousand dollars a month. We can live three months, and that only, without large support from the Pacific." He suggested that, "twenty-five thousand dollars a month, paid regularly while the war lasts, from California, would make our continuance on our present magnificent scale of beneficence a certainty. We could make up the other twenty-five thousand a month here." He said that "the Board imperatively urge me to go out to California and tell her all we owe her for past favors. . . . When California needs my presence for such an object she will ask for it . . . God bless California." Henry had sent his telegram on 23 October. By 9 November the San Francisco group had mobilized yet another campaign to keep the Sanitary Commission afloat.[17]

Most writers in discussing the work of the United States Sanitary Commission have been content merely to spell out the details of this first effort at organized charitable works on a grand scale. Few have looked behind the good works to study the philosophical thinking which lay behind the ministrations to the suffering of the war and the efforts to help individuals mired in the armies and the wounded in the hospitals lost to their own kindred. Fortunately, intellectual historian George M. Frederickson has probed beneath the surface to take a more definitive look at the philosophy behind this impulse to such service. For some time the lengthening casualty lists brought no profound speculation about the meaning of suffering but only an attempt to bring relief to the numerous wounded men in the armies and hospitals. Frederickson calls the United States Sanitary Commission, "the largest, most powerful, and most highly organized philanthropic activity that had ever been seen in America."[18] The commission had popular favor, more so than the Christian Commission[19] which tried to combine the alleviation of suffering with the exposition of the conservative Christian Protestant position in theology. Eventually the work of the Sanitary Commission became a kind of tradition or legend "particularly because it seemed to show that amidst all the brutality of war the North had exhibited a humane and philanthropic spirit."[20]

At first glance this great work appears to be the simple expression of an almost spontaneous reaction to the suffering of the men in the Northern armies both in the camps and on the actual battlefields of the bloody war. Frederickson believes that the Sanitary Commission did provide an outlet for the longings of the North, especially for the women, to alleviate suffering. But "it is significant . . . that the commission on the whole was staffed not by a cross section of the American public but by members of the highest social class."[21] We have seen that when things were going badly on the Peninsula in 1862 appeals were made for women to nurse the sick and wounded and those who responded were the elite of New York intellectual and social life—Mrs. Bellows, Mrs. George Strong, and so on, who even took their servants with them to staff the hospital ships that brought the wounded back from that ill-fated McClellan expedition against Richmond. 'The Sanitary Commission was a predominantly upper-class organization, representing those patrician elements which had been vainly seeking a function in American society."[22]

But what really distinguished the members of the commission was not their birth but their social philosophy. 'The organization was ruled in a supremely authoritarian manner by a small number of men—designated as the commissioners. While this body included scientists and experts on military and public health, it was dominated by intellectuals with more general interests—men who took time from their Sanitary duties to write and speak on the broadest political and social questions."[23] Henry Bellows, who still maintained his New York pulpit during the war in spite of an extraordinary schedule of work for the commission, had a weekly podium from which he could speak his views to many of the most distinguished citizens of the city. In September 1861 Bellows more than hinted that he stood against the perfectionist and millenialist strains in American reform. He opposed the spirit of the times, which tended to see a philanthropic meaning in the war, and he attacked those "ideals or abstract aspirations, which clothed now in the garb of religion, and now of philanthropy, are nevertheless revolutionary and anarchical."[24] Bellows was a different kind of theologue than the usual preachers. Charles J. Stillé, the official historian of the Sanitary Commission, said of Bellows, 'he had the clearest perception of what could and could not be done . . . "[25]

Even more fiercely conservative than Bellows was George
Templeton Strong, the treasurer of the organization. The secretary
of the commission, Frederick Law Olmsted, was no more of a
humanitarian than Bellows or Strong. He had traveled extensively in
the South before the war, and his books contain some of the best
descriptions of the antebellum South. But he certainly did not agree
with the abolitionists in their attempts to portray the terrible
sufferings of the slaves. He was concerned more about the slaves'
unprofitableness than with their slavery. Stillé, the member of the
commission who later became its historian, found no expression
more distasteful than the concept of humanitarianism. Stillé believed
that men could be driven to devotion by something more than the
vague sentiments of humanitarianism. He evidently believed that
one responded to this as a duty that came from some divine
command. So these patricians who ruled the Sanitary Commission
took their philosophical point of view not even as the humanitarian
alleviation of suffering but as obedience to duty divinely
commanded. The only exception to this point of view was that of
Dr. Samuel Gridley Howe. Howe had taken time from his great
work with the blind, deaf, and dumb to support many humanitarian
crusades, but he rapidly lost interest in the commission once it was
formed and took little active part in it.

Thus the Sanitary Commission was ruled by a conservative
elite. It would be wrong to state that there was not some sense of
Christian charity in the minds of these men, "yet there is evidence
that the commission's work was regarded not only as a duty, but as a
heaven-sent opportunity for educating the nation."[26] The work of
the commission was a great teacher as to how to do a necessary job.
"The work of the commission was as much an attempt to revise the
American system of values as to relieve the suffering of the
wounded."[27] If one examines the large body of literature that was
published by the commission one readily discovers it stated that "its
ultimate end is neither humanity nor charity. It is to economize for
the National service the life and strength of the National soldier."[28] If
one puts this more bluntly it says that the soldier's life was being
saved so that he could die a useful death on some future battlefield.
Frederickson believes that it was not a spirit of the acceptance of war
that motivated the commissioners such as Henry Bellows, but that
the agonies of war were welcomed as a test of personal courage and
as a good in themselves. Bellows believed that a large dose of
suffering would be good for the Northern souls for they had suffered
little up until the beginning of the war. George Templeton Strong

concurred with Bellows in this philosophy of suffering. In his diary Strong wrote, "The logic of history requires that we suffer for our sins far more than we have yet suffered. Without the shedding of blood there is no remission of sins."[29]

George M. Frederickson summarizes the attitudes in these words: "Men like Bellows, Strong, and Stillé welcomed the sufferings and sacrifices of the hour because they served the cause of discipline in a broader sense than demanded by purely military requirements. An unruly society, devoted to individual freedom, might be in the process of learning that discipline and subordination were good in themselves, and the commissioners wanted to play their role in teaching a lesson."[30] Frederickson also believes that the commission conceived of itself "less as a benevolent enterprise than as a barrier between the irresponsible benevolence of the people and the army." Bellows believed that the army would suffer greatly from irresponsible benevolence in the hospitals and on the battlefield without the barrier of the government-recognized commission to block and channel such efforts. Therefore, the commission with its professionals who knew what they were doing prevented the people from swamping and interfering with the army.

The Good Samaritans were not volunteers but paid agents of the Sanitary Commission. This concept was highly criticized, but it was based on the idea that the work was so full of drudgery and tedium that only someone dependent on the small pay would be willing to persist in the work month after month. Walt Whitman was especially critical of the work of the commissioners. He termed them "well paid & (hirelings as Elias Hicks would call them—they seem to me always as a set of foxes & wolves)—they get well paid & are always incompetent and disagreeable—"[31]

George M. Frederickson concludes in assessment of the work of the Sanitary Commission: "With all their ulterior motives, the commissioners undeniably performed a valuable work. If it was justifiable for the North to subordinate all considerations to the winning of the war, the methods of the commission were, on the whole, appropriate to the occasion. A nation engaged in total war cannot afford the luxury of too much democracy or humanitarianism; military efficiency must be the paramount consideration."[32] I believe that this is a somewhat cynical analysis of the work of the commission working on assumptions not current a hundred years ago about the equality of all people. (We have still only reached the concensus that equality exists in the division of rights—human rights, but certainly there is no equality of abilities as yet achieved.) Bellows, Strong, and the other elitists had witnessed at first hand the corruption in their own city, they had seen the mobs burn and kill, and the police rendered incapable of much action by internal police-political squabbles. After the battle of Gettysburg they had their convictions in this regard strengthened when it was necessary to bring troops from the Gettysburg battlefield in order to put down the Draft Riots in New York City.

CHAPTER NINE

Approaching Its Natural Conclusion

How Heavy the Harness Is

If 1863, a year that was decisive in the Civil War, was a busy one for Bellows in his work with the Sanitary Commission, it was no less busy in his church. There were debts to be paid. In spite of the war it was decided in January 1863 that there ought to be a campaign to pay off the debt on the "Beefsteak Church." A subscription list was drawn up. Henry S. Gair, Charles C. Goodhue, John C. Lloyd, and Benjamin F. Wheelwright gave $1,000 each; Peter Cooper gave $700, and Henry Bellows, Charles C. Butler, John Armstrong, Dortman B. Eaton, N. A. Murdock, William F. Cary, George E. Stone, and Benjamin G. Arnold gave $500 apiece. Ten persons gave $250 each and there was a long list of those who gave $100 or less, eighty-eight names in all for a total of $15,050. The list is a fine compendium of names of active parishioners in 1863.

Twenty-six year old Louisa Lee Schuyler, whose family gave rather generously to the subscription, added twenty dollars of her own to the list, and penned a short note to Dr. Bellows. "I wish I could tell you how the memory of your preaching, of words spoken years ago, has remained with me & influenced my life. The little good there may be in it I feel to be due, in large measure, to your teaching, example, and friendship."[1]

There were also improvements to be made in the church. One commemorated a former minister, William Ware, the first minister of All Souls, who had died in 1852, at the age of fifty-five. He had contributed so much to the life of the church that the congregation wanted to do something to commemorate his ministry. The project had originally begun in 1855. On the last Sunday in February 1863, eleven years later, a beautiful plaque in memory of William Ware was ready for dedication.[2]

There were new parishioners, such as Herman Melville, an obscure writer of South Sea romances. After he married the daughter of the Chief Justice of the Massachusetts Supreme Court on 4 April 1847, the newlyweds established a home at 103 Fourth

Avenue (now Park Avenue South) with Herman's brother Allan and his bride. This house was some blocks from the Church of the Divine Unity, where they rented a pew for the second half of the year 1849, paying $14.15 for the privilege.[3] Early in October 1850, Melville bought a farm at Pittsfield, Massachusetts, and he moved there with his mother, sisters, his wife and his first son Malcolm. In Pittsfield, Melville finished his novel *Moby-Dick*, which was published also in England under the title of *The Whale*. But it was too symbolic and too existential for nineteenth-century readers, and as Melville lapsed into obscure writings so did his reputation, which was not enhanced by *Pierre, or The Ambiguities*, which was published in 1852.

In the spring of 1863, Melville, now a ruined man in reputation and in finances, sold the Pittsfield farm to his brother Allan and bought a house at 104 East 26th Street. This was the home in which Herman and Elizabeth lived until his death. It was only six short north and south blocks from Bellows's new All Souls Church at 20th Street and Fourth Avenue. Church records indicate that the family attended Bellows's church and that on 28 January 1865 "Mrs. E. S. Melville" rented pew #209 in the gallery of the church which was valued at $200, the third least expensive pew available with an annual rental of $17.50.[4]

On Sunday morning, 29 March 1863, those parishioners who attended church were asked to consider a letter which, in his usual fashion, Bellows had left with the sexton. It told the story of the building of the San Francisco church under the able leadership of Thomas Starr King whose efforts had made it possible for California by that time to give half a million dollars to the work of the U.S. Sanitary Commission. Bellows mentioned that some former members of All Souls were active in the San Francisco church—Robert B. Swain, Edward Tompkins, and E. Lambert. Bellows stated that he felt that the sister Unitarian churches would probably like to help in giving a marble baptismal font to the San Francisco church, but that he wanted *"our own particular congregation to do it, on its own independent account."* He wrote that the piece of marble was ready to ship, and that the gift would come as a complete surprise to the people of the San Francisco church. He began the subscription, as was his custom, with an amount he hoped would be equaled by a number of his fellow parishioners—$25. A total of $600 was needed to buy, ship, and carve the font. The amount was completely subscribed by such men as Nathaniel B. Currier, D. B. Eaton, Isaac Green Pearson, Moses H. Grinnell, Charles C. Goodhue, and others.[5]

Amid all of his other worries, Bellows was also concerned about Eliza's physical condition. She was forty-five years of age, and she was obviously going through serious mental and physical trials. The little respite from thinking about her own ills which had occurred with the hospital ship experience the previous year during the Peninsula Campaign had not lasted. Bellows wrote to his sister Eliza at Walpole preparing her for the summer months ahead when Eliza would probably be at the ancestral homestead. "Eliza is more seriously unwell that is at all common with her. I think it probable that some constitutional changes may have commenced, from which she is likely to suffer a good deal for the next two or three years." He felt that, "under these circumstances, I shall think it my duty to consult her ups & downs of feeling as much as possible & cannot tell how, when, or where her health may make it necessary for us to go or stay."

He doubted whether she would get to Walpole during the summer months; at least it would be uncertain. There had been some changes proposed in the Walpole Homestead, and Bellows wanted his sister to have them stopped if it was at all possible, for such construction work would simply add to Eliza's confusion at the estate. It is obvious that Bellows was carrying not only a heavy patriotic load but an immense family strain on his broad shoulders.[6]

Back at work in New York for the fall season, Bellows wrote: "I am really surprised when I get back to find how heavy the *harness* is I habitually wear. By a blessed oblivion, the moment I slip off the yoke, I forget that it has a galling weight—& when I wear it hardly know how heavy it is." But he realized that "putting it *on* freshly gives me a realizing sense that my daily life for ten months is one of severe mental & physical toil." The work on the interior of the church had been completed. The organ gallery had been moved "forward a foot which improves their position very decidedly; also built a roof on the organ to prevent *sound* escaping up into the attic—also moved the base pipes out into the open part. The outside is cleaning slowly—will take a month longer." He was to open the church services for the fall the following Sunday, 20 September. The family were in good health.[7]

Mrs. George Schuyler (Eliza Hamilton) was fatally ill. "It is indeed most sad to think that so vital a soul as hers is about to leave us. Her friendship has been so precious to me that I can hardly contemplate her loss with composure. . . . She talks of death with all the cheerful courage & calmness with which any other long journey might be spoken of. She watches her own soul & all its motions with a candid curiosity, under the portentious circumstances in which she is placed." Then he wrote his high opinion of her, "you know what I think of her—on the whole the most richly gifted of all the women I have known, equally rare in original & cultivated graces, in mental power, oral elevation & spiritual insight—as strong as gentle, as clear as deep—as much a delicate, modest woman, as a richly furnished strong & brave companion." He continued, "My friendship with her has been equally of the mind & heart. She has sympathized with my political, my religious & my personal feelings. Rarely has a more dignified & perfect friendship existed than ours." Bellows went on to say that this friendship of twenty-five years had been so deeply meaningful to him.

His ruminations about Mrs. Schuyler also give some interesting sidelights into Bellows's religious ideas. Mrs. Schuyler had "begged me not to *undervalue* my *Unitarianism*. She was bred an *Episcopalian* & has found great comfort in *our* faith. She has, I think, noticed my own dissatisfaction with some of the views connected with Unitarianism. I value her testimony on the subject extremely. She says from her death-bed in full view of both systems that her comfort comes from *our* view that it is higher, more supportive & more scriptural. It did me great good to hear this."[8]

Just before Christmas Eliza Schuyler passed away. Louisa Schuyler wrote to Bellows, "It is over now—at eight o'clock this morning perfectly quiet & peaceful—life breathed away so gradually that we could not tell when was the last breath. She asked to be lifted into the chair in which my grandmother died—& did not speak again after she was placed in it. Sunday morning, the resurrection."[9]

The first indication that serious trouble was brewing in the relationship of the First and Second Unitarian churches in New York and the new Third church founded by Octavius Brooks Frothingham is indicated in a letter to Bellows about their joint Christmas service. Samuel Osgood in a letter to Bellows noted that Frothingham was dedicating his new church building on Friday, 25 December. He added this for Bellows's eyes only: "I am not sorry to be spared the probable trial of hearing him deny the Gospel & church of Christ to set up his dreary & egotistical mysticism & humanism. You must choose between the two services. I advise you to go if they will let you speak out the Gospel like a man. But if you consent to sit & hear Deism & Naturalism on Christmas day, God help you."[10]

It was a moot choice. Frothingham had decided to conduct the ceremony himself instead of following the usual custom of inviting the neighboring Unitarian ministers to participate. Therefore, he regarded the general invitation which his trustees had sent to the other churches as sufficient. Osgood and Bellows did not feel this way. Bellows wrote to Frothingham and complained that this sort of invitation was not sufficient. Did Frothingham want to create a division in "our New York column?" Frothingham wrote back an almost flippant letter and promised that if the pulpit chairs were done, Bellows could have one of them. Frothingham later termed this a warm personal invitation. But Bellows did not see it that way. He did not like this belated and grudging token of respect, and therefore stayed away from the ceremony. His daughter Annie did attend.[11]

There then ensued a somewhat bitter and acrimonious correspondence between Bellows and Frothingham. Bellows wrote, "I did not come to the Dedication because your reply to my serious note seemed to me trifling, & wanting in the frankness I expected. I could not have come without feeling that I had forced my way into your pulpit, over which I conceive you to have exclusive control." Bellows continued, "Your notions of ministerial comity differ so essentially from my own, that I do not think it probable that we can by correspondence arrive at any mutual understanding on the subject. I am truly anxious, however, on every account—not to widen the difference which already exists." The acrimony had reached a difficult stage, for Bellows wrote: "If you think it worth while to submit the points at issue, & the correspondence between us to a third party, say Dr. Hedge, I will agree to abide by his decision, & to acknowledge myself 'incoherent, loose, petulant' or whatever else he may adjudge, if you will agree to acknowledge yourself to have violated the general usages of our churches, & to have given just cause of offense by your course, at your cornerstone laying, and your Dedication; if the umpire so decides." Bellows then proposed the method of settlement, "He shall decide the case on a statement of the facts made by yourself, and another made by me, both of which shall be endorsed by your own Board of Trustees as correct—according to their best knowledge—&, besides, by our recent correspondence." He gave Frothingham the right to select another "if Dr. Hedge does not suit you, will you name any man of ripe experience & character who does; say Dr. Stearns of Cambridge. I do not wish to make too much of this, Nay I do not wish to put you in the wrong. If the matter can stop here without having uncomfortable feelings in your heart, I am perfectly willing to forget it."[12]

Frothingham replied by letter the next day sensibly rejecting the offer. He felt "that it makes a small business into a great importance, involves an innocent man in a private controversy, tends to make a private matter public, and gives an official and state character to that which simply concerns us two." Frothingham went on to say that he did not see what would be gained by submitting the question to a third party. He protested that he could not be accused of violating the general usages of the churches when he did not know what those usages were. Frothingham saw no precedents that he ought to follow. He continued: "My complaint, Dr. Bellows, is not that you show a disposition to interfere with my personal rights—but that you put a certain [interpretation] on my part & conduct which I do not comprehend." He accused Bellows of deliberately trying to create division in the liberal church. He said that although he disliked the letter and Bellows's attitude he had always tried to be a gentleman, and had "never intentionally wounded either you or Dr. Osgood by my professional or official behaviour. Indeed I have more than once regarded clerical etiquette when it went against my personal feeling to do so."

His conclusion was good advice. "Let the matter drop and be forgotten. My personal regard and affection for you remain what they have always been, sincere and cordial. . . . Our ministerial chain cannot suffer from being broken, so far as I am concerned. I am and shall continue to be."[13] And there evidently the matter was ended.

Actually the quarrel was more than a personal slight of Bellows by Frothingham. Bellows and Osgood did not believe in the kind of Unitarian church that Frothingham had created. Bellows and Osgood both felt that Frothingham had come into New York under the false colors of starting a church in typical Unitarian tradition, and that it turned out to be exactly the kind of liberalism that Bellows was fighting within the denomination, and here it was right in his own "bishopric." As the successor to Parker, a position which Parker himself had suggested when he sailed away to die in Italy in 1860, Frothingham carried on for twenty years in New York. Later, after the National Conference was formed, Frothingham was so angry at Bellows's influence at the conference that his church dropped the name Unitarian and became The Independent Liberal Church. Eventually the church building was sold and Frothingham moved to Lyric Hall which became a center famous for his preaching. He preached eloquently in the style of Edward Everett without pulpit and without manuscript. Around him developed an unusual congregation made up of prominent writers, thinkers, and reformers. It became in large measure a church of the unchurched. Frothingham's influence was extended by the weekly printing of his sermons, which found readers all over this country and in various parts of Europe. He also for many years was the art critic for the *New York Tribune*. He excelled in writing biography, as his life of Theodore Parker attests.

In 1879 Frothingham was struck with a dread disease, locomotor ataxia. He resigned his charge, for it was clearly impossible for him to continue his preaching. He went to Europe, then returned to Boston to live. During this period he wrote lives of George Ripley and William Henry Channing, and published his volume called *Boston Unitarianism*. He died on 27 November 1895, having just completed his seventy-third year.[14]

Frothingham's influence on the two more typical Unitarian churches in New York City was never great. They went their way and he went his. Bellows came into conflict with him after the founding of the National Conference of Unitarian Churches in 1865 when the Free Religious Association broke away from this Conference and Frothingham became its first President. But this conflict was ideological. What disturbed Bellows more than anything else was that in his conservative position of ecumenicism and rapport with other Christians there should be a Unitarian in the city who claimed to be a Unitarian but not a Christian. Frothingham's church's dropping the name Unitarian helped the other two churches a great deal.

California Calls

January 1864 was the twenty-fifth anniversary of Bellows's ordination and installation at All Souls. He wrote to Orville Dewey, "I think the love of you & yours did as much to overcome my reluctance to take the post as any thing & I associate with you all the labors & hopes & fears & joys of my earlier ministry." Bellows felt that it was a "blessed blindness" that he so little knew the immensity of the task he was undertaking twenty-five years before.[1]

As if to mark the occasion, on Sunday morning 17 January, Bellows was given a signal honor. He was asked to preach in Washington in the House of Representatives, "where a brilliant & large audience had assembled, filling floor & galleries." He preached on the religious aspects of the war from an old manuscript of the previous May, but it "could not have been better fitted for the time & place." He felt that "the whole affair went off satisfactorily."[2]

Henry Bellows's article on the Sanitary Commission appeared the same month in the prominent quarterly magazine, "The North American Review."[3] In this article Bellows particularly documented the struggles which the commission had with government inefficiency and red tape. Enough time had passed so that Bellows was able to be frank in this article. Most of those who had been so inept in the Army were no longer on the scene.

There was, however, still criticism of the U.S. Sanitary Commission, all sorts of rumors flowed about vast amounts of money spent, and the salaries of the officers. Henry Bellows wrote a letter to Henry Ward Beecher hoping that Beecher would help to bring to the public the actual facts. Bellows stated that the Board of the Commission and the Standing Committee and the officers "give their services gratuitously, they are refunded their traveling expenses, in part—nothing more." He continued, "their agents 200 in number whose pay averaged two dollars per day," 14/15 of all of the money of the commission is spent in supplies "and goes on to the backs, and into the mouths of the soldiers." Bellows also indicated that "the cost of collecting and distributing the supplies is less than three percent." Bellows estimated that ten percent of the cost of care of the sick & wounded had been thrown upon the Sanitary Commission. As a sample they had spent $75,000 at Gettysburg. The Pacific Coast had sent about $700,000 out of the million dollars in cash the Sanitary Commission had received.[4]

On 12 February 1864, Thomas Starr King wrote Bellows what proved to be his last letter to his mentor. It must have been received by Bellows about the time that the sad news arrived by telegram of King's death. King reported that "our church is finished & dedicated . . . it is noble & beautiful." He continued that he still wanted "to see a tower 180 ft. by the side of it, & then I shall feel that I have built my monument in our uncertain sands." (Strange that neither Bellows nor Starr King built the planned towers to their respective churches.)

Starr King was also able to report that the baptismal font given by the members of All Souls had been dedicated the previous Sunday, 7 February. "The font, equisitely carved, & with your inscription around its base, in black German text with illuminated Old English Capitals, was placed in the church. A glorious carved canopy thirty-two ft. high has been given by a friend of mine & yours, not a parishioner, to surmount it." King closed with a prophetic question, "When will you look upon the font yourself? This year?"[5]

On 4 March 1864, a telegram arrived at New York that drastically changed the course of the life of Henry Bellows. It was from James Otis of San Francisco, and it read: "T. Starr King died very suddenly this morning. Illness diptheria. Sick only a few days. Was conscious to the last & happy to go. You cannot realize our loss."[6]

Baptismal Font in the First Unitarian Church of San Francisco, Given by the members of All Souls Church, 1864, Courtesy of the San Francisco Church

On 7 March a telegram was sent from San Francisco to Henry Bellows. It was signed by four men, Robert B. Swain, George C. Sreve, James C. Otis, and M. S. Macondra. It read:

His death was a wonderfully triumphant indication of his character, his life, his religion—resigned, trustful & conscious to the last moment—he calmly made every preparation & yielded his soul to God! No man but yourself can now complete the work he so nearly finished. We require a successor for a few months at least. You alone can represent the departed. You alone can fill the void & heal the mangled hearts. Otherwise, the glorious fruits of his labors, of which he was so hopeful—& just before the ripening of which he died—may perhaps be lost forever. Could he whisper to you from the grave a voice would be heard saying—"My flock is without a shepherd. Listen to the calls. Thousands will welcome you to the field of your best friend's labors, untiring solicitude, earnest cares & interested hopes. Answer."[7]

On 8 March Bellows was on his way to Philadelphia for business with the Sanitary Commission and the upcoming Sanitary Fair in that city. He wrote to Eliza, "I can't enter on the *great* subject. You may believe it occupies my mind *somewhat;* but I thank God I am not so much my own law & my own master, as to feel that the *decision* rests primarily with me. Thus Providence will guide & I shall follow with difficulty, its intimations."[8] By the next day Bellows had more or less reached a positive conclusion about going to California. He wrote to Eliza from Philadelphia and summarized his feelings: "So far as my parish is concerned, I think I can be spared from April 1 to October 1. Six months—three of which from July 1 to Oct. 1 are of little parochial importance. The other three are." He had thought of a substitute preacher: "my plan would be to get a *first-class— second-rate* man (first-rate is not attainable) to come & live in my place & do my whole work. . . . My plea with the parish would be that a vacation from *writing sermons* & a change of climate & work *might be* the means of prolonging my usefulness & health in New York."

He wrote that he found "greater difficulty in leaving the Sanitary Commission—not perhaps in their objections but in my own feeling that my judgment is the real balance wheel of the concern & that every day questions arise which it might be dangerous to leave to those unaccustomed to this kind of responsibility." He was also concerned about his family's welfare: "In regard to the family things can go on as usual. The Californians won't allow me to be straitened in a pecuniary way & I should see no special occasion for your not freely consulting your own inclination in regard to the summer—always assuming that you abandon the idea of going with me—which I do not regard as being as wild as you do." He suggested to Eliza that "six months of new life in another climate & away from housekeeping, with two sea voyages of twenty-three days might set up your nervous system for five or ten years. I wish you would consider it." Having made up his mind, Bellows enclosed a note to be given to Mr. Prichard to call a meeting of the Church Trustees so that he could explain the matter to them.[9]

Meanwhile Robert Swain kept up a barrage of telegrams imploring Bellows to come to San Francisco if only for one month.[10] "You promised to come if California needed you. California needs you now."[11] And another on 15 March, "Come by all means & do as you please afterwards. The interests of the commission demand your pressure as much as anything. Mrs. King sends cordial thanks."[12]

Bellows talked informally to the trustees on Friday evening, and on Sunday afternoon, 13 March 1864, a meeting of the congregation of All Souls Church was held in the church for the purpose of reading the letter from San Francisco. Dr. Bellows had asked that the meeting be called. The Minutes tell the story. "Dr. Bellows said that after full consideration of this call, he had decided, in view of the very important service he might render, by his presence in California, to liberal Christianity, as well as to other objects which he had much at heart [the Sanitary Commission], that it was his duty to ask the society to give him a leave of absence until the first of October, next, for the purpose of going there."[13] The society agreed to his request.

Bellows telegraphed to San Francisco, "The force of my desire to meet your wishes has overcome the great obstacles in my way. I leave on the steamer of the twenty-third inst. I have solemnly pledged myself to return in six months & this must be explicitly understood. If not, tell me not to come."[14]

One of Bellows's concerns would be to find a successor to King for the San Francisco church. He asked some ministers to meet in Boston with him on this matter. Charles H. Brigham, the minister in Taunton, Massachusetts, wrote that he would be unable to attend that meeting. But he offered some suggestions as to King's successor if it was not to be Bellows himself. "We have no man in our body, unless it be yourself, who can in all respects, or even in most respects, make good the loss we have sustained." He continued, "There are some who will do for the pulpit, but they cannot have the outside & secular influence; others, who will be good outside, but will fail in the pulpit. Stebbins is an instance of the former class, and Edward Hale of the latter class. Collyer would be a good man, if he had more education and more eloquence of manner." He trusted that if he were asked Bellows would "find it in his heart to stay with them in California." He also suggested that two ministers of differing capacities might go out "who might help one another, and, together, supply in a measure King's large place."[15]

Writing from Boston to Annie, Bellows told her some good news. Russell had talked to the professors at Harvard, and at least two of them had encouraged him to go to California. "Russy will come to New York April 1, & we shall *all go to California together.*" She was to tell Uncle Frank Bellows who worked for the Pacific Mail line that he had better procure staterooms for four "before it is too late." He also told Annie, "I have sent for Mr. Stebbins of Portland to meet me here & think if he can be had, he is the best man to hold my place in my absence."[16]

Five days later Bellows wrote to Edward Everett Hale, "Every thing is arranged between Stebbins & myself. He comes into my house & pulpit early in April with the hearty good will of the people, & will be transplanted to San Francisco into ground I shall prepare for him with equal cordiality on their part."[17]

Horatio Stebbins, having accepted Bellows's offer to fill his shoes in the New York City parish, and then probably to go on to San Francisco, was having some qualms about leaving Portland. Yet everything was in readiness. He promised to be in the All Souls pulpit on the Sunday after Bellows left for San Francisco, 10 April. His great concern was whether he should ship his household furniture and his books to New York or not.[18]

By 24 March Bellows had engaged two staterooms on the *Champion,* each having three berths. Mrs. Bellows, Annie, and Catherine, the maid, would occupy one, and Bellows, Russell, and Rev. H. C. Badger who was to do work for the Unitarian Association in the West were to occupy the other. Bellows pleaded with Russell to get to New York as quickly as possible to help him expedite the preparations.

As the sailing date approached Robert Swain sent another encouraging telegram to Henry Bellows. "I wish I could tell you how the expectation of your coming rejoices the people of the State. You will soon be received to grateful hearts and open arms. God grant you a safe and pleasant passage. Can you canvass the fire-field for a successor for us before leaving. King thought well of Everett Hale, & was about writing. You know what we want & will know better after arrival." The message of this telegram, with its suggestion that Bellows look around for a permanent minister for the San Francisco church, is surprising, since Bellows had already assured Horatio Stebbins that he was going to San Francisco in six months. Evidently Robert Swain knew nothing about Bellows's arrangements with Stebbins, an indication of the confidence with which Bellows did everything, for he pulled it off without a hitch.[19]

Bellows wrote to Edward Everett Hale and enclosed the telegram from San Francisco, and added this note, "My dear Hale, I think Stebbins all things considered, the better man for King's place." But he showed his admiration for Hale. "He has not half your organizing genius—but they want for a time in his pulpit, a man whose power is *preaching* & no man who *does* what you can *do*, can keep his power there, if he has it." Bellows continued, "I am satisfied with our choice, even if you could be spared, which you can't. What would become of Boston! I thought it my duty to send you this expression of their good will. Stebbins won't go, if they really don't want him. I certainly can't *crowd* him on them. But when they know all they will want him."[20] Now the choice of Stebbins was "our" choice!

A sea voyage and a trip across Panama were usually involved in 1864 in a trip to California before the completion of the continental railroad in 1869. It was a venturesome trip. Before he left Bellows drew up a will—just in case. He left every thing to "my beloved wife" and her heirs. And he appointed his half-brother, Frank Bellows, as executor. As a codicil he added that "in case of accident to my whole family, involving the loss of us all, by shipwreck or otherwise, I do give & bequeath all my property of every kind & nature to Francis W. E. Bellows, my brother, for his own use & comfort with a request that he will aid my brothers & sisters & their children, out of my bequest to him, according to his own sense of justice & duty." It was signed 3 April 1864.[21]

Another telegram from Robert Swain arrived. It is dated in San Francisco 8 April 1864 and was meant to be a farewell bon voyage greeting. "Prayers too from every heart on the western edge of the continent are offered for a safe voyage for yourself & family. May smooth waters & pleasant breezes favor you. Love from Mrs. King, Robert B. Swain."[22]

George Strong bade Bellows goodbye on 3 April. "We shall miss him sorely these coming six months, for he is most useful and efficient. He has foibles, and they lead many people to underrate him. Though public spirited and unselfish, farsighted and wise . . .

he is conceited and likes to be conspicuous. But what a trifling drawback it is on the reputation of a man admitted to be sagacious, active, and willing to sacrifice personal interests in public service, to admit that he knows, after all, that he is doing the country good service, and that he likes to see his usefulness made manifest in newspapers."[23]

West Coast Interlude

The Bellows family sailed for Panama on 4 April 1864 on the ship *Champion* after a gala farewell reception given by the parish on the evening of 30 March. On 12 April, the *Champion* was at Inagua in the West Indies, and Henry wrote to his brother Frank that they had had a stormy first two days at sea. "It was really alarming," Bellows wrote. "We were all very sick, but have got bravely over it." They had been delayed on the voyage and had put in at this small port to fill their water tanks, and Bellows and the children went ashore to see the scenery. This "is our first view of the tropics," he wrote. There were 875 "souls [aboard the] *Champion*, crowded almost beyond endurance, with a most promiscuous crew but they behave admirably well."[1]

On 22 April, Horatio Stebbins wrote to Bellows about the happenings at All Souls. He had been detained a week because both he and his little daughter had been ill with "a heavy cold" and the "threat of lung fever." He had preached on Sunday 17 April for the first time, and after church a large group had gathered around him, "and I had a reception." He mentioned the funeral of Mrs. Kirkland which took place the Sunday before his arrival. He commented that "a good parishioner and most benign looking man tells me that he was mad on the occasion, at Osgood's Episcopal strut through the Broad Aisle!" Stebbins was looking forward to going to California, but he realized that he needed a colleague to help with what must be an intolerable burden in the new country. He had heard some bad things said about King. "I inferred however that it was the whim and growl of some pietistic copperhead."[2]

On 28 April, Frederick Law Olmsted, one of Bellows's closest friends in spite of their differences on the Sanitary Commission, wrote Bellows one of his longest and rarely friendly letters. He was completely bogged down with work trying to run the Mariposa Company. The letter was largely to temper some of the enthusiasm that Olmsted knew Bellows would have for California and for Thomas Starr King. In regard to California Olmsted wrote, "I think you will be disappointed with California in many respects." He described San Francisco as "an ordinary western large town taken up and thrown down on the Pacific shore a little worse and a little more disjointed, perhaps, for the jar—of the absolutely superficial, unrooted and veneered character of all that you see of all that which looks like civilization (in its radical sense) in California." Olmsted found that no Californian really wanted to live all of his life there. Obviously Olmsted—a very cultured man—found the pioneer country a little thin in what he termed civilization and culture, although he wrote that he was living very comfortably at Bear Valley.

In regard to Starr King, Olmsted warned Bellows that the name King in California "has not the talismanic influence which you might be apt to suppose and of which you will probably be assured." Olmsted felt that a very large assemblage of people had "yielded themselves wholly captive to his eloquence and are really his disciples." They give an "appearance of great reverence for his memory, of respect for his religious principles, and of enthusiastic devotion to his political faith." Olmsted continued, "yet between the bigots and the traitors I believe a majority of the people of the state secretly or openly hate and detest his memory and will do and are doing their best to prevent the continued living of his influence."

Olmsted felt that this word of caution would help Bellows when he arrived in San Francisco. He wrote that people would never admit this fact. "King presented the works of his faith to them in such an altogether lovely, and in such an uncombative form, that they dare not avow themselves (even to themselves) to be believers, after the way in which they were educated, in its tendency and relationship to infidelity and wickedness." Olmsted was trying only to give a realistic picture so that Bellows would not go overboard in his optimism either about California or about Thomas Starr King. He added that he hoped that when Bellows got settled that he could show him the Yosemite Valley.[3]

On 30 April, Bellows sent a telegram for Horatio Stebbins to share with the people of All Souls: "Just arrived. All in perfect health. Give my people my love & blessing."[4] A few days later, in a letter, Bellows described their arrival: "We came up this interesting Bay, and through the Golden Gate, Saturday afternoon, in a fine clear air, and anchored about 6:00 P.M. at the P[acific] Mail S. S. Co's wharf." He was impressed with the view of Telegraph Hill and Russian Hill as they passed through the Golden Gate. He found the villages across the Bay much like Staten Island. There had been a drought in California and the hills were not green but very brown.[5]

Having arrived on a Saturday evening, Bellows preached at the San Francisco church the next day, both morning and evening. The sermon had been prepared in advance. It was a double sermon which began in the morning and then was concluded in the evening. It is forty-seven pages in its printed form in rather small type. The sermons were called, "In Memory of Thomas Starr King."[6] It was a fitting appreciation of Thomas Starr King by the man who perhaps knew him the best and had influenced his life more than any other. Bellows had encouraged King to preach in New York the first time he had met him; he had tried to secure the pulpit of the Second Church for him; he had literally sent him to California. Now he would say all that he had to say in his heart.

It must have been a long and emotional experience for those who crowded the San Francisco church that Sunday morning and evening. Their faith in Starr King was being vindicated by the greatest churchman among the Unitarians, the mentor of their lost pastor, and certainly his great admirer. It was a fine way for Bellows to introduce himself to the San Francisco community one day after his landfall.

It did not take Henry Bellows very long to get into the swing of things, even in the political sphere. Evidently one thing the Californians of all parties agreed upon was that they were opposed to a proposed tax on mining stocks. Bellows wrote to his friend Samuel P. Chase, Secretary of the Treasury, a letter about the matter. "Leading men of all parties unite in thinking the proposed tax on the mining stocks, most perilous to the loyalty, and unfavorable to the development of California. Tax the actual wealth of the Pacific, but in heaven's name don't tax enterprise, risk, and hope, without at one blow you wish to kill the goose that lays the golden eggs."[7]

Bellows was in the pulpit for four Sundays. Then desiring to get away from the pressures, he decided to spend the next two weeks traveling in the mountains. He had grown to like the country and compared it to England, "its meadows full of scattered trees, old oaks chiefly—with no under brush, but when you look about for the houses corresponding to the landscape you don't find them." He found the scenery somewhat monotonous. "I don't see the great fascination yet of this region—& I think I see it under great advantages. I feel no temptation to exchange New York for San Francisco."[8]

On 1 June, Henry Bellows with his party took the boat up the

San Joaquin River to Stockton. They ate well in the evening and Bellows had a good sleep that night, walked around Stockton, and then bought passage on the stage for Murphy's Hotel which was sixty miles distant. The pride of Stockton was the State Lunatic Asylum which held 540 patients, with ample room for about half that number. Bellows found a kind of gentleness about the discipline at the institution that seemed very humane to him. He commented that the great cause of insanity in California was "the absence of home relationships & conjugal intercourse & the bad vices that grow out of this deterioration."[9] They left the next day by way of Murphy's Hotel for the big trees.

On 3 June, the party arrived at Murphy's Hotel after "sixty-five miles on a very decent road." His traveling companions, Annie, Mrs. King, Russell, and Charlie Low were doing well. Murphy's was a very comfortable hotel in a village of about 300 or 400 people. They rode among the gold mines all day. "The whole country is scarred & skinned with these defacing operations," Bellows wrote.[10]

In the morning the party explored some of the surface mines in the area. Bellows was impressed with how much water the mining operation required and how much devastation was left when it was all over. His description of the mining process of washing the dirt and extracting the gold would do justice to a mining engineer. The mining business had become, he wrote, "a dull, systematic, methodical business." After this excursion and lessons in mining procedures the party went by stage to the big trees. "I have never seen a forest of such peculiar glory," he wrote, "Had there been no big trees—at the end of the route, the trees on the way would have repaid the journey." Some of them were 200 to 250 feet high, and up to eight feet in diameter.

But the trees that most amazed him were the "species of Sequoia, or 'gigantia Washingtonia,' of which the big trees are specimens." They are "evergreens of a rare species, of which four localities are now known." He noted that "these big trees are bare of branches say for 150 feet—they spread very little at the root, being an almost uniform size for the first 100, or even two hundred feet & then gradually tapering off to the top which is from 300 to 450 feet in height." He noted that the ordinary diameter was about fifteen feet but some were twenty-five feet or in several instances even thirty feet. "The size is not easily realized—because the ordinary trees are all so large & because the general features of the landscape are so vast." He found that he "had formed no proper notion of them." He was also amazed that their "seed is no bigger than turnip seed, almost the least of seeds." During all this sightseeing, he did not, however, get away from business: "I preached yesterday morning on the stump of the old tree round which a little house has been built—the whole floor being the solid root of the tree—we had about *thirty* hearers & there was room for a hundred more. My text was *the mustard seed* which tho the least of all seeds, becomes the greatest of herbs."[11] That Sunday afternoon they drove down to Murphy's Hotel.

The next stop was to be the Yosemite Valley, and this was to be a trip in the saddle. They found good horses and took three guides with them into the valley. After riding seventeen miles they came to Black's, a rude ranch where they had an excellent supper, after which they were put into what was called a room, "where Russ & I shared the bunk bed in the house with the bed-bugs, some visible & others rather felt than seen." The second day "the trail became heavily wooded & more difficult." But they still made seventeen miles again. At noon Mrs. King declared herself too tired to go further. There were no accommodations but a miner's hut and no food. Mrs. King stayed there with Annie, Russell, and Charlie Low, and Bellows went on with the rest of the party twenty miles further. The other four came the next morning. They stayed at a very rude hotel where the only partitions were of canvas.

The next morning after they had traveled ten very difficult miles, "the Yosemite Valley suddenly broke upon us from the most commanding mountain height & asserted every foot. You look down into a valley of ten miles long, where a solid piece of mountain ground about ten miles long & two & half broad of irregular dimensions, has suddenly sunk about 4,000 feet, straight into the earth leaving sharp precipices of rock, all around it." (Bellows was wrong in his geological theory, for the Yosemite is the result of glaciation and not of faulting.) "The falls are truly beautiful rather than grand," he wrote. A guide from Mr. Olmsted approached the Bellows and offered an invitation from Olmsted that they return to the north by way of Bear Valley. Bear Valley was a trip of two and a half days, and then it was two and a half days more back to San Francisco.[12]

The Bellows party decided to make the trip to Bear Valley. Having arrived, Bellows wrote one of the longest letters of his life (twenty pages) to the Standing Committee of the Sanitary Commission in New York City. He did this partly for the record, but also being with Olmsted brought to the forefront of his mind the work of the Sanitary Commission. It was a good opportunity to send best wishes to those in the East. He described the Mariposa Estate as being "in the foot hills of the Sierra Nevada" with an average height of about 5,000 feet. The estate "is about twenty miles long & six or eight broad. It is a wild mountain region. . . . The landscape is monotonous, yet impressive." He was a little concerned, for "in this settlement, there is *no* society for Olmsted or his family. The only really attractive person I have seen is the *black-smith,* who goes to the legislature & is really a commanding figure & character." The veins of gold-bearing quartz on the Mariposa Estate had been worked for fourteen years now, sometimes vigorously, sometimes not at all. Bellows was impressed with the prodigious effort and cost of getting the gold-bearing rock out of the ground and the gold out of the rock. He was surprised to find that the laborers were chiefly from Cornwall in England with a few Chinese and Americans. Again, his description of the crushing and refining process would make a mining engineer proud. The real problem that Olmsted and others faced was, whether, when a mine or vein began to get thin, they should go on and hope that it would become richer again or quit and take their profits or losses. Bellows was concerned that the owners of the Mariposa Estate would give Olmsted enough time to make the operation profitable. He felt that Olmsted himself would get little out of it. The salary sounded large when offered, but the costs of living were fantastic.[13]

Five days later Bellows was back in San Francisco writing again to the Standing Committee and enclosing the twenty-page letter he had written at Mariposa. He told the members of the committee that he was meeting some underground opposition in California. "Secret & subtle means have been taken to misrepresent & prejudice the community. Open assaults are carefully avoided & every handle carefully covered up. But the attempt to injure our great influence here is very patent. I have no doubt of my ability to head off the whole danger & that without any open break with the Christian Commission." The opposition to the Sanitary Commission came not only from the underground copperheads but also from the Christian Commission which was working in many ways with the soldiers and sailors just like the Sanitary Commission.[14]

While Bellows had been away at Mariposa and the Yosemite, Horatio Stebbins had written him a letter that brought him up-to-date on what was happening at All Souls. Dr. Eliot of Saint Louis had preached on 12 June "stating the claims of Washington University." Stebbins was concerned that Charles Brooks had a letter from his son Charles in California which gave the impression "that Hale had been already called or was the choice of the people in San Francisco." He was also disturbed that Bellows had commented about the amount of work to be done in the San Francisco church. "King who always found his life in losing it, killed himself," and Stebbins was not anxious to follow in his footsteps that way. In fact, Stebbins had become a bit indignant at Bellows: "Holding the delightful position of a *candidate* for the pulpit in San Francisco, not knowing even if I shall be *asked*, much less if I shall go. My noble friend, you cannot be indifferent to this aspect of the subject." Stebbins continued, "After all I have done, acting in accordance with the judgment of wise and good men, acting with simplicity and singleness of purpose, with perfect disregard of personal comfort, I am promoted? to the dignity of waiting to see if they want me! . . . The position is one of exceeding awkwardness and entirely false to me."

Stebbins also felt that he could not wait in New York City all summer to know if the people of San Francisco wanted him. "I was within an inch of telegraphing to you, that I withdraw entirely. But I am unwilling to act in any manner to embarrass you, and it is against my principles to *flare up*." He did not wish to be urged upon the San Francisco parish. He would look for a parish in the East, if necessary.[15]

Bellows spent his time between Sundays (when he usually occupied the San Francisco pulpit) traveling "about the state a great deal, making Sanitary & patriotic speeches. . . . California is by no means the panacea for all human wants. Doubtless it is easier to get a living here than at home; wages are thrice as high & labor is in demand. The soil is productive. Things grow here if only a little water finds its way to them, with prodigious vigor." He was also able to report that Eliza "likes San Francisco—for its picturesqueness, & its abundant flowers & its freedom from cares. She visits a great deal about the parish (I go nowhere) & saves me a world of trouble in that way."[16]

On 10 July the San Francisco parish was to meet, and Robert Swain was very concerned that the proposition that Horatio Stebbins be called should be presented in the proper way. He wrote a note to Bellows in which he suggested that it must be apparent that the parish was not committed to anyone in any way, that Bellows had looked around at the suggestion of the trustees, and had consulted the brethren in Boston for a successor before leaving New York. On this basis Bellows had sounded out the brethren, had some recommendations to make, but no one was committed to anything or anybody.[17]

The parish voted to call Horatio Stebbins to the pulpit of the San Francisco church. It was a well-engineered job by Bellows and Swain—accomplished because there was much understanding between all of the parties concerned. Stebbins did not understand church politics enough to believe that it would all come about. Stebbins received a letter from Bellows and also a telegram from the San Francisco trustees dated 15 July, and had answered and immediately accepted the offer of the San Francisco pulpit. Stebbins admitted to Bellows that he did not understand how the call had been brought about. "Now that the thing is settled, I am now persuaded of our inability to understand the elements of the case when we are so widely separated, and each one exposed to influences which the other does not know." Stebbins proposed to sail for San Francisco on 13 August so that he could meet Bellows there and Bellows could properly introduce him to the parish.[18]

Early in July, Bellows wrote an analysis of the prospects for the Unitarian cause in the West, with particular attention to San Francisco. He believed that "a *second* society in San Francisco is more practical than a *first* society in any other part of the state." He needed a bright and attractive man to start this second church. Rev. H. C. Badger had been acting as his personal secretary. He was loathe to release Badger from these duties, and he doubted if he was the man to start a second society. "I am going into Nevada Territory (about the most lively part of the whole Coast) in a few weeks, & shall have fresh impressions of the prospects of our cause there. I expect, however,to find a whirlwind of speculation before which religion quails & subsides—except in the strongest hands." He had also heard that "Nevada Territory is a hateful region for men of refinement & sensibility."

Bellows hoped through Hale's encouragement to raise a Starr King professorship for Antioch College before leaving San Francisco, although he had found the place essentially a poor region. Actually, he could not understand how the Sanitary Commission had done so well in this area. He felt that the liberal religious cause "have now a new & glorious race before them. If our Unitarian Body can now rise to its duties, Generously plant one foot here on the Pacific, & another in the heart of the West, it may stride over the continent scattering its blessings every where."[19]

On Wednesday, 14 July, Bellows left on another extensive trip of exploration, this time to Lake Tahoe and the Nevada country. His purpose was threefold—first, to see a country largely unknown; second, to see if funds could be raised for the Sanitary Commission; and third, to explore the possibilities of establishing liberal Christianity in this outpost of the West. The trip began on a steamer to Sacramento, with the first fifty miles a race with the rival steamship line. He traveled all over the Nevada territory and missed preaching "not a single Sunday." This is another of Bellows's magnificent letters, of interest chiefly to persons concerned with conditions in the Nevada Territory in 1864.[20]

To the members of the Standing Committee of the Sanitary Commission Bellows gave a more detailed account of his efforts on their behalf. He had spoken at Lake Tahoe, Carson City (the capital, where "the convention now in session to form a state of the territory, adjourned to hear me"), at Gold Hill, at Silver City, at Dayton, and at Virginia City ("first to a church that could not hold half the people that came . . . & then in the largest theater . . . when the crowds went away unable to get in"). He added to his friends on the commission, "It is about the hardest work I ever did in my life, to ride about over the desert of dust mountains & talk an hour & a half in a hot church or hall every night, not to speak of talking all day to people who want to know personally the San'[itary] Commission missionary!" He added that there "are only 50,000 people in the whole Nevada Territory crowded into a few rude mountain mining towns—the oldest about four years old." The Gould and Curry mine employees had given to the Sanitary Commission "the largest bar or brick of silver ever cast in the Territory. It weighs 200 pounds. It is engraved with a Sanitary Commission inscription. I propose to exhibit it in San Francisco for a few days, & hope when it reaches you you will have it exhibited for their gratification in N.[ew] York or elsewhere. They have a notion that it ought to make something for the S. C. by exhibition at one of our great fairs. . . . It is worth about $4,200 in gold." Bellows was leaving the same day for San Francisco, "250 miles, half by stage." He was going by the route of the Donner Pass over the Sierras.[21]

If Bellows had any thought that the large sums of money that came to the Sanitary Commission from California came spontaneously from the hearts of loyal citizens he had that bubble burst soon after he arrived on the scene. Instead of spontaneity he discovered that the businessmen of San Francisco had developed almost a shakedown technique to be certain that every responsible and well-heeled citizen gave generously to the work of the commission. To the members of the Standing Committee back in New York, Bellows gave in detail the techniques by which the fundraising worked. He was involved in trying to set up an efficient organization for the 1865 campaign before he sailed for the East coast. Bellows described the method. 'They have a way of banding together four or five gentlemen, & sitting down before a refractory non-payer until he surrenders in the terms they consider he ought to subscribe to the Sanitary Fund. In this way once a year they go through the city, & get the monied men fully committed. Those who do the work *one* season are generally fully satisfied with their disagreeable experience, & back out the next. The committee is then filled up with fresh *victims*, who go through the same bitter, but useful labor. The question now is *next year's committee*." Bellows also discovered that the Christian Commission had thoroughly organized California in the same manner, and that one of the best fundraising techniques was a monthly pledge system.[22]

Horatio Stebbins and his family arrived in San Francisco on Tuesday 6 September, "in fair health & good spirits." Bellows took them right "to our excellent hotel" (Lick House). Bellows wrote "they have seemed *at home*, almost at once." They wasted no time in installing Stebbins as minister of the church. This event took place on 11 September 1864. With this event completed, Bellows felt his "ministerial burden lifted off." However, on 18 September Bellows was to preach his farewell discourse to the "noble & beautiful congregation, to which I have already become sincerely attached." There was much that he appreciated in California. "I have a feeling that I shall miss something of animation and fresh young life and plastic, pliable hearts, when I return to my old, fixed Society."[23]

Stebbins was "surprised & delighted with the church, the vigor & majesty of the congregation, the appearance of the city & the promise & prospect before him." His wife, children, and sister also appeared to be happy with the move. Bellows was to sail in two weeks. Russell had decided to stay on a few months to work for the Sanitary Commission.[24]

On 9 September 1864, which was the fourteenth anniversary of the admission of California into the Union, the Society of Pioneers took advantage of the fact that Henry Bellows, the famous orator from the East, was in San Francisco. They asked him to be the orator of the day. There was a long line of marchers down the streets of San Francisco made up of the men who comprised the California

Pioneers. Henry Bellows rode with the Chaplain. In his speech Bellows said that he deplored the leveling of the hills in San Francisco. He said that the city could have been as beautiful as Sydney, Australia. He deplored the charging of tolls to travel on the roads in the Nevada Territory. "The intervals between the toll-gates hardly gave my host time to button up his pocket." He spoke of the desolation caused by the gold mining, the eroding of the hills, the scarred terrain as the mines scraped the vast quantities of minerals from the soil, and left a desert. He even added a plea for the

Certificate showing Henry Bellows to be an honorary member of the Society of California Pioneers, Courtesy of the Bellows Family

reelection of President Lincoln in their divided country. In many ways it was a very critical address.[25]

On 22 September, twenty-two citizens of San Francisco commissioned Bellows to deliver to President Lincoln in Washington "a gold specimen with a box of California gold and workmanship, which you will receive through the kindness of Rev. Dr. Bellows." The presentation essay that accompanied the gift said that the articles were "of small intrinsic value, though the specimen is unique and the most beautiful bit of gold in its native state, we have ever seen." They sent it as "a slight token of our cordial and unqualified approbation of your official conduct; and of our profound thankfulness that during these years of our national peril, our President has been always and eminently true to our country and to humanity." They wished that his leadership would continue until "the destruction of slavery and the restoration of peace and national unity."[26]

The Bellows family had "a smooth & pleasant passage over the Caribbean Sea," after the usual hectic and exhausting trip across the Isthmus of Panama. Bellows escaped seasickness entirely, and Mrs. Bellows and Annie "almost entirely." Then they suddenly moved from the tropical heat into the northern cold, and Bellows added, "I have not been warm since we arrived!" They reached Sandy Hook on Saturday evening, 15 October, but the pilot felt that it would be dangerous to go into the port. At 5:00 A.M. on Sunday morning the ship moved into New York. "It was light when we reached quarantine. Staten Island looked almost fairy-like in its beauty." They landed at 9:30 A.M., and "then came the great fight about their baggage."

They arrived at their home before time for church. Dr. Dewey had come "to fill the pulpit, & I let him." Bellows was "hungry, chill[ed] & out of all gear." Bellows had, however, written a sermon for the occasion, and he gave it in the evening "to a full house." Bellows wanted to avoid a scene, and "to slip in without too much agitation." He "gulped down [his] emotion & made a calm appearance, although fearfully excited within. After church, every body stopped & we had a repetition of the leave-taking—only joy took the place of sadness—I don't know which is hardest to bear. The people are unaffectedly glad to see us back, & give us a new place in their warm hearts." But Bellows felt that "dislocation, as if a geological *fault* has acted itself out in my moral stratification, affects me, I can hardly find my way to Heaven from this new-old-spot."[27]

Looking Toward New Fields

Upon returning to New York, Bellows discovered that in his absence the work of the Sanitary Commission had gone very well. George Strong reported on 18 October 1864 of a speech by Bellows about his trip. "The doctor delivered a most interesting and instructing monologue on his observations and experiences of the last six months in California, Oregon, and Washington Territory, held the floor without much interruption from half past seven until five minutes ago (11:30 P.M.) and was not in the least tedious or prosy." Strong realized that Bellows had "gone deep into the philosophy of California manners and morals, and his view of the probable future of the Pacific States is not discouraging. He expatiates on the Yosemite Valley, the marvelous trees, 'the cascades' of the Columbia, and the like. Olmsted is living in great state and dignity as chief of Mariposa."[1]

Bellows spent all of the last week of October 1864 in Washington. Many decisions had been postponed during his absence, so that "I am if possible more pressed with work than ever." There was a meeting of the entire commission, and it was revealed that the expenses had been averaging a quarter of a million dollars a month, which Bellows described as due "to the necessity of *buying stores*, chiefly anti-scorbutics." The commission was doing much with onions and molasses and fresh fruits and vegetables to combat the existence of scurvy among the troops. Bellows felt that the expenditures were too high, "but it is hard to go backwards." He found that the commission and the staff now lacked balance among the personnel, but he felt that that was "not strange considering the balance-wheel man was in California!" He had come very near to going down to Virginia to Grant's headquarters to look into some matters about "some improved plans about the treatment of prisoners in Rebel hands."

Bellows had also had a visit with President Lincoln on 27 October, "& in the presence of the Secretary of State, delivered the *gold Box*, reading the letter to him & making a suitable speech about the donors, their former democratic character, & the loyalty of California." The President "expressed himself as heartily gratified." They then got into a discussion about mining in the West about which Bellows obviously knew a lot. They talked about "the state of art & science in Cal.[ifornia] & the political prospects."

Bellows noted in Washington that "the election is occupying every moment of the spare time of patriotic men." Bellows himself had spoken in New York at the eighteenth ward meeting after his return, and he was scheduled to speak again on 3 November "to a public meeting in Cooper Institute, & Friday night to a political assembly of loyal women in the Church of the Messiah." On Saturday he was to attend a celebration of the birthday of William Cullen Bryant at the Century Club together with Mrs. Bellows and Annie. He also was to meet with the trustees of the Mariposa Company "to make a report on my observations on the mine." He was also preparing for a meeting early in December with the Boston clergy "to hear my report about Cal.[ifornia]."[2]

Bellows was pleased with the reelection of Abraham Lincoln whom he admired so much and for whom he had campaigned ardently. He also noted that it was not only the men who were active in politics this year but the women, who, although they had no vote, made it a point to attend the campaign meetings. Bellows himself had addressed 3,000 people at the Cooper Institute and had talked for an hour and a quarter "at one of the most successful campaign meetings." He found "the meetings of the opposition . . . comparatively small & spiritless." Bellows's opinion of the opposition is illustrated in these words, "It was nevertheless feared that the sullen, ignorant masses of foreigners, cooperating with the spoil-hunters in the Democratic party, would manage by appeals to mean & culpable considerations, the fatigue at high places, & the unscrupulous promise of a fall in the cost of all necessary articles of living, on the McClellan election, to bring out a favorable vote in his favor. Great anxiety existed on this point."

Bellows had been surprised at the popular majority with which Lincoln had won the election. Only three states had not given Lincoln a majority. The administration had expected that violence might break out in New York City and they had sent "Gen. Butler with five thousand to N.[ew] York to preserve order." Bellows had talked with Butler several times and found him fearless and with "Napoleonic energy." He felt that the victory had "called forth an almost religious joy in the people. So happy, so relieved, so thankful seem the virtuous & patriotic portion of society, that the intelligence, the unselfishness & the worth of the nation has triumphed; that we have a country, & a policy & a government."

Bellows had also participated with other prominent New Yorkers in the reception and entertainment of Professor Goldwin Smith of Oxford University, "the ablest & most efficient exponent of our principles, & friend of the American cause in England. He came on to see for himself how the state of public sentiment was."

Smith spoke at several of these meetings, "explaining his own
relations to the liberals in England; his views of our cause; his
increased faith in it, since he had seen it with his own eyes & the
confidence in the improvement in English feeling after the sublime
results of the election, became known there." These meetings also
convinced Bellows of something he had missed in the rawer West,
"the *charms of the educated refined society* of New York." He felt
that this was "the chief advantage of our life over that of S.[an]
Francisco."

By this time Bellows was beginning to feel at home again in New
York City. "I find already the absorbing cases of home & parish,
commission & country, society, art & other interesting things, taking
me out of my California rut & putting me on the old familiar track
again. I am writing sermons as usual, flavored a good deal with our
Pacific experience, but not directly on the subject." He had not even
had time to look at his California letters "to put them into some
shape."[3]

Bellows more and more began to think about his own Unitarian
denomination. He probably had visited more churches and knew
more about the strengths and weaknesses of the denomination than
any other person. Beginning about this period in late 1864 one gets
the impression that Bellows conceived of himself in a new and
important role in the rejuvenation of the Unitarian movement, and
in this work he was to show a breadth of spirit that the interpreters of
the history of the times have often overlooked.

Frederic Henry Hedge had written to Bellows about the coming
meeting with the Boston clergy and had evidently complained about
the radicals within the denomination. Bellows hoped that his address
would have "an important influence upon the future of our
denomination." Then he commented to Hedge, "The real life in our
body is in the *heretical* wing. If we cut *it* off, there is nothing to move
with! My theological instincts and my Christian feelings are outraged
by the *Rationalism* of our young men—but as my whole practical
nature & working instincts are equally outraged by the paralytic
imbecility of our sounder & more Christian wing, I am not willing to
rely on *that* for the future." He continued, "We must solve our
difficulties by ignoring our theological differences, & finding *in
work*, a way out of our heresy & our deadness. I am persuaded that
Rationalism is *not a working power*, even at its liveliest state, & I
think our young men, noble & earnest as many are, will find it out,
when they attempt *work* on a grand scale—outside the little field of
N.[ew] Eng.[land] where what comes up is due to the general

husbandry of the past, more than to the labor of the present farmer." Then he went on to express his hopes as to what he could do for the Unitarian movement. "I foresee that I am to do something for our body if I live, through the union in me of an actual faith & an organizing spirit & faculty. I have *staved* off the responsibility as long as I could but it presses me sorely & I do not obey the call of God."[4]

Bellows made his projected trip to the Boston area. He lectured in Portland, Maine. On 4 December he preached in Thomas Starr King's old pulpit at the Hollis Street Church while Rev. George Cheney preached at All Souls. Bellows made an address on Tuesday evening, again at the Hollis Street Church, on Unitarian prospects on the Pacific Coast. It was a most productive session in Boston, and a great deal of enthusiasm was aroused for a rejuvenation of the denomination.

A special meeting of the American Unitarian Association was held at the Hollis Street Church in Boston on 6 and 7 December "to awaken interest in the work of the Association by laying before churches the condition of our funds and the demand for our labor." There was a large group of ministers and laymen in attendance "and the tone of the meeting was hopeful and enthusiastic. After Dr. Stebbins, the president, had stated the purpose of the meeting, Dr. Bellows urged the importance of a more effective organization of the Unitarian body. His success with the Sanitary Commission had evidently prepared his mind for a like work on the part of Unitarians, and for a strong faith in the value of organized effort in behalf of liberal religion."[5]

Bellows's speech aroused great enthusiasm, and the group resolved to raise $100,000 for its work during the next year. Bellows then suggested that a committee be appointed to plan for a convention in New York City early in 1865. He was promptly appointed chairman of this committee.

Bellows had a chance to slip off to Walpole for the first time since his return from California to see all of the Bellows clan and to renew his closest friendships with his family. On Saturday night he took the train back to New York and gave an extemporaneous sermon on Sunday morning, and probably, as was often his custom, dug a sermon out of the sermonic barrel for the evening service.

Duties on the Sanitary Commission were pressing, and the third week in December found Bellows at City Point and then at the headquarters of the Union Armies. On 21 December, a Wednesday evening, he wrote from aboard a Sanitary Commission barge at City

Point. He had had supper at Fortress Monroe on Tuesday. It was raining heavily and the sea was rough, but they had embarked for City Point sailing about eighty miles up the James River. "The old plantations are mostly in ruins," he noted. Bellows found life very comfortable on board the Sanitary Barge except that the sleeping was uncomfortable on a cold December night. He found it impossible to get warm in bed, although he wore all his underclothing.

The crisis that had called Bellows down to the headquarters of the Army was what Bellows termed a "mischievous slander." This grew "out of the presence of some Refugee women sent aboard our boat by the Provost-Marshall & kept there ten days, until the low-mouthed scoundrels on the wharf circulated the report that our agents & officers were *keeping* disreputable women on the Sanitary barge—& the reputation of Dr. McDonald & Dr. Sivalin was rapidly going down to our vast discredit. We have had to examine many witnesses & establish the fact of perfect innocency in our agents—which is now done."[6]

Bellows did not make it home to New York City until the morning of 26 December. He described his trip as "a disagreeable journey." He had gone close enough to the front so that he could "see the batteries of the enemy, the spires of Petersburg, & the suburbs of Richmond, all visible from a tower which I did not ascend." He had gone into the famous Dutch Gap "where shells exploded & shells not exploded, were strewn about. It was a *dangerous* neighborhood but not the less interesting on that account." Bellows believed that Grant wanted Lee to stay where he was until Sherman came up from the South.

Bellows had had an hour's conversation with General Grant. "He is a plain, quiet man, of *little* language & little manner, but with a solid sort of look, as if he kept up a calm, steady thinking. I should think him a man *without pride of opinion* & therefore without motive to refuse or oppose counsel & assistance from any quarter; a man capable of *taking advice,* which is a great point." Bellows felt that Grant even enjoyed Sherman's successes. Bellows doubted that Grant had "great *positive* power. Some men are great from the *absence* of weakness, vanities, & self-conceit, pretension & self-seeking. I think that Grant is like *an apple* stuck with cloves—that is he draws the spicy folks about him, & forms an innocent, pure & simple centre for such a concentration of ability."[7]

Strong reported that "Bellows thought the General might have taken 'just a little too much soup.' According to his [Bellows's] judgment, much of Grant's strength lies in his singleness of purpose, his entire devotion to his work, his freedom from political aspirations, and his readiness to avail himself of the talent and energy of any subordinate without pausing to consider whether his own personal renown may not be thereby endangered."[8]

Writing a New Year's Day letter on 2 January 1865 (New Year's Day came on Sunday so it was celebrated on Monday), Bellows felt that the bottom was dropping out of the Confederacy. "We have therefore a more confident feeling that the war is approaching its natural conclusion, & that the next active campaign will finish it & that must be by the middle of next summer. I think 4th July next will see us victors, & the nation essentially at peace."[9]

Early in 1865 the Sanitary Commission was at the apex of its usefulness. Its average monthly expenditures were around a quarter of a million dollars, it maintained a force of more than five hundred in the field, it was supporting a vast number of convalescent homes and lodges, it had its own flotilla of steamers, its own hospital cars, and its own wagon trains. It was also apparent to most observers that time was swiftly running out for the Confederacy.

CHAPTER TEN

Morning Is Breaking
All Around

Finding a Creed

With the civil strife apparently concluding in a matter of months,
and with the United States Sanitary Commission well organized and
efficient in the field, Bellows could now turn his energies to the
reorganization of the Unitarian denomination into a Unitarian
Church of America.

The plan which Bellows had proposed in Boston for the
rejuvenation of the denomination had received a diverse reception.
Some of the men applauded, but some were highly skeptical that the
denomination could make a great effort. Bellows hoped that Edward
Everett Hale and Charles Henry Brigham who agreed most closely
with his plan could both come to New York the first week in January
1865 to discuss it in depth. Bellows had heard from some trustworthy
sources "that the larger plan *we* proposed struck the majority of our
ministers as quixotic, & that they anticipated nothing but failure
from its undertaking." This did not surprise Bellows. If anyone
proposed something large it was immediately suspect.[1]

On 12 January 1865, an invitation went out from Henry W.
Bellows in New York notifying the members of the committee that
they had been appointed, and that there would be a meeting at
Bellows's home at 59 East 20th Street on Wednesday 25 January at
10:00 A.M. Bellows wanted to know if he could count on each
person's attendance. In regard to the coming convention, Bellows
suggested to Hale that he expected "little from the preliminary
meeting" except some suggestions as to time and method of
organization. Bellows also expected the attendance at the meeting of
the committee to be small, for some of the men could not come from
a distance. But he felt that the conference would test the mettle of the
Unitarian cause. "If we are impotent, we are to show it, & make way
for those who have the future in their loins. The sooner we are
known to be as a denomination, childless—'No son of ours
succeeding,' the sooner the name of liberal religion will pass into the
hands of another dynasty." Bellows felt that the convention was the
place in which Unitarians would catch the pulse of their conscience.[2]

Bellows was also beginning to feel that if the denomination was to become a national church it must define its beliefs. He wrote, "I am persuaded that history shows no progress in any sect not built upon *dogma,* & that, *inconvenient* as it is, we must *find* & enunciate *our creed.* And it must be a creed we can feel the importance of pushing, —nay of invading with." He showed that his intention was not dogma but people. "It is the *people* we are after. We must then have a *pronunciamento,* or creed. We want to mark what part of old theology has stranded & can't go down the stream any further, & bid the people come with axe & saw & hack & cut away, till the ark can float again."[3]

Bellows had in mind something more than just the reorganization of the Unitarian churches. He confided to Russell: "The times seem ripe for a great movement of the *Liberal Christian Church of America.*" He was moving in his thinking beyond denominational strength. "I am persuaded that some millions of our fellow citizens & fellow Christians are not only impatient of the existing ideas & expressions of the popular religious creeds & the Ministerial Body in general, but are longing for some National Church." He defined this church as one "while allowing the fresh air of intellectual liberty to blow in at the doors, & the present lights of science and experience to shine in at its windows, would be, nevertheless, eminently Christian, worshipful & tender, humane & devout, tolerant yet earnest; in short a Church in which the open avowed Creed should be in congruity with men's opinions on other subjects; science, politics, art, business, pleasure & this life's honest legitimate concerns." He noted that in the search of people for a meaningful religion "there is a strange fumbling round, which is exhibited in Spiritualism & Secularism, that indicates the need of some great movement to create & grade a road for the unchurched and dissatisfied & creedless millions, to advance upon."

Bellows went on to say that he did not believe that the Unitarians, Universalists, Hicksite Quakers, Spiritualists, Parkerites, and so on "can meet this want, by peddling about their separate or conjoined creeds. They have proved themselves *outside* the great popular church by their petty piddling operation for fifty years past." He continued, 'They are not *a* Church, or *the* Church, but a criticism, a commentary, a protest, a negation. They made themselves & others so uncomfortable in Christendom & the Church that they were either left behind or jumped out, & having got into a side-road, they have been vainly trying to lead the travel their way."

But, he said, "the people mean-while went on upon the old road, & in the old coach—& they have the right-of-way, and the old stopping-places, and the dear familiar prospects, and the original way-bill, & the tested driver." Bellows believed that "the Christian Unction, the original impulse, the Holy Spirit, the true symbols, the real demands of the Christian Church, never have been in the hands of the liberals. They are still with the great popular sects, whose religious instincts have kept them near the old covenant & the old symbols."

Bellows explained further: "My theory of the National Church of America is the *old* Church inspired with the *new liberty & motion of life*. In losing the liberals out of it, it has lost the spice & spirit of the new era. We want to return into the Church, & to carry back with us all the freedom, all the inspiration, all the science, taste, culture we have gathered in our exile, & look again at the old symbols in the light of all this experience, not to disown them, but to re-interpret . . . them in a fresh & larger & more earnest spirit."

What Bellows thus wanted was a "creed . . . in strict accordance with the historical past—growing out of it, as a flower from its root—but which shall be accompanied by an interpretation so broad & generous that it shall at once liberalize the views & satisfy the free longings of the millions." He wanted this to be not a Unitarian but a Christian Creed. He wanted it to be not negative "but affirmative." He sensed that "millions of Trinitarians are waiting to *hear* it." He believed that it is only in such churches "that the great Reformation is to be ultimately effected." He wanted to mix the liberals and the orthodox, and felt that unless this was done "we are both lost." He proclaimed "We are the *leaven*, they are the *flour*. You can't live on *leaven*, but you can't live on flour *without* leaven." He felt that the liberals must do the leading simply because they had "no ecclesiastical character to lose." He felt that with this Unitarian leaven there could be a new kind of church in America, "something different from either element." This could be the church universal.[4]

In keeping with this larger liberal church of which he dreamed, Henry Bellows had a conference late in January with Rev. Henry Blanchard of Brooklyn, a Universalist. Bellows had asked Blanchard for a list of the "liberals" in the Universalist denomination to whom he could turn if his Universal Christian Church were to be more than just Unitarian. Blanchard supplied him with a list of twenty-three names of ministers all along the East Coast whom he believed could be called the liberals in the Universalist denomination. The list included:

J.E. Brice of Middletown, Conn., J. Hazard Hartzell of Buffalo, N.Y., E.W. Reynolds of Watertown, N.Y., W.P. Payne of Clinton, N.Y., Richmond Fisk of Lockport, N.Y., A.J. Canfield of Williamsburgh, N.Y., William Spaulding of Salem, Mass., W.T. Stowe of East Lexington, Mass., Thomas Gorman of Malden, Mass., J.G. Bartholomew of Roxbury, Mass., R.A. Ballou of Boston, G.W. Skinner of New Bedford, Mass., T.E. St. John of Worcester, Mass., Charles J. White of East Boston, Mass., W.E. Gibbs of West Cambridge, Mass., J.F. Powers of East Cambridge, Mass., Harvey Hersey of Provincetown, Mass., Clark R. Moor of Cambridgeport, Mass., Charles Leonard of Chelsea, Mass., L.W. Burnington of North Adams, Mass., A.J. Patterson of Portsmouth, N.H., Amory Battles of Bangor, Maine, and E.C. Bolles of Portland, Maine.[5]

Henry Bellows was now prepared to approach the church body nearest his own if the conference adopted his ideas of ecumenicity.

On 1 February 1865, an official printed notice went out to all the Unitarian congregations inviting them to send their pastor and two delegates to meet in New York "to consider the interests of our cause and to institute measures for its good." It proposed, "We wish now to hold such a convention for a more thorough organization of the Liberal Church of America." They begged the churches to send "the strongest, wisest, and most prudent men of our body." The date was fixed for 10:00 A.M. on Wednesday, 5 April, and no place for the meeting was given except New York.[6]

Bellows was also very concerned about the credentials of the delegates to the meeting. If money were going to be raised, the churches ought to understand that the meeting would be a legal one and well conducted. He asked Hale to consult four or five men about the specifics of the credentials and to set up some standards. He also believed that there had to be a definite program for the meetings, and he set to work with his usual efficiency preparing such a program.[7]

Having sent out the preliminary notice of the meeting of the New York Convention of the Unitarian Churches, Bellows then wrote a much longer explanation of the purposes of the meeting which was printed, signed by himself, Hale, and A.P. Putnam, and sent to all of the churches. We know that Bellows wrote it, for on his copy he wrote, "Page proofs of my address to the churches." Bellows thus spoke for this subcommittee.[8]

After the letter of explanation went out it was not long before Bellows began to get reactions. Samuel Joseph May of Syracuse wrote, "But do you not mean to invite our Universalist brethren to cooperate with us, and become one with us?" May, of course, did not know that Bellows had already written to get a list of the more liberal of the Universalist brethren. Samuel May pointed out that the Universalist body was larger than the Unitarians, and "there are no greater differences of doctrinal belief between their body and ours—than between the various portions of our own body." May mentioned that the Universalists had been able to convert a class of the working people that the Unitarians had never touched. He suggested that the Unitarians had taken away the greatest Universalist, Thomas Starr King, and he mentioned several other prominent Universalists.

May also wanted to know if Bellows wanted "our noble women to be represented at the convention?" He felt that they were for the most part more interested in Christianity than the men, and understood it better. May began to raise some theological questions with which the convention was going to have to struggle. "I cannot see how anyone can properly be called a Christian," he wrote, "who does not profess to believe that Jesus Christ was an authoritative teacher of true religion, a teacher sent from God." He made an even more difficult standard of judgment—"nor do I think that any one should be considered a *true* Christian who has not become Christ-like."[9]

On 20 February, Bellows was in Boston addressing a group of fifty ministers at the Hollis Street Church. After his address on the uniting of the right and left wings of the Unitarian denomination, there was a three-hour discussion. Bellows summarized the results. "A very few are anxious to divide; the great majority to hold together. I think there will be no split. The older men are shy about committing themselves to the convention, chiefly because they don't know what it may pledge them to do." He continued, "They have had misgivings that there was 'a cut in the meal,' some scheme for entrapping them into more discipline, & still they were prepared to endure. The young men however are full of zeal, enthusiasm & spirit, infectious in their desire to seize this opportunity, & they will push the older men in spite of themselves on to the good work."[10]

To Russell, Henry Bellows was a bit more explicit about the meeting in Boston. He listed four groups into which the Boston ministers appeared to be divided. First, *"the elder men*, old-fashioned Unitarians, very *ethical* in their humor—preaching the doctrine of self-culture & personal righteousness." This group was associated with Boston respectability, and little disposed to undertake great things. These men were "spiteful towards the transcendental or radical wing, and pretty jealous of any thing which don't originate in Boston." He listed Dr. Gannett as the head of this group and George Ellis, Samuel Lothrop, James Thompson, and Edward Hall of Worcester as specimens of it.

The second group was "a pretty large section of Radicals—transcendental in their philosophy, unhistorical in their faith—men like Frothingham, Longfellow, Potter of New Bedford, a strong body of young men just out of Divinity Studies—who really think Xity [Christianity] only one among a great many other religions." He found these men shy about the convention "thinking some test may be applied, some *creed* slipped around them. They take a great alarm at any suggestion of any standard of faith—however generous, but are partly willing to co-operate on some platform of *Work* which has no doctrine in it."

The third group were a *"small section* of Evangelicals—who believe that Jesus Christ was a strictly miraculous person & a savior indeed, of whom Rufus Ellis, Mr. Sears & a very few others are samples." These men want to secede "& are disposed to deny any fellowship with the looser & more liberal party. The fourth group were "another set of *Broad Church men,* like J. F. Clarke, Dr. Hedge, E. E. Hale—& numerous others—who recognize the elements of truth in all the other sections, & believe in the possibility of welding them together." Bellows made it clear that "with this party I belong & am working. With it, too, must necessarily work all of each of the other sections."

He felt that the convention would be significant because there were to be two laymen for every minister present. "It may be said to be the first chance for the lay element in our Denomination to develop its consciousness, & learn to articulate its experience or its wants . . . I think there must be a healthier tone of thought & one of a more practical character." Bellows believed that without this kind of interchange "the pulpit and the pews are getting alienated from each other, & the ministers correspondingly ineffective and unsustained." The very idea of a convention has aroused the laity as nothing Bellows had even dreamed."[11]

Word was moving throughout the denomination that Henry Bellows was going to try to impose a creed upon the convention.

A. P. Putnam of Brooklyn found this highly amusing. He wrote to Bellows, "Does not all this carping about the matter that gets into our papers, indicate *sickness*?" He felt that the persons who opposed any basis of organization misunderstand the purposes of the conveners of the convention. "They cannot seem to distinguish between a creed in the obnoxious sense of that word, & a statement of faith that shall serve for the purpose of information & as a rallying-cry."[12]

Meanwhile, some of the more conservative Boston churches had been having internal struggles with the issue of whether or not to send delegates to the convention. Hale reported to Bellows that Rufus Ellis at the First Church in Boston had called a parish meeting, had "read the 'call' and asked what they would do." There was dead pause, "after which with due nagging the parish was silently made to vote it would not send any delegates,—*four* bold inquirers steadfastly voting that they would." The next week Hale put a hundred copies of Bellows's sermon on the First Church literature tables, and Dr. Stebbins preached in the afternoon about the convention. A group of younger parishioners kicked up such a fuss "that a meeting was called the next week and now they propose to recalcitrate and . . . to let us have two delegates."

At the Second Church in Boston, Chandler Robbins "attempting the same game was unhorsed the first time." Even "the smallest country parishes are choosing their men." And Hale whispered to Bellows that he would not be surprised if his friend Cyrus Bartol who generally was against the whole thing "writes to reserve a room in Hotel Bellows."[13]

Bellows was delighted that "the laity are kicking up behind." He was concerned about the "faithlessness & blindness of our clergy whose spiritual eyes are so bandaged up with their Kentucky-cave-life-in-a-small-pond-under-ground, that they don't know day-light when they come to it. The morning is breaking all around, & they sleep in midnight stupor." He was pleased that the laity would not countenance this siesta. Bellows almost wished that they had called an entirely lay convention "to take denominational matters into their own hands. It would have been a rich joke!"

A committee from the five New York parishes was meeting on Tuesday evening "to make outward arrangements for the convention." Room space had been engaged at Irving Hall, and they had hired the old Church of the Messiah for the three days of the convention for committee meetings. Bellows felt that the central location of the old Messiah building would make it a better place for the business than All Souls. He suggested that the laymen were afraid of "too much clerical talk." And for this reason Bellows felt that it was "important to have an order of *business* arranged before hand, and a business Committee packed, & put into the Presiding officer's *head*, to report the first things, after officers are elected."

Bellows felt that "even more important than what we do, is *the perfecting of the organization by which any thing can be done.*" He believed that "to organize in an effective way will be our greatest triumph!" Bellows believed that the first and the main task of the convention would be to organize effectively and if this were not accomplished, little would ever get done.

The second consideration was to keep "Religious work (what is peculiar to the Church) . . . prominent!" He did not want the Conference to become another Freedman's organization, a Sanitary Commission, "or general civilizers." He felt that "the nation so far as it is emancipated wants a *Church, a worship* & a *Christian Cultus.*" The third duty of the Conference was to understand that it was the newly settled continent that they wanted to organize for liberal Christianity. He felt there was "more room than we can occupy, & yet all our boys want to be back-woodsmen & shoot Indians & hack down forests." Frothingham had gone on to Boston that week and flung "his fire-brands into [the Boston] Ministerial Union." Bellows feared that "if anyone can detract from the convention, he can, with his 'glittering generalities'."[14]

By 17 March it was apparent to Bellows that "we shall have the weight of the Denomination in the convention." The tide had turned. It was therefore doubly important that this opportunity was not to be missed. "It is all important that we should keep a disputatious, carping & personal *spirit* out of the meeting & prove to the world that the Unitarian Convention did not come together at N[ew] York, like the Democratic Convention at Charleston, to *split.*" It would be difficult for the Unitarians to show that they were the church to which the liberal Christians should come if they were purely a disputatious body and not able to run their own business meetings.

Bellows also felt that in order to appeal to these persons what was needed was "a platform of principles, sentiments, ideas—as *definite* & as *evangelical as our Body* will *bear—& no more so.*" He was concerned that this kind of a platform be brought forward at some stage of the convention. Bellows believed that it should be possible to offer a platform that both Gannett at one extreme and Frothingham at the other could accept. He sensed that it might disrupt the meetings to bring this controversial question up at once, but that a time should be set aside when it would be discussed. Bellows then outlined to Hale exactly what would be done at each hour of the convention. If the convention were of no consequence, it would not be because of bad planning on the part of Bellows' committee.[15]

The planners wanted nothing to be left to chance. James Freeman Clarke even read his entire opening address to Edward Everett Hale so that he could be certain that the tone and the thrust was what was wanted at the opening of the convention.[16] The sermon was then sent on to Bellows, who wrote, "I like Bro[ther] Clarke's sermon prodigiously."[17] Bellows also informed Hale that he ought to have a long talk with Governor John Albion Andrew of Massachusetts who had been chosen to be the presiding officer of the convention. His presence lent dignity to the office, for Andrew had been closely connected with James Freeman Clarke and his church in Boston. This had deepened the religious and humanitarian side of his nature. He was active in social causes, so that he would have the support of the liberals and the social radicals. He had been active in the nomination of Abraham Lincoln for President, and had been elected the governor of Massachusetts on the same ticket which made Lincoln President. In 1864 he had been reelected governor. He was an ideal choice for many reasons to be the presiding officer.[18]

Bellows also had enlisted the services of one of his leading laymen, a lawyer, Dortman B. Eaton, in whom Bellows had great faith; and he promised that he would "be thoroughly acquainted with my views & feelings & one of the delegates from our Church will be ready to do any nice service in debate which may be required."[19]

The day before the convention opened Bellows wrote to his sister, Eliza Dorr, that he had great hopes for its success. "If it succeeds, as I hope, it will be worth five years of life to put order into the chaos of our cause & get some tangible platform for our Unitarian brethren to stand on. We have been all over the lot quite long enough. I wish with all my heart it were successfully over." On a more personal note Bellows was delighted with the progress of the Union armies before Richmond, and noted to Eliza Dorr that "this is the anniversary of my parting with my people a year ago, to sail next day, April 4th, for California. It has been a rich year. How pleasant the thought of some rest is; this summer!"[20]

The Triumph of Our Denominational Life

"For the first time in the history of the Unitarian body in this country the churches were directly represented at a general gathering."[1] Actually, there were two hundred and twenty-two churches who sent three hundred and eighty-five delegates to the convention. Only men could be official delegates, but there were many women present. This was one of the first times in Unitarian circles the laymen of the churches actually had more representation than the clergy. Bellows had purposely seen to it that this came about so that in the organization of a national denomination the business skills of the laymen could be tapped.

The evening before the convention began, Dr. James Freeman Clarke gave the sermon which Bellows had already previewed. In it Clarke called for a new spirit of inclusiveness, a broad and tolerant catholicity, and the union of the Unitarian churches on the basis of all the work that had to be done. The next day, 5 April, the convention met at the Broadway Atheneum, formerly Dr. Osgood's church. Bellows had set the scenario well, and for the first part of the convention, at least, things went according to schedule. The Honorable John A. Andrew, the Governor of Massachusetts, was elected to preside over the convention. Among the vice presidents elected were William Cullen Bryant of Bellows's church and Bellows's former colleague, Dr. Orville Dewey. Edward Everett Hale was made secretary.

Among the less controversial business of the conference was approval of the efforts of the Unitarian Association to secure the sum of $100,000 for expansion, and the churches were urged to contribute to this fund. They agreed to seek a like sum for the endowment of Antioch College, and they commended to men of wealth the financial needs of the Meadville Theological School and the Harvard Divinity School. They decided that a denominational paper was needed which was to be launched under the title of *The Liberal Christian*. A resolution which anticipated merger with the Universalist body was presented, and James Freeman Clarke, Samuel J. May, and Robert Collyer were appointed a committee to seek more unity—at least through correspondence—with the other liberal *Christian* faiths such as the Methodists, Congregationalists, Universalists, and others.

We have already seen in the preparation for the conference that contrary to what historians have usually said about Henry Bellows, he did not belong to the ultraconservative wing of the Unitarian movement. His mood was conciliatory. He felt that all elements

James Freeman Clarke, D.D., Courtesy of the Unitarian Universalist Association

within the denomination would have to be brought to a more common ground theologically, and if not theologically, at least in the pursuit of good works. Conrad Wright has written: "Historians have generally ranked Bellows with the conservative wing of the denomination. But it was never his way to adhere to any extreme position, whether of the right or of the left, if it were possible to find a middle ground." Wright calls Bellows "an inveterate middle-of-the-roader."[2] When Bellows died, Cyrus Bartol, who knew him so well, commented that "his talent, his temper, was to mediate, harmonize, reconcile . . . He had no notion of letting an enterprise he was embarked in, by following extreme counsels, or by any exclusive tendency, go to excess."[3]

Bellows believed that Unitarianism was so narrowly parochial that it would take a great deal of effort to overcome the apathy of the conservative Boston-based right wing. He actually feared this apathy and unconcern about growth in conservative ranks more than he feared the criticism of the radicals. The Boston conservatives were strongly in favor of congregational polity, which gave them complete independence, and in many ways blocked any firm attempt for the churches to work together. Bellows had run into this separatism and unconcern for denominational needs in 1850 when he tried to raise some money among the Boston ministers and churches for Antioch College.

Bellows identified himself with what he called the Broad Churchmen—ministers who felt that there were differences within the denomination which ought to be recognized and cherished, but which should not split the Unitarians into warring segments. Bellows was not certain that this Broad Church party within the denomination was large enough to carry the day, but he felt that the effort should be made.

As Bellows had anticipated, when the suggestion was made at the convention for some statement as to what the Unitarians really stood for, cries of "creedalism" and "coercion" were thrown at Bellows' party. Bellows did not want a creed. His own church in New York had no basis for being a church member except a simple confession about the nature of Jesus Christ which a person made in complete freedom to the minister. Bellows wanted the denomination to stand for something more than freedom itself. He believed that in the atmosphere of freedom it would be possible for churchmen to make a general statement which could be accepted by almost everyone at the convention. He felt that to organize a national church upon no statement at all except that everybody believed in freedom would be building upon the sands, and would not constitute a church at all. Freedom was to be the means, not the end.

Yet, the minute that some concise statement was proposed, Bellows was accused of trying to creedalize the new church and to impose his ideas upon the others. Nothing like this was on his mind at all, as so many of his statements in his letters indicate. As Stow Persons interprets the history, "On the second day a committee dominated by Bellows presented a plan for the organization of a National Conference of Unitarian Churches. The proposed constitution stated that its members were disciples of 'the Lord Jesus Christ, dedicated to the advancement of his Kingdom'." But as Persons states, "short as these phrases were, they were sufficiently offensive to the radicals to launch a struggle which culminated two years later with the virtual secession of several promising young men from the Unitarian denomination."[4] Persons does not mention that the Free Religious Association never really amounted to anything significant in the Unitarian movement, and many who joined it still kept their loyalty to the Unitarian Association and even to the National Conference.

Since the draft for the "creed" which was proposed by Bellows at the convention is preserved in Bellows's own hand, it is interesting to see exactly what kind of theological doctrines Bellows was seeking for the convention to approve. There was a provision that no person had to accept the conclusions of the convention. They simply indicated that a majority believed that these were truths that united them. One of the problems, of course, in the statement was the phraseology and the number of typical Christian words which are used, but which Bellows did not use in any creedal or Trinitarian sense.

The convention, Bellows claimed, "assembled in the name of Almighty God, the Universal Father, and of Jesus Christ, our Lord and Savior." Note that the third person of the Trinity is absent, and that Bellows in his interpretation of Jesus in no sense implied that Jesus was uniquely divine as contradistinct from other human beings. He also indicated that the convention wanted to establish "communion and fellowship among Christians." Bellows had no concept that the National Council would include non-Christians. He was aiming at the more liberal of the Protestant sects. He wanted to unite "upon the sole basis of a common faith in the Gospel of Jesus Christ, subject to the free interpretation of every individual disciple." There certainly is not much problem here about the willingness to allow latitude of belief.

Then he gave his title of the proposed church organization: the Liberal Christian Church of America, a title that was not adopted at the convention. Bellows was too broad for the majority of Unitarians in 1865. He believed that large numbers of people still wanting to keep their own church bodies and organizations also wanted to reach out to join with others. He felt that the truths of the Christian religion are "capable of being fully expressed in verbal propositions." Bellows went on to claim that the "fundamental object of the Gospel of Christ is to establish the *Kingdom of God,* the reign of justice, truth, purity & goodness in the hearts and lives of individual men, and of humanity which is corporate Man." He continued, "salvation by Christ, is the reign of the Kingdom of God, and is independent of time and place, of life & death, of here and hereafter."

Bellows felt that "the Church visible is that external institution, founded on the historical Christ, which has had hitherto, & will continue to have the special function of carrying on his work of direct appeal, warning, & instruction in righteousness, and in his name communicating his life and spirit to the world." He believed that "the Church invisible is identical with the Kingdom of God." Bellows felt that no other basis than this was necessary for union of the churches. He felt that Unitarians and Trinitarians could unite in such a creed. He believed that the function of the Liberal Christian Church of America would be to "build up the Kingdom of God, and promote the reign of the Gospel." He pointed out again that the existence of this new church body in no way would "interfere with any existing Denominational organizations. They will continue to work in their own way as long as they choose." He wanted the Gospel of Christ "to subdue into itself and unto God the whole mind, the whole heart, and the whole soul of humanity."[5] Bellows had most of the convention with him on this matter. And essentially the constitutional statement was not a creed at all. It was more a statement of faith, and it could be changed by any future convention (as it was). A creed is usually considered to be binding and unchangeable. Bellows had nothing like that in mind.

Of the radicals, Octavius Brooks Frothingham presented the greatest problem, partly, I suspect, because Bellows, along with Samuel Osgood, had been having misunderstandings with Frothingham almost from the moment he came to New York City. There is no reason to suspect that Bellows would get any better cooperation from Frothingham in this matter, which was ideological rather than a matter of comity. Bellows expected Frothingham to disrupt the proceedings, even though his tone at his Boston speech had been conciliatory. But Frothingham made it clear that he would not disrupt the proceedings but that if he did not like what happened at the convention, he would withdraw.

At the opening session held at the Broadway Atheneum, after Edward Everett Hale had presented a series of routine resolutions dealing with the organization of the convention, A. A. Low, of the Church of the Savior in Brooklyn, tried to get a creedal basis for the convention adopted with a series of resolutions. Low's conservatism was of a very Christian kind. He had objected to Clarke's opening sermon as being far too conciliatory. Bellows felt that this move on Low's part was an attempt to split the convention. The conservative tone of the resolutions did not bother him. But he felt that the move was against the cooperative spirit he hoped would be apparent. Bellows immediately intervened, and the resolutions were ruled out of order by Governor Andrew. They were later introduced again, but this time they were laid on the table where they remained to the very end of the convention. Then they were referred to the Council which the conference set up, and disappeared forever. Bellows had been afraid that since Low was such an outstanding member of the greater New York community, no one would oppose him, so he performed the disagreeable task himself.

More to Bellows's liking than the Low resolutions were those that had been prepared in advance by the business committee. These were adopted in the afternoon of the first day's session. One dealt with the obligation of Unitarians to organize nationally on a more comprehensive plan. The second stated that any decisions and resolutions adopted by the convention should be distinctly understood to represent the opinions only of the majority and not of all persons present. Things were going according to the plans which Bellows and Hale had drawn up.

The rest of the afternoon was devoted to reports of the work of the American Unitarian Association, the Western Conference and other organizations within the denomination. Some later accused Bellows of engineering the convention. He certainly planned well. Governor Andrew was a good parliamentarian and kept things in order and according to schedule, and either Bellows or Hale was constantly on the convention floor to prevent any more surprises such as that engineered by A. A. Low. But, as Conrad Wright put it, "if Bellows was a strong leader of the convention, as doubtless he was, he was a leader by the consent of his followers, and it was their objectives as much as his that were achieved."[6]

On Wednesday afternoon the task was to set up the permanent organization of the National Conference. The committee on organization was to consist of twelve delegates with Bellows as chairman. There is no record of its discussions. The drafts of the constitution and bylaws were presented on Thursday morning. The constitution was simple enough, for it consisted of the aforementioned preamble and eight simple articles. The conference was to be called "The National Conference of Unitarian Churches," not quite the broadness that Bellows had wanted even in the name. He wanted to get beyond the term Unitarian and make all Liberal Christians feel welcome. But the name was rejected by the conference not because of the word Christian, but because so many of the laymen, as both Henry Bellows and his daughter Annie said in letters, had a strong loyalty to the name Unitarian, especially by those who had come out of orthodox Christian backgrounds. Therefore, Bellows' predictions came true that they could not get everything that was wanted, but they would settle for the best that could come out of the conference.

So by and large Bellows was pleased at the end of the sessions. Three-quarters of the Unitarian churches had been represented at the conference in New York City. The desires of the majority had carried the day. There was now an organization not of individuals as the American Unitarian Association had always been, but a new denomination which was composed of churches. If what was accomplished fell short of Bellows' fondest expectations, it must be remembered that it accomplished much.

By 11 April Bellows was still "not yet over the fatigue of the Victory, which cost us so much spiritual blood!" Yet, he rejoiced that they had lived to see the "triumph of our Denominational Life!" He felt that the "outsiders estimate the results even more fully than we do." He commented that "All orthodoxy was down on us last Friday, as if a Monitor had suddenly sailed into Norfolk Harbor & drawn the fire of every battery." He regretted that "Frothingham *joined* the enemy, altho on a different tack—& shot all his guns into the convention & into me—poor innocent! last Friday morning." Yet, Bellows was not worried. "The only service he can render to our cause is by vigorously attacking it & showing the world how different we are from himself. It would be for our interest to pay him for a constant attack." Bellows continued, "The more enlightened Orthodox men, are I hear, rejoiced at the stand we took; knowing very well that we stand between them & general skepticism like an outer sea-wall."[7]

To Russell, Henry Bellows confided that there were half a dozen ministers who stayed away from the convention: Dr. Furness, Putnam, Weiss, the two Ellises, and Chandler Robbins. He called these "the only absentees of any note." He also commented about the relative strength of the radicals, "The radicals were *no-where* & were as much amaz'd at their insignificance, as Lilliput must have been on his first visit to Brobdingnag." He felt that "the laity proved intensely *conservative*, full of sound, solid sense, with no disposition to be blown about by every wind of doctrine. An organization was effected of a wholly satisfactory character—& a conservative *preamble*, but with full independence in the individual churches." He concluded on a positive note, "The greatest surprise was expressed to find our Body so united, so practical, so Christian, & so willing & anxious to *work on a larger scale*. The convention was an *absolute & entire success*."[8]

The convention was ended, and Octavius Brooks Frothingham took the occasion of his Palm Sunday sermon to express to his congregation the dashing of his hopes for the Unitarian denomination.[9] He had realized that he had hoped too much to come out of the convention just as the people of Jerusalem hoped too much of Jesus on Palm Sunday. He spoke of how churches "from Maine to Missouri" had responded to the call and had sent delegates to New York City. "The feeling was cordial, the hopes were high." Men who had not attended a religious convention for years were present. Frothingham continued with his comparison to Palm Sunday: "They came; they deliberated; they had the prayer and the hymn; they shouted hosannahs; they have gone. What remains? A piece of ground covered with dry leaves." He felt that "The Liberal Body shrunk from its own principle, and disowned the purport of its summons. It met to protest against the prevalent sectarianism" and "it made a longer stride toward sectarianism than it had ever made before." He claimed "there has never been a convention so narrow and blind and stubborn as it was." Worst of all "instead of the Liberal Church in America which we thought we were to have, we have the old Unitarian Association, made more Unitarian than ever." He believed that the attempts to make "Liberal Christianity a sect, was a mistake particularly deplorable just now, and calculated, if persisted in, to destroy completely the intellectual and moral influence of the body." He felt that "Unitarianism" could never be a popular form of religion. He did not think that Unitarians could "have a large influence," nor "will they be able to effect much in Christendom."

Surprisingly, with much of what Frothingham said Henry Bellows would have been in agreement. It was Bellows who proposed the Liberal Christian Church of America but found the laymen at the convention too enamored of the name Unitarian, so many of them

having adopted it after leaving another sect of Christianity. It was
Bellows who wanted to invite the Universalists. He would have
agreed about stating publicly what the church really believed, as
Frothingham advocated. What Bellows was not prepared for was the
savagery of the attack which was to last for some years from
ministers such as O. B. Frothingham and to lead to the
establishment of the Free Religious Association.

The War Has Left Things Changed

Abraham Lincoln was shot by John Wilkes Booth at Ford's Theater
shortly before 10:00 P.M. on 14 April. He died the following
morning, and the nation was plunged into despair. At first many
Americans had not appreciated the leadership of the Illinois
peacemaker, but Bellows, through his contact with Lincoln in
connection with the Sanitary Commission, had learned to love and
respect the President. Mrs. Bellows described the feelings of the
hour: "The blackness of darkness covered all our hearts & homes!
Almost for the first time did I feel timid, even more than in those
days of riot, & feel nervous & tremblingly anxious to keep together,
lest more Southern villains should be lurking near us." Then she
described her husband's reaction: "After the first shock of the
dreadful news, Henry sat down to give expression to his feelings for
himself & for the crowded congregation which today came to hear
him give voice to what was burning in their hearts, & it is almost
needless to tell *you* that he did it in his own great way—a way to give
relief & comfort to all who heard."

Mrs. Bellows described the decoration of the church interior,
"Our pulpit was covered with two flags joined together in such a way
as to indicate the American Eagle with wings unstrung & drooping!"
The church had been draped in black. Mrs. Bellows explained that
"this expression of the universal sorrow is every where displayed—in
private dwellings as well as public ones." She commented that "the
sudden revulsion of feeling from exultant joy to bitter woe &
indignation seemed after the first paralyzing shock almost to
threaten the sanity of the public mind, & people feel as if unusual
self-control were needed to prevent in themselves & those they meet
any extreme expressions of opinion & feeling, until all the dreadful
facts of this dire tragedy shall be known and comprehended."[1]
Henry's sermon on Lincoln was printed in the *Evening Post* on
Monday evening, and then incorporated into a book.[2]

Henry Bellows was very close to the brother of Lincoln's assassin, Edwin Booth, the actor, and his mother. They lived at 28 East 19th Street, very close to All Souls Church and the parsonage. On 17 April, Bellows wrote a letter to a Mr. Kennedy in charge of New York police, and suggested that "the police should keep a special eye on the premises of no. 28 E. 19th—the home of Mrs. Booth and her son, Edwin, the mother & brother of the wretched assassin of our good & lamented President," to protect them from "excitable persons." Bellows found that Mr. Booth, whom he had visited earlier in the day, was "dreadfully affected by his brother's crime. He is a loyal man & deserves sympathy in this great misfortune."[3]

Bellows and others went by train to Washington on 18 April to attend Lincoln's funeral. Moses Grinnell was also on board. On Wednesday 19 April, they learned that members and officers of the Sanitary Commission had places on the official program and were expected to attend the ceremonies in the East Room of the White House. Strong reported, "We went in a body to the office of the Secretary of the Treasury in the Treasury Building . . . & a little before twelve we marched to the White House through the grounds that separate it from the Treasury, were shown into the East Room and took our appointed places on the raised steps that occupied three of the sides—the catafalque with its black canopy and open coffin occupying the center. I had a last glimpse of the honest face of our great and good President as we passed by. It was darker than in life, otherwise little changed . . . Of the religious service, the less that is said, the better, for it was vile and vulgar; Bishop Simpson's whining, oratorical prayer most nauseous."[4]

Bellows described the President's funeral in the East Room. "About 800 *representative* men gathered round his ashes, making in their very presence . . . the most impressive of all burial solemnities." He felt that "the actual service was common-place, & did not *voice* the occasion, but it could not belittle or stifle it. It was in itself too great & too speaking for that! The grief was genuine, profound & all pervading." Bellows saw the new President, Andrew Johnson, in both public and private meetings. "He was *morally sober* . . . and showed no weak signs of exhilaration at his sudden elevation to such a dizzy height."[5]

On Friday 21 April, Bellows, Strong, Binney, and Stillé met with the new President, Andrew Johnson. They had a brief interview in which Bellows told the new President who they were and what they did, and the President replied in substance that he knew all about the commission and would further it with all of the means in his power. It was a brief interview and the group were impressed with Johnson.[6]

When the war ended there was the problem of demobilization of the large civilian army, some 2,500,000 men. This was many times the size of any military force ever assembled in the world before. The Sanitary Commission in its role during the war had been in correspondence with the grass roots of the nation, and now it began to fulfill the duties of what today would be called the Veterans Administration. They created and introduced government military records. Their careful registering of the soldiers formed the basis of the pension system for Civil War veterans.

Although some of the work of the Sanitary Commission continued, Bellows was able to announce the new directions in an official statement on 20 May 1865. He stated that henceforth the Sanitary Commission would devote itself "first—to getting invalid soldiers and occupants of our hospitals comfortably home; secondly—to securing bounty and pension, and back pay to them and their families; thirdly—to procuring employment for the partially disabled; fourthly—to providing asylums for those without friends and utterly unable to take care of themselves." Bellows suggested that in this "just and grateful work" they would need continued financial support, and he urged the local chapters to keep their organizations intact.[7]

Nine months later, on 20 February 1866, Bellows finally received from the Cashier of the United States Sanitary Commission, Mr. Charles C. Lathrop, the final statistics about the money raised by the commission during the war. "The total amount of *money* received by the commission from all sources to Jan'y 1st, including interest, sales of property, supplies etc. is $4,918,305.26. The estimated cash value of *supplies* received as per financial statement published to July 1/65 is $10,000,000."[8] This was but a statistical summation of the healing work that the Sanitary Commission did during the Civil War. Yet the entire sum of money raised for binding up the wounds of the war was in total less than the cost of the war for a single day.

One of the lasting effects of the work of the Sanitary Commission was that it demonstrated that an organized effort was more effective in social amelioration than the disorganized goodwill of individuals. "It is appropriate that Bellows, who had defended the doctrine of institutions against the individualists and the millenialists in his prewar speculations, should have headed an organization which did much to teach Americans the practical value of institutions as opposed to spontaneous action."[9] As Bellows himself expressed it, the war was "God's method of bringing order out of chaos."[10] Dr. Frederickson commented "he might have added that the commission had been one of God's instruments."[11]

It was in this field of philanthropy that the Sanitary Commission had its most lasting effect. Much previous philanthropy had been inspired by utopic ideals of social reform. There had also been present a more conservative kind of philanthropy which had been an individual proposition. Money was given for specific purposes named by the donor. But the Sanitary Commission had put between the givers and the recipients an elite board of directors which would decide, on some more rational basis than individual whim, who would receive the gifts. There was also a kind of tough-minded realism about suffering. The more conservative upper social classes could now find a case for administering relief to the unfortunate people of the lower classes.

Service by many people in the employ of the Sanitary Commission had placed an emphasis on professionalism in the social-service field. Louisa Lee Schuyler of Bellows's church, who as a young woman was the corresponding secretary of the Women's Central Association of Relief in New York City, is a typical example of one who made an entire career on the basis of this new professionalism. She turned her energies in 1872 to organizing the New York State Charities Aid Association, an organization modeled on the Sanitary Commission. It was concerned more with the efficiency of the labors of those who worked in the field of social service than with the alleviation of suffering.

Also active in this application of the new "scientific methods" of social-service work were Joseph Tuckerman of Boston and New York, and Mrs. Charles Lowell who founded the Charity Organization Society of New York the year of Henry Bellows's death in 1882. "The goal for Mrs. Lowell was a hard-working capitalistic society, saved from materialism, corruption, and bad taste by an aristocracy subservient to the highest principles." Thus the Sanitary Commission was a pioneer in the organization of planned charitable enterprises which have had so much influence in the United States.[12]

Much to Henry Bellows's joy, early in June 1865 an announcement was sent out that Antioch College would reopen again on 12 September. The bulletin contained the information that "the Unitarian friends of the college have just endowed five professorships with one hundred thousand dollars, the institution is wholly out of debt, and by its constitution cannot run into debt." Although a new president had not yet been chosen, the new professors had been selected. Among them was the Reverend Austin Craig as Bellows Professor of Moral and Intellectual Philosophy.[13]

On 23 June Bellows was in Yellow Springs, Ohio, staying at the Yellow Springs House and attending the meetings of the board of trustees. Annie accompanied her father on the trip. It was a typical Bellows trip to Buffalo and Niagara Falls, to lecture in Elmira, and then to head for New York City, stopping off at Binghamton to visit the Inebriate Asylum.

Bellows commented to his wife, who had gone to Walpole for the summer months, that things had gone well at the Antioch meetings. The Unitarians had come up with one hundred thousand dollars, the result of the efforts stimulated by Bellows and the National Conference. The Unitarians now had seven of the thirteen trustees, which, Bellows wrote, "throws the Institution into our full power." They made the appointments to the professorships, but they did not appoint a president. That matter was left in the hands of Edward Everett Hale, E. W. Clark, and Henry Bellows "with full powers." Bellows felt that the Unitarians now had a powerful body to represent them on the board of the college. These included: A. A. Low, H. P. Kidder, E. W. Clark, Artemas Carter, O. W. Steele, President Hill of Harvard, Edward Everett Hale, Jon Kebler, William Channing Russell,[14] Eli Fay, and Henry Bellows. Bellows commented, "Such a body of wealth, influence & sense could make things go."[15]

Rev. T. B. Forbush of West Roxbury was elated at the announcement that Antioch was now under Unitarian control. But he was concerned as to where the young ministers were to come from who would staff the new churches in the "great south and west." Forbush related to Henry Bellows some incidents in the Boston Ministerial Association in recent months which disturbed him greatly and which he believed militated against the entry of young people into the Unitarian ministry. He cited a few instances for Bellows's ear. Recently the Boston Association (evidently before the convention) had heard it argued that the denomination must be divided. Some of the conservatives said "they could no longer have fellowship with certain ministers whom they declared not Christian." This discussion went on for months. They also declared that they could not "exchange with certain brethren on account of their 'infidelity'." They wanted "to limit the influence of these brethren so far as was possible." When young Stebbins had been ordained at Charlestown, Dr. Gannett and Dr. Ellis had protested against it "on the ground of heresy."

The board of the American Unitarian Association was dominated by these conservatives. Forbush asked, "How can honorable and high-minded young men be expected to enter the ministry? Will any such man put himself in a position where he must be watched & probed thus?" Dr. Stearns at the convention had declared that "You must give young men elbow room if you want them in the ministry." Forbush knew that he would get a sympathetic ear from Bellows in this matter, for Bellows now had come to represent the mediating Broad Church point of view, and as such he became the acknowledged leader of the Unitarian denomination.[16]

By the end of August Bellows was convinced that he "had more of the peace of God this summer than ever before! The close of the war, the essential winding up of the Sanitary Commission, the maturity of my children, the beauty of the season, the fair health of my wife, and a certain willingness to *rest* without too much thought of the future, have together made my life more reposeful & permitted me a gentle consciousness of what I was enjoying, that marks out this summer as one of the most blessed of my life." He continued, "I have had daily my two or three hours of necessary business & ecclesiastical correspondence, the business of the S. Com. [Sanitary Commission], the Chairmanship of the 'Council' of the Unitarian body, the concerns as chief trustee of Antioch College occupying me just eno[ugh] to keep rudder way on my vessel." He had also read a "few pleasant books, Hedge's *Reason in Religion*, Forsyth's *Cicero*, *Horace Mann's Life*, Lord Derby's *Homer*, . . . the Galsworthy's, Arnold's Essays." He continued, "horseback with my children & drives have filled up the early morning & the late afternoon. I have preached only three half-days here, & spent one Sunday (on my way to Saratoga) with the young church at Montpelier; made one drive with Eliza five & twenty miles into Vermont to see 'the Irelands'—so the time has sped away."[17]

Bellows's life had changed drastically during the year 1865. He wrote, "I find the old torrent of work hurrying me on, in spite of all resistance. True the Sanitary [Commission] does not ride me—But I am deeply busy with my parish, writing sermons & lectures, holding Bible classes & visiting sick & sad." Bellows also felt that the war had changed the complection of his own environment. "The war has left things changed. People are a good deal more open to change &

direction & the rushing worldliness & pride of life about us makes sober & thoughtful people pause to ask what is to be done to help the cause of society & truth & Christian worth. I must do my part in this."[18] Another change was that Russell was now home from California and had enrolled for some courses in theology at the Union Theological Seminary in New York City.

At this stage in his life Bellows saw fit to buy from Joseph Allen and W. R. Alger their shares in the *Christian Examiner*. What prompted Bellows to do this is something of a mystery since the paper had been a steady loser monetarily. More importantly, Bellows had an opportunity to define what he meant by the word Christian in the *Christian Examiner*. It is one of the simplest and yet most profound of Bellows's comments on what it meant to be a Christian. "What is *Christian?* is, then, the important point to decide in determining the bounds within which *examination* or discussion is to be allowed or encouraged in our Journal. Of course, we cannot adopt a dogmatic standard—as we have refused always to acknowledge a *creed*. And yet we cannot properly decline the general judgment of the Christian world in respect of what makes or leaves a man *Christian*." He continued, "I assume that to declare oneself a disciple of Jesus Christ, & to exhibit his spirit is the sole universally recognized conviction of a right to claim the Christian name to those who claim it, & exhibit ordinary evidences of the Christian character & spirit. If, therefore, any man calling himself a Christian, & especially a Christian minister, sends an intelligent, scholarly, reverential article to us, I know not how we can decline it on the leave of doctrine or tendency."[19]

Now Bellows had a bit of parish work to do. Mrs. King after her husband's death had enjoyed being Thomas Starr King's widow for a while. But then she had fallen in love and was evidently living with a Mr. Norris whom she had met in San Francisco. Henry gave his opinion of this affair to Cyrus Bartol in Boston where Mrs. King's largest group of friends lived: "My private opinion is that she intends to marry Mr. Norris (now in New York) in the course of a few weeks or months. He is an excellent man—of large fortune & good repute, of suitable age & an old & dear friend of Mrs. King's." Bellows added, "if she *can* give up her place as King's widow, this is a good opportunity—and with my views of her character (which is what you know it to be) I think the sooner she is under some honest man's protection the better for her dignity & the peace of her friends. I hope for King's sake her friends in Boston will treat her kindly."[20]

Meanwhile, there was disquieting news from San Francisco. Horatio Stebbins had turned out to be anything but a Starr King or a Henry Bellows, and there were murmurings against his ministry. Charles Lowe, the Secretary of the American Unitarian Association, wrote to Henry that he had talked with George Hepworth about the possibility of going to the West to work in conjunction with Stebbins. Lowe wrote, "It is evident that persons in San Francisco (I know not how influential they may be) are very much dissatisfied & are very earnest in their desire to have Mr. H[epworth]. I have no doubt either that he would do vastly more for the outward prosperity of their church than Stebbins or Ames." Lowe felt that "the unpleasant part of the condition of California affairs is pretty widely known & undoubtedly much exaggerated by malicious misrepresentations." Lowe also pointed out to Bellows that these same persons were talking about Bellows. "They accuse you of acting the Pope over them."[21] It did little good to point out again and again that Bellows had told the San Francisco church that they were under no obligation to take Stebbins.

The situation in San Francisco publicly surfaces in an article which appears in the Bellows Papers from an unidentified San Francisco paper. The author begins by pointing out that Unitarians live in San Francisco; they also live in New York; "and one man among them is greater than his fellows, and his name is Bellows; and this man sitteth firmly on the back of the Unitarians, and whither he would that they should go thither, goadeth he them. And the Unitarians reasoned one with another, and said, 'Behold now what manner of man is this Bellows? For he saith unto one Unitarian, go, and he goeth, and to another come, and he cometh. Go to, let us make him a Pope and we will bow down to him and serve him, and his letters shall be encyclical letters.' And it was so." The article, in the same biblical phraseology, goes on to record that when King died, Bellows came to San Francisco. The people shouted, "Long live the King." And "Bellows sent Horatio to reign in his stead." The account then went on to relate that there was only one account of Horatio's success, but alas there were many empty pews. It was a nasty article, hitting Bellows at his most vulnerable spots. But it did indicate one thing: that the great promise that Bellows had for the San Francisco church and for Horatio Stebbins in particular were overly optimistic.[22]

Soon, however, the news from San Francisco was improving. Robert B. Swain, Bellows's close friend, reported that the desire to call George Hepworth had been made by one indiscreet young man who was now ashamed of himself. Swain wrote, "Stebbins is steadily gaining permanent strength, and is now I think beyond the reach of danger. Ames works in harness with him admirably well, and between the two they are doing good service." But Swain was a little irked at Mrs. Thomas Starr King. She had written him from New York "in rather desponding mood." But Swain believed that her unhappiness came from within. He was, however, "a good deal annoyed on hearing that she has *encouraged* rather than *denied* a rumor that I made her a proposal and that my illness last summer arose from my disappointment." Swain maintained he could not be *"weak* enough for anything so silly." He felt "the statement is wickedly false." The failure to deny it was "dishonest." He maintained that he, eligible man though he was, had not the slightest intention to remarry, and he believed that Mrs. King was not suited to him in any way. He added that he wanted to end his exile in San Francisco and return to New York, and was grieved by the recent death of Robert Minturn, one of his close friends.[23]

In early April 1866, Henry Bergh, one of Bellows's most distinguished parishioners, was able to report to Bellows that he had worked hard to get his bill on the prevention of cruelty to animals through the New York legislature. It had already passed the state senate, and had been reported to the lower house. Bergh hoped that Bellows would use his strong influence to get the bill on the agenda and passed through the legislature.[24]

Roswell Cheney McCrea has said of Bergh that "the early history of the anti-cruelty movement in this country is his biography." Henry Bergh was the son of a wealthy New York shipbuilder, Christian Bergh. Henry studied at Columbia College but he never graduated; he and his brother managed the New York shipyard. But after his father's death he had a comfortable income, and he spent the next three years traveling in Europe. While he was in Europe in 1863, he was appointed the head of the legation at St. Petersburg, but he soon resigned because Mrs. Bergh could not stand the cold Russian winters. It was while he was in Russia that Bergh became interested in the prevention of cruelty to animals. He often intervened on the streets when he saw acts of cruelty being performed on animals, a kind of conduct that was probably countenanced only because of his diplomatic connections. He also became acquainted with the Earl of Harrowby who was President of the Royal Society for the Prevention of Cruelty to Animals. He returned to New York shortly after the Civil War, resumed his place in a pew at Henry Bellows's church, and enlisted the aid of his minister in forming such a society in the United States. On 6 February 1866, he delivered a lecture in Clinton Hall giving statistics relating to the cruelty practiced on animals and with a view to organizing a society. A week after he asked Bellows to use his strong influence, on 10 April 1866, the New York state legislature passed an act which granted a charter for just such a society.

On 21 May 1866, a meeting was held for the purpose of organizing a Society for the Prevention of Cruelty to Animals. Mayor Hoffman was chosen as the temporary chairman, and he remarked that, although the city had its share of charities, "no society had yet been established to take care of the poor beasts who had neither voices nor votes." A letter from Dr. Bellows was read, for he could not be present, in which Bellows said that he felt that the future of the society would depend almost entirely upon "the zeal and efficiency of the President and Secretary, and it is very important that they be persons who can give their whole time to its business . . . A dozen fearless arrests will do more to effect a reform than a dozen public meetings," if the heart of the executive officer were in the matter. He suggested that Henry Bergh had exactly the qualifications to be the executive officer of the society. Bellows felt that within three months the society would "make itself most beneficially felt in the removal of much brutalizing and shameful indecency and cruelty from the streets, piers and ferries of this city." A letter from Peter Cooper was also read endorsing Henry Bergh, who then upon motion was unanimously elected President of the society. Bellows was elected one of the vice-presidents.[25]

By 1 June 1866, however, Henry Bergh realized that he could scarcely run his Society for the Prevention of Cruelty to Animals as an all-male organization. He wanted female patronesses, and he wrote a letter to Bellows asking for names that he might improve a letter with "that felicitousness of expression which your friends and the public recognize you the possessor of, in such an eminent degree."[26]

Radicals Outside Our Camp

On Russell's twenty-fifth birthday Bellows wrote to his son: "How much confidence & peace I have in your character & temper. You have not been merely a *promising*, but a *performing* boy from the beginning. We have not waited for you to outgrow your faults in order to enjoy you." He praised Russell, "You have been eminently *satisfactory*, and at the completion of your first quarter-century, I think it is fair to tell you that I am now in the full enjoyment of your society, sympathy & affection." Henry even said of Russell, "I am not looking forward to any *improvement* in conditions which are perfectly satisfactory already."[1] Henry was proud of his son, who evidently had performed well for the United States Sanitary Commission on the Pacific Coast after Henry himself had left San Francisco. A small diary now in the Bellows Papers tells something of the details of Russell's travels throughout Northern California.[2] Later Bellows was not to feel so happy about his son. They parted ways when Russell swore allegiance with the new intellectual movement in the Unitarian body with which his father was scarcely sympathetic.

To celebrate Russell's twenty-fifth birthday the Bellowses gave a dinner party, which Bellows described as a "curious & wholly original sort of festival." They invited William Cullen Bryant, Dr. Samuel Osgood, Dr. Cyrus Bartol, Rev. John White Chadwick, and Miss Elizabeth Bartol in addition to the members of the Bellows family. The Bartols had spent a week with the Bellowses.

The next day at 8:30 P.M. Bellows officiated at a wedding in "the big Room" of the parish house. It was none other than the wedding of Mrs. Julia Wiggin King, "consenting to play the bride," and Mr. William Norris "the groom." There were many guests, and Bellows indicated that there were "a great many *hidden* tears in it, I can tell you." So came to a conclusion an alliance that had bothered all of Mrs. Thomas Starr King's friends for some months.[3] But the wedding did not end the gossip.

Mrs. King and Mr. Norris—obviously living together—were in New York City and had come to Bellows to have him marry them. Bellows was reluctant to do this, and he was angry when Mrs. King chose to be married while Bellows had a houseful of prominent guests. Mrs. King was very anxious when she arrived back in San Francisco to make it appear as if her wedding in New York had been a sumptuous social affair. However, she knew that Robert Swain had corresponded with Bellows on the matter.

On 24 May 1866, Robert Swain wrote to Bellows telling him that the steamer bringing the Norrises had arrived a few days previously. Mrs. Norris had immediately contacted Mr. Swain, ostensibly to greet him, but primarily to know if he knew the truth from correspondence with Henry Bellows. Swain told her that he had recently received a letter from Henry Bellows. Then there developed a little cat-and-mouse game. Mrs. Norris wanted to see the letter so that she knew exactly what Bellows had written to Swain about the wedding [unfortunately this letter is not extant]. Swain promised to show it to her. But to Bellows he wrote: "She then said, 'Did he write you about our wedding?' I replied, 'Yes,' he wrote *something*. 'I want you to tell me all of the particulars,' she replied. 'I want you to let me see this letter'." Swain promised that he would put it "in his jacket some day when I am coming to see you."

Swain wrote, "Now there is some rich fun in prospect—I understand her game perfectly. The wedding at your house was a *managed* thing & the accidental presence of Bryant and others, happy accessories. She wants to boast that they were married in your home by special invitation under the sanction of your church & your social position." But Swain knew that she could not claim this if he knew the facts. Swain vowed *"She shall never have an item* . . . She will be greatly perplexed and I shall enjoy the developments, thanks to you. Her shrewdness in the matter was very keen—but I have the inside track, and I propose to keep it."[4] Bellows even failed to keep an accurate record of the marriage, for it was entered in the All Souls Marriage records as of 25 January 1866, and although he got the name of William Norris correct, he entered Julia Wiggin King as Juliet G. Fay.[5] This could only have been done purposely for the writing is in Bellows's hand.

Late in April 1866, Bellows was in Washington for a busy weekend. He lectured at the Unitarian church on the evening of 27 April. "The church was choke-full." He described the lecture as *"theological."* He was also having fun hobnobbing with the Washington famous: Grant, Sherman, Howe, Sumner, Chief Justice Chase, and Senator Sprague. The new President had indicated that he wished to talk with Bellows at his convenience, but Bellows wished to wait until he could have the President's ear for an entire evening.[6] But the appointment was arranged for that very evening, and Bellows had a special interview with the President "& a long, frank & full conversation of an hour & a half." The Secretary of the Treasury alone was present in addition to Bellows and President Johnson. Bellows found the President "a very remarkable man—full of ability, broad in his vision, & as it seems to me wholly honest in his purposes." Then he added, "I never heard half as much, nor half as well said from Mr. Lincoln. Indeed, he would be considered a very remarkable talker any where. He is able to offer very solid reasons for every thing he says & does." Bellows felt that his trip to Washington was a learning experience in which he would try to form "correct opinions."[7]

A few days later Bellows summarized for Edward Everett Hale the points that he had covered in his talk with President Johnson. He had told the President that "the Congress was a war congress, and wishes to settle Reconstruction in the spirit & on the basis of the war." But Bellows, although he believed this was natural, felt that it was not possible, "because the spirit which sustained the war dries up & sinks with the return of peace, & all the economic & business interests clamor for speedy tranquilization of the vacillating in suspended elements in the problem." Bellows told the President that he felt that the country wished the South back "on *some* terms, & will soon wish it back on *any* terms—sooner than leave it with grounds of complaint & causes for commercial non-intercourse."

Bellows believed that since the President was a Southerner and had been a slave holder, "he inherits all that feeling about States Rights & local self-government which has grown up out of the necessity of protecting slavery." Yet, he believed that the President was a Southerner who comprehended the North. "My fear is that he judges the average sentiment of the country more accurately than we do." Bellows also felt that Johnson didn't think much of the Negro. "But he is a practical statesman, & more practical than Congress, whose practical wisdom is a good deal quenched by idealism & moral & personal excellence & tone. Is that not dreadful to say!" Bellows also felt that Secretary of State William Seward was "*not* guiding & governing the President;—nobody does or can."[8]

Bellows was doing some thinking about the new National Conference. He had concluded that the conference ought to be smaller, and probably it ought not to be a conference of local churches as of local area groups. "The real subject at our conference really ought to be *local organization*," he wrote to Edward Everett Hale. "It is this for which our denomination is suffering." He had written on this subject for the next issue of the "Inquirer."[9]

But his chief concern about the national organization was the quality of the ministers that the denomination was sending out to the churches. He wrote to A. A. Livermore at Meadville about the matter. He felt that the efforts to organize the whole denomination would not come about "until our separate churches have a warmer & more cooperative church life, until a church means more & does more for the members—our rich laity will not much care whether there are any *more* ministers of the same tepid & cold sort that we have so many of, or not." Bellows felt that the future of the Unitarian movement depended upon "a reorganization of our individual churches." He hoped that the Syracuse Convention to be held in October would get at the heart of the matter. "But there is great discouragement in the apparent apathy of the best laymen & the worthiest ministers." He continued, "The old crop of our clergy—excellent as ethical & even Scriptural teachers—had no sympathy with the wants of the common people in this raw, democratic country. They were proper, passionless, half-English, old-style thinkers," who did not really understand the needs of the pew. Bellows felt that unless there was "a new breed with a different sentiment . . . our denominational life will prove a failure, & go *out* with a fetid smell very soon."[10]

Bellows was getting somewhat apprehensive about the Syracuse Conference. He asked Hale if there was anything that he could do in order to prepare for it. "We must expect more freedom of debate than we had last year, & that no small *jealousy* exists of a few of us—who must strive not to *force* the Body into any measures against its will." Bellows continued his emphasis that the problem of organization in the denomination was in the individual church "which is almost without form & void in our modern Unitarian churches." He was setting down the details of the organization of such a church, "fixing the duties & *place* & rights of the Minister, the duties & authority of the Standing Committee, or Trustees, the relations of the members to each other & their modes of co-operation & mutual *edification*, the place of *the* Church, whether identical with or distinct from the Congregation." Bellows continued, "He who will produce the model of a *working* Church whose success is not due to special ministerial gifts or talents, but to measures & methods & rules of general application, & capable of being taught & *learned—he* will be the real savior of the Unitarian Body. Get this *unit*, & we shall have *something* to add & combine." Bellows wished that the organization within the local churches could be the central topic at the convention.[11]

The Syracuse Convention was held on 10/11 October. Bellows gave what he termed "my political address" on Friday evening. "The hall was full & I had a very flattering reception & good deliverance." He believed that the success of the convention "was so nearly perfect that I can only thank God for it with all my heart. I could hardly have believed it possible that so much progress in sound, practical wisdom could be attained in so short a period. I consider the National Conference as firmly established, and the Unitarian Body as thoroughly consolidated." He also believed that "the scheme of *local* organization is adopted & will go through, I hope."[12] This was what Bellows felt about the convention. What actually happened?

Even though Henry Bellows was writing home that everything was going well at the Syracuse Convention, he and his friends had their hands full with vociferous opposition from the radicals. Between the end of the New York Convention and the Syracuse Convention, the questions which separated the various types of Unitarian belief had been freely debated in the denomination. On the first day of the conference Francis E. Abbot, then the minister at Dover, New Hampshire, proposed a new preamble to the Constitution. In his wording Abbot sought to argue that, because there was difference of opinion wherever there was "perfect freedom of thought," the progress of the whole movement was "hindered by common creeds and statements of faith." Abbot wanted the churches to unite in common *work*, and he wanted to see the name changed to "The National Conference of Unitarian and Independent Churches."[13]

Russell Bellows was somewhat more detailed in his description of what had happened at the conference. The "Radicals in the person of young Rev. Mr. Abbot . . . introduced a proposed substitute for the present Preamble & Art 1st of the Constitution of the Conference. It was the old subject & question, with which you are perfectly familiar—viz., shall Jesus Christ be distinctly recognized as our Lord & Master & Head of the Church, or shall we, to suit certain persons, a minority, adopt a Preamble which fails to give such explicit recognition." Russell stated the matter quite succinctly. In the debate which followed Abbot's motion "in which our strongest, ablest men participated, Mr. Burleigh of Florence, Massachusetts, was present & spoke in *favor* of the proposed amendment with considerable power & eloquence. But his speech had little influence. Father followed him in a very earnest speech, in which he answered him completely. Speaking on that question occupied the whole session, from 2:00 to 5:00 P.M., & was threatening to take up the evening session also, but was finally closed shortly after five, by the strong vote of 157 against to ninety in favor of the Amendment." That vote was closer than Bellows had hoped. Russell felt that the "speakers preserved an excellent temper all through the debate, but the earnestness was most intense on both sides."[14]

On the motion of James Freeman Clarke the name was changed, however, to "The National Conference of Unitarian and

Other Christian Churches," which was actually the broader kind of name that Bellows had wanted at the New York Convention. When the Radical ministers boarded their train for Boston, they held a consultation and determined to organize an association that would give them the liberty they desired. A meeting was held at the home of Cyrus Bartol on 5 February 1867 to consider what should be done. A new Free Religious Association was planned, and the organization was perfected at a meeting in Horticultural Hall in Boston on 30 May 1867. O. B. Frothingham was elected president of the new organization. The purpose of the association was "to promote the interests of pure religion, to encourage the scientific study of theology and to increase fellowship in the spirit."[15]

Dr. William Greenleaf Eliot of Saint Louis also had a practical suggestion for Bellows. He wrote that he believed that now "we are in a most hopeful condition—for the first time a *Church*." He felt that they were both stronger and more free. What was now needed was a "Common Prayer Book & Hymnal." He felt that this should be prepared under the direction of the Council, "*to be recommended* for general use" and that if this service book were "at once adopted by twenty or thirty of our leading churches, it would rapidly win its way." He wanted the preparation of such a service book to be given to "wise men, not *all* of them from Boston." He felt that the Hymnal and Service Book should be printed at conference expense with a free gift to all churches to try and then to be sold at cost. He felt that such a book bearing an imprint as being approved by the National Council of Unitarian Churches "would materially aid to check those absurd experimenters in theology who now compromise our cause."[16]

The first week in November, Bellows was in Boston helping to organize the local conference that had been authorized by the Syracuse Convention. But he also had some good times. He met with his Harvard classmates at a dinner party which celebrated the thirty-fourth year since their graduation. "There are forty-seven living out of seventy-one, & *twenty-four* were present. Some I had not met since we graduated! We had a boyish rollicking time, singing our college songs, & telling our old stories & calling each other Bill & Harry & Tom & Dick. It was thoroughly charming."[17]

In November 1866, Bellows began an ambitious plan for improving the Unitarian publications in New York City. At the parsonage that evening "a few gentlemen" of All Souls Church met and established a New York Unitarian Publication Society "to increase the circulation of the *Christian Inquirer*, the *Christian*

Examiner & the literature of the denomination." They proposed to form a stock company under the laws of New York State with a capital of $25,000 in shares of $100. They hoped to maintain "a *depot* of Unitarian books & tracts . . . & bring the utmost business tact & energy to the increase of the circulation of our periodicals." Over the next few months the entire $35,000 in stock was subscribed, and Bellows was elected president of the new organization. Naturally, Bellows was the largest subscriber with ten shares. Ten gentlemen bought five shares each, and a long list of persons bought from one to three shares until the total was subscribed.[18]

In November 1866, Bellows called together the Unitarian Churches in New York City, and under the mandate of the Syracuse Conference began the organizing of a local New York City Conference of Unitarian Churches. Rev. Octavius Brooks Frothingham was absent, later adamantly maintaining that he had never known that the meeting called for 19 November was for such an important purpose. He had spent that morning writing a review of Stillé's *History of the Sanitary Commission,* rather than attending. "Had I received the smallest intimation that any special business was to be brought before the association—had the faintest hint been thrown out that a matter so important as the establishment of a local conference was to be considered, no thing would have kept me away." John W. Chadwick had met Frothingham on the way to Boston and he, too, had had no conception that so important a matter was to be discussed without calling a special meeting.

Frothingham was opposed to such an organization. He was by the terms of his conscience unable to affiliate with the National Conference any longer. "You know that I . . . could not accept the Preamble of the Constitution of the conference, that I have earnestly protested against the attempt at organization on sectarian principles however attenuated, or for sectarian ends, however plausible;—that the . . . movement was unpleasant to me." Frothingham did not wish to make a public issue of the matter and therefore wrote Bellows a private letter, in which he concluded, "Nothing would give me greater pleasure than to join with our churches in some good social work that might justify our own faith here in New York; and I shall be always glad to feel that in many respects we are one if we cannot be one in this particular enterprise."[19]

Bellows's response to this opposition was indicative of his deep feeling for organization. He wrote to Edward Everett Hale that he did "not [have] much hope of the conference in this neighborhood. We have a set of flabby noddles here without *snap,* or capacity of work, or talent for business:—(I mean our ministers—) & I can get nothing out of them. They leave all the work to me." Bellows acknowledged that the split had come. "The Radicals are preparing to pitch their tent (*one* will hold them) outside our Camp! Frothingham announces his secession in a private note of Friday last." He also supposed that "Chadwick will go with him, altho I trust his *Society* will not. I am not very sorry. I think we shall gain more than we lose & I am not a bit frightened."[20]

Frothingham was, however, conciliatory in a note which he wrote shortly to Bellows. He believed that Bellows and his friends had a right to do their work, and he concluded, "If the 'Radicals' organize they will simply organize to do the work which you leave undone—while you do the work which they leave undone. Let us shake hands in good faith and feeling."[21]

There was dissension also within the right wing of Unitarianism. On 19 December Rufus Stebbins wrote to the proprietors of the *Christian Examiner* that he had been a subscriber to the denominational journal for thirty years "through all its ebbs and flows." But in the past few years it had not represented what he believed was Unitarianism. It contained "self-contradictory articles, nullifying each other's statements . . . Ability is a good thing in a periodical, but a tolerable consistency is better."[22] Bellows's hope of bringing all wings of the denomination together was rapidly evaporating as the left and the right demurred from the organization of the National Conference.

CHAPTER ELEVEN

Troubles and Strife

Tired Down to the Bottom

Cyrus Bartol at this juncture felt that his sympathies were not with his friend Bellows and the National Conference of Churches but with the dissident group. Bartol was one of those ministers who dreaded any shackles upon his free faith. He wrote Bellows a very apologetic letter in which he expressed his affection for his friend but informed him that he must put his sympathies with the dissidents.[1] Bellows responded to Bartol's affectionate letter, saying he thoroughly understood the "public attitude of antagonism to so old & beloved a friend as I am." He too felt sorrow that in this matter their ways must part. Particularly did he regret separating from his friend on what was "the gravest question of the day." But, he continued, "pained beyond expression as I am at your position of leader in what must end in secession, I am not consciously affected in my tender friendship & complete trust, & I am ready to say that *nothing* you can do or say, will touch the life of so perfect & full a love as ours has been." He understood how Bartol was led by his own beliefs to the position he now maintained.

This was one of the most severe tests that Bellows ever had to live up to his doctrine of the rights of others to have their own convictions, a doctrine he had sought to evince in the preamble to the constitution of the National Conference, and in regard to which he had failed for this dissident group of Unitarian ministers.[2]

Charles Lowe, the Secretary of the American Unitarian Association, was also concerned about the sectionalism among Unitarians. He shared with Bellows the vision of a great national Unitarian body. He felt that the sectionalism was most manifest right in the seat of Unitarianism, in Boston itself. He wrote, "I think I needn't tell you anything about that Boston Association. You know well enough that this, which ought to be the place where we should go for our best encouragement in everything good, is, on the contrary, the place where we find criticism, distrust & coldness. So marked is this that I believe our earnest workers dread to go before it with any of their plans." But Lowe reassured Bellows that

340

these dissidents did not represent the true Unitarian sentiment in New England. "There is such a general spirit of cordiality & interest in your plans & success that it has given a good deal of pain here to have it intimated that our N.[ew] E.[ngland] brethren are harboring suspicions against us." Lowe went on to reassure Bellows that he had the unwavering support of most of the New England ministers.[3]

Charles Chauncey had been at the meeting at Dr. Robbins's home when Dr. Ellis had berated "not only 'the *Liberal Christian*' but all Liberal Christians, liberal movements, views, sympathies." Chauncey protested that Dr. Ellis was not a true representative of the Boston Association. He hoped "Mr. Putnam did not take that meagre and chilly meeting at Dr. Robbins's as significant of the feeling of his brother ministers in this vicinity." He wished success to the *Liberal Christian*, and agreed to contribute to its columns.[4]

Bellows believed that the decision of the Radicals not to cooperate with the National Conference was a tempest in a teapot, and "not important enough to command the attention of serious & active men. Not that great talent, worth & sincerity are not employed in it but that none of these things disjoined from practical sense & wide human sympathies, move the world." Bellows felt that he had "no quarrel with the radicalism or the breadth of liberality—or the freedom of inquiry of these gentle men. My quarrel is with the narrowness of their foundations & the exceptional & cliquish character of their thinking." He felt that "they are neither philosophers, statesmen, nor men of affairs;—to say nothing of their theoretical *un*-Christianity." The Radicals' thin intellectualism disgusted Bellows. He regarded their whole scheme as "the fantasy of recluses & men without wide sympathies—a sort of emasculated clan, eunuchs in the kingdom of God, who are not only without the great passion that begat the shaping movements of the world, but without the power of generating their species after one cross with each other."[5]

On 10 March 1867, Edward Everett Hale wrote Bellows that on that Sunday evening he had attended a large Unitarian gathering, part of the new missionary program of the National Council. The Music Hall had been full of people in spite of what Hale called "such a night,—which would have emptied any theater . . . men making naturally a large proportion of the assembly." There had been no speaker from outside of Boston. Hale believed that the people were ready to undertake a "religious crusade—which will bring the irreligious and Godless part of this land into line & relation with

Christ & God." He believed that there were more than fifty ministers ready to take a decided stand. "But the congregations, as Hepworth told them tonight, are mostly in advance of the ministry."[6]

Bellows's reply was equally ecstatic. "Thanks be to God, my dear Hale, for the meeting you report & the interpretation thereof. . . . You speak my inmost mind when you say that the people are beginning to be interested in Liberal Christianity as *a religion*: not merely as a philosophy or a political crusade disguised in church robes. If I were ten years younger, so help me God, I would start a Unitarian crusade, in the open fields."[7]

All of this worry and anxiety was telling on the health of Bellows. As early as 22 February he was writing to Eliza Dorr that "I am radically *tired out*, not sick, & with no seated disease—but simply in pressing need of absolute & protracted rest. Nineteen years of uninterrupted toil, aggravated by the unusual labors & anxieties of the war & the strain of public and professional responsibility, has used up all my *reserve forces*." He believed "the last year has been full of indications of impaired digestion, fixed fatigue, & weariness of spirit, accompanied with active signs of cerebral exhaustion, sleeplessness, nervous fancies & semi-inflammation of all the alimentary canal." His physician felt that he should not let this condition mature, and had advised "a year's rest without cares, or preaching, or responsibilities of any kind, will probably change my whole alimentary system & set me up for ten years renewed work, & prolong my life." In spite of the pressure of personal, church, denominational, and public affairs, Bellows concluded, "I must go away, as soon as I can, & have accordingly, within a day, asked my people for a *year's vacation*, beginning with May 1."

Bellows felt that the church might be reluctant to let him go for so long. It was a matter in which no one else could make a judgment for him. Henry wrote that "*my wife is anxious for me to go*, but is unwilling to go with me. Whether her reluctance will yield to my wishes I cannot yet say. I shall not force her altho very desirous to have her go!" He planned to take Russell and Annie. They too needed a change. "Nanny keeps me continually anxious, & Russ has recently alarmed us not a little by a kind of nervous syncope which indicates alas! that he has his mother's constitution, & *must* not be pushed either in study or anything else." Bellows felt that everything seemed to point to a European tour. He had been planning this for ten years. He himself felt that he had outlived a sense of anticipation of such a tour, but that he might get satisfaction "in the reflected pleasure of my children, & the prospect of invigorating my own youth."[8] With Eliza Dorr's husband near death, Bellows had pondered his duty, but felt that he had to consider his own health.

By the middle of March Mrs. Bellows had decided to make the trip to Europe with the rest of the family. "I had so much pain in making up my own and my wife's mind to go, that it has not been an inviting subject to write about," Henry told Cyrus Bartol. He had wished that something more interesting than a trip to Europe had presented itself. "Yes, I confess that curiosity & love of journeying & leisure are nearly extinct in my bosom; that *work* is my pleasure, & *Walpole* my magnet in vacation. But I am *tired* down to the bottom; my nerves play me wakeful tricks, & I feel shattered in various ways, too seriously, not to think it highly necessary to try a full year's rest from professional & public cares."[9]

Before leaving for Europe Bellows penned a last letter to Catharine Sedgwick, slowly dying at the home of her niece in Boston. Bellows hoped to come to Boston to see her before he left. He had just come from a meeting of the Mission School "where three hundred and fifty poor little girls, have the care of a set of young ladies belonging to our church, who spend about four hours every Saturday morning, in teaching them sewing, & good morals & manners. It is a beautiful sight to look into their young faces, which poverty & filth cannot wholly obscure, & in which so much possibility of virtue & happiness slumbers."

Bellows addressed the group every Saturday morning on some moral subject. The previous week he had spoken about controlling the temper and this day it had been about cleanliness, next week selfishness. He told Catharine that he too thought "a good deal about the sunset of life—for my own most active days are rapidly passing away. I hope that I may have as cheerful & hopeful a decline as you are having." He felt that Catharine with her "love of many which has *not waxed cold*, could make the winter of life tolerable . . . God bless you my dear friend."[10]

In view of the approaching trip which would certainly strain Bellows's finances to the limit, a group of ten members of the church got together and presented Bellows with a purse of $5,000. They were Thomas Christy, B. G. Arnold, Charles E. Butler, Elliot C. Cowdin, Charles C. Goodhue, W. A. Murdock, W. H. Fogge, John Armstrong, and K. W. and E. N. Goddard. The purse was handed to Bellows by Mr. Prichard, the president of the board of trustees. Bellows, pleased, replied to the group, "I am never surprised by any thing my faithful parishioners do for their pastor! I am so accustomed to indulgence & magnanimous treatment from you, that my habitual feeling of grateful affection cannot be much exalted by exceptional favors." He rejoiced that in this list of eleven names he saw the names "of those friends whose love & approbation I most value."[11]

The receipt of this gift climaxed a very busy April. Henry's brother-in-law, Joseph Dorr, had quietly passed away at Walpole the first of the month and Bellows had gone for the funeral. He had traveled to Germantown for an ordination and dedication ceremony just before Good Friday, and was shortly to make a trip to Boston, where he consulted with Samuel Shaw, a Boston lawyer, about some of the matters regarding the family property in Boston in the light of his forthcoming tour of Europe. It was necessary that Bellows appoint a guardian for the Boston properties for which he was responsible. Shaw sent on a bond to Bellows for him to sign.[12]

Consulting Samuel Shaw about the appointment of a guardian led to a most interesting set of letters that lay unrecognized in the Massachusetts Historical Society until 1975. Among the members of Bellows's congregation were Mr. and Mrs. Herman Melville. Melville was in obscurity, having written a few early books which were popular—romances of the South Seas. His novels, *Moby-Dick* and *Pierre*, had been failures, and in December 1866 he had taken a job in the New York Customs office. Mrs. Melville sometime early in May consulted Bellows about the problems of living with Herman, and confided to him that she wished to leave her husband. Surprisingly, she proposed that Bellows arrange a kidnapping of her—"seemingly against her will." Bellows dutifully wrote of the plans to Samuel Shaw, his lawyer and her half-brother. Shaw replied in a long letter which sheds more light on the Melville household problems that had only been hinted at prior to the discovery of Shaw's letter.[13]

We do not have a transcript of the meeting of Elizabeth Melville with her minister, nor do we have Henry Bellows's letter to her brother Samuel in Boston. But the seven-page letter of Samuel Shaw in reply to a letter from Bellows which takes up the matter of the Melville family problems in detail, is an astounding letter! For what Elizabeth Melville in her desperation proposed to her minister was that he or some of her friends "make a sudden interference and carry her off, she protesting that she does not wish to go and that it is none of her doing." In short, she proposed to her minister that he or some of her friends kidnap her and send her to Boston, she seeming to be against the whole matter but actually having planned it all. Her half-brother, Samuel Shaw, opposed this action (as probably also did Bellows) because he felt that his sister should make up her own mind. It was a personal matter and she herself must make the decision and not have others influence her. He proposed that "she should come to Boston as if on a visit, which would give her ample opportunity for preparation without exciting premature suspicion, and that when here her friends should inform her husband that a separation, for the present at least, has been decided on." Shaw wrote Bellows that Elizabeth would be given good legal counsel and care at his home in Boston.

Shaw also confided to Henry Bellows that the Shaw family had long known about the family difficulties, "which has been a cause of anxiety to all of us for years past." He also informed Bellows that the Melville family, "though not till quite recently, have expressed a willingness to lend their assistance." He also stated that his sister believed her husband to be "insane." This is the first time, I believe, that this word has been used by the family of Herman Melville in extant manuscripts to describe his despondent state of mind. Shaw mentions in his letter to Bellows that his sister had consulted Dr. Augustus Kinsley Gardner who was a specialist in New York City on childbirth and "Insanity," having served on the staff of several "Lunatic Asylums." Perhaps Elizabeth consulted him in regard to both of his specialties. Gardner was also a distant relative of Bellows on his mother's side of the family, and attended All Souls Church.

Bellows, as a practical man as well as a minister, must have listened sympathetically to Elizabeth's plan, put his tongue in his cheek, and passed on her suggestions to her brother. There can be no doubt that he agreed with her brother's letter that the matter had to be resolved by her and not by outsiders upon whom, of course, would fall the blame for the separation. On 18 May, the Bellows party sailed for Europe on the *Ville de Paris*.

Two days after the ship sailed Elizabeth Melville wrote the recently discovered letter to her minister. He had called the previous Saturday, but she was not at home. She had wanted to go to his home and at least say goodbye to him. "I also wanted to thank you for the active interest you took in my behalf. I do so now—most sincerely—and whatever further trial may be before me, I shall feel that your counsel is a strong help to sustain, more perhaps than any other earthly counsel could." She expressed appreciation that his long talk with her "has been a great comfort." Her natural piety came out when she added: "I lay to heart your encouraging words, and pray for submission and faith to *realize* the sustaining power of the Master's love, and to approach his Table in the very spirit of his last command."[14] Even if Henry Bellows had not been able to arrange her "kidnapping," at least he had given her some strength by his counseling to better bear her troubles with Herman.

It was in this atmosphere of tense family relationships that the Melvilles' oldest son, Malcolm, shot himself on 11 September 1867. (Whether it was a suicide or an accident will never be known although when the family requested it, the court determined that the death was accidental.) Malcolm was just eighteen years old at the time. He had been too young to fight in the Civil War but appeared to be enamored of the colorful uniforms. He belonged to a boys' regiment and loved to wear the uniform and to carry his pistol. We might ask now with this new evidence of the family difficulties if Malcolm's death was partly the result of the tensions in the home rather than that Malcolm's death caused the tensions. It certainly caused the Melvilles, especially Herman, to further withdraw from society.

For the time he was to be away Bellows arranged a distinguished list of Unitarian preachers to occupy his pulpit at All Souls Church. Most of them preached several Sundays and remained in New York to do parish work. Others were available for a single Sunday only. William R. Alger, (Horatio's cousin) began the ministerial procession in the pulpit on 19 and 26 May. He was followed by a most distinguished procession: Orville Dewey, Ednah D. Cheney, Alonzo Hill, and Rufus Ellis. (There was a summer vacation for eight Sundays.)

When the church opened again in the fall, Robert Collyer began the fall season. He was followed by William G. Eliot, Alger again, Edward Everett Hale, Frederick Henry Hedge, Ezra Stiles Gannett, Charles Everett, James Freeman Clarke, Orville Dewey, George Briggs, Samuel Lothrop, Alfred P. Putnam, and William Henry Furness. While Bellows was on his sabbatical in Europe and the Near East, All Souls did not want for the best Unitarian preaching offered in this country.[15]

Several years after his European trip Bellows advised Edward Everett Hale, who had not been well, to take a similar European trip. "And if you do go," he warned Hale, "don't imitate *my* example; but really sever off from all literary propensities. I wish I had done so, even now that it is all over. I am sure anybody will feel your right to any amount of rest. Don't take it in dribbles, but one good draught. Spend next winter in Egypt in a darbeha!"[16]

A Rich Rewarding Journey in the East

Bellows preached his farewell sermon on 12 May 1867, and on the following Saturday their ship, the *Ville de Paris*, departed for Europe. It was a ten-day trip, and the ship arrived in Brest on 28 May.

If Bellows were taking this trip for a rest he certainly gave little indication of it from the hectic pace of the trip and its extensiveness. Bellows sat down many evenings after a long day when the rest of the party had gone to sleep from sheer exhaustion and wrote long letters home. These letters were conceived primarily to be read to his parishioners, but they appeared in two volumes of travels prepared for publication by Henry's colleague, Dr. Samuel Osgood of the Second Church. The first volume was printed before Bellows returned in the fall of 1868, and the second a short time after he returned.

These two volumes,[1] which were published by Harper and Brothers, total 982 pages, and were considered models of their kind. Unfortunately, they never sold very well, and although Bellows continued for several years to receive royalties, these were quite small. Anyone who wishes to understand the conditions of Europe, Egypt, and the Middle East in 1867/68 will find some keen insights in these volumes. Bellows interviewed many of the greats of his day including Unitarians and religious liberals wherever he could find them. In some areas they also show some of his thinking about various social and religious problems. The titles of the sections of the books indicate the extent of the travel by the Bellows party, which included Mrs. Bellows, Russell, and Annie, and at times others. The first section is about the ocean trip. There are five chapters about Paris and France, one on Amsterdam, six chapters on Germany, two on Austria (especially about the Alpine regions), ten chapters about Switzerland, seven more about Germany with trips to Heidelberg, Hamburg, Berlin, Wittenberg and Halle, Dresden, Prague, and two chapters on Vienna.

The second volume takes one first to Venice, then to Bologna, Padua, Rome, Naples, and Messina. From Messina the party embarked for Egypt. There are ten chapters about Egypt which are highly interesting, for the party hired a small steamship and took a trip up the Nile as far as Assuan (Aswan) where now the high dam has been built. They took a ship across to Syria and rode horseback down the coast of Syria to Phoenicia and the Holy Land. They spent time in Jerusalem, Bethlehem, Jordan, the plains of Jericho,

Nazareth, Esdraelon, Safed, Mount Hermon, and then the party rode back to Syria, Damascus, and Beirut. They embarked again by ship to Cyprus and sailed through the Dardanelles to Turkey. Thence they traveled to Greece. From Athens they went by ship to Corfu, Florence, and Paris. The second volume ends with a short trip into Belgium and Holland.

It is not within the scope of this book to trace all of Bellows's travels or even to trace his opinions on religious matters, though there are many such in the two volumes. But a few insights are helpful, and I have included these plus a few comments from the letters of this period which are not contained in the travel books.

Bellows used the occasion of his fifty-third birthday on 11 June 1867 to write to his brothers and sisters. He recalled that three years previously he had celebrated his fiftieth birthday in the Valley of the Yosemite. This "is all a dream the way life passes by," he mused. Seeing all of the old sights of Paris had reminded him of life's brevity. In Paris he had also seen thousands upon thousands of tombs, "generally *in the shape of dog kennels.*" Yet, in spite of these reminders of death this was perhaps the first and last year that he did not write sentimentally about the death and greatness of his twin brother, Edward Stearns Bellows.[2]

Since Bellows had partly gone to Europe for his health he went through the usual procedure of visiting the various spas and mineral springs. These were the social gathering places of Europe in this decade, and the spas were as much for social contact and gambling for bored wealthy persons as for curing disease. Since Bellows's problems were largely of the intestinal tract it seemed to him appropriate that he should drink the waters and take the baths. He wrote to Eliza Dorr, "The whole business is treated much more *medically* than with us. People do not drink the waters *at random* but follow careful medical advice—which I think is the only prudent way."[3]

Bellows was a true Protestant and fearful of the Catholic Church. This attitude crops up in the most unexpected places. On this trip he traveled extensively in Catholic countries. He felt that Catholicism was strong because "it is a unit." And he contrasted this unity with the apparent weakness of Protestantism, "Protestantism, with a hundred times the wealth, intelligence, public spirit and administrative ability, by reason of its sectarian jealousies and division can have no parallel successes, and is losing rapidly its place in legislative grants and public policy," he wrote. He expressed his fears, "There is an apathy about the Roman Catholic advances in the United States among American Protestants which will finally receive a terrible shock. There is no influence at work in America so hostile to our future peace as the Roman Catholic Church. The next American war, I fear, will be a religious war—of all kinds the worst. If we wish to avert it, we must take immediate steps to organize Protestantism more efficiently and on less sectarian ground."[4]

In Munich Bellows felt that "the chief charm of the cathedral service was the music from a full choir, accompanied by the organ and a complete orchestra. They sang the music of Pergolese and Palestrina, and never have I realized so perfectly what sacred music was and ever should be." He felt the music was "strictly religious." This led him to compare this beautiful music with "the music of the modern church," which he described as "characteristically barbarous." He described modern church music as being "dull, monotonous and inartistic droning of hymns . . . by a feeble choir or an undrilled congregation."[5]

In December Charles Lowe, the Secretary of the American Unitarian Association, wrote to Bellows that the association had voted "That Rev. Dr. Bellows be authorized to act as representative of the Association during his residence abroad in all ways by which the interests of Liberal Christianity may be served; especially in cultivating cordial & friendly relations between the Unitarian Church of America and the liberal religious thinkers of Europe, to the end that our mutual sympathy may be strengthened & our efficiency increased."[6] Bellows actually was doing exactly this—visiting with all of the liberal ministers of the Continent whom he could meet. But, in view of his proposed extended trip to England, the action of the American Unitarian Association made his visit more an official than a personal one.

In the journeys to the Near East one gets the impression not of a sick man traveling for his health, but one driven with ambition and with passable health. On the way down the Syrian coast the party hit terrible weather in late February, and the entry in the book is typical of Bellows. Everyone else was huddled in the tents, "and two giving audible proofs of a sound nap, while the wind raves about and the rain drums on the tent, and the sides flap as my pen runs on." Was Bellows asleep? No, he was writing a book, and certainly not under the best of conditions. "I am sitting with my feet in a puddle, all feeling being happily out of them from cold, and the candle is at its last gasp, I must drop my quill and tumble into bed with my clothes on. Truly it is not wholly pleasant to travel in Syria in February. Yet it is not without its great pleasures even now. Goodnight." How many men would sit up and write a book under such circumstances? It gives some measure of the character and the determination of the man.[7]

One of the most interesting aspects of Bellows's personality was that although he was liberal in most areas of life, his attitudes toward sex and the relationships between men and women were strictly monogamous and typical of the times. He constantly commented in his trips through Islamic countries that the backwardness of those countries was due to polygamy. On the trip up the Nile in January 1868, their little flotilla stopped at the Nile port of Assiout, and there the American consul, Mr. Weser (he was also the English and Russian Consul) invited all of the Bellows group to a party at his home. One of the items on the program was what today would be called a "belly dance." Bellows tried through his disgust to describe what he saw, and his prejudices shine strongly through his words.

"The dancing consisted in very graceless gyrations, which were made slow or fast as the music guided, and in swayings or contortions much more suited to the circus or the gymnasium than the saloon [he meant salon]. The principal feat consisted in convulsing the trunk of the body until it trembled like jelly, or worked like yeast, while the feet and hands were kept perfectly still." He found that the dancer exhibited an extraordinary and almost incredible control of muscles which are usually wholly automatic and beyond our influence, except as they act in connection with limbs or head. "The effect, however, was painful, not to say disgusting . . . There was a possibility of abandon and orgiastic fury in the creature's movements and mien that kept us in a constant apprehension that the utmost limits of decency would be passed." The party was spared, for "the presence of some American ladies restrained her, although it became very apparent to what inflammatory uses Oriental dancing was put among the natives, and how readily and naturally it served the worst purposes." Bellows was uncomfortable! "I confess I have never felt myself in a less pleasant predicament, nor felt a more grateful relief than in getting into fresh air after such an experience of Oriental degradation." He added that the native guests and the host "seemed to be wholly unaware of any thing out of the way in the entertainment."[8]

Eliza Bellows did not make the trip to Egypt and the Near East, preferring to remain in various hotels with her friends in Europe while Henry and the two children made the arduous trip. This was probably a wise decision in the light of her very poor mental and physical health. But she was kept informed of what was happening to the party by frequent letters.

Bellows had hoped to get back to the church by the end of the summer. But it seemed important that he should make an extended visit to England. His leave had been extended by the church to the middle of September in order that this might be possible. He felt that "it will be a comfort to get back to one's own tongue, and to feel that one has again joined the noble race of Anglo-Saxons! I don't think we fully appreciate how much nobler, from a moral & spiritual point of view, they are, than any other race—& how fortunate we are in being born of them."[9]

While Bellows was in Florence in 1868 Hiram Powers, the great American sculptor, was working there. James F. Drake of All Souls gave Powers a commission so that Bellows sat for a portrait bust. Bellows so much enjoyed sitting for Powers that he wrote a series of eight articles about the sittings, seven of which were published in *Appleton's Popular Journal of Literature, Science and Art* in 1868.[10] The Powers bust was finished in due time and two copies of it were made. One copy was eventually given to the Century Club of New York City by Russell Bellows and the other was given to the American Unitarian Association by the descendants of Bellows's family through his second wife, Anna Peabody Bellows. The original portrait bust was eventually given on permanent loan to the All Souls Church in New York City where it rests in the vestibule of the church sanctuary. The bust itself gives something of the regal Roman look to Bellows that so characterizes the statuary of the period.

In June 1868, the Bellows party landed in England and Henry and his family began a round of lionizing that he had seldom known even in his own land. The British were impressed that the famous Dr. Bellows had been the President of the United States Sanitary Commission. The Unitarians of England in a church which was not at all prosperous were happy to find a Unitarian hero whom they could exhibit to the people of Great Britain. A great Collation was given for Henry Bellows on 4 June 1868. There was a long series of toasts, one of which was "to Dr. Bellows—the eloquent Champion of Liberal Christianity, and the thrice welcome Representative of the Unitarian Churches of America."[11]

Bellows himself described his reception. 'The whole Unitarian denomination have risen to welcome me, & have demanded my clerical services with the utmost eagerness." Bellows found this lionization so "exhausting to my nervous strength that I am afraid of

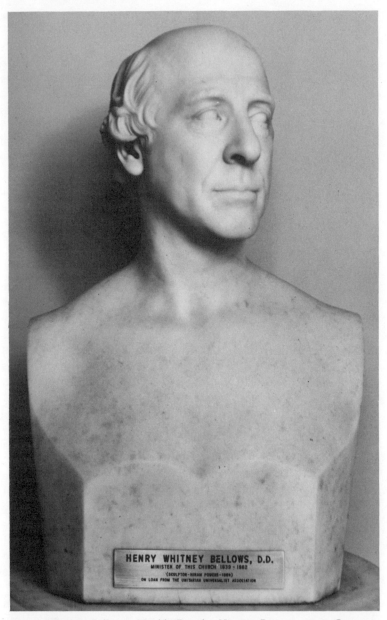

Henry Whitney Bellows, Marble Bust by Hirman Powers, 1868. On permanent loan to the Unitarian Church of All Souls by the Unitarian Universalist Association

exposing myself to it any longer—lest I should lose all the advantages of my year's rest from professional duty." He wanted a month of quiet after he returned before climbing into the All Souls pulpit again. He wished to stay in New York for as short a time as possible and go to Walpole until the church opened. He felt that Mrs. Bellows had never been as well as before her recent sickness at Rome. She as well as his two children needed the rest. He hoped to have a month in Walpole before he resumed preaching.[12]

As a souvenir the British Unitarian Association presented him with a book of pictures of as many Unitarian ministers as it was possible to collect. The Secretary of the British Unitarian Association wrote to each of the ministers and asked for a standard-sized picture; most of the ministers responded.[13]

After Bellows had returned to America and looked back upon his experience with the British Unitarians he realized that he had been "admitted into the inner councils of *both* schools of policy & opinion" there. He did his "utmost to knit them together, to animate them to more zealous cooperative work & greater forbearance with each other." He wanted Unitarians to "occupy more religious *room* in the religious life of England."

One of these schools of British Unitarian thought was represented by James Martineau, brother of Harriet Martineau who accompanied Charles Follen on a trip West (See *Liberals Among the Orthodox*, p. 213). "The theological school of Martineau & Taylor in London is thoroughly committed to the purely speculative & critical training. Much learning has made them very impractical & very theoretic. But they are possessed of the *purest* spirit & are admirably thorough. I found the product of their labors on the whole a very encouraging one. I liked the men themselves highly, but I do not think them judicious leaders of our ecclesiastical movements. They are philosophers & sages, not *Statesmen* or *Churchmen*."[14]

There was a strong effort among American Unitarians to get James Martineau to come to America to preach at the National Conference in October. Bellows naturally seemed to these enthusiasts to be the man to put pressure on the reluctant Martineau—who did not like sea voyages. Bellows's reluctance to invite Martineau seemed a little strange, and finally Bellows had to explain his reasons to a friend,—"I could not have become a very earnest advocate of his visit, owing to no want of love, respect or interest, but from doubts of the wisdom of his coming to America, after the kind of part he played during the war. Not only he, but the majority of the influential Unitarian ministers & laymen were on the *Southern* side. Mr. Adams, our minister, ceased his attendance on Martineau's preaching because of his anti-Northern sympathies & expressions." Bellows went on to say that Martineau in this respect only represented the general attitude in England toward the Northern side of the struggle. He had learned to like Martineau personally, and felt that he understood his position enough to even forgive his illusions. "He is formed to charm & instruct & to *sway* but not to organize & lead men. He is the *handsomest* creature I saw in England!"[15]

The Bellows party departed for New York on Saturday 8 August on the steamer *China*, and landed at New York on Tuesday 18 August. Three days later they were able to escape from the city without a whirl of social engagements and go to Walpole for a month's rest.

The Osgood Affair

A week after arriving at Walpole Bellows made an important decision, and wrote Thomas Christy, the president of the board of trustees of the church. Mrs. Bellows's ill health was "so much impaired by nervous debility—the result of many years of anxious dutifulness to her family"—that Bellows felt he did not dare to move back into the parsonage. He described it as "one of the gloomiest & most inconvenient & laborious houses to dwell in." It had "tremendous flights of stairs" and useless crannies. It was difficult to light, had a "genuine lack of air & sunshine." Bellows felt that living in this house had done a great deal in "breaking down my wife's health." He concluded that it was his duty to leave the parsonage, and he apologized if this conclusion would "be troublesome to the society." He wanted the approval of the trustees in his move. He hoped they could put the space in the parsonage to other uses. He also raised the financial problem which this entailed for him and for the society. He explained to Mr. Christy that he had never been able to live on his salary without the income from his wife's estate which amounted to about $3,000 annually. He needed some extra salary for a rented house. He reminded Christy that on 2 January he would have been the minister at All Souls for thirty years.[1]

In a less official letter on the same day written to his dear friend, Mrs. David Lane, Bellows was even more explicit about the old

Samuel Osgood, D.D., Courtesy of the Unitarian Universalist
Association

parsonage. "My wife with her continual delicacy, has for years been
sinking under the weight of her domestic cares; my daughter has
been running up & down from the fourth story until her health is
uncertain, & I have been shuddering in that dreadful hole (called my
study) where neither light nor air could come, & where gas lamps
made my winter noon-tide." He continued, "The general effect of
the outrageous structure upon domestic quiet & home happiness is

indescribably bad. There is *no* parlor, for the drawing room cannot be warmed in winter. The only sitting-room is the dining room, which has no closets big enough for a dinner-set, & which can only be reached from the kitchen by a circuitous journey."

Bellows complained, "We wash by gas-light & dry our clothes *six* stories off. We have no sunlight in the kitchen, so that it is a wonder our servants ever stay a month, & they won't without additional wages & the best not at all. It is a most costly place to light and heat & is not light nor warm after all is done. It cannot be kept clean, nor ventilated, nor made free from damps." How they had stayed in the parsonage for twelve years seemed a miracle to him.[2]

All Souls trustees met on 3 September 1868 and quickly responded to Bellows's letter. They decided to make his salary the sum of $8,000 annually when he moved out of the parsonage. Mr. Christy suggested that there had been some offers for the rental of the property, and the standing committee was authorized to consult with a real estate broker to determine the value of the parsonage.[3] The board met again before the annual meeting, and they resolved to recommend to the congregation that they raise Bellows's salary to $7,500 and that when he vacated the parsonage, it be raised to $10,000.[4] In order to cover these costs the rental value of the pews was to be raised to twenty-four percent and the assessment on the pews owned at sixteen percent of their value.[5]

In spite of his "vacation," Bellows was immediately involved in church business, for the Convention of the Unitarian and other Christian Churches had been scheduled to be held in New York City early in October. Edward Everett Hale wrote to Bellows the day after his arrival from England that "We have appointed the convention in New York, in the wish that it may always be there;—to retain its metropolitan central and effective character." Hale also felt that the spirit of the planning meeting was a good one. He wanted Bellows to come to Boston on 30 September for a meeting of the council.[6]

Samuel J. May welcomed Bellows home from Europe and his pilgrimage but reminded him, "you have come home to work harder, if possible, than you ever have done, to have more demands, of a greater variety, made upon you and be driven to answer them." May then proceeded to tell Bellows that the first thing he must do "is to mend 'the left wing' of our denomination, so that it may not fall off wholly from the body. You are said to have struck it a harder blow than any one else in 1865, and, I believe, you can do more than any one else to mollify the pain that was then given, if they are willing to be soothed and conciliated."[7]

The session of the National Conference was held from 7 to 9 October. Another attempt was made to bring about a reconciliation between the extremes of the Unitarian movement. James Freeman Clarke introduced a resolution that embodied a "freedom clause." But such a broad invitation to freedom was not acceptable to the majority of the delegates. Edward Everett Hale finally introduced the following resolution which was adopted:

> To secure the largest unity of the spirit and the widest practical co-operation, it is hereby understood that all the declarations of this conference, including the preamble and constitution, are expressions only of its majority, and dependent wholly for their effect upon the consent they command on their own merits from the churches here represented as belonging within the circle of our fellowship.

The freedom clause "that we heartily welcome to that fellowship all who desire to work with us in advancing the kingdom of God" in Clarke's resolution was thus defeated.[8]

The conference involved a long and arduous three days for all concerned, but it was especially difficult for Bellows, who gave the opening address at the convention. He wrote Mrs. Bellows, who had remained at Walpole, when it was all over, "I have been inexpressibly thankful for the evidence I see of returning vigor, earnestness & order in the Unitarian body. It is plain that the filaments organic life and growth are knitting in the frame of our denomination, as the bones traceable in a foetus!" He stated that he had "never expected to see in my time such a wondrous development of wisdom & cooperative life in our Body. I would not wonder if ten years hence it were one of the best organized & most compact religious bodies in the church."[9]

If Bellows was overjoyed at the results of the National Conference, others were not. Rufus Ellis, the Minister of the First Church in Boston, was one of these. Holding an extremely orthodox Unitarian position, he admitted, "I have no influence beyond my own church & a small circle of friends" so that he could do nothing. But he believed that so many concessions had been made to the Radicals that he seemed "to be shut out from all further cooperation with Unitarians." Ellis went on to suggest that his church in Boston still used its ancient Covenant as a basis for membership. He claimed that "the doctrine of the Nicene Creed is not unwelcome to me." He felt that the Nicene Creed emphasized the sonship that entered "into the very absoluteness of Being before creation & out of all relations to time." He liked that doctrine as well as the Apostles' Creed.

Ellis wanted to withdraw his support from the National Conference and also from the local conferences which it had set up.[10] Bellows had probably expected this kind of reaction from Rufus Ellis, who correctly, as he said, represented very few persons but himself and a few of his parishioners. But Bellows's great hope was to keep the bonds of the Unitarian body together, liberals as well as the most orthodox conservatives.

Russell Bellows's theological education had been postponed by the trip to California in 1864 and his subsequent work there with the United States Sanitary Commission and the European trip. His health was never robust, and he did not appear to be able to stand the rigors of a full theological course. So he took a few courses at Union Theological Seminary in New York City. Thus only partly equipped for the ministry, he was nevertheless called to be the minister of Bellows's home church at Walpole, New Hampshire. His first sermon was delivered on 18 October 1868. Bellows wrote to his son several days later and said he hoped that Russell was "happily launched upon your chosen voyage & that the timbers were pronounced sound & the vessel shapely trim, & full of promise."

Young Bellows had preached on "the Convention," and his father warned him that other subjects would be more difficult. Henry wrote that the *"commonest"* themes are the best. "I never preached on *small* subjects," wrote Henry. "My first sermons grappled with immortality, the problem of evil, the conflict of business cares and religious consecration; the dark ways of God; and the great themes of *repentence* & newness of life."[11]

On 23 October the Board of the New York and Hudson River Conference met in New York City. The wording of the resolution is perhaps significant: "Voted, that Mr. Russell N. Bellows, *having applied through his father* for license from this organization to preach—this conference being fully satisfied of his Christian character, & his qualifications for the Christian ministry, do grant the petition, & do most affectionately commend our young brother to the hearty confidence & favor of our churches." The document is signed by Henry W. Bellows, President. If any young man ever came into the ministry tagging his father's coattails it was Russell Nevins Bellows.[12]

Although things were going well in the denomination and at All Souls Church, there were unmistakable signs that the Church of the Messiah was in bad shape, psychologically and financially. Samuel Osgood was not an appealing preacher or minister; he spent a great deal of his time participating in the social life of the city. The church had gone so badly in debt in erecting its new edifice that the society was threatened with financial collapse. On 14 October 1868, the trustees of the Church of the Messiah met and "resolved that the Pastor of this Society be authorized to arrange for a meeting of the Boards of Trustees with such other members of each Society as they may please to invite to confer together upon the future welfare of our cause in this city."[13] The resolution really meant to consider the situation of the Second Church.

On 21 November 1868, Bellows attended a second meeting in his own parlor on the subject of the crisis in the Church of the Messiah. There were twenty men present. "They owe $100,000 on their church which has cost over $250,000," Bellows recounted to his wife. "It was felt after mature discussion that the only course was for Dr. Osgood to retire. And he has accordingly sent in his resignation." The All Souls people were to "endeavor to pay a certain portion of the debt & to aid them in calling another minister who can build them up into strength & self-supporting ability."

The suggestion that he resign or retire, as it was more politely put, came as something of a surprise to Dr. Osgood who felt that his good friend Dr. Bellows had betrayed him. Bellows wrote, "I expect no little abuse & trouble about the Osgood affair." He also reported that Mrs. Osgood had called upon him and had "spent five minutes of womanly vituperation upon me, for having lent myself to the project for *resigning* her husband . . . It seems to fall to me to do all the disagreeable things!"[14]

As Bellows expected, the matter did not end there. Dr. Osgood was "a good deal pained." He resented that Bellows had recommended to his parishioners that they ask Osgood to resign. Osgood felt that Bellows "was eventually urging my dismissal instead of leaving to me the grace of free action. I resigned before hearing any word of disaffection. I am a good deal pained by your disparaging course & your taking the liberty which you dissuaded me from taking & said that you should not take. The whole record does not seem to me to be straight-forward."[15]

Not content merely to write one "official" letter, Samuel Osgood wrote another more vituperative letter to Bellows. "The thing that cuts me to the heart," he wrote, "is that you tried virtually to have me dismissed from my post by asking our trustees to request me to resign after leaving the choice freely to me with the assurance that nothing more was to be said by either of us at the meeting." Then Osgood reminisced about their friendship. "I have loved you & believed wholly in your integrity. Yet I am most shaken in my convictions & am only comforted by the opinion that I have always done my best to serve you & that I have done nothing to bring on this harsh rebuke without a word of sympathy or of recognition of my peculiar & mental trials from you." He wanted a meeting with Bellows, with Frederick Farley as intermediary.[16]

Bellows fortunately kept a copy of his answer to Dr. Osgood. "I cannot afford to let you take this unfriendly tone of correspondence with me, & I have too much respect for your essential principles of Christian character to believe that you mean to keep it up. If I have injured you, let the injustice be clearly pointed out, and I will not only confess, but apologize and to the best of my ability atone for it."

Bellows suggested a plan: "Let us call in our brother ministers and let them hear your grievance and I will abide by their decision. Better still, why not come up & see me & have a calm talk over this trying crisis & see just what grounds of complaint there are?" Bellows concluded, "You have known me for thirty-five years, & must be able to have some confidence that I would not willfully & knowingly injure you. I certainly cannot believe that you wish to injure me." He suggested that he would call at the Osgoods' if he were welcome and that he would be at his home that evening if Osgood wanted to visit him.[17] Actually, before Bellows had suggested the possibility of Dr. Osgood's resignation to his trustees he had privately suggested it to Osgood himself before the meeting, but Osgood had simply shrugged the thought off as being inappropriate.

Osgood proposed to Bellows that they both meet with Dr. Frederick Farley on Monday 7 December at 10:00 A.M. at his home. "My self-respect does not allow me to enter your house until the wrong of November 22 is explained & apologized for." Osgood wanted to "meet as Christian ministers & let God rule our minds." He also accused Bellows of meddling in the affairs of the Church of the Messiah: "Our people have their affairs in their own hands & regret having been persuaded to take another attitude." The more he thought about the matter the more Bellows seemed a meddler and in the wrong.[18]

Bellows evidently told Farley that he saw no need for the meeting. But Osgood was insistent. Osgood also admitted to Bellows that he had written to "a few leading clergy in Boston of my affairs for counsel & stated the facts without professing to understand the motive for your urging my people to take the initiative against me." Osgood now believed that his own people did not want him to resign, and they had suggested that he withdraw his letter of resignation wholly. He stressed to Bellows that "a handsome sum of money was subscribed." He reiterated his loyalty to the Unitarian cause.[19]

Most of Bellows's letters to Osgood were not preserved, but in a letter to his wife, Bellows showed how he was suffering from the misunderstanding. "I have suffered more than you would have believed possible from the Osgood imbroglio—I mean in my feelings. It seems impossible for threatened parties to behave in disinterestedness; or for for self-saving persons to appreciate courage & fidelity." Bellows felt that he had "been made the scapegoat of the whole difficulty, & all the results of *his* disqualifications & the ruin of his parish, somehow on me, as if *his* leaving* were *my fault,* because I have been compelled to bring our old & dreadful sore to surgical relief at last." Yet he felt deeply for Osgood. "His distress & that of his family, brought to me in every way, has filled me with real grief & hung on me almost as if I were really the cause of it."[20]

The interview with Osgood was held on Monday morning as scheduled. Evidently Farley either could not attend or refused to be present, for Bellows says that the interview was with Osgood "& his wife alone!" Bellows found himself in an unenviable position, in Osgood's own home. He commented, "The case had to be dealt with, as if they were both *children,* to be soothed and treated with something short of the real truth! I think the end will be a patching up of the matter for a year, perhaps." Bellows felt that the anger of Osgood's "people seems to be aroused & this shows itself in a spunky determination *not* to give in to the counsel they sought from us. But I think the case is past doctoring!"[21]

Evidently Bellows had suggested that the whole matter of the meeting of 21 November never be mentioned. Osgood agreed. "Our trustees concur in your suggestion that the meeting of November 21 had better pass without record & the whole matter run like water into the ground." Osgood still insisted that the trustees "in no way formed the idea of my resigning." They were rather insulted at the idea that it had been in their minds that their minister resign. Someone was not being completely candid with Osgood. Then he added, "So let the matter drop & the strife end. I have had my say & so leave it there." He hoped that with Bellows's help they could reduce the debt on the Church of the Messiah.[22]

Bellows's reply evidently accepted the pleas of Osgood and offered to help. Osgood proposed that he would try to raise $50,000 within a month, and wished Bellows's blessings on such a campaign.

He added that "to leave the post would be a small matter, but to go under a cloud & with the church in danger is a bitterness that I pray not to know."[23] Bellows put his pocketbook where his mouth was, and sent a letter to Osgood making a personal pledge for the liquidation of the debt on the Church of the Messiah. This letter is lost, but Osgood replied, "I passed your offer of kindness to our financial committee & offered myself a subscription of the same amount, but the conviction was that we ministers had little enough for themselves, & ought not to tax thousands thus." Osgood expressed his thanks to Bellows for the material signs of backing in the enterprise.[24]

All of this effort and conflict was wearying for Bellows. At the end of the year he wrote to Russell, "The more I taste of public life and conspicuous position, the less I like it. I suppose Providence gives us the spur of ambition & the love of power & influence to use as for some ends of its own. But however much the race horse may in his youth & prime enjoy the course, his taste for it gives out sooner than his riders." He went on to say that he presumed a "quiet field of labour" was much to be desired, and he hoped that Russell was happy in the tiny Walpole Church. "Without any great demands of the public, a Minister may try to build up a church & a small community in the order of the divine kingdom, is as happy & useful a sphere as a man can desire, provided he is wide awake & has no disposition to adopt the sleepy standards about him."[25]

I Don't Like to Mix In

Bellows spent New Year's Day in New York while Russell and Mrs. Bellows were still in Walpole. On the thirtieth anniversary of his ordination, on 2 January 1869, Bellows wrote to his wife to recall their first meeting at the social affair after the solemn ceremonies of ordination in the Chambers Street church. He wrote that it was a terrible New Year's Day in New York with sleet on the streets. Yet "some seventy persons called" at the Bellows parsonage, "mostly in carriages." Annie had helped her father in receiving the visitors.[1]

Bellows devoted himself quite seriously to the work of the parish this particular winter. He conducted a weekly Bible class of seventy teenage girls, and a class of young men who met every other Friday evening. There were four religious schools for children run by the church, and the enrollment numbered over 800 children with about 100 teachers. But the Osgood affair still rankled in his heart in spite of these successes. He wrote to some friends in Charleston,

South Carolina, "For the first time in my life I have suffered from virulent & secret misrepresentation. But I am quite content to fall back on my *character* for open dealing & truth—& let slanderers say their fill."[2]

Bellows was not well the last week in December and the first week in January. "My duties & my cares are more than I can safely attend to, & my bowels have been out of order & seem obstinately deranged. They especially try me at night (not with calls) but with sleeplessness & *malaise,*" he explained to his wife. This sickness more than ever convinced him that he should move out of the parsonage and live in the country near New York City. Before another autumn he hoped to see the family settled in the environs of New York, "& to begin a more placid & quiet existence." He missed the circle of his family, and Mr. B. G. Arnold had offered to build Bellows a house on some property he owned.[3]

The annual meeting was held on Tuesday evening, 12 January 1869. As was his custom, Bellows did not attend. But Mr. Prichard visited him the next day to inform him that the congregation at the suggestion of the trustees had voted to raise Bellows's salary from $5,000 to $7,500 while he continued in the parsonage and when he left it they would raise his salary to $10,000 per year, a munificent sum in those days of the late 1860s with no income taxes to worry about. Mr. Prichard also informed Bellows that Mr. Arnold had a house on some land "out on the East River" which he thought Bellows could have. "I shall go out & see it as soon as the present tenant makes up his mind to leave, as he thinks he will. It looks as if we could really accomplish something, & be easy in our circumstances too; that is with reasonable carefulness." Henry wrote to Mrs. Bellows that he was "more & more satisfied every day, that I cannot prudently *live* in New York, much better than *you* can, & that wisdom & peace will both be served by our retiring a few miles from the city. But we need only *try it for a year,* & if it don't work, we can come back to New York. There is nothing desperate about the step therefore;—as it involves no great risk."[4]

Writing to Orville Dewey in January Bellows recalled that it had been about twenty years since Dewey had left New York for his Sheffield retirement. He commented that he now was just about as old as Dewey had been then. "I begin to realize what sort of necessity it was that drove you out of the city & from your important & valued post here!" Bellows felt that he was a good deal older at fifty-four than Dewey had been at the same age. "With a more active exterior temperament I have rushed through so much labour of body

& mind, of heart & will." He commented, "nobody can ever know the fearful drain of the War, when for four years I had a great parish, and a greater public-Work both on my brain & hands. I think I crammed *ten* years into the four, & shall never recover the vigour I then squandered. I don't regret it; but I foresee a limit to my work, & sometimes I think it is nearer than others suspect."

The European tour had rested him but now that he had returned to his duties, "fatigue & exhaustion" had taken over his body and mind, and he was "obliged to use self-serving methods to get along with it at all." He missed his family (still in Walpole). And his "denominational position and responsibilities are always costing me distress, & requiring the utmost reliance on a sentiment of duty & fidelity to earnest convictions, to carry me through."[5]

Eliza was thinking of returning to New York, but Bellows was plainly worried about her return to the complexities of the city. "It is clear that you possess a very sensitive & exquisite cerebral organization," he wrote, "which is yet sound & capable of affording you great happiness, when calm & not over-tasked. It *has* been greatly over-wrought—& is liable to fall either way, into gloom or into feverish heat." He felt that it was "a very sacred duty to protect it from either, & I am confident that persistent *rest*, will bring you into a condition to enjoy & to give joy to me, for many years—should our lives be spared." He further shared with Eliza, "I shall want your care, your society, your sympathy, when the strain on my life is over, & nobody can tell how soon that may be."[6]

The situation at the Church of the Messiah continued to decline, and the *Liberal Christian* late in January contained an article about the sad state of the church. On 25 January 1869, Henry Bellows wrote a most confidential letter to Samuel Osgood, of which he kept a copy. He wanted to do nothing "to widen the breach which recent circumstances have opened." Bellows assured Osgood that he sought "no information about the internal affairs of your church, and believe very little that busy-bodies say." Then Bellows did a very interesting thing; he went back into the history of both the First and Second Churches and said, "It did no damage to William Lunt or William Ware, when in a manly way facing the discouraging aspects of their ministry in New York, they bravely left their posts to successors whom it was hoped might do better."

He pointed out that "they had reputations, as you have, independent of their failure in the pulpit. Was it not a mistake to regard a proposal for your resignation as an indignity or a wrong? Would it not have been better for all, had it come fully & decisively some time ago?" These were rather plain words bluntly spoken in confidence and probably resented. This was almost too frank a letter for Osgood to understand. But Bellows was being honest and working not for his ego but for what he felt was the good of the whole Unitarian movement in New York City.[7]

Osgood was beginning slowly to realize that his usefulness in the Church of the Messiah was about at an end. Replying to Bellows he began, "In what remains of my ministry here, I desire very much to keep the dignity of the pastoral office not only for my sake & yours, but for him who comes after me & our profession in general." He hoped that Bellows would regard him as the "head of the Parish" and not listen to gossip about him.[8]

By the end of January Osgood was feeling a little more charitable to Henry Bellows. He wrote, "I have been strangely mystified, but have not removed the sentiment of forty years, nor been driven from the feeling that you did not mean to be wholly if at all unfriendly when you dealt so harshly with me & my professional problem. I have had this feeling & have put it into writing."[9]

By the first part of February Henry was writing to Eliza that he hoped that she could come to the city for a few experimental weeks to see how it reacted on her nervous system. He had not yet done anything about moving from the parsonage, but he promised that he would not do anything rash. Professor Cutler of Harvard had visited Bellows in New York, probably to pursue the idea of the presidency of Harvard for his friend. But Bellows was tired. "My audacity is over, I find myself growing cautious & purposive."[10]

February was a busy month for Bellows. He preached at the Conference at Yonkers on 11 February, went on to Boston and preached for Edward Everett Hale on Sunday 14 February. Then he went westward to Springfield, Vermont, where he met Eliza, who came from Walpole to meet him; they returned to New York together. There was a Harvard dinner at Delmonico's on Tuesday evening, 23 February. The evening was filled with speeches. Bellows was the first speaker after the dinner at 9:00 P.M. He made "a light rambling speech, full of recollections of Cambridge forty-one years ago, 1828, when I entered, with sketches of the college, professors, customs, goodies, cake-vendors, habitués, stag-dinners." He continued, "I sketched the dependence of Boston Society on Cambridge by showing that nobody could be born, baptized, educated, married, purged, bled, vomited, sued, convicted . . . buried, or even secured possession of property without the leave of an *alumnus* armed with a college diploma—& made in fine, intermingled with some serious passages, a pleasant . . . after-dinner speech, which set the company in an academic humour that did not fail or flag during the evening."[11] There were sixteen toasts, and everyone went home well pleased with Harvard.

The first week in March, Bellows returned to the now-familiar City of Washington. This time he joined an excursion train to attend the inauguration of President Ulysses Simpson Grant on Thursday, 4 March 1869. He found the city crowded—especially with blacks, and commented that they came out to honor the General because this was the first time there was any semblance of universal suffrage in the country. He found the crowds oppressive, tried to get into the Senate chambers—but they were too full—and did not go to the Inaugural Ball. General Grant rode alone on a horse in the procession without a military escort. Bellows had dinner with Secretary of State Seward. Everyone was curious whom Grant would appoint in Seward's place in the new administration. 'Thousands of office-seekers are waiting to know into whom to plunge their expectant claws. This terrible thirst for place is one of the worst features of the country. I wish that we paid our legislators in nothing but honor & made it easier to get a living in any other way, than the government clerkships."[12]

On 18 March, Samuel Osgood wrote Bellows a confidential letter in which he explained that he had finally decided to resign as the pastor of the Church of the Messiah. He enumerated his reasons: 1. the terrible debt on the church which he was in no position to arouse enough loyalty to get it repaid; 2. He had consulted with his doctor, Dr. Parker, who had advised him to give up this "double load of thought & anxiety"; 3. He felt that it would be unfair to ask his personal friends to pay large sums toward his staying when that was at best problematical; 4. The Unitarian movement had changed so much that he saw no hope of improving the state of the Church of the Messiah; and 5. He began to see that he represented a point of view which was not popular among Unitarians. In the field "of faith & feeling" he was out of step with "some if not most of our New York Unitarians."[13]

Late in March the Bellows family finally found a house to their liking, at No. 232 East 15th Street, only five short north and south blocks from the church. A professional builder had built it for his own use, and it had cost more than Bellows was paying for it. The builder's health had failed, and he was pleased to find a purchaser. Bellows asked some of the church trustees to look at it to see what they thought of the building and the price, and they had agreed that it was a good bargain. Bellows paid $42,000 for it of which $20,000 was to be paid down on 10 April, and he had a mortgage for $22,000, of which $15,000 could be considered a permanent mortgage if he liked. The $7,000 had to be paid off in one or two years. Bellows had sold some stocks and bonds to raise the $20,000. He calculated that the house would cost him $3,500 per year, and while that was not equal to the increase that the parish would give him of $2,500, he felt that the increased cost was worth it in the increased health possibilities to his family. He told Russell that he thought the house a good financial investment.

Actually the cost of this home was a financial noose around Bellows's neck for the rest of his life. He lived in close company with the social and financial elite of the city, and in many ways was expected to live in the same manner as they did. Yet, even a salary of $10,000, with no income taxes, meant that with such standards Bellows was always trying to earn more money through lecturing, and he was constantly pressed to meet the debts of a family that also adopted the standards that they saw around them—so difficult to maintain even on a large minister's salary.[14]

Easter Sunday in 1869 fell on 28 March, and Bellows reported that in spite of a bad rain the attendance at the morning service was large. The evening services were also drawing full attendance now that Bellows was giving a course of lectures. He remarked about these lectures, "They are only old sermons a little revamped & mixed in with extempore matter & cost me no special effort. I hope a good deal from them—as they strike deliberately a little lower key than the concert-pitch of our church & meet a want of average minds & hearts." He commented, "We carry often-times too fine goods to the market—broad cloth where the people really want satinet." Osgood had now resigned and was going to Europe alone, as his wife was not in good health. "I feel sadly for his disappointment," Bellows wrote, "but what can knock the nonsense out of some folks!"[15]

By 1 April 1869, Bellows had two main thoughts on his mind. The first was the surprise announcement that Charles W. Eliot had been appointed President of Harvard, which post, of course, Bellows himself had coveted highly. He wrote to Edward Everett Hale an analysis of his future brother-in-law—an opinion that with the years he was to drastically change. "I am not greatly surprised at Mr. Eliot's nomination. I know nothing of him personally. But my impression is that he is altogether too much of a drill-sergeant & routinist to give any inspiration to Harvard. His name will add nothing to its prestige."

The second thing on Bellows's mind was helping the Church of the Messiah find a replacement for Samuel Osgood. The church was worth $300,000, but there was a debt of $110,000 on it. Its morning congregation now was around 250 persons and the evening congregation 175 on a good day, compared with Bellows's almost full houses (1,200 persons). Bellows felt that a second-rate man could do nothing with the church, and that they desperately needed a first-rate preacher and administrator. There had been some talk of selling the church, and Bellows felt that "there are men there spiteful and reckless enough to sell out, to gratify their cupidity or their caprice."

He believed that only two men were capable of building the Church of the Messiah. "We want a man, respected & honored for his general abilities, culture and position." He felt that George Hepworth might be able to draw a good crowd around him and keep up the Unitarian prestige in New York. But the man Bellows really wanted was Edward Everett Hale. "If *you* could come, you would soon have a strong collection of thoughtful, able people around you, & would be able to carry forward the cause with wonderful vigor. I really think together *we* could change the whole aspect of our Unitarian national prospects." All Hale needed to do was to give the word that he was interested and Bellows would "put the machinery in gear, & do my best to bring it before you in formal shape."[16]

Hale responded that although he was flattered that Bellows thought him the man for the pulpit of the Messiah he was not well. He needed to take care of himself carefully for the next year so that he would have ten more years of usefulness. He suggested Robert Collyer of Chicago, and believed that George Hepworth was probably the best man for the church and hoped that it could be arranged that Hepworth would preach at the Messiah in May.[17]

Bellows felt that Hepworth should be secured at once to fill the pulpit of the Church of the Messiah. Yet he was loath to interfere in the affairs of the church. "I don't like to *mix* in," he wrote Hale, "because I have already roiled the waters, & I think it best to keep out of the whirlpool. But I shall do my utmost, in a quiet way, to bring about that result."

The third week in April was spent moving from the parsonage to 232 East 15th Street on Stuyvesant Square. "The health of my family requires more light, air & comfort . . . There, if it please God I hope to end my days,"[18] which he did.

Osgood was receptive to the idea of Hepworth replacing him in the Messiah pulpit. "Hepworth is crude but wide-awake . . . Let him try," Osgood wrote to Bellows in a goodbye letter the day before he sailed for Europe.[19] Several persons had suggested that Osgood might make a good editor of new literary review. But Bellows was opposed to this: "As to Osgood, his behavior has been so childish & weak in all his recent difficulties, that I couldn't trust him at the head of any review that was supposed to be the organ of Liberal Christian thought. He's a mere baby, with certain powers of mischief, which he will not hesitate to employ. If he don't placard our Body as a *failure* all over England & Europe (simply because he is a failure) we may thank our stars, & not his good will.[20]

There was a meeting at Bellows's home on Thursday 20 May to talk about the debt of the Church of the Messiah. The result of this meeting was that a group of the members of the First Church (All Souls) got up a subscription of $20,000 for a loan to the Second Church (Church of the Messiah). It was a fine vote of confidence.[21]

A. A. Livermore was celebrating his quarter of a century in the Unitarian ministry, largely as an educator of ministers at Meadville Theological Seminary. He had invited Bellows to be present at the celebration but Bellows had planned a trip to Chicago to help dedicate the new Church of the Unity. He had also agreed to be at the Antioch Commencement, so a trip to Meadville was impossible.

Bellows felt that one of the great Unitarian events in the entire history of the West was the dedication of the new Church of the Unity in Chicago. Robert Collyer's new edifice was "gloriously situated in one of the finest squares in the city." It would seat normally 1,100 people, but on the occasion of the dedication more chairs and benches had raised the number of the congregation to 1,500 persons. Bellows described the interior as "one of the finest audience chambers in the country, much finer in every way, than the Ch[urch] of the Messiah. It is spacious, airy & has as elegant & fascinating a roof as I have seen in any of our churches." Bellows had preached the sermon, and had closed it with a plea that the people free the church from debt. (It had cost $165,000 and was in debt $113,000.) Robert Collyer followed Bellows "with a touching address & then commenced one of the most exciting scenes of a people gradually melting into a large & contagious liberality."

Collyer's fundraising effort "lasted one hour & in that time under various appeals conducted in Mr. Collyer's own inimitable way, $70,000 were subscribed as free offerings toward the debt, leaving the church with a moderate mortgage of $43,000 only—& not a pew *sold*, or to be sold!" Bellows felt that "this splendid success was wholly unexpected & stands an unrivaled experience in church history in our denomination, or perhaps any other." In the afternoon Brother Staples (Carleton A. Staples) was installed as the Minister of the Third Unitarian Church in Chicago, and in the evening there was an assemblage in the new church at which Bellows made the closing speech, "all ended with proud gratitude & joy as one of the brightest days in the history of the denomination."[22]

Bellows continued on his journey, preaching at Indianapolis on the following Sunday, 27 June, and then attending meetings of the trustees of Antioch College. Mrs. Bellows left for Walpole on Saturday, 3 June, and by 12 June, after preaching the previous day, Bellows himself headed for Walpole for the summer vacation. It was not to be a good nor a happy summer.

CHAPTER TWELVE

A Green Old Age

Never Fully at Home in the Flesh

When Bellows arrived in Walpole he found his wife "in her chamber & much in the condition she was last summer, dependent, restless, & incapable of much house keeping or other care. I am afraid she is going to have a trying summer."[1] Within the course of the next ten days Mrs. Bellows's condition deteriorated so badly that it was thought best to take her to Northampton to put her in the care of a specialist there. The doctor described Mrs. Bellows's "trying condition as wholly due to physical derangement, & is trying to bring back the action of the skin & the due balance of the other organs. Let us be patient & give him a fair trial, while we hope *every thing* & trust all to the Great Disposer."

Bellows was also worried about Annie's health. She was completely apathetic to almost everything, seemingly living in another world. Bellows commented, "I have been making Nannie a close study—walking with her & trying to get at her inmost condition. She seems in a strange apathy & will-less sort of state." He proposed to Annie that she go off on a trip with some of the cousins in the Adirondacks, and that seemed to brighten her smile.[2]

Annie went on the trip, and her father wrote her giving her an analysis as to what he believed to be wrong with her mother. "I am deeply convinced that your mother is the unconscious victim of *too much liberty;* of desires too freely allowed; of caprices too easily admitted; of a will (which because not worldly or foolish) we have thought needed no restraint!" Henry Bellows continued the analysis, "She has had *her own way* until opposition, defeat, trifling irregularities, & little unavoidable annoyances have grown to seem mountains in her morbid & exaggerated mind." Eliza had been "guilty of forgetting under what restraints of their own feelings, wishes, wills, *most people* providentially live,—how little freedom to do as they choose, & act upon their feelings most people can be allowed by their providential circumstances."

Bellows felt his own responsibility in the matter. "I now feel how weak & wrong I have been—more to blame than dear mother herself—altho God knows in what ignorance & unconscious

371

innocency of purpose I have acted." He concluded, "my conviction is that your mother must now submit to a full year of separation from her family, live under medical care & moral restraint, & settle the tone of her mind on an entirely new basis. I have written her a tender but wholly plain letter, setting forth her case to her fully & explaining it in detail. She has too much sense not to see it."[3]

Bellows had gone down to visit Mrs. Bellows on the occasion of their thirtieth wedding anniversary on Friday 13 August. But she had seemed to wither under his tender ministrations. "She had improved considerably to appearance when I arrived, but seemed to go backwards every moment I stayed, so that it was a kind of misery to see her—bad for me & worse for her. I resolved not to see her again for at least two months & told her so. She is very acquiescent in my judgment."[4] He resolved not to bring her to New York during the coming fall, but to leave her in Northampton where she was happy and well taken care of.

Bellows preached at Greenfield, Massachusetts, at a meeting of a local Unitarian Conference on Wednesday evening 18 August. He went back to Walpole for a few short days. Then on 24 August he received a telegram from Dr. Denniston in Northampton "advising me that I had best come down, and not knowing just what to expect." Russell accompanied his father.

It was not mental illness, but the physical condition of Mrs. Bellows which had alarmed the doctor. "I found your mother sicker than I have ever known her to be under an acute attack of inflammation of the whole intestinal canal," Bellows wrote to Annie. "It had set in very suddenly & unexpectedly, & gone a great way before attention was called to it, & in forty-eight hours has so weakened her strength that when the necessary reaction comes, the doctor fears her vigour may not be able to rally to resist the prostration sure to follow the inflammation. There is nothing to do but wait."

The doctor expected the culmination of the disease on Saturday. Mrs. Bellows now was not as conscious of the pain as she had been previously. Bellows himself was not allowed to see her. Russell went into the room for a moment and held her hand. Nothing could be done by the family because of her mental condition except "to exaggerate her trials." Bellows was looking forward to the time when it was safe and he could be with Eliza "all the time." He hoped that Annie would not feel that she should come immediately to Northampton. "I hope you, like Russ & myself, will be able to look at the case with calmness & submission. If the good God chooses to take our precious one to his own rest, by this sharp attack, it will not be without its alleviations. Her interest in life is so small! her prospects so feeble . . . that if a gracious Providence brings her sorrows & sicknesses to an end, I shall endeavor to swallow all selfish grief, & to share the joy of her release from a weary weight of weakness & mental distress."[5]

Bellows visited Eliza late in the evening of 26 August. "Perhaps if she *wished* to live, her chances would be increased," he wrote, "but she does not, & seems almost to dread the possibility of recovering!" Eliza at first did not want Henry to visit her to see her suffering, "but I think she found comfort to some degree in my tenderness & in my prayers." Her cheeks were drawn, and Bellows thought that she looked ten years older than she was. The doctor still gave her very little chance to live, one in ten perhaps.[6]

By Friday evening Bellows wrote to James Freeman Clarke, "The struggle is over! & my dear wife's suffering body at rest, & her pure spirit with God." He set the funeral date for the following Wednesday at 4:00 P.M. at their home at 232 E. 15th Street. He asked James Freeman Clarke to be present if possible, and to officiate at the funeral services.[7] On Saturday they brought Eliza's last remains to the house "she had chosen so lately." The funeral had been moved up to Monday at 3:00 P.M.

Bellows wrote to Cyrus Bartol that he had been preparing for this possible event for most of two years. "The grief of *losing* my wife has had its chief sharpness in these long years when I have seen how little life was worth to her, & felt how she was fading away! I merely close up a long account with sorrow in shutting the lid upon that dear frame. I have been too sad for too long, to expect to be very glad again in this world!"[8]

Annie arrived in New York, and Mrs. Bellows was laid out "in my front room overlooking the park—in the place where Lizzie loved to be." On Sunday evening Bellows was still waiting to hear from James Freeman Clarke, and Bellows had asked Robert Collyer who happened to be in New York to conduct the service with Dr. Frederick Farley assisting.[9] The funeral service in New York was followed by the trip to the family plot in Greenwood Cemetery where Eliza was put to rest beside her three deceased children.

Cyrus Bartol wrote a beautiful obituary which is in the Bellows Papers. Bartol wrote that Mrs. Bellows had "preserved a wonderful simplicity which no affected or conventional ways of the world could hide or seemed ever able even to touch." He found her a rare combination of "unusual feminine delicacy . . . with so much almost masterly strength of intellect and will." Bartol, as would be expected, had a spiritual rather than a psychological explanation for Eliza's illnesses, writing with many circumlocutions about her "nervous temperament."[10]

The longest, most personal, and perhaps the most accurate assessment of Eliza's life was made by Bellows himself when he opened up his heart to his old friend Orville Dewey. Although written shortly after the committal, it shows an objectivity about the meaning of his wife's life that others would scarcely grasp. "I have *had* my worst pangs of separation & sorrow in the necessities of nervous weakness & decay which have for *several years* made our lives more or less distinct! I have lost my wife *again* & *again*, in the successive eras, when her debility has compelled her temporarily to leave me, & when I have suffered all the worst pangs of bereavement in the terrible feelings that we could not safely share each other's cares & presence!" He continued, "The tears I have shed & the agony I have suffered as the inevitable conviction has, by one proof after another, come upon me, that *she* could never again be my real companion, has been for five years the chief sadness & gloom of my lot." He explained, "To love with the whole heart, to respect & reverence a wife as I did, & yet see her fading away, losing balance & self-control, threatened with mania & incapable of fulfilling or bearing the ordinary duties of wife & mother—is a fate compared with which Death is a small evil!" He was moved by shock. Yet he felt that death had emancipated Eliza's tangled nerves, and that she was now healthy and "back among us!" He continued the vision: "We think of her, we converse with her, we enjoy her, as we have not been able to do, I had almost said, for ten years!"

Bellows felt that this whole problem of Eliza's health went back to the difficulties which she had had with the birth of their first child and his subsequent early death. Yet she had bravely used her nervous energy for her husband and the children as they arrived, and two more had died in infancy. Bellows went into a paean of ecstasy about Eliza's character for Dr. Dewey. It is summed up in this sentence, "I cannot exaggerate the respect she exacted from me by her native dignity & elevation of spirit—her truth & singleness of soul!" He described his attitude as one of *"Respect, perfect respect."*[11]

To his close friend, William Silsbee, he wrote some additional words:

She was never fully at home in the flesh, or this bustling, imperfect world. Haunted by an ideal of Moral Perfection, controlled by a despotic conscience, without relish for the conventions & shows of society, with a restless, nervous necessity for action, life below was a ceaseless conflict & struggle, in which she found less content & repose, than those who loved & respected her fully, could have desired. But she kept *on*, never surrendering to her own debility or nervous irritation, always making Duty & usefulness her pole star.[12]

Work is always good therapy for grief, and Bellows had plenty of work in his denomination. His efforts to put some life into the Unitarian movement in the United States had certainly produced results in the four and a half years since the organization of the National Conference of Churches in New York in April 1865. In 1869 the Secretary of the Association, Charles Lowe, was able to make a report on this progress. It was a very thorough report, for it was an appeal for funds. The second Sunday in November each year in many of the churches was designated as "A.U.A. Sunday." Lowe reported that more aid had been given to "feeble societies."

There also had been "missionary effort in places where no society exists"; there had been instituted some "theater preaching," in which Bellows himself had been active, aid had been given to the theological schools; the work of the mission in India had been continued; the Mission to Seamen had been carried on; there had been cooperation with the work of the African Methodist Church, "Christian teaching of the coloured people"; the publishing work had been carried on to such an extent that tracts were circulating on the average of 1,000 per day. Bellows and all those associated with the Unitarian movement might well look with pride at the rebirth of the Unitarian movement which had so badly lagged just prior to the Civil War and now was resurrected.[13]

On Wednesday, 6 October 1869, the Rev. Stephen H. Camp was installed as the Minister of the Third Unitarian Society in Brooklyn. As usual, the Unitarians made something of an installation. Edward Everett Hale was the preacher of the evening, and Henry Bellows gave the installation prayer. The Rev. A. P. Putnam gave the address to the people and the Rev. John White Chadwick extended the right hand of fellowship.[14]

On 28 October 1869, Bellows received a letter from the office of Drake Brothers at 16 Broad Street that they had just received a bill of lading from Hiram Powers in Florence, Italy, "consigning to us a marble bust of yourself." Drake Brothers expressed the hope that Bellows would let Moses H. Grinnell know when the bust was arriving, and they would see to it that "we shall not have the

trouble . . . that we did with the original sent us by our brother."
This bill of lading refers to the copy of the Hiram Powers bust
ordered by Bellows.[15]

Bellows found it very difficult to adjust to his parish duties after
Eliza's death. He himself was bothered with poor health. As usual
his remedy was a trip on horseback which he took the middle of the
month. In early November Russell Bellows gave up his work at the
Unitarian Church in Walpole. The National Conference was held in
Quincy, Massachusetts, with Bellows in attendance.

In November George Hepworth took up his duties as the new
minister of the Church of the Messiah. Hepworth had been born in
Boston in 1833. His parents were Unitarians. He graduated from the
Harvard Divinity School in 1855. His first parish was on Nantucket
Island. In 1858 he was installed as the minister of the newly
organized Church of the Unity in Boston. During the Civil War on a
leave of absence he went with the 47th regiment to Louisiana as a
chaplain. He was especially interested in bringing the Unitarian
religion to a larger audience, and in 1867 he instituted theater
preaching in Boston.

In June 1867, Hepworth advertised in the *Christian Register*
that he was establishing a Unitarian seminary in Boston which would
prepare men for Unitarian evangelism. The response was far greater
than anyone expected. That fall, twenty-three men from all over the
United States lived together in a "common house." George
Hepworth acted as the president, and there was one other resident
professor, the Rev. Charles Taylor Canfield. The rest of the teaching
duties were performed by distinguished Unitarian ministers: Ezra
Stiles Gannett, Edward Everett Hale, Samuel H. Winkley, and John
H. Morison of Milton. The curriculum was very simple, consisting
of biblical studies and the practical ways of delivering a message.
Students spent large amounts of time working in local parishes. The
first commencement was held on 18 June 1868. A few days later in
Hepworth's church the graduates were ordained as "Unitarian
evangelists." The second year thirty-five highly qualified students
were admitted.

But already attempts to merge the Boston School with the
Harvard Divinity School were in progress. Hepworth had made his
point about practical studies for the ministry. The demise of the
school occurred about the same time as his call to the Church of the
Messiah in New York City. But there were plans for the merger even
before Osgood resigned at the Messiah.[16] Bellows had pushed the

Church of the Messiah to call Hepworth, feeling that the popular appeal of his preaching might help the struggling church to attract more members and to pay off its mountainous debt.[17]

On 1 December 1869, Bellows joined with Frederick A. Farley, Alfred P. Putnam, and the newly arrived George Hepworth to protest the editorial policies of the *Liberal Christian*. These four ministers believed that its editor, James Freeman Clarke, had been too liberal in allowing Radicals in the denomination to express their point of view in the paper. Their letter stated "that the *Liberal Christian* was established to give an unqualified support to a form of positive, historical Christianity, & was conducted distinctly on that platform during its whole career as the *Christian Inquirer*; & that it was designed to keep it on that same basis when it changed its name & enlarged its size & capital." It had not been intended as an "objective" paper. "But it was intended to allow respectful & decorous articles from Radical Sources, admission into its columns under certain restrictions—but not under editorial patronage & responsibility." The four ministers felt that under Clarke's management "the paper is gradually but steadily losing this character—that its policy is devious, unsettled, & self-neutralizing; that he holds or attempts to hold an even balance between the Historical believers in our Body, and the left wing, or theistic & Radical party, which leaves it wholly in doubt where the policy of the paper, or of the Unitarian Body is."

The ministers did not question Clarke's motives. "We do not propose to give any *new* policy to the paper," they wrote, "but simply to restore it to its *original* policy; one of avowed & positive Christian faith, in the historical meaning of that word; with generous liberality & forbearance towards doubters, or inquirers, or rationalistic & theistic minds." They wanted a man at the helm in sympathy with this avowed point of view, and asked for Clarke's resignation. The letter is obviously the work of Bellows, and the three signers could be expected with their points of view to agree with him. New York Unitarianism at this time was far more avowedly Christian than Boston Unitarianism.[18]

A letter from Hiram Powers gave sympathy to Bellows in his bereavement. Powers trusted that the bust had arrived long before his letter. He gave instructions for lighting the bust. "It should have a single light for it, and not too low, it ought to cast shadows from the eyebrows over the nose downwards. Hold a light at different elevations before it." Powers also instructed Bellows to keep the bust covered with gauze in the summertime, and to clean it with spirits of lime and water, and not to use soap on the marble.[19] He also included a bill for 102 pounds, 10 shillings.

On 17 December 1869, Charles Lowe wrote to Henry Bellows that he had received a letter from Samuel Osgood "stating that he withdraws from the denomination. I shall not however, feel it my duty," wrote Lowe, "to give publicity to it, leaving him to do this as he may prefer." This was a new turn of events. Osgood's bitterness toward Bellows and his trustees now was turned against the denomination, and somewhat in spite, perhaps in a true sense of accommodation to his own spiritual nature, he joined the Episcopal Church.[20] It was a symbolic close to an unhappy year for Bellows.

The Life of a Widower

Thus ended the decade of the 1860s, certainly the most important decade in Henry Bellows's life. The decade had begun with the opening of the Civil War, the establishment of the Sanitary Commission, the trip to San Francisco, the extended trip to Europe and the Near East, and had ended with Mrs. Bellows's untimely death in the last year of the decade. Bellows now faced the new decade of the seventies a widower.

In the middle of February 1870, Bellows wrote an article for the *Liberal Christian* on the subject "Harmony in the National Conference." He explained to Edward Everett Hale the reasons for this article which soon was to appear, that the article continued "my deliberate view of the policy our Body ought to propose. It is my *necessary* conviction as well as my calmest sense of what *wisdom* requires. I want to get theological *disputation* out of the Nat[ional] Conference, and the A.U.A." He felt that the way to do this was "to favor the *two* vents, the "Free Religious operation on the *left* & 'the Evangelical Unitarian operation' on the *right*—where extremists can have their say & unite in as much, or as little as will satisfy them to enjoy fellowship with their own class & emphasize their own faith or doubt—& then come to the National Conference as to a common ground, where there is no excuse for nasty & acrimonious debate—but ample room for practical, ministerial & denominational work & counsel." He made his own position clear: "I wish to identify myself with the moderates & middle men & with the Nat[ional] Conference."[1]

Charles Lowe was in complete disagreement with the idea that a new conservative organization should be organized within the

Unitarian denomination as a "safety valve." Lowe wrote to Bellows, "I cannot for my life see how it is possible to make it other than destructive in spirit." Lowe felt that if Dr. Putnam and Dr. Bellows were to be in charge of this new organization "there would be nothing to fear." "But," he continued, "human nature is a persistent kind of thing, & from what we know of it it is pretty safe to predict more than you allow for. There will be men prominent on one side & the other, able to say thorny things & prone to say sharp things."[2]

It was now five and one-half years since Bellows had turned over the duties of minister of the San Francisco parish to his hand-picked choice, Horatio Stebbins. The news from San Francisco had been most discouraging, and as his reporter was Robert B. Swain—one of the dissidents—the news must have troubled Bellows a great deal because he had such high hopes for the future of the church in the West. In the middle of March 1870, Robert Swain wrote Bellows another discouraging letter outlining the problems in the San Francisco church. Describing the spirit in the church he said, "We seem to be dead here now, poor timber in the board of trustees; a lifeless congregation; antagonism between the society and the pastor's family—but little inspiration from the pulpit, and I think great discouragement there." Swain wrote, "How it will end I can't tell. Mr. Stebbins informs me that he is very solicitous about the health of his wife. The trouble is more mental than physical. Unless a change soon takes place for the better she may seek refuge in an insane asylum."[3]

Because the church was closed for repairs in the middle of June, Bellows was relieved of his duties and was able to go to Sheffield, Massachusetts, to visit the Deweys for several days over Sunday 19 June. It was always refreshing and invigorating for him to spend a few quiet days with the Deweys which involved long hours of conversation with the man whom he considered to be his mentor and advisor. He also attended a meeting of the board of trustees of Antioch College at the end of June in Yellow Springs, Ohio, came back to New York, and then went up to Dobbs Ferry for a few days with the George Schuylers.

An unidentified Unitarian minister wrote to Bellows in July in response to his article in the *Liberal Christian* and suggested that the denomination ought to purge those who did not believe as Bellows and others did about the position of Jesus Christ in the Church. Bellows replied by expressing his doctrine of what the Unitarian Church was all about. "The Unitarian Church," he wrote, "springing up as a citadel of spiritual freedom & the rights of private judgment surrendered or threatened everywhere else. The chief service it has rendered has been to keep religious liberty alive & to make it *consistent* with *Christian piety & faith.*" He continued, "the last part of the work has been the most uncertain & the most difficult, & when achieved, will be [a] grand triumph of the body."

Bellows used an analogy: "To give up the essential principle of *utter freedom,* in order to secure a more easy victory for our cause, would be like throwing over the *passengers* to lighten the ship threatening to founder. I would sooner go down with the vessel, were I the *captain,* than throw any lawful passengers over the bulwarks." He continued: "Therefore, as one of the officers aboard our Unitarian craft, I stand with my cutlass raised to defend even the most disagreeable & repulsive, in their rights—knowing the getting into harbour is not half so important as being honest, faithful & noble in our engagements & to our principles implied or expressed. I have not studied the Unitarian cause for thirty-five years without understanding something about it." He believed "that Channing was a safe leader & I am following him. He would have died sooner than have spoken a word against the absolute right of private judgment, & befriended Parker, when he had almost no other friend."

Bellows declared, "I intend to preach what I believe (& I believe more than most) with all my heart, but I will not deny to any other Unitarian born in our ranks or claiming the name, the right to do the same, however he may differ from me." He continued, "nor will I exclude him by any formal & authoritarian definition, out of the Body or out of my sympathy—to save the name of our Body with orthodoxy. This is just the offense that drove me out of the pale of the orthodoxy of fifty years ago. Nobody will catch me in the folly or crime of repeating that old bigotry & self-righteous exclusiveness."[4] Anyone who felt Bellows wanted to exclude those who disagreed with him from the denomination or the National Council, ought to read these passionate words on the right of private judgment as expressed in this letter to an unknown correspondent.

During August Bellows organized a party of eight to take a journey to the Adirondacks; Mr. and Mrs. George Schuyler, Georgina Schuyler, Mary Richards, Annette Rogers, and Russell, Annie, and Henry Bellows made up the party. "We spent *three* days going & coming—*seven* in the mts. & *seven* on the lakes, camped out *five* nights." They traveled through the mountains in wagons, stopping at farmhouses and inns; they ascended several mountains "living roughly but very substantially on trout, venison, chicken, eggs, pan-cakes & *hot* bread; everything was primitive and rude, but clean & tolerable." They enjoyed even more than the mountains the boating on the lakes "in tiltish canoes." The guides portaged the canoes from one lake to another. They sang, talked over their experiences, and Bellows read poetry aloud.[5] It was a wonderful relaxation in the company of good friends.

Bellows found it difficult to get back to work in New York that fall. His mood had gone sour. "It is always a trying time to come back," he wrote, "back to a home which has lost its centre; back to a life which is no longer crowned with *hope;* back to work that in so many ways disappoints; back to cares to which I ever feel less equal; back to fewer old friends & less & less understanding new ones!"[6]

The two volumes of Henry Bellows's travels to Europe, Africa, and Palestine had been in print now for well over a year. Bellows asked Harper & Brothers for a statement as to the sale of the book. They responded that 127 copies of Volume I had been sold and 134 copies of Volume II since their last statement. They accordingly sent him a royalties check for $45.68, scarcely any financial reward for what had been an extended labor on Bellows's part. It is strange indeed that the books did not sell better. His chapters on Egypt were written long before Egyptian travel became popular. They were well written and full of interesting material, but like so many good books they never appealed to the public. Copies today are found mostly in large libraries.[7]

Russell was having difficulties finding a significant life work, and this worried his father exceedingly. He had been the minister at Walpole for only a few months when he was forced by ill health to leave the post. Then he had hoped to found a fifth Unitarian church in Manhattan, but this project had fallen through. Now he was to assist his father with the *Liberal Christian.* Bellows described his son's malaise in these words: "I *must* keep [him] near me, for my own & his sister's sake, & whose health does not permit him to engage in any severe head-work." Bellows told what he had in mind for Russell. "He will be Asst. Editor, & if the paper flourishes, he will have the benefit of it. Meanwhile he has a moderate salary & gives all his time to it. He will do all the drudgery & office work. If he can *stand* it, he has many qualifications for it, & of course we shall work very easily together." Bellows had been persuaded to lend his name to the paper as its editor. He doubted if his name had much influence, and described it as "an influence which my brethren *suppose* dwells in my name. I never thought it a name to conjure with;—but if *it* will work when I am asleep, I am glad to know it, & *it* may do all it *will*. I shall try to do some real work."[8]

Charles Lowe had asked and then ignored Bellows's advice, and now decided to take the Somerville Church and leave the Secretaryship of the American Unitarian Association. The new Secretary elected was the Rev. Rush R. Shippen, who had preceded Robert Collyer at the Chicago Church of the Unity and succeeded Edward Everett Hale at The Church of the Unity in Worcester, Massachusetts. In this position he had come into conflict with Bellows, who had urged him to resign his position there for the good of the church. Like Osgood, Shippen quite naturally had been somewhat resentful of Bellows's interference in his professional affairs. He now wrote to Bellows to explain that he had no animosity for what had happened in the past. "I trust that we may so cordially cooperate, that when honestly compelled to differ in judgment we may . . . show how much we are at home with each other by frank opposition, without even a suspicion of unfriendliness or personal bias."[9] He believed that he needed Bellows's help and cooperation in his new position.

On 9 July Bellows preached his last sermon before the summer recess, and looked forward to going to Walpole for the summer. He got back to New York only a week prior to this time, having given four lectures at Meadville and taken in the May meetings in Boston. He then went to Chicago for eight days during which time he had given four sermons and one lecture; then went to Antioch College for the trustees' meeting. He spent one night at the Grinnells' and one at the Schuylers' up the Hudson River at Irvington. His favorite parishioner, Moses Grinnell, was, he wrote, "pretty much broken up & ruined, I fear by political ambition, social extravagance, luxurious living, & recklessness of money affairs! This is entre nous. But they have enough to live on."

The Grinnells were going to Europe in the fall. The Schuylers he found in exactly the opposite situation. "What a contrast their cozy, thoughtful, high-toned home is! Splendid girls! Wish they were pretty—nobody can fill 1st Mrs. George Schuyler's place, but *Mary* Hamilton is delightful, & always improving." In this letter to Dewey, Bellows playfully referred to his residence at Walpole as that of "H.W.B. D.D. Prince, cardinal of the Reformed Church Catholic!"[10]

Bellows had projected the idea of a horseback trip through Vermont to be undertaken during the last two weeks of August, and had written to ask William Weeden in Providence and Edward

Everett Hale to join Russell and himself in such a venture. But the trip did not materialize, and Bellows spent the summer "leading a quiet—half-busy, & half-idle life. Editorial & self-imposed duties have kept me from *rusting.*" He declared, "Work is my life, & I should be miserable in my solitude, without it. For *solitary,* every man of my years must be—no matter how many children & friends he has about him—if he has lost his wife! I think I shall miss mine more & more, till we meet again!"[11] Included among his summer visitors were Mr. and Mrs. George Schuyler who spent four days with Bellows.

Bellows went with Annie to Sheffield to visit with the Deweys for several days before going down to New York to open the fall services at the church on 17 September 1871.

The great Chicago Fire of 8 October 1871 had destroyed the new beautiful edifice that Bellows had helped Robert Collyer dedicate in 1869. Collyer's flock was decimated and scattered. The whole north end of the city was in shambles. In a very sad letter Collyer told Bellows of his determination not to leave the people if he could last without a salary for an entire year. He had "got what is left of the poor scattered flock to meet me on the sidewalk there in front of the church, and we had prayed together and wept all the tears left in our hearts and I had spoken to them and told them nothing should part us." They went "away feeling almost happy again." The whole country responded to the plight of the people in Chicago, and much relief had been sent both in money and supplies.[12]

As head of the United States Sanitary Commission Bellows also undertook to gather together in New York City dry goods to be sent to Chicago. Mrs. Stevenson of All Souls was appointed to approach the sellers of dry goods in the city to ask for donations of their merchandise to be forwarded to Chicago. "With our earnest hope that the liberality of our citizens will not give out while the distress lasts."[13]

But Mrs. Stevenson met refusal, and Bellows described the refusal thus. He "sent her to the leading dry goods men, to ask assistance. She reported a *universal refusal* on the ground that they had done all they could or were committed to other channels of relief. My own people are working to furnish Robert Collyer & his brother ministers in Chicago, with the means of clothing the poor and aiding the modest and uncomplaining destitute." Bellows had also written to the Chamber of Commerce urging them to erect "one hospital of a temporary character & one the army plan, with beds for 3,000 in Chicago, as the best means of alleviating the distressing sickness sure to follow so dreadful an exposure, such a fearful shock to the nerves, such irregular living & such crowded homes, as the Chicago disaster has occasioned. I do not yet know what limitations their funds are under, nor what ear they may lend to my counsel."[14]

The Hepworth Affair

Bellows had not approved of George Hepworth's sermon at All Souls when he had preached there earlier on the meaning of the communion service. Now, on Christmas Day, 1871, Bellows had a second unpleasant experience. He had agreed to share the Christmas service with George Hepworth in the Church of the Messiah. The congregation of All Souls was invited to join with them. Hepworth was to preach the sermon. The subject announced in the papers for the occasion, "Church All-in-All," had worried Bellows. So when he met Hepworth at the church before the service he asked his colleague what he was going to say. Bellows reported, "He said he was coming out with *a statement of faith, which did not stop short of the Deity of Christ.*"

Bellows said that he begged Hepworth "to pause," and "asked him if he had considered his duty to the position; his implied obligation to address to Unitarian doctrine, the discourtesy of springing a Revolution upon a popular congregation on a festival day; the exposure to suspicion of undermining the cause he was set to defend & betraying the fortress of which he was commander?" Bellows said that Hepworth "would not listen—pleaded conscience, conviction." Bellows told him, "I could not compromise myself by participating in any such public service, nor spoil my day by listening to any thing so painful." Hepworth begged Bellows "to hear & then strike." "But," said Bellows, "I thought it best not to gratify his vanity by sitting & hearing him break down our chief distinctive doctrine, & so, bade him good morning & came home." Bellows added, "I shall wait to see how explicit it really was & how his people take it—if there are any *people* left to know white from black or one dogma from another in the congregation. Of course I am dreadfully disgusted and angry. I hope it will end in his precipitate leaving. He has been only weakness & solicitude to me, ever since he came."[1] This was the man whom Bellows thought, other than Robert Collyer, was the only man who could handle the Church of the Messiah. Now he wanted Hepworth's leaving more than anything else.

Rush R. Shippen, the new Secretary of the American Unitarian Association, gave his interpretation of George Hepworth's sermon a

George Hepworth, Courtesy of the Unitarian Universalist Association

few days later. "What tune is Mr. Hepworth's trumpet playing? The *Times* report of his last Sunday's sermon may be taken simply as extreme Right Wing Unitarianism, although its logic is flimsy & weak, and the whole affair open to criticism. Mr. Hale just now says, he is disposed to ask Mr. Hepworth for a copy for print—to show that Unitarians accept every plea for the Divinity (not Deity) of Christ." Shippen added this bit of news, "from Mr. Hepworth's talk in the rooms of the A.U.A. a few weeks since, I imagine he means to transfer his fellowship to the orthodox ranks." On that occasion Hepworth "frankly declared himself weary of the rush of concession which Unitarianism has come to be—weary of the personal abuse he has received among us—as finding more fellowship among the liberal orthodox, & ready to go to them tomorrow."

But Shippen also had a less charitable explanation as to why Hepworth was leaving the Unitarian ranks. It was the same problem that led Osgood away. "I imagine that the ugly debt upon his church has more to do with his change of mind & heart, than any improved interpretation of the Gospel of John." Things were not going well for the Church of the Messiah. Would Bellows dare to make any more recommendations to them as to how to conduct their affairs?[2]

Shippen spoke further of the conference earlier with Hepworth in which Bellows's colleague had spoken "as if to prepare me for his intended change." Hepworth also "spoke only in friendly terms of [Bellows & he] said nothing had marred your personal harmony & he had no grievance against you. Only that you & he were such *different* sort of men that you could not work together. Said he was very lonely in New York—exchanged only one Sunday in all the year." The final words of the interview were, "Shippen, it's no use. I'm tired of the whole concern. It's gone too long thus." Shippen had offered to come down to preach at the Church of the Messiah to "tell your people what I believe are the grand affirmations of the Unitarian faith . . . He said, 'Yes,' but remember my congregation is mostly *Orthodox*. You must not pitch into them." Shippen felt that there was something politic and Jesuitical in Hepworth's attitude, and that, "He is not to be trusted."[3]

Bellows was very loath to again enter into the affairs of the Church of the Messiah. He wrote to Edward Everett Hale, "My unhappy mediation in the Osgood case, makes me shrink from any intermeddling—such as really belong to my relations to the cause . . . Mr. Hepworth doesn't seek my counsel, & keeps as far aloof as he can from every thing common & co-operative."[4]

Edward Everett Hale was not as upset as Bellows about the prospects of Hepworth's taking the church with him over into orthodoxy. He summed it up thus: "I should suppose that the men who carried the Church of the Messiah to the point where he found it, are not the men to be now persuaded that they have never understood the New Testament." Hale felt that Hepworth would resign. He had only promised to go to New York for two years. That time was now up. Hale felt that such a resignation should be accepted. But his concern was an even deeper one. "This calls up again the lamentable question who we have in a pulpit who has any popular power of appeal and at the same time believes anything worth believing. That is the old ground which we have gone over so often together,—and of which I am afraid you know the barrenness as well as I." Hale believed "that New York is the most attractive point in the country,—and that if the church debt can in any way be handled every young man in the country would like to try the position." Hale wished Charles Lowe were still Secretary of the American Unitarian Association "and could go [to New York] tonight."[5]

Early in January 1872 Bellows described what happened at the annual meeting of the Church of the Messiah. Hepworth had not only decided that he himself would go over to orthodoxy but he attempted to carry the church with him by electing three new orthodox trustees. On the present board of nine trustees there were already three orthodox and six Unitarian trustees, and if the three Unitarian trustees whose terms were expiring could be replaced at this meeting with three orthodox ones, he would have a majority of the board of trustees, which, although it would not indicate complete control, would be well on the way. Bellows wrote about George Hepworth: "He has been double & treacherous & has tried to carry the church over with him, & came very near doing it." Bellows described how the revolution had been thwarted, "By rallying all the *legal* votes & excluding all others, the annual meeting which Hepworth tried to convert into a *mass* meeting, was made a severe & crucial test of legal strength. . . . The vote at last, 300 being present (many of my own serious men going to give moral effect to the right side) was about seventy votes, only *four* majority for the Unitarian side." But, as Bellows explained, "this was enough, & the victory . . . was for honour & our cause. The church is now in the hands of six Unitarian & three orthodox trustees & these last will probably resign."

After the unfavorable vote George Hepworth did resign, but his resignation was not accepted. Bellows felt that this resignation was inevitable.[6] Finally, of course, Hepworth did resign, and Bellows reported to the American Unitarian Headquarters in Boston about the "Hepworth Affair." "I hope you are as little interested as we are by the flutter Mr. Hepworth has caused!" He expressed what was on many minds, "So long as he has landed outside the denomination." He believed that what the Church of the Messiah now needed was "a scholar & a gentleman & a full blown Unitarian."[7]

Bellows had long believed that Hale himself should be the minister of the Church of the Messiah, but had been previously rebuffed by Hale's claim of ill health. Rush R. Shippen, the

Secretary of the American Unitarian Association, also believed that Hale was the man for the pulpit.[8] The matter rested for the time being.

The late winter and spring of 1872 were normal ones for Bellows. He went to the funeral of his Aunt Louisa Knapp in Walpole on 19 March 1872. In April he preached in the Music Hall in Boston and attended a lecture by Ralph Waldo Emerson called "Literature." He also took a trip in April with Russell to Charleston, South Carolina. Anniversary week, the last week in May, found him in Boston for the annual meeting of the A.U.A.

Then in late June Bellows sailed for England to deliver a lecture on John Howard. He had been invited by the International Prison Congress to lecture on this pioneer prison reformer. The Congress lasted from 3 July through 13 July.

The steamer *Java* left New York City on Wednesday, 19 June 1872, with Bellows, Russell, and Annie aboard. The trip took a little longer than the usual run because the ship "sailed south 150 miles, out of our way, to avoid ice, of which," Bellows wrote, "we have not seen an ounce." The *Java*, advertised to be the fastest ship across the Atlantic, was delayed on this trip, but Bellows described it as "extraordinary in comfort and quietness."[9]

On 5 July Bellows gave his discourse on John Howard.[10] He had condensed it from four hours into two hours—still rather long for a lecture. "Archbishop Manning presided. All my London friends came & the discourse was a real success, the only thing enthusiastically rec'd during the Congress. It will be printed in London."[11] He had "doubted somewhat whether the occasion justified the labor . . . spent upon it. But the writing of it educated me on the subject for which I had to read many volumes. What I should not otherwise have had patience to grapple with."[12]

By 11 July, the Bellowses had finished their London visit and headed for the Continent—Antwerp "with its pictures and churches," Cologne, the Rhine, on to Zurich and the snow-capped Alps. They spent days riding horseback at Interlaken in the shadow of the Jungfrau. Then they went down the Rhone and eventually to Paris which Bellows found "brilliant & novel." Then back to England and a quick excursion into Scotland.[13]

The Bellows party arrived home from Europe on the *Algeria* on Saturday 21 September. No church service had been scheduled for the following day, so Bellows was able to go immediately to Walpole where his sister, Eliza Dorr, was seriously ill. Returning to New York for the fall season after his visit with Mrs. Dorr, he spent Tuesday evening and all day Wednesday at a Unitarian Conference on Staten Island. He stayed at the Goodhues', "an elegant place in full view of the lovely bay. . . . He has one beautiful daughter of *nineteen* to inherit all his wealth. She is a lovely creature with more genius than her parents. If I were of Russell's age, I should be head & ears over in love with such a fine creature!"

Bellows found the conference "largely attended & was full of spirit & life." He found that the attendance was about "one man to a dozen" women, but he did not complain about this. "It was amusing to me to see that almost all the pillars of *all* the Unitarian societies in Brooklyn, Yonkers, Staten Island, had been reared under my ministry in New York, & still feel like parishioners. I really felt my heart all too small to slice up among the hundred fine women that claimed my pastoral blessing & affection!"[14]

Then Bellows was called immediately to Walpole, for his sister was dying. Eliza Dorr had been, next to his deceased twin, his closest relation; and for many long years he had written to her, cared about her, and worried about her health. Now she was gone.[15]

Even though the Bellows household was without a wife and mother, Bellows and the grown-up children did all that they could to make it into a family place. Bellows wrote to Orville Dewey about their Christmas celebration of 1872: "I had thirty people under my roof last night. We sat down twenty-one to dinner—quite a patriarchal occasion!" On Christmas Day he had had Mr. Powers, a visiting lecturer, preach. Dr. Chapin, the Universalist, and Mr. Frothingham had been present and Bellows wished that they hadn't been, for Powers's sermon was very poor. "It never *grew* out of any *root*—had no main ideas compelling its form & progress;—was a piece of literary carpentry. . . . I had an awful twinge of doubt whether he could do anything else! Meanwhile, he is earnest, Christian, sweet & simple—and I still *hope!*"[16]

Bellows found this particular winter especially dark and gloomy. "The winter has been a laborious & severe one in every way for me, I begin to feel faded—disposed to lie on the sofa a couple of hours in the afternoon—a very unusual indulgence for me. The life in New York is burdened as much by what are called its pleasures, as by its duties." He added regarding his official duties, "I really have to fight for a chance to stay at home to dine—at least half my days of late being ended with some state-dinner where some complex sense of obligation or higher policy compelled to overcome my disinclination to, & go—often at a cost of nervous energy which a good *preach,* would not exceed. I shall clearly have to *shut down* on this ever increasing exaction."[17]

Bellows had a broken vacation in the summer of 1873; he was called back to New York City five times for deaths and necessary business. He always came back to New York in the fall "with mingled gladness & sadness—feeling the creases of the old harness now stiff & weather-shrunk & of the difficulties of pulling the load—but yet with a readiness to give my last strength to the effort."[18]

That fall proved to be utterly exhausting to Bellows, and early in December he realized that he could not go on with his duties any longer without an extended rest. Reluctantly, for he had had a short leave of absence to go to England only a year before, he asked the board of trustees and the church for an extended leave of absence in order that he might go South to seek restored health. On 10 December 1873, the trustees voted to grant him leave and to bear the cost by voluntary subscriptions in the parish among the members. Nathan Chandler, president of the board, presented Bellows with a resolution commending his search for health. The leave was to begin immediately following the morning service on 21 December. Again, as when the parish voted to let him go to San Francisco for six months, they made it quite plain that they expected their beloved pastor back again. They trusted that the rest would lead "under Providence, to his complete restoration, not only for his sake and ours, but for the cause of that Unitarian Christianity of which in this city, and in our generation, he has been the chief human support."[19] It was apparent that he was being released temporarily and reluctantly.

All over the country, 1873 had been a difficult year financially. On 6 November Bellows had written to William Prichard that he knew "the difficulty of collecting church & other dues." But even though he felt "a great reluctance to state my own necessities," he wanted to be paid. The church was actually $1,500 behind in paying Bellows's salary. Bellows stated to Mr. Prichard that he needed $500 immediately to meet living expenses. On the last day of November he had to pay his real estate taxes of $535. And he needed the final $1,000 of his salary by 28 November. He concluded, "I am very sorry to bother you—who have so often strained yourself for my relief—but I am a poor creature to be in debt, or fail of obligations. It worries me beyond measure." The treasurer obviously got the money somewhere.[20]

Another little-known parishioner was also in financial trouble. In a letter dated 29 December 1873, Elizabeth Shaw Melville (Mrs. Herman Melville) indicated that the Melville family was also in financial trouble. She too wrote the treasurer:

> Perhaps the giving up my pew (209 gallery) at this time requires some explanation. I have no desire to leave Dr. Bellows's church and shall ask the privilege of still occupying seats in the gallery without *for the present* holding myself responsible for pew rent. The 'notice' (in compliance with the rules) was prompted by an unwelcome necessity which I trust will be temporary, and I shall wish to become a legitimate pew holder again at the earliest possible moment, feeling that now, more than ever, we need to strengthen the bond that holds our beloved church together.[21]

The "unwelcome necessity" persisted for some time, and the Melvilles did not rent a pew again until fourteen years later when Herman Melville himself rented pew #138 (on the ground floor rather than in the gallery). It was valued at $800. But this apparent prosperity did not last and in March 1890, Mrs. Melville rented one valued at $250 which she retained until her death in 1906.

The Pillow and Staff of My Remaining Pilgrimage

Henry Bellows took his daughter Annie with him and headed for the warmer climate of the Southern states. By mid-January 1874, they were ensconced in a comfortable room in the Saint James Hotel in Jacksonville, Florida. They had "become exclusively acquainted with the 100 people in the house." Bellows expected to be stationary there for a month at least. He had learned to take walks, but Florida was cold in January, and he wrote, "I write in my *overcoat*, & I have a fire in my room." But he expected the chilly weather soon to disappear. He was faced with the problem that people wanted to meet and talk with him "who come & introduce themselves under some sort of pretense & want to know about Unitarianism." Bellows was quite surprised at this interest. One Methodist editor told him that "the thinking people . . . in all sects were substantially Channing Unitarians or Parkerites." Bellows liked this because he found "no hostility & no rooted prejudice to contend with."[1]

Although Bellows did not find the weather springlike, "nothing inviting in the sky or air," nevertheless he settled into a routine. He read many hours each day, walked two hours, wrote one hour, and spent "an hour at every meal protracted by pleasant chat." In the evening he mixed "with the social circle in the general parlor." And he slept a "full eight hours." This regimen left "several hours for lounging on the balconies, dressing & dreaming." He found his companions at Jacksonville generally those "people with pulmonic or with nervous diseases, or of persons accompanying them. The greater part of the invalids" were "men & women who like [himself] have been nervously exhausted with professional or business cares." "On the whole," he added, "it is an interesting clan. . . . There is no public bar, no noise, no confusion, cleanliness, order & comfort prevail." He said that the "keepers are not flashy, be-ringed & fast working publicans, but plain, quiet, domestic landlords with nothing but their industry & desire to please to distinguish them from the company." He found the colored servants preferable to those of the North.

There were a great many people from the West (Pennsylvania, Ohio, and Illinois). Bellows felt that they were "wonderfully behind-hand in theology—not narrow in spirit, but totally hide bound in their training. We little know," he added, "how efficacious the pulpit has been in inculcating the notion of verbal inspiration, the personality of the devil, & the existence of hell-fire." He believed that "these people are systematically taught not to [question] any of these sacred notions. . . . The old Calvinism has been driven out of New England & out of northern cultivated & thinking circles, but it exists . . . among the best people in the middle & Southern states." He added, "How confident & how little affected by modern thought lawyers & statesmen are in their ideas, in this and other Southern . . . sections." He thought that "the old theology, not able to bear the topical & free atmosphere of the North has merely settled into the South."

Bellows was careful not to *"shock"* his friends, and always prepared for a discussion of his Unitarian ideas with "a previous course of science & sympathy & fellowship with their devout and positive religious principles & experiences." He added, "I really find them well disposed towards me universally—and often unconscious of the incompatibility of their notions with mine." When asked to preach, in the public parlor, he declined and urged that a Methodist pastor, Dr. Abel Stevens, be given the task. Bellows felt that he would do more good with this select company "by personal intercourse & conversation," than by preaching. He hoped to stay at

Jacksonville for a month at least, so congenial did he find the atmosphere.[2]

Later in the month Bellows moved to Magnolia, Florida. It was now five weeks since he and Annie had left New York. But in typical Bellows fashion the party was growing (two nieces had joined them). He began his stay in the Florida resort the fourth week of January. This time the setting was not a hotel. The guests lived in cottages set among the "orange trees in full bearing." There were also cactus, palms, and Spanish bayonet bushes and the typical live oak trees of the Deep South "from which hang long grey mosses, ten & twenty feet in sweep." The cottages were right next to "the broad Saint John's River, four miles wide." The group boated daily on the river and watched the steamers go by. The temperature was mild, and Bellows said he wore "the clothing of June." There were about fifty people in the enclave, and although each group lived in a separate cottage Bellows found that taking the meals together "at a common table, a common hotel" to which the cottages were attached was most agreeable. Evenings were spent in the hotel until it was time for bed.[3]

The first indication of an event that was to occur in the near future is indicated in a letter of 5 February 1874, when Bellows commented on the people who were shortly expected to arrive at Magnolia. Mrs. Ephraim Peabody was to be there in a few days as was William Silsbee. Bellows felt that spring was blossoming all around him, the birds were coming back. He had read almost all of the fourteen volumes of Walter Scott's novels that he had brought with him. He found them "wholesome, instructive, learned & full of dramatic action—without much however of . . . moral speculation —but always heroic & noble in spirit."[4]

On Sunday 8 February Bellows conducted a private worship service in one of the rooms for a small group of persons. He read from the Bible, read a sermon by William Ellery Channing, and the group sang some hymns. Bellows remembered that this was the day at All Souls in New York when young Francis Greenwood Peabody would preach in his pulpit.

Mrs. Ephraim Peabody had arrived at Magnolia the previous day with her daughter, Anna, and her son-in-law, Charles W. Eliot, and his son Charles, Junior. The young boy was "a serious invalid, crippled [at] the knee joints & obliged to live in a wheeling chair." Bellows described Mrs. Peabody as "a pleasant woman, an old acquaintance & as dear Ephraim Peabody's widow (he died . . . 18

years ago) very interesting to me—as he was a special friend & one whom I altogether admired. He preached my Ordination Sermon."[5] Bellows obviously liked Magnolia—the atmosphere, the climate, and the people.

By 10 February he was taking walks with the Silsbees, Mrs. Grier (widow of the Supreme Court justice), Miss Peabody, and Charles W. Eliot. Charles Eliot had married Miss Peabody's sister Ellen Derby Peabody who had died in the same month that Charles W. Eliot had been invited to be the President of Harvard. This is the first indication that Bellows and Anna Peabody were together in anything approaching an intimate social situation—if walking together through the woods in a party of six is intimate. They also went rowing together on the cove. Bellows found that he was a little tired of so many people, "getting a little more bookish," and he remarked that "society can easily exhaust its charms." He wrote, "I can stand only about so much of its vacancy & absurdness. Compared with the company of a good book, it is fearfully empty."[6]

Russell reported to his father that Francis Greenwood Peabody's preaching was "wonderfully fresh & refreshing." Bellows read these parts of Russell's letter "to Peabody's mother & sister (& to Mr. and Mrs. Silsbee) . . . What a precious fellow he [Peabody] must be," Bellows commented.

Even though he was a thousand miles away from New York, Bellows could not keep his mind off matters that affected All Souls Church. He wrote to Nathan Chandler, the president of the board of trustees, in March that he thought it might be a good idea to sell the present church edifice and buy the Church of the Messiah, that church being on hard times. The boards of the two churches had had two meetings by the time that Nathan Chandler wrote back to Bellows. Chandler wrote, "I think I may say for *our* board, that, pecuniarily, we did not find their condition nearly as desperate as we had feared, in short, with a good united society, the financial situation need cause no very serious anxiety." Chandler, however, was "sorry to say they do not seem to be 'all of one mind,' in several respects and herein lies their greatest difficulty, but . . . I think in regard to 'consolidation' whatever, I think we are all *entirely* in accord with you." (Bellows's letter to Nathan Chandler is not extant so we do not know exactly what it was with which the board agreed.)

Most of the All Souls people, said Chandler, felt that their church at 20th Street ought to be "a mile or so further up town, and certainly the Church of the Messiah is excellently located for us, and has great advantages over ours in having a large and convenient

Sunday School room." But, Chandler added, "it appears as if they would make another attempt to go on by themselves, and it looks as if the church might be kept out of the market for considerable time."[7]

Even though he was lounging in ease in Florida Bellows could not keep his mind off the concerns of the denomination, either. He wrote to A. A. Livermore at Meadville that he was spending his ease with "Ephraim Peabody's widow, daughter, & grandson (son of President Eliot)." However, Bellows felt that he would "never be young again." He hoped to have a "mellow if not *green* old age with less care & more meditation. Thirty-five years in New York have pretty much used me up," he wrote. Putnam in Brooklyn and others had written to him of stormy weather ahead in the denomination. "The changes, the divisions, the peculiarities of our day are not unmanageable," Bellows wrote. The problems facing the Unitarian denomination were not unique. "It is a world-wide controversy. God is in it, & over it, & I am not afraid of it." Bellows was mellowing. God was in his heaven, and all would be well in the National Conference because somehow it was run by cosmic forces beyond man's control.[8]

Early in April, further pursuing his rest cure, Bellows and his party moved from Magnolia, Florida, to Aiken, South Carolina, a well-respected spot used by those seeking to move North with the spring. It was three days' journey from Magnolia to Aiken. There he met his friends, the William Weedens from Providence, Rhode Island.

A week later he left for Charleston, South Carolina, with Mr. and Mrs. Weeden, purportedly to see Fort Sumter and historic Charleston, actually to be with Miss Peabody in whom he had become vitally interested. "I have seen a great deal of Anna Peabody," he wrote to Annie, "& find her charming—full, as Russ says, of sweetness & light—a wholly superior character, of a finer dignity, delicacy, & pride of spirit than I had guessed. If she were of my mind I can't say what [would] happen. But I cannot flatter myself that she shares my admiration, or feels towards me, as I do towards her. I think I ought frankly to say to you my dear daughter, that her society is very . . . attractive & holds me here in spite of myself for a few days."[9]

Bellows was in love again. First it had been William Ellery Channing's daughter, Mary—at a distance. Then it was Eliza Townsend with whom he fell in love on the evening of his ordination in New York, and with whom he had lived for thirty years, and who had borne him five children, of whom only two had lived. And now he was writing to one of these surviving children, his daughter Annie, telling her that he had fallen in love again, a man of sixty who considered himself long past his prime, in love with a young woman of thirty-six years, and like a young swain he was prolonging his vacation and pursuing her to Charleston.

Within a few days he reported to his son that, "it looks *very nearly certain* that Annie Peabody & I shall be formally engaged." He felt "as if it were *already* so in every thing but *words.*" But he realized that he had no right to say that he had her pledge "until a distinct absolute verbal promise has come." Anna wanted to consult her brother, Robert Peabody, the architect, in Boston. Bellows had no wish to hurry her in so important a matter, although his "suspense & anxiety" had "nearly made him sick." He paid her this compliment, "She has been all that a delicate, noble, deep woman could be in my wooing & seems to me just the person to satisfy my judgment, meet my wants, & fill my heart—besides giving new dignity & happiness to our home." He beseeched Russell to keep this matter utterly quiet because "Anna is thirty-six." The Weedens were leaving for Baltimore, but he was staying in Charleston until this matter was settled in some way.[10]

Bellows let no grass grow under his feet in the pursuit of his beloved. Three days later he reported to Russell that "things again look favorable. I am sure Miss Peabody is meditating surrender! She confesses her interest & seems awaiting only letters from her brother to come to a definite decision. I feel almost certain it will be favorable." He added, "Indeed any other thought is becoming insupportable, for my whole heart & mind & conscience are in the scale, & success is necessary to my peace. I should *survive* defeat, but it would be nearly as *bitter* as death." This scarcely sounds like a man of sixty speaking of love.

Then Henry talked "turkey" with his son who was of course very much interested in the practicalities of his father marrying a young woman. Bellows assured Russell that in any will he would settle upon his new wife only what he had derived from his own father's estate and not what he had derived from Eliza's estate. He also promised that if Miss Peabody should have a child when they were married, he would purchase a life insurance policy for his education. He assured Russell that he thought first of his own children. He hoped that Russell would love "Miss Peabody as a dear *sister*" when he got to know her.[11]

Anna Langdon Bellows, Courtesy of the Bellows Family

Russell (working on the *Liberal Christian* in New York) wrote to his sister, Annie, that he felt that their father "was treading on pretty delicate & dangerous ground." Both the children wished their father "had let well enough alone." Russell even said that Miss Peabody was much more of his own style than of his father's. Russell felt "that it was a pretty *risky* matter, and that there were so many possible momentous consequences bound up in it." Under these circumstances he felt at first that he could "hardly favor it." But he added, "this thought was entirely independent of Miss P, and would be equally true, *whoever* the lady was." Russell sermonized, "marriage is always a pretty *blind* business, and a second marriage seems blinder still!" As to Miss Peabody herself, Russell found her "a very noble, lovely woman . . . and if anybody must come into the family, it would be difficult to select a finer, nobler woman."[12] Things did take time, for Miss Peabody wanted to consult not only her brother, Robert, but also President Eliot, her brother-in-law, who would not be home from Europe for a week.

Yet, on the same day that Russell was writing his letter to Annie, Bellows was writing the news to Russell that "Miss Anna H. Peabody is engaged to marry me. The event happened at 12½ today & makes Charleston and No. 4 Meeting Street a sort of sacred place." Bellows felt that Anna would balance his own nature, that it would be a good partnership. "She will be the counterpart of my impulsive, emotional nature—the balance wheel. . . . I feel that she is to be the pillow & staff of my remaining pilgrimage, I, the devoted servant of her simple tastes & dignified character." He continued, "I feed upon her as one starving feeds upon his first loaf. She has restored my attachment to life, and made my future attractive. I think I shall live ten years longer for her sake! . . . I hope the middle of June will see us married, and . . . at Walpole for a couple or more of solid restful months, & then we will all begin anew at New York."[13]

Now that the engagement was a fact the aura of secrecy could be broken and Bellows could announce its reality to his closest friends. To the Bartols he wrote that "after a whole winter's watching" he could not find a fault in Anna Peabody, "except her unnatural willingness to marry an old fellow like me!" He was *awfully happy*."[14]

Mrs. Ephraim Peabody, who watched all of this romance as a sort of helpless chaperone, wrote in her unpublished autobiography about the courtship of Dr. Bellows with her daughter at Magnolia, Aiken, and Charleston. When they arrived at Magnolia she "saw Dr. Bellows in the distance whom [she] had not seen for years." She "got Anna to run & call him." This, after the romance "was remembered & alluded to." She talked with Dr. Bellows about her son's ordination (Francis Greenwood Peabody's) which struck her that "it was very natural." She continued the story, "One night he pushed me into my chamber & began to talk of A. [Anna]. I determined not to worry myself for I did not think she would consider the matter at all." Annie and Henry Bellows gave up their bedroom to Mrs. Peabody because she was in a wheelchair and their room was on the ground floor. Mrs. Peabody and Anna then went to Charleston, but Bellows pursued. "He brought champagne to the

Russell Nevins Townsend Bellows, Courtesy of the Massachusetts Historical Society

table and was generally delightful. Before Mr. Weeden left town he got him to select a diamond ring, being pretty sure of success."[15] Bellows wanted to be married before his birthday on 11 June when he would be sixty years of age, but plans could not be made for a wedding by that date, so the wedding date was set for 30 June.

Anna wanted a quiet private wedding in the Peabody home in Boston. Bellows wanted to take his bride to Walpole and be alone with her except for the servants for a week, and then he hoped that his children could join them. He made it clear to Russell and Annie that he could "not have more than one *head* of the house" and that must be his wife. Bellows also was practical with his children. He said that Miss Peabody had "a little fortune—say $18,000 in her own right" and that upon her mother's death "a handsome sum further."[16]

Obviously the Peabody and Bellows clans were worried about the appearance of a new wife who was just a few years older than Bellows's children, neither of whom was married and both of whom spent a great deal of time in the New York and Walpole homes. Mrs. Peabody, after receiving a letter from Annie Bellows, wrote to her that she appreciated her "delicate position . . . the dread of a stranger in your pleasant home," and Annie's deep feelings "of being supplanted." But Mrs. Peabody assured Annie that with Bellows's "great big heart . . . there can be no thought of a second place. The more he loves her, the happier he is, the more he will love you." She explained that because Anna could calm her mother down without a word, "she will have a most tranquilizing effect on your too excitable papa. I tell her she will have to dash him with cold water all his days."

The important thing in this letter is that Mrs. Peabody gives us some insights into the character of Anna. "She was not handsome like her sister [Mrs. Charles W. Eliot]. . . . She was not introduced into society as Ellen was, for her father was not living, & she went as she could." She was the pet of her father, and he called her "poor Anna—a little tenderness over her deafness." She did all sorts of things for her sister. Then came Ellen's illness. At "first it was thought best to leave the children . . . with Anna while they went abroad." But then the Peabody home was broken up and the whole family went to the south of England where the three little boys lived with Mrs. Peabody and Anna, and Charles Eliot and Ellen went traveling in search of Ellen's health. When they went to the Pyrenees, little Robert was "taken fearfully ill . . . Anna watched him like a true mother." For months the little child was ill "till finally . . . in Paris he breathed his little life away on her bosom."

Anna kept house for the Eliot family. They took a house in the country, and both the boys were very sick. "Night & day again Anna was at work," caring for Charles and Samuel Eliot. In March 1869, Charles W. Eliot was elected president of Harvard University to succeed Thomas Hill, and was inaugurated on 19 October 1869. Ellen Derby Peabody Eliot died in March leaving the two small boys. "Anna had four houses on her hands at one time." She arranged President Eliot's house in Cambridge, "bought every carpet, opened all the furniture again . . . & arranged his home . . . The house in Boston had to be dismantled," and the summer house gotten ready for rental.

Then Anna and Mrs. Peabody went to Europe. There they met Robert Peabody, the architect, and traveled through the north of Italy with him.

At this juncture Anna got the "frightful Roman fever," and for six weeks "trembled between life & death." It was concern at this time over her daughter's condition that was the cause of Mrs. Peabody's lameness, which confined her to a wheelchair the rest of her life. She said "such anxiety & distress went to my *bones*. . . . When she [Anna] rose from that sick bed her figure was gone—she was the stout woman you see, her hair was all gone . . . she returned home so changed!" That summer she kept house for Charles Eliot. That fall Anna went back to care for her mother, because the lameness had endured. Both Robert and Francis, her brothers, became engaged at this time. She traveled with her mother seeking a cure, eleven months in Clifton, "200 invalids & not a healthy friend," and then they went to Santa Cruz accompanied by Miss Bartol and a maid. Then they took the trip to the South in 1874. "We were sent where she was to find rest & happiness I trust. She called your father to speak to me," Mrs. Peabody wrote to Annie Bellows, "so that he says she ran after him."

Mrs. Peabody then proceeded to tell Annie Bellows that "if anybody is to be pitied in this business, will you remember *me*?" The home in Boston was unfit for her because it was all stairs. Robert had planned a one-floor home for her in Brookline, but Anna was to have been a part of that picture, and this had to be given up. "I shall never have my own belongings around me again and must henceforth be left to hirelings."[17] Obviously Anna had been under some pressures not to consider seriously marriage with Henry Bellows.

The wedding plans were thrown into an uproar because of the sudden death on 19 June of Dr. Derby, Mrs. Peabody's only brother, and "very dear to her and Anna." The family decided not to postpone the wedding, but to make it simpler. The next day

Anna's trousseau arrived from Paris in "apple-pie order. Three silk dresses, & two house dresses & a traveling dress & I don't know how many summer dresses—nor how many skirts, underclothes, hkd, [handkerchiefs], stockings, gloves, neckties, neck-ornaments, bonnets, etc. . . . The wedding dress is of creamy heavy silk, with a tail that reaches almost to Walpole, & festooned with orange blossoms . . ."[18]

The wedding took place as planned, at Robert Peabody's home in Brookline at 6:00 P.M. on 30 June. About sixty guests were present. Anna's brother, Francis Greenwood Peabody, who was now settled at Cambridge, married the couple. Those closest to the two families were present including "about sixty of her nearest & my dearest friends." The couple left for Providence at 9:30 P.M. where Bellows's friend Weeden had put his empty house and servants at their disposal. They reached Walpole the very next day. "The dear old home had been put into Pinkie order" by the two Bellows children, and "trained servants were waiting to do [their] bidding & the whole establishment [was] in smooth working order." Bellows added that "Anna is charmed with her first view of her country Home." Bellows wished that he could stay there always.[19]

CHAPTER THIRTEEN

As Life Wears to Its Close

The Sweetest of Cries

In late September Henry and Anna left Walpole for Boston to settle Mrs. Peabody in "her house on W. Cedar Street." From there they proceeded to New York. Annie had returned to the city already and Russell was to remain at Walpole for a month writing sermons in the hope of finding a church settlement in the fall. Bellows's approach to another winter's work in New York was far better than it had been a year ago when he had returned tired and worn." I am confident of strength, sufficient (with care), to carry me through the winter's work. My vigor has sensibly increased this summer. I feel moved to work,"[1] he wrote to Orville Dewey.

The denomination was now beginning to look forward to the fall convention of the National Conference of Churches in October, and George Batchelor, one of the ministers in Salem, expressed to Bellows, who was president of the governing council, reasons for believing that the conference had lost the power that it had displayed in the late sixties in uniting and furthering denominational advance. Batchelor believed that "the 'radicals' who attend the conference [do not] expect to ask for, or obtain the abolition of the Preamble." His own Unitarian conference in Essex County in Massachusetts he believed "represents as active a form of radicalism as we are likely to deal with in practical form, and I am sure that nobody here *asks* or expects the Unitarian body to surrender its Christianity."

Batchelor pleaded with Bellows to give some further leadership in this matter. "There need be no conflict, there ought to be none. It only needs some man of sufficient influence to plant himself on *both sides.*" As Batchelor put it, "to claim all the conservative deserves, viz—the right to a full and clear expression of his Christian faith—and also for the radical, to defend his right to work with the others for common and desirable ends, without also assenting to some doctrine which has no relation to the ends he would work for."[2]

Bellows offered to do what Batchelor had hoped at the forthcoming conference. "I will consider carefully what I can *say before* the Saratoga Convention—(in the paper)—to aid in rekindling the enthusiasm which you think it in our favor to arouse. And should there be any necessity *in* the convention of quelling discontent among the friends of soul liberty, if others fail, I trust I shall not of doing my part towards that necessary result."[3]

Bellows was pleased the way things went at the National Conference meetings at Saratoga. He was encouraged to find that he could stand "such a drain on heart & mind." He found that the conference had aroused all of his powers. After ten years of service he gave up the chairmanship of the council "with a grateful feeling." "It was my child," he wrote Dewey. He felt that "the most difficult & critical work is *over*. The conference is a vital, powerful reality, & if I am not wholly blind, it *carries* with it & in it, the triumph of our cause."[4]

Robert Collyer had been at the Church of the Messiah preaching and had drawn full crowds both morning and evening. The Upper Church, as it was often called, was contemplating calling Mr. Collyer, and Jackson S. Schultz, an All Souls Trustee from 1872 to 1875 and now of the Second Church, wrote a very unofficial letter to Bellows asking his opinion of Mr. Collyer, and whether he [Bellows] would feel that he could encourage Collyer to come to New York. He wrote, "You may take a larger view of the subject & consider the whole cause both at Chicago and here and may come to a different conclusion—and whatever that may be I shall try to think right." Schultz continued, "I can't help but think so far as the cause in this city is concerned Mr. Collyer would help us."[5]

A call was indeed extended in October to Robert Collyer to become the minister of the Church of the Messiah. But the people of Chicago quite plainly did not want Collyer to leave them. Artemas Carter wrote as chairman of a three-man committee for the Unity Church in Chicago. They had held a public meeting to discuss the matter, and various sentiments had been expressed. "The love and affection of his people towards him are all that any minister could ask—that they do most earnestly and sincerely desire him to remain with them—that they know of no reason why he should leave."[6]

Five days later Collyer wrote to Bellows that he could not accept the call to New York. "Perhaps I ought not to have thought of it," he wrote. He confessed that for a year he had been thinking about a change on the ground "that some other man could do a better work here and perhaps I could do better work in some other place." He heard the cries of grief when he contemplated leaving Chicago. The other two churches in Chicago were without pastors at the time, and this influenced Collyer's decision. The churches proposed getting together and giving Collyer larger audiences and a larger salary. So Collyer decided not to leave Chicago, and he added a personal note to his friend Bellows, "I can truly say that one item in the temptation to come to New York was that you are there."[7] This was a vital decision on Collyer's part. The next five years at the Church of the Messiah were to be some of the most critical in the life of the church, which narrowly avoided being closed.

After he received Collyer's letter of refusal, Mr. Colton visited Bellows, who wrote: "The general sentiment he thinks will now be to sell their church to us for a moderate figure, say, $250,000 & ask us to settle a colleague with me, to take the brunt of the pastoral work & preach evenings, until he made a name & was able to preach mornings too." Bellows wrote about the meeting, "I was *cautious*, but the plan does not strike me badly, & shall want some formal move—which may or may not come."[8] The merger move never materialized.

On 3 November Bellows and about twenty of William Cullen Bryant's closest friends called on him "to congratulate him on his octogenarian honors." Bryant was "in excellent condition, good health, fine spirits, and evidently highly gratified with the attention he rec'd." Bellows hoped that some of the rest of his contemporaries would have the same freshness and zest for life at the age of eighty as Bryant had. The visit and birthday made Bellows ponder, for Bryant was two decades older than he was.[9]

At the annual meeting of the society held on 12 January 1875 (which Bellows evidently did not attend), there were several resolutions, but one expressing the feeling that the society was declining because not enough pastoral work was being done by the minister irked Bellows.[10] There was much discussion of the matter by the small group present. Warm affection was expressed for their pastor, but they resolved to meet again on the second Tuesday in February to further discuss the matter.

Bellows was obviously upset by this implied criticism, for he wrote his son, "I judge that they look for, or desire, more *visiting* in the society than I can give . . . I told them that the moment they thought the interests of the church likely to flourish better in younger hands, I would retire. This brought out expressions of warm attachment & determination to stand by their minister in 'his declining years'."[11]

Russell was concerned that after all of these years as minister of All Souls Church such "nit picking" at the annual meeting could so concern and upset his father. He felt that persons who had done the criticism meant well, but that "the expression was bungling & the ignorance necessarily dense." Russell questioned the value of the Wednesday class that Bellows had conducted and the importance of the afternoon or evening service to the life of the parish, and doubted their vitality. The Sunday morning service was important. He also felt that his father should put "extra time & work upon the *younger* elements of the congregation where if *anywhere* they are needed."[12]

Bellows began to think that "the little stir among the people will do good." Mr. Goddard had come and spent an hour with Bellows on Saturday evening, "& was very tender & genial." He had stated to Bellows that "the whole aim of the resolutions was to get at [Bellows's] wishes, & to give [him] the opportunity of asking for an assistant." He assured his pastor that persons in the parish were willing to underwrite the cost of an assistant at $2,500 per year. Most important, Mr. Goddard assured Bellows that "there was a universal devotion to [him] in the parish & a firm desire to *keep* [him] as long as they could."[13]

By 1875 Bellows was realizing that continuing as the owner and editor of the *Liberal Christian* was more than he could undertake. Under various names he had published this paper for a quarter of a century, often filling many of the pages himself. When Rev. Charles Wendte proposed to Bellows in May 1875 that there ought to be a union of the *Liberal Christian* with the *Liberal Worker,* Bellows was amenable to the idea. He felt that the *Liberal Christian* was no longer needed in New York, "the *Christian Register* covering the ground." He wrote to Wendte that he was "prepared to negotiate with any responsible parties who want to consider the matter. The *Liberal Christian* is wholly & absolutely under my control as a property." True, it had a debt of $2,200, but he felt that this should not be a barrier to merger. "The good will of the paper with its hard-earned constituency of 2,500 or 3,000 (I don't know which) must be worth more than enough to pay its small debt." He felt that this debt would have to be paid in any such merger, as his "personal sacrifice of labour & work for twenty-five years should free [him] from any new loss."[14] It seemed like a good opportunity to lessen that work load that so plagued his health. But nothing ever came of his proposed merger with the *Liberal Worker.*

On the first anniversary of the marriage of Anna and Henry, 30 June 1875, Bellows looked back and commented that, "if a good Providence guided me, it did in the choice of my wife. The day proved an unalloyed joy & some of repose to me, & every day makes me more sensible of the wisdom . . . of the choice I made, & of the loveliness of her simple, devoted & wise heart & character." He continued, "I feel at the end of the first year, as if I had only *begun* to sound the depths of her unaffected goodness, truth, & sweetness . . . I bless God with ceaseless gratitude for this most precious gift."[15]

At Walpole there was great happiness, for Anna was near the point of confinement with her first baby. This coming blessed event brought some rather contradictory feelings to Bellows. His wife was scarcely older than his own children from his first marriage. Now there was to be a little child again in the household, and he was to be the parent rather than Russell or Annie. He commented, "you can easier imagine that I describe the curious mixture of youthful hopes & *aged* recollections; of a life nearly lived out, & a life beginning;—of a father's & a grandfather's feelings—that agitate & thrill & pain my bosom—as I look forward to the prospect of again holding a *young* child & my own, in my arms!" He commented, "it seems partly *out* of nature, & partly *super* natural. I think that I understand Abraham's feelings when Isaac was about coming into the world! It will be a great relief to me when Anna is safely through with her trial."[16]

On 13 August, the sentimental side of Bellows came out when he wrote to Russell, vacationing at Mount Desert Isle in Maine, that this was the day thirty-six years ago when he and Eliza Townsend had been married. "I often see her in my dreams, looking as she was in her comparatively young & well years. I can ever recall her fidelity, untiring devotion to us all, her superiority to the worldliness about her, her elevation of tone, love of nature & absolute truth of soul, without fresh gratitude & a surge of feeling that is not always controllable." He found that he "could not sleep this morning with thinking of her."[17]

By 18 August Bellows was still waiting for the birth of the child. "All things are ready. Dr. Draper is at Mrs. Wrights, our nurse is a prudent efficient woman. Dr. Twitchell [of Keene] is waiting only a telegraphic tick to come up. There is a general expectation in town almost amounting to impatience."[18] Henry was "hourly expecting [his] wife's confinement. She is now in the beginning of labour & before this closes, I may add a postscript of importance, at least to us. It is an anxious hour; but I busy myself to keep away too painful thoughts & too much weakening & sympathies." Then he added a postscript: "Henry W. Bellows, Jr. has just come into the world; & his mother is comfortable & happy. I am proud & glad & grateful

Henry Whitney Bellows with his son, Henry Whitney Bellows, Jr. (taken about 1876 when his son was about a year old), All Souls Archives

beyond words!"[19] "The sweetest of cries is in my ears; that of a newborn babe, just born!—ten lbs., well-formed, healthy & stout—its mother comfortable & too blessed for words! & too proud & happy to do anything but bless God & think of the dear friends who are ready to echo my joy."[20]

Sort of a Fossil

Russell Bellows was in Washington preaching to a dissident group which had separated from the Washington Church. The minister of that church, Frederic Hinkley, had not been a success, and after a ministry of five years had resigned. There was some talk of Russell becoming the minister of the main Washington Church rather than just of the splinter group to which he was preaching. His father wrote him a rather frank letter to show Russell exactly where his qualities and his deficiencies lay in the profession of the ministry. His father thought the Washington Church "in many respects suited to your capabilities if not your tastes. You would find in Boston & immediate neighborhood a chance for a culture theological & pulpit-wise, which you lack—but also a demand you are not over-able to meet—exchanges a plenty—but a sense of scholastic defect—which will never be made up until you conquer your distaste or inadequacy to sober & systematic reading."

Then Henry analyzed his son. "I never knew a fellow with so much thought & mental training, so little furnished book-wise & so little disposed to sober & hard reading. If you do not conquer this you will rue it. You have too little *abandon* & *drive* of nature to trust very much to inspiration & invention." He continued in this vein, "You must have knowledge & profit by other men's thoughts. Your sermons ought to be illustrated by historic references & literary ornament & be each one a work of reading & preparation of facts as well as thought & experience. You don't know how to study."

"This," he confessed, "is partly an unhappy *heritage* from me—which I have overcome practically by steady & sober reading—but have never overcome in any way to make me an authority, a systematic theologian, or a *final* teacher in any thing. With my faculties I ought to have had a *first* rate education—& have been enough of a scholar to know things at first hand. But I . . . succeeded too early & too easily to make this apparent."

Bellows concluded, "It is not too late for you to repair at least something of your early successes."[1] Russell actually did a good job in Washington bringing back together the two dissident groups.[2]

Bellows late in his life reserved his more philosophical letters for Orville Dewey. In such a letter Bellows discussed the basis for faith and belief. "After men are once brought into *obedience* to moral law & spiritual realities, I think, Naturalism or Deism a very good faith," he wrote. "Indeed, such men are free from *all* bonds of system. But how few such there are? I cannot but feel therefore, a sort of pain in the criticism I am compelled to pass upon popular orthodoxy—a feeling that I am perhaps putting down the only shelter the majority of people can accept."

He wrote that he began "to understand how intelligent, wise & strong men, learned in history and philosophy, can maintain the *orthodox* symbols. I even think *us* shallow & hasty in our effort to empty them of meaning, or deny them intelligibility." He cautioned, "Clearly, the *simplicity* we are driving towards, will be a severe trial for the next generations of liberals. It will be a good deal if religion, as Rousseau hoped it would be with society, returned to its material state! Whether this may not be too much like *vulgar savageness* in one case, & too much like the simplicity of *troubling one's head with nothing*, in *religion*, who can predict? I feel no want myself—but I begin to feel some anxiety for others."[3]

Bellows was a rememberer of anniversaries and quite sentimental about them. On his and Anna's second wedding anniversary on 30 June 1876, the Bellowses were in Walpole and Henry thought about the meaning of the day. "Anna was saying only yesterday, that never had one word or look from *you* detracted from the happiness & repose of her lot since she entered the family." Bellows had spent the day before the anniversary celebration in writing a "versified history (in twenty-six verses) of 'our Wooing'—a wedding present for my wife. She was much pleased."[4]

Money had always been a problem for Bellows. He lived life well and in grand style. He had a family that was dependent upon him, a house in New York City on which he paid about $550 per year in taxes, and another house in Walpole. Neither of his children had married, and they were constantly asking him for money. Even with a salary of $10,000 per year and some extra income, times were difficult. Obviously in July 1876 he had been losing some sleep over the matter, for he wrote to Russell, "My money affairs give me no small solicitude day & night; for I foresee my inability to meet them, or to continue our present rate & style of living." He wrote about a remedy, "Some decisive change must be made this fall or we shall plunge into a disgraceful & inexcuseable bankruptcy. . . . I would even sell my house & live in an *apartment*—if this were not a ruinous period for selling any property. That would be a great hardship—but better than our present steady excess." He wanted to talk this matter over with the whole family when Russell came up from New York. "It is really absolutely necessary to face the whole facts, with unflinching firmness and real action."[5] Very little was done to curb expenses, though, and the family somehow muddled through until the end of Bellows's life.

In November 1876 at a meeting of the Council of the National Conference of Unitarian and Other Christian Churches, it was decided to have a Ministers Institute on the alternate years when the National Conference, which now met biennially, did not hold its sessions. The committee consisted of Bellows, Rev. James De Normandie, Rev. George A. Thayer, Rev. S. R. Lathrop, and Rev. Joseph May. The planning for this and succeeding conferences was to be one of Bellows's great contributions to the denomination in the last few years of his life.[6]

But there was new unhappiness in Bellows's life; another of his old friends was mortally ill. This time it was the second Mrs. George Schuyler. Her sister, the first Mrs. Schuyler, had died of cancer, and now on 18 January 1877, Bellows saw Mary Schuyler alone. "For the 1st time she told me she had her sister's disease & had had it *four years* & now the end was coming & she was glad of it. She was brave, but looks very sick & wilted. I think her fortitude & interest on others, very wonderful under this silent unmentionable trouble."[7]

At the end of January 1877 Mary Schuyler wrote to her pastor from her home on West 31st Street. "I cannot look forward to going through the many months which may be before me of weariness and weakness without having the spiritual helps and strength which those who are accustomed to it know best how to give." She asked Bellows if he would be willing every week or ten days to "have some prayer or service" with her. She felt that this would be imposing upon his own health but could think of no one else capable of doing this for her.[8] She did indeed linger for many months, and as one looks at Bellows's busy calendar of the year 1877, one wonders how he ever found the time to perform this service which she asked.

The Schuyler family was one of the few families of Dutch background who were attracted to Unitarianism. Another Dutchman, Augustus Blauvelt[9] sought out Bellows's counsel because he found that he no longer could believe the old Calvinistic religion of the Dutch Reformed Church. Bellows invited him to dinner at his home several times, and they had long discussions about religion. After the first meeting Bellows wrote to him that he found his nature very compatible. "I doubt if two perfect strangers ever coalesced more heartily or more suddenly! The only difference, I judge, is what belongs to our dissimilar training & antecedents. I was *born* free & you have bought your freedom with a great price." Bellows continued, "I fancy your imagination is still a little enthralled by old conceptions. How could it be otherwise? But I dare say I am without some valuable experiences of a religious or theological kind, which an orthodox nurture might have given me. Let us profit by each other's separate wealth, & make common stock of the whole!"[10]

Bellows stressed how much one gives up to accept a "free" religion. Having come into contact with minds "born free" Bellows commented to Blauvelt, "I think you will not at once realize how much you give up, as well as how much you *take* on." He believed that "freedom has its own burdens, & bondage its own sweets. Especially, we are apt to forget, that a horse that would *pull* must *stay in harness*—he can roll more quickly out!"[11]

Russell Bellows had been working on the *Inquirer* for his father, and in early 1877 he evidenced a desire to try to run the paper entirely by himself. Russell, therefore, bought from William Potts his half interest in the paper for the sum of $500. For this he received "my one-half undivided interest in the subscription list of the newspaper known as the *Inquirer*, and formerly known as the *Liberal Christian*, including all good will & all receipts from and after this date for subscription and advertising excepting a margin up to twenty-five percent on advertising bills already charged." It sounded like a fine business deal, but largely what Bellows received was a small subscription list, an ailing newspaper, and the debts. Bellows had never really been able to make the paper a go financially, but Russell hoped by revising its format and putting in considerably more time than his father had been able to do, it might be made a life work for him. Unfortunately young Bellows had more time but not the genius of his father.[12]

James Freeman Clarke complained to Bellows about the new tone of the *Inquirer*, and the short shrift a recent sermon he had delivered had received in the pages of the paper. Bellows assured him that only those writings which had his initials were his personal responsibility. He had turned the paper over to his son, Russell, and he wrote, "my son's views are different from my own, as Minister's sons are apt in these days to differ from their fathers. It is natural after my long control of the paper, that I should be held responsible for its views, but I must bear that as I do not wish to put myself in open hostility to my son's opinions. I suppose he is a reverential disciple of the left wing, & thinks his father, a sort of fossil—but he is too honest & good to be shoved further away by open opposition."[13]

Yet, two weeks later Bellows wrote his friend Bartol that under Russell's direction the paper was doing quite well. "It looks now as if the paper were on a good tack. . . . I think Russell has great wisdom, although I sometimes differ with him. But I am too conscious of the influence of habit and age, not to be willing to have young men, if sound in heart & life, hold opinions different from my own. They may easily be better ones, if I *don't* like them!"[14]

Late in June 1877, Bellows gave an address to the Divinity School reunion at Harvard. He himself was terribly impressed with the reception that his address had among those who heard it. He wrote from Cambridge, "I think I have not seen such enthusiasm, gratitude, pride & pleasure, around anything I did, & I don't remember any occasion, where such unanimity & . . . from the most opposite classes of minds, seemed to prevail. . . . There was a clamor for me to go on, when I prepared to stop at the expiration of an hour & a quarter, & I completed the 1-1/2 hours."[15] Bellows's growing age was not dimming his proclivity for long-windedness.

After this successful experience Bellows traveled to Sheffield, Massachusetts, to see Orville Dewey on his way back to Walpole. He was there on 4 July. Bellows was discouraged by Orville Dewey's physical condition. "The dear old doctor is manifestly weaker & sadder . . . is anxious to depart. He said today, 'I am more afraid of *life* than of *death*'!" Dewey at eighty-four was very weak and tired of life. The next day Bellows went over to Stockbridge to spend some time with Henry D. Sedgwick before returning to his vacation home at Walpole.[16]

Toward the end of the month Mrs. George Schuyler died at the Schuyler's seaside home. George himself was suffering from the gout, and he wrote to Bellows in response to a letter of sympathy which Henry had sent to him on the sad occasion. About his wife he wrote, "to be able to face for so many years such a painful end, without losing a particle of her interest in all that was worth being interested in, was the natural result of a character of uncommon disinterestedness, and also the religious views free from all dogmas, simple, trustful, and are sufficient for the trials she was called upon to endure."[17] The granddaughter of Alexander Hamilton had many of the qualities of her grandfather.

At about the same time Orville Dewey wrote to Bellows that he was in much pain and had a great dread of it. "I sympathize deeply with your dread of pain," Bellows wrote, "having had a great immunity from it all my life & not being able to understand the equanimity with which many people less disciplined, seem to encounter it." Bellows remarked that Eliza, his first wife, was able to "sit down in the dentist's chair with a smiling indifference to that torturous engine, which reminded me of the stoicism of an Indian chief!" He himself, he added, could not face that "nerve-punching inquisitor, without shaking in [my] shoes."

Bellows also commented pointedly to Dewey that Eliza Schuyler (the first Mrs. George Schuyler) had a similar horror of pain, but "she *learned* to *bear* it, & even derived spiritual aid from the tortures she suffered! She had a notion that she entered more closely into the communion of suffering with the Master." Bellows added, "I can't believe that physical pain, though it may nurture heroism, & so, moral strength, is necessary to spiritual growth." He then told his friend Dewey that if he could stand quinine, he could use it, but not to continue to use it over a week.[18]

On Sunday 12 August 1877, Bellows preached at a special missionary service at Saratoga Springs. It was a part of one of the experiments being conducted by the American Unitarian Association in order to popularize the Unitarian faith. It was out and out a missionary effort at one of the popular American spas, and Rev. Rush Shippen, the secretary of the association, wrote to Bellows that many things were lacking at Saratoga for a completely successful missionary effort; there was no suitable hall and the singing was poor. But he told Bellows that he would have some large advertising placards printed and some small handouts prepared to announce his preaching.[19]

The preaching went well at Saratoga. "I had a great audience yesterday," Bellows wrote, "morning and evening in the Great Hall used at the convention, & a fine soil in which to plant the seed of the new, fresh gospel." In spite of Shippen's caution, "The arrangements were satisfactory as to music, & pulpit, & lively interest accompanied my efforts."

Bellows commented that "instead of attacking orthodoxy or naming it, I undertook to cut *under* it, & show the people a free, rational faith, in dead earnest, which would meet their moral & spiritual wants, without compromising interference in blinding the instincts of truth." His efforts were well received. "Many people," he said, "strangers & acquaintances, stopt to thank me, & one gentleman from Vermont said, 'I never hear anything I can believe in my state. It is refreshing to get a whiff of sense & truth in the name of Religion. The Gospel is dumb in my region'."[20]

Russell was having difficulties keeping the *Inquirer* going. Neither he nor his father completely trusted William Potts from whom Russell had bought a half interest. The editor of the *Christian Register*, the Rev. Thomas J. Mumford, had recently died, and Henry suggested to Russell that "$2,500 and the *Inquirer's* list, would make you editor, if the thing were fully engineered." Bellows suggested to his son that it might be possible thus to combine the two denominational papers. Now was the time to suggest this plan to the Boston denominational paper before Mumford's place was filled.

He questioned somewhat whether Russell could live with the editorial policies of the *Christian Register*. "Perhaps you think the *Register* pledged to a policy you could not assume," he wrote. "I think it is only pledged to the broad interpretation of the Unitarian organizations & its faith; that any editor who wished to ignore our past or cut loose from it, would be out of place. But I can't believe that either you or I would find it difficult to devise a policy that would be equally acceptable to the enlightened Unitarians of both the past schools." And he added dejectedly, "There really seems only *one* school now,"[21] and it was not Henry's school of thought.

Russell was still procrastinating as to his eventual career (actually this kind of process went on for his entire adult life). His father wished that he would make up his mind, and cautioned against feeling that any religious newspaper had in it the makings of financial success. "The *Register* is barely self-supporting," he wrote to Russell, "notwithstanding its prestige. The *Index* never had a leg to stand on. No Unitarian Review or Free Religious magazine has ever got roots in fertile soil. The place for such influence as they exert is in the general organ of news & literature not in *special* papers. . . . Why waste the fresh & vigorous part of your life in such a forlorn hope?"[22]

As Bellows had already indicated, he believed the Unitarian movement was foundering. He blamed the failure on the "times." For example, Rush R. Shippen, the Secretary of the American Unitarian Association, wrote Bellows in September of 1877 indicating that two churches in which Bellows was very interested were in trouble. The church in Newark, New Jersey, wanted enough money from the association to pay a minister's salary. Local initiative was at a low ebb in Newark, and Shippen wrote to Bellows that "they deem the mission *our* affair rather than theirs, and that in helping it at all they have conferred a favor." At the same time the Harlem Church was getting nowhere in becoming self-supporting, and they too expected the association to underwrite their expenses. They had written to Shippen, "It is a burning shame that our church should be closed for want of the paltry sum of $1,000." Shippen wondered if either of these churches could stand financially on its own.[23]

Bellows was one of the originators and was on the planning committee of the Minister's Institute which met on alternate years with the meetings of the National Conference of Churches. The institute met in Springfield the second week in October 1877, and proved to be particularly meaningful to Bellows.[24] Bellows felt that "the general success of the institute had been far above any body's expectation both in attendance, interest, satisfaction & profit. Things have gone differently from what was expected by any of us. The papers have been better, more careful, scholarly, & important & more carefully & respectfully listened to . . . an immense amount of comparison of views has been exchanged."

William Henry Channing preached on Monday night at the Springfield church, a sermon which Bellows characterized as "of a highly exalted but very visionary character—in which mysticism, French generalization & Millenarianism were mixed up . . . & to the edification of the devout I doubt not. It was all in the air & had no feet if it had lighted. It was curiously out of place in a scientific meeting."[25]

Bellows presided at the opening business session on Tuesday morning. This was followed by the opening address, "The Metaphysics of Theism," by Professor Frederick Henry Hedge at noon. Bellows called Hedge's address "highly intellectual but very equivocal in its Christian elements." Hedge talked against personal immortality, and many thought that he "had tested the liberality of the institute. It was having a fearful strain on our candor—a sort of doctrine of *despair* cheerfully taught—as if . . . he liked living on only in his influence on the earth." The lecture prompted a long discussion.[26]

Bellows believed that his friend Hale, who preached on Tuesday evening, "did a great deal worse. Instead of preaching, as he was asked, he took the liberty of introducing a lecture on what he called "Our Modern Christology" . . . which had a wonderful appearance of knowledge, audacity, particularity—& definiteness, oversimilitude & importance—but which the real radicals present knew to be stolen scraps, made up facts. . . . It was tremendous impudence, really addressed to the ignorant & unlearned, over the heads of the institute—it was as bold as if nobody knew any better."

Bellows believed that Hale was "a great master in narrative & fiction, but [he thought] it finished a large part of what remains of confidence in the genuineness of the man himself."

Of the papers read at the conference Bellows felt that that of Joseph Henry Allen of the Harvard Divinity School on "The Messiah and the Christ in History" and of the Rev. Edward B. Hall on "St. Paul and the Development of the Early Church" were "really *great* in the serious, solid character of their thorough preparation, admirably arranged method, reverent didactic manner & the importance of their views; they came up to the level of our proper aim." Bellows felt that the paper of the Rev. Andrew Preston Peabody, on the subject "Pastoral Duty and Ministerial Piety," was "Grandfatherish, & wise & good—but his discourse aimed at the feet & not the head & was hardly worthy even of his usual style & force."

Dr. Minot Judson Savage of the Church of the Unity in Boston "gave a vigorous paper with much that was true . . . & nothing that was very comprehensive or showed the experienced minister, or practitioner." Bellows commented, "He reads, but he does not think. He is too hasty & too much under the influence of his last books . . . He is an attorney, not a judge. He has a concept of being more of a man than he is and fed upon his popular success. The subject was too big for him & he too young for it."

What interested Bellows most about the institute was a private discussion which the ministers had on Wednesday when the usual visitors were not invited, "on the plan & order of the institute." Bellows opened the business at the request of the committee, "with an account of the plans we had formed." Bellows explained that it was·the hope of the committee to keep the preaching, which would be open to the public, separate from the institute and "popular in character." He believed the "machinery should be as simple as possible, nothing but a standing committee with full powers—of seven persons, & the two sec's ex-officio thrown in." The whole subject was discussed for two hours, "with great interest." Some wanted more and some wanted less debate at the institute. They all agreed that the purpose of the institutes should be "scientific theology."

The institute then named a new committee consisting of Nathaniel Thayer, James De Normandie, Henry Bellows, Joseph Henry Allen, Edward B. Hall, Rufus Ellis, and Francis Greenwood Peabody with George Batchelor and Rush R. Shippen as the two executive ex-officios. The institute concluded its meetings on Friday with Bellows giving a morning lecture on "The Art of Preaching."[27]

In the fall of 1877, all of the publishing enterprises in which Bellows had taken an interest over the years were terminated when the *Inquirer* was merged with the *Christian Register*. George Ellis of the *Christian Register* and Russell Bellows of the *Inquirer* drew up the final contract. The *Register* took over the *Inquirer's* subscription list and the advertising already contracted for, and Russell assumed all debts exclusive of those due to the subscribers. It was an inauspicious ending to all of the energies which Henry Bellows had put into the publishing enterprises for the Unitarians during most of his lifetime. He had worked without pay, usually making up the deficits himself over the years. But the subscription lists never became large enough to keep the enterprises going.[28]

On 3 November 1877, a second boy was born to Anna and Henry Bellows. They gave him the name Robert Peabody Bellows; the Peabody in honor of Anna's father, Ephraim Peabody. Bellows was overjoyed when he wrote, "we had a little boy born into our arms, this *very morning*! . . . My wife is very comfortable & happy & I am very proud & glad, & the child a good healthy, fat little atom, who looks like his brother Henry, & on whom we begin at once to build new hopes!"[29]

Mine Eyes Have Seen the Salvation

Early in 1878 William Silsbee, his wife, and daughter Annie got together with the Bellows family for a visit. Late in February 1878, Henry wrote to his friend how good it was to see them and how nice it was that spring that year appeared to be coming so early. This thought led him to some other ideas; "I sometimes think," he wrote, "it is one of the proofs of immortality that we are *willing* to have the year hurry on so swiftly, & for the sake of summer *greet* the long winter, as if it did not cost us a large slice out of the last quarter of our loaf of earthly existence. Even old men do not *grudge* its passing away . . . & it must be because we carry the instinct of a timeless being within us, & can well afford to make light of the waste of our years."

He continued, "Not that I do not nightly reflect upon the blessing of each passing day, & count over its precious privileges of romantic love, & mental stimulus, of knowledge gained, & curiosity gratified, & services rec'd & rendered—& even with an added & growing feeling of gratitude—as life wears to its close." Bellows wrote, "amid all that, I am *satisfied*, to hear the time approach as it does so swiftly, when time shall be no more, Silsbee, because *immortality* is so strong & clear in my hope, & so truly a part of my happiness & being."[1]

Another intellectual activity which meant a great deal to Bellows was a series of meetings of the clerical members of the Century Club of which Bellows had been one of the founders. They got together "for free discussion on questions of common professional interests." The list included "Dr. Adams, & Hitchcock & Washburn & Polter & Vincent & Booth—all wise & strong men—Presbyterians, Episcopalians & Congregationalists; about ten, & I the only professed liberal." Bellows wrote, "We have talked over without gloves, *Future Retribution & Inspiration!* It is the very first chance I have ever had to measure ideas with these representatives of the established & popular sects. They are vastly freer than we think—but with streaks of old-time prejudices that seem like bits of bone in your mouth, when you think you have only soft food."

Bellows described his clerical friends as having "modern *coats* & medieval *trousers!* and you have a painful sense that they don't quite dare to state their *whole* minds. They are still badly bound up in their Scripture systems & phraseology, but they are panting for freedom & puzzled with their own thots, & very curious about ours." He found that they questioned him with an eagerness that he found surprising; "I have not felt the coldness of a single shoulder, nor noticed the rise of an eye-brow!"

Bellows felt that this kind of an experience with the more orthodox ministers was the opening of a new era of understanding between the sects. "I think the old theology is passing away as a sentiment of living force, among educated men, under forty," he wrote. The old theology "was based on the Sovereignty of God, or divine decrees. It was assumed that we had authoritarian accounts (Independent of Reason or conscience or human approval) of God's will & law, and that alone being fixed & unalterable & we had nothing to do but accommodate ourselves to it as we best could."

He contrasted this with "the modern theology [which] begins at the other *end* of the scale—with *man* & proceeds from the known to the unknown, from the finite to the infinite—& *not* from an *assumed* knowledge of God to a proper view of man & his prospects as going downwards instead of upwards. I think this change has now become a fixed fact, in *tendency* at least; & that it is a change as important as any the world has seen."[2]

Bellows was much interested in art, the theater, and in music. He wrote to Parke Godwin, Bryant's son-in-law and literary heir, that uninvited he had visited the studio of a Mr. Minor whom he believed to be a major American artist. He believed that Minor's picture *Autumn* should be given serious consideration to be included in the selection of American pictures that was being gotten together to send to the Paris Exhibition. Parke Godwin was a member of the selection committee. The description of the picture shows some of Bellows's artistic criteria:

> Tired as we all must be of the gaudy, sensational pictures of our Autumn scenery, which certain artists, chiefly *foreigners,* have painted for a quarter of a century, it was a great surprise & delight to behold our early November woods painted in their grave colors, the leaves still clinging to the branches, & the shadowless light of noon day, falling upon & tangled in with them—full of brilliancy, without one false note of glaringness, & strong & broad, without one sacrifice of the whole effect to any detail or ambition of technical display . . . as if Inness's merits had been separated from his defects in Minor's picture—which has much of the merit of Corot's style without any imitation of it.[3]

By the end of March Bellows was in Boston for business sessions of the executive committee of the National Council. Rush R. Shippen was preaching at All Souls. Henry wrote to Russell, that he was "pretty well worn out from the winter's work; digestion imperfect & sleep restless, & night-*marish.*" Bellows related a typical anxiety dream—but it was an ecumenical one. When he got into the pulpit in the dream he couldn't find the prayer book, then he couldn't find his sermon. So he called Russ from the congregation, and sent him home for a sermon. Once he got the sermon he couldn't find his voice. In his dream Bellows saw Phillips Brooks in the congregation, and called him up and asked him to read the sermon. Brooks "read it so fast, I lost my breath & exploded with a gasp that waked me up in terror. Strange how often this or a similar distress connects itself with the pulpit in my dreams."[4] Every minister or speaker must have similar anxiety dream states.

Bellows was in a melancholy mood on 12 April 1878, Russell's thirty-fifth birthday. As Bellows put it, "Half the ordinary human life has gone by for him." What he did not say in the letter was that Russell had not yet found himself in any profession, either the ministry or writing. At other times Bellows had expressed his disappointment in Russell—of whom he probably expected too much.[5]

Rush R. Shippen of the American Unitarian Association and Bellows were still interested in keeping the Harlem Unitarian Church alive. Naturally Shippen looked to Bellows as the Unitarian leader in

New York to give him advice. The church had fallen $1,600 into debt, largely through careless financing. Shippen had a personal conference with the two leading laymen of the church, a Mr. Butler and a Mr. Carlin. They had enough money to take care of the running expenses of the church with a gift of $500 pledged by Bellows. The American Unitarian Association was going to give another $100 to take care of the interest on the $1,600 debt.

But Shippen had wider concerns. The American Unitarian Association lacked the funds necessary to keep every struggling church alive. He indicated to Bellows that in the current year the association was giving $5,000 to New Orleans, $5,000 to the Third Society in Chicago, and $2,000 to save the "Wilmington church from the hammer."

Shippen added that the Harlem Church "ought to rejoice in being kept alive at all, with so promising a future, with this $1,600 accumulated by their own neglect, they ought to be happy that they have not forfeited entirely the confidence of outside friends . . . it is rather forcing us to the wall. And while I have no desire to give up, but feel that it is one of the cases to carry through while the American Unitarian Association has life left to do it."[6]

The first week in May of 1877 found Henry and Anna Bellows making a trip to Washington, Baltimore, and Philadelphia. Bellows acted "like an experienced papa, taking a well-grown daughter on a round of visits to the neighboring sights!" But "she enjoyed the *show* & I enjoyed her delight. Better than all, I took her away quite an obstinate dyspeptic, & brought her home *cured*." He preached at the Baltimore church on Sunday 5 May and commented that he was not bothered by the poor acoustics of the church. He claimed that it was because of the echo some preachers like "John Ware, Mr. Weld, Edward Hale shout and drown their words in their own noise, & of course, find few churches without echoes—least of all the Baltimore!"

Coming back to New York on Tuesday evening, the following night, 8 May, Bellows and the remaining members of the United States Sanitary Commission met at Bellows's home and disbanded the Sanitary Commission, "which has had so many odds & ends of work left in its hands, as never get to be able to close its life . . . As one of the serious labours of my life, I naturally feel a good deal of interest in the *closing* scenes of the commission's existence!"[7]

Thus seventeen years after its birth the United States Sanitary Commission officially closed itself down. Bellows had tried for some years to get the United States government to join the Geneva

Convention of the International Red Cross, for the Sanitary Commission was doing the work on the battlefields of the Civil War that the International Red Cross had been established to do in 1864. He had never gotten any show of interest from the Congress in regard to America's affiliation with the international body. So he literally gave up, and probably the feeling then current that America would not need the International Red Cross because in what was conceived to be an age of progress there was never going to be another war. Clara Barton, a Universalist from Oxford, Massachusetts, finally persuaded the United States to join the International Red Cross as Bellows lay on his deathbed less than five years later. She receives credit for the establishing of the American Red Cross, and Bellows's memory is largely absent from the official histories.

Bellows's most famous parishioner, William Cullen Bryant, went into New York from Roslyn on the morning of 29 May and spent the morning at the office of the *Evening Post* conferring with the members of his staff. After lunch, Bryant was driven in his carriage to Central Park where a bust of Giuseppe Mazzini, the Italian patriot, by the sculptor G. Turini, placed at the park entrance on the West Drive opposite 67th Street was to be dedicated. It was a hot day, and Bryant took shelter under the trees with the other participants until the program began. There were several preliminary addresses before Bryant's part on the program. Finishing his address he returned to his seat and listened to an address in Italian by one of the sponsors of the affair. James Grant Wilson, a Civil War General and author, suggested that the two go to his home for some refreshment. Bryant refused the proposal of a carriage, and the two walked to Wilson's home at 15 East 74th Street. Wilson had tried to hold an umbrella over Bryant's head, but he refused that also.

When they arrived at Wilson's home, Wilson went in to open the inner door. While he was unlocking the door Bryant fell backwards and struck his head on a paving stone. He was carried unconscious into the parlor, but soon recovered and insisted that he go to his own New York home at 24 West 16th Street, where he was put in the care of his niece. The condition was considered serious but the self-reliant Bryant even refused to let his pulse be taken.[8]

Bellows was in Boston for some ministerial meetings at the time. He was in suspense about Bryant's condition on 31 May; "the suspense," he wrote, "attending Mr. Bryant's condition. . . . I rather expect to find him *dead* or dying tomorrow. The papers hold out hopes of his recovery, but I have *less* than his doctors, which can seldom be measured by what they confess. Well, it is hardly to be wished that he should survive any serious shock to a brain as old as his." Bellows continued, "When he falls the column will shake the best part of the country. His is a great fame, made solidly by serious, faithful persistent strides, under a real inspiration. . . There is nothing to decay in his work—no careless phrases, no fashion of passing thought or utterance, no extravagance, no sentimentalism, no sing song music." Bellows believed that Bryant's "themes have been, if somewhat few, universal in their interest. He has dealt with nature in her inner spirit & her most significant roles and fortunes. He said what he felt & saw . . . & not to tickle others."

Bellows also had a criticism, "He has not dealt with humanity, except as he has seen it reflected in Nature's face, not with man at work with man, or in conflict with him, but in communion with mother nature. There is little individuality in any of his few men & women. I don't know that he has created one *personality* in all his poetry." Bellows went on, "but for pure & genuine sentiment, & for delicate unaffected presentation of the influence of Nature, who exceeds him!"[9] Bellows was obviously preparing his own mind for what he knew inevitably was in the offing, a funeral sermon about his parishioner and friend.

Bryant wanted something very simple for his funeral. He had told his daughter, Julia, that he wanted his funeral to be conducted as quietly as possible with burial beside his wife at Roslyn. Shortly before the poet's death, Bellows was consulted, and "protested [this simplicity] on the ground that Bryant 'was a public man and a private funeral would be inappropriate'."[10] A compromise solution was arranged. The body would be taken to the church before the service, there would be no procession, no pallbearers in the church, and the audience would be dismissed following the sermon. Bryant's daughter, Julia, felt that even this would be inappropriate, but was overruled by the others. Meanwhile, Bryant's life was ebbing away, and he died in his sleep on the morning of 12 June.

On 13 June, Bellows wrote, "Bryant is gone! & I am full of preparation for his funeral tomorrow in our church."[11] Julia reluctantly agreed to the desire of Bryant's friends that a funeral service be conducted at the Church of All Souls, and, indeed the rite, despite efforts made to preserve dignity, was of such a character that Bryant would have been horrified.

It seems that an hour before the service was to begin at ten o'clock on the morning of June 14th, the church was surrounded by a multitude of people. When the coffin was brought to the church from the Bryant home, police were unable to clear a passage, and it was forced through the crowd. When the doors were opened, the people pushed forward, the police being unable to control the mob, and the church was immediately filled, with a crush of standees in the aisles, in the balcony, and in the lobby outside the auditorium.[12]

The coffin was placed before the pulpit and covered with a black shroud. It had been requested that there be no flowers, and there was only one floral piece, a white bouquet given by Bryant's employees. There were two other baskets of flowers on the communion table. The "Andante" from Beethoven's Seventh Symphony was played as an organ prelude (a popular use of the organ at that time was to play symphonic music), and a quartet sang a hymn. Bellows used the King's Chapel Service for the dead, and offered a prayer. There was another hymn. Bellows then gave his address which ended with a quotation from Bryant's poem, "June." The service ended with the choir singing Bryant's hymn, "Blessed Are They that Mourn," and the recital of the Lord's Prayer.

In the funeral oration, Bellows stated that Bryant "had never been a communicant in any church until he joined ours, fifteen years ago."[13] He commented that from that time on Bryant appeared at church morning and evening in regular attendance until the last

Henry Whitney Bellows preaching at the Funeral of William Cullen Bryant in All Souls Church, June 11, 1878, From Frank Leslie's Illustrated Magazine, *June 29, 1878, All Souls Archives*

month of his life. Bellows attributed this regular attendance to the fact that Bryant in the last twenty years of his life had shown "an increasing respect and devotion to religious institutions and a more decided Christian quality in his faith." Bellows commented that Bryant's last years were his devoutest and most humane years.

One must remember the difference between actually joining a church and owning a pew in a church. For many years Bryant had owned a pew at both the First Church and the Second Church, alternating his attendance between the two churches depending upon who was the minister. When Bellows came to New York, Bryant's devotion was to the First Church or All Souls. But he evidently never joined the church until about 1863. (The church has no known records of actual church membership during these years, only pew records.)

Bellows painted Bryant's character as that of a man who found it difficult to be with people. "The editorial profession enabled his shy and somewhat unsocial nature to work at arm's length for the good of humanity and the country." Bryant, he said, knew his own personal limitations and respected them. "He loved and honored human nature; he feared and reverenced his Maker; he accepted Christianity in its historic character; he believed in American institutions; he believed in the church and its permanency, in its ordinances and its ministry; and he was no backward-looking praiser of the times that had been and a mere accuser and defamer of the times that are."

A special train took the remains and the members of the funeral party to Roslyn. Bryant's grave was beside that of his wife Frances in the village cemetery. For the graveside ceremony Bellows chose passages from Bryant's own poems about death. The coffin was lowered into the ground, and girls from the Sunday school class of the Roslyn church walked in a circle around the grave and threw in flowers.

Bellows, personally, was impressed with the funeral services. After he returned from Roslyn on the private train with perhaps fifty other persons he wrote, "The funeral in our church was very impressive from the solid worth & high position of the dense crowd of citizens of all religious names & all sorts of societies, who gathered to honor Bryant's memory. I have never seen such an assembly in New York!" The family had asked that Bellows do the entire service in the church and at graveside, and this pleased Bellows and simplified the funeral. Bellows indicated that the selections which he had read at the graveside from Bryant's poems which spoke of death had been collected together by Bryant's own brothers, and Bellows thought that they were "wonderfully apt & impressive." He liked the simple touch of the young girls filling the grave with flowers after the service.[14]

Bellows left the day after the funeral to give the Baccalaureate at Cornell. Here he was greeted by his friend William Channing Russell, the son of Lucy Channing Russel, who had told the neighbors of William Ellery Channing's speech in the Russel home in 1819, and now was the President of Cornell College. (He had added an extra "l" to his father's name.) Bellows went on to Yellow Springs, Ohio, to give a graduation address at Antioch College. From these familiar places he went to an even more familiar one, and visited Orville Dewey at Sheffield, Massachusetts. He found Dewey *"weaker* than I feared, extremely feeble, emaciated, & dead-eyed, disposed to lie upon the couch most of the time & capable of only short interviews." Bellows commented, "He looked death-struck to me," although "very affectionate." Bellows was very worried that Dewey was not convinced of the reality of immortality. He did not feel that Dewey "could be any more *certain,* than *we* are certain of the immortal witness of Spirit & personal Spirit, to its own eternity."[15]

From Sheffield, Bellows went on to the homestead at Walpole. There he wrote that he finally was unwinding and beginning to get some rest. "I am slowly subsiding into indolence & wholesome stupidity; have had more than a fortnight of struggle with my active habits and the momentum of the machine. At length, the heat of the year's campaign, dies down, & I begin to cool off in brain & to grow indolent & apathetic. I *hate* it—but it is very wholesome! Not that I ever *feel* well in vacations. My artificial life has become normal, & I *feel* best when hardest at work & most driven."[16]

It was an unusually quiet summer for Bellows. In July he did almost nothing but rest. In August he preached at Charlestown, New Hampshire, in Worcester, in Newport at the Channing Memorial Church, and again at the "popular preaching" of the denomination at Saratoga Springs.

The third week in September, just before the fall season began at the New York church, he spent the week at the Convention of the General Conference at Saratoga, "a busy & exhausting week." But Bellows somehow got through it "without damage to health or activity." On Monday 16 September on the way to Saratoga a train from Boston in which there were "thirteen cars from Boston full of Unitarians . . . the passenger train had a collision with a cattle train, twelve miles this side of Albany . . . which spoiled *two* engines, crumpled up the *tenders*, & wrecked the baggage car." The accident, Bellows claimed, "occurred purely from carelessness. We were half an hour behind time—& the brakes on our express train had been rendered knowingly useless, by interposing a Pullman car (breaking the steam-connection between the engine & the cars) at the head of the train." When the engineer saw the freight train coming he *could not* stop. The freight train reversed its engine a mile away. The engineers and the firemen jumped for their lives just before the crash. It was startling but not terrific, and all that really happened was the loss of three hours on the way to Saratoga.

At the conference Brooke "Herford of Chicago gave an excellent opening sermon, Clarke a glorious essay on the New Theology, & Carroll Everett a still more consummate discourse on the New Ethics." Bellows felt that there was a new spirit in the conference. There were 2,500 people present. But "the quality of the delegates . . . the earnest desire to go to work—the harmony, breadth & elevation of sentiment—were beyond any thing we have previously known. It was a true Pentecost." Bellows also was happy with the business sessions of the conference which had "carried all the points [he] had desired to put through, though not without some earnest debate." He commented, "I never *felt* so sure our dark days were over, & our cause likely to advance rapidly. . . . 'Mine eyes have seen thy salvation'."[17]

Saving the Second Church

Bellows continued to interest himself in the affairs of the Second Church. That society was without a pastor, in serious danger of going out of existence, and was trying to sell the church building to pay off the debt. Dexter A. Hawkins, a lawyer and active member of the church, wrote Bellows about an offer of which there is no record in All Souls minute books. "When we offered the property as a free gift to your society, provided you would move up there and carry on Unitarian worship in that building, it seemed to us to be the only way to save the property to the denomination, and, in fact, though not in name, save the society. We could then have brought a large additional strength to your society, with the additions we should have brought to it (it seemed to us), would have had no difficulty in clearing the property entirely of any debt." Mr. Hawkins continued his argument, "One strong society is far better than one middling one and one foundering one; and while it was great mortification to us to be under the necessity of nominally going out of existence, yet the satisfaction in seeing a strong Unitarian church worshiping in the building erected by us, would have been some compensation."[1]

Having worked so hard over the years in the establishment and maintenance of all four of the New York Unitarian churches, Bellows was not content to sit idly by and watch the Church of the Messiah go out of existence by having the building sold to another denomination. It is interesting that Bellows would take this attitude, because from his own point of view, All Souls stood to gain a great deal. Many of the members of the Church of the Messiah would undoubtedly gravitate toward the First Church if the Second Church went out of existence. But Bellows believed that there was a need for more than one strong Unitarian church in New York City. "The cause," as he frequently called it, loomed larger in his mind than his own parochial interests. He made a trip to Boston and talked with Rush R. Shippen, the Secretary of the American Unitarian Association. He suggested that one way to wake up the denomination to the possible demise of the Church of the Messiah was to hold a convention, at least of the Eastern churches, in the building of the Church of the Messiah, and thus to awaken interest in saving the church.

Rush R. Shippen went to work on the project with enthusiasm. He secured James Freeman Clarke to preach at such a convention, and got indications from Hale, Ware, Savage, Brooks, Dole, May, and Abbott that they personally would be present. He wanted to be certain that the real leaders of the denomination were present. The committee from the Church of the Messiah was enthusiastic about the project also; its members wanted Dr. Edwin Hubbell Chapin, the prominent Universalist minister, and some other Universalists and Swedenborgians to be invited. Shippen wrote, "We do not propose to go to New York for social junketting, but for an earnest practical meeting. I have specially left Wednesday afternoon open for a meeting of more practical sort to consider Church of Messiah affairs." He wanted to depend upon New York for the audience, and not "all the world."

Shippen also proposed that the Church of the Messiah write to the churches of the Eastern seaboard states and ask them to send their pastor and one or two lay delegates to the convention. And he added significantly, "I have not said to the Messiah committee that we propose to save their church; for they would too easily lie back on the denomination. But as the meeting approaches I will ask them to have all their figures & facts ready for private report." He continued, "my hope is that our meeting will rally and encourage them to do their best. And if *they* can come anywhere near saving the church, the denomination might join hands to do the rest."[2]

The convention was held early in December, and Bellows felt that "the names of the men present are themselves proof that we had a good time." Bellows wrote to Orville Dewey, "What a storm for a *convention* in the *Church* of the *Messiah* round which storms have hung so long . . . Clarke's sermon on the *Equivalents* in modern times of the old words of faith & the old historical facts was original & suggestive. Dole's paper was a little young but beautiful & able and well rec'd." The debates morning and evening had been "capital." Bellows remarked, "There is always more light than heat, & more theology than religion on these occasions." About the most important subject of the conference Bellows said, "I think there is one *chance* in ten that the Church of the Messiah may be saved. The display of interest by outsiders was encouraging. Plans are on foot to pay off the 1st mortgage of $68,000. Whether it can be managed is doubtful—but there is more chance than there was a week ago."[3]

Dexter A. Hawkins was appointed the chairman of a special committee at the Church of the Messiah to raise the funds. The committee began its work by publishing a financial statement. They laid the present financial condition of the church to the fact that when the church at Madison Avenue and 28th Street was sold in 1864 "we instructed the architect to give us a church and a chapel at a cost at the outside of $120,000 . . . When the buildings were half erected we discovered that the architect had planned a structure that would cost $320,000, instead of $120,000." The building committee had "stopped work at once, and ordered him to change the plans so as to reduce the cost to the lowest possible limits. The result was the present church, chapel and vestry, at a cost of $245,000 instead of $120,000. . . . This brought us in debt $165,000 instead of $40,000."

The report continued: "Notwithstanding the defection of two of our pastors [Osgood and Hepworth], we reduced the debt by 1 January 1875, to $100,000." Then Hawkins's committee gave a complete account of their present debts, the total amount owed being $122,741. Hawkins also pointed out that during the past seven years the society had raised for annual expenses declining amounts ranging from $12,707 in 1872 to $6,561 in 1878. But, he pointed out, it had been an average of $10,661 over the seven-year period. It was a depressing financial statement for a church. No wonder Bellows felt that one chance in ten to save the church was an optimistic estimate of the odds.[4]

A few days after the publication of this distressing report Hawkins wrote to Bellows to present a plan to liquidate the debt. He proposed that the Church of the Messiah members would raise $50,000 among themselves. He further proposed that the Church of All Souls contribute all the bonds originally taken by their members amounting to $22,000. He also suggested that the denomination through the American Unitarian Association contribute $50,000. This would liquidate the debt. He commented to Dr. Bellows, "Your people will not feel the $22,000 because it is bonds, and you are numerous and strong. Our people will lift a heavier burden in taking $50,000 from their small numbers than any Unitarian society has yet done. . . . But, they are willing to do it to save the extinction of our society & prevent this injury to the cause that would result from such a catastrophe in the metropolis of the country."[5] Hawkins enclosed the 11 December financial statement for Bellows. During the holidays the matter rested.

In January 1879 Bellows and the congregation of All Souls celebrated the occasion of the fortieth anniversary of his ordination and his assumption of the pastorate of the church. Bellows used the occasion to preach two consecutive sermons on 5 and 12 January containing his recollections of the history of the church. These were later printed by the congregation and widely distributed, and have constituted until recently almost the entire available knowledge of the past history of the church. The congregation was pleased with what constituted a major historical and recollective effort on Bellows's part. They sent their pastor some verbal tokens of their esteem and drew up a formal letter of appreciation. They felt that the discourses were "of permanent interest, not only as setting forth the history of the society, but because they narrate the growth of liberal ideas and a spirit of toleration in this community."[6]

Bellows soon began to have hopes for the Church of the Messiah. On the occasion of his fortieth anniversary he asked his own people to subscribe $22,000 by giving up their bonds and making gifts. They had already succeeded in getting more than half of the amount by 1 February 1879. The Church of the Messiah members themselves had subscribed $58,000, and the American Unitarian Association had agreed to give $25,000. It looked hopeful. "I feel most deeply grateful," Bellows wrote, "for the chance & the hope of seeing this awful reproach carried away, of a lost church in our little beleaguered fellowship."[7]

Early in February he also attended a meeting of the leading clergy of 300 churches "to consider the tenement house question &

the relationship of religious teachers to it." He commented that "half our population lives in *tenement* houses . . . often 2,000 in one great house; often ten in one room—& the death rate instead of being fifteen–twenty in 1,000—is often forty–fifty–sixty. But the loss of life is nothing to the loss of virtue, decency, civilization. Morality & Religion are powerless in the presence of such debasing & barbaric conditions." The subject was discussed by experts, and all present agreed "to preach a sermon" on the situation, to "arouse a simultaneous alarm & effort at reform."[8]

On 12 February Henry and Anna attended a party in celebration of Peter Cooper's eighty-ninth birthday. "It was a great occasion. . . . The Chancellor of the Board of Regents in gown & cap conferred the degree of L.L.D. upon the old gentleman, for his service to the cause of education." And Peter Cooper made "a nice written speech."[9]

On 19 February Bellows wrote to Orville Dewey that he thought he could "now say that the Church of the Messiah is *safe!*" There had been a meeting on 18 February of the representatives of the three parties at Bellows's house. Present were Rush R. Shippen of the American Unitarian Association, five trustees of the Church of the Messiah, and seven All Souls people, "& we all & each agreed to furnish the quota. The money is raised in the Church of the Messiah—$58,000; and can be collected in a week, the AUA is ready with its $35,000 [up $10,000], our bond-holders for $22,000 have about half *given* in their bonds, & we have pledged ourselves to buy out the rest at such a price as they may demand." The American Unitarian Association was to take "a silent & permanent mortgage (that is without interest) on the church for the joint sum of its contribution & ours ($57,500) to guard against all possible perversion." Bellows added, "We are all much elated."[10]

Bellows and Shippen of the American Unitarian Association were beginning to plan who should be asked to candidate at the shortly-to-be-saved Church of the Messiah. Shippen wrote to Bellows that he favored Brooke Herford of Chicago, if Chicago could spare him. But he felt that Herford "is really the needed ballast to our Western Unitarianism." His second choice was Charles Beard, the leading Unitarian preacher in England at the Liverpool church. Shippen's two top choices were a former Englishman and an Englishman.[11] The church finally ended up with a Welshman. People in New York City have a tendency to go abroad not only for symphony conductors but also for ministers of leading pulpits.

Bellows had some other suggestions, having been through a list of all the ministers: Lathrop of Syracuse, De Normandie of Portsmouth, Thayer of South Boston, and Dole of Jamaica Plain. But more than anything else Bellows hoped for an able and friendly colleague in the city. There had been too many changes and struggles in the Church of the Messiah. Writing to Orville Dewey, he commented, "I am ready & glad to think our churches may be on the terms they were when you & I were here side by side without one moment's conflict or coolness, or sense of separate interests."[12]

By 5 March, Shippen had somewhat changed his opinions about the Church of the Messiah pulpit. He wanted to be considered as a candidate for the post himself. He wrote to Bellows and quoted Ephraim Peabody of King's Chapel as saying that "while a few men can fulfill a successful life ministry in one place, most men achieve their best results by a succession of ten-year settlements—each one a preparation for better service in the next—and the last the crown and culmination of all that went before." Shippen mentioned to Bellows that he had been eight years in Chicago, twelve years in Worcester, and now had served eight years as Secretary of the American Unitarian Association. Shippen said although he did not want to seek the Messiah pulpit for himself, he felt that he was ready for it. But the Church of the Messiah was now looking again at Robert Collyer as it had some years before. Shippen wrote: "Until it is clear that Mr. Collyer cannot be had, & that there is no Starr King at command," he would be available.

Therefore, he concluded, "if the place & the people should *seek me*, I have such profound faith in the future possibilities of the opening, that God helping me I believe that by faithful administration in pulpit, Sunday school & social life, I could lead them forward to a growing & healthy & strong career."[13]

Not having heard from Bellows after a week about his proposal that he be considered for the pastorate of the Church of the Messiah, Shippen was bewildered. "The silence grows pathetic! Is it ominous. . . . You always reply so promptly." He confessed that he probably should not have written in such a personal vein to Bellows. But if Collyer was not available—and he still believed that Collyer was the best man for the position—why should they not consider him? "It has been my good fortune to fill the two churches in Worcester & Chicago so that the *houses* had to be enlarged! It would be a pity not to have that happen to Messiah! I wouldn't spoil it."[14]

In order to prepare his address on the history of the Second Church which he was to deliver at the special ceremonies on 18 and

19 March, Bellows read for the second time, after a lapse of thirty years, Channing's 500-page volume of *Essays, Sermons and Reviews*. He got completely lost in reading Channing, and again began to think of Channing's importance in New York Unitarian history. A great deal of this crept into his address. In fact, he spent most of his time praising Channing and Orville Dewey. "I rejoice to say," he wrote to Dewey, "that the book not only justifies his great place in the church & the world, but I think it is more rare and wonderful than his reputation." He continued, "Strange to say, he shows the acquaintance of a man of the world, with all that is outside his profession, & exhibits a knowledge of great human passions & appetites which his fastidious purity & self-consecration have hidden from uncritical eyes."[15]

A special series of commemorative services were scheduled for Tuesday and Wednesday, 18 and 19 March 1879. 19 March was the fifty-fourth anniversary of the founding of the church in 1825. On Tuesday evening, 18 March Bellows was the featured speaker at the service.[16] Because his address was to be of major importance, the rest of the service consisted only of a hymn by William Lunt, the first settled minister of the Second Church, two anthems by the choir, and a prayer by Frederick A. Farley of Brooklyn. Bellows's discourse runs over forty printed pages, so one can imagine the length of time it took to deliver it. Bellows, in his address, pulled out all of the ecclesiastical and rhetorical stops that he knew. This was his opportunity to try to bring the people of this church to reason, so that with their pulpit vacant they would this time choose the right man and not be led astray as they had so many times before.

He began with rejoicing that the church had been saved. He praised the liberality of a few great men of wealth without whose gifts the debt could not have been lifted. Bellows made it quite clear that he also felt that his own parish's efforts were likely to be underrated because it had loaned the money years ago, and now had given up these loans of $22,000 as a gift. "I insist," he proclaimed, "that the conduct of the First Unitarian Church towards the Second, in its distress, and now for its deliverance, is worthy to be written in the brightest letters in the chronicles of our church histories."

Bellows also praised the courage of the American Unitarian Association in contributing one-third of all its capital to a single Unitarian church. This act was unprecedented, he said. He pointed out that "the American Unitarian Association is a missionary body, and it only rightly estimates its true duty and office in making great account of the maintenance and spread of our visible churches. The diminution of their number in New York would have been a calamity not easily overstated. . . . The AUA had the courage of its convictions," he said. The First Church in Providence had also been especially generous. But, he cautioned the congregation,

> the courage of the AUA still waits its vindication from the proven success which this church has yet to exhibit, in the wisdom of its choice of a new pastor, in its discreet and cautious self-management, in its stableness of purpose, its seriousness of spirit, and its power to gather in and hold and bless a congregation of united, docile and Christian worshipers. This is the only proof the denomination will accept of the prudence and wisdom of the course the association has taken.

Leaving the subject of the redemption from debt Bellows then went on to tell the history of the Second Church, its founding as an "Upper Church" from the First Church on Chambers Street, and its vicissitudes.

Finally Bellows waxed eloquent in one of the greatest passages he ever wrote, which is quoted in full because it is as true today as it was in 1879:

> Plainly, your future prosperity depends upon your being a Unitarian society, pure and simple, without compromises and without suspicion of wavering; upon your reliance upon the solidity, stableness, soundness of principle, clearness of views, and manifest seriousness and piety of your future minister—and on the patient and persistent method he pursues in building you up, not in puffing you up by false inflations. Pardon the fears we have lest you should be tempted to fall back into sensational ways, to put your trust in those princes whose royalty consists only in their scented breath and tricks of rhetoric, and who are better fitted to conduct caucuses than churches, and to fill theaters than sanctuaries. If you aim only at immediate success, a success of crowds, a success of music, a success of anything less than religious life, your well-filled churches fail in the midst of the most prosperous appearance with crowds of attendants, with ministers whose names are in every newspaper, and who are covered with academic degrees conferred by the reporters. Churches succeed too, when *religion* does *not* succeed at all—succeed by the suppression of Christianity, its perversion or its caricature. If you wish to avoid both these failures—the splendid failure of a church going to the hammer when its seats are crowded, or the mournful failure of a church shining like a sea-shell in purple and gold, when the spirit of religion is dead, or has crept out of its original home, you have only to fall in with the doubtless honest, but as doubtless mistaken notions of those who will tell you that your first need is *a minister who will draw*. What you

want is a minister who will make *religion* draw, and hold together what it draws! You want, first of all, a truly religious, a consecrated, an unfeignedly Christian man; not a fanatic, a sentimentalist, or an actor; not a man who thinks the power of religion lies in its forms or its vestments, but one that thinks it is the spirit of truth, of holiness and of righteousness; a man who regards religion as the principal thing, and watches for human souls to convert them to its peace, its joys and its ennobling gifts.

Bellows hoped that in their new minister they would find "a man of this spirit." He concluded this monumental address saying that he had "spoken with the plainness and authority of the oldest settled minister of our common faith here on the ground . . . who feels the sacredness of the cause for which our churches stand in the metropolis of America." He stated the challenge this way, "Let me see a vigorous, faithful, serious, consecrated minister placed at your head, and wisely and tenderly building up your church, and faith and life."

The next day Bellows wrote to Orville Dewey to give him a firsthand account of the ceremonies at the Church of the Messiah. Bellows told Dewey that his bust was "set against a screen of crimson velvet & surrounded (not touched or obscured) by delicate green leaves & flowers." Channing's portrait had been placed on an easel, "similarly garlanded." Bellows revealed to Dewey that his historical discourse had taken an hour and three-quarters to deliver, "with careful estimates of the services of Channing . . . & of your own ministry—with briefer accounts of Mr. Lunt, Dr. Osgood & the other ministers." The audience was "not so numerous as we had hoped." He said that "George W. Curtis made the best speech I ever heard him utter." Having shared these good things with Dewey, Bellows remarked that, "something worse than financial trouble has afflicted the 2nd Church! That we could retrieve. But it has *lost* by death & dispersion pretty much *all* that made it once great. It must be *another* congregation—little flavored with the old blood."[17]

CHAPTER FOURTEEN

The Old Warrior

I Begin to Feel My Limits

Robert Collyer had been called to be the minister of the Church of the Messiah, and after much persuasion had accepted. Bellows believed that Collyer was too showy and not the man for the job. Brooke Herford, vacationing in England, wrote to Bellows to reassure him that his colleague in Chicago was really more the man for the job than Bellows believed. "You fear that his work is that of a *flashy attractiveness* without the necessary element of *quiet religious power & permanent holding*" was the way in which Herford described Bellows's feelings. Herford then went on to tell Bellows of his own experience with Collyer in Chicago where they had worked together for three and one-half years: "When I came over [from England], I was by no means sure that the glamour which I had felt in his occasional society & speech would withstand the test of close & constant contact. But it *has* done."

He continued, "Indeed, considering how long he has been at Unity Church, & how he has been feeling for years the *strain* which has obliged him at last to make a change—there is still a wonderful freshness & vitality in his work & his influence, there. . . . Below the surface of the humorous lecturer etc.—there is a great strong heart of faith (growing more conservative), and a solid, broad *sense* which constantly comes out in counsel. Yes, and an amazing width of *culture*, too,—strong & real even if not very systematic." Herford described Collyer's talents, "Though nothing of an *organizer*, his church is the most active in *good works* of any of ours in the West (not in mere bazaars etc. but in *mission* work, such as the industrial school which his people have kept up thro' all these hard times). So much so, that Unity Ch[urch] will feel his loss in its *workings* less than most of our churches would feel the departure of its minister."[1]

Whether this personal word from Collyer's colleague in Chicago reassured Bellows there is no indication, nor do we know whether Bellows had expressed his opposition or doubts publicly about Collyer's fitness for the task so that someone pressed Herford to write to Bellows. Bellows had watched many tragedies at the Church of the Messiah with its ministers; he had lived through forty years of their problems. He had suggested in his address that after the debt was lifted they ought not to go after the popular preacher, yet this is exactly what they had done. He was justifiedly worried about the church's future. Fortunately for the Church of the Messiah Collyer turned out to be an excellent choice. He served as minister of the Church of the Messiah from 1879 until 1896 and then after Minot J. Savage had been the minister for ten years and had a nervous breakdown, Collyer stepped in again and served for one more year as the minister.

Although Bellows was now sixty-five years of age his ability to play with his children seemed to grow rather than to abate. He wrote to Dewey that the family was going to celebrate young Henry's fourth birthday on 26 August (his birthday was 25 August but a little cousin, Stuart, had a fourth birthday on 27 August so they compromised on 26 August). Bellows said: "[This] is the chief event of the summer . . . I have written 'a baby Pinafore'—a parody on the comic opera, which we shall sing (my organist comes from New York to help us!) & Russell from Newport, & Miss Bessie Hobbs from Waltham, & I have four nephews & nieces (Hattie's children, *here*) to help along. Pretty occupation for a Bishop of sixty-five." But in spite of the fun Bellows also was beginning to feel more and more the wear and tear of such an active life. "I begin to *feel* of my limits to see how they will bear the armour of another year's campaign! I am conscious of a little more shrinking from the battle, every season. But I suppose it will go on a little while longer!"[2]

Herford's letter must have had some effect on Bellows, for late in August he wrote a letter to Robert Collyer welcoming him to New York City and offering him the hand of a brother minister. Collyer realized that Bellows did not really want him to leave Chicago and come to New York. He wrote to Bellows, "You have also in your mind the frank and manly affirmation that you did not want me to make this change but I have kept saying to myself he will see the pleading in my eyes and hear it in my voice to sort of creep into his heart when I get down there. And he will take me in and his loving kindness will be all I can hope for and inspire and help me beyond all other things I shall find in my new field of labor." So when Bellows wrote to him, Collyer was overjoyed with the words of welcome.[3]

Bellows discovered that working for Civil Service reform inevitably meant becoming enmeshed in politics. Early in October 1879 the Civil Service group in which Bellows was active met to decide what their attitude should be toward the candidates in the coming election. "Whether we can honorably & conscientiously support the *least bad* of the *availables* or must stick to the *best*, available or not. It is maintained plausibly & even with truth, that the failure to elect a Republican ticket in New York *this fall*, endangers if it does not abandon the success of a Republican election in the coming Presidential campaign—an evil greatly to be deplored." The group decided, "We are enjoined by all the Republican organs to sacrifice our civil service scruples—to the exigencies of the election." Bellows felt that President Hayes had been "baffled & annulled—by the necessity of keeping harmony in the party." He went on to say that he would "maintain as President of the Club . . . the duty of maintaining our principles of anti-*machine* & anti-*available* nominations, in short of insisting upon the rights of intelligence & conscience, *within* the parties." He maintained, "*I* will not vote for men who tend to degrade politics by ignoring the claims of competency, integrity & energy in favor of mere *availables.*" He then went on to say that one should vote for such party candidates as he honestly could and to scratch the rest.[4]

The Minister's Institute was held in October 1879 at Providence, Rhode Island. Bellows termed it "a glorious success!" There were 150 ministers in attendance. He declared the essays "right noble, ripe & round & bristling with scholarship." These lectures were all given in the forenoons and there were debates each afternoon "led by picked men." Bellows felt that "the scientific spirit prevailed as never before, in the meetings of the institute proper, & it became a *school* where the best men taught 'eager pupils'." Rabbi Evthreit had held a large audience spellbound for two and a half hours while he talked about the Old Testament. Bellows also found "the orthodox clergy (who were steadily present from the City of Providence) greatly impressed with the scholarship, earnestness, openness & reverence of the discussions . . . It was a much more satisfactory meeting than Springfield, excellent as that was. As father of the scheme I am unspeakably grateful & proud of the child of my faith and hope."[5]

At the end of October Bellows made an assessment of how Robert Collyer was doing at the Church of the Messiah. The "pews are selling & letting fast . . . There is an excellent feeling & promise & he seems satisfied. I don't believe in the movement fully, but I shall gladly be proved a bad prophet. He at least is sweet & fraternal & I enjoy him & see him often."

Bellows had just spent several days in Boston and Cambridge in regard to the work of the Harvard Overseers, to which he had recently been elected by popular vote of the alumni. However, since he was not a resident of Massachusetts there was a problem. He wrote, "My *election* is still in dispute—but meanwhile I have my seat & have to attend to its duties only the more assiduously from being doubtful in my tenure of it." He felt that nothing but goodwill existed to his presence on the board, "But the statutes are, I think, *against it*. Yet it is doubtful *what* the final report will be on my case! It is only as involving a policy of *nationality* in the University as against *state-rights* that it is important . . . The alumni are resolved to make legal by sturdy appeals to legislative action. Personally it is a great annoyance to me to be an Overseer." He was called to Boston every few weeks on business, and the position took much time and strength.[6]

The Harlem church was in financial trouble, a seemingly persistent condition. The American Unitarian Association gave them an annual subsidy of $500. But their debt seemed constantly to grow. They had a $12,000 mortgage on the church, and two houses which were supposed to be rented did not bring in any income because one tenant failed to pay his rent and the other house was left empty. There was a strong feeling in New York and at headquarters in Boston that many people were moving into the Harlem area who were out of easy access to the Church of the Messiah or of All Souls and could be attracted to the Harlem church. There appeared to be a need for a church in this area of the city.

Russell Bellows had labored for some time with this church, but he had quit in despair. Now a Mr. Carlin was the minister. The congregation liked him, but the necessary financial support was still not coming from them. Rush R. Shippen of the American Unitarian Association wondered if the Harlem church expected to be bailed out by the association as had the Church of the Messiah. Shippen proposed to Bellows that when he preached for Putnam in Brooklyn on 16 November the leaders of the two New York churches and the leaders of the Harlem church should get together with him for a conference.[7]

By November Bellows had sized up Collyer's capacities and limitations as well. "Mr. Collyer has come, & got warm in his seat," he wrote to one of his former parishioners who had moved West. "He has a house full of people, and I dare say orders off some of my less fixed attendants. He is heartily welcome to as many as he attracts. You know that old brooms must get accustomed to being left hanging to the wall." Bellows continued, "but I must not do my people injustice! The truth is, they stick like burrs, & I see no signs of neglect. Mr. Collyer draws a different class from mine—people to whom familiarities & departures from pulpit etiquette are not offensive who like a laugh in summertime—& a proof that the minister doesn't feel the least 'stuck-up' in the pulpit."

Bellows also meditated on his own pulpit philosophy. "Well! I'm too old for their tricks, & was bred in a different school. But I don't mean to disparage Collyer, who is a genius in his way & a hearty, humane & religious spirit, very attractive & loveable. But he will strike a *wholly new* layer in New York—& it won't be what we commonly call the Unitarian folk." He continued in this vein, "Perhaps you who were brought up in the old way will say—so much the better! The Unitarians are too rational, too respectable, too cold! Well! They may be." Was Bellows becoming too complacent about his Unitarianism when he wrote, "But I like their kind, & the older I grow, the better pleased I am with the sort of folks that grow on our own vine. I am confident that there are no people on the planet wider-minded, purer-hearted, honester & more to be respected & loved, than just these chilly, egotistical, rational Unitarians."[8]

Bellows by special invitation gave the address at the Thanksgiving Service at Temple Emanu-El, then located at the corner of Fifth Avenue and 43rd Street (now located at Fifth Avenue and 65th Street). This congregation was of the Reformed Jewish faith. The secretary of the synagogue wrote to Bellows that they "were fully aware of the dogmatic differences that divide the denomination of which you are so illustrious a representative, and the congregation which we asked you to address." In a letter sent to Bellows after the event, the secretary of the board of trustees, Myer Sterze, further commented, "We know also that one of the cardinal principles underlying our faith, and upon which it rests, like a rock, is the firm conviction that finally mankind will worship in one Temple, to one God, and under the aegis of one common Brotherhood."[9] He commented that each group should work out in its own way the methods of worshiping God (a good Unitarian principle). The congregation wished to publish Bellows's address and requested a copy. The service was typical of the Reformed faith, the reading of the Thanksgiving proclamation, Prayers, Hymns, Adoration, and the Kaddish. Bellows's address was titled *Religious Toleration.*[10]

Bellows had prepared for this occasion well. He had read about the Feast of the Tabernacles in Smith's *Dictionary of the Bible*, and he had consulted Joseph Henry Allen's *Hebrew Men and Times*. He began his address by pointing out the origins of Thanksgiving in the Hebrew Feast of the Tabernacles. He praised the congregation for their belief that "the Lord our God is one Lord." He said, "One thing, perhaps the most characteristic and vital of all belonging to the Old Testament, its heart and soul—the proper unity of God,—the Christian church has left unappropriated and unhonored." It was in this common belief in the unity of God that Bellows felt his greatest sympathy with the Jewish congregation. He praised the Jewish people for having stuck to this belief: "In fidelity to the unity of God, you held the fort against the polytheism of ancient nations and the tritheism of the historical Christian church. You held it at a cost that never has been paid for any truth before nor since; for a longer time; and it was worthy of your national sacrifice." Bellows prophesied that the day would come when:

> philosophers and sages and saints will count as among the most shocking, deplorable and mortifying of all events in Christian history, the persistent persecution and ostracism that for almost the whole history of the church have been visited upon the people who could not become Christians without acknowledging another and a visible God, and who for this have been hated, despised and persecuted, until at last not religious charity, but political necessity, has secured them partial toleration.

Bellows realized how difficult it is for the Jewish religion, which holds that its law came down directly from God Almighty, to be tolerant at the same time of other beliefs. Yet people are becoming more tolerant, said Bellows. He quoted Gibbon's sarcastic yet true remark that "the various modes of worship which prevailed in the Roman world were all considered by the people as equally true, by the philosophers as equally false, and by the magistrates as equally useful, and thus toleration produced not only mutual indulgence, but even religious concord." And then Bellows said, "Thank God the toleration of indifference or universal skepticism is not the only kind possible. There is a toleration which springs from humility, the due knowledge of human limitations, and the loftier and nobler conception of the divine nature and character. There is a toleration which springs from a better acquaintance with the slow development of the human race . . . and above all by a better notion of the relation of the present to the past."

He thanked the congregation for the invitation to speak to them. "I know very well," he said, "that you are no more old-fashioned or orthodox Jews, and I am just as little an old-fashioned or orthodox Christian, and you have had not a great way to stretch your hand, nor I a great way to extend mine." He concluded his address by declaring, "It is going to appear that *God is himself tolerant*, and that he has always allowed himself to be served by truth of heart and purpose, in spite of errors of opinion."

It was a significant address on an important ecumenical occasion, and Bellows did not trust to an extemporaneous speech but carefully wrote out his address.

In December Bellows traveled to Washington on Civil Service reform business, and met with the President of the United States. "I have formed a higher idea of Pres. Hayes from seeing & talking with him, in the presence of his chief cabinet officers," he wrote. He felt that talking man-to-man with the President had given him new insights; "tete-a-tetes have their advantages."

Bellows also reported that 104 pews had been purchased or rented in the Church of the Messiah since Robert Collyer came. "They seem content, purposive & happy, & New York & Brooklyn have welcomed him warmly." He didn't "see any evidence of declining interest in [his] people." And fortunately the First Church was not "affected by the revival of the Messiah church, otherwise than favorably."

On a more personal note in his own immediate family, "the little children are growing in health & promise." Little Robert with his curls had become very attached to his father. Bellows spoke about "the tenderness these little folks have given to my old heart." He found young Henry to be a "very *thinking* child & *original* in all his ways. He mixes up his theology with his Mother Goose & startled me with the question—'I *know* there's a real Santa Claus—but is there a *real* God'?" His mother had overheard him preaching a sermon. "Think of the state of a child's mind of four years cavorting with theology, nursery rhymes, British politics & African jungle hunts at the same time!"[11]

The courts of Massachusetts now decreed that under the laws of the Commonwealth an Overseer of Harvard must be a resident of the state. This decision embittered many Harvard alumni, including Bellows himself. He wrote a rather pointed letter to Edward Everett Hale in response to Hale's condolences about the court defeat. Bellows wrote, "It's not my fault, but my misfortune that I was made the victim of the ill-considered revolution. But I think that it will finally come to this. There may be two or three overseers *at large* (to pacify the alumni & to represent the natural idea) added to the board, from whom eligibility is removed by act of legislature. That would be my remedy."[12]

A week later Charles W. Eliot reported to his brother-in-law that "a bill to make non-residents eligible for the overseers is well advanced in the legislature." Eliot had met with the Governor, the President of the Senate, and the chairmen of several important committees, and "was told that the bill would go through without any opposition." Eliot added, this "is a good year to try such a measure, for Harvard is strongly represented in the State-House."[13] Three days later Eliot wrote to Bellows again and assured him that the work that Bellows had done in regard to the endowment for the Divinity School was much appreciated. He mentioned the large gift of $75,000 from Mrs. Tileston of All Souls and said that many more $1,000 and $500 subscriptions were coming in. Eighteen persons had subscribed $1,000 each and twenty-six persons $500 each. Eliot added, "I hope you will go to the Harvard dinner & tell them some of your opinions about the Board of Overseers & the nationality of the university."[14]

On 6 March 1880, the baby whose imminent arrival Bellows had hinted to his friends some months previously was born. She was named Ellen with the middle name of Derby from Anna's familial line. To have a little girl gladdened the heart of Bellows, who would attain his sixty-sixth birthday some four months later. His friend William P. Tilden, a Unitarian minister in Boston, congratulated him on the new arrival, "A *daughter!* How tenderly Hennie & Bob-o-link will love their little sister. We can see them looking up at the awfully cunning little toes, and softly kissing the cheek of down."[15] Henry described Ellen as "a healthy, happy, sweet child—over whose cradle I bend in grateful love, many times a day." Anna was nursing Ellen, "without harm to herself."[16]

During the year 1880 Unitarians throughout the country celebrated the centennial of William Ellery Channing's birth at Newport, Rhode Island, on 7 April 1780. It was agreed that a new church should be erected in Newport, to be called the Channing Memorial Church. The local congregation raised some of the money, but other amounts were subscribed throughout the country. Bellows reported that "we have subscribed about $3,000 in our church towards the *Memorial Church*; & it is likely to go through." He was also confident that "there is a great interest reviving in Channing from the stir now making."[17]

Bellows reported to Orville Dewey that interest in Channing was aroused "in many different places. In London, Montreal, Chicago, Cincinnati, Washington, Brooklyn, Newport, there have been celebrations in which statesmen, judges, divines of many sects, have lead crowds of enthusiastic disciples or beneficiaries, in all-day-long testimonies to the beauty & benignity, and sanctity of Channing's life & writings." This upsurge had surprised "even those best prepared." Two thousand people came to the meetings at Newport from all parts of New England.

The Brooklyn celebration "was a thing wholly exceptional in spirit and fervour . . . Similar accounts come from London & the great western cities." Bellows felt that "our liberal Christianity was after all, the *very thing* good people wanted!" And in his enthusiasm, he expressed a great deal of wishful thinking: "They will see that the old regime of Trinitarian & Calvinistic theology is pretty much over, & will feel inclined to say little about the awful infidelity of Unitarianism." Bellows congratulated Dewey for having been so close to Channing, and that he had "lived to see such a day as the 7th of April!" He wrote, "few have done as much as you to make that day possible. God knows how *unwilling* controversy has been . . . to all our leaders. But this battle made our peace."[18]

The Wade School of Religious Philosophy

A young man from Oswego, New York, Charles E. Perkins, had been writing to Bellows about becoming a Unitarian minister. Now he wrote Bellows asking for a photograph. Bellows's reply was revealing. He wrote that he had been "over my few photographs to find one that will not prejudice you against your yet unseen friend." So long as Perkins did not see this photograph Bellows felt that the young man could give "unbridled rein to your fancy & make me what your benevolence will. But when you come to study my picture, I'm afraid you will say, 'Well! it's not what I should have expected'." Bellows did not think that life had breathed on him unkindly. "For a man in the *last* half of his *last* decade—I am in vigorous health, I can work six hours a day & play then three more! I can walk my four miles without much fatigue." He had many plans for the future: "I have a great deal of reading & writing to do,—a large correspondence, much public responsibility—many social duties, frequent public appearances to make—an intellectually exacting congregation—a wide literary & artistic acquaintance—& a deep concern for all the political, social & religious life of the city & nation. You will find evidence of this in my bare crown, my deep-graved wrinkles & my battered face." But he hoped that one would "see behind all evidence of settled tranquility—the fruit of a most happy & fortunate life—passed amidst great interests & earnest thots & labors."[1]

On 29 May 1880, Bellows received an invitation to give the oration to the alumni of the Harvard Divinity School, at a convocation to be held on Tuesday evening, 29 June. F. W. Hooper of Keene, New Hampshire, wrote to Bellows that the Honorable Horatio Colony, President of the Alumni, would give an address of welcome. This was to be followed by Bellows's oration, and then "a short *original poem* by Theodore C. Williams of Cambridge, Mass." Williams, a graduate of Harvard, was orator of the class of 1876. He had taught three years and was now a student at the Harvard Divinity School. "He is very promising." Hooper hoped that there would be 200 people present, graduates of the school, and some people of Keene.[2] The reference to Theodore Chickering Williams is interesting for in three years Williams was to become Bellows's successor at All Souls, and was to be known primarily as a poet and hymn writer.

Henry and Anna Bellows were invited to George F. Baker's summer home at Atlanticville, New Jersey, in early June. Anna was worn out from bearing her third child. It was an enjoyable stay, but it was cold. Bellows wrote his usual letter to his children contemplating his birthday on 11 June. The summer was spent at Walpole, as usual.

Toward the end of the summer, Bellows spent several days with Cyrus Bartol who had bought seventy-five acres of land at Manchester, N.H., and was in the midst of developing it into home sites. Bellows admired Bartol's business acumen and predicted that with such foresight, he might make his daughter a millionaire if he just held on to the land long enough. Then he went over to Portsmouth to see De Normandie. Edward Hall of Worcester was also in attendance to work on the program for the Saratoga conference. He went sailing three afternoons, sunned on Rye Beach, boated out to the Isle of Shoals, went to Boston and back to Walpole, a trip which he found exhilarating.[3]

By the middle of September Bellows was back in New York to begin the season's work at All Souls, leaving the family behind to enjoy the country air of Walpole. He wrote, "I am just going to begin again the work of my life—to open the dear old church & to hold forth the word of life to the people I have long tried to lead in the paths of truth & holiness. It is always a solemn & trying moment with me, & especially when every year is so uncertain, & my strength & ability to work are so soon to leave me." He continued in a self-critical vein, "I see all the defects & limitations of my ministry, lament my mistakes, & yet see how hopeless it is now to correct them. No man knows *how* God is using him & his limitations are overwhelmed by the wisdom which is *over* him. It is not that my ministry has not been a successful & prosperous one for *me*, but I lament that it has not been efficacious to the extent of my desires for others." Bellows felt that it was "useless to repine, & I must not complain because God did not give me greater power & skill to fulfill purposes that he will accomplish by better instruments in his own time."

Bellows reminded himself that so many of his friends of middle age were passing away one by one. "I sometimes fear our congregation has seen its best days, & I grieve as I look forward to its possible decline, when soon I must resign my leadership to become only a memory! But all is in the hands of the Infinite Wisdom & Goodness." He dreaded also the coming conference at Saratoga for he foresaw a crisis in the denomination. He felt a "lack of coherency, cooperation and zeal." He felt that if the conference wanted to, it "could correct our mistakes & organize ourselves efficiently—but I doubt if this will exists, & so I cannot foretell what a week may bring forth."[4]

The next day, Bellows, accompanied by Russell and Annie, went to the conference where they spent five days at the United States Hotel. There were 600 delegates present and 2,000 volunteer attendants. Bellows was still chairman of the council and so he had "the chief responsibility." He commented that it was a "very spirited & successful meeting & gave us all much encouragement." He had come home "dreadfully tired with the speeches" and "all of the social excitement." He remarked that "the better time you have the more emptied of all energy and life" you become.

He and his two oldest children returned to New York to find that Anna had come down alone from Walpole with the three younger children. Bellows described Ellen at seven months as "a

lovely piece of good nature, happiness & health. She has never had a
drop of food except from her mother who, for the first of her three
children, has been able to keep on nursing—which made her proud
and happy."⁵ Annie, Henry's daughter, went back to Walpole to
enjoy the October foliage.

In October Bellows made a long journey to dedicate two
churches, the first in Auburn, New York, where he was also invited
to address the students at the Auburn Seminary (an orthodox
Protestant seminary now merged with Union Theological Seminary
in New York City) and the second in Cleveland, Ohio, where he
found the new church "a beauty of stone . . . & all paid for, & every
pew taken."⁶ He also believed Mr. Hosmer to be a fine minister.
This last visit to Cleveland was to be an important event, for in
Cleveland he met Mr. Jeptha Homer Wade, whom he interested in
Meadville Theological School, and with whom he was to have
dealings for the remaining year of his own life.

The trip had been almost too much for Bellows's health. He was
ill for ten days at the beginning of December, and went away to
Lakewood with Anna and the baby to stay for five days. He returned
to New York in much better health. But he was confined to the house
and commented, "I lie on the sofa & am *told* to be quiet."⁷

On 24 December, Charles W. Eliot wrote to Bellows that the
"money for the Divinity School was obtained and $10,000 over."
Eliot commented that "it was an excellent committee, and the cause
was good."⁸ So once again Bellows had been successful in
contributing to the health of an institution in which he believed, and
certainly the Harvard Divinity School was one closest to his heart.

Bellows did not have a good December; he did not write a single
sermon. He was afflicted with "nervous dyspepsia," and what he
called "Job's ills [boils]—which have beset me behind and before."
On 28 December Dr. Edwin Chapin, the minister of the Fourth
Universalist Church of New York, and much beloved by many in all
denominations, died; he was just the same age as Bellows. Bellows
commented about him, "I have never been intimate with him. His
breeding placed him in another circle."

Bellows felt that Chapin was "a thoroughly good fellow,
devout, sincere, and wondrous eloquent. But he was *coarse*, &
mingled so much that was doubtful and low tone, with his ordinary
social intercourse, that I eventually gave him a wide berth." Bellows
wrote that he would "miss his kind, genial, hearty voice. He was
very unsectarian & had the good will of all the clergy." About

Chapin's preaching, he commented, "I'm afraid he did not preach very *instructively*. He was more or less an emotional rhetorician—who fed himself in the aromatic thought or *language* of modern times—& buried in a sort of sacred obscurantism, all definite lines of doctrine! I think he contributed nothing to the *thought* of this community tho a good deal to its *delight*."[9]

All of his illness and gradual loss of strength and power led Bellows to contemplate his future as the minister of the Church of All Souls. On 9 January 1881, in place of the morning sermon Bellows read a "deliberate Apostolic Epistle" to his congregation. This address "concerned the whole conduct of our affairs—Sunday school, charities, pulpit & pastoral work. But the nub of the whole was the declaration, that the interests of the congregation, & my own health & comfort, required the appointment of a *curate, assistant, colleague,* or whatever he might be called, to preach in the second service, to preside in the S[unday] school, & to fill in & fill out, all the deficiencies & growing negligencies in my work."

Bellows proposed to support his colleague by deducting from his salary the cost of such assistance, although if one looks at Bellows's financial situation, which is spoken of despairingly in his letters, one wonders how he could even have contemplated this drop in level of his salary. As an alternate plan Bellows declared his "deliberate purpose to resign & retire—to make way for a full successor." He did all of this under the advice of his physician, Dr. Draper, and after he had talked over the matter with his wife and older children. All of this came "after several weeks of painful deliberation." The annual meeting was to be held on 11 January, and Bellows hoped that the congregation would take some action officially.

He commented that among the congregation "there is a good deal of flutter & surprise & agitation of heart," and he hoped that there would be "some earnest . . . *frank* discussion of these alternatives." Yet he did not think the people would let him go. He found preaching "much more exhausting than formerly & it always takes me two days to get over Sunday!" He believed that he had "used up [his] *capital* of nervous power, too freely, & must put myself on half or quarter rations!"[10] He had had these "fits of nervous exhaustion" before, one in 1848 when he went to Europe, one in 1867 when he went to Europe and the Near East, and one in 1873, when he went South for his health and met Anna.

A good deal of the energy of the last year of Bellows's life was devoted to the proposed establishment of a Unitarian Theological School in Cleveland, Ohio. Although Bellows had been very active and successful in raising money for his own Harvard Divinity School he also realized that there was need for another theological seminary with less academics and more practical training for the ministry than at Harvard. We have seen that Bellows also had been active in gaining support for the Meadville Theological School. The proposition of the Wade Theological School came from his visit to Cleveland where he met the aging wealthy philanthropist, Jeptha Homer Wade.

Jeptha Homer Wade was a financier and one of the founders of the American commercial telegraph system. He was born at Romulus, in Seneca County, New York, on 11 August 1811. As a young man he learned the trade of a carpenter. He became interested in art, however, and studied with Randall Palmer, a local portrait painter. From 1837 until 1842 he traveled through New York, Louisiana, and Michigan as an itinerant portrait painter. When the telegraph was invented in 1844, Wade began to study its commercial possibilities, and built a one-line telegraph system from Detroit to Jackson, Michigan. Other "Wade" lines followed in quick succession between Midwestern cities. His line and those of others were gradually consolidated until in 1856 most of them were combined into the Western Union Telegraph Company with Wade as general agent. He also pushed a line into the Far West, from Salt Lake City to San Francisco, which was completed in 1861. In 1866 he became general manager of the enlarged Western Union.

In 1856 he established his residence in Cleveland, and became very closely identified with many business enterprises in Cleveland, organizing in 1867 The Citizens Savings & Loan Association. He was also active in railroad building and management. He was modest, easily approached, and an interesting conversationalist who never lost his interest in painting and music.[11]

Bellows visited Wade while at the dedication of the Cleveland church, and developed a deep personal relationship with him. In fact, it appeared that whenever Bellows negotiated with Wade, large things appeared about to happen; when others took over, they failed.[12]

Bellows approached Wade, hoping to get a large endowment for Meadville. It soon became apparent that Wade wanted to endow a theological seminary, but that he wanted it to be in Cleveland and not in an obscure Pennsylvania town such as Meadville. He owned a large area of land in the very heart of Cleveland, and it was part of this tract which he proposed to donate for a merged school. The school was to be built on a parcel of land consisting of eight acres, in the very center of a hundred-acre tract that Wade was donating to the city. This same tract of land now houses the Cleveland Museum of Art, so it was indeed a central location.

Like most wealthy men, Wade found it difficult to know how to give away his money. Everyone wanted his money and the pressures were intense. He wrote, "there are two very difficult things to do—one is to make a fortune [which he seems to have accomplished rather easily], and the other is to know what to do with it."[13] He wanted to do something for which the people of Cleveland would remember him. He desired to help the Unitarian cause because his late only son was interested in the Unitarian religion. Whether he understood the internal conflicts within Unitarianism when he proposed the gift is somewhat doubtful. But before the whole affair was over he certainly understood these conflicts for they, along with Bellows's death, torpedoed the entire project.

A factor that undoubtedly interested Wade was, he wrote to Bellows, that "Mr. Case left property worth about $1,000,000 to establish the 'Case School of Applied Science' to be located here" (that is, on land adjacent to that owned by Wade). "It is expected and almost certain that the Western Reserve College will be moved from Hudson to this city." He continued, "if your institution should also come here and be made equal to the others, would not that reap advantages by being together? And would it not make Cleveland such an educational center as to attract endowments and support that could hardly be expected if separate and in country villages?"[14] Wade wanted to make his gift equivalent to that of Case. That was a mighty proposition.

Bellows very shortly realized that this merger in Cleveland was going to be a more difficult proposition than simply to receive a check from Wade for the half-million dollars first proposed. There was Meadville to be considered, and probably this was the tenderest proposition of all, for very few men in that school would want to move to the city of Cleveland. But Bellows soon discovered that it was Wade himself who constituted the most serious problem. Wade had some very strange ideas of his own as to what constituted the basis of a theological school to be erected in his memory.

On 24 November, just after receipt of Wade's letter of 22 November, offering to endow the school, Bellows wrote to A. A.

Livermore, the President of Meadville, that he wished he "were able to see you & the Huidekopers brothers, face to face, & say what I must now imperfectly *write*." He told Livermore that all of this had to be kept in confidence. He sent copies of Wade's letters and hoped that all of the questions would be asked at this time. He indicated that there might be some trouble with Wade. "He is a level-headed, generous, noble-minded man—but *daft* on *Spiritualism*, & with most of the limitations of self-educated or *non*-educated men who have become rich, & are growing old." Bellows found "the pecuniary possibilities . . . to be very *tempting*."[15]

The great question mark in the whole transaction was the attitude of the people at Meadville, both the board of trustees and the professors. None of the residents at Meadville could be expected cheerfully to be uprooted from their lovely rural surroundings and move to the large city of Cleveland. On 27 November 1880, an informal meeting of the trustees was assembled. The trustees seemed cordial to the idea although probably not a single one of them ever expected the idea of moving to Cleveland to come to fruition. However, they raised the usual objections to the merger of schools or the going out of existence of a school and moving to a new location.

There was the problem of the appointment of a new board of trustees, and who was to decide who the trustees were to be. There were the usual legal problems connected with endowments, particularly since Ohio was a different state from Pennsylvania, with different laws. Their conclusion was that they would yield in the decision to the larger Unitarian body, namely the Council of the National Conference of Unitarian Churches and the American Unitarian Association. These two boards met in Boston on 13 December 1880 and found the proposition satisfactory, even with the inclusion of a chair on the study of spiritualism. They also appointed a committee consisting of Henry Bellows, H. P. Kidder, and Alfred Huidekoper (later replaced by Grindall Reynolds) to consult with Jeptha Wade.

This committee met with Wade in Cleveland on 16 January 1881. Bellows described the visit in at least two letters, one to Dewey and one to Hale. To Dewey he wrote that Wade was a little less enthusiastic than he once was "to turn over half a million dollars, to a theological school, sustained by a sect as small & unpopular as ours—& to a school which must continue to be small for his life-time." Bellows was "not *certain* that the plan will work & [we] must cultivate patience & submission."[16]

At the meeting "all did not run smoothly" because Wade, probably on the advice of his lawyer, had some new conditions to make "not in the original proposal." He also proposed to give another quarter of a million dollars over a five-year period if it were to be matched by the Unitarians. And Bellows doubted whether "in our languid body, it could be carried out at all." This proposal had awakened adverse feelings among the Meadville people.

Bellows also began to see that Wade's proclivity as a moneymaker was at work. He had control of 400 acres on Euclid Avenue. He proposed to give 100 of these to the city for a park and for the theological school. But he proposed to subdivide the other 300 acres, and recoup all of his generosity by selling this land at a good profit. Western Reserve College had purchased forty acres directly opposite Wade's holdings. Bellows commented that it was good financially for Jeptha Wade, "since it would make that end of the city an academic centre, & soon draw homes & buildings to the neighborhood. I think he means to play off the park bequest against the scheme of the citizens,—to force them by a regard to their interests, to assume a burden which no doubt they might otherwise shrink from shouldering."

This kind of scheming irritated Bellows, and he was sorry to be a part of it. Bellows said that he was "not disposed to hurry, coax, flatter, or beg. It is bad policy & bad morals." Bellows had been perfectly frank with Wade and had told him how few Unitarians there were so that the school would never be large. Bellows was not "*discouraged,* but [could] only see difficulties to be overcome with a patient spirit." Wade had proposed that the Unitarians should advance a quarter of a million dollars to match his quarter of a million, and that this should include the endowments both of Meadville and Antioch. Bellows wrote Hale to see if the Antioch funds could be transferred.[17]

With these mounting complications Bellows began to wonder if the struggle was worth the price. He wrote that "nothing would induce me to stick at it, instead of backing out & letting it gracefully fall through, except the feeling that even if it shortened my life & burdened my decline, it is a cause worth laboring, suffering & dying for—& one in which it would not be unwise on me to engulf myself what remains of my nearly finished career."[18]

The matter lay in quiescence until the end of June when Edward Everett Hale, who was in Ohio on other matters, visited Cleveland at Wade's request to talk over the matter of the school. Wade obviously wanted to proceed with his development plans. Hale was enthusiastic after the meeting, for it seemed as if some of the difficulties could be overcome in the financing of the school. Wade said that eight acres had been set aside for the school in his park area. And he proposed that the endowment of the school be $500,000, of which Wade would give half; Meadville was to give $150,000, and the American Unitarian Association $100,000. Hale did not know where this money would come from, but made a counterproposal that the American Unitarian Association should raise $5,000 each year which would be the equivalent of a $100,000 endowment. To this Wade agreed. Everything seemed to be moving again.[19] The Wade School was to be a broader school than just a seminary. The breadth was suggested by the six areas of the professorships that Hale listed for Wade:

1. The Christian religion;
2. the Comparative Study of Religious Systems;
3. the Literature of Religion and the arts of expression;
4. the History of Religion;
5. the Mutual Relations of Body, Mind, and Soul (this was evidently Hale's concession to the study of spiritualism);
6. Social Science, and the care of the suffering classes.

Hale saw no reason why the plan could not now go through.[20]

A meeting of the committee of Bellows, Kidder, and Alfred Huidekoper was called for in Boston on 29 July. It was unfortunate, indeed, that Huidekoper was prevented from attending because of illness. He was replaced by Grindall Reynolds, a Meadville trustee, but one of the few on the board who really favored the plan to move to Cleveland. This committee drew up a document, and Hale secured Wade's consent with a visit to him in Cleveland. But Wade had a new condition. He reserved the right to retract his gift if at the end of three years the Unitarians had not raised their full $250,000. With this new condition in mind, Bellows and Reynolds met at Walpole on 29 and 30 August with Dorman B. Eaton, a prominent New York lawyer, and an active member of Bellows's church. Eaton insisted that it was legally unsound for a document to be worded as a contract between Wade and the American Unitarian Association. Thus, on Eaton's advice, the new document was made binding only on Jeptha Wade.

The change angered Wade exceedingly. He wrote to Bellows, "very likely your lawyer is an able one as you suggest but seems to be on the wrong side." He said that he could not execute the document because he was obligated to pay the $250,000 "as may be needed or asked for by said association." But the American Unitarian Association "don't agree to pay *anything.*" He was worried about how such an agreement could be enforced. "Certainly *I* shall not try to enforce it. . . . You speak of bringing the same lawyer here to arrange with me further details. I can only say it would be a waste of time. We shall have to get at it in some other way or drop the subject."[21]

After Bellows received Wade's letter he wrote to Hale that "Eaton was so obstinate in his conviction that it could not be binding—that I yielded to what I all the while felt to be unpolitic & now the fat is in the fire." There was a meeting of the Meadville trustees on 22 September and Bellows suggested to Hale that "it is evident that he finds you a better man to deal with than any one of us—and if only you could think the matter of sufficient importance, to go straight to Cleveland & get your paper signed & bring it to Meadville . . .it would be a great victory & perhaps save the enterprise." Bellows said he would go himself, but felt Hale the better man for the job.[22]

On 22 September 1881, Wade's new proposal was presented to the trustees of the Meadville Theological School. It contained the following proposals, among others: "The new school was to be called, 'The Wade School of Religious Philosophy'."

The school was to be open to all who wished to study there with "no pledge of doctrinal opinion" on the part of any student. "A chair of spiritualism might be added to the faculty."[23]

Under the guiding hand of Grindall Reynolds the objections of the Meadville trustees were kept to a minimum. The trustees felt that the Professor of Spiritual Philosophy must be appointed with great care. But the most significant proposal or condition was "that the school should be a Christian theological school, and so declared in its charter, and its initial trustees should be appointed by the American Unitarian Association "as men with fidelity to the Christian purposes of the school."

We now see two currents then strong in Unitarian circles coming into conflict. There was the Christian faction of the Unitarian body represented by Bellows, Hale, Meadville, and others. But there was also the non-Christian Free Religious Association, and the Western Unitarian Conference which had spread its influence in the West with a philosophy largely based upon transcendentalist opinions. Wade's point of view was more in sympathy with the latter view.

Bellows had gotten himself in deeper than he realized. In most cases he had been able to act as mediator between the two groups, and this was a part of his great genius as a churchman. But how could he tolerate that Meadville would be allowed to break with the Christian tradition? Yet he felt that compromise was possible. He, therefore, began to push to eliminate the sectarianism from Meadville's proposal, while at the same time retaining Christianity as the school's base. Christianity, he thought, was not yet "played out," and if the school refused to call itself Christian, then he would sacrifice the whole scheme—[24] a fact which indicates how strongly he felt about the issue.

It was actually Bellows who made the compromise that appeared to assure the school's foundation. He convinced both Wade and Hosmer in December that as one of its functions the school would be termed "The Wade Theological School" so long as theology was defined as "what will promote knowledge of God and the good of man." But immediately a dispute arose as to the selection of the trustees. By Ohio laws three-fifths would have to be Ohio residents, and Meadville favored a plan that the American Unitarian Association and the National Conference should have a say in their selection. Wade wanted none of these restrictions.

The last letter that Bellows wrote on the subject was on 16 January 1882, when he wrote to Grindall Reynolds that he thought the plan of a Boston lawyer, Charles Allen, that Unitarians should maintain control of the board of trustees in order that it not be taken over by trinitarians was the only sensible answer. Bellows advised Grindall Reynolds that this ought to be broken to Wade gradually.[25]

With Bellows's death at the end of January 1882, the matter seemed to become more and more snarled in controversy. The Meadville trustees became concerned that the school would lose its Christian emphasis. Edward Everett Hale took over the leadership. But, compared to Bellows, he was clumsy in trying to get the Antioch endowment for the Cleveland project. The whole scheme for raising fifty percent of the denomination's endowment was not even submitted to Wade for his approval. Hale drew up a plan to pack the board with people already on Antioch's board of trustees, and Wade felt that this was an attempt to exclude him and anyone of his choosing from running the school. The bitterness grew, and Wade began to feel that he was being used to get his money for sectarian purposes. By 1884 the whole idea of the school died inconspicuously. As Exoo put it, "the unexpected and untimely death of Henry W.

Bellows was without a doubt a decisive turning point in swinging fate against the school, for Bellows was a virtuoso of the art of compromise. After his passing, negotiation became less adroit and more open."[26] It was the passing of a dream, and one can only regret that Bellows's final energies were expended in such a misguided project doomed to failure almost from the start.

Our Generation Is Thinning Out

Early in 1881, Bellows, in quest of an assistant to help with the work load at the church, made a trip to the Harvard Divinity School. But he met with disappointment. "The men who could be *useful*," he wrote, "are men who have too much independence, to take a subordinate position. I saw & talked with all the senior class in the Divinity School, in hope of finding *one* whom I might utilize. But the three who seemed *fit* had fixed purposes of *paddling their own canoes*. I was even glad to *find* this spirit, & that *money* did not tempt them." Bellows determined that he would "have to wait on Providence."

Just to be certain that he kept in preaching trim while in Boston, Bellows went to hear Phillips Brooks in his "beautiful church." He found Brooks "so manly, so competent, & so persuasive a preacher—with such a grand sort of voice, & with such . . . directness & simplicity."[1]

On 12 February 1881, Bellows went to the Hewitts' to join a group of men in a celebration of the ninetieth birthday of Peter Cooper. There were twenty-four men present at the celebration, and Bellows remarked to Dewey that many of them were over eighty years of age—S. B. Ruggles, Thurlow Weed, Robert Stuart, Wilson G. Hunt, Hamilton Fish, Governor Tilden, W. E. Dodge, and Dr. Weisse were from seventy to seventy-five years of age. "Every head was gray," Bellows wrote, "except one, & he [George W. Childs] wore a wig." General Patterson, who was eighty-nine, gave an after-dinner speech. "Mr. Cooper spoke very clearly, & with a wonderful memory, quoting poetry quite at length, & giving quite an unexpected account of his *religious views* (the company was mainly orthodox), with a fine tribute to Channing & his influence."

Bellows felt that Peter Cooper was "the *first* to set the example of large benefactions in his *own life time."* Bellows also found a curious contradiction in "the Pickwickian seriousness of theological standards! Here were men who affect to think a Trinitarian & Calvinistic faith indispensable, speaking of a pure theist, who discards everything supernatural in Deity, as the *holiest* & *best* man in the community. And this after an open declaration of his faith, in all its naked simplicity! It is a very funny world!"[2]

Late in February Hamilton Fish, Jr., of Troy, New York, accepted Bellows's invitation to come to All Souls for a period of a month to see if he would be interested in being Bellows's assistant minister. Fish promised not to go to New York with his "mind made up to decline an invitation." He agreed to "undertake the Sunday school and Bible class work which you have laid out." He also was very concerned about the title of assistant. "I should naturally prefer, in making any more or less permanent engagement, the name of a *colleague* to that of an *assistant.*" Fish said he would defer to Bellows and said that he had no desire "to alter well-established methods of work." He expected to have liberty in his preaching and he felt that there would be no problem in this regard. He believed that the people would listen to and respect the preaching of a colleague more than that of an assistant. He also agreed to stay with the Bellowses for the month although his wife could not accompany him.[3]

Immediately upon his return Bellows was caught up in the work of the parish. He preached at the Good Friday and Easter services, and had two funerals. On Easter Sunday he "baptized eighteen persons & children, & among them our darling Ellen Derby." He wrote, "The little children were wild to get papa back, & I have enjoyed them almost as a new possession!" He had taken young Henry "to the Academy of Fine Arts, & he looked at every picture with eager interest & criticized the subject . . . of many with a miraculous sort of intuition." Young Henry had been very excited about his visit to the museum. He found Robert a different sort of child than Henry, "solid, prosaic; handsome, but less interesting." Little "Ellen is now weaned & creeping about, the sweetest-tempered thing alive."

He was concerned about the impression which Rev. Hamilton Fish had made on the congregation during his month's stint in All Souls while Henry was away. "Mr. Fish made a *fair* impression in his month's supply. He is excellent in the Bible class & Sunday school where I greatly need effective superintendence. In the pulpit he is above the average of going preachers—but not very much. I don't fancy he can add much strength to All Souls, by his preaching. I can't say what the people will decide." He figured that the matter would "hang along for a while," and probably the people would force him to make the decision. He thought that Mr. Fish might be tried for a year.[4] But nothing came of it.

At the end of May, Bellows was in Boston with Russell attending the last May meetings of the American Unitarian Association that he was to attend in his life. He stayed at the Parker House, and made three public appearances. The first and the most important was on the evening of 24 May. Rush R. Shippen spoke of his ten years of service as the secretary of the association, for he was now going to the Washington church. Bellows felt that he spoiled his report "by going out off his beat to fight with science & free religion in a futile way," although the matter appeared to be popular. Brooke Herford "followed with a capital speech," telling of the difficulties of Western Unitarianism. Bellows followed, and concluded the meeting "with an explanation of the difficulties with which the liberal faith has to contend in the nature of things." He was happy that his words had been well received.[5]

Bellows characterized the week as being full of "excellent speaking—without whinings & old-fashioned self-accusations." He felt that the new Secretary, Rev. Grindall Reynolds, was a great improvement over Shippen. Bellows admitted to Dewey that in his four speeches he had spoken extemporaneously, an art at which he was now very adept. He returned to New York on 27 May "limp as if broken on the wheel."[6]

Bellows's last traditional birthday letters were written from Walpole on 11 June 1881. In a letter to Dewey he again remembered his brother Edward who had died forty-four years previously at the age of twenty-three, and said that his affection for him was "still so vital! I see this again & compare thoughts & feelings & renew our tie of brotherhood, as one of the fond expectations of my heart, as it beats more slowly towards the journey's end." Yet, in spite of being sixty-seven years old, Henry wrote that he had "no great hankering after a life protracted by any self-serving process—& after usefulness & enjoyment are gone would quite as soon be under what Dr. Holmes calls 'green blankets' as under less certain *comforters* of *purely* human texture."[7] To Russell he wrote a very businesslike letter giving his future schedule, and concluded about his birthday, "It is hard for me to realize how near through with human life I am! I contemplate the end without reluctance or dismay; conscious that the declining years of life are 'full of labour & sorrow' & are not to be desired in any long-protracted form."[8]

During the last year of his life Bellows was very worried about his daughter Annie's health. He had taken her South to Aiken, South Carolina, but she had not really improved. He called her condition "a low & somewhat threatening condition." He explained this by saying that "she inherits from her mother a tendency to *melancholy* which has been exasperated by a poverty of the blood that has showed itself this winter in a series of ulcers, very painful and depressing in their influence. I fear the poor child has a small chance of ever being well—& it afflicts me seriously."[9] It is true that Annie like her mother was never very well. But she lived a life of almost sixty-one years until 1906.

The family (including his grown daughter Annie and son Russell) were constantly living beyond their means. Mixing as they did with the social elite and the wealthy in New York City it was difficult to not ape the wealthy in material desires and to keep up with them, particularly in dress. On 19 June 1881, Bellows wrote a pointed letter to Annie in which he said that the whole family must tighten their belts. "The expenses of the family are beyond my means," he wrote, "& are growing larger with all the doctors' bills. I have one bill of $300 to pay for you, now, & another milliner's bill of over $90—& no money to do it with. We have got to come to a general stand—& consider what we can *all* do to limit expenses, & to serve the common good of the family. Self-indulgence, or disregard of the domestic order & common comfort cannot safely be indulged in by any of us. But we have so much in our love for each other & mutual respect that we must try to live more on that."[10]

In the middle of August 1881, Bellows spent three hot days at Lake Winnipesaukee where the Unitarians held a week's camp meeting. He felt that this kind of popular religion was "distasteful." He was impressed with "this imitation of Methodistic methods—& at the steam which we cold Unitarians are able to get up under pressure!" But the thermometer stood at ninety-four degrees, and three days was all that Bellows could stand. "After two public addresses of a formal sort, & some platform speeches—I left with a sense of having got out of a repugnant business."

He then visited Cyrus Bartol, in Manchester, Massachusetts. Bellows described their friendship in these words: "I have been his close friend for nearly fifty years—a curious friendship, since we are opposites in everything except mutual liking." He spent four days with the Bartols. Bartol was "sharp at a bargain, & is said to have made a quarter of a million dollars, in speculating in lots and acres, that were deemed nearly worthless until he clapped his poetic eyes upon their capabilities!" Bellows did not have Bartol's abilities in the subdivision of property.

From the Bartols he went to Lowell to preach. "Ugly, Noisy, Busy Lowell," he complained. From there he went to Manchester, New Hampshire. "Manchester in England is bad enough—but Manchester in N. Eng. is worse! Materialism, fat & kicking, new riches, flaunting & vulgar! This is the name for the general effect." He then went on his annual week's visit with Dr. Henry Hedge to visit William Weeden, "who has an ancestral seat near Narragansett Pier—on Point Judith. This is the place where the geologic wall of rocky coast beginning in Labrador & coming down almost unbroken to this point and bids adieu to cliffs & stones. It leaves a continuous coast of sand thence to *Florida!*"

It was at this point, on the last rock, that Weeden had his summer home. Edward Everett Hale lived next door. Weeden was a "rich manufacturer of Providence, who having made his fortune early, knows how to use it, & how to share his resources with men that interest his mind." Bellows enjoyed the time with Weeden, Hedge, and Hale, and wrote that he "had a week of rich social engagement." Then he went to Newport, and read a paper before the Town and Country Club on "Some Sources of Power in the Fine Arts, & Especially Music," and met a great many friends. He felt that the materialism which he had seen at Lowell was "in its aesthetic *flower* at Newport." He came home to Walpole "with a real sickness for the simplicity of these wild hills—where fashion has seldom set her foot."

When he arrived he discovered his friend Rabbi Gustav Gottheil domiciled in his house. Gottheil was "a German from Berlin, thirteen years settled on a great synagogue at Manchester, England, & now, since eight years, ruler of the *Temple* Emannuel—the chief synagogue of America." Bellows admired the rabbi because "he is a most learned scholar and a most loveable man—& is more agreeable to me as a religious companion than any other clergyman in our city."

Bellows thought about his work for the beginning of the coming fall season. He was to give an address at the memorial services for the Universalist minister, Dr. Chapin. He was to preach at the dedication of the William Ellery Channing Memorial Church at Newport on 18 September. On 3 October he was to give the opening address at the Minister's Institute at Princeton on "Man." Meanwhile, he had to get his family back to New York. But he added, "I am pretty nearly ready for all three engagements."[11] It sounded like a rather busy and exhausting schedule for a man in the last year of his earthly life with very little diminution for what Bellows called old age.

The first item on Bellows's agenda for the fall was the service at the Church of the Divine Paternity in honor of Edwin Chapin. Bellows complained that it "was over three hours long." But there was "a great audience crammed the building & it was necessary to speak very loud." He felt that "the exercises were . . . creditable to the Universalists." Bellows himself spoke the last hour, and commented that he hoped "it was not as great a trial to the audience as it was to me—for I had to strain my voice to the utmost to be heard, & was completely exhausted by it."[12] He was still tired the next day.

One of the frankest and perhaps one of the bitterest letters of Bellows's life was written to his son on 27 September 1881. Russell Bellows had written a long letter to his father expressing sympathy for some of the new movements in Unitarianism. Russell could scarcely have expected his father to agree with him. Bellows lashed out, "I understand you are prepared to say, with Gannett, Hosmer & the free religionists in general—that Historic Christianity is played out, & the *profession* of it & the *sticking* to the name is a pretence & a fraud; that we are about to make *new departures*—which will burn our ships behind us, & the whole cargo of Christian traditions & symbols—& that the *school* [Wade Theological School] wanted is in this interest. Very well." Bellows was not in favor of building the proposed school upon the new Naturalism but upon the Christian traditions.

Bellows continued, "I am a Christian in faith & theory, an accepter & teacher of historic Christianity; & altho I am free to cancel all the misgrowths & accretions & monstrosities of the Christian Church system—yet beneath *all*, I feel that the most saving truth[es] have been & continue to be in action. I wish no break of *continuity*; no rejection or denial of Christian faith & symbols—but only such enlargement of view & purification of feeling—as will enable the world to profit by the more spiritual conception of Christ's teachings, we are able to form & entertain."

He continued, "I fully believe that we need absolute freedom, & absolute courage of inquiry & absolute good faith in confession—but all I am able to use or understand, does not weaken my attachment to the Christian name & faith, nor my conviction that they will outlast all free Religion, which in my judgment has no future, & no institutional power in it." Bellows went on to add that if the relationship to Christianity were taken out of the plan for the Wade school, "I shall have nothing to do with it."[13]

Then something very mysterious and unexpected happened. Russell Bellows sent a letter of resignation as minister of the Harlem church to the chairman of the board of trustees. Elijah Dunbar wrote Russell as to what happened at the special meeting which was held in the Chapel of the Fourth Unitarian Church in Harlem on the evening of 27 September. Dunbar wrote, "I have never seen so many out to a business meeting before. Mr. Wilson was called to the chair." Russell's letter was then read. "For a few moments no one moved or said a word. All was quiet. At last Mr. Wright moved that your resignation be accepted but made no remark. No one could be found to second it."

Without a second there was no motion before the Harlem congregation. The chairman then asked the people to give their views on the subject without a motion. Mr. Knox wanted Russell Bellows to withdraw his resignation and remain as pastor. But he made no motion. Mr. Wright made a speech in which he praised Bellows for his talents and character, "but thought as you wished to leave it was better you should. . . . He believed that if all our people would make it a point to attend church every Sunday . . . you would come back and the congregation would grow." Others spoke in the same vein. A motion was then made that Russell Bellows be asked to withdraw his resignation. There was then a unanimous vote in favor of this resolution. Dunbar hoped that Bellows would remain as their pastor. Dunbar also wanted his letter kept a secret.[14]

However, Russell made the resignation stick, and the *Christian Register* for 27 October 1881, through its New York correspondent, commented that "the little society seemed to flourish well under his steering, and the energy and zeal Mr. Bellows brought to a difficult task won warm encomiums from the people. Liberal religion has never taken very firm root in the upper part of the island, but the struggle has been bravely maintained by a few, aided not a little by the older and wealthier Unitarian churches of this city; and let us hope it may go on to complete success."[15]

Henry Bellows attended the ceremonies attendant upon the dedication of the William Ellery Channing Memorial Church at Newport, Rhode Island, on Tuesday evening, 18 October. Bellows found it a very meaningful affair, "the nearest thing to Channing himself!" There were many present who had known Channing. Frederick A. Farley, aged eighty-two, William Furness, aged seventy-nine, F. H. Hedge, aged seventy-six, John H. Morison, and Mr. Stebbins who were over seventy. Bellows had enjoyed Dr. Morison's short speech above all "because it had that atmosphere of Channing's *presence* in it, that nobody else communicated." He also was impressed with the church itself, although it was not as yet finished inside. It was "as beautiful as any church in America," he wrote. 'The spire is the loftiest and most sightly in town—& distantly seen, is beautiful; & more beautiful near at hand." Bellows believed that his sermon went well although "it had the disadvantage of being written a month beforehand (in expectation that the dedication would occur Sept 14)" and Bellows found that the sermon had *"cooled"* for him.[16]

That Glorious and Inspiring Beyond

It was toward the end of his life that Bellows first came into contact with Clara Barton, a Universalist from North Oxford, Massachusetts. It seems very strange that Clara Barton and Bellows had never met. A great deal of her personal reputation came through her service in the Civil War, yet she was never associated with the United States Sanitary Commission. She saw a need for ministering to suffering on the battlefields, devised her own plan, and carried it out. She disliked working for an organization and preferred being independent.

For four years after the war Miss Barton superintended a search for missing soldiers. Her health failed, and she went abroad, and soon was in the midst of war again, the Franco-Prussian war. She became associated with the International Red Cross at Geneva. When she returned to America she sought to establish the American Red Cross under official government recognition. The United States had failed to ratify the International Red Cross Convention in 1864 although the government was officially represented at the convention. In 1866, Bellows and others organized the American Association for the Relief of Misery on the Battlefields. This was the first Red Cross organization in this country, and its sole purpose was to secure American ratification of the Red Cross Convention. But Bellows and his associates were unable to arouse public interest, and the organization went out of existence in 1871.

Miss Barton succeeded where Bellows had failed. She wrote a pamphlet called "The Red Cross of the Geneva Convention, What Is It?" She was not successful with the Hayes administration. But she had success with President Garfield. On 21 May 1881, the American Red Cross was organized with Miss Barton as President. But Garfield was assassinated before he could recommend adoption of the treaty. Secretary of State Blaine and President Arthur secured its confirmation by the Senate in March 1882, just two months after the death of Bellows.

There are two letters from Clara Barton to Henry Bellows in the Bellows Papers written in November and December of 1881, just before Bellows's death, and just before Miss Barton's successful work to establish the American Red Cross through American adoption of the Geneva Convention. Bellows had written her an encouraging letter and she hoped "that we might have commenced an acquaintance to continue long and pleasantly." She continued, "I have always wanted to know you and have regarded it as a privation that I did not." She described the recent resolutions signed by the Grand Army, and the ex-president of Yale, the current president of Yale, and others urging that the Senate favor the treaty. "What I most desire," she added, "is a line from Dr. Bellows. It need not be formal, nor addressed to anyone but myself." She wanted a kindly word and "experiences of your sympathy with, and interest in the movement, —*our* movement, —for you have labored in it as well as I, and *first*—and I *wish* you would claim and occupy your place. I want you there."

In December Clara Barton thanked Bellows for his excellent letter, and asked that he send her some names of persons in positions of authority who also might write. Bellows must have rejoiced that his dream was becoming a reality, and that younger hands had taken up the task that he was laying down.[1]

Bellows's last Thanksgiving was spent quietly with his family—as he desired. He called it "a purely domestic Thanksgiving." The three little children had stayed up until the dinner was served at 6:00 P.M., "& behaved themselves in a charming way." The children sat at the table with the others, but instead of the usual Thanksgiving fare they ate "bread and milk." And Bellows added, "Is not this a proof of a wise mother's discipline?"[2]

In the middle of December Bellows made his last journey to Cleveland to talk with Wade about the new theological school, and then went on to Saint Louis to preach on Friday evening, 16 December, at the Saint Louis church. He had troubles with drafts in the sleeping cars. He found the people of Saint Louis "very proud of [their city]."[3] In spite of a heavy cold Bellows got through the sermon splendidly. He found "thoughtful people of all persuasions" were at the service. He believed it "was an opportunity to be prized & I had made a preparation adequate to it—& managed to satisfy both extremes by breadth, candor & simplicity of treatment." He and Anna had seen the Saint Louis Museum, the work of her brother, the architect, Robert Peabody. Bellows felt that "he has lifted the whole style of architecture in Saint Louis," but he worried about his cold and voice.[4]

His sermon at the dedication of the new church was published in full in the *Saint Louis Globe-Democrat*, which Bellows termed "A Republican paper." But Bellows was ailing with his cold and throat and was not able to participate in all of the accolades which were given him in connection with his visit. But, in typical style, he preached once on Sunday and once on Monday.[5] On Wednesday he and Anna left for New York with a stopover at Cincinnati. The highlight of his trip was a conviction that "the Cleveland business [Wade] was substantially advanced, & is likely now to come surely to a point." His view of Robert's new church and Museum of Fine Arts had uplifted him. But he was glad to be *"safe home, & find the children well."*[6]

Late in December 1881, less than six weeks before his death, Bellows wrote that he had "a fair measure of strength . . . On the whole I am better than a year ago and hope to be allowed a few more years of work. On the 2nd of January I shall complete the forty-third year of my ministry, a long settlement in one post, for which I am profoundly grateful."[7] He had written to Mrs. Ephraim Peabody, his wife's mother, "I mean to enjoy all I can while life lasts by taking as bright and cheerful views of passing events and conditions. But all the while I have in view that glorious and inspiring beyond, where we shall escape lameness [Mrs. Peabody's infirmity], weariness, separation and decay. Let us cherish the hope of that emancipating hour when we shall be free from infirmities and rejoice among the angels in heaven."[8]

On Sunday 15 January, he wrote what proved to be his last letter to Orville Dewey. He commented, "We are all well here—as for myself tho not in full strength, I am in fair working order." He then proceeded to discuss Renan's *Marcus Aurelius* which he had just been reading, and the place of philosophy in Roman society.[9]

On Tuesday evening, 17 January, Bellows participated in his last public ceremony, the installation of the Rev. George W. Gallagher as minister of the Fourth Unitarian Church on 128th Street—the Harlem church—in Manhattan. The right hand of fellowship that evening was given by his son, Russell, the former minister of the church. Rev. Robert Collyer gave an address to the people, and Dr. Bellows gave the charge to the minister. There is no record of what he said. It was, like much of his preaching at the time, extemporaneous. Daughter Anna Bellows at least has given us one phrase from his charge. He spoke of himself as an "old warrior putting on the armor of a young soldier."

On 19 January he went to a wedding in Brooklyn, and "returned so ill that he never arose from his bed of sickness again."[10] The records of the family are somewhat vague about the exact nature of Bellows's illness. Russell says that it was "an acute trouble, the precise nature of which his physicians did not discover until after his death."[11] This does not tell us much. But his fatal disease was undoubtedly a blockage of the intestines, an area in which he had constantly suffered all of his life. If it was cancer, we must remember that "cancer" was a word scarcely spoken in Bellows's day, although he discussed the matter freely with the two Mrs. George Schuylers both of whom had died from the same disease.

Bellows lingered for only ten days, gradually becoming weaker and weaker. On 28 January, his physician, Dr. W. H. Draper, issued a report on Dr. Bellows's health, obviously to be read to the congregation on Sunday 29 January. "Dr. Bellows passed a comfortable night. There is not material change in his condition since yesterday morning—the obstructed bowel remains unrelieved."[12]

His daughter Annie spent all of that last Sunday with him in his room at the time of the church service, five blocks away. "He was too weak to talk, and lay there quite silently. But, as he heard the church bells ring at the usual hour when he went into the pulpit, he lifted his arm with a gesture of appeal and sorrow. No words were necessary to explain his feelings as the hand slowly fell to his side with a long-drawn sign of pain and submission."[13]

Writing a week after his father's death to Orville Dewey, Russell Bellows gave a more personal account of the last days of Henry on this earth.

He knew to the end just where he was & how fast he was nearing the everlasting gates. *No acute pain,* only discomfort and a desire for the inevitable end. His peace of mind and soul in view of death was very beautiful,—and somewhat surprising in one so strong in *body* and with no *desire* to leave this world. But his *acquiescence* to the Divine Will was perfect and unswerving. He had no "leave takings," no talk *about religion,* only one *extended* conversation of any kind. Then he spoke of writing to "Dewey, Silsbee and Weeden" the next day. This was on Saturday, two days only before his release.[14]

At almost the same hour that Bellows was passing away, his close friend Orville Dewey, destined to live only two months longer, was thinking about him in Sheffield, hoping to hear some word. It did not arrive at 11:00 A.M. by the Albany mail. Dewey wrote in his letter, which, of course, Bellows never read, "I feel as if your difficulty were partly in me. Is it not because you are a part of me?" And he added these words, "You have taught men how to live; are you now to teach them how to die—with what resignation, with what calmness, with what trust in God?" And while Dewey was writing these prophetic words they were an apt description of the mind of Bellows as he slipped off into eternity.[15]

Funeral services for Dr. Bellows took place at 9:00 A.M. on Thursday, 2 February 1882. "Long before the hour appointed for the service, the beautiful audience-room of All Souls was filled with a hushed multitude. The organ's dirge was broken only by muffled sobs and the soft tread of those who bore in the sleeping form of the beloved pastor."[16] Many ministers of all denominations from New York and neighboring cities were present. There was a delegation from the Century Club, and another from the Union League Club. There were many prominent citizens present: Peter Cooper, Dr. Walcott Gibbs, George William Curtis, John T. Agnew, David Dudley Field, Parke Godwin, and many others. Lilies of the valley and violets lay in banks at the foot of the altar, and on "the coffin-lid was only a bunch of feathery palms with a few snowy flowers."

Edward Everett Hale gave the eulogy. It was typical Hale oratory which spoke in general terms, but at times was quite specific. "Never was a body of people . . . so linked together personally, organically, I may say, with the thought and life and mind of their minister for well-nigh half a century, as was this congregation with Henry Whitney Bellows. They were life of his life." Hale maintained that whoever would analyze the life of the pastor "will have to go back to that eternal secret, always old and always new, that he lived in the presence and the love of God. God was with him by day and by night. God was his strength and comfort." Hale maintained that Bellows would never leave us, and concluded with the thought that "in the host of heaven we know that there is one more who with those larger powers which he has taken on, loves us with the same love with which he has always loved us, and who will minister to us in this faithful ministry."

The mortal remains of Henry Bellows were taken immediately to the train which took the coffin and the mourners to Walpole. Services were conducted in Walpole on Friday, 3 February, at the Unitarian church by the pastor whom Bellows had described as a "little man," the Rev. William Brown.

Bellows was buried in the family plot at the cemetery to the right of his first wife, Eliza Nevins Townsend Bellows, in whose grave also are the remains of their three children who died in infancy (Edward Stearns Bellows, Eliza Bellows, and Mary Davis Bellows) and Francis William Greenwood Bellows (1880). Behind his grave was that of William Benjamin Allen and the Rev. John Bellows.[17]

There is one empty grave site in the plot, and it would seem fitting that here should rest the remains of Henry's twin brother, Edward Stearns Bellows. It was the goal of Henry all of his life to go to Michigan to recover the remains of his brother and transfer them to Walpole. They do not lie in the same plot, but they occupy the same place in eternity.

Henry Bellows's final will and testament had not been drawn up until he was near the end of his life, and he knew it, on 24 January 1882, just six days before he died. William Prichard drew up the will from an earlier one made in January 1878. In his final will Henry left to Russell and Anna, the children of his first marriage, the lot and house at 232 East 15th Street (which still had a $10,000 mortgage on it), the farm and forty acres of land in Walpole (also subject to some mortgages), and the undivided half of George Bellows's interest in their father's estate. The household goods were divided between his older children and his second wife. The California silver was bequeathed to Russell, and if he died without issue it was to go to Robert Peabody Bellows. (It is now in the Red Cross Building in Washington.) Eliza's silver tea set went to Annie.

To his wife he left the original share of his father's estate, and the share of his brother Alexander Hamilton Bellows. Russell and Mrs. Bellows were to be the executors of the will. Lastly, he appointed his wife guardian of his three young children.

Anna Peabody Bellows and the three children: Robert, Ellen and Henry. (Taken three or four years after Dr. Bellows' death, 1885-1886). Courtesy of the Bellows Family

To those who did not know Henry Bellows it seemed a strange will. It left almost everything to his older children, Russell and Anna. But this was because most of Bellows's worldly possessions came from their mother, his first wife, Eliza Nevins Townsend, from her wealthy family. Henry had lived very well during his lifetime, had been very generous with his money as well as with his energies. But so little was left to his second wife who had three small children to care for that the people of All Souls took it upon themselves to raise a subscription of $50,000 with which an annuity was bought for the benefit of Anna Peabody Bellows and the three children.[18]

Almost immediately after the death was announced, letters of condolence began to come in addressed to Mrs. Bellows and to Russell. A large portion of the 2 February edition of the *Christian Register* was devoted to an account of Bellows's life written by Edward Everett Hale, together with many letters of appreciation of his life and work, even before this issue of the *Christian Register* was printed.

The First Congregational Society met on Wednesday, 1 February, "at the earliest moment of the death of their minister," and gave utterance to their own "deep feelings of personal bereavement and to their heartfelt sympathy with his family in their great loss." For the time being the society omitted "all reference to his noble character and life-long service to his church and his country."[19] This simple message expressed how the church felt about Dr. Bellows and his sudden demise.

The copy of the bust of Henry Bellows by Hiram Powers was offered by Russell Bellows to the Century Club which had been one of the great interests of his father. The Century Club adopted a Resolution regarding the life of Bellows, and A. D. MacDonough of the club wrote that "the club will with pleasure receive and care for it for such time as you may wish to leave it in their charge." The bust still remains at the Century Club. The original bust given to the American Unitarian Association by Robert Peabody Bellows is now on permanent loan to the Unitarian Church of All Souls of New York City, and is proudly displayed in the church vestibule.

At the May meetings of the American Unitarian Association held on 25 May 1882, a portion of the day was set aside for a memorial address which was delivered by Frederic Henry Hedge—who knew Bellows so well. Hedge termed Orville Dewey, who had died in March, "the honey-lipped Nestor." "But Bellows, he said, "has had in all our annals no equal as a man of action." He mentioned Channing "whom we regard as our father in the faith." But on this day Hedge said, "we commemorate the disciple and brother by whose organizing genius that faith has been made to take itself a body as compact as our unformulized [sic] theology and the right to differ, which we claim, will allow."

Hedge termed Bellows "our Bishop, our metropolitan," although he admitted that the terms had no place in Unitarian polity. He felt that Bellows had this position of leadership, "by no robbery, but by universal consent of the brethren." It fell to Bellows as "a native gift . . . He ordered us hither and thither, and we surrendered ourselves to his ordering." Hedge mentioned the National Conference of Churches and the Minister's Institute as examples of Bellows's ordering his brethren to do things. He termed Bellows "our Unitarian missionary" whose journeys far exceeded those of Saint Paul.

Hedge considered Bellows a man who sought popularity and who achieved it. But he did not feel that this was hypocrisy, but "pure affability." He was a "rare combination of the consecrated soul with the boon companion,—the enthusiast with the man of the world."

Hedge then went on to develop the theme of a consecrated soul which he had mentioned as a quality of Bellows's character. "If he shone as a man of the world in worldly converse, he had none the less his conversation in heaven." He mentioned his service during the Civil War, and how amazingly he had continued to be the pastor of All Souls Church during all of these other events. He recalled "his amazing activity . . . even in his dreams, I think, he must have been at work . . . Often his sermons were written at one sitting. But haste was not apparent in them."

As to deep reflection in Bellows's life, Hedge was uncertain. "Long, deep, silent brooding, I suppose, was not in his nature." But Hedge termed him "a diligent reader. He found time to acquaint himself with almost every significant book that came from the press."

Hedge continued: "The one talent denied him was that of repose. He could not do nothing! He could not lie by. Of leisure, he had no experience, no relish, scarcely knew what it meant." Hedge mentioned his breakdown and subsequent journey to Europe. "But the tour is turned to new toil. Half the night is spent in bringing to protocol the observations and events of the day . . . The written sheets are sent home, are committed to the press; and, when the journey is ended, behold! it is a book."

Hedge mentioned his extemporaneous preaching. He suggested that only for the exceptional preacher was this a safe method of speaking. He said that he had known only two preachers who were safe in this area. "One of these was the late Father Taylor [the Boston seaman's chaplain], and the other was our brother Bellows." Hedge concluded, "We do not claim for him the vision of a seer; we do not claim for him the penetration of the great original thinker, nor the erudition of the deep-read scholar, nor even the insight of the emancipated critic." But he said that Bellows, unlike Channing, had left no written word which would secure a long future. "The best that can be said of any man may surely be said of him,—that he was one of those 'who passing through the valley of Baca, make it a well.' It is good to celebrate such: it is better, so far as our meaner gifts and feebler will may suffice, to follow them."[20]

Frederic Henry Hedge then went on to speak of the death that same year of Ralph Waldo Emerson. Although Emerson was eleven years Bellows's senior, their respective lives and viewpoints indicate the inner struggle going on within intelligent minds in the middle years of the nineteenth century about the role of institutions in human society. Emerson spoke out for the free spirit untrammeled

The Bas-Relief of Henry Whitney Bellows by Augustus Saint-Gaudens in the sanctuary of All Souls Church

by institutions. Emerson was not the rebel Thoreau was. Thoreau more closely resembled Bellows's parishioner Herman Melville in reactions against human institutions that resulted in war, slavery, and violence. But essentially he claimed that there was no need for the church.

Emerson left the ministry of the Second Church in Boston as a young man evidently disillusioned with the institution of the church. In spite of this he continued to be a Unitarian minister and to preach all of his life. It has been said that a study of his diaries shows that after the Sundays on which he himself preached, the church appeared to be a fairly decent and important human institution, but on the Sundays when he was not in the pulpit his opinions of the church were more negative. Whether or not fame is the most important consideration of greatness, Emerson is one of the most famous of Unitarians, known not only in America but throughout the civilized world.

Bellows's contribution, as Hedge pointed out, was on a far different level than that of Emerson. Bellows was primarily an institutionalist. He believed in, helped establish, and fought for the organization of the church not only on a local level but nationally, and was an effective Unitarian emissary internationally.

In many ways the ideas of the two men were closer than is at first apparent if one were but to contrast their ideas and careers. Both wanted human beings to be honest. Emerson felt that the church was not honest, and Bellows believed that this honesty was the most important task of the church—to state its position honestly, and not to overstate it or, in connection with the controversy with the Free Religious Association, to understate it. The main difference was that Emerson felt that individuals could go the religious route alone seeking to enter directly into contact with the Eternal. Bellows believed that also, but he also believed that organizing men and women into a human institution called the church was not only helpful but essential for religion and its perpetuation.

Emerson got the most plaudits for his efforts—largely literary reputation—but Bellows's ideas and leadership meant more to the Unitarian movement than did Emerson's. It is strange that in considering this part of our American history and particularly our Unitarian history that far more importance should be given to the philosopher than to the churchman. Perhaps this biography of Henry Whitney Bellows, magnificent doer, consummate churchman, will do something to right this unbalance.

In 1886 a life-size bas-relief of Henry Whitney Bellows by Augustus Saint-Gaudens[21] was unveiled in the church with special ceremonies. The opening address was given by Dr. Theodore Chickering Williams, the new minister of the church. There were addresses by Robert Collyer and Horatio Stebbins. Edward Everett Hale gave an oration. Francis Greenwood Peabody gave the prayer. The relief was presented to the church by Mr. William Prichard and the unveiling was done by Henry Bellows's two sons, Henry W. Bellows, aged eleven, and Robert P. Bellows, aged nine.

On the marble mounting of the relief were carved these words written by Henry Bellows's brother-in-law, Charles W. Eliot, President of Harvard University:

HENRY WHITNEY BELLOWS
Born in Boston, June 11, 1814. Died in
New York, Jan. 30, 1882.
For forty-three years minister of this Church,
to which he gave the name All Souls.

———

A preacher, strong, fervent, uplifting,
A courageous thinker,
A persuasive orator.

———

A patriot, loving freedom, indignant at wrong,
A life-long philanthropist.
President of the
United States Sanitary Commission 1861–1878.

———

An ardent, generous friend; joyous with the
joyful, tender with the sorrowful.
A devout Christian, trusting in God,
and hoping all things of men.

Officers of the Unitarian Church of All Souls, 1837–1881.

1837 President: Robert Ainslie,
1837–1843
Treasurer: John T. Balch,
1836–1839
Secretary and Clerk: Charles
S. Francis, 1830–1868
Trustees: (three elected each
year for three-year term)
Robert Ainslie
Daniel Low, 1837–1838
Thomas Tileston

1838 Trustees:
Joshua Brooks
George Winston Gray
Robert Schuyler
Joel Stone, 1838–1840

1839 Minister: Henry Whitney
Bellows, 1839-1882
Treasurer: William F. Cary,
1839–1840
Trustees:
Edward Anthony
William F. Cary,
1839–1841
Joseph W. Haven

1840 Trustees:
Robert Ainslie
H. M. Hayes, 1840–1841
John Thomas

1841 Treasurer: Joel Stone,
1841–1844
Trustees:
J. B. Bright
William C. Langley
Jeremiah Smith, 1841–1842
Joel Stone
Benjamin F. Wheelwright,
1841–1842

1842 Trustees:
Gilbert Allen
Robert Schuyler
Thomas W. Storrow

1843 President: Robert Schuyler,
1843
Trustees:
Irving Curtis, 1843–1844
Moses H. Grinnell
Jeremiah Smith
William Taggard

1844 President: Moses H.
Grinnell, 1844–1859
Treasurer: Charles S.
Francis, 1844–1857
Trustees:
Pierre M. Irving
John Thomas
Andrew Thorp

YEAR OF
ELECTION:

1879   Secretary and Clerk: William
      T. Wardwell
    Trustees:
      Nathan Chandler
      Emerson Foote
      J. Harsen Rhoades

1880   President: J. Harsen Rhoades
    Secretary and Clerk: Henry
      D. Sedgwick
    Trustees:
      Benjamin G. Arnold
      Saul B. Dana
      Henry D. Sedgwick

1881   Treasurer, Secretary and
      Clerk: Emerson Foote
    Trustees:
      George F. Baker
      Addison Brown
      William M. Prichard

APPENDIX B

Church Membership Criteria

IN THE EARLY PART of the year 1846 the church went through a period of discussion about the Covenant or Bond of Union which had been adopted on 30 January 1821, under the leadership of Henry Ware, Jr. The Covenant adopted at that time was typical of Unitarian covenants of the period—very conservative. They professed "our faith in Jesus Christ and our subjection to the laws of his Kingdom." They received "the Scriptures of the Old and New Testament as our rule and guide of life." They agreed to observe the ordinances "which He has appointed." They expected to "receive its rewards hereafter, through riches of divine favor manifested by Jesus Christ."[1] But since no one had signed the covenant since 1824, twenty-two years before, the congregation had no real basis of membership in the church that was relevant.

The Covenant was far too conservative to serve as a basis for joining the church for many persons twenty-five years later, and too specifically represented conservative Unitarian thinking in 1821. The subject came up late in the year 1845 and by February 1846 a new basis for joining the church had been adopted by the congregation. Section II of the Bylaws of the society had indicated that there was to be a separate body called 'The church." It was to have no power. That remained in the hands of those who owned and rented pews (the society), who alone (the males) possessed a vote at congregational meetings. The Bylaws stated that 'The pastor, and the communicants of this society, constituting the church, may prescribe their own rules of order and discipline; but it is expressly understood that no subscription or assent to any covenant other than that approved by this society, and to be found in its records, shall be required as a qualification for church-Membership."[2] The church was the religious body whereas the society was the governing body. Persons could belong to either one or the other or both.

In the Minute Book (Volume II) there are two sets of recommendations that evidently came before the church for ratification.[3] One is dated 1846, and contains a draft of a new constitution for the church. This document states that "this church on the 30th day of January 1821" adopted a covenant, "which constitution & covenant have practically been inoperative, the date of the last signature being December 9, 1824, and the whole number of signatures only forty-seven," that "at a meeting of the pastor and the communicants of the society" held in the church [the date is left blank] voted to abolish the old constitution and covenant, and then proceeded to adopt the following rules and regulations:

There was to be "no form of admission" required "to the rite of communion." It continued, "All Christians of any denomination who love & honour the memory of our Lord & Savior Jesus Christ shall have free access to the communion." Any member of the church who was also a member of the society could vote at the meetings of the church. The pastor was to preside at all meetings (and had a "casting vote"). He was required to keep a record of the proceedings "& a list of the members who are also members of the society," and to report back to the church on important matters. There was to be an annual meeting following the last communion day each year. The document goes on to name the church officers and their duty and collections for the poor on communion Sundays.

There is also a document which is a report of the committee appointed to consider the reorganization of the church. It is not dated, but I take it to be a preliminary report, and the forementioned document to be the actual rules which were adopted. The committee recommended that "the method of uniting with this church shall continue to be optional with the candidate, and that the signature of no creed or profession whatever shall be required." The committee recognized that some of the members wanted a more formal token "or a more precise bond of union with this church." Therefore, it was recommended that "as many as can see their way clear . . . subscribe to the original covenant of this church." Evidently that portion of the church who wanted a more formal creed was one Henry W. Bellows who signed the original covenant on 21 February 1846, the only person to sign. Bellows obviously was pushing for a general statement of faith rather than such a free basis of membership as was adopted. Later when he was active in organizing the National Conference of Churches he was able to have such a general statement adopted, much to the displeasure of some ministers who founded the Free Religious Association calling the covenant a creed. Bellows felt that a church should make clear the parameters of its beliefs even if the details were not spelled out. He would have appreciated the present covenant of All Souls which replaced the "no covenant" of his congregation which was adopted in 1922: "In the freedom of the truth and in the spirit of Jesus we unite for the worship of God and the service of man."

This second document also gives us a bit more insight as to how one joined "the church." No one was to be excluded from communion, and "all those who now [considered] themselves members of this church shall be required to inform the pastor of this fact & that all those who propose uniting with us shall previously signify it to the pastor—that he may enter their names upon the church records." This was the basis of church membership when Herman Melville first rented a pew in 1849, and it was the basis of membership in the church when he joined the church some time before 1 January 1884. We cannot be more specific about when Melville became an actual member because we have not found Dr. Bellows's "Membership Book."

In *Liberals Among the Orthodox* I stated on pages 10 and 11 that I did not believe that there was any indication of a basis for joining the church from the time that the Ware Covenant went out of usage until the congregation adopted the present Bond of Union in 1922: "In the freedom of the truth, and in the spirit of Jesus, we unite for the worship of God, and the service of man." I am happy to correct this now. I am especially appreciative of Dr. Joyce Kennedy of Mount Saint Vincent University in Halifax, Nova Scotia, who prodded me to do some extra work on this subject. This became very important when I discovered during the course of the research for this book that Herman Melville rented a pew in the Church of the Divine Unity during the last half of the year 1849. What kind of a church was Melville willing to join? To rent a pew one did not have to subscribe to anything doctrinal. But one hardly would rent a pew in a church totally alien to one's religious beliefs. The church which Melville attended while he was writing *Moby-Dick* was obviously broad enough for his religious tastes, and when he brought his bride Elizabeth Shaw to New York in 1847 Melville found himself at home in the Church of the Divine Unity.

Notes

Abbreviations Used

BP—Bellows Papers at the Massachusetts Historical Society, Boston

MHS—Massachusetts Historical Society

HWB—Henry Whitney Bellows

EB—Eliza Bellows (Mrs. Henry Bellows)

Anna B.—Anna Bellows (daughter)

RNB—Russell Nevins Bellows (son)

WS—Rev. William Silsbee

OD—Dr. Orville Dewey

CAB—Dr. Cyrus Augustus Bartol

TSK—Rev. Thomas Starr King

EEH—Dr. Edward Everett Hale

JFC—Dr. James Freeman Clarke

SO—Dr. Samuel Osgood

FLO—Frederick Law Olmsted

Preface

1. Thomas Bellows Peck, *The Bellows Genealogy or John Bellows*, (Keene, N.H.: Sentinel Printing Co., 1890), pp. 283–320. This extensive account was written by HWB's son, Russell Nevins Bellows.

2. George H. Williams, "James Luther Adams and the Unitarian Denomination," *Andover Newton Quarterly* 17 (January 1977), 3: 176–177.

3. Loren Eiseley, *All the Strange Hours: The Excavation of a Life* (New York: Scribners, 1975), pp. 189–190.

Chapter 1—The Church Is My First Bride

Born and Bred an Unitarian

1. Peck, *The Bellows Genealogy*, pp. 283–320.

2. Anna L. Bellows, *Recollections of Henry Whitney Bellows* (New York: New York League of Unitarian Women, printed by the Branch Alliance of All Souls, 1897), p. 4.

3. Emily R. Barnes, *Narratives, Traditions, and Personal Reminiscences Connected With the Early History of the Bellows Family and the Village of Walpole, New Hampshire* (Boston: George H. Ellis, 1888), pp. 281–287.

4. HWB, "The Round Hill School," *Harvard Register*, 3 (1881): pp. 3–7.

5. Joseph E. Cogswell with a note appended by George Bancroft to John Bellows, 22 August 1828, BP, MHS.

6. Peck, *The Bellows Genealogy*, p. 285.

7. HWB to Edward Bellows, 14 October 1833, BP, MHS.

8. HWB to his parents, 6 November 1833, BP, MHS.

9. HWB, New Orleans, to Edward Bellows, Cambridge, 17 March 1834, BP, MHS.

10. HWB to Edward Bellows, 30 April 1834, BP, MHS.

11. *General Catalogue of the Divinity School of Harvard University,* published by the University, Robert S. Morrison, editor, 1919, pp. 44–50.

12. Dewey had gone to Williams College (A.B., 1814), then to Andover Theological Seminary where he was graduated in 1819.

13. HWB to WS, Barnstable, Mass., 12 February 1837, BP, MHS.

14. John Butler, Adrian, Mich., to John Bellows, Walpole, 16 April 1837, BP, MHS.

15. HWB to Andrew Lipscomb, Tuskeegee, Ala., 7 August 1860, BP, MHS.

16. HWB to WS, Cincinnati, Ohio, 25 July 1837, BP, MHS.

Candidating in New York

1. HWB to Ephraim Peabody (copy), 4 October 1837, BP, MHS.

2. HWB to John Bellows, Walpole, N.H., 25 January 1838, BP, MHS.

3. Ibid.

4. HWB to WS, Pittsburgh, Penn., 28 March 1838, BP, MHS.

5. HWB, Augusta, Ga., to Jacob N. Knapp, Walpole, N.H., 22 November 1837, BP, MHS.

6. HWB, Mobile, Ala., to John Bellows, Walpole, N.H., 25 June 1838, BP, MHS.

7. Mobile Alabama Congregational Church trustees to HWB, 11 May 1838, BP, MHS.

8. HWB to WS, 2 August 1838, BP, MHS.

9. C. Dellington to HWB, 17 May 1838, BP, MHS.

10. Cincinnati trustees to HWB, July 1838, BP, MHS.

11. HWB to Jacob Knapp, 21 April 1838, BP, MHS.

12. HWB to Charlotte Silsbee, 26 October 1838, BP, MHS.

13. Henry Ware, Jr., to HWB, dated only Thursday afternoon, 1838, BP, MHS.

14. Mrs. Saint John to HWB, 7 August 1838, BP, MHS.

15. John N. Bellows to HWB, 12 September 1838, BP, MHS.

16. HWB to Charlotte Silsbee, 26 October 1838, BP, MHS.

17. George F. Simmons to HWB, 28 October 1838, BP, MHS.

18. Cf. Curtis Dahl, "New England Unitarianism in Fictional Antiquity: The Romances of William Ware," *New England Quarterly* 48 (March 1975), 1: 104–115.

19. In keeping with the style of the day, the Second Church chose a new name. It now became the Church of the Messiah, and was dedicated as such

on 2 May 1839. It remained the Church of the Messiah until the early part of this century when John Haynes Holmes secured a change of name to The Community Church of New York City.

I Accept Your Invitation

1. HWB to Mrs. Dorr, Boston, Mass., 6 November 1838, BP, MHS.
2. HWB to WS, 18 November 1838, BP, MHS.
3. HWB to Mrs. Dorr, 13 November 1838, BP, MHS.
4. HWB to WS, 18 November 1838, BP, MHS.
5. Ibid.
6. John Bellows to HWB, 19 November 1838, BP, MHS.
7. All Souls Minute Book, Volume I, pp. 279–280. I have labeled all of the minute books "All Souls Minute Books" even though the name All Souls was not applied to the church until 1855.
8. Robert Ainslee to HWB, 4 December 1838, BP, MHS.
9. All Souls Minute Book, Volume I, pp. 280–283.
10. Mary Hustace Hubbard, "A History of the First Congregational Church," unpublished manuscript, All Souls archives, n.d., p. 2. Hereinafter referred to as Hubbard, "First Congregational Church."
11. Bound in All Souls Minute Book, Volume I, p. 283.
12. Hubbard, "First Congregational Church," p. 2.
13. Jonathan Goodhue, *Diary*, New York Society Library, n.d.
14. HWB, *The First Congregational Church in the City of New York. A Sketch of Its History with a Review of His Own Ministry*, "Addressed to his Parishioners, January Fifth and Twelfth, 1879, on the occasion of the Fortieth Anniversary of his Settlement." Printed, not published, by The Church of All Souls, New York, 1899, pp. 12–13. Hereinafter referred to as *Fortieth Anniversary Sermons*.
15. HWB to Mrs. Dorr, 3 January 1839, BP, MHS.
16. HWB to John Bellows, 3 January 1839, BP, MHS.
17. HWB to Mrs. Dorr, 3 January 1839, BP, MHS.
18. HWB to WS, 5 January 1839, BP, MHS.
19. HWB, 6 January 1839. Untitled manuscript sermon in BP, MHS.
20. All Souls Trustees to HWB, 8 February 1839, BP, MHS.
21. HWB to WS, 7 March 1839, BP, MHS.
22. HWB to WS, 9 March 1839, BP, MHS.
23. HWB to WS, 23 January 1839, BP, MHS.
24. HWB to his father, Walpole, N.H., 1 February 1839, BP, MHS.
25. HWB, *Fortieth Anniversary Sermons*, pp. 13–14.
26. Ibid., p. 14.
27. Ibid., p. 15.

28. Ibid., p. 13.
29. Hubbard, "First Congregational Church," p. 1.
30. Ibid.

My Old Flame
1. John Bellows to HWB, 17 May 1839, BP, MHS.
2. HWB to Mrs. Dorr, Walpole, N.H., 13 February 1838, BP, MHS.
3. HWB, "Respectibility, Or Holiness," a sermon delivered before the Young Men's Benevolent Society in Boston, Mass., Sunday evening, 9 December 1838. (Boston: Weeks, Jordan, and Co., 1839).
4. HWB to Charlotte Silsbee, 27 December 1838, BP, MHS.
5. HWB to WS, 5 January 1839, BP, MHS.
6. HWB to Mrs. Dorr, 18 January 1839, BP, MHS.
7. Mrs. George Lee to HWB, 28 January 1839, BP, MHS.
8. HWB to Mrs. Dorr, 25 February 1839, BP, MHS.
9. HWB to WS, 5 January 1839, BP, MHS.
10. Mrs. A. M. Ireland to HWB, 4 April 1839, BP, MHS.
11. HWB to EB, 2 January 1869, BP, MHS.
12. HWB to Eliza Townsend, 22 February 1839, BP, MHS.
13. Eliza Townsend to HWB, 25 February 1839, BP, MHS.
14. HWB to WS, 13 April 1839, BP, MHS.
15. HWB to Mrs. Dorr, 24 April 1839, BP, MHS.
16. HWB to his mother, 27 April 1839, BP, MHS.
17. HWB to Mrs. Dorr, 31 May 1839, BP, MHS.
18. SO, Niagara Falls, N.Y., to HWB, 31 July 1839, BP, MHS.
19. HWB to his mother, 5 August 1839, BP, MHS.
20. HWB to Mrs. Dorr, 11 August 1839, BP, MHS.
21. HWB, Walpole, N.H., to the Townsends, 4 September 1839, BP, MHS.

Chapter 2—The Channing of His Time?
We Never Worshiped There Again

1. HWB, *Fortieth Anniversary Sermons*, pp. 4–5.
2. Hubbard, "First Congregational Church," p. 1.
3. Ibid., p. 1.
4. HWB to "My Dear friend," 4 November 1839, BP, MHS.
5. Cf. Walter Donald Kring, *Liberals Among the Orthodox: Unitarian Beginnings in New York City, 1819–1839,* (Boston: Beacon Press, 1974), pp. 176–185. Hereinafter referred to as Kring, *Liberals Among the Orthodox.*
   Cf. also Douglas C. Stange, "The Making of An Abolitionist Martyr: Harvard Professor Charles Theodore Christian Follen 1796–1840," *Harvard*

Library Bulletin, (January 1976), XXIV: 1. A fine article on Follen's place in the antislavery movement and his relationship to the New York church.

 6. HWB to WS, Savannah, Ga., 24 January 1840, BP, MHS.

 7. EB to HWB, 18 and 19 February 1840, BP, MHS.

 8. EB to HWB, 22 and 23 February 1840, BP, MHS.

 9. EB to HWB, 24 and 25 February 1840, BP, MHS.

10. HWB to EB, 26 February 1840, BP, MHS.

11. HWB to WS, 8 June 1840, BP, MHS.

12. HWB to EB, 26 February 1841, BP, MHS.

13. HWB, Niagara Falls, N.Y., to his mother, 29 June 1841, BP, MHS.

14. HWB to Orville Dewey in Paris, 22 November 1841, BP, MHS.

15. HWB to OD, 22 March 1842, BP, MHS.

16. HWB to WS, 29 March 1842, BP, MHS.

17. HWB to his mother, 12 April 1842, BP, MHS.

18. John White Chadwick, *William Ellery Channing* (Boston: Houghton Mifflin, 1903), p. 421.

19. Jonathan Goodhue, *Diary,* New York Society Library, n.d.

20. HWB, "A Discourse Occasioned by the Death of William Ellery Channing, D.D." (New York: Charles S. Francis and Co., 1842).

21. Ibid., p. 23.

22. Ibid., p. 24.

23. HWB to OD, Rome, 10 January 1843, BP, MHS.

24. HWB, "Sermon Preached at the Ordination of Mr. Dexter Clapp, Over the Unitarian Church at Savannah, Georgia" (New York: Charles S. Francis and Co., 1843).

25. HWB to EB, 25 November 1843, BP, MHS.

26. All Souls Minute Book, Volume I, p. 334.

27. HWB to WS, 20 October 1843, BP, MHS.

28. HWB, *Fortieth Anniversary Sermons,* p. 16.

29. Hubbard, "First Congregational Church," p. 4.

30. Ibid., p. 4.

31. HWB, *Fortieth Anniversary Sermons,* p. 17.

32. HWB to WS, 20 October 1843, BP, MHS.

33. Hubbard, "First Congregational Church," p. 4.

The Walls Are Very Insecure
 1. All Souls Minute Book, Volume I, pp. 338–339.

 2. Ibid., p. 342.

 3. Ibid., p. 350.

 4. HWB to John Bellows, 14 January 1844, BP, MHS.

5. Jacob Landy, *Minard Lefever* (New York: Columbia University Press, 1970). This is the authoritative biography. Unfortunately at the time that the book was written the author did not know that Lafever also designed the second edifice of the First Congregational Church. I brought it to his attention in 1976 when this volume was in preparation.

6. All Souls Minute Book, Volume I, p. 354. The plans and specifications of Mr. Lafever were adopted by the trustees on 12 June 1844.

7. Transcribed in All Souls Minute Book, Volume I, p. 369.

8. HWB to WS, 10 March 1845, BP, MHS.

9. All Souls Minute Book, Volume I, p. 371.

10. Allan Nevins and Milton Halsey Thomas, eds., *The Diary of George Templeton Strong (New York: Macmillan, 1952),* 1: 267–268. *Hereinafter referred to as Strong, Diary.*

11. *A Picture of New York in 1846 with a short account of Places in its vicinity: designed as a Guide to Citizens and Strangers: with numerous engravings, and a map of the City* (New York: Charles S. Francis and Co., 1846), pp. 133–134.

12. Henry Arthur Bright, *Happy Country This America: The Travel Diary of Henry Arthur Bright* (Columbus, Ohio: Ohio State University Press, 1978), p. 73.

13. HWB, *Fortieth Anniversary Sermons,* p. 19. List of subscribers in BP, May 1845.

14. All Souls Minute Book, Volume I, p. 389.

15. All Souls Minute Book, Volume II, p. 8.

16. Benjamin Armitage to his brother Enoch in Manchester, England, 9 December 1845. Armitage Papers, Manuscript Division, New York Public Library.

A Changing Minister in a Changing New York

1. Cyrus A. Bartol to EB, 2 December 1845, BP, MHS. This letter is unsigned, but the handwriting and language are unmistakable.

2. Samuel A. Eliot, *Heralds of a Liberal Faith* (Boston: Beacon Press, 1910), 2: 20.

3. HWB to CAB, 7 January 1846, BP, MHS.

4. CAB to HWB, 15 January 1846, BP, MHS.

5. HWB to CAB, 10 February 1846, BP, MHS.

6. Robert Greenhalgh Albion, *The Rise of New York Port (1815–1860)* (New York: Charles Scribner's Sons, 1967), pp. 258–259, 275.

7. Edward Robb Ellis, *The Epic of New York City* (New York: Coward-McCann, 1966), p. 257.

8. George Willis Cooke, *Unitarianism in America* (Boston: American Unitarian Association, 1902), p. 445. (Reprinted by Ames Press, New York, 1971.)

9. Cf. William S. Osborne, *Caroline M. Kirkland* (New York: Twayne Publishers, 1972) for the interesting careers of William and Caroline Kirkland.

10. HWB to OD, 4 November 1846, BP, MHS.

11. HWB to OD, 29 November 1846, BP, MHS.

12. HWB to CAB, 2 June 1846, BP, MHS.

13. HWB to OD, 29 November 1846, BP, MHS.

14. Original Sunday School Book, All Souls archives.

15. HWB, *On the Alleged Indefiniteness of Unitarian Theology,* a tract published by the Unitarian Association of the State of New York, January 1847.

Putting His Stamp on the Parish

1. HWB, *"A Discourse in Memory of Thomas Starr King Given to His Flock in San Francisco,"* 1 May 1864, morning and evening (San Francisco: Frank Eastman, 1864).

2. HWB, *Restatements of Christian Doctrine in Twenty-Five Sermons* (New York: D. Appleton and Company, 1860).

3. HWB, "Relation of Christianity to Human Nature," A Sermon Preached at the Ordination of Mr. Frederick N. Knapp as Colleague Pastor of the First Congregational Church in Brookline, Mass., on Wednesday, 6 October 1847. (Boston: Wm. Crosby and H. P. Nichols, 1847.)

4. Communication to HWB from the All Souls trustees, 18 February 1848, BP, MHS.

Chapter 3—Indications of Reality

Revolution in France, Riots in England

1. CAB to HWB, 28 March 1848, BP, MHS.

2. HWB to WS, 2 April 1848, BP, MHS.

3. Elihu Townsend to HWB, 18 April 1848, BP, MHS.

4. Printed copies of these letters are mounted in a large scrapbook found in 1975 in the Walpole, N.H. attic.

5. Letter of Saturday, 22 April 1848.

6. Letter of 25 April 1848.

7. Ibid.

8. Letter of 28 April 1848.

9. Letter of 12 May 1848.

10. Letter of 23 May 1848.

11. Second letter of 23 May 1848.

12. First letter of 23 May 1848.

13. Letter of 7 June 1848.

14. First Letter of 20 June 1848.

15. Second letter of 20 June 1848.

16. Third letter of 20 June 1848.

17. Fourth letter of 20 June 1848.

18. Letter of 29 June 1848.

19. Letter dated July 1848.

20. Letter of 23 July 1848.

21. Letter of 30 July 1848.

22. Second letter of 30 July 1848.

23. Letter of 4 August 1848.

24. First letter of 17 August 1848.

25. Second letter of 17 August 1848.

26. Third letter of 17 August 1848. At this point the letters in the scrapbook end. Many of these had been published in the *Inquirer* weeks after Bellows had returned to the United States.

27. Cf. Samuel A. Eliot, *Heralds of a Liberal Faith,* Volume III, *The Preachers* (Boston: The American Unitarian Association, 1910), pp. 37–40.

28. Frank Bellows to HWB, 23 May 1848, BP, MHS.

29. Mrs. Kirkland wrote a book about her trip with the Bellowses. Caroline M. Kirkland, *Holidays Abroad or Europe from the West* (New York: Baker and Scribner, 1849).

She Sank Very Suddenly

1. Russell Nevins to HWB and EB, which he reconstructed from his diary, 28 October 1848, BP, MHS.

2. HWB to his mother, 23 October 1848, BP, MHS.

3. HWB to CAB, 1 November 1848, BP, MHS.

4. Ibid.

5. SO to HWB, 21 November 1848, BP, MHS.

6. Cf. Kring, *Liberals Among the Orthodox,* pp. 33, 37, 105, 256–259, for a more thorough treatment of Goodhue's life.

7. This letter is loose in the Goodhue Diary, New York Society Library.

8. HWB, "The Christian Merchant: A Discourse Delivered in the Church of the Divine Unity on the Occasion of the Death of Jonathan Goodhue." (New York: Charles S. Francis and Co., 1848.)

9. HWB to OD, 18 December 1848, BP, MHS.

10. OD to HWB, 2 January 1849, cited in Mary E. Dewey, ed., *Autobiography and Letters of Orville Dewey, D.D.* (Boston: Roberts Brothers, 1883), p. 206.

11. HWB to OD, 18 December 1848, BP, MHS.

12. Dewey, *Autobiography and Letters,* pp. 102–103.

Trembling and Rejoicing in Responsibility
1. Rufus P. Stebbins to HWB, 9 December 1845, BP, MHS.
2. For an account of the Huidekoper family consult Arthur S. Bolster, *James Freeman Clarke, Disciple to Advancing Truth* (Boston: Beacon Press, 1954), p. 105ff. Clarke married Anna Huidekoper.
3. Frederic Huidekoper to HWB, 12 April 1849, BP, MHS.
4. Kring and Carey, "Two Discoveries Concerning Herman Melville," *Proceedings* of the Massachusetts Historical Society, Volume 87 (1975), published 1976.
5. HWB to OD, 3 May 1849, BP, MHS.
6. SO to HWB, 3 May 1849, BP, MHS.
7. HWB, "A Sermon occasioned by the Late Riots in New York, preached in the Church of the Divine Unity," Sunday morning, 13 May 1849. (New York: Charles S. Francis and Co., 1849.)
8. HWB to EB, 30 May 1849, BP, MHS.
9. HWB to CAB, 15 June 1849, BP, MHS.
10. HWB to EB, 29 June 1849, BP, MHS.
11. HWB to OD, 24 October 1849, BP, MHS.
12. Ibid.
13. HWB to Mrs. Dorr, 7 November 1849, BP, MHS.
14. HWB to CAB, 8 November 1849, BP, MHS.
15. HWB to WS, 8 November 1849, BP, MHS.
16. HWB to his mother, 15 November 1849, BP, MHS.

Unagitated by Abolitionist Fever
1. Ellis, *The Epic of New York City*, p. 258.
2. HWB to CAB, 9 March 1850, BP, MHS.
3. George Simmons to HWB, 8 November 1845, BP, MHS.
4. HWB, *Fortieth Anniversary Sermons*, pp. 25–26.
5. Moses H. Grinnell to HWB, 3 March 1850, BP, MHS.
6. HWB to CAB, 9 March 1850, BP, MHS.
7. Letters to Messrs. Thomas and Grinnell by John W. Cory, 18 March 1850, BP, MHS.
8. N.B.—there is no indication in the All Souls Minute Book that the church trustees took any official action.
9. HWB to CAB, 25 March 1850, BP, MHS.
10. Board of Directors of the New York Unitarian Association to HWB, 9 May 1850, BP, MHS.
11. Conrad Wright, *The Liberal Christians* (Boston: Beacon Press, 1970), p. 75.

12. Some modern writers are not happy to label Henry Bellows a moderate in regard to the slavery issue. Douglas C. Stange in the article "From Treason to Antislavery Patriotism: Unitarian Conservatives and the Fugitive Slave Law" in the *Harvard Library Bulletin* 25 (October 1977) 4: lists Bellows as a "conservative" in these matters. Dr. Stange is quite critical of Bellows, Orville Dewey, and other Unitarian ministers for being lukewarm on the slavery issue, and one gets the impression from this article that it was only the abolitionists who were opposed to slavery. Bellows wanted to preserve the Union, and he hoped that slavery could be eradicated slowly, perhaps by purchase of the freedom of the slaves. The abolitionists wanted to drive in and free the slaves regardless of the consequences. If Bellows is to be termed a conservative because he did not like this dangerous method, then everyone is a conservative to Dr. Stange except the abolitionists.

13. Wright, *The Liberal Christians*, p. 70.

14. The *Christian Inquirer*, 22 December 1849.

Chapter 4—Going Beyond Channing

Four Long Nines

1. HWB to his mother, 1 April 1850, BP, MHS.
2. HWB to CAB, 25 March 1850, BP, MHS.
3. HWB to EB, 3 July 1851, BP, MHS.
4. HWB to his mother, 4 August 1851, BP, MHS.
5. SO to HWB, 26 August 1851, BP, MHS.
6. HWB to CAB, 8 September 1851, BP, MHS.
7. HWB to CAB, 1 November 1850, BP, MHS.
8. HWB to OD, 31 March 1851, BP, MHS.
9. Ibid.
10. SO to HWB, 26 August 1851, BP, MHS.
11. HWB to CAB, 7 November 1850, BPQ MHS.
12. CAB to HWB, 10 November 1850, BP, MHS.
13. CAB to HWB, 7 February 1851, BP, MHS.
14. HWB to WS, 5 February 1851, BP, MHS.
15. HWB to OD, 26 March 1851, BP, MHS.
16. HWB to CAB, 11 June 1850, BP, MHS.
17. HWB to OD, 11 Junen1850, BP, MHS.
18. HWB to CAB, 21 September 1851, BP, MHS.
19. HWB to John Bellows, 18 December 1851, BP, MHS.
20. HWB to WS, 6 January 1852, BP, MHS.

Beautiful Garments of Real Relief

1. HWB to EB, 23 January 1852, BP, MHS.

2. HWB to EB, 28 January 1852, BP, MHS.

3. HWB to Mrs. Dorr, 16 February 1852, BP, MHS.

4. HWB to John Bellows, 17 February 1852, BP, MHS.

5. HWB, "Religious Liberty: The Alleged Failure of Protestantism: A sermon Preached in the Unitarian church at Waahington, on Washington's Birthday, 22 February 1852." (Washington: Kirkwood and McGilll, 1852.)

6. HWB to "My dear Friend," 3 March 1852, BP, MHS.

7. HWB to OD, 13 April 1852, BP, MHS.

8. HWB to EB, 18 April 1852, BP, MHS.

9. HWB to EB, 21 April 1852, BP, MHS.

10. HWB to CAB, 3 May 1852, BP, MHS.

11. HWB to CAB, 12 May 1852, BP, MHS.

12. HWB to "My dear Friend" (perhaps CAB), 13 June 1852, BP, MHS.

13. HWB to EB, 3 August 1852, BP, MHS.

14. HWB to EB, 5 August 1852, BP, MHS.

15. HWB to CAB, 10 August 1852, BP, MHS.

16. HWB to Mrs. Dorr, 3 October 1852, BP, MHS.

17. HWB to John Bellows, 19 October 1852, BP, MHS.

18. Ibid.

Our Church Was Sold Last Night

1. HWB to John Bellows, 19 October 1852, BP, MHS.

2. Printed in the *Inquirer*, 13 November 1852.

3. George T. Curtis to HWB, 7 November 1852, BP, MHS.

4. HWB to George T. Curtis, 10 November 1852, BP, MHS.

5. HWB, *Fortieth Anniversary Sermons*, p. 19.

6. HWB to CAB, 4 January 1853, BP, MHS.

7. List of donors to the new church, dated 29 March 1853, BP, MHS.

8. HWB to CAB, 18 April 1853, BP, MHS.

9. HWB to John Bellows, 18 April 1853, BP, MHS.

10. C. F. Choate to HWB, 13 April 1853, BP, MHS.

11. Peck, *The Bellows Genealogy*, p. 319.

12. HWB, "The Ledger and the Lexicon, or Business and Literature in Account with American Education," Phi Beta Kappa Oration, Harvard University, 26 July 1853.

13. HWB to RNB, 22 July 1853, BP, MHS.

14. HWB to his mother, 7 August 1853, BP, MHS.

15. HWB to CAB, 18 August 1853, BP, MHS.

16. HWB to CAB, 22 September 1853, BP, MHS.

17. HWB to John Bellows, 2 November 1853, BP, MHS.

18. HWB to CAB, 3 December 1853, BP, MHS.

19. Ibid.

20. HWB to John Bellows, 7 December 1853, BP, MHS.

A Friendly Criticism

1. HWB to CAB, n.d. (early January 1854), BP, MHS.

2. Nicholas Dean to HWB, 12 January 1854, BP, MHS.

3. Ibid.

4. *Dictionary of American Biography* 6:2, pp. 240–243.

5. HWB to EB, 11 January 1854, BP, MHS.

6. HWB to EB, 12 January 1854, BP, MHS.

7. HWB to EB, 14 January 1854, BP, MHS.

8. HWB to CAB, 6 February 1854, BP, MHS.

9. HWB, "Unitarianism in Boston: A Friendly Criticism," 24 March 1854. Printed not published (New York: Charles S. Francis and Co., 1854).

10. HWB to CAB, 28 March 1854, BP, MHS.

11. Sermon in the Harvard Divinity School Library with a note to CAB by HWB.

12. HWB to CAB, 28 March 1854, BP, MHS.

13. George Lee Schuyler to HWB, 14 March 1854, BP, MHS.

14. HWB to George Lee Schuyler, 18 March 1854, BP, MHS.

15. George Lee Schuyler to HWB, 26 March 1854, BP, MHS.

16. William Ellery Sedgwick to HWB, 25 May 1854, BP, MHS.

17. Peck, *The Bellows Genealogy*, p. 281.

18. HWB to the Bartols in London, 28 June 1854, BP, MHS.

19. HWB to the Bartols in Europe, 16 July 1854, BP, MHS. When I visited the homestead in company with Henry Bellows's daughter, Ellen Endicott, and his granddaughter, Mrs. Anne Tower, the present owner, neither the vista nor the feelings had changed in a century and a quarter.

Chapter 5—Seasons of Duty

Cupolas Here, Cornices There

1. Strong, *Diary*, Volume 2, pp. 178–179.

2. HWB to the Bartols in Europe, 16 July 1854, BP, MHS.

3. HWB, *Historical Sketch of Colonel Benjamin Bellows*, An Address at Walpole, N.H., 11 October 1854 (New York: John A. Gray, 1855).

4. Dewey, *Autobiography and Letters*, pp. 89–91.

5. HWB to CAB, 11 April 1855, BP, MHS.

6. HWB, "A Sermon Preached at the Installation of Adams Ayer" (Brattleboro, Vt.: O. H. Platt, 1855, printed for private distribution).

7. HWB to EB, 27 June 1855, BP, MHS.

8. Charles S. Francis to HWB, 20 July 1855, BP, MHS.

9. HWB to EB, 4 September 1855, BP, MHS.

10. HWB to EB, 28 September 1855, BP, MHS.

11. HWB to EB, 10 October 1855, BP, MHS.

12. HWB to EB, 15 October 1855, BP, MHS.

13. HWB to John Bellows, 7 November 1855, BP, MHS.

14. HWB to CAB, 29 November 1855, BP, MHS.

Father of All! Thy Children Come

1. Octavius Brooks Frothingham, the son of Nathaniel Langdon Frothingham, had successfully led the North Church in Salem, Mass., since 1847. Early in 1855 Frothingham accepted a call from the newly organized Unitarian society in Jersey City, and was thus a neighbor of the New York and Brooklyn ministers.

2. Program of Dedication, All Souls Minute Book, Volume 2, p. 139.

3. *Journal of Commerce*, 27 December 1855.

4. Ibid.

5. Strong, *Diary*, Volume 2, p. 233.

6. *Journal of Commerce*, 27 December 1855.

7. Strong, *Diary*, Volume 2, p. 233.

8. "A Sheep Among Shepherds," an article by "Mintwood," *New York World*, 11 December 1870.

9. *Journal of Commerce*, 27 December 1855.

10. AB, *Recollections of HWB*, p. 11.

11. HWB, *Fortieth Anniversary Sermons*, p. 42.

12. AB, *Recollections of HWB*, p. 10.

13. All Souls Minute Book, Volume 2, pp. 141–142.

14. "List of enrollees for the series of Pastoral Lectures," 3 February 1856, BP, MHS.

15. HWB to CAB, 12 March 1856, BP, MHS.

Present Excitements

1. Frederic Henry Hedge to HWB, 22 April 1856, BP, MHS.

2. HWB to Frederic Henry Hedge, 29 April 1856, BP, MHS.

3. EEH to HWB, 16 May 1856, BP, MHS.

4. EB to HWB, 22 June 1856, BP, MHS.

5. HWB to EB, 25 June 1856, BP, MHS.

6. OD to HWB, 15 June 1856, BP, MHS.

7. HWB to OD, 9 July 1856, BP, MHS.

8. Ibid.

9. Ibid.

10. Strong, *Diary*, Volume 2, p. 362.

11. All Souls Minute Book, Volume 2, p. 152.

12. N.B.—Bellows later in 1879 incorrectly recalled this as a Thanksgiving Day sermon. It was Palm Sunday.

13. HWB, "The Relation of Public Amusements to Public Morality Especially of the Theatre to the Highest Interests of Humanity" (New York: Charles S. Francis and Co., 1857).

14. HWB, *Fortieth Anniversary Sermons*, p. 24.

15. CAB to HWB, 30 April 1857, BP, MHS.

My Track Made of Iron
1. HWB to OD, 22 June 1857 (incorrectly dated Monday the 23rd, Monday being the 22nd), BP, MHS.

2. OD to HWB, 24 June 1857, BP, MHS.

3. HWB to EB, 2 July 1857, BP, MHS.

4. Horace Mann to HWB, 22 September 1857, BP, MHS.

5. HWB to EB, 4 November 1857, BP, MHS.

6. HWB to EB, 12 November 1857, BP, MHS.

7. Strong, *Diary*, Volume 2, p. 386.

8. All Souls Minute Book, Volume 2, p. 161.

Chapter 6—The Suspense of Faith

The Weakest Part of My System
1. *Quarterly Journal* of the American Unitarian Association, Volume 1, p. 530.

2. Ibid., p. 531.

3. Ibid., p. 531.

4. Ibid., p. 532.

5. Ibid., p. 533.

6. Ibid., p. 534.

7. Ibid., p. 541.

8. Ibid., p. 543.

9. HWB to CAB, 2 July 1858, BP, MHS.

10. CAB to HWB, 3 July 1858, BP, MHS.

11. Mrs. George Schuyler to HWB, 6 July 1858, BP, MHS.

12. HWB to EB, 21 July 1858, BP, MHS.

13. HWB to EB, 22 July 1858, BP, MHS.

14. HWB to EB, 8 October 1858, BP, MHS.

15. HWB to "My dear Friend" (unidentified), 19 November 1858, BP, MHS.

16. HWB to EB, 10 November 1858, BP, MHS.

17. HWB to "My dear Friend" (perhaps OD), 19 November 1858, BP, MHS.

18. HWB to EB, 24 January 1859, BP, MHS.

19. HWB to CAB, 4 May 1859, BP, MHS.

20. HWB to EB, 18 June 1859, BP, MHS.

A New Catholic Church

1. HWB to CAB, 22 June 1859, BP, MHS.

2. HWB, "The Suspense of Faith," An Address to the Alumni of the Divinity School of Harvard University (New York: Charles S. Francis and Co., 1859).

3. HWB, *Fortieth Anniversary Sermons*, p. 24.

4. Letter signed "An humble but earnest layman of the church," to HWB, 10 July 1859, BP, MHS.

5. The *Quarterly Journal*, 1 October 1859, Volume 7, pp. 13–20.

6. Mrs. George Schuyler to HWB, 31 July 1859, BP, MHS.

7. *Harpers Weekly* Magazine, 27 August 1859, pp. 548–549.

8. Clifton J. Phillips, *Puritan and Unitarian Views of Church and Society*, unpublished thesis, Starr King School of the Ministry, Berkeley, California, 1944, p. M4.

A Sequel to the Suspense

1. HWB to CAB, 22 September 1859, BP, MHS.

2. HWB, "A Sequel to 'The Suspense of Faith'," Addressed to his own Congregation, Sunday, 25 September 1859, on the Reopening of All Souls Church after the summer vacation (New York: D. Appleton and Company, 1859).

3. HWB, *Restatements of Christian Doctrine in Twenty-Five Sermons* (New York: D. Appleton and Company, 1860).

4. HWB to WS, 22 November 1859, BP, MHS.

5. HWB to CAB, 26 December 1859, BP, MHS.

6. HWB to CAB, 12 December 1859, BP, MHS.

7. CAB to HWB, 29 December 1859, BP, MHS.

8. Frederic Henry Hedge to HWB, 7 April 1860, BP, MHS.

A Church of the Unchurched

1. H. A. Marriner to HWB, 31 July 1859, BP, MHS.

2. H. A. Marriner to HWB, 2 August 1859, BP, MHS.

3. HWB to "Dear William" (probably William Silsbee), 9 August 1859, BP, MHS.

4. The Antioch Senior class to HWB. (The letter was signed by C. W. Christy, Rebecca Rice, and Olympia Brown. Olympia Brown was ordained by the Universalist Church in 1863, the first woman in the United States to be ordained to the ministry of a regularly constituted ecclesiastical body, and was later active in the women's suffrage movement.) 9 August 1859, BP, MHS.

5. James Eastwood to HWB, 17 August 1859, BP, MHS.

6. Paul Revere Frothingham, "Octavius Brooks Frothingham," in Samuel A. Eliot, ed., *Heralds of a Liberal Faith*, Volume 3, *The Preachers* (Boston: The American Unitarian Association, 1910), pp. 121–122.

7. J. Wade Caruthers, *Octavius Brooks Frothingham, Gentle Radical* (University, Ala.: University of Alabama Press, 1977). A fine new biography of Frothingham which has a good balance of understanding.

8. Octavius Brooks Frothingham, *Recollections and Impressions* (New York and London: G. P. Putnam's Sons, 1891), p. 103.

9. SO to HWB, 23 August 1859, BP, MHS.

10. HWB to Mrs. Dorr, 24 February 1860, BP, MHS.

11. HWB to WS, 22 November 1859, BP, MHS.

12. TSK to HWB, 2 December 1859, BP, MHS.

13. HWB to EB, 7 December 1859, BP, MHS.

14. TSK to HWB, 26 December 1859, BP, MHS.

15. TSK to HWB, 2 January 1860, BP, MHS.

16. HWB to RNB and Anna B., 11 January 1860, BP, MHS.

17. HWB to George Bellows, 18 February 1860, BP, MHS.

Chapter 7—Our Commission Is Ordered by the Government
Last Days of Peace

1. Abraham Lincoln, "The Address of the Honorable Abraham Lincoln in vindication of the Policy of the framers of the Constitution and the principles of the Republican Party," 27 February 1860, Young Men's Republican Union with notes by Charles C. Holt & Cephas Brainerd (New York: G.F. Nesbitt & Co., 1860), p. 22.

2. HWB to Mrs. George Schuyler, 5 March 1860, BP, MHS.

3. Quoted in William Day Simonds, *Starr King in California* (San Francisco: Paul Elder and Co., 1917), pp. 15–16.

4. Robert B. Swain to HWB, 29 April 1860, BP, MHS.

5. HWB to EB, 21 June 1860, BP, MHS.

6. HWB to EB, 22 June 1860, BP, MHS.

7. HWB to Andrew Lipscomb, 7 August 1860, BP, MHS.

8. RNB to HWB, 23 September 1860, BP, MHS.

9. HWB to RNB, 26 September 1860, BP, MHS.

A Crisis of Extreme Interest

1. Anna B. to RNB, 20 May 1860, BP, MHS.

2. HWB to RNB, 31 October 1860, BP, MHS.

3. HWB to CAB, 7 November 1860, BP, MHS.

4. HWB to RNB, 11 November 1860, BP, MHS.

5. HWB to Mrs. Dorr, 3 December 1860, BP, MHS.

6. HWB to CAB, 12 December 1860, BP, MHS.

7. Mrs. George Schuyler to HWB, 30 December 1860, BP, MHS.

8. Harvard Class standing, 1860–1861, BP, MHS.

9. HWB to RNB, 1 January 1861, BP, MHS.

10. HWB to CAB, 8 January 1861, BP, MHS.

11. HWB to RNB, 9 January 1861, BP, MHS.

12. HWB to CAB, 13 February 1861, BP, MHS.

13. RNB to EB, 8 March 1861, BP, MHS.

14. HWB to CAB, 17 March 1861, BP, MHS.

15. HWB, *Fortieth Anniversary Sermons*, p. 27.

16. Ibid., pp. 27–28.

17. Ibid., p. 28.

18. HWB, "Duty and Interest Identical in the Present Crisis," a sermon in All Souls Church on Sunday morning, 14 April 1861. (New York: Mynkoop, Hallenbeck & Thomas, 1861.)

19. HWB, "The State and the Nation—Sacred to Christian Citizens." Sermon preached in All Souls Church, 21 April 1861 (New York: James Miller, 1861), pp. 6–7.

20. George M. Frederickson, *The Inner Civil War: Northern Intellectuals and the Crisis of the Union* (New York: Harper and Row, 1965), pp. 70, 71. I am deeply indebted to Professor Frederickson's analysis of Henry Bellows's position in this political area, and also with regard to the philosophy behind the work of the United States Sanitary Commission.

The Air Is Thick with Bayonets

1U HWB to RNB, 19 April 1861, BP, MHS.

2. HWB, "The State and the Nation—Sacred to Christian Citizens."

3. George E. Manning, Jr. to HWB, 26 April 1861, BP, MHS.

4. EB and HWB to RNB, 28 April 1861, BP, MHS.

5. HWB, Order of meeting flr 29 April 1861, BP, MHS.

6. Marjorie Greenbie, *Lincoln's Daughters of Mercy* (New York: G. P. Putnam's Sons, 1944), p. 66.

7. Ibid., p. 67.

Just a Fifth Wheel?
1. Moses H. Grinnell to Abraham Lincoln, 14 May 1861, BP, MHS.
2. HWB to EB, 16 May 1861, BP, MHS.
3. HWB to EB, 20 May 1861, BP, MHS.
4. HWB to EB, evening letter, 20 May 1861, BP, MHS.
5. HWB to EB, 21 May 1861, BP, MHS.
6. Greenbie, *Lincoln's Daughters of Mercy*, p. 72.
7. Ibid., p. 76.
8. HWB mo RNB, 23 May 1861, BP, MHS.
9. HWB to RNB, 26 May 1861, BP, MHS.
10. Ibid.
11. HWB to EB, 5 June 1861, BP, MHS.
12. HWB to RNB, 11 June 1861, BP, MHS.
13. Greenbie, *Lincoln's Daughters of Mercy*, p. 78.
14. Document No. 1., "Plan of Organization" of the United States Sanitary Commission, dated by HWB as 13 June 1861, BP, MHS.
15. HWB to RNB, 16 June 1861, BP, MHS.
16. Ibid.
17. Anna Bellows, *Recollections of Henry Whitney Bellows*, p. 20.
18. HWB to RNB, 7 July 1861.

Chapter 8—The Making of a Marvel

Things in a Higgledy-Piggledy State
1. FLO to May Cleveland Olmsted, 14 November 1860, cited in Laura Wood Roper, *FLO: A Biography of Frederick Law Olmsted* (Baltimore: The John Hopkins University Press, 1973), p. 151.
2. Ibid.
3. There were 387 killed, 1,582 wounded, and 12 missing, Boatner, *Civil War Dictionary* (New York: David McKay Company, Inc.), p. 104.
4. HWB to EB, 25 July 1861, BP, MHS.
5. HWB to "My dear Friend" (unidentified), 5 August 1861, BP, MHS.
6. HWB to EB, 6 September 1861, BP, MHS.
7. HWB to EB, 12 September 1861.
8. HWB to CAB, 13 September 1861, BP, MHS.
9. HWB to EB, 14 October 1861, BP, MHS.
10. HWB to EB, 17 October 1861, BP, MHS.
11. HWB to RNB, 12 October 1861, BP, MHS.

Great Events Are Happening Every Day
1. Cf. Benjamin P. Thomas and Harold M. Hyman, *Stanton: The Life and Times of Lincoln's Secretary of War* (New York: Alfred A. Knopf, 1962).

2. HWB to EB, 25 January 1862, BP, MHS.

3. Strong, *Diary*, Volume 3, p. 204.

4. Ibid., p. 207.

5. HWB to EB, 7 March 1862, BP, MHS.

6. Strong, *Diary*, Volume 3, p. 213.

7. TSK to HWB, 18 March 1862, BP, MHS.

8. HWB to RNB, 10 May 1862, BP, MHS.

9. HWB's list of persons in Rev. Dr. Bellows's Party, 6 May 1862, BP, MHS.

10. HWB to Katy Vose, 7 May 1862, BP, MHS.

11. EB to "Dear Friends," a kind of journal of her activities for several days, dated 9 May 1862 on first page, BP, MHS.

12. HWB to EB, 10 May 1862, BP, MHS.

13. HWB to Dr. Van Buren, copy in HWB's handwriting, 13 May 1862, BP, MHS.

14. EB to Anna B., 23 May 1862, BP, MHS.

15. William Greenleaf Eliot to HWB, 23 May 1862, BP, MHS.

16. HWB to EB, 29 June 1862, BP, MHS.

17. HWB to EB, 1 July 1862, BP, MHS.

18. HWB to TSK, 4 July 1862, BP, MHS.

19. Robert Swain to HWB, 22 July 1862, BP, MHS.

20. HWB to EB, 1 September 1862, BP, MHS.

21. HWB to EB, 3 September 1862, BP, MHS.

22. Parke Godwin and James McKaye to HWB, 6 September 1862, BP, MHS.

23. Boatner, *The Civil War Dictionary*, p. 21.

24. HWB, "The United States Sanitary Commission," in *Johnson's Universal Encyclopedia*, and also printed for private distribution. (New York: G. P. Putnam's Sons, n.d.), p. 22.

25. TSK to HWB, 18 September 1862, BP, MHS.

26. Robert Swain to HWB, 18 September 1862, BP, MHS.

27. TSK to HWB, 28 September 1862, BP, MHS.

28. TSK to HWB, 10 October 1862, BP, MHS.

29. HWB to RNB, 12 December 1862, BP, MHS.

30. Strong, *Diary*, Volume 3, p. 277.

Some Hard Nuts to Crack

1. HWB to Thomas Hill, 27 March 1862, BP, MHS.

2. Thomas Hill to HWB, 5 April 1862, BP, MHS.

3. HWB means the denomination called "Christian."

4. HWB to Thomas Hill, 11 April 1862, BP, MHS.

5. HWB to RNB, 11 April 1862, BP, MHS.

6. HWB to Thomas Hill, 16 May 1862, BP, MHS.

7. HWB to EB, 26 June 1862, BP, MHS.

8. Samuel B. Parkman to HWB, 20 October 1862, BP, MHS.

9. HWB to CAB, 24 October 1862, BP, MHS.

10. TSK to HWB, 28 October 1862, BP, MHS.

11. TSK to HWB, 31 October 1862, BP, MHS.

12. TSK to HWB, 24 November 1862, BP, MHS.

13. William Cullen Bryant to HWB, 27 November 1862, BP, MHS.

14. TSK to HWB, 10 December 1862, BP, MHS.

15. HWB to RNB, 9 November 1862, BP, MHS.

Only a Drop in the Bucket

1. General W. S. Rosecrans to HWB, 31 January 1863, BP, MHS.

2. Strong, *Diary*, Volume 3, p. 294.

3. HWB, "Speech of the Rev. Dr. Bellows, President of the United States Sanitary Commission, Made at the Academy of Music, Philadelphia, Tuesday evening, February 24, 1863." (Philadelphia: Philadelphia Agency of the United States Sanitary Commission, 1863.)

4. William H. Seward to HWB, 11 March 1863, BP, MHS.

5. HWB to EB and Anna B., 19 April 1863, BP, MHS.

6. HWB to Mrs. Dorr, 26 June 1863, BP, MHS.

7. Mrs. George Schuyler to HWB, 3 July 1863, BP, MHS.

8. HWB to Mrs. Dorr, 5 July 1863, BP, MHS.

9. HWB to "Dear Friend," 6 July 1863, BP, MHS.

10. HWB to EB, 8 July 1863, BP, MHS.

11. HWB to CAB, 4 August 1863, BP, MHS.

12. FLO to HWB, 10 August 1863, BP, MHS.

13. HWB to CAB, 19 August 1863, BP, MHS.

14. EB to HWB, 29 August 1863, BP, MHS.

15. HWB to EB, 10 October 1863, BP, MHS.

16. HWB to RNB, 13 October 1863, BP, MHS.

17. HWB telegram and the appeal dated 9 November 1863, BP, MHS.

18. Frederickson, *The Inner Civil War*, p. 98.

19. The Christian Commission was modeled after the pattern of the United States Sanitary Commission. Support came from the more conservative and evangelical denominations in America. It combined field service with evangelism. At no time did its scope of work approach that of the United States Sanitary Commission.

20. Frederickson, *The Inner Civil War*, p. 99.

21. Ibid., p. 99.

22. Ibid., p. 100.

23. Ibid., p. 100.

24. HWB, "The Valley of Decision: A Discourse of September 26, 1861, On the Occasion of the National Fast" (New York: H. B. Price, 1861).

25. Charles J. Stillé, *History of the United States Sanitary Commission* (New York: Hurd & Houghlin, 1868), p. 70.

26. Frederickson, *The Inner Civil War*, p. 102.

27. Ibid., p. 102.

28. "Statement of the Objects and Methods," Sanitary Document No. 69 (New York: 1863), p. 5.

29. Strong, *Diary*, Volume 3, pp. 274–275.

30. Frederickson, *The Inner Civil War*, p. 106.

31. Walt Whitman, *Correspondence*, ed. Edwin H. Miller (New York: 1861), Volume 1, pp. 110–111.

32. Frederickson, *The Inner Civil War*, p. 109.

Chapter 9—Approaching Its Natural Conclusion

How Heavy the Harness Is

1. Louisa Lee Schuyler to HWB, 18 January 1863, BP, MHS.

2. Cf. Kring, *Liberals Among the Orthodox*, p. 203, for a picture of the plaque, and pp. 116–203 for the life and ministry of William Ware. Unknown until it turned up in the reading of the Bellows Papers is a twelve-page letter from Mrs. Mary Ware to HWB. The letter gives a very good analysis of the character of her husband.

3. All Souls Treasurer's Book, 1841–1856, p. 92.

4. All Souls Pew Records, 1863–1866, p. 52.

5. HWB to the congregation, 27 March 1863, BP, MHS.

6. HWB to Mrs. Dorr, 20 May 1863, BP, MHS.

7. HWB to RNB, 17 September 1863, BP, MHS.

8. HWB to RNB, 25 October 1863, BP, MHS.

9. Louisa Lee Schuyler to HWB, 20 December 1863, BP, MHS.

10. SO to HWB, 19 December 1863, BP, MHS.

11. O. B. Frothingham to HWB, 24 December 1863, BP, MHS.

12. HWB to O. B. Frothingham, 30 December 1863, BP, MHS. All these letters should be compared with the account of the events as recalled by Frothingham in his book, *Reflections and Impressions*, written twenty-five years later, in which he gives an inaccurate and one-sided version of the affair.

13. O. B. Frothingham to HWB, 31 December 1863, BP, MHS.

14. Cf. *Dictionary of American Biography*, Volume IV, Part I, p. 44. Also cf. J. Wade Caruthers, *Octavius Brooks Frothingham: Gentle Radical* (University, Ala.: University of Alabama Press, 1977).

California Calls

1. HWB to OD, 2 January 1864, BP, MHS.

2. HWB to EB, 18 January 1864, BP, MHS.

3. The *North American Review* 202: 153–194. HWB's name does not appear as the author of the article nor does his name appear in the index. This is not surprising since no names appear in the *Review* nor are any names attached to any of the articles.

4. HWB to Henry Ward Beecher, 8 February 1864, BP, MHS.

5. TSK to HWB, 12 February 1864, BP, MHS.

6. Telegram from James Otis to HWB, 4 March 1864, BP, MHS.

7. Robert B. Swain, George Sreve, James Otis, and M. A. Macondra to HWB, 7 March 1864, BP, MHS. The text is also copied into the All Souls Minute Book, Volume 2, p. 231.

8. HWB to EB, 8 March 1864, BP, MHS.

9. HWB to EB, 9 March 1864, BP, MHS.

10. Robert B. Swain to HWB, telegram, 10 March 1864, BP, MHS.

11. Robert B. Swain to HWB, telegram, 12 March 1864, BP, MHS.

12. Robert B. Swain to HWB, telegram, 15 March 1864, BP, MHS.

13. All Souls Minute Book, Volume 2, p. 232.

14. Copy of telegram in RNB's hand on letter of 7 March from San Francisco, BP, MHS.

15. Charles H. Brigham to HWB, 16 March 1864, BP, MHS.

16. HWB to Anna B., 17 March 1864, BP, MHS.

17. HWB to EEH, 22 March 1864, BP, MHS.

18. HWB to RNB, 24 March 1864, BP, MHS.

19. Robert B. Swain to HWB, telegram, 31 March 1864, BP, MHS.

20. HWB to EEH, 1 April 1864, BP, MHS.

21. Will of HWB, dated 2 April 1864, and codicil dated 8 April 1864, BP, MHS.

22. Robert B. Swain to HWB, telegram, 3 April 1864, BP, MHS.

23. Strong, *Diary*, Volume 3, p. 425.

West Coast Interlude

1. HWB to Frank Bellows, 12 April 1864, BP, MHS.

2. Horatio Stebbins to HWB, 22 April 1864, BP, MHS.

3. FLO to HWB, 28 April 1864, BP, MHS. He uses the contemporary spelling of Yosemite—Yo Semite.

4. HWB to Horatio Stebbins, telegram, 30 April 1864, BP, MHS.

5. HWB to "Dear Brothers and Sisters," 3 May 1864, BP, MHS.

6. HWB, "In Memory of Thomas Starr King—a discourse Given to his Flock in San Francisco, Sunday morning and evening, May 1, 1864" (San Francisco: Frank Eastman, 1864).

7. HWB to S. P. Chase, 5 May 1864, BP, MHS.

8. HWB to Hamilton Bellows, 1 June 1864, BP, MHS.

9. HWB to EB, 2 June 1864, BP, MHS.

10. HWB to EB, 3 June 1864, BP, MHS.

11. HWB to EB, 4 June 1864, BP, MHS.

12. HWB to EB, 9 June 1864, BP, MHS.

13. HWB to "The Standing Committee" of the Sanitary Commission, 17 June 1864, BP, MHS.

14. HWB to "The Standing Committee," 22 June 1864, BP, MHS.

15. Horatio Stebbins to HWB, 12 June 1864, BP, MHS.

16. HWB to Mrs. Dorr, 30 June 1864, BP, MHS.

17. Robert B. Swain to HWB, 10 July 1864, BP, MHS.

18. Horatio Stebbins to HWB, 17 July 1864, BP, MHS.

19. HWB to someone connected with Antioch, probably EEH, early June 1864, BP, MHS.

20. HWB to Frank Bellows 17 July 1864, BP, MHS.

21. HWB to "The Standing Committee," 27 July 1864, BP, MHS.

22. HWB to "The Standing Committee," 11 August 1864, BP, MHS.

23. HWB to Mrs. Dorr, 11 September 1864, BP, MHS.

24. HWB to CAB, 12 September 1864, BP, MHS.

25. HWB, "Oration on the Occasion of the Fourteenth Anniversary of the Society of California Pioneers" (with poem by Bret Harte), (San Francisco: Alta, California Book and Job Office, 1864).

26. Letter to Abraham Lincoln from twenty-two citizens of San Francisco (signed by them), 22 September 1864, BP, MHS.

27. HWB to RNB, 19 October 1864, BP, MHS.

Looking Toward New Fields
1. Strong, *Diary*, Volume 3, pp. 501–502.

2. HWB to RNB, 2 November 1864, BP, MHS.

3. HWB to RNB, 13 November 1864, BP, MHS.

4. HWB to Frederic Henry Hedge, 13 December 1864, BP, MHS.

5. Cooke, *Unitarianism in America*, p. 188.

6. HWB to EB, 23 December 1864, BP, MHS.

7. HWB to Joseph and Mrs. Dorr, 26 December 1864, BP, MHS.

8. Strong, *Diary*, Volume 3, p. 533.

9. HWB to RNB, 2 January 1865, BP, MHS.

Chapter 10—Morning Is Breaking All Around
Finding a Creed

1. HWB to EEH, 31 December 1864, BP, MHS.

2. HWB to EEH, 16 January 1865, BP, MHS.

3. Ibid.

4. HWB to RNB, 30 January 1865, BP, MHS.

5. Henry Blanchard to HWB, 31 January 1865, BP, MHS.

6. "National Convention of Unitarian Churches," notice of the New York meeting, 1 February 1865, BP, MHS.

7. HWB to EEH, 4 February 1865, BP, MHS.

8. HWB's copy of the proof of the letter to the churches, 5 February 1865, BP, MHS.

9. Samuel May to HWB, 9 February 1865, BP, MHS.

10. HWB to EB, 21 February, 1865, BP, MHS.

11. HWB to RNB, 1 March 1865, BP, MHS.

12. A. P. Putnam to HWB, 9 March 1865, BP, MHS.

13. EEH to HWB, 10 March 1865, BP, MHS.

14. HWB to EEH, 13 March 1865, BP, MHS.

15. HWB to EEH, 17 March 1865, BP, MHS.

16. EEH to HWB, 25 March 1865, BP, MHS.

17. HWB to EEH, 27 March 1865, BP, MHS.

18. Cf. *Dictionary of American Biography*, Volume I, Part 1, pp. 279–281.

19. HWB to EEH, 27 March 1865, BP, MHS.

20. HWB to Mrs. Dorr, 3 April 1865, BP, MHS.

The Triumph of Our Denominational Life

1. Cooke, *Unitarianism in America*. The story of the Conference is one of the few parts of Bellows's career that is amply documented. Cooke has an account in pp. 190–195, from which some of my information is taken. The account usually used has been Stow Persons, *Free Religion: An American Faith* (New Haven, Conn.: Yale University Press, 1947). But this account is written largely from the point of view of the radicals who formed their own Free Religious Association. Conrad Wright, first in the Unitarian Historical Society *Proceedings*, Volume XV, Part II, 1965 (published in 1968), and then reprinted in the *Liberal Christians* (Boston: Beacon Press, 1970), pp. 81–109 has brought the whole matter, particularly HWB's role, into better perspective.

2. Conrad Wright, *The Liberal Christians*, p. 84.

3. Cyrus A. Bartol, "Henry Whitney Bellows," *Unitarian Review* 17 (1882): 234.

4. Stow Persons, *Free Religion*, p. 15.

5. HWB, "Statement of Faith of the National Liberal Christian Church of America," 7 April 1865, BP, MHS.

6. Conrad Wright, *The Liberal Christians*, p. 102.

7. HWB to EEH, 11 April 1865, BP, MHS.

8. HWB to RNB, 12 April 1865, BP, MHS.

9. O. B. Frothingham, "The Unitarian Convention and the Times" (New York: C. M. Plumb & Co., 1865).

The War Has Left Things Changed
1. EB to her sister, 16 April 1865, BP, MHS.

2. HWB, *Our Martyr President—Abraham Lincoln: Voices from the Pulpit of New York and Brooklyn*, Sermon 3 by HWB, pp. 49-63 (New York: Tibbals and Whity, 1865).

3. HWB to Police Chief Kennedy, 17 April 1865, BP, MHS.

4. Strong, *Diary*, Volume 3, p. 589.

5. HWB to CAB, 26 April 1865, BP, MHS.

6. Strong, *Diary*, Volume 3, p. 591.

7. "Official Statement of the Workings of the Sanitary Commission," 22 May 1865, bulletin, BP, MHS.

8. Financial statement in BP by Charles C. Lothrop, cashier, 2 February 1866.

9. Frederickson, *The Inner Civil War*, p. 111.

10. HWB to RNB, 7 September 1862, BP, MHS.

11. Frederickson, *The Inner Civil War*, p. 111.

12. Ibid., p. 214.

13. Antioch College announcement, June 1865, BP, MHS.

14. William Channing Russell was the son of William and Lucy Channing Russel, founders of All Souls, and now evidently spelling the name with a double "l."

15. HWB to EB, 24 June 1865, BP, MHS.

16. T. B. Forbush to HWB, 1 July 1865, BP, MHS.

17. HWB to "My dear Friend" (perhaps Bartol), 29 August 1865, BP, MHS.

18. HWB to Mrs. Dorr, 5 November 1865, BP, MHS.

19. HWB to Joseph Allen, 11 November 1865, BP, MHS.

20. HWB to CAB, 16 November 1865, BP, MHS.

21. Charles Lowe to HWB, 5 January 1866, BP, MHS.

22. Newspaper clipping in BP, unidentified and undated.

23. Robert B. Swain to HWB, 15 February 1866, BP, MHS.

24. Henry Bergh to HWB, 4 April 1866, BP, MHS. Cf. *Dictionary of American Biography*, Volume I, Part 2, pp. 215–216, article by Roswell Cheney McCrea. Cf. also Gerald Carson, *Men, Beasts, and Gods* (New York: Charles Scribner's Sons, 1972), pp. 95–106.

25. Unidentified newspaper clipping in BP, 22 May 1866, MHS.

26. Henry Bergh to HWB, 1 June 1866, BP, MHS.

Radicals Outside Our Camp

1. HWB to RNB, 12 April 1866, BP, MHS.
2. Diary of RNB, 1864–1865, BP, MHS.
3. HWB to "My dear Friend," 13 April 1866, BP, MHS.
4. Robert B. Swain to HWB, 24 May 1866, BP, MHS.
5. All Souls Marriage Records, Volume 1, p. 94.
6. HWB to EB and RNB, 28 April 1866, BP, MHS.
7. HWB to EB and RNB, dated incorrectly as Saturday morning, 19 April 1866. It was probably written Sunday morning, 29 April 1866, BP, MHS.
8. HWB to EEH, 3 May 1866, BP, MHS.
9. HWB to EEH, 5 September 1866, BP, MHS.
10. HWB to A. A. Livermore, 22 September 1866, BP, MHS.
11. HWB to EEH, 25 September 1866, BP, MHS.
12. HWB to EB, 13 October 1866, BP, MHS.
13. Cooke, *Unitarianism in America*, p. 201.
14. RNB to EB, 11 October 1866, BP, MHS.
15. Cooke, *Unitarianism in America*, pp. 202–203.
16. William Greenleaf Eliot to HWB, 1 November 1866, BP, MHS.
17. HWB to Mrs. Dorr, 4 November 1866, BP, MHS.
18. "Organization of the New York Unitarian Publication Society," in HWB's handwriting, 13 November 1866, BP, MHS.
19. O. B. Frothingham to HWB, 29 November 1866, BP, MHS.
20. HWB to EEH, 3 December 1866, BP, MHS.
21. O. B. Frothingham to HWB, 5 December 1866, BP, MHS.
22. Rufus Stebbins to HWB, 19 December 1866, BP, MHS.

Chapter 11—Troubles and Strife

Tired Down to the Bottom

1. CAB to HWB, 4 February 1867, BP, MHS.
2. HWB to CAB, 6 February 1867, BP, MHS.
3. Charles Lowe to HWB, 19 February 1867, BP, MHS.
4. Charles Chauncey to HWB, 20 February 1867, BP, MHS.

5. HWB to EEH, 23 February 1867, BP, MHS.

6. EEH to HWB, 10 March 1867, BP, MHS.

7. HWB to EEH, 10 March 1867. It must be 11 or 12 March, BP, MHS.

8. HWB to Mrs. Dorr, 22 February 1867, BP, MHS.

9. HWB to CAB, 18 March 1867, BP, MHS.

10. HWB to Catharine Sedgwick, dated, Saturday 22 March (must be 23 March if it was a Saturday) 1867, BP, MHS.

11. HWB to eleven benefactors, 19 April 1867, BP, MHS.

12. Samuel Shaw to HWB, 1 May 1867, BP, MHS.

13. Shaw's letter (6 May 1867), BP, MHS, is given in full in Walter D. Kring and Jonathan Carey, "Two Discoveries Concerning Herman Melville," *Proceedings* of the MHS 87 (1975): 137–141 (published in 1976). Dr. Hershel Parker, noted Melville scholar, has called this "the most important biographical article that has yet appeared on Melville," and the Melville Society is preparing a book on the basis of this find in the Bellows Papers.

14. This letter of 20 May 1867, BP, MHS, is printed in full in the above *Proceedings* article.

15. List of preachers in HWB's handwriting, BP, MHS.

16. HWB to EEH, 10 April 1869, BP, MHS.

A Rich Rewarding Journey in the East

1. HWB, *The Old World in Its New Faces: Impressions of Europe in 1867#1868* (New York: Harper and Brothers), Volume 1, 1868, Volume 2, 1869. 982 pages total.

2. HWB to "Dear Brothers and Sisters," 11 June 1867, BP, MHS.

3. HWB to Mrs. Dorr, 17 July 1867, BP, MHS.

4. HWB, *The Old World in Its New Faces*, Volume 2, pp. 84–85.

5. Ibid.

6. Charles Lowe to HWB, 12 December 1867, BP, MHS.

7. HWB, *The Old World in Its New Faces*, Volume 2, p. 242.

8. Ibid., pp. 153–154.

9. HWB to CAB, 30 May 1868, BP, MHS.

10. HWB, "Seven Sittings with Powers, the Sculptor," *Appleton's Popular Journal of Literature, Science, and Art.* The first five are in Volume 1, the last two in Volume 2, 1868.

11. "Sentiments at the Collation, 4 June 1868," BP, MHS.

12. HWB to Frank Bellows, 16 July 1868, BP, MHS.

13. This presentation album showed up recently in the Bellows homestead at Walpole, N.H. Through the generosity of HWB's granddaughter, Mrs. George W. Tower, it now rests in the Andover Harvard Library at Harvard Divinity School. When she and the author found the presentation booklet it would probably have been passed over except that, having read the Bellows

Papers about the presentation album, I immediately knew what it was. Since the volume has probably scarcely been opened since Bellows's death, the pictures are in mint condition, and they represent a beautiful historical source book about the Unitarian ministers of England in 1868. In addition to the ministers, the book contains an unmarked photo that looks surprisingly like HWB's parishioner William Cullen Bryant, an unidentified woman, Mrs. Gaskell, Cardinal Antonelli, and HWB's distant relative John Bellows (not Henry's brother) of Gloucester, England.

14. HWB to A. A. Livermore, 29 August 1868, BP, MHS.

15. HWB to "My dear Friend," marked "Private," 3 September 1868, BP, MHS. "My dear Friend" is unidentified.

The Osgood Affair

1. HWB to the Trustees of the First Congregational Church, 28 August 1868, BP, MHS.

2. HWB to Mrs. David Lane, 28 August 1868, BP, MHS.

3. All Souls Minute Book, Volume 2, p. 296.

4. Ibid., pp. 297–299.

5. Ibid., p. 297.

6. EEH to HWB, 19 August 1868, BP, MHS.

7. Samuel J. May to HWB, 2 October 1868, BP, MHS.

8. Cf. Cooke, *Unitarianism in America*, pp. 204–205.

9. HWB to EB, 8 October 1868, BP, MHS.

10. Rufus Ellis to HWB, 10 October 1868, BP, MHS.

11. HWB to RNB, 21 October 1868, BP, MHS.

12. License of RNB to preach, 23 October 1868, BP, MHS.

13. SO to HWB, 16 October 1868, BP, MHS. The Minutes of All Souls Church make no record of this event.

14. HWB to EB, 22 November 1868, BP, MHS.

15. SO to HWB, 23 November 1868, BP, MHS.

16. SO to HWB, 28 November 1868, BP, MHS.

17. HWB to SO, copy, 28 November 1868, BP, MHS.

18. SO to HWB, 5 December 1868, BP, MHS.

19. SO to HWB, 6 December 1868, BP, MHS.

20. HWB to EB, 7 December 1868, BP, MHS.

21. Ibid.

22. SO to HWB, 8 December 1868, BP, MHS.

23. SO to HWB, 11 December 1868, BP, MHS.

24. SO to HWB, 24 December 1868, BP, MHS.

25. HWB to RNB, 30 December 1868, BP, MHS.

I Don't Like to Mix In
1. HWB to EB, 2 January 1869, BP, MHS.
2. HWB to "Dear Friends All," 4 January 1869, BP, MHS.
3. HWB to EB, 11 January 1869, BP, MHS.
4. HWB to EB, 13 January 1869, BP, MHS.
5. HWB to OD, 22 January 1869, BP, MHS.
6. HWB to EB, 24 January 1869, BP, MHS.
7. HWB to SO, copy, 25 January 1869, BP, MHS.
8. SO to HWB, 25 January 1869, BP, MHS.
9. SO to HWB, 27 January 1869, BP, MHS.
10. HWB to EB, 2 February 1869, BP, MHS.
11. HWB to RNB, 25 February 1869, BP, MHS.
12. HWB to RNB, 4 March 1869, BP, MHS.
13. SO to HWB, 18 March 1869, BP, MHS.
14. HWB to RNB, 24 March 1869, BP, MHS.
15. HWB to RNB, 29 March 1869, BP, MHS.
16. HWB to EEH, 1 April 1869, BP, MHS.
17. EEH to HWB, 6 April 1869, BP, MHS.
18. HWB to EEH, 10 April 1869, BP, MHS.
19. SO to HWB, 11 May 1869, BP, MHS.
20. HWB to EEH, 19 May 1869, BP, MHS.
21. List is in the BP,, MHS, dated June 1869.
22. HWB to EB, 21 June 1869, BP, MHS.

Chapter 12—A Green Old Age

Never Fully at Home in the Flesh
1. HWB to Hamilton Bellows, 14 July 1869, BP, MHS.
2. HWB to EB, 27 July 1869, BP, MHS.
3. HWB to Anna B., late July or early August 1869, BP, MHS.
4. HWB to "My dear Friend" (perhaps OD), 17 August 1869, BP, MHS.
5. HWB to Anna B., 25 August 1869, BP, MHS.
6. HWB to Mrs. Dorr, 7:00 A.M., 27 August 1869, BP, MHS.
7. HWB to JFC, 27 August, Friday night, 1869, BP, MHS.
8. HWB to CAB, 28 August (should be 29 August), 1869, BP, MHS.
9. HWB to Mrs. Dorr, 28 or 29 August 1869, BP, MHS.
10. Newspaper clipping in the BP, MHS, "Eliza N. Bellows," signed CAB.
11. HWB to OD, 7 September 1869, BP, MHS.
12. HWB to WS, 8 September 1869, BP, MHS.

13. Charles Lowe, printed report of the "American Unitarian Association," 1 October 1869, BP, MHS.

14. Installation program of the Third Unitarian Society in Brooklyn, 6 October 1869, BP, MHS.

15. Drake Brothers to HWB, 28 October 1869, BP, MHS. Cf. also letter of Dr. Richard Wunder, Senior Research Fellow of the Smithsonian Institution, to the author, 16 February 1972, regarding the identification of the two busts. All Souls archives.

16. George Hunston Williams, ed., *The Harvard Divinity School: Its Place in Harvard University and in American Culture* (Boston: Beacon Press, 1954), pp. 92–99.

17. Cf. *Dictionary of American Biography*, Volume IV, Part 2, pp. 569–570.

18. Four New York Ministers to "The Publication Society," 1 December 1869, BP, MHS.

19. Hiram Powers to HWB, 1 December 1869, BP, MHS.

20. Charles Lowe to HWB, 17 December 1869, BP, MHS.

The Life of a Widower
1. HWB to EEH, 23 February 1870, BP, MHS.
2. Charles Lowe to HWB, 28 February 1870, BP, MHS.
3. Robert B. Swain to HWB, 13 March 1870, BP, MHS.
4. HWB to "Dear Friend," 14 July 1870, BP, MHS.
5. HWB to "Dear Friend" (perhaps CAB), 4 September 1870, BP, MHS. (For anyone interested in the Adirondack Lakes region in 1870, there are many long letters about the area.)
6. HWB to Mrs. Dorr, 27 September 1870, BP, MHS.
7. Harper & Brothers to HWB, 30 November 1870, BP, MHS.
8. HWB to OD, 10 April 1871, BP, MHS.
9. Rush R. Shippen to HWB, 13 June 1871, BP, MHS.
10. HWB to OD, 8 July 1871, BP, MHS.
11. HWB to Mrs. David Lane, 4 September 1871, BP, MHS.
12. Robert Collyer to HWB, 17 October 1871, BP, MHS.
13. HWB in a note about Mrs. Hoge of Chicago who was collecting dry goods, 13 October 1871, BP, MHS.
14. HWB to Miss Collins in Chicago, 24 October 1871, BP, MHS.

The Hepworth Affair
1. HWB to "My dear Friend" (perhaps OD), Christmas Day, 1871, BP, MHS. Cf. HWB to Rush R. Shippen, 28 December 1871, AUA Papers, Harvard Divinity School Library.
2. Rush R. Shippen to HWB, 29 December 1871, BP, MHS.

3. Rush R. Shippen to HWB, 30 December 1871, BP, MHS.

4. HWB to EEH, 3 January 1872, BP, MHS.

5. EEH to HWB, 5 January 1872, BP, MHS.

6. HWB to EEH, 9 January 1872, BP, MHS.

7. HWB to George William Fox, 17 January 1872, AUA Papers, Andover-Harvard Theological Library.

8. Rush R. Shippen to HWB, 26 January 1872, BP, MHS.

9. HWB, off Queenstown, Ireland (now Cobh), to Mrs. Dorr, 28 June 1872, BP, MHS.

10. HWB, "John Howard: His Life, Character and Services," an address delivered before the International Prison Congress in London, 3–13 July 1872 (London: Office of the Congress, 1872).

11. HWB to OD, 2 August 1872, BP, MHS.

12. HWB to CAB, 6 August 1872, BP, MHS.

13. HWB to Hattie Wheelock, 19 August 1872, BP, MHS.

14. HWB to Mrs. Dorr, 9 October 1872, BP, MHS.

15. HWB to Hattie Wheelock (Mrs. Dorr's daughter), 17 October 1872, BP, MHS.

16. HWB to Orville Dewey, 26 December 1872, BP, MHS.

17. HWB to CAB, 7 March 1873, BP, MHS.

18. HWB to A. A. Livermore, 23 September 1873, BP, MHS.

19. Nathan Chandler to HWB, 10 December 1873, BP, MHS.

20. HWB to William Prichard, 6 November 1873, BP, MHS.

21. Elizabeth S. Melville to William Prichard, 29 December 1873. Mr. Prichard put a note in the upper right-hand corner of the first page of the letter: "Mrs. [Herman] Melville," and appended the date, "31 Dec. 1873." Her letter must have been written on 29 December and he noted the cessation of holding the pew as of 31 December. All Souls archives.

The Pillow and Staff of My Remaining Pilgrimage

1. HWB to RNB, 16 January 1874, BP, MHS.

2. HWB to RNB, 18 January 1874, BP, MHS.

3. HWB to Roxy Vose, 30 January 1874, BP, MHS.

4. HWB to RNB, 5 February 1874, BP, MHS.

5. HWB to RNB, 8 February 1874, BP, MHS.

6. HWB to RNB, 10 February 1874, BP, MHS.

7. Nathan Chandler to HWB, 19 March 1874, BP, MHS.

8. HWB to A. A. Livermore, 22 March 1874, BP, MHS.

9. HWB to Anna B., 13 April 1874, BP, MHS.

10. HWB to RNB, 17 April 1874, BP, MHS.

11. HWB to RNB, 20 April 1874, BP, MHS.

12. RNB to Anna B., 22 April 1874, BP, MHS.

13. HWB to RNB, 22 April 1874, BP, MHS.

14. HWB to CAB, 23 April 1874, BP, MHS.

15. Mary Jane Derby Peabody, unpublished autobiography in the Derby-Peabody Papers, MHS.

16. HWB to RNB and Anna B., 26 April 1874, BP, MHS.

17. Mrs. Ephraim Peabody to Anna B., 29 April 1874, BP, MHS.

18. HWB to RNB and Anna B., 20 June 1874, BP, MHS.

19. HWB to OD, 4 July 1874, BP, MHS.

Chapter 13—As Life Wears to Its Close

The Sweetest of Cries

1. HWB to OD, 26 September 1874, BP, MHS.

2. George Batchelor to HWB, 24 August 1874, BP, MHS.

3. HWB to George Batchelor, 28 August 1874, BP, MHS.

4. HWB to OD, 26 September 1874, BP, MHS.

5. Jackson S. Schultz to HWB, 27 September 1874, BP, MHS.

6. Artemas Carter, Murray Nelson, and George Payson to HWB, 16 October 1874, BP, MHS.

7. Robert Collyer to HWB, 21 October 1874, BP, MHS.

8. HWB to RNB, 21 October 1874, BP, MHS.

9. HWB to OD, 5 November 1874, BP, MHS.

10. All Souls Minute Book, Volume 2, p. 405.

11. HWB to RNB, 27 January 1875, BP, MHS.

12. RNB, Washington, to HWB, 28 January 1875, BP, MHS.

13. HWB to RNB, 1 February 1875, BP, MHS.

14. HWB to Charles Wendte, 22 May 1875, BP, MHS.

15. HWB to RNB, 29 June 1875, BP, MHS.

16. HWB to OD, 18 July 1875, BP, MHS.

17. HWB to RNB, 13 August 1875, BP, MHS.

18. HWB to RNB, 18 August 1875, BP, MHS.

19. HWB to EEH, 25 August 1875, BP, MHS.

20. HWB to OD, 25 August 1875, BP, MHS.

Sort of a Fossil

1. HWB to RNB, 21 October 1875, BP, MHS.

2. Cf. Laurence C. Staples, *Washington Unitarianism* (Northampton, Mass.: Metcalf Printing & Publishing Co., 1970), p. 56.

3. HWB to OD, 7 April 1876, BP, MHS.

4. HWB to RNB, 30 June 1876, BP, MHS.

5. HWB to RNB, 13 July 1876, BP, MHS.

6. George Batchelor to HWB, 2 November 1876, BP, MHS.

7. HWB to Anna B., 19 January 1877, BP, MHS.

8. Mrs. George Schuyler to HWB, 27 January 1877, BP, MHS.

9. Dr. Augustus Blauvelt was born in Covert, Seneca County, New York, 7 April 1832. He was graduated from Rutgers in 1858 and from the Dutch Reformed Theological Seminary in New Brunswick, New Jersey, in 1861. He had pastorates in Philadelphia and the Madison Street Chapel in New York. From 1862 to 1864 he was a missionary in China. He was the minister of the Dutch Reformed Church at Bloomington, N.Y., from 1866 until 1871. After that time he devoted himself to literary work. The degree of Doctor of Divinity was conferred upon him by Rutgers University because of certain articles he had written in defense of Christian truth. He later wrote some articles in which he expressed some Unitarian views, and he was deposed from the ministry of the Protestant Reformed (Dutch) Church in 1877. The biographical account in Appleton's says that "incessant labor and mental anxiety resulted in loss of health and he became insane." (*Appleton's Cyclopedia of American Biography* [New York: 1877], Volume I, p. 290; and *Biographical Record; Theological Seminary, New Brunswick, New Jersey, 1784-1934*, p. 109.) He was corresponding with Dr. Bellows about his Unitarian views early in 1877, and shortly after Bellows's death in 1882 he was given money to do missionary work for the American Unitarian Association. In 1883 he declared himself a Unitarian minister, and was listed in the AUA Yearbook until his death at Binghamton on 14 April 1900. One wonders whether the judgment "insane" had to do with his psychological or theological health.

10. HWB to Augustus Blauvelt, 1 February 1877, BP, MHS.

11. HWB to Augustus Blauvelt, 13 February 1877, BP, MHS.

12. Deed of William Potts to RNB, 10 February 1877, BP, MHS.

13. HWB to JFC, 9 May 1877, BP, MHS.

14. HWB to CAB, 22 May 1877, BP, MHS.

15. HWB to RNB, 27 June 1877, BP, MHS.

16. HWB to RNB, 4 July 1877, BP, MHS.

17. George Schuyler to HWB, 20 July 1877, BP, MHS.

18. HWB to OD, 23 July 1877, BP, MHS.

19. Rush R. Shippen to HWB, 7 August 1877, BP, MHS.

20. HWB to "Dear Children," 13 August 1877, BP, MHS.

21. HWB to RNB, 31 August 1877, BP, MHS.

22. HWB to RNB, 4 September 1877, BP, MHS.

23. Rush R. Shippen to HWB, 6 September 1877, BP, MHS.

24. Fortunately we have preserved in the BP a long letter from Dr. De Normandie of Portsmouth, N.H., 13 September 1877, outlining the

tentative program of the committee meeting, which HWB could not attend. Also a letter from HWB to RNB of some fourteen pages, 11 October 1877, giving HWB's reaction to the Conference.

25. HWB to RNB, 11 October 1877, BP, MHS.

26. Ibid.

27. Ibid.

28. Contract between George Ellis and RNB, 1 October 1877, BP, MHS.

29. HWB to George (unidentified), 3 November 1877, BP, MHS.

Mine Eyes Have Seen the Salvation

1. HWB to WS, 15 February 1878, BP, MHS.

2. HWB to OD, 25 February 1878, BP, MHS.

3. HWB to Parke Godwin, 26 January 1878, BP, MHS.

4. HWB to "Dear Children," 22 March 1878, BP, MHS.

5. HWB to OD, 12 April 1878, BP, MHS.

6. Rush R. Shippen to HWB, 24 April 1878, BP, MHS.

7. HWB to "Dear Friend" (unidentified), 8 May 1878, BP, MHS.

8 .This story in detail is related in Charles H. Brown's *William Cullen Bryant* (New York: Charles Scribner's Sons, 1971), pp. 518–521.

9. HWB to "My dear Friend" (perhaps OD), 31 May 1878, BP, MHS.

10. Charles H. Brown, *William Cullen Bryant,* p. 520.

11. HWB to "Dearest Friend" (unidentified), 13 June 1878, BP, MHS.

12. Charles H. Brown, *William Cullen Bryant,* p. 521.

13. HWB, "In Memoriam: William Cullen Bryant," Funeral Oration (New York: Religious Newspaper Agency, 1878).

14. HWB to "My dear Friend" (probably OD), 14 June 1878, BP, MHS.

15. HWB to CAB, 1 July 1878, BP, MHS.

16. HWB to OD, 13 July 1878, BP, MHS.

17. HWB to OD, 23 September 1878, BP, MHS.

Saving the Second Church

1. Dexter Hawkins to HWB, 9 November 1878, BP, MHS.

2. Rush R. Shippen to HWB, 22 November 1878, BP, MHS.

3. HWB to OD, 12 December 1878, BP, MHS.

4. Financial Statement, Church of the Messiah, 11 December 1878, BP, MHS.

5. Dexter Hawkins to HWB, 16 December 1878, BP, MHS.

6. HWB's copy of this resolution in BP, MHS. Also recorded in The All Souls Minute Book, Volume 2, pp. 486–487. The resolution was signed by Henry D. Sedgwick, secretary.

7. HWB to Anna B., 2 February 1879, BP, MHS.

8. HWB to "Dearest Chuck" (unidentified), 5 February 1879, BP, MHS.

9. HWB to Anna B., 13 February 1879, BP, MHS.

10. HWB to OD, 19 February 1879, BP, MHS.

11. Rush R. Shippen to HWB, 27 February 1879, BP, MHS.

12. HWB to OD, 28 February 1879, BP, MHS.

13. Rush R. Shippen to HWB, 5 March 1879, BP, MHS.

14. Rush R. Shippen to HWB, 13 March 1879, BP, MHS.

15. HWB to OD, 9 March 1879, BP, MHS.

16. HWB, "Address at the celebration of the lifting of the debt of the Church of the Messiah, 18 December 1879, The Unitarian Traditions of New York" (no indication of publisher).

17. HWB to OD, 20 March 1879, BP, MHS.

Chapter 14—The Old Warrior

I Begin to Feel My Limits

1. Brooke Herford to HWB, 13 August 1879, BP, MHS.

2. HWB to OD, 25 August 1879, BP, MHS.

3. Robert Collyer to HWB, 1 September 1879, BP, MHS. (Collyer never went to school, so his punctuation is almost nonexistent, and his letter is reproduced as it is.)

4. HWB to "My dear Friend." This is usually OD but on political matters it is often William Weeden of Providence. 8 October 1879, BP, MHS.

5. HWB to OD, 25 October 1879, BP, MHS.

6. Ibid.

7. Rush R. Shippen to HWB, 31 October and 1 November 1879, BP, MHS.

8. HWB to Mr. or Mrs. Adee, 17 November 1879, BP, MHS.

9. Special communication from Myer Sterze, the secretary of the board of trustees of Temple Emanu-El, New York City, to HWB, 2 December 1879, BP, MHS.

10. HWB, "Religious Toleration, a Discourse given in Temple Emanu-El, New York, on the Day of National Thanksgiving, November 27, 1879, by Henry W. Bellows, Minister of the First Congregational Church, New York. Published at the request of the Congregation" (New York: G. P. Putnam's Sons, 1880).

11. HWB to OD, 23 December 1879, BP, MHS.

12. HWB to EEH, 2 February 1880, BP, MHS.

13. Charles W. Eliot to HWB, 10 February 1880, BP, MHS.

14. Charles W. Eliot to HWB, 13 February 1880, BP, MHS.

15. W. P. Tilden to HWB, 16 March 1880, BP, MHS.

16. HWB to "Dear Friend," 27 March 1880, BP, MHS. Ellen Derby

Bellows Robinson Endicott was the last survivor of HWB's children. She died on 6 August 1972 at the age of ninety-two, intelligent and active to the end. The author knew her and visited with her at the Walpole home. She had three children by her first husband (Dr. Samuel Robinson, a Boston chest surgeon), Anne (Mrs. George W.) Tower, Katharine L. Robinson (a painter), and Thomas L. Robinson (the former owner of a newspaper in Charlotte, N.C., and former vice president and general manager of the *New York Herald Tribune*. These three children of Ellen Endicott are still living (1979) and have been of inestimable help in the preparation of the biographical material and by supplying photographs.

17. HWB to Charles Wendte, 3 April 1880, BP, MHS.

18. HWB to OD, 11 April 1880, BP, MHS. Bellows spoke at the Newport celebration. HWB, "William Ellery Channing: His Opinions, Genius and Character," given at Newport, R.I., 7 April 1880 (New York: G. P. Putnam's Sons, 1880).

The Wade School of Religious Philosophy

1. HWB to Charles A. Perkins, 20 May 1880, BP, MHS.

2. F. W. Hooper to HWB, 29 May 1880, BP, MHS.

3. HWB to OD, 4 August 1880, BP, MHS.

4. HWB to Mrs. Bellows, 19 September 1880, BP, MHS.

5. HWB to Mrs. Adee, 2 October 1880, BP, MHS.

6. HWB to OD, 23 October 1880, BP, MHS.

7. HWB to OD, 13 December 1880, BP, MHS.

8. Charles W. Eliot to HWB, 24 December 1880, BP, MHS.

9. HWB to WS, 28 December 1880, BP, MHS.

10. HWB to "Dear Friend" (probably OD), 10 January 1881, BP, MHS.

11. Cf. *Dictionary of American Biography*, Volume X, Part 1, p. 306.

12. The history of the proposed Wade Theological School has been written by George D. Exoo in "Cerebral Seminary: The Story of the Wade Theological School," in *The Proceedings of the Unitarian Historical Society* in Volume XV, Part II, 1965 (published in 1968). Here I have given only a summary of this important concern of the last year of HWB's life.

13. Alfred Huidekoper to Grindall Reynolds, 22 November 1882, AUA Papers, Andover-Harvard Theological Library.

14. Jeptha Homer Wade to HWB, 6 November 1880, BP, MHS.

15. HWB to A. A. Livermore, 24 November 1880, BP, MHS.

16. HWB to OD, 21 January 1881, BP, MHS.

17. HWB to EEH, 22 January 1881, BP, MHS.

18. HWB to Anna B., 16 January 1881, BP, MHS.

19. EEH to HWB, 29 June 1881, BP, MHS.

20. EEH to Jeptha Homer Wade, copy sent to HWB, 7 July 1881, BP, MHS.

21. Jeptha Homer Wade to HWB, 12 September 1881, BP, MHS.

22. HWB to EEH, 16 September 1881, BP, MHS.

23. Jeptha Homer Wade to Grindall Reynolds, 21 September 1881, AUA Papers, Andover-Harvard Theological Library. Quoted in full in Exoo, "Cerebral Seminary."

24. Exoo, "Cerebral Seminary," pp. 52–53.

25. HWB to Grindall Reynolds, 16 January 1882, AUA Papers, Andover-Harvard Theological Library.

26. Exoo, "Cerebral Seminary," p. 57.

Our Generation Is Thinning Out
1. HWB to "Dear Friend" (perhaps OD), 2 February 1881, BP, MHS.

2. HWB to OD, 13 February 1881, BP, MHS.

3. Hamilton Fish, Jr. to HWB, 22 February 1881, BP, MHS.

4. HWB to OD, 18 April 1881, BP, MHS.

5. HWB to Mrs. Bellows and Anna B., 25 May 1881, BP, MHS.

6. HWB to OD, 28 May 1881, BP, MHS.

7. HWB to OD, 11 June 1881, BP, MHS.

8. HWB to RNB, 11 June 1881, BP, MHS.

9. HWB to Frederic Henry Hedge, 13 June 1881, BP, MHS.

10. HWB to Anna B., 19 June 1881, BP, MHS.

11. HWB to Andrew Lipscomb, 21 August 1881, BP, MHS.

12. HWB to Anna B., 12 September 1881, BP, MHS.

13. HWB to RNB, 27 September 1881, BP, MHS.

14. Elijah Dunbar to RNB, 28 September 1881, BP, MHS.

15. The *Christian Register*, 27 October 1881.

16. HWB to OD, 22 October 1881, BP, MHS.

That Glorious and Inspiring Beyond
1. Clara Barton to HWB, 19 November 1881, and another undated letter, probably in December 1881, BP, MHS.

2. HWB to "Dear Friend" (unidentified, perhaps OD), 27 November 1881, BP, MHS.

3. HWB to RNB and Anna B., 16 December 1881, BP, MHS.

4. HWB to "Dear Children" (RNB and Anna B.), 16 December 1881, BP, MHS.

5. HWB to Anna B. and RNB, 18 December 1881, BP, MHS.

6. HWB to OD, 23 December 1881, BP, MHS.

7. Quoted in Peck, *The Bellows Genealogy*, p. 316.

8. Ibid., p. 317.

9. HWB to OD, 15 January 1882, BP, MHS.

10. Anna Bellows, *Reminiscences of Henry W. Bellows*, p. 27.

11. Peck, *The Bellows Genealogy*, p. 317.

12. Dr. W. H. Draper, progress report, 28 January 1882, BP, MHS.

13. Anna Bellows, *Reminiscences of Henry W. Bellows*, p. 27.

14. RNB to OD, 8 February 1882, BP, MHS.

15. OD to HWB, 11:00 A.M., 30 January 1882, BP, MHS.

16. Most of this material is taken from the *Christian Register*, Thursday, 9 February 1882, 61:6. It contains not only an account of the funeral but the address of EEH, an article ("Personal Immortality") by HWB, and an extract from his earliest published work, "Respectability or Holiness," 1838.

17. Later other burials were added to the plot, so that today it is almost full, except for one grave. Added were these persons: Thorndike Howe Endicott (1965), Ellen Derby Bellows Endicott (1972), Russell Nevins Bellows (1914), Anna Langdon Bellows (1906), Anna Huidekoper Peabody Bellows (1920), Henry Whitney Bellows, Jr. (1893), Robert Peabody Bellows (1957), Harriet Augustus Bellows Allen (1897), Mary Elizabeth Bellows (daughter of John Bellows, 1891), and Mary Nichols Bellows (wife of John Bellows, 1887).

18. A copy of HWB's will is in the BP, MHS. 24 January 1882. A list of those who subscribed the $50,000 is in the All Souls archives.

19. William Wardwell, secretary of the board of trustees, to RNB, 1 February 1882, BP, MHS.

20. Speech of Frederic Henry Hedge, UUA *Reports* for 1882, pp. 20–27.

21. Unfortunately this work by Saint-Gaudens is almost unknown. Louise Tharp does not mention it in her definitive work on Saint-Gaudens (Louise Hall Tharp, *Saint-Gaudens and the Gilded Era* (Boston: Little Brown, 1969), although a plaster cast is in the Saint-Gaudens National Monument at Cornish, N.H. This cast was made for a traveling exhibition of Saint-Gauden's sculpture by the Metropolitan Art Museum.

Appendix B: Church Membership Criteria

1. Cf. Kring, *Liberals Among the Orthodox*, pp. 89–90, for the full account and text of the first Covenant.

2. Bylaws of the First Congregational Church of the City of New York, 1843, All Souls archives.

3. These documents were found loose in the second volume of the All Souls Minute Book. I presume that they were not entered on the records of the society because the church was a separate entity. Unfortunately neither the minutes of the meeting supposedly kept by Bellows nor the "list of members" has been found.

Bibliography

Bibliographical Note

THIS BIOGRAPHY OF Henry Whitney Bellows has been written from hitherto largely unexplored primary resources. The chief source is the Bellows Papers in the Massachusetts Historical Society which consists of some sixty-six boxes of family correspondence, of which approximately the first half covers the period of Bellows's life. These papers were given to the Society in 1933 by Bellows' son, Robert P. Bellows, and his daughter Mrs. Ellen Bellows Endicott.

Newly cataloged are the American Unitarian Association letters in the Andover-Harvard Library. In these papers there are 383 letters from Bellows to whoever was the Secretary of the American Unitarian Association at the time. Extensive reading of these letters shows that in many cases they are repetitive of the material in the Bellows Papers. The AUA letters are pasted into books which makes machine copying a major problem.

The most important extant account of Bellows's life and personality is in *The Bellows Genealogy, Or John Bellows* by Thomas Bellows Peck et al (Keene, N.H.: Sentinel Printing Co.). The article is thirty-seven pages long and was written by his son Russell. More helpful are the two sermons which Bellows preached on the occasion of his fortieth anniversary in 1879 and which were printed by All Souls Church. A little booklet by his daughter Anna Bellows and a book by his cousin Emily Barnes on some recollections of his youth in Walpole are helpful.

The best modern interpretation of Bellows is that by Dr. Conrad Wright of the Harvard Divinity School in several articles in *The Liberal Christians* in which Wright assesses Bellows's views on slavery and his work with the National Conference of Unitarian Churches.

There is also extensive material by Bellows in the United States Sanitary Commission Papers in the New York Public Library. These papers were organized by Bellows and others after the Civil War, but constitute material about a very specialized part of his career too detailed for a biography such as this.

There is some question as to what has happened to a large collection of Bellows's manuscript sermons. Russell Bellows mentions in Peck, *The Bellows Genealogy*, p. 315, that Bellows left "some twelve hundred manuscript sermons and lectures." However, in the Bellows Papers there are only several dozen of these manuscripts. What happened to the rest is at present unknown.

Since there is no general bibliography of Henry Bellows's printed material in circulation it seems appropriate to list all of the known writings but to omit a general bibliography which can be found in the footnotes. The list of printed works is extensive, but some may have been inadvertently overlooked. Not included are the many articles which he contributed to the *Christian Examiner* and the *Christian Inquirer*.

Note on Bellows's Magazine Publishing and Editing

The *Christian Inquirer* was started in New York on 17 October 1846 as a weekly newspaper with four six-column pages. It was managed by the New York Unitarian Association under Bellows's editorship. On 22 December 1866, the *Christian Inquirer* became the *Liberal Christian*. On 2 December 1876 it became the *Inquirer* and continued until the end of 1877.

The *Christian Examiner* was a monthly magazine rather than a newspaper. It was begun in 1831 and had successive prominent editors. It was purchased in 1865 by James Walker, who brought it to New York with Bellows as editor. It was discontinued with the December issue in 1869.

For further information on Unitarian newspapers and magazines consult George Willis Cooke, *Unitarianism in America* (Boston: The American Unitarian Association, 1902; reprinted by the Ames Press, New York, 1971), pp. 447–452.

List of Publications by Henry Whitney Bellows

Books

Re-Statements of Christian Doctrine, in Twenty-Five Sermons. New York, London: Appleton and Co., 1860.

The Old World in Its New Faces: Impressions of Europe in 1867–1868. New York: Harper and Brothers, 2 volumes, 1868–1869.

Twenty-Four Sermons Preached in All Souls Church New York, 1865–1881, selected and edited by Russell N. Bellows. New York: published by the editor, 1886.

Addresses

"The Ledger and the Lexicon: Business and Literature in Account with American Education," Phi Beta Kappa oration at Harvard University, 6 July 1853. Cambridge, Mass.: Bartlett, 1853.

"Historical Sketch of Colonel Benjamin Bellows, Founder of Walpole, New Hampshire," 11 October 1854. New York: John A. Gray, 1855.

"Address in Behalf of the United States Inebriate Asylum." New York: M. B. Wynkoop, 1856.

"The Relation of Public Amusements to Public Morality, Especially of the Theatre to the Highest Interests of Humanity." Delivered at the Academy of Music, New York City. New York: Charles S. Francis and Co., 1857.

"Treatment of Social Diseases," Lowell Lectures. Boston: 1857.

"Influence of Theological Theories upon the Practical Conduct of Life," in *Religious Aspects of the Age*. New York: Thatcher & Hutchinson, 1858.

"The Relation of Liberal Christians to a True Theology and a Higher Religious Life," address delivered at the 23rd anniversary of the American Unitarian Association. Boston: AUA, 1858.

"the Suspense of Faith," an address delivered to the alumni of Harvard Divinity School, Cambridge, Mass., 19 July 1859. New York: Charles S. Francis and Co., 1859.

"A Sequel to 'the Suspense of Faith'," delivered in All Souls Church, 25 September 1859. New York: Appleton and Co., 1859.

"Italian Independence," an address of 15 April 1860. Printed in *Pulpit and Rostrum*. New York: H. H. Lloyd & Co., 1860.

Liberty and Union, One and Inseparable," delivered at the Republican Union Festival, Washington, D.C., 22 February 1862. New York: G. P. Putnam & Sons, 1862.

"In Memory of Thomas Starr King," given in the First Unitarian Church, San Francisco, 1 May 1864. San Francisco: F. Eastman, 1864.

"Oration to the California Pioneers at the Celebration of the Fourteenth Anniversary of the Admission of California to the Union," 9 September 1864. San Francisco: Alta California Book and Job Office, 1864.

"Public Life in Washington, or the Moral Aspects of the National Capital," an address read 7 May 1866. New York: James Miller, 1866.

"Address Before the College of Physicians and Surgeons at Their Annual Commencement," 14 March 1867. New York: John F. Trow & Co., 1867.

"Some Thoughts on the Organizing Principle in Christianity," an address given before the British and Foreign Unitarian Association, London, 3 June 1868. London: Edward T. Whitfield, 1868.

"John Howard: His Life, Character and Services," an address delivered before the International Prison Congress in London, 3–13 July 1872. London: Office of the Congress, 1872.

"Our American Sunday," a paper read at the National Conference of Unitarian and Other Christian Churches, 25 October 1872. Boston: AUA, 1872.

"Civil Service Reform," an address read at the first quarterly meeting of the Civil Service Reform Association of the City of New York, 18 October 1877. New York: Civil Service Reform Association, 1877.

"The First Congregational Church in the City of New York, a Sketch of Its History with a Review of His Own Ministry, January 5th and 12th, 1879, on the Occasion of the Fortieth Anniversary of His Settlement." Printed, not published, by the Church of All Souls, New York, 1899.

"The Unitarian Traditions of New York," a discourse given 18 Mach 1879 at the Church of the Messiah in commemoration of the fifty-fourth anniversary of the founding of the church and of the recent redemption of the church from debt, memorial booklet published by the church, 1879, pp. 9–50.

"William Ellery Channing, His Opinions, Genius and Character," a discourse given at Newport, R.I. on the celebration of the centenary of his birth, 7 April 1880. New York: G. P. Putnam & Sons, 1880.

Sermons

"Respectability or Holiness," a sermon delivered before the Young Men's Benevolent Society in Boston, Mass., 9 December 1838. Boston: Week, Jordan and Co., 1839.

"A Sermon Preached November 26, 1843 at the Ordination of Mr. Dexter Clapp over the Unitarian Church at Savannah." New York: Charles S. Francis and Co., 1843.

"Relation of Christianity to Human Nature," a sermon preached at the ordination of Rev. Frederick N. Knapp, Brookline, Mass., 6 October 1847. Boston: Wm. Crosby and H. P. Nichols, 1847.

"Faith in Christianity As a Fact," Sermon XII in *Sermons on Christian Communion*, edited by T. R. Sullivan. Boston: Wm. Crosby and H. P. Nichols, 1848.

"A Sermon Occasioned By the Late Riot in New York," 13 May 1849. New York: Charles S. Francis and Co., 1849.

"Religious Liberty, the Alleged Failure of Protestantism," a sermon preached at the Unitarian Church in Washington, D.C., on Washington's birthday, 22 February 1852. Washington, D.C.: Kirkwood and McGill, 1852.

"Unitarianism in Boston: A Friendly Criticism," a sermon preached at All Souls Church in New York. New York: printed, not published, Charles S. Francis and Co., 1854.

"Worship, the Want of Our National Church," a sermon delivered at the installation of Adam Ayer as the associate pastor of the Unitarian Church in Charlestown, N.H., 7 June 1855. Brattleboro, N.H.: O. H. Platt, 1855.

"The Christian Liberal," a sermon delivered at the Western Unitarian Conference at Buffalo, N.Y., 13 June 1855. Buffalo, N.Y.: Steam Press of Thomas & Lathrops, 1855.

"Some of the Points of Difference Between Unitarian and Orthodox Christians." Boston: American Unitarian Association, 1855.

"Religious Education from Within and from Above," a sermon delivered at the ordination of Stephen Barker as minister of the First Congregational Society in Leominster, Mass., 2 September 1857. Boston: Crosby, Nichols and Co., 1857.

"The Importance of a Positive and Distinct Theology," preached at All

Souls Church, New York, 30 January 1859, and in Cincinnati, Ohio, 24 April 1859. Cincinnati: Robert Clarke & Co., 1859.

"Christian Unity with Reference to the Sermon of Dr. Van Renselear on the Death of Bishop Doane . . . and to the Address of Henry Whitney Bellows on 'the Suspense of Faith'." New York: 1859.

"The Broad Church, Some Considerations on the Suspense of Faith." Boston: 1859.

"the Crisis of Our National Disease," sermon preached on the day of the national fast, 4 January 1861, *Fast Day Sermons*. New York: Rudd and Carleton, 1861.

"The Demoralization of the National Soul," a sermon preached at All Souls Church, 25 January 1861, from *Spirit of the Pulpit*, pp. 9–14.

"The Advantage of Testing Our Principles, Compensatory of the Evils of Serious Times," sermon preached at the Second Unitarian Society of Philadelphia, 17 February 1861. Philadelphia: C. Sherman and Son, 1861.

"Duty and Interest Identical in the Present Crisis," sermon preached at All Souls Church, 14 April 1861. New York: Wynkoop, Hallenbeck & Thomas, 1861.

"The State and the Nation—Sacred to Christian Citizens," sermon preached at All Souls Church, 21 April 1861. New York: Charles S. Francis and Co., 1861.

"How Are We to Fulfill Our Lord's Commandment, 'Love Your Enemies' in a Time of War?'", sermon preached at All Souls Church, 2 June 1861. New York: Baker and Godwin, 1861.

"The Valley of Decision, a Discourse Given on the Occasion of the National Fast," preached in All Souls Church, 26 September 1861. New York: H. B. Price, 1861.

"The Supernatural, A Discourse at the Installation of the Rev. William Henry Channing as Pastor of the Unitarian Church in Washington, D.C.," 9 December 1861. Washington, D.C.: Henry Polkinhorn, 1861.

"Orthodoxy and Liberal Christianity Compared and Contrasted." Boston: American Unitarian Association, 1861.

"The War to End Only When the Rebellion Ceases," preached 30 April 1863. New York: Anson D. F. Randolph, 1863.

"The National Instinct, Our Guide Through the War," an address on the occasion of Thanksgiving, 26 November 1863. New York: James Miller, 1863.

"The New Man for the New Times," a sermon preached at All Souls Church on New Year's Day, 1865. New York: James Miller, 1865.

"The Reformed Church of Christendom, Or the Duties of Liberal Christians to the National Faith at This Crisis of Opinions," a sermon preached at All Souls Church, 8 January 1865. Boston: American Unitarian Association, 1865.

"Death of Abraham Lincoln—Our Martyr President," in *Voices from the Pulpits in New York and Brooklyn*, sermons from Easter Sunday, 1865, pp. 49–63. New York: Tibbals and Whitney, 1865.

"The Sovereignity and Fatherhood of God," preached during Bellows's visit to England. London: Edward T. Whitfield, 1868.

"The Unitarian Denomination," a sermon preached at the third meeting of the National Conference of Unitarian and Other Christian Churches in New York, 6 October 1868. New York: 1868.

"Church and State in America," a sermon preached at the installation of Rev. Frederic Hinckley in Washington, D.C., 25 January 1871. Washington, D.C.: Philp and Solomons, 1871.

"Costliness of God's Moral Government," a sermon preached in All Souls Church, 24 September 1871. Baltimore: John P. Des Fornes, 1871.

"A True Theology the Basis of Human Progress," a sermon preached in Boston at the Hollis Street Church, 1871. Boston: American Unitarian Association, 1872. In *Christianity and Modern Thought*.

"Patterns: Or Precision in Thought, Word and Deed," preached 23 March 1872. New York: published by the *Liberal Christian*, 1872.

"The Battle for Civilization," two sermons preached at the services of dedication of the Fourth Unitarian Church of Chicago by Henry Whitney Bellows and James Freeman Clarke, 27 April 1873. Chicago: Fergus Printing Co., 1873.

"Memories of Departed Worth," a sermon preached at All Souls Church, 2 December 1877. New York: 1877.

"The Nature and Claims of Jesus Christ," a sermon at the ordination of Rev. J. M. W. Pratt at the First Unitarian Church in Wilmington, Del., 28 January 1878. Baltimore: James & Webb, 1878.

"The Old Theology and the New," a sermon preached at All Souls Church. New York: G. P. Putnam & Sons, 1878.

"The Glory of Youth," a Baccalaureate sermon given at Cornell University and Antioch College, June 1878. Ithaca, N.Y.: Cornell University Press, 1878.

"Three Distinctive Principles of Liberal Christianity," a sermon preached at the installation of Rev. Clay MacCauley in Washington, D.C. Washington, D.C.: Gibson Brothers, 1878.

"Christ and Abraham." New York: G. P. Putnam's Sons, 1879.

"Religious Toleration," a discourse given at Temple Emanu-El, New York City, Thanksgiving Day, 27 November 1880. New York: G. P. Putnam & Sons, 1880.

"Patriotism and Piety, the Inspiration and Guardian Powers of the Nation," a Thanksgiving sermon, 25 November 1880. New York: in *New York Herald Tribune*, Extra No. 79., 1880.

"Before and After the President's Death," two sermons preached in All Souls Church about James A. Garfield, 18 and 25 September 1881. New York: G. P. Putnam & Sons, 1881.

"God the Father the Only Intelligible Object of Worship." London: Phillip Green, 1894, and in *Dogma and Doctrine*, New Series, London: British and Foreign Unitarian Association, 1906.

"Thorns in the Flesh—a Sermon on the Uses of Bodily Pain," dedicated to the permanent invalids in private homes and hospitals, n.d.

Funeral Sermons

"A Discourse Occasioned by the Death of William Ellery Channing," preached at a union memorial service at the Church of the Messiah, New York City, 13 October 1842. New York: Charles S. Francis and Co., 1842.

"The Christian Merchant," delivered at the Church of the Divine Unity at the funeral of Jonathan Goodhue. New York: Charles S. Francis and Co., 1848.

"Memorial to William Ware," a sermon preached on the Sunday following the news of Ware's death, 29 February 1852. New York: John A. Gray, 1852.

"Address at the Funeral of Robert C. Goodhue," preached in All Souls Church, 9 April 1862. New York: John A. Gray, 1862.

"Address at the Funeral of Mrs. George L. Schuyler," preached in All Souls Church, 22 December 1863. New York: David G. Francis, 1864.

"Services at the Funeral of the Late Professor James J. Mapes," 13 January 1866. New York: 1866.

"A Testimony of Ninety Years, In Memory of Jacob Newman Knapp," who died at age ninety-five, 27 July 1868. Preached in Walpole, N.H., 13 September 1868. Cambridge, Mass.: John Wilson and Son, 1868.

"A Finished Life," an address at the funeral of Mrs. Mary Bellows, who died 31 July 1869, with other notes of her life. Cambridge, Mass: John Wilson and Son, 1870.

"An Address at the Funeral of Mr. Edward J. Kuntze," at the hall of the YMCA in New York City, 13 April 1870, reprint from the *Liberal Christian*, 1870.

"Address at the Funeral of Mrs. Lucy Elliot Smith," at Fort Washington, N.Y., 5 November 1870. New York: E. B. Tripp & Co., 1870.

"Address at the Funeral of Mrs. Caroline C. Cornell," 9 December 1870. New York: E. B. Tripp & Co., 1870.

"Address at the Funeral of Mrs. Laura Wolcott Gibbs," at All Souls Church, 13 December 1870. New York: privately printed.

"In Memoriam Sarah Bedell, Wife of Peter Cooper." New York: printed for private circulation, 1870.

"Address at the Funeral of Mr. Henry T. Tuckerman," 21 December 1871 (with portrait). New York: G. P. Putnam & Sons, 1872.

"Preparing for Old Age," a sermon delivered at All Souls Church after the death of Mrs. Louisa Bellows Knapp in Walpole, N.H., age eighty-six. Cambridge, Mass.: John Wilson and Son, 1872.

"Essential Goodness the Reality of Religion," a memorial sermon preached in the First Unitarian Church of Concord, N.H., Sunday, 16 March 1873, following the death of the Honorable Adams Bellows. Concord, N.H.: Republican Press Association, 1873.

"Address at the Funeral Service for Inspector James Kelly," 5 November 1874. New York: Evening Post Steam Presses, 1874.

"Oration at the Funeral of William Cullen Bryant," at All Souls Church, 14 June 1878. New York: Religious Newspaper Agency, 1878.

"In Memoriam Mrs. Charles E. Miller." New York: 1879.

Articles

"Testimony of Four Witnesses to the Divine Goodness," American Unitarian Association. Boston: James Munroe & Co., 1845.

"On the Alleged Indefiniteness of Unitarian Theology," American Unitarian Association of the State of New York, Tract No. 1. New York: 1847.

"The Pro-Slavery Testimony of the Northern Conscience Cross-Questioned." New York: 1855.

"Suggested Reading for Their Congregations," with Samuel B. Osgood. New York: privately printed, July 1856.

"Appeal in Behalf of Antioch College." New York: John A. Gray, 1858.

"Relation of the Unitarian Faith to the Current Creeds of Christendom," in *Tracts for the Times.* Albany, N.Y.: 1860.

"Cities and Parks: with Special Reference to the New York Central Park," *Atlantic Monthly,* April 1861, pp. 416–429.

"Unconditioned Loyalty," no title page. New York: Anson D. Randolph, 1861. 10,000 copies circulated by the United States Sanitary Commission.

"Claims of Antioch College upon the Unitarian Denomination." Boston: A. Mudge and Son, 1865.

"Seven Sittings with Powers, the Sculptor," *Appleton's Journal of Literature, Science, and Art,* June to September 1869.

"Christianity and Modern Thought." Boston: American Unitarian Association, 1872.

"The Sacrificial Element in Christianity," in *Pulpit Teachings on Great Subjects* 1:2. New York: G. P. Putnam & Sons, 1877.

"An Appeal on Behalf of the Further Endowment of the Harvard Divinity School of Harvard University." Cambridge, Mass.: John Wilson and Son, 1879.

"Historical Sketch of the Union League Club of New York, Its Origin, Organization, and Work, 1863-1879." New York: privately printed and distributed, 1879.

"The Round Hill School," *Harvard Register*, 3 (1881): pp. 3-7.

"Some Considerations of the Proposed Union of the Meadville Theological School with a Possible New School of Theology to be Founded at Cleveland, Ohio, by the Munificence of John H. Wade; with the Outlines of a Plan for the New School, and a Consideration of the Obstacles to be Overcome to Meet the Conditions of Mr. Wade's Proposal." New York: privately printed, 29 July 1881.

"The Break Between Modern Thought and Ancient Faith and Worship." Boston: The American Unitarian Association, 1891.

Introductions

"Introduction" to *Christian Aspects of Faith & Duty*, by John James Taylor. New York: James Miller, 1865.

"Introduction" to *Modern Materialism in Its Relation to Religion & Theology*, by James Martineau. New York: G. P. Putnam & Sons, 1877.

"Introduction" to *The Institute Essays*, Providence, R.I. Boston: George Ellis, 1880.

United States Sanitary Commission

"Speech of the Rev. Dr. Bellows, President of the United States Sanitary Commission," Philadelphia, 24 February 1863. Philadelphia: Philadelphia Agency of the U.S. Sanitary Commission, 1863.

"Origin, Struggles and Principles of the U.S. Sanitary Commission," *North American Review*, January 1864, pp. 153-194. This article is not signed by Bellows, but his authorship is mentioned in letters in the Bellows Papers.

"Sanitary Commission, No. 95., Provision Required for Disabled Soldiers and Sailors," 15 December 1865.

"How and Where the Money Goes," Correspondence between Bellows and Henry Ward Beecher, U.S. Sanitary Commission, California Branch, 1864.

"The United States Sanitary Commission," reprinted from *Johnson's Universal Encyclopedia*, for private distribution. New York: G. P. Putnam & Sons, 1865.

"United States Sanitary Commission, Statement of Receipts and Disbursements," from 27 June 1861 to 14 May 1878.

Index

Abbot, Francis E.: 336
Academy of Music, NYC.: 175, 256
Academy of Music, Philadelphia: 263
African Methodist Church: 375
Agnew, Dr. Cornelius Rae: 236, 242, 264
Aiken, South Carolina: 395, 398, 459
Ainslee, Robert: 20, 46, 475
Alcott, Bronson: 170
Alger, William: 176, 328, 346
All Souls Church, NYC. (First Congregational Church): 11, *132*, 155, dedication 153-155, comments on architecture, 155-160, *156*, 157, Belltower 157, *158*, 236, 312, 323, 351, 384, 394, 405, 423, *424*, 428, 430, 439, 442, 443, 445, 446, 448, 467, 469, 470
All Souls Mission School: 343
All Souls Parsonage: 111, 149, *150*, *151*, 162, 323, 355-356, 368
"The Alleged Indefiniteness of Unitarian Theology": 68-70
Allen, George: 127
Allen, Gilbert, 475
Allen, Horatio: 77, 127, 476
Allen, John: 476
Allen, Joseph Henry: 328, 417, 441
Allen, William B.: 64, 468, 476
American Red Cross: 463-464
American Unitarian Association: 99, 166, 183, 285, 302, 314, 317, 319, 320, 327, 329, 349, 351, 382, 388, 421, 428, 431, 432, 433, 451, 453, 454, 455, 458, 470
Andrew, Gov. John Albion: 313, 314, 319
Battle of Antietam (Sharpsburg): 255
Antioch College: 135, 136, 137, 139, 140, 152, 176, *177*, 189, 205, 217, 239, 256, 257, 258, 294, 314, 325, 326, 327, 369, 370, 382, 426, 452, 455
Arnold, Benjamin G.: 127, 274, 343, 363, 477, 478
Apollo Hall, NYC.: 48, 50
Armitage, Benjamin: 57

Army of the Potomac: 243, 252, 263
Armstrong, John: 343, 477
Astor, John Jacob: 50
Astor Place Opera House: 98
Astor Place Riot: 98-99, 103
Atlantic Monthly: 240
Ayer, Adams: 149

Bache, Prof. Alexander: 235, 236, 242
Badger, H.C.: 285, 294
Baker, George F.: 445, 478
Balch, John T.: 475
Baldwin, Isaac: 6, 7
Baltimore Sermon: 197
Bancroft, George: 3, 4
Barnes, Mrs. Emily (HWB's cousin): 2
Bartol, Cyrus Augustus: 7, 58-60, *59*, 61, 90, 113, 175, 184, 185, 186, 204, 311, 316, 332, 337, 340, 373, 374, 413, 445, 459, 460
Bartol, Elizabeth Howard (Mrs. Cyrus): 58-60
Barton, Clara: 422, 463-464
Basilica of San Giovanni Battista, Monza, Italy: 157
Batchelor, George: 403-404, 417
Beach, Moses Yates: 63
Bear Valley, Calif.: 291
Beecher, Henry Ward: 152, 281
"The Beefsteak Church": 135, 162, *156, 157*, 274
Bellows, Alexander Hamilton (HWB's brother): 1, 4, 5, 186-187, 468
Bellows, Anne Hurd Langdon (HWB's stepmother): 2, 219
Bellows, Anna Langdon (HWB's daughter): 76, *89, 100, 143*, 211, 290, 300, 342, 371, 372, 373, 380, 388, 391, 396, *397*, 400, 401, 446, 447, 466, 468
Bellows, Anna Peabody (HWB's second wife): 406-407, 410, 445, 446, 447, 465, 468, *469*, 469
Bellows, Colonel Benjamin: 146
Bellows, Betsy Eames (HWB's mother): 1

531

Bellows, Edward Stearns (HWB's twin brother): 1, 5, 8, 9, 26, 99-100, 458, 468
Bellows, Edward Stearns (HWB's first child): 42, 468
Bellows, Eliza Eames Dorr (HWB's sister): 1, 5, 388-389
Bellows, Eliza Townsend (HWB's first wife): 26, 30, 30, 32, 33, 41, 78, 110-111, 143, 168, 178, 187, 249, 250, 268, 276, 300, 322, 342, 350, 353, 354-355, 362, 364, 365, 370, 371, 372, 376, 378, 407, 468
Bellows, Eliza (HWB's daughter): 88-89
Bellows, Ellen Derby Robinson Endicott (HWB's daughter): 443, note 443, 446, 457, 469
Bellows, Francis Greenwood (HWB's half-brother): 2, 5, 88, 89, 468
Bellows, George Gates (HWB's half-brother): 2, 5, 212
Bellows, Harriet Augusta (HWB's half-sister): 2, 5
Bellows, Henry Whitney Jr. (HWB's son): 407, 408, 437, 442, 457, 469, 474
Bellows, John (HWB's father): 1, 2, 3, 5, 41
Bellows, John Nelson (HWB's half-brother): 1, 4, 5, 6, 13, 118, 144, 151, 152, 153, 468
Bellows, Louisa (Mrs. Jacob Knapp, HWB's aunt): 2
Bellows, Mary Anne Louisa (HWB's sister): 1, 2
Bellows, Mary Davis (HWB's daughter): 76, 89, 100, 101-102, 468
Bellows, Percival Langdon (HWB's half-brother): 2, 5, 130
Bellows, Robert Peabody (HWB's son): 418, 442, 457, 468, 469, 470, 474
Bellows, Russell Nevins Townsend (HWB's son): 43, 76, 100, 143, 185, 186, 211, 218, 220, 234, 285, 290, 331-332, 342, 351, 358, 362, 372, 376, 380, 381, 383, 388, 394, 396, 397, 398, 399, 400, 403, 405-406, 409, 410, 412, 413, 415, 418, 420, 439, 446, 458, 459, 461, 462, 466, 467, 468, 470
Bergh, Henry: 330-331
Birmingham, England: 79
Blackwell, Dr. Elizabeth: 217, 229
Blanchard, Henry: 307
Blauvelt, Augustus: 411-412, note 411

"Bleeding Kansas": 169
Bond of Union, All Souls: 479-481
Booth, Edwin: 323
Booth, John Wilkes: 322
Boston Unitarian Seminary: 376
Boynton, Ray: 476
Briggs, George Ware: 87-88, 346
Brigham, Charles H.: 176, 284, 305
Bright, J.B.: 475
British Unitarian Association: 353, note 353
Broadway Atheneum: 314, 319
Broadway, NYC.: 49, 102
Brooklyn, Third Unitarian Society: 111
Brooks, Charles Timothy: 8, 292, 428
Brooks, Joshua: 475
Brooks, Phillips: 420, 456
Brown, Addison: 477, 478
Brown, Olympia: note 205
Brownson, Orestes: 224
Bryant, William Cullen: 17, 75, 80, 213, 217, 260, 261, 262, 300, 314, 332, 405, 422-426, 424
Bull Run, First Battle of: 243
Bull Run, Second Battle of: 254
Butler, Charles: 154, 189, 274, 343, 476, 477

California: 248, 260, 263, 268, 269, 275, 283, 285, 286, 287, 288, 289, 299, 313, 328
California Society of Pioneers: 296-298, 297
Cameron, Simon: 235, 246
Camp, Stephen H.: 375
Canfield, Charles Taylor: 376
Carson City, Nevada: 295
Catholicism: 348-349
Cary, William F.: 127, 274, 475, 476
Central Park, NYC.: 80, 240
Century Club, NYC.: 76, 300, 351, 419, 467, 470
Chadwick, John White: 332, 338, 339, 375
Chandler, Nathan: 390, 394-395, 477, 478
Channing Memorial Church, Newport, R.I.: 426, 443-444, 460, 462-463
Channing, Mary Eustis: 26, 27, 29, 32, 46, 395
Channing, William Ellery: 8, 13, 26, 28, 43, 44, memorial service 44-45, 62, 119, 189, 190, 380, 393, 426, 433, 443-444, 470

Channing, William Henry: 190, 280, 416
Chapin, Edwin H.: 125, 389, 428, 447-448, 460-461
Charlestown, N.H. Unitarian Society: 149, 426
Charleston, S.C.: 395
Chase, Salmon P.: 232, 233, 289, 333
Cheney, George: 302
Chauncey, Charles: 341
Chicago Fire, 1871: 383-384
Chicago Unitarian Church: 176, 252
The Christian Commission: 269, note 269, 292, 296
The *Christian Examiner*: 328, 337-338, 339
The *Christian Inquirer*, sometimes called just the *Inquirer*, later named the *Inquirer*: 65, 79, 92, 106-107, 182, 337-338
The *Christian Register*: 376, 406, 415, 418, 462, 469
Christy, Thomas: 343, 354, 476, 477
Church of the Divine Paternity (Fourth Universalist):461
Church of the Divine Unity, NYC.: 55, 56, *56*, 125, 126
"Church of the Holy Zebra": 135, 159
Church of the Messiah (Second Church) NYC.: 17, note 17, *40*, 57, 130, 277, 311-312, 358, 359, 362, 364, 365, 366, 367, 368, 369, 376, 377, 384-386, 394-395, 404-405, 427-435, 54th anniversary 433-435, 436, 437, 438, 439, 442
Church of the Savior, Brooklyn: *52*, 68, 319
Church of the Unity, Boston: 376, 417
Church of the Unity, Chicago: 369, 370, 382, 404-405, 436
Church of the Unity, Worcester, Mass.: 168, 382
Church (HWB's concept of): 305-307, 317-318, 379-380
Cincinnati Congregational Unitarian Church: 12, 210
Civil Service Reform: 437-438, 442
Clapp, Dexter: 45
Clapp, Theodore: 107
Clarke, James Freeman: 65, 197-198, 217, 218, 310, 313, 314, *315*, 319, 336, 346, 357, 373, 377, 412, 427, 428, 429
Cleveland, Ohio: 447, 449, 450, 451, 453, 454, 455
Cleveland Museum of Art: 450

Collamore, Ebenezer: 476
Collyer, Robert: 285, 314, 346, 368, 369, 373, 382, 383, 404-405, 432, 436, 437, 438, 439, 440, 442, 466, 474
Compromise of 1850: 104
Cooper, Peter: 17, 127, 148, 180, *181*, 213, 227, 274, 431, 456-457, 467
Cooper Union: 180, 181, 213, 230, 300
Cooper Union Address: 213-215
Cornell University: 426
Covenants of All Souls: 479-481
Cowdin, Eliot C.: 343, 477
Currier, Nathaniel: 127, 275, 476, 477
Curtis, George T.: 125-126
Curtis, George W.: 435, 467
Curtis, Irving: 475
Curtis, Joseph: 148
Curtis, Paul A.: 127, 476

Dales, James G.: 129, 476
Dana, Saul B.: 477, 478
Dean, Nicholas: 127, 135, 151, hymn 154, 155, 156, 173, 476
Dewey, Orville: 8, 14, 17, 18, 19, 21, 22, 33, 36, 37, *38*, 38, 39, 41, 43, 45, 65, 66, 71, 75, 92-93, resignation 93-94, 96, 97, 101, 107-108, 120, 169, 176, 180, 298, 314, 346, 363, 374, 379, 409, 413, 414, 426, 431, 432, 433, 435, 467, 470
Dietz, William H.: 476
Disciples of Christ Denomination: 136, 177, 257, 258
Divinity School Address: 190, 197
Dix, Dorothea: 232, 233, 235, 243, 266
Doctor of Divinity (HWB Harvard): 146
Dorr, Joseph: 5, 343, 344
Camp Douglas: 252
Douglas, Stephen A.: 213
Drake, James E.: 351, 375
Draper, Dr. William H.: 448, 466

Eaton, Dorman B.: 274, 275, 313, 453, 454
Egyptian "Belly Dance," HWB's reaction: 350
Eliot, Charles W.: 367, 393, 394, 39% 400-401, 443, 447, 474
Eliot, William G.: 251, 256, 292, 337, 346
Ellis, George: 310, 320, 341, 418

Ellis, Rufus: 310, 311, 320, 327, 346, 357-358, 417
Emerson, Ralph Waldo: 25, 43, 116-117, 169, 190, 217, 388, 471, 473
England: 79-81, 351, 388
Trip to Europe and Middle East: 347-348, 379, 381, 388
Everett, Carroll: 427
Everett, Charles: 346
Everett, Edward: 279
Evthreit, Rabbi: 438

Farley, Frederick A.: 111-112, 154, 156, 360-361, 373, 377, 433, 463
Federal Street Church, Boston: 8, 44
Fifth Avenue Hotel, New York City: 216
Fillmore, Millard: 118
First Church in Boston: 1, 311
Fish, Hamilton Jr.: 457-458
Florence, Italy: 83, 351
Fogg, William H.: 343, 477
Follen, Charles Theodore Christian: 16, 17, 19, 20, 23, 25, 41, 108, 190
Follen, Eliza Cabot: 41
Foote, Emerson: 477, 478
Forbush, T.B.: 326-327
Fortieth Anniversary Sermons: 430
Fortress Monroe: 249, 303
Fourth Universalist Church, NYC.: 125, 447-448
France: 81-82
Francis, Charles S.: 51, 55, 150, 172-173, 174, 182, 475
Frasee & Pearson: 53, 54
Frederickson, George M.: 223, 269, 270, 272, 325
Free Religious Association: 280, 322, 337, 454, 480
Fribourg, Switzerland: 86
Frothingham, Nathaniel: 21
Frothingham, Octavius Brooks: 154, note 154, 156, 190, 206, 207, 207, 208, 209, 277-280, note 278, 310, 313, 318, 321, 337, 338-339, 389
Frye, Jed: 477
Fugitive Slave Law: 104
Furness, William Henry: 11, 20, 21, 113, 114, 320-321, 346, 463

Gannett, Ezra Stiles: 57, 178, 310, 313, 327, 346, 376
Gardner, Dr. Augustus Kinsley: 345
Genoa, Italy: 83

Geneva Convention: 247, 421-422, 463, 464
Geneva, Switzerland: 86-87, 248
Gettysburg, Battle of: 265-266, 273
Gibbs, Dr. Walcott: 228, 236, 242
Goddard, J. Warren: 477
Godwin, Parke: 254, 419-420, 467
Goodhue, Charles C.: 343, 389
Goodhue, Jonathan: 21, 44, 91-92
Goodhue, Robert Clarkson: 258, 274, 275
Gottheil, Rabbi Gustav: 460
Grant, Ulysses Simpson: 303, 304, 333, 366
Gray, George Winston: 475
Green, Walter C.: 476
Greenfield, Mass.: 372
Greenwood Cemetery: 373
Grinnell, Moses: 49, 103-104, 127, 129, 148, 152, 153, 154, 163, 164, 174, 231, 275, 323, 375, 382, 475, 476, 477
Grinnell Minturn & Co.: 172

Hale, Edward Everett: 167, 167, 168, 285, 286, 293, 294, 305, 308, 310, 311, 313, 314, 319, 326, 334, 335, 338, 341, 346, 357, 365, 367, 368, 376, 378, 382, 383, 386, 387, 416-417, 428, 442, 452-453, 454, 455, 460, 467, 469, 474
Hall, Edward B.: 21, 417, 445
Hamlin, Hannibal: 227
Hammond, Dr. William A.: 248
Harlem Unitarian Church: 415-416, 420-421
Harper's Weekly Magazine: 198
Harris, Dr. Elisha: 227, 229, 233, 236, 242
Harsen, Dr. Jacob: 233
Harvard College: 4, 5, 9, 185, 218, 220, 221, 234, 257, 285, 365, 367, 394, 401
Harvard Divinity School: 6, 7, 8, 21, 137, 186, 190, 314, 376, 413, 417, 443, 447, 456
Harvard Overseers: 439, 442-443
Haven, Joseph W.: 475
Hawkins, Dexter A.: 427, 429
Hayes, H.M.: 475
Hayes, Rutherford B.: 442
Hayward, Stella: 26
Hedge, Frederic Henry: 65, 166, 186, 204, 217, 278, 301, 310, 346, 416, 460, 463, 470-473

Hepworth, George: 329, 330, 342, 368, 376, 377, 384-387, *385*, 386, 429
Herford, Brooke: 427, 431, 436, 437, 458
Hicksite Quakers: 306
Hill, Alonzo: 346
Hill, Thomas: 257, 258, 326, 401
Hollard, Frederick W.: 21
Hollis Street Church, Boston: 302, 309
Holmes, Oliver Wendell: 260, 261
Hooker, General Joseph: 264
Hosmer, Frederick Lucian: 447, 455
Hospital Transport Service: 248
Howard, John: HWB's discourse on: 388
Howe, Dr. Samuel Gridley: 237, 271, 333
Hubbard, Mary Hustace: 20
Huidekoper, Alfred: 451, 453
Huidekoper, Frederic: 94, 95
Huntington, Frederick Dan: 166

Inebriate Asylum, Binghamton, N.Y.: 253, 326
Independent Liberal Church, NYC.: 279
International Prison Congress: 388
International Red Cross: 422, 463
Ireland, Mrs. A.M.: 29
Ireland, George: 71
Ireland, George Jr.: 476
Irving, Pierre: 475
Italy: 81-83
The *Inquirer*: 412, 415, 418

Jacksonville, Florida: 391-393
Jersey City Unitarian Church: 206
Johnson, Andrew: 323-324, 333, HWB's attitude towards 334

Kennedy, Joyce: 481
King, Mrs. Julia Wiggin: 284, 286, 328, 330, 332-333
King, Thomas Starr: 70, 71, 72, 75, 96, 149, 209, 210, 216, 217, 248, 253, 255, 256, 259, 260, 261, 275, 281, death 282-283, 285, 286, 287, 288, 289, 293, 294, 309, 329, 432
Kirkland, Caroline (Mrs. William): 65, 78, 79, 88, note 88, 127, 229
Kirkland, Prof. William: 65, 92
Kossuth, Louis: 115, 120
Knapp, Frederick Newman: 72

Knapp, Jacob Newman (HWB's uncle): 2
Knapp, Louisa (HWB's aunt): 388

Lake Leman, Switzerland: 86
Landy, Jacob: 51, note 51
Lane, David: 476
Lane, Mrs. David: 354
Langley, William C.: 475
Lee, Mrs. George: 28, 29
Lee, General Robert E.: 247, 255, 265, 303
Lefever, Minard: 50, 51, life 51-52, 53, 54, 127
Lexington (Steamship): 16, 41
The *Liberal Christian*: 314, 341, 364, 377, 378, 379, 381, 397, 406, 412-413
The Liberal Christian Church of America: 306, 308, 317
The *Liberal Worker*: 407
Lincoln, Abraham: 213-215, 216, 218, 219, 224, 231, 233, 234, 235, 236, 245, 246, 250, 253, 265, 298, 299, 300, 322-323, 333
Lincoln, Robert: 220, 221, 234
Livermore, Abiel Abbot: 8, 334, 395, 450-451
Liverpool, England: 79
London, England: 80-81
Longfellow, Henry Wadsworth: 111, 260, 261
Longfellow, Samuel: 310
Lothrop, Samuel K.: 20, 21, 154, 155, 310, 346
Low, A.A.: 319, 326
Low, David: 475
Lowe, Charles: 329, 340, 349, 375, 378-379, 382
Lowell, Mass.: 460
Lowell, Mrs. Charles: 325
Lowell, James Russell: 260
Lowell Lectures: 177
Lunt, William: 16, 37, 364, 433, 435

McClellan, General George: 243, 244, 245, 247, 253, 254, 255, 261, 264, 265, 300
McKaye, James: 255
Macondra, M.S.: 283
Magnolia, Florida: 393-395, 398
Mann, Horace: 135, 136, 137, 139, 140, 176, 177, 204-205, 217
Mardi (Melville): 96
Mariposa Estate: 292

Mariposa Mining Co.: 267, 268, 300
Martineau, Harriett: 353
Martineau, James: 353-354
Massachusetts Historical Society: 344
Mauran, Orondontes: 17
May, Samuel Joseph: 108, 177, 309, 314, 356, 411, 428
Meadville Theological School: 75, 94, 99-100, 314, 382, 395, 449, 451, 452, 453, 454, 455
Medical College, NYC.: 134, 148
Medical Department, U.S. Army: 245, 248, 254
Melville, Elizabeth Shaw: 95, 96, 274, 344-346, 391, note 391, 481
Melville, Herman: 96, 97, 274, 275, 344-346, 473, 480, 481
Melville, Malcolm: 347
Mercantile Library Assn., NYC.: 124
The Minister's Institute: 411, 416, 438, 460
"Mintwood": on All Souls Church 159-162, on HWB 160-162
Mission to Seamen: 375
Mobile, Alabama: 11, 104
Moby-Dick (Melville): 96, 275, 344, 481
Mott, Dr. Valentine: 227, 229
Mould, Jacob Wrey: 131, 135, 147, 153, 157, 158, 163
Murdock, Uriel A.: 477
Murdock, W.A.: 343
Murphy's Hotel: 290, 291

Nahant Beach, Mass.: 111
Naples, Italy: 84-85
National Asylum for Inebriates: 153
National Conference of Unitarian Churches: 279, 280, note 314, 317, 319-320, 326, 334, 335, 375, 480, became
National Conference of Unitarian and Other Christian Churches: 336-337, 338, 339, 340, 341, 356-357, 403, 404, 416, 420, 426, 451, 455
Nevada Territory: 260, 295
Nevins and Townsend: 129
Nevins, Russell Hubbard (Mrs. HWB's uncle): 127, 129, 130, 133
Newberry, Dr. John: 235, 242
New York Bank for Savings: 49
New York City Unitarian Convention: 302
New York Conference of Unitarian Churches: 308, 338
New York Customs Office: 344

New York Draft Riots: 266-267, 273
New York Evening Post: 16, 322, 422
New York and Hudson River Conference: 358
New York Infirmary: 227
New York, New Haven and Hartford Railroad: 146
New York Public Library: 172
New York State Charities Aid Assn.: 325
New York State Unitarian Association: 62, 106
New York Sun: 63
New York Tribune: 268, 280
New York Unitarian Publication Society: 337-338
New York University Chapel: 148, 153
Niblo's Hall: 131, 133, 134
Nightingale, Florence: 227, 243
Norris, William: 328, 332-333
The North American Review: 281
Norton, Andrews: 190
Nuthall, Prof. Thomas: 4

Olmsted, Frederick Law: 219, 240, 241, 242, 243, 248, 254, 267, 268, 271, 287, 288, 291, 292, 299
Omoo (Melville): 96
Oregon Territory: 299
Osgood, Samuel: 8, 33, 65, 90, 97, 101, 112-113, 120, 130, 131, 154, 155, 170, 208, 278, 279, 314, 318, 332, 355, 358-362, 364, 365, 366, 367, 368, 369, 376, 378, 382, 429, 435
Otis, James C.: 282
Oxford, England: 80

Paestum, Italy: 85
Palfrey, John C.: 7
Panama: 286, 287
Paris, France: 81
Parker, Theodore: 8, 140, 190, 217, 218, 279, 280, 306, 380
Parkman, John: 156
Parkman, Samuel P.: 259
Peabody, Andrew Preston: 218, 417
Peabody, Anna: 393, 394, 395, 396, 398, 400-402, becomes Mrs. HWB
Peabody, Ephraim: 10, 20, 21, 57, 170, 393-394, 418, 432
Peabody, Mrs. Ephraim (Mary Jane Derby): 393, 395, 398, 400-401, 403
Peabody, Francis Greenwood: 393, 394, 398, 402, 417, 474
Peabody, Joseph: 476

Peabody, Robert: 396, 398, 401, 402, 465
Pearson, Isaac Greene: 53, 173, 182, 275, 476
Perkins, Charles E.: 444
Persons, Stow: 317
Phoenix Bank: 64
Phi Beta Kappa Address: 129, 130
Philadelphia Sanitary Fair: 283
Phillips, Clifton J.: 199
Pierre, Or the Ambiguities: (Melville): 275, 344
Pisa, Italy: 83
Pittsfield, Mass.: 275
Pope, General John: 254
Powers, Hiram: article by HWB: 351, 352, 375-376, 377, 378, 470
Prescott, William H.: 111
Prichard, William M.: 182, 284, 343, 390, 391, 468, 474, 476, 477, 478
Protestantism: 118-119
Putnam, A.P.: 308, 311, 346, 375, 377, 379, 395
Putnam, George: 57, 320, 341

Quincy, Josiah: 3, 7

Redburn (Melville): 96
Republican Party: 219, 438
Reynolds, Grindall: 451, 453, 455, 458
Rhoades, J. Harsen: 477, 478
Rider, William: 127
Ripley, George: 280
Riverside, Conn.: 121-122, 123
Robbins, Chandler: 311, 320, 341
Rome, Italy: 84
Roper, Laura Wood: 240
Rosecrans, General W.S.: 261, 263
Round Hill School: 3, 4, 9
Russel, Lucy Channing: 103, 426
Russel, William W.: 103
Russell, Salem T.: 477
Russell, William Channing: 326, 426

Saint-Gaudens, Augustus: 472, 474
Saint Peters Church, Rome: 84
Salem, Mass. North Church: 206
San Francisco, Calif.: 284, 288, 289, 294, 295, 296, 297, 298, 329, 378, 390
San Francisco Unitarian Church: 209, 217, 259, 275, 281, 282, *282*, 286, 289, 293, 294, 379
San Joaquin River: 290
Saratoga Springs, N.Y.: 414, 426, 446
Savage, Minot Hudson: 417, 428, 437

Sawyer, Nathaniel: 77
Schulz, Jackson S.: 477
Schuyler, Eliza (1st Mrs. George): 170, 184, 198, 276-277, 411, 414
Schuyler, George: 127, 129, 140-144, *141*, 240, 379, 380, 382-383, 413
Schuyler, Georgina: 380
Schuyler, Mary (2nd Mrs. George): 411, 413
Schuyler, Louisa Lee: 227, *228*, 230, 231, 274, 325
Schuyler, Mrs. Philip: 22, 31
Schuyler, Robert: 49, 50, 127, 146, 475
Second Church in Boston: 473
Secretary of War: 245
Sedgwick, Catharine: 17, 343
Sedgwick, Henry D.: 228, 413, 477, 478
Sedgwick, Robert: 127
Sedgwick, William Ellery: 144
"Sequel to the Suspense of Faith": 199-203
Sequoia Trees: 290-291
Seward, William H.: 120, 214, 216, 218, 219, 231, 246, 263, 268, 299
Shaw, Samuel: 344-345, note 344
Sherman, General William T.: 303, 333
Shippen, Rush R.: 176, 382, 384, 388, 414, 415-416, 417, 420-421, 428, 431, 432, 439, 458
Silsbee, William: 8, 91, 113, 120, 374, 393, 394, 418
Simmons, George Frederick: 13, 14, 104
The Sketch Club: 37, 75
Skiddy, Francis: 476
Slavery: 11, 12, 103-109, note 108, 169, 214, 221
Smith, Jeremiah: 76, 475
Society for the Prevention of Cruelty to Animals: 330-331
Soldier's Relief Committee of San Francisco: 269
South Congregational Unitarian Church, Boston: 168
Spiritualism: 306, 451
Sparks, Jared: 111
Sreve, George C.: 283
Stanton, Edward McMasters: 246, 250, 251
Staples, Carleton A.: 370
Staten Island Ferry: 103
Staten Island, N.Y.: 227, 298, 389
Stearns, John G.: 476

Stebbins, Horatio: 285, 286, 287, 288, 292, 293, 294, 296, 329, 330, 379, 474
Stebbins, Rufus Phineas: 8, 94, 206, 339
Stillé, Charles J.: 271, 323, 338
Stockton, Calif.: 290
Stone, Joel: 475
Storrow, Thomas W.: 475
Strong, George Templeton: 54, 102-103, 170, *171*, 172, 179, 180, 236, 242, 246, 247, 248, 263, 271, 272, 273, 286-287, 299, 303, 323
Sumner, Charles: 111, 169, 333
Sumter, Fort: 216, 221-223, 224, 395
"Suspense of Faith": 24, 149, 191-197, 199, 204
Swain, Robert B.: 217, 253, 255, 256, 275, 283, 284, 285, 286, 293, 294, 329-330, 332-333, 379
Syracuse Conference: 177
Syracuse Convention: 335-337
Switzerland: 85-87

Taggard, William: 49, 475
Lake Tahoe: 295
Taylor, Father Edward: 217
Temple Emanu-El, NYC.: 440-442
Theatre, Lecture on the: 174-176
Third Congregational Unitarian Church, NYC.: 206, 277
Third Unitarian Church, Chicago: 370
Thomas, John: 17, 77, 127, 475, 476
Thorp, Andrew: 475
Tileston, Thomas: 475
Tileston, Mrs. Thomas: 443
Townsend, Elihu (Mrs. HWB's father): 17, 49, 50, 77, 78, 127, 129
Townsend, Mrs. Elihu (Mrs. HWB's mother): 122
Transcendentalism: 23, 24, 25, 190, 454
Tucker and Dodd: 53, 54
Tuckerman, Joseph: 325
Twenty-Five Doctrinal Sermons: 203-204
Typee (Melville): 96

Union Theological Seminary: 328, 358
Unitarian Denomination: 189, 301, 302, 305, 306, 307, 309-310, 312, 313, 314, 320, 335, 358, 375, 377, 395, 415, 451, 452
U.S. House of Representatives: 280-281

United States Sanitary Commission: 233, 235, 236, 238, 240, 242, 243, 244, 245, 246, 247, 248, 249, 250, 251, 252, 253, 254, 255, 256, 260, 261, 263, 266, 268, 269, philosophy of 269-273, 274, 275, 281, 283, 292, 294, 295, 296, 299, 302, 304, 305, 312, 322, 324-325, 327, 358, 378, 383, 421, 422, 463
Unity Sunday School: 67-68
Universalists: 125, 306, 307, 308, 309, 327, 358, 378, 383, 421, 422, 463

Van Buren, Dr. W.H.: 233, 236, 248
Vaux, Calvin: 240

Wade, Jeptha Homer: 447, 449, 450, 451, 452, 453, 454, 455
Wade School of Religious Philosophy: 449, 454, 455
Walker, James: 184, 186
Walpole, N.H. Church: 358, 362, 376, 381, 389
Walpole, N.H. Homestead: 139, *140*, 144, note 145, 244, 276, 354, 370, 371, 382, 400, 402, 403, 407, 426, 445, 446, 468
War Department: 242, 243, 244, 246, 326
Ward, George C.: 477
Ward, James O.: 127
Wardwell, William T.: 477, 478
Ware, Henry Jr.: 7, 13, 21, 60-61, 218
Ware, Henry Sr.: 7, 16, 190
Ware, William: 15, 19, 20, 21, 22, 37, 38, 75, 76, 274, note 274, 364
Washington Territory: 299
Webster, Daniel: 106, 125-126, 137, 140
Weeden, William: 120, 382, 395, 396, 399, 402, 460
Western Reserve College: 452
Western Sanitary Commission: 251, 252, 255
Western Unitarian Conference: 319, 454
Wheelwright, Benjamin: 127, 173, 274, 475, 476, 477
White-jacket (Melville): 96
Whitridge, Thomas: 257
Willard's Hotel, Washington, D.C.: 232, 242
Williams, John E.: 127, 228
Williams, John W.: 476
Williams, Theodore Chickering: 445, 474

Wilton, N.H. Unitarian Church: 144,
  151
Women's Central Relief Association:
  229, *229, 230,* 230, 236, 238
  240, 243
Whittier, John Greenleaf: 260, 261
Wright, Conrad: 107, 315, 319

Yorktown, Va.: 249
Young Men's Benevolent Society,
  Boston: 26
Yosemite Valley, Calif.: 291, 292

Zurich, Switzerland: 85

Date Due

Demco 293-5